Computer System Validation

Pharmaceutical, Biologics, and Medical Device Regulations and Guidance Documents Concise Reference

Computer System Validation: Pharmaceutical, Biologics, and Medical Device Regulations and Guidance Documents, Concise Reference,

Pharma
Logika
Books

PharmaLogika Books
PO Box 901
Raleigh, NC 27602-0901
www.pharmalogika.com

ISBN-13: 978-1-937258-25-2

Authors: Mindy J. Allport-Settle and Dr. Kirstin A. Counts
Published by PharmaLogika Books.
Printed in the United States of America.

Please direct all inquiries to

info@PharmaLogika.com

For information on our other available titles and services, visit us

www.PharmaLogika.com

CONCISE REFFERENCE

COMPUTER SYSTEM VALIDATION

PHARMACEUTICAL, BIOLOGICS, AND MEDICAL DEVICE REGULATIONS AND GUIDANCE DOCUMENTS

MINDY J. ALLPORT-SETTLE
DR. KIRSTIN A. COUNTS

Pharma Logika Books

CSV

Table of Contents

Regulations

Guidance Documents

Chapter 11
SaMD: Application of Quality Management System

Chapter 12
Software as a Medical Device (SaMD): Clinical Evaluation

CSV

Chapter 1
Introduction

About This Book

First and foremost, this book is a unified reference source for current Computer System Validation practices as mandated by Title 21 of the United States Code of Federal Regulations (21 CFR). In addition to the regulations defining these requirements, the pertinent guidance documents and published questions and answers available at the time of publication are also presented. The included Code of Federal Regulations Title 21 Overview is designed to provide a foundation for understanding the background of the FDA and its regulations.

Due to the global nature of the pharmaceutical and medical device industries and the rapidly progressing digital information environment, it is necessary to consider regulations and industry standards beyond the borders of a single country or a single organization. Computerized systems are an integral part of the global pharmaceutical landscape, requiring the consideration of regulations and guidance from around the world. With that in mind, several regulations and guidance documents from the European Union have been included, along with a recommended reading list of additional resources is included at the end of the guidance document section.

This book is intended to be used both as a reference for experienced industry representatives and as a training resource for those new to the industry. As governance over computerized systems in pharmaceutical and medical device manufacturing advances, resources such as these will continue to provide perspective on the requirements and subsequent rationale of our current era.

Included Documents and Features

FDA Regulations

- Code of Federal Regulations Title 21 Overview
- Part 11 (21 CFR § 11)
- Part 820 (21 CFR § 820)

European Union Regulations

- Annex 11: Computerised Systems
- Annex 15: Qualification and Validation
- GMP Medicinal Products for Human and Veterinary Use: Chapter 4

Guidance Documents

- Software as a Medical Device: Key Definitions
- Software as a Medical Device: Possible Framework for Risk Categorization and Corresponding Considerations
- Software as a Medical Device: Application of Quality Management System
- Software as a Medical Device: Clinical Evaluation
- Changes to Existing Medical Software Policies Resulting from Section 3060 of the 21st Century Cures Act
- Computerized Systems Used in Clinical Investigations
- Computerized Systems Used in Clinical Trials
- Deciding When to Submit a 510(k) for a Software Change to an Existing Device
- Guidance for the Content of Premarket Submissions for Software Contained in Medical Devices
- Cybersecurity for Networked Medical Devices Containing Off-the-Shelf (OTS) Software
- Policy for Device Software Functions and Mobile Medical Applications
- General Wellness: Policy for Low Risk Devices
- Blood Establishment Computer System Validation in the User's Facility
- Medical Device Data Systems, Medical Image Storage Devices, and Medical Image Communications Devices
- Off-The-Shelf Software Use in Medical Devices
- Data Integrity and Compliance with Drug CGMP: Questions and Answers
- Qualification and Classification of Stand Alone Software
- Notice to sponsors on validation and qualification of computerised systems used in clinical trials
- Q&A: Good Clinical Practice (GCP)—selected Questions

Reference Tools

- Combined glossary
- Abbreviation Quick Reference List
- General index for all standards and guidance documents

About the Reference Tools

FDA and CGMP Overview

This overview provides a brief history of the FDA. It explains what good manufacturing practices are, why we have them, and how they came to be. The overview also lists all of the titles within Title 21 of the U.S. Code of Federal Regulations.

Combined Glossary

The Combined Glossary collects definitions written into each regulation and guidance and presents them alphabetically rather than by document.

When a word or term is defined multiple times in the regulation and guidance documents, each definition is provided with its corresponding document reference. The source for each entry is bracketed (i.e., [21 CFR § 11]) for ease of reference. While the definitions are similar from one regulatory or guidance document to the next, they are not always identical.

General Index for all standards and guidance documents

The index is composed of a list of both words and terms specific to good manufacturing practices. It is a tool that assists in cross-referencing the various regulations and guidance documents.

CSV

Chapter 2

Computer System Validation: The Basics

Regulations, Guidance, and Accepted Frameworks

For decades, Computer System Validation (CSV) has been the method implemented by the life sciences industry to ensure the quality, safety, and integrity of computerized systems. CSV is an adaptation of the validation principles utilized in mechanical engineering where verification and validation activities establish that a mechanical system is fit for purpose, meaning that all stated specifications and requirements are met and fulfilled.

The life sciences industry includes pharmaceutical, biologics, medical device development and manufacturing, clinical research organizations (CROs), and a variety of associated business providers. Here, validation and verification have been integrated with qualification activities into the Software Development Lifecycle (SDLC) to address the critical demands of these regulated environments.

The ultimate purpose of CSV is to ensure patient protection while safeguarding a company's intellectual property, employees, reputation, and financial interests. It begins with a clear understanding of regulation and guidance provided by governing bodies such as the US Food and Drug Administration (FDA), the European Medicines Agency (EMA), and the UK's Medicines and Healthcare products Regulatory Agency (MHRA).

In the United States, the primary regulations governing CSV are provided by the FDA in the *Code of Federal Regulations, Title 21 Food and Drugs, Part 11 Electronic Records; Electronic Signatures* (21 CFR Part 11 or 21CFR11) and *Part 820 Quality System Regulation* (21 CFR Part 820 or 21CFR820). (Part 820 is specific to Medical Devices but is used as guidance for other factions of the life sciences industry, such as Pharmaceuticals and CROs.) The EMA utilizes *Eudralex Volume 4, Annex 11 Computerised Systems* (Annex 11). Both sets of regulations codify the applicable laws set out by their governing bodies and are designed to provide the base requirements meant to protect patient safety.

> The ultimate purpose of ***Computer System Validation*** is to ensure patient protection while safeguarding a company's intellectual property, employees, reputation, and financial interests.

In industry, these regulations are viewed by many as single sources of truth, and in a sense, they are. However, in practice, clear-cut interpretation and application of these truths can be somewhat elusive. Regulations simply state the rules and requirements set forth by law. They do not provide precise directives for obtaining a state of compliance, nor do they offer instructions or templates for implementation.

It is critical to recognize that the application of regulations such as 21 CFR Part 11 or Annex 11 does not dimmish responsibility for any other requirement. A system can only be proven fit for purpose and successfully validated in a regulated environment when all requisite components have been defined and successfully tested. For example, a computer system that supports clinical studies must follow 21 CFR Part 11 as well as the regulations applicable to Good Clinical Practice (GCP), Good Documentation Practice (GDP), protection of Personal Health Information (PHI), and any other applicable regulation, guidance, or law relevant to the use of the system.

To help the industry interpret these regulations, the agencies have clarified their "current thinking" on them through guidance documents, workshops, and conferences, which allow for the practical application of these regulations to change as the needs of the industry change.[1] The agencies also encourage opinions and feedback from the industry during open comment periods for draft guidance. The FDA, specifically, will accept appropriately submitted comments on any guidance document at any time as detailed in 21 CFR 10.115(g)(5).[2]

Several professional organizations produce additional guidance for CSV. Unlike the agencies, these professional organizations also provide specific frameworks for successful implementation, such as the *Good Automated Manufacturing Practice* (GAMP® 5) series produced by the International Society for Pharmaceutical Engineering (ISPE) and the *Technical Information Report 45* (TIR 45) produced by the Association for the Advancement of Medical Instrumentation (AAMI). While guidance produced by professional organizations is not mandatory for compliance, they provide common structure and logic for developing quality systems, software lifecycles, and control processes that the agencies recognize, accept, and follow. Other professional organizations associated with CSV include the International Organization for Standardization (ISO), the International Electrotechnical Commission (IEC), and the International Medical Device Regulators Forum (IMDFR), among others.

A Brief History of CSV Regulation and Guidance

In 1997 the FDA issued and made effective 21 CFR Part 11. These regulations applied to all FDA program areas and "were intended to permit the widest possible use of electronic technology, compatible with FDA's responsibility to protect the public health."[3] They outlined circumstances for application, defined pertinent terminology, and dictated the requirements associated with electronic documentation and electronic signatures. Specifically, 21 CFR Part 11 was put forth to establish the "criteria under which the agency considers electronic records, electronic signatures, and handwritten

21 CFR Part 11
applies to all FDA program areas

1 United States, FDA. About FDA Guidance Documents. Retrieved March, 2021, from https://www.fda.gov/regulatory-information/search-fda-guidance-documents

2 Comments can be submitted online at regulations.gov. Official information related to the comment submission for guidance documents can be found in 21 CFR 10.115(h) and can be accessed online at https://www.ecfr.gov/current/title-21/chapter-I/subchapter-A/part-10/subpart-B/section-10.115

3 United States, FDA. (2003, August). Guidance for Industry Part 11, Electronic Records; Electronic Signatures — Scope and Application. Retrieved from https://www.fda.gov/regulatory-information/search-fda-guidance-documents/part-11-electronic-records-electronic-signatures-scope-and-application

signatures executed to electronic records to be trustworthy, reliable, and generally equivalent to paper records and handwritten signatures executed on paper."[4]

In the field, Part 11 compliance proved to be especially cumbersome, particularly in the areas of validation, audit trails, record retention, record copying, and legacy systems. Most critically, there were concerns that Part 11 compliance would unnecessarily restrict the use of electronic technology, significantly increase compliance costs, and discourage innovation and technological advances without providing a significant public health benefit. In response, the FDA withdrew and later reissued its early guidance pertaining to Part 11.[5] It continues to produce updated guidance as technology changes.

Annex 11 in Volume 4 of the EU GMP Guidelines similarly defines electronic records and electronic signatures. Its first iteration was published in 1991. Subsequent versions of these guidelines have since been released in response to technological advancements. Its most recent revision went into operation in June 2011.

The Software Development Lifecycle

Terminology

The terms Validation, Qualification, and Verification are often used interchangeably and are sometimes presented as a single concept. However, these three terms are not equivalent. Instead, they represent three distinct groups of activities related to software usability in a regulated environment.

The FDA defines Validation as "confirmation by examination and provision of objective evidence that software specifications conform to user needs and intended uses, and that the particular requirements implemented through software can be consistently fulfilled."[6] Validation utilizes results and documentation obtained through verification activities as evidence, but it requires additional testing (e.g., simulated use environments and usability testing). It proves that results, as experienced by the user, meet the specified requirements in the initial Validation Plan.

What sets Validation apart from Qualification and Verification is the level of documentation. Validation requires a more extensive document set and is a separate activity unto itself. For clarification, it is essential to remember that Validation is both the overarching point of the entire effort and a description of individual results within the process. Simply validating a single phase of the development process through verification or qualification is insufficient to achieve a truly validated system.

---

4 21CFR11.1(a)

5 United States, FDA. (2003, August). Guidance for Industry Part 11, Electronic Records; Electronic Signatures — Scope and Application. Retrieved from https://www.fda.gov/regulatory-information/search-fda-guidance-documents/part-11-electronic-records-electronic-signatures-scope-and-application

6 United States, FDA. (2002, January). Guidance for Industry: General Principles of Software Validation. January 2002. Retrieved from h at https://www.fda.gov/regulatory-information/search-fda-guidance-documents/general-principles-software-validation

Qualification, as it relates to CSV, is defined in guidance as the "action of proving and documenting that equipment or ancillary systems are properly installed, work correctly, and actually lead to the expected results."[7] Inside a formal CSV process, qualification exists in two places:

1. an individual process within the larger Validation effort that proves the success of a given phase (i.e., Installation Qualification, Operation Qualification, and Process Qualification)

2. a separate process in which qualification serves as an abbreviated version of validation for circumstances requiring a less rigorous degree of documentation, such as the qualification of a macro (i.e., a set of functions that perform a specific calculation) or a COTS (commercial off-the-shelf) system.

Verification, as described by the FDA, "provides objective evidence that the design outputs of a particular phase of the software development life cycle meet all of the specified requirements for that phase."[8] Therefore, verification is the result of testing. Evidence is built through specific documentation of actions such as static analysis, dynamic analysis, walkthroughs, and inspections during each step and activity.[9] Verification activities are intended to confirm that the software meets its stated design specifications and intended purpose in isolation away from the production environment.

WATERFALL

Computer System Validation processes have historically been structured around the Waterfall Methodology, a project management approach utilizing a downward, linear flow of sequential phases where the product of each phase feeds the next. It is a hierarchical approach that moves from highest-level concepts down to more detailed and refined concepts.

> ***Excessive documentation*** has become the Achilles' heel of the Waterfall Method in the current era

The Waterfall Model is the traditional process model utilized in software engineering. Dr. Winston Royce is credited with the first printed diagram of what would eventually become known as the Waterfall Model in his 1970 paper entitled, "Managing the Development of Large Software Systems." In this paper, Royce built the method's foundation and proffered his view that "management of software is simply impossible without a very high degree

7 European Union, EMA, GCP IWG. (2021, March). Guideline on computerised systems and electronic data in clinical trials. EMA/226170/2021. Retrieved from https://www.ema.europa.eu/en/documents/regulatory-procedural-guideline/draft-guideline-computerised-systems-electronic-data-clinical-trials_en.pdf

8 United States, FDA. (2002, January). Guidance for Industry: General Principles of Software Validation. January 2002. Retrieved from at https://www.fda.gov/regulatory-information/search-fda-guidance-documents/general-principles-software-validation

9 United States, FDA. (2002, January). Guidance for Industry: General Principles of Software Validation. January 2002. Retrieved from https://www.fda.gov/regulatory-information/search-fda-guidance-documents/general-principles-software-validation

of documentation."[10] The application of Royce's philosophy on documentation became the cornerstone of Validation practices for regulated industries. As technology has accelerated and expanded, so has the magnitude of compulsory documentation. Subsequently, the burden of excessive documentation has become the Achilles' heel of the Waterfall Method in the current era.

Figure 1 demonstrates an example of a fundamental Waterfall sequence.

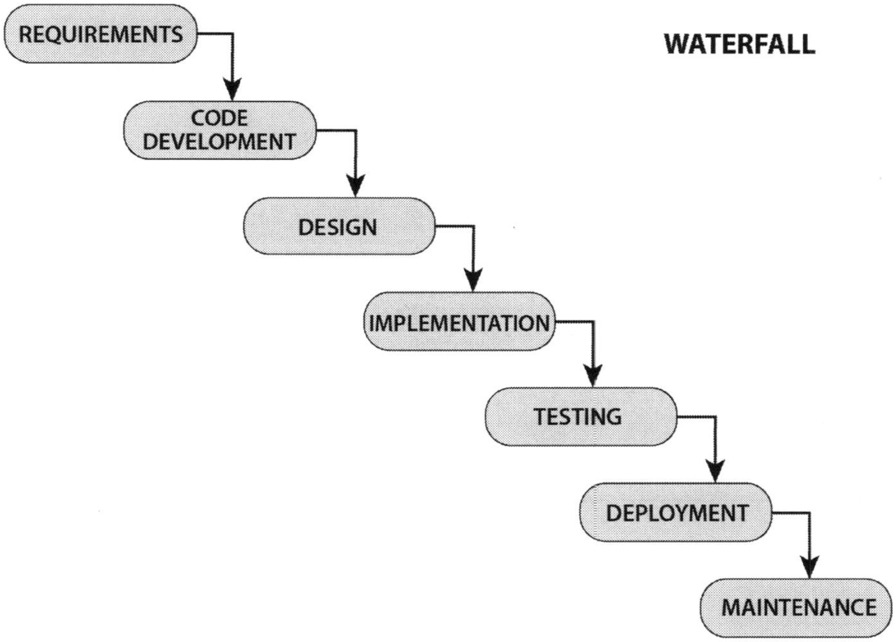

Figure 1 Waterfall Example

V-Model of Validation

In CVS, Waterfall is the foundation of the larger Validation process. The V-Model of Validation expands the process to meet the demands set by regulation. A basic V-Model is illustrated in Figure 2. In this example, the familiar downward flow defines the project and drives it toward implementation. It is then paired with its mirror image—an upward, sequential progression of testing and integration designed to qualify (e.g., Installation Qualification, Operational Qualification, Performance Qualification, or IQ/OQ/PQ) each initial phase.

The CSV process begins with a Validation Plan represented at the highest level on the left side of the V-Model diagram. Each subsequent phase becomes more detailed and specific until the

10 Royce, W. (1970, August). Managing the Development of Large Software Systems. Proceedings, IEEE WESCON, 1-9. Retrieved from at http://www-scf.usc.edu/~csci201/lectures/Lecture11/royce1970.pdf

project reaches implementation. Thorough documentation defining each phase is required. The right side of the diagram moves upward from implementation toward the Validation Report. These phases represent testing and evidence collection activities, which provide the evidence to support the corresponding step on the left. The entire purpose of the Validation Report is to describe everything that happened from implementation to plan completion, including failures in testing and deviations from the original Validation Plan. The Validation Report tells the story of the process and ties together the evidence proving that the system is fit for purpose.

Figure 2 illustrates a typical Software Development Lifecycle V-model demonstrating the linear progression of phases and the relationship between phases.

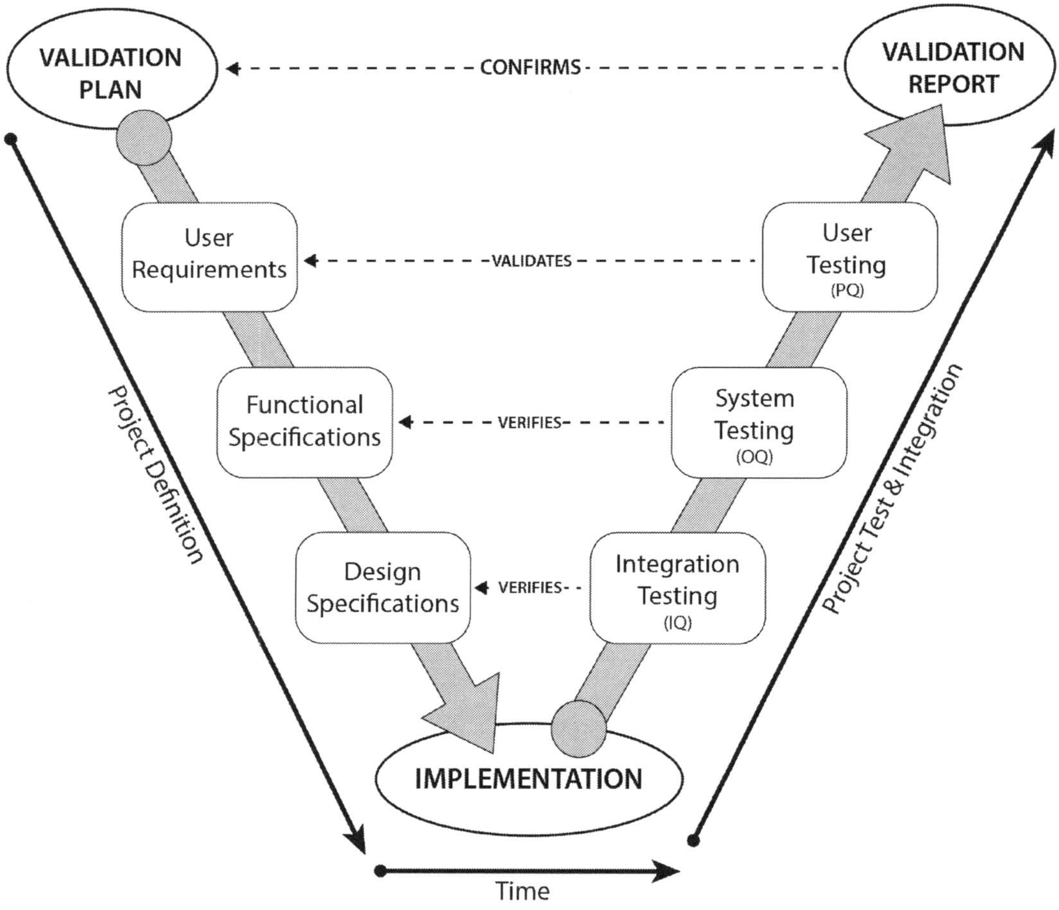

Figure 2 Software Development V-Model

CSV Limitations

As technology advances, the computerized systems associated with the pharmaceutical and medical device industries inevitably become more complex and highly integrated. As a result, the quantity of information collected, managed, and stored by these systems continues to expand at a rapid pace.

One of the most significant obstacles associated with CSV in practice is the proliferation of common misunderstandings and excessive interpretation of regulations. Additionally, a focus on fictional scenarios and "what ifs" rather than factual instances of agency findings can result in lost revenue for the manufacturer. Critical to Pharmaceutical Research and Development (R&D), commercial development, and sales is a proper understanding of what the regulations require and how those requirements can be met with modern, agile, and ever-changing technology. This is especially true of operations that support technology. Minutiae-driven scrutiny by internal quality groups can produce a form of "analysis paralysis" that can stunt the growth of a company's pipeline and endanger patients by inhibiting the timely delivery of revolutionary products.

The price (for both companies and patients) of slow development pipelines can be attributed, in part, to lagging technology. Lagging technology can be blamed for target acquisition and slow trial development due to fear of mishandled results secondary to failed CSV rather than the actual results of studies that rely on CSV to document results.

The Future

Agile and Computer System Assurance

It is no secret that technology moves faster than laws and regulations. As software development companies moved into the highly regulated life sciences environment, they brought newer, more streamlined Agile Methodologies, initiating a conceptual shift in industry and the bodies that govern it toward a model known as Computer System Assurance (CSA). CSA is structured around faster development cycles that utilize risk analysis. In response, regulators and regulations have found it necessary to catch up with technological advancements, leaving companies to navigate through uncharted territory. Consequently, industry professionals have been effectively stuck between shifting regulatory interpretations and conventional corporate paradigms.

While it may seem that regulatory requirements and corporate expectations are at odds with one another, they are not. Ultimately, industry and agencies are aligned: patient safety must remain paramount, and research and the resultant life-improving products must make it to market faster. Therefore, regulations must not hinder business, and businesses must not injure patients.

CSA relies on 80% testing and 20% documentation. CSA depends upon a system of controls that compare documented risks to the evidence that specific risks have been considered and mitigated (where mitigation is necessary). These controls can be evidenced through many control frameworks (such as SOC2 Type 2, HITRUST, HIPAA, and others) that third-parties can easily audit. This type of repeatable control and audit structure also allows for the use of third-party, cloud-based platforms and greater reliance on vendors. By spreading out responsibilities in this manner, companies will be able to accelerate innovation and compliance, resulting in better outcomes for patients and companies alike.

A hallmark of Agile Methodologies is the sprint. Sprint cycles are iterative and allow for failures to be identified and addressed as development continues, reducing time and required documentation while maintaining traceability.

As of the writing of this book, the FDA has delivered public presentations at conferences with specific talking points supporting its acceptance of the concept of Computer System Assurance,[11] but has not released any formal guidance. Its issuance is anticipated on the Federal docket register in 2021.[12]

Figure 3 illustrates a sample Sprint Cycle. The overall process begins with a validation plan and ends with a validation report. The cycle of development, testing, and integration repeats as often as required to address failures and changes until the software is ready for delivery.

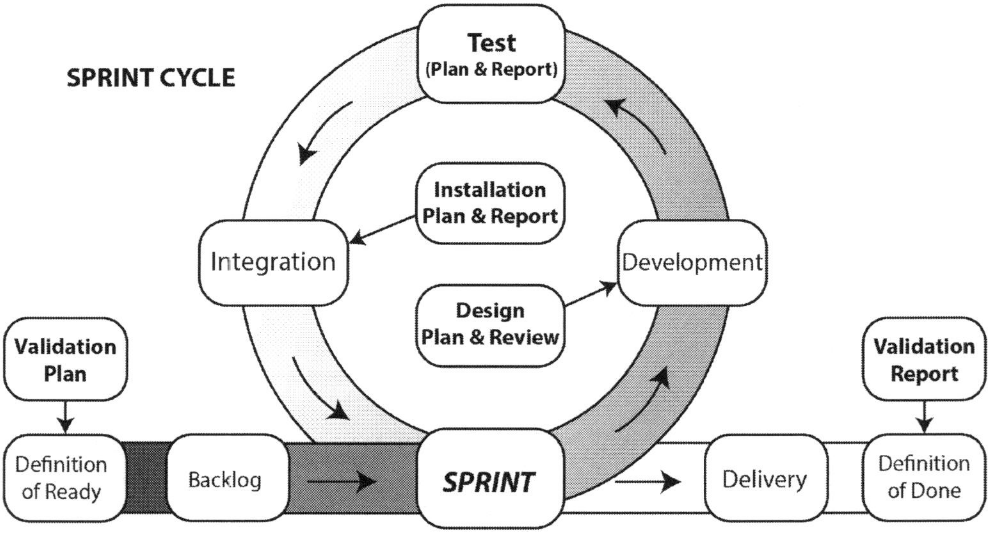

Figure 3 Sprint Cycle

AGILE/WATERFALL HYBRID

Companies evolving from Waterfall to Agile will benefit from a temporary hybrid bridge. This Hybrid Methodology begins to build a continuous integration and continuous development

11 United States, FDA. Regulatory Information. Retrieved January 2021 from https://www.fda.gov/regulatory-information/search-fda-guidance-documents

12 United States, FDA. News & Events for Human Drugs. Retrieved January 2021 from https://www.fda.gov/drugs/news-events-human-drugs guidance-documents

mindset within the organization. Rather than having an initial approved Validation Plan that ends with a final approved Validation Report, these reports are continuously updated as test cycles are opened and closed. This allows the company to evolve toward an Agile mindset while retaining more familiar Waterfall knowledge. This hybrid approach is a corporate transformation toolset, allowing evolution to Agile Methodology.

While computer system validation methodology has been the standard in the industry for several decades, a shift has begun. The goal is to integrate Agile methodologies into the regulated environments of pharmaceuticals and medical devices without endangering patients. The ultimate result of this integration is yet to be fully realized; however, companies and governing bodies are moving in that direction.

Figure 4 illustrates an example of a Hybrid flow in a GxP System.

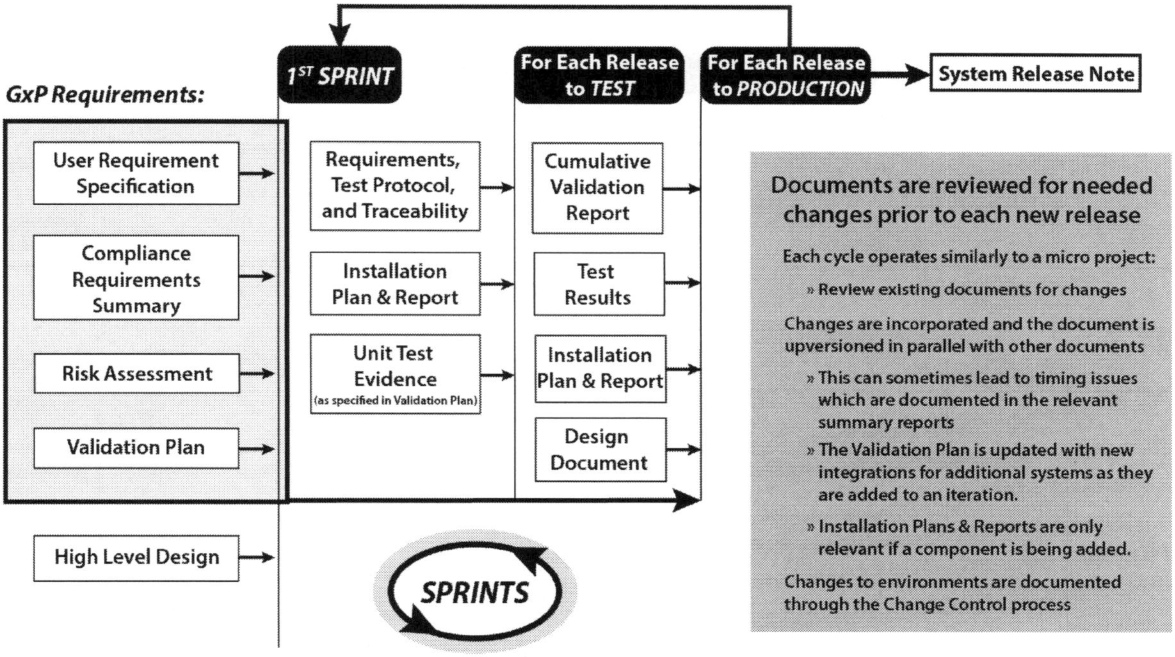

Figure 4 Agile/Waterfall Hybrid

CSV

Chapter 3
United States Code of Federal Regulation Title 21 Overview

The Food and Drug Administration (FDA)

The United States Food and Drug Administration (FDA) is responsible for protecting and promoting the nation's public health.

The programs for safety regulation vary widely by the type of product, its potential risks, and the regulatory powers granted to the Agency. For example, the FDA regulates almost every facet of prescription drugs, including testing, manufacturing, labeling, advertising, marketing, efficacy, and safety. FDA regulation of cosmetics, however, is focused primarily on labeling and safety. The FDA regulates most products with a set of published standards enforced by a combination of facility inspections, voluntary company reporting standards, and public and consumer watchdog activity.

The FDA frequently works in conjunction with other Federal agencies, including the Department of Agriculture, Drug Enforcement Administration, Customs and Border Protection, and Consumer Product Safety Commission.

Historical Origins of Federal Food and Drug Regulation

Historically, there were few federal laws regulating the contents and sale of domestically produced food and pharmaceuticals before the 20th century (with one exception being the short-lived Vaccine Act of 1813). Some state laws provided varying degrees of protection against unethical sales practices, such as misrepresenting the ingredients of food products or therapeutic substances.

The history of the FDA can be traced to the latter part of the 19th century and the U.S. Department of Agriculture's Division of Chemistry (later Bureau of Chemistry). Under Harvey Washington Wiley, appointed chief chemist in 1883, the Division began conducting research into the adulteration and misbranding of food and drugs on the American market. Although they had no regulatory powers, the Division published its findings from 1887 to 1902 in a ten-part series entitled Foods and Food Adulterants. Wiley used these findings and alliances with diverse organizations (such as state regulators, the General Federation of Women's Clubs, and national associations of physicians and pharmacists) to lobby for a new federal law to set uniform food and drugs standards to enter into interstate commerce.

Wiley's advocacy came at a time when the public had become alert to hazards in the marketplace by journalists and became part of a general trend for increased federal regulation in matters pertinent to public safety during the Progressive Era.[1] The 1902 Biologics Control Act was put in place after diphtheria antitoxin was collected from a horse named Jim, who also had tetanus, resulting in several deaths.

The 1906 Food and Drug Act and Creation of the FDA

In June 1906, President Theodore Roosevelt signed into law the Food and Drug Act, also known as the "Wiley Act," after its chief advocate.[2] Under penalty of seizure of goods, the Act prohibited the interstate transport of food that had been "adulterated." The term "adulterated" meant the use of added fillers, a reduction in "quality or strength," the addition of coloring to conceal "damage or inferiority," the use of "filthy, decomposed, or putrid" substances, and formulations with additives shown to be "injurious to health." The Act applied similar penalties to the interstate marketing of "adulterated" drugs, in which the "standard of strength, quality, or purity" of the active ingredient was not either stated clearly on the label or listed in the United States Pharmacopoeia or the National Formulary. The Act also banned "misbranding" of food and drugs.[3] The responsibility for examining food and drugs for such "adulteration" or "misbranding" was given to Wiley's USDA Bureau of Chemistry.[4] Strength, quality, identity, potency, and purity (SQuIPP) are currently the key product safety standards, with only two measures added since the 1906 Act.

Wiley used these new regulatory powers to pursue an aggressive campaign against the manufacturers of foods with chemical additives. The Chemistry Bureau's authority was soon checked by judicial decisions and by the creation of two separate organizations within the USDA: the Board of Food and Drug Inspection in 1907 and the Referee Board of Consulting Scientific Experts in 1908. A 1911 Supreme Court decision ruled that the 1906 act did not apply to false claims of therapeutic efficacy,[5] in response to which a 1912 amendment added "false and fraudulent" claims of "curative or therapeutic effect" to the Act's definition of "misbranded." However, these powers continued to be narrowly defined by the courts, which set high standards for proof of fraudulent intent.[6] In 1927, the Bureau of Chemistry's regulatory powers were reorganized under a new USDA body, the Food, Drug, and Insecticide organization. This name was shortened to the Food and Drug Administration (FDA) three years later.[7]

The 1938 Food, Drug, and Cosmetic Act

By the 1930s, muckraking journalists, consumer protection organizations, and federal regulators began mounting a campaign for stronger regulatory authority by publicizing a list of injurious products which had been ruled permissible under the 1906 law. The list included radioactive beverages, cosmetics that caused blindness, and worthless "cures" for diabetes and tuberculosis. The resulting proposed law was unable to pass through the Congress of the United States for five

1 History of the FDA at www.FDA.gov.
2 History of the FDA at www.FDA.gov.
3 ext in quotation marks is the original text of the 1906 Food and Drugs Act and Amendments.
4 History of the FDA at www.FDA.gov.
5 United States v. Johnson (31 S. Ct. 627 May 29, 1911, decided).
6 History of the FDA at www.FDA.gov.
7 Milestones in U.S. Food and Drug Law History at www.FDA.gov.

years. However, it was rapidly enacted into law following the public outcry over the 1937 Elixir Sulfanilamide tragedy, in which over 100 people died after using a drug formulated with a toxic, untested solvent. The only grounds on which the FDA could seize the product was misbranding. The product was branded as an "Elixir." An "elixir" was defined as a medication dissolved in ethanol, not the diethylene glycol used in the Elixir Sulfanilamide.

President Franklin Delano Roosevelt signed the new Food, Drug, and Cosmetic Act (FD&C Act) into law on June 24, 1938. The new law significantly increased federal regulatory authority over drugs by mandating a pre-market review of the safety of all new drugs and banning false therapeutic claims in drug labeling without requiring that the FDA prove fraudulent intent. The law also authorized factory inspections and expanded enforcement powers, set new regulatory standards for foods, and brought cosmetics and therapeutic devices under federal regulatory authority. This law, though extensively amended in subsequent years, remains the central foundation of FDA regulatory authority to the present day.[8]

Early FD&C Act amendments: 1938-1958

Soon after passage of the 1938 Act, the FDA began to designate certain drugs as safe for use only under the supervision of a medical professional, and the category of "prescription-only" drugs was securely codified into law by the 1951 Durham-Humphrey Amendment.[9] While pre-market testing of drug efficacy was not authorized under the 1938 FD&C Act, subsequent amendments such as the Insulin Amendment and Penicillin Amendment did mandate potency testing for formulations of specific lifesaving pharmaceuticals.[10] The FDA began enforcing its new powers against drug manufacturers who could not substantiate their drugs' efficacy claims. The United States Court of Appeals for the Ninth Circuit ruling in Alberty Food Products Co. v. United States (1950) found that drug manufacturers could not evade the "false therapeutic claims" provision of the 1938 Act by simply omitting the intended use of a drug from the drug's label. These developments confirmed extensive powers for the FDA to enforce post-marketing recalls of ineffective drugs.[11] During this era, much of the FDA's regulatory attention was directed toward the abuse of amphetamines and barbiturates, but the Agency also reviewed some 13,000 new drug applications between 1938 and 1962. While the science of toxicology was in its infancy at the start of this era, rapid advances in experimental assays for food additive and drug safety testing were made during this period by FDA regulators and others.[12]

Good Manufacturing Practices vs. Current Good Manufacturing Practices

The terms "Good Manufacturing Practices (GMPs)" and "Current Good Manufacturing Practices (CGMPs or cGMPs[13])" are often used interchangeably both in industry and by FDA inspectors.

---

8 History of the FDA at www.FDA.gov.

9 History of the FDA at www.FDA.gov.

10 Milestones in U.S. Food and Drug Law History at www.FDA.gov

11 History of the FDA at www.FDA.gov.

12 History of the FDA at www.FDA.gov.

13 The lower case "c" was coined in industry to differentiate between the law, emphasized with capital letters, and the current accepted industry practice not mandated by law..

"Good Manufacturing Practices" generally refers to the legal mandates detailed in Title 21 of the Code of Federal Regulations (21CFR). "Current Good Manufacturing Practices" refers not only to the legal requirements but to the guidance provided by the FDA and the standards practiced in industry that are not memorialized as law.

Organizational Structure

The FDA is an agency within the United States Department of Health and Human Services responsible for protecting and promoting the nation's public health. It is organized into the following subdivisions, each focused on a major area of regulatory responsibility:

- ❑ The Office of the Commissioner (OC)
- ❑ The Center for Drug Evaluation and Research (CDER)
- ❑ The Center for Biologics Evaluation and Research (CBER)
- ❑ The Center for Food Safety and Applied Nutrition (CFSAN)
- ❑ The Center for Devices and Radiological Health (CDRH)
- ❑ The Center for Veterinary Medicine (CVM)
- ❑ The National Center for Toxicological Research (NCTR)
- ❑ The Office of Regulatory Affairs (ORA)
- ❑ The Office of Criminal Investigations (OCI)

How does the FDA communicate with Industry?

Code of Federal Regulations[14]

The Code of Federal Regulations (CFR) is the codification of general and permanent rules and regulations (sometimes called administrative law) published in the Federal Register by the executive departments and agencies of the Federal Government of the United States. The CFR is issued by the Office of the Federal Register, an agency of the National Archives and Records Administration (NARA).

The CFR is divided into 50 titles that represent broad areas subject to Federal regulation. Title 21 is the portion of the Code of Federal Regulations that governs food and drugs within the United States for the Food and Drug Administration (FDA), the Drug Enforcement Administration (DEA), and the Office of National Drug Control Policy (ONDCP).

It is divided into three chapters based on the governing regulatory entity:

Chapter I — Food and Drug Administration

Chapter II — Drug Enforcement Administration

Chapter III — Office of National Drug Control Policy

14 Available CFR Titles on GPO Access at http://www.access.gpo.gov/nara/cfr/cfr-table-search.html#page1

Guidance Documents

Guidance documents represent the Agency's current thinking on a particular subject. They do not create or confer any rights for or on any person and do not operate to bind FDA or the public. An alternative approach may be used if such approach satisfies the requirements of the applicable statute, regulations, or both. For information on a specific guidance document, please contact the originating office. Another method of obtaining guidance documents is through the Division of Drug Information.

Federal Register

The Federal Register (since March 14, 1936), abbreviated FR or Fed. Reg. is the official journal of the United States' federal government containing most routine publications and public notices of government agencies. It is a daily (except holidays) publication.

The Federal Register is compiled by the Office of the Federal Register (within the National Archives and Records Administration) and is printed by the Government Printing Office.

There are no copyright restrictions on the Federal Register as it is a work of the U.S. government. It is in the public domain.[15]

Citations from the Federal Register are [volume] FR [page number] ([date]), e.g., 65 FR 741 (2000-10-01).

Direct Communication and Letters

The FDA interacts with consumers, health professionals, and industry representatives through letters, meetings (requested by either the FDA or the industry representatives), and telephone calls.

While not all questions can be answered over the phone, the FDA prefers telephone interactions over physical meetings (when a teleconference can reasonably replace a face-to-face meeting).

www.FDA.gov

The FDA maintains a website at www.fda.gov that is focused on three key audiences:

- ❑ consumers
- ❑ health professionals
- ❑ industry representatives

Through collaboration with users in testing site-wide designs, FDA.gov provides online access to its guidance documents, communication with industry, consumers, and health professionals. Information is categorized by topic, with related subjects consolidated in sections on the site.

Additionally, FDA.gov provides a search engine for Title 21 of the CFR that makes finding keyword references throughout the title more accessible.

15 The Federal Register at the GPO, online in both text and PDF, from 1994 on.

Conferences

The FDA routinely sends speakers to industry conferences where they are available to answer questions on their particular area of expertise.

False Statement to a Federal Agency

The U.S. Code of Federal Regulations (CFR) makes it a federal crime for anyone willfully and knowingly to make a false or fraudulent statement to a department or agency of the United States. The false statement must be related to a material matter, and the defendant must have acted willfully and with knowledge of the falsity. It is not necessary to show that the government agency was, in fact, deceived or misled. The issue of materiality is one of law for the courts. The maximum penalty is five years' imprisonment and a $10,000 fine.

A person may be guilty of a violation without proof that he or she had knowledge that the matter was within a federal agency's jurisdiction. A businessperson may violate this law by making a false statement to another firm or person with knowledge that the information will be submitted to a government agency. Businesses must take care to avoid exaggerations in the context of any matter that may come within the jurisdiction of a federal agency.

CFR Title 21

Food and Drugs: Parts 1 to 1499[16]

Chapter I — Food and Drug Administration, Department of Health and Human Services

Subchapter A- General

(1) General enforcement regulations

(2) General administrative rulings and decisions

(3) Product jurisdiction

(4) Regulation of Combination Products

(5) Organization

(7) Enforcement policy

(10) Administrative practices and procedures

(11) Electronic records; electronic signatures

(12) Formal evidentiary public hearing

(13) Public hearing before a public board of inquiry

(14) Public hearing before a public advisory committee

(15) Public hearing before the commissioner

(16) Regulatory hearing before the food and drug administration

(17) Civil money penalties hearings

(19) Standards of conduct and conflicts of interest

(20) Public information

(21) Protection of privacy

(25) Environmental impact considerations

(26) Mutual recognition of pharmaceutical good manufacturing practice reports, medical device quality system audit reports, and certain medical device product evaluation reports: United States and the European community

(50) Protection of human subjects

(54) Financial disclosure by clinical investigators

(56) Institutional review boards

(58) Good laboratory practice for nonclinical laboratory studies

(60) Patent term restoration

(70) Color additives

16 All of the 21CFR regulations can be searched online for no charge at https://www.ecfr.gov/cgi-bin/ECFR?page=browse

(71) Color additive petitions

(73) Listing of color additives exempt from certification

(74) Listing of color additives subject to certification

(80) Color additive certification

(81) General specifications and general restrictions for provisional color additives for use in foods, drugs, and cosmetics

(82) Listing of certified provisionally listed colors and specifications

(83-98) [reserved]

(99) Dissemination of information on unapproved/new uses for marketed drugs, biologics, and devices

Subchapter B – Food for Human Consumption

(100) General

(101) Food labeling

(102) Common or usual name for nonstandardized foods

(104) Nutritional quality guidelines for foods

(105) Foods for special dietary use

(106) Infant formula requirements pertaining to current good manufacturing practice, quality control procedures, quality factors, records and reports, and notifications

(107) Infant formula

(108) Emergency permit control

(109) Unavoidable contaminants in food for human consumption and food-packaging material

(110) Current good manufacturing practice in manufacturing, packing, or holding human food

(111) Current good manufacturing practice in manufacturing, packaging, labeling, or holding operations for dietary supplements

(112) Standards for the growing, harvesting, packing, and holding of produce for human consumption

(113) Thermally processed low-acid foods packaged in hermetically sealed containers

(114) Acidified foods

(115) Shell eggs

(117) Current good manufacturing practice, hazard analysis, and risk-based preventive controls for human food

(118) Production, storage, and transportation of shell eggs

(119) Dietary supplements that present a significant or unreasonable risk

(120) Hazard analysis and critical control point (HACCP) systems

(121) Mitigation strategies to protect food against intentional adulteration
(123) Fish and fishery products
(129) Processing and bottling of bottled drinking water
(130) Food standards: general
(131) Milk and cream
(133) Cheeses and related cheese products
(135) Frozen desserts
(136) Bakery products
(137) Cereal flours and related products
(139) Macaroni and noodle products
(145) Canned fruits
(146) Canned fruit juices
(150) Fruit butters, jellies, preserves, and related products
(152) Fruit pies
(155) Canned vegetables
(156) Vegetable juices
(158) Frozen vegetables
(160) Eggs and egg products
(161) Fish and shellfish
(163) Cacao products
(164) Tree nut and peanut products
(165) Beverages
(166) Margarine
(168) Sweeteners and table syrups
(169) Food dressings and flavorings
(170) Food additives
(171) Food additive petitions
(172) Food additives permitted for direct addition to food for human consumption
(173) Secondary direct food additives permitted in food for human consumption
(174) Indirect food additives: general
(175) Indirect food additives: adhesives and components of coatings
(176) Indirect food additives: paper and paperboard components
(177) Indirect food additives: polymers
(178) Indirect food additives: adjuvants, production aids, and sanitizers
(179) Irradiation in the production, processing and handling of food

(180) Food additives permitted in food or in contact with food on an interim basis pending additional study

(181) Prior-sanctioned food ingredients

(182) Substances generally recognized as safe

(184) Direct food substances affirmed as generally recognized as safe

(186) Indirect food substances affirmed as generally recognized as safe

(189) Substances prohibited from use in human food

(190) Dietary supplements

(191-199) [reserved]

Subchapter C – Drugs: General

(200) General

(201) Labeling

(202) Prescription drug advertising

(203) Prescription drug marketing

(205) Guidelines for state licensing of wholesale prescription drug distributors

(206) Imprinting of solid oral dosage form drug products for human use

(207) Requirements for foreign and domestic establishment registration and listing for human drugs, including drugs that are regulated under a biologics license application, and animal drugs, and the National Drug Code

(208) Medication guides for prescription drug products

(209) Requirement for authorized dispensers and pharmacies to distribute a side effects statement

(210) Current good manufacturing practice in manufacturing, processing, packing, or holding of drugs; general

(211) Current good manufacturing practice for finished pharmaceuticals

(212) Current good manufacturing practice for positron emission tomography drugs

(216) Pharmacy compounding

(225) Current good manufacturing practice for medicated feeds

(226) Current good manufacturing practice for type A medicated articles

(250) Special requirements for specific human drugs

(290) Controlled drugs

(299) Drugs; official names and established names

Subchapter D - New Drugs and Over-the-Counter Drug Products/Drugs for Human Use

(300) General

(310) New drugs

(312) Investigational new drug application

(314) Applications for FDA approval to market a new drug

(315) Diagnostic radiopharmaceuticals

(316) Orphan drugs

(317) Qualifying pathogens

(320) Bioavailability and bioequivalence requirements

(328) Over-the-counter drug products intended for oral ingestion that contain alcohol

(329) Nonprescription human drug products subject to section 760 of the Federal Food, Drug, and Cosmetic Act

(330) Over-the-counter (OTC) human drugs which are generally recognized as safe and effective and not misbranded

(331) Antacid products for over-the-counter (OTC) human use

(332) Antiflatulent products for over-the-counter human use

(333) Topical antimicrobial drug products for over-the-counter recognized as safe and effective and not misbranded

(335) Antidiarrheal drug products for over-the-counter human use

(336) Antiemetic drug products for over-the-counter human use

(338) Nighttime sleep-aid drug products for over-the-counter human use

(340) Stimulant drug products for over-the-counter human use

(341) Cold, cough, allergy, bronchodilator, and antiasthmatic drug products for over-the-counter human use

(343) Internal analgesic, antipyretic, and antirheumatic drug products for over-the-counter human use

(344) Topical OTIC drug products for over-the-counter human use

(346) Anorectal drug products for over-the-counter human use

(347) Skin protectant drug products for over-the-counter human use

(348) External analgesic drug products for over-the-counter human use

(349) Ophthalmic drug products for over-the-counter human use

(350) Antiperspirant drug products for over-the-counter human use

(352) Sunscreen drug products for over-the-counter human use [stayed indefinitely]

(355) Anticaries drug products for over-the-counter human use

(357) Miscellaneous internal drug products for over-the-counter human use

(358) Miscellaneous external drug products for over-the-counter human use

(361) Prescription drugs for human use generally recognized as safe and effective and not misbranded: drugs used in research

(369) Interpretative statements re warnings on drugs and devices for over-the-counter sale

(370-499) [reserved]

Subchapter E - Veterinary Products/Animal Drugs, Feeds, and Related Products

(500) General

(501) Animal food labeling

(502) Common or usual names for nonstandardized animal foods

(507) Current good manufacturing practice, hazard analysis, and risk-based preventive controls for food for animals

(509) Unavoidable contaminants in animal food and food-packaging material

(510) New animal drugs

(511) New animal drugs for investigational use

(514) New animal drug applications

(515) Medicated feed mill license

(516) New animal drugs for minor use and minor species

(520) Oral dosage form new animal drugs

(522) Implantation or injectable dosage form new animal drugs

(524) Ophthalmic and topical dosage form new animal drugs

(526) Intramammary dosage form new animal drugs

(528) New animal drugs in genetically engineered animals

(529) Certain other dosage form new animal drugs

(530) Extralabel drug use in animals

(556) Tolerances for residues of new animal drugs in food

(558) New animal drugs for use in animal feeds

(564) [reserved]

(570) Food additives

(571) Food additive petitions

(573) Food additives permitted in feed and drinking water of animals

(579) Irradiation in the production, processing, and handling of animal feed and pet food

(582) Substances generally recognized as safe

(584) Food substances affirmed as generally recognized as safe in feed and drinking water of animals

(589) Substances prohibited from use in animal food or feed

(590-599) [reserved]

Subchapter F - Biologics

(600) Biological products: general

(601) Licensing

(606) Current good manufacturing practice for blood and blood components

(607) Establishment registration and product listing for manufacturers of human blood and blood products

(610) General biological products standards

(630) Requirements for blood and blood components intended for transfusion or for further manufacturing use

(640) Additional standards for human blood and blood products

(660) Additional standards for diagnostic substances for laboratory tests

(680) Additional standards for miscellaneous products

Subchapter G – Cosmetics

(700) General

(701) Cosmetic labeling

(710) Voluntary registration of cosmetic product establishments

(720) Voluntary filing of cosmetic product ingredient composition statements

(740) Cosmetic product warning statements

(741-799) [reserved]

Subchapter H - Medical Devices

(800) General

(801) Labeling

(803) Medical device reporting

(806) Medical devices; reports of corrections and removals

(807) Establishment registration and device listing for manufacturers and initial importers of devices

(808) Exemptions from federal preemption of state and local medical device requirements

(809) In vitro diagnostic products for human use

(810) Medical device recall authority

(812) Investigational device exemptions

(813) [reserved]

(814) Premarket approval of medical devices

(820) Quality system regulation

(821) Medical device tracking requirements

(822) Postmarket surveillance

(830) Unique device identification

(860) Medical device classification procedures

(861) Procedures for performance standards development

(862) Clinical chemistry and clinical toxicology devices

(864) Hematology and pathology devices

(866) Immunology and microbiology devices

(868) Anesthesiology devices

(870) Cardiovascular devices

(872) Dental devices

(874) Ear, nose, and throat devices

(876) Gastroenterology-urology devices

(878) General and plastic surgery devices

(880) General hospital and personal use devices

(882) Neurological devices

(884) Obstetrical and gynecological devices

(886) Ophthalmic devices

(888) Orthopedic devices

(890) Physical medicine devices

(892) Radiology devices

(895) Banned devices

(898) Performance standard for electrode lead wires and patient cables

Subchapter I - Mammography Quality Standard Act

(900) Mammography

Subchapter J - Radiological Health

(1000) General

(1002) Records and reports

(1003) Notification of defects or failure to comply

(1004) Repurchase, repairs, or replacement of electronic products

(1005) Importation of electronic products

(1010) Performance standards for electronic products: general

(1020) Performance standards for ionizing radiation emitting products

(1030) Performance standards for microwave and radio frequency emitting products

(1040) Performance standards for light-emitting products

(1050) Performance standards for sonic, infrasonic, and ultrasonic radiation-emitting products

Subchapter K - Tobacco Products

(1100) Tobacco products subject to FDA authority

(1105) General

(1107) Establishment registration, product listing, and substantial equivalence reports

(1140) Cigarettes, smokeless tobacco, and covered tobacco products

(1141) Cigarette package and advertising warnings

(1143) Minimum required warning statements

(1150) User fees

Subchapter L - Regulations under Certain Other Acts

(1210) Regulations under the federal import milk act

(1230) Regulations under the federal caustic poison act

(1240) Control of communicable diseases

(1250) Interstate conveyance sanitation

(1251-1269) [reserved]

(1270) Human tissue intended for transplantation

(1271) Human cells, tissues, and cellular and tissue-based products

(1272-1299) [reserved]

Chapter II Drug Enforcement Administration, Department of Justice

Controlled Substances

(1300) Definitions

(1301) Registration of manufacturers, distributors, and dispensers of controlled substances

(1302) Labeling and packaging requirements for controlled substances

(1303) Quotas

(1304) Records and reports of registrants

(1305) Orders for schedule I and II controlled substances

(1306) Prescriptions

(1307) Miscellaneous

(1308) Schedules of controlled substances

(1309) Registration of manufacturers, distributors, importers and exporters of List I chemicals

(1310) Records and reports of listed chemicals and certain machines; importation and exportation of certain machines

(1311) Requirements for electronic orders and prescriptions

(1312) Importation and exportation of controlled substances

(1313) Importation and exportation of list I and list II chemicals

(1314) Retail sale of scheduled listed chemical products

(1315) Importation and production quotas for ephedrine, pseudoephedrine, and phenylpropanolamine

(1316) Administrative functions, practices, and procedures

(1317) Disposal

(1321) DEA mailing addresses

(1322-1399) [reserved]

CHAPTER III OFFICE OF NATIONAL DRUG CONTROL POLICY

(1400) [reserved]

(1401) Public availability of information

(1402) Mandatory declassification review

(1403-1499) [reserved]

REGULATIONS

21CFR

Chapter 4

Part 11 Electronic Records; Electronic Signatures

[Code of Federal Regulations]
[Title 21, Volume 1]
[Revised as of April 1, 2019]
[CITE: 21CFR11]

Title 21—Food and Drugs
Chapter I—Food and Drug Administration
Department of Health and Human Services
Subchapter A—General

PART 11 ELECTRONIC RECORDS; ELECTRONIC SIGNATURES[1,2]

SUBPART A—GENERAL PROVISIONS

SEC. 11.1 SCOPE.

(a) The regulations in this part set forth the criteria under which the agency considers electronic records, electronic signatures, and handwritten signatures executed to electronic records to be trustworthy, reliable, and generally equivalent to paper records and handwritten signatures executed on paper.

(b) This part applies to records in electronic form that are created, modified, maintained, archived, retrieved, or transmitted, under any records requirements set forth in agency regulations. This part also applies to electronic records submitted to the agency under requirements of the Federal Food, Drug, and Cosmetic Act and the Public Health Service Act, even if such records are not specifically identified in agency regulations. However, this part does not apply to paper records that are, or have been, transmitted by electronic means.

(c) Where electronic signatures and their associated electronic records meet the requirements of this part, the agency will consider the electronic signatures to be equivalent to full handwritten signatures, initials, and other general signings as required by agency regulations, unless specifically excepted by regulation(s) effective on or after August 20, 1997.

---

1 Authority: 21 U.S.C. 321-393; 42 U.S.C. 262. / Source: 62 FR 13464, Mar. 20, 1997, unless otherwise noted

2 21CFR§11 can be accessed online at https://www.accessdata.fda.gov/scripts/cdrh/cfdocs/cfcfr/CFRSearch.cfm?CFRPart=11

(d) Electronic records that meet the requirements of this part may be used in lieu of paper records, in accordance with 11.2, unless paper records are specifically required.

(e) Computer systems (including hardware and software), controls, and attendant documentation maintained under this part shall be readily available for, and subject to, FDA inspection.

(f) This part does not apply to records required to be established or maintained by 1.326 through 1.368 of this chapter. Records that satisfy the requirements of part 1, subpart J of this chapter, but that also are required under other applicable statutory provisions or regulations, remain subject to this part.

(g) This part does not apply to electronic signatures obtained under 101.11(d) of this chapter.

(h) This part does not apply to electronic signatures obtained under 101.8(d) of this chapter.

(i) This part does not apply to records required to be established or maintained by part 117 of this chapter. Records that satisfy the requirements of part 117 of this chapter, but that also are required under other applicable statutory provisions or regulations, remain subject to this part.

(j) This part does not apply to records required to be established or maintained by part 507 of this chapter. Records that satisfy the requirements of part 507 of this chapter, but that also are required under other applicable statutory provisions or regulations, remain subject to this part.

(k) This part does not apply to records required to be established or maintained by part 112 of this chapter. Records that satisfy the requirements of part 112 of this chapter, but that also are required under other applicable statutory provisions or regulations, remain subject to this part.

(l) This part does not apply to records required to be established or maintained by subpart L of part 1 of this chapter. Records that satisfy the requirements of subpart L of part 1 of this chapter, but that also are required under other applicable statutory provisions or regulations, remain subject to this part.

(m) This part does not apply to records required to be established or maintained by subpart M of part 1 of this chapter. Records that satisfy the requirements of subpart M of part 1 of this chapter, but that also are required under other applicable statutory provisions or regulations, remain subject to this part.

(n) This part does not apply to records required to be established or maintained by subpart O of part 1 of this chapter. Records that satisfy the requirements of subpart O of part 1 of this chapter, but that also are required under other applicable statutory provisions or regulations, remain subject to this part.

(o) This part does not apply to records required to be established or maintained by part 121 of this chapter. Records that satisfy the requirements of part 121 of this chapter, but that also are required under other applicable statutory provisions or regulations, remain subject to this part.

[62 FR 13464, Mar. 20, 1997, as amended at 69 FR 71655, Dec. 9, 2004; 79 FR 71253, 71291, Dec. 1, 2014; 80 FR 71253, June 19, 2015; 80 FR 56144, 56336, Sept. 17, 2015; 80 FR 74352, 74547, 74667, Nov. 27, 2015; 81 FR 20170, Apr. 6, 2016; 81 FR 34218, May 27, 2016]

Sec. 11.2 Implementation.

(a) For records required to be maintained but not submitted to the agency, persons may use electronic records in lieu of paper records or electronic signatures in lieu of traditional signatures, in whole or in part, provided that the requirements of this part are met.

(b) For records submitted to the agency, persons may use electronic records in lieu of paper records or electronic signatures in lieu of traditional signatures, in whole or in part, provided that:

(1) The requirements of this part are met; and

(2) The document or parts of a document to be submitted have been identified in public docket No. 92S-0251 as being the type of submission the agency accepts in electronic form. This docket will identify specifically what types of documents or parts of documents are acceptable for submission in electronic form without paper records and the agency receiving unit(s) (e.g., specific center, office, division, branch) to which such submissions may be made. Documents to agency receiving unit(s) not specified in the public docket will not be considered as official if they are submitted in electronic form; paper forms of such documents will be considered as official and must accompany any electronic records. Persons are expected to consult with the intended agency receiving unit for details on how (e.g., method of transmission, media, file formats, and technical protocols) and whether to proceed with the electronic submission.

Sec. 11.3 Definitions.

(a) The definitions and interpretations of terms contained in section 201 of the act apply to those terms when used in this part.

(b) The following definitions of terms also apply to this part:

(1) *Act* means the Federal Food, Drug, and Cosmetic Act (secs. 201-903 (21 U.S.C. 321-393)).

(2) *Agency* means the Food and Drug Administration.

(3) *Biometrics* means a method of verifying an individual's identity based on measurement of the individual's physical feature(s) or repeatable action(s) where those features and/or actions are both unique to that individual and measurable.

(4) *Closed system* means an environment in which system access is controlled by persons who are responsible for the content of electronic records that are on the system.

(5) *Digital signature* means an electronic signature based upon cryptographic methods of originator authentication, computed by using a set of rules and a set of parameters such that the identity of the signer and the integrity of the data can be verified.

(6) *Electronic record* means any combination of text, graphics, data, audio, pictorial, or other information representation in digital form that is created, modified, maintained, archived, retrieved, or distributed by a computer system.

(7) *Electronic signature* means a computer data compilation of any symbol or series of symbols executed, adopted, or authorized by an individual to be the legally binding equivalent of the individual's handwritten signature.

(8) *Handwritten signature* means the scripted name or legal mark of an individual handwritten by that individual and executed or adopted with the present intention to authenticate a writing in a permanent form. The act of signing with a writing or marking instrument such as a pen or stylus is preserved. The scripted name or legal mark, while conventionally applied to paper, may also be applied to other devices that capture the name or mark.

(9) *Open system* means an environment in which system access is not controlled by persons who are responsible for the content of electronic records that are on the system.

Authority: 21 U.S.C. 321-393; 42 U.S.C. 262.
Source: 62 FR 13464, Mar. 20, 1997, unless otherwise noted.

Subpart B—Electronic Records

Sec. 11.10 Controls for closed systems.

Persons who use closed systems to create, modify, maintain, or transmit electronic records shall employ procedures and controls designed to ensure the authenticity, integrity, and, when appropriate, the confidentiality of electronic records, and to ensure that the signer cannot readily repudiate the signed record as not genuine. Such procedures and controls shall include the following:

(a) Validation of systems to ensure accuracy, reliability, consistent intended performance, and the ability to discern invalid or altered records.

(b) The ability to generate accurate and complete copies of records in both human readable and electronic form suitable for inspection, review, and copying by the agency. Persons should contact the agency if there are any questions regarding the ability of the agency to perform such review and copying of the electronic records.

(c) Protection of records to enable their accurate and ready retrieval throughout the records retention period.

(d) Limiting system access to authorized individuals.

(e) Use of secure, computer-generated, time-stamped audit trails to independently record the date and time of operator entries and actions that create, modify, or delete electronic records. Record changes shall not obscure previously recorded information. Such audit trail documentation shall be retained for a period at least as long as that required for the subject electronic records and shall be available for agency review and copying.

(f) Use of operational system checks to enforce permitted sequencing of steps and events, as appropriate.

(g) Use of authority checks to ensure that only authorized individuals can use the system, electronically sign a record, access the operation or computer system input or output device, alter a record, or perform the operation at hand.

(h) Use of device (e.g., terminal) checks to determine, as appropriate, the validity of the source of data input or operational instruction.

(i) Determination that persons who develop, maintain, or use electronic record/electronic signature systems have the education, training, and experience to perform their assigned tasks.

(j) The establishment of, and adherence to, written policies that hold individuals accountable and responsible for actions initiated under their electronic signatures, in order to deter record and signature falsification.

(k) Use of appropriate controls over systems documentation including:

(1) Adequate controls over the distribution of, access to, and use of documentation for system operation and maintenance.

(2) Revision and change control procedures to maintain an audit trail that documents time-sequenced development and modification of systems documentation.

Sec. 11.30 Controls for open systems.

Persons who use open systems to create, modify, maintain, or transmit electronic records shall employ procedures and controls designed to ensure the authenticity, integrity, and, as appropriate, the confidentiality of electronic records from the point of their creation to the point of their receipt. Such procedures and controls shall include those identified in 11.10, as appropriate, and additional measures such as document encryption and use of appropriate digital signature standards to ensure, as necessary under the circumstances, record authenticity, integrity, and confidentiality.

Sec. 11.50 Signature manifestations.

(a) Signed electronic records shall contain information associated with the signing that clearly indicates all of the following:

(1) The printed name of the signer;

(2) The date and time when the signature was executed; and

(3) The meaning (such as review, approval, responsibility, or authorship) associated with the signature.

(b) The items identified in paragraphs (a)(1), (a)(2), and (a)(3) of this section shall be subject to the same controls as for electronic records and shall be included as part of any human readable form of the electronic record (such as electronic display or printout).

Sec. 11.70 Signature/record linking.

Electronic signatures and handwritten signatures executed to electronic records shall be linked to their respective electronic records to ensure that the signatures cannot be excised, copied, or otherwise transferred to falsify an electronic record by ordinary means.

Authority: 21 U.S.C. 321-393; 42 U.S.C. 262.
Source: 62 FR 13464, Mar. 20, 1997, unless otherwise noted.

Subpart C—Electronic Signatures

Sec. 11.100 General requirements.

(a) Each electronic signature shall be unique to one individual and shall not be reused by, or reassigned to, anyone else.

(b) Before an organization establishes, assigns, certifies, or otherwise sanctions an individual's electronic signature, or any element of such electronic signature, the organization shall verify the identity of the individual.

(c) Persons using electronic signatures shall, prior to or at the time of such use, certify to the agency that the electronic signatures in their system, used on or after August 20, 1997, are intended to be the legally binding equivalent of traditional handwritten signatures.

(1) The certification shall be submitted in paper form and signed with a traditional handwritten signature, to the Office of Regional Operations (HFC-100), 5600 Fishers Lane, Rockville, MD 20857.

(2) Persons using electronic signatures shall, upon agency request, provide additional certification or testimony that a specific electronic signature is the legally binding equivalent of the signer's handwritten signature.

Sec. 11.200 Electronic signature components and controls.

(a) Electronic signatures that are not based upon biometrics shall:

(1) Employ at least two distinct identification components such as an identification code and password.

(i) When an individual executes a series of signings during a single, continuous period of controlled system access, the first signing shall be executed using all electronic signature components; subsequent signings shall be executed using at least one electronic signature component that is only executable by, and designed to be used only by, the individual.

(ii) When an individual executes one or more signings not performed during a single, continuous period of controlled system access, each signing shall be executed using all of the electronic signature components.

(2) Be used only by their genuine owners; and

(3) Be administered and executed to ensure that attempted use of an individual's electronic signature by anyone other than its genuine owner requires collaboration of two or more individuals.

(b) Electronic signatures based upon biometrics shall be designed to ensure that they cannot be used by anyone other than their genuine owners.

SEC. 11.300 CONTROLS FOR IDENTIFICATION CODES/PASSWORDS.

Persons who use electronic signatures based upon use of identification codes in combination with passwords shall employ controls to ensure their security and integrity. Such controls shall include:

(a) Maintaining the uniqueness of each combined identification code and password, such that no two individuals have the same combination of identification code and password.

(b) Ensuring that identification code and password issuances are periodically checked, recalled, or revised (e.g., to cover such events as password aging).

(c) Following loss management procedures to electronically deauthorize lost, stolen, missing, or otherwise potentially compromised tokens, cards, and other devices that bear or generate identification code or password information, and to issue temporary or permanent replacements using suitable, rigorous controls.

(d) Use of transaction safeguards to prevent unauthorized use of passwords and/or identification codes, and to detect and report in an immediate and urgent manner any attempts at their unauthorized use to the system security unit, and, as appropriate, to organizational management.

(e) Initial and periodic testing of devices, such as tokens or cards, that bear or generate identification code or password information to ensure that they function properly and have not been altered in an unauthorized manner.

Authority: 21 U.S.C. 321-393; 42 U.S.C. 262.
Source: 62 FR 13464, Mar. 20, 1997, unless otherwise noted.

21CFR

Chapter 5
Part 820 Quality System Regulation

[Code of Federal Regulations]
[Title 21, Volume 8]
[Revised as of April 1, 2017]
[CITE: 21CFR820]

Title 21—Food and Drugs
Chapter I—Food and Drug Administration
Department of Health and Human Services
Subchapter H—Medical Devices

Part 820 Quality System Regulation[1,2]
Subpart A—General Provisions

Sec. 820.1 Scope.

(a) Applicability.

(1) Current good manufacturing practice (CGMP) requirements are set forth in this quality system regulation. The requirements in this part govern the methods used in, and the facilities and controls used for, the design, manufacture, packaging, labeling, storage, installation, and servicing of all finished devices intended for human use. The requirements in this part are intended to ensure that finished devices will be safe and effective and otherwise in compliance with the Federal Food, Drug, and Cosmetic Act (the act). This part establishes basic requirements applicable to manufacturers of finished medical devices. If a manufacturer engages in only some operations subject to the requirements in this part, and not in others, that manufacturer need only comply with those requirements applicable to the operations in which it is engaged. With respect to class I devices, design controls apply only to those devices listed in §820.30(a)(2). This regulation does not apply to manufacturers of components or parts of finished devices, but such manufacturers are encouraged to use appropriate provisions of this regulation as guidance. Manufacturers of blood and blood components used for transfusion or for further manufacturing are not subject to this

1 Authority: 21 U.S.C. 351, 352, 360, 360c, 360d, 360e, 360h, 360i, 360j, 360l, 371, 374, 381, 383; 42 U.S.C. 216, 262, 263a, 264. / Source: 61 FR 52654, Oct. 7, 1996, unless otherwise noted.

2 21CFR§11 can be accessed online at https://www.accessdata.fda.gov/scripts/cdrh/cfdocs/cfcfr/CFRSearch.cfm?CFRPart=820

part, but are subject to subchapter F of this chapter. Manufacturers of human cells, tissues, and cellular and tissue-based products (HCT/Ps), as defined in §1271.3(d) of this chapter, that are medical devices (subject to premarket review or notification, or exempt from notification, under an application submitted under the device provisions of the act or under a biological product license application under section 351 of the Public Health Service Act) are subject to this part and are also subject to the donor-eligibility procedures set forth in part 1271 subpart C of this chapter and applicable current good tissue practice procedures in part 1271 subpart D of this chapter. In the event of a conflict between applicable regulations in part 1271 and in other parts of this chapter, the regulation specifically applicable to the device in question shall supersede the more general.

(2) The provisions of this part shall be applicable to any finished device as defined in this part, intended for human use, that is manufactured, imported, or offered for import in any State or Territory of the United States, the District of Columbia, or the Commonwealth of Puerto Rico.

(3) In this regulation the term "where appropriate" is used several times. When a requirement is qualified by "where appropriate," it is deemed to be "appropriate" unless the manufacturer can document justification otherwise. A requirement is "appropriate" if nonimplementation could reasonably be expected to result in the product not meeting its specified requirements or the manufacturer not being able to carry out any necessary corrective action.

(b) The quality system regulation in this part supplements regulations in other parts of this chapter except where explicitly stated otherwise. In the event of a conflict between applicable regulations in this part and in other parts of this chapter, the regulations specifically applicable to the device in question shall supersede any other generally applicable requirements.

(c) Authority. Part 820 is established and issued under authority of sections 501, 502, 510, 513, 514, 515, 518, 519, 520, 522, 701, 704, 801, 803 of the act (21 U.S.C. 351, 352, 360, 360c, 360d, 360e, 360h, 360i, 360j, 360l, 371, 374, 381, 383). The failure to comply with any applicable provision in this part renders a device adulterated under section 501(h) of the act. Such a device, as well as any person responsible for the failure to comply, is subject to regulatory action.

(d) Foreign manufacturers. If a manufacturer who offers devices for import into the United States refuses to permit or allow the completion of a Food and Drug Administration (FDA) inspection of the foreign facility for the purpose of determining compliance with this part, it shall appear for purposes of section 801(a) of the act, that the methods used in, and the facilities and controls used for, the design, manufacture, packaging, labeling, storage, installation, or servicing of any devices produced at such facility that are offered for import into the United States do not conform to the requirements of section 520(f) of the act and this part and that the devices manufactured at that facility are adulterated under section 501(h) of the act.

(e) Exemptions or variances.

(1) Any person who wishes to petition for an exemption or variance from any device quality system requirement is subject to the requirements of section 520(f)(2) of the Federal Food, Drug, and Cosmetic Act. Petitions for an exemption or variance shall be submitted according to the procedures set forth in §10.30 of this chapter, the FDA's administrative procedures. For guidance on how to proceed for a request for a variance, contact Division of Regulatory Programs 2, Office of Regulatory Programs, Office of Product Evaluation and Quality, Center for Devices and Radiological Health, Food and Drug Administration, 10903 New Hampshire Ave., Bldg. 66, Rm. 1438, Silver Spring, MD 20993-0002.

(2) FDA may initiate and grant a variance from any device quality system requirement when the agency determines that such variance is in the best interest of the public health. Such variance will remain in effect only so long as there remains a public health need for the device and the device would not likely be made sufficiently available without the variance.

[61 FR 52654, Oct. 7, 1996, as amended at 65 FR 17136, Mar. 31, 2000; 65 FR 66636, Nov. 7, 2000; 69 FR 29829, May 25, 2005; 72 FR 17399, Apr. 9, 2007; 75 FR 20915, Apr. 22, 2010; 80 FR 29906, May 22, 2015; 85 FR 18442, Apr. 2, 2020]

SEC. 820.3 DEFINITIONS.

(a) *Act* means the Federal Food, Drug, and Cosmetic Act, as amended (secs. 201-903, 52 Stat. 1040 et seq., as amended (21 U.S.C. 321-394)). All definitions in section 201 of the act shall apply to the regulations in this part.

(b) *Complaint* means any written, electronic, or oral communication that alleges deficiencies related to the identity, quality, durability, reliability, safety, effectiveness, or performance of a device after it is released for distribution.

(c) *Component* means any raw material, substance, piece, part, software, firmware, labeling, or assembly which is intended to be included as part of the finished, packaged, and labeled device.

(d) *Control number* means any distinctive symbols, such as a distinctive combination of letters or numbers, or both, from which the history of the manufacturing, packaging, labeling, and distribution of a unit, lot, or batch of finished devices can be determined.

(e) *Design history file (DHF)* means a compilation of records which describes the design history of a finished device.

(f) *Design input* means the physical and performance requirements of a device that are used as a basis for device design.

(g) *Design output* means the results of a design effort at each design phase and at the end of the total design effort. The finished design output is the basis for the device master record. The total finished design output consists of the device, its packaging and labeling, and the device master record.

(h) *Design review* means a documented, comprehensive, systematic examination of a design to evaluate the adequacy of the design requirements, to evaluate the capability of the design to meet these requirements, and to identify problems.

(i) *Device history record (DHR)* means a compilation of records containing the production history of a finished device.

(j) *Device master record (DMR)* means a compilation of records containing the procedures and specifications for a finished device.

(k) *Establish* means define, document (in writing or electronically), and implement.

(l) *Finished device* means any device or accessory to any device that is suitable for use or capable of functioning, whether or not it is packaged, labeled, or sterilized.

(m) *Lot* or *batch* means one or more components or finished devices that consist of a single type, model, class, size, composition, or software version that are manufactured under essentially the same conditions and that are intended to have uniform characteristics and quality within specified limits.

(n) *Management with executive responsibility* means those senior employees of a manufacturer who have the authority to establish or make changes to the manufacturer's quality policy and quality system.

(o) *Manufacturer* means any person who designs, manufactures, fabricates, assembles, or processes a finished device. Manufacturer includes but is not limited to those who perform the functions of contract sterilization, installation, relabeling, remanufacturing, repacking, or specification development, and initial distributors of foreign entities performing these functions.

(p) *Manufacturing material* means any material or substance used in or used to facilitate the manufacturing process, a concomitant constituent, or a byproduct constituent produced during the manufacturing process, which is present in or on the finished device as a residue or impurity not by design or intent of the manufacturer.

(q) *Nonconformity* means the nonfulfillment of a specified requirement.

(r) *Product* means components, manufacturing materials, in-process devices, finished devices, and returned devices.

(s) *Quality* means the totality of features and characteristics that bear on the ability of a device to satisfy fitness-for-use, including safety and performance.

(t) *Quality audit* means a systematic, independent examination of a manufacturer's quality system that is performed at defined intervals and at sufficient frequency to determine whether both quality system activities and the results of such activities comply with quality system procedures, that these procedures are implemented effectively, and that these procedures are suitable to achieve quality system objectives.

(u) *Quality policy* means the overall intentions and direction of an organization with respect to quality, as established by management with executive responsibility.

(v) *Quality system* means the organizational structure, responsibilities, procedures, processes, and resources for implementing quality management.

(w) *Remanufacturer* means any person who processes, conditions, renovates, repackages, restores, or does any other act to a finished device that significantly changes the finished device's performance or safety specifications, or intended use.

(x) *Rework* means action taken on a nonconforming product so that it will fulfill the specified DMR requirements before it is released for distribution.

(y) *Specification* means any requirement with which a product, process, service, or other activity must conform.

(z) *Validation* means confirmation by examination and provision of objective evidence that the particular requirements for a specific intended use can be consistently fulfilled.

(1) *Process validation* means establishing by objective evidence that a process consistently produces a result or product meeting its predetermined specifications.

(2) *Design validation* means establishing by objective evidence that device specifications conform with user needs and intended use(s).

(aa) *Verification* means confirmation by examination and provision of objective evidence that specified requirements have been fulfilled.

(bb) *Human cell, tissue, or cellular or tissue-based product (HCT/P) regulated as a device* means an HCT/P as defined in 1271.3(d) of this chapter that does not meet the criteria in 1271.10(a) and that is also regulated as a device.

(cc) *Unique device identifier (UDI)* means an identifier that adequately identifies a device through its distribution and use by meeting the requirements of 830.20 of this chapter. A unique device identifier is composed of:

(1) A device identifier —a mandatory, fixed portion of a UDI that identifies the specific version or model of a device and the labeler of that device; and

(2) A production identifier —a conditional, variable portion of a UDI that identifies one or more of the following when included on the label of the device:

(i) The lot or batch within which a device was manufactured;

(ii) The serial number of a specific device;

(iii) The expiration date of a specific device;

(iv) The date a specific device was manufactured.

(v) For an HCT/P regulated as a device, the distinct identification code required by 1271.290(c) of this chapter.

(dd) *Universal product code (UPC)* means the product identifier used to identify an item sold at retail in the United States.

[61 FR 52654, Oct. 7, 1996, as amended at 78 FR 58822, Sept. 24, 2013]

Sec. 820.5 Quality system.

Each manufacturer shall establish and maintain a quality system that is appropriate for the specific medical device(s) designed or manufactured, and that meets the requirements of this part.

Subpart B—Quality System Requirements

Sec. 820.20 Management responsibility.

(a) Quality policy. Management with executive responsibility shall establish its policy and objectives for, and commitment to, quality. Management with executive responsibility shall ensure that the quality policy is understood, implemented, and maintained at all levels of the organization.

(b) Organization. Each manufacturer shall establish and maintain an adequate organizational structure to ensure that devices are designed and produced in accordance with the requirements of this part.

(1) Responsibility and authority. Each manufacturer shall establish the appropriate responsibility, authority, and interrelation of all personnel who manage, perform, and assess work affecting quality, and provide the independence and authority necessary to perform these tasks.

(2) Resources. Each manufacturer shall provide adequate resources, including the assignment of trained personnel, for management, performance of work, and assessment activities, including internal quality audits, to meet the requirements of this part.

(3) Management representative. Management with executive responsibility shall appoint, and document such appointment of, a member of management who, irrespective of other responsibilities, shall have established authority over and responsibility for:

(i) Ensuring that quality system requirements are effectively established and effectively maintained in accordance with this part; and

(ii) Reporting on the performance of the quality system to management with executive responsibility for review.

(c) Management review. Management with executive responsibility shall review the suitability and effectiveness of the quality system at defined intervals and with sufficient frequency according to established procedures to ensure that the quality system satisfies the requirements of this part and the manufacturer's established quality policy and objectives. The dates and results of quality system reviews shall be documented.

(d) Quality planning. Each manufacturer shall establish a quality plan which defines the quality practices, resources, and activities relevant to devices that are designed and manufactured. The manufacturer shall establish how the requirements for quality will be met.

(e) Quality system procedures. Each manufacturer shall establish quality system procedures and instructions. An outline of the structure of the documentation used in the quality system shall be established where appropriate.

SEC. 820.22 QUALITY AUDIT.

Each manufacturer shall establish procedures for quality audits and conduct such audits to assure that the quality system is in compliance with the established quality system requirements and to determine the effectiveness of the quality system. Quality audits shall be conducted by individuals who do not have direct responsibility for the matters being audited. Corrective action(s), including a reaudit of deficient matters, shall be taken when necessary. A report of the results of each quality audit, and reaudit(s) where taken, shall be made and such reports shall be reviewed by management having responsibility for the matters audited. The dates and results of quality audits and reaudits shall be documented.

SEC. 820.25 PERSONNEL.

(a) General. Each manufacturer shall have sufficient personnel with the necessary education, background, training, and experience to assure that all activities required by this part are correctly performed.

(b) Training. Each manufacturer shall establish procedures for identifying training needs and ensure that all personnel are trained to adequately perform their assigned responsibilities. Training shall be documented.

(1) As part of their training, personnel shall be made aware of device defects which may occur from the improper performance of their specific jobs.

(2) Personnel who perform verification and validation activities shall be made aware of defects and errors that may be encountered as part of their job functions.

CH 5

Subpart C—Design Controls

Sec. 820.30 Design controls.

(a) General.

(1) Each manufacturer of any class III or class II device, and the class I devices listed in paragraph (a)(2) of this section, shall establish and maintain procedures to control the design of the device in order to ensure that specified design requirements are met.

(2) The following class I devices are subject to design controls:

(i) Devices automated with computer software; and

(ii) The devices listed in the following chart.

Section	Section
868.681	Catheter, Tracheobronchial Suction.
878.446	Glove, Surgeon's.
880.676	Restraint, Protective.
892.565	System, Applicator, Radionuclide, Manual.
892.574	Source, Radionuclide Teletherapy.

(b) Design and development planning. Each manufacturer shall establish and maintain plans that describe or reference the design and development activities and define responsibility for implementation. The plans shall identify and describe the interfaces with different groups or activities that provide, or result in, input to the design and development process. The plans shall be reviewed, updated, and approved as design and development evolves.

(c) Design input. Each manufacturer shall establish and maintain procedures to ensure that the design requirements relating to a device are appropriate and address the intended use of the device, including the needs of the user and patient. The procedures shall include a mechanism for addressing incomplete, ambiguous, or conflicting requirements. The design input requirements shall be documented and shall be reviewed and approved by a designated individual(s). The approval, including the date and signature of the individual(s) approving the requirements, shall be documented.

(d) Design output. Each manufacturer shall establish and maintain procedures for defining and documenting design output in terms that allow an adequate evaluation of conformance to design input requirements. Design output procedures shall contain or make reference to acceptance criteria and shall ensure that those design outputs that are essential for the proper functioning of the device are identified. Design output shall be documented, reviewed, and approved before release. The approval, including the date and signature of the individual(s) approving the output, shall be documented.

(e) Design review. Each manufacturer shall establish and maintain procedures to ensure that formal documented reviews of the design results are planned and conducted at appropriate stages of the device's design development. The procedures shall ensure that participants at each design review include representatives of all functions concerned with the design stage being reviewed and an individual(s) who does not have direct responsibility for the design stage being reviewed, as well as any specialists needed. The results of a design review, including identification of the design, the date, and the individual(s) performing the review, shall be documented in the design history file (the DHF).

(f) Design verification. Each manufacturer shall establish and maintain procedures for verifying the device design. Design verification shall confirm that the design output meets the design input requirements. The results of the design verification, including identification of the design, method(s), the date, and the individual(s) performing the verification, shall be documented in the DHF.

(g) Design validation. Each manufacturer shall establish and maintain procedures for validating the device design. Design validation shall be performed under defined operating conditions on initial production units, lots, or batches, or their equivalents. Design validation shall ensure that devices conform to defined user needs and intended uses and shall include testing of production units under actual or simulated use conditions. Design validation shall include software validation and risk analysis, where appropriate. The results of the design validation, including identification of the design, method(s), the date, and the individual(s) performing the validation, shall be documented in the DHF.

(h) Design transfer. Each manufacturer shall establish and maintain procedures to ensure that the device design is correctly translated into production specifications.

(i) Design changes. Each manufacturer shall establish and maintain procedures for the identification, documentation, validation or where appropriate verification, review, and approval of design changes before their implementation.

(j) Design history file. Each manufacturer shall establish and maintain a DHF for each type of device. The DHF shall contain or reference the records necessary to demonstrate that the design was developed in accordance with the approved design plan and the requirements of this part.

Subpart D—Document Controls

Sec. 820.40 Document controls.

Each manufacturer shall establish and maintain procedures to control all documents that are required by this part. The procedures shall provide for the following:

(a) Document approval and distribution. Each manufacturer shall designate an individual(s) to review for adequacy and approve prior to issuance all documents established to meet the requirements of this part. The approval, including the date and signature of the individual(s) approving the document, shall be documented. Documents established to meet the requirements of this part shall be available at all locations for which they are designated, used, or otherwise necessary, and all obsolete documents shall be promptly removed from all points of use or otherwise prevented from unintended use.

(b) Document changes. Changes to documents shall be reviewed and approved by an individual(s) in the same function or organization that performed the original review and approval, unless specifically designated otherwise. Approved changes shall be communicated to the appropriate personnel in a timely manner. Each manufacturer shall maintain records of changes to documents. Change records shall include a description of the change, identification of the affected documents, the signature of the approving individual(s), the approval date, and when the change becomes effective.

Subpart E—Purchasing Controls

Sec. 820.50 Purchasing controls.

Each manufacturer shall establish and maintain procedures to ensure that all purchased or otherwise received product and services conform to specified requirements.

(a) Evaluation of suppliers, contractors, and consultants. Each manufacturer shall establish and maintain the requirements, including quality requirements, that must be met by suppliers, contractors, and consultants. Each manufacturer shall:

(1) Evaluate and select potential suppliers, contractors, and consultants on the basis of their ability to meet specified requirements, including quality requirements. The evaluation shall be documented.

(2) Define the type and extent of control to be exercised over the product, services, suppliers, contractors, and consultants, based on the evaluation results.

(3) Establish and maintain records of acceptable suppliers, contractors, and consultants.

(b) Purchasing data. Each manufacturer shall establish and maintain data that clearly describe or reference the specified requirements, including quality requirements, for purchased or otherwise received product and services. Purchasing documents shall include, where possible, an agreement that the suppliers, contractors, and consultants agree to notify the manufacturer of changes in the product or service so that manufacturers may determine whether the changes may affect the quality of a finished device. Purchasing data shall be approved in accordance with 820.40.

Subpart F—Identification and Traceability

Sec. 820.60 Identification.

Each manufacturer shall establish and maintain procedures for identifying product during all stages of receipt, production, distribution, and installation to prevent mixups.

Sec. 820.65 Traceability.

Each manufacturer of a device that is intended for surgical implant into the body or to support or sustain life and whose failure to perform when properly used in accordance with instructions for use provided in the labeling can be reasonably expected to result in a significant injury to the user shall establish and maintain procedures for identifying with a control number each unit, lot, or batch of finished devices and where appropriate components. The procedures shall facilitate corrective action. Such identification shall be documented in the DHR.

Subpart G—Production and Process Controls

Sec. 820.70 Production and process controls.

(a) General. Each manufacturer shall develop, conduct, control, and monitor production processes to ensure that a device conforms to its specifications. Where deviations from device specifications could occur as a result of the manufacturing process, the manufacturer shall establish and maintain process control procedures that describe any process controls necessary to ensure conformance to specifications. Where process controls are needed they shall include:

(1) Documented instructions, standard operating procedures (SOP's), and methods that define and control the manner of production;

(2) Monitoring and control of process parameters and component and device characteristics during production;

(3) Compliance with specified reference standards or codes;

(4) The approval of processes and process equipment; and

(5) Criteria for workmanship which shall be expressed in documented standards or by means of identified and approved representative samples.

(b) Production and process changes. Each manufacturer shall establish and maintain procedures for changes to a specification, method, process, or procedure. Such changes shall be verified or where appropriate validated according to 820.75, before implementation and these activities shall be documented. Changes shall be approved in accordance with 820.40.

(c) Environmental control. Where environmental conditions could reasonably be expected to have an adverse effect on product quality, the manufacturer shall establish and maintain procedures to adequately control these environmental conditions. Environmental control system(s) shall be periodically inspected to verify that the system, including necessary equipment, is adequate and functioning properly. These activities shall be documented and reviewed.

(d) Personnel. Each manufacturer shall establish and maintain requirements for the health, cleanliness, personal practices, and clothing of personnel if contact between such personnel and product or environment could reasonably be expected to have an adverse effect on product quality. The manufacturer shall ensure that maintenance and other personnel who are required to work temporarily under special environmental conditions are appropriately trained or supervised by a trained individual.

(e) Contamination control. Each manufacturer shall establish and maintain procedures to prevent contamination of equipment or product by substances that could reasonably be expected to have an adverse effect on product quality.

(f) Buildings. Buildings shall be of suitable design and contain sufficient space to perform necessary operations, prevent mixups, and assure orderly handling.

(g) Equipment. Each manufacturer shall ensure that all equipment used in the manufacturing process meets specified requirements and is appropriately designed, constructed, placed, and installed to facilitate maintenance, adjustment, cleaning, and use.

(1) Maintenance schedule. Each manufacturer shall establish and maintain schedules for the adjustment, cleaning, and other maintenance of equipment to ensure that manufacturing specifications are met. Maintenance activities, including the date and individual(s) performing the maintenance activities, shall be documented.

(2) Inspection. Each manufacturer shall conduct periodic inspections in accordance with established procedures to ensure adherence to applicable equipment maintenance schedules. The inspections, including the date and individual(s) conducting the inspections, shall be documented.

(3) Adjustment. Each manufacturer shall ensure that any inherent limitations or allowable tolerances are visibly posted on or near equipment requiring periodic adjustments or are readily available to personnel performing these adjustments.

(h) Manufacturing material. Where a manufacturing material could reasonably be expected to have an adverse effect on product quality, the manufacturer shall establish and maintain procedures for the use and removal of such manufacturing material to ensure that it is removed or limited to an amount that does not adversely affect the device's quality. The removal or reduction of such manufacturing material shall be documented.

(i) Automated processes. When computers or automated data processing systems are used as part of production or the quality system, the manufacturer shall validate computer software for its intended use according to an established protocol. All software changes shall be validated before approval and issuance. These validation activities and results shall be documented.

Sec. 820.72 Inspection, measuring, and test equipment.

(a) Control of inspection, measuring, and test equipment. Each manufacturer shall ensure that all inspection, measuring, and test equipment, including mechanical, automated, or electronic inspection and test equipment, is suitable for its intended purposes and is capable of producing valid results. Each manufacturer shall establish and maintain procedures to ensure that equipment is routinely calibrated, inspected, checked, and maintained. The procedures shall include provisions for handling, preservation, and storage of equipment, so that its accuracy and fitness for use are maintained. These activities shall be documented.

(b) Calibration. Calibration procedures shall include specific directions and limits for accuracy and precision. When accuracy and precision limits are not met, there shall be provisions for remedial action to reestablish the limits and to evaluate whether there was any adverse effect on the device's quality. These activities shall be documented.

(1) Calibration standards. Calibration standards used for inspection, measuring, and test equipment shall be traceable to national or international standards. If national or international standards are not practical or available, the manufacturer shall use an independent reproducible standard. If no applicable standard exists, the manufacturer shall establish and maintain an in-house standard.

(2) Calibration records. The equipment identification, calibration dates, the individual performing each calibration, and the next calibration date shall be documented. These records shall be displayed on or near each piece of equipment or shall be readily available to the personnel using such equipment and to the individuals responsible for calibrating the equipment.

Sec. 820.75 Process validation.

(a) Where the results of a process cannot be fully verified by subsequent inspection and test, the process shall be validated with a high degree of assurance and approved according to established procedures. The validation activities and results, including the date and signature of the individual(s) approving the validation and where appropriate the major equipment validated, shall be documented.

(b) Each manufacturer shall establish and maintain procedures for monitoring and control of process parameters for validated processes to ensure that the specified requirements continue to be met.

(1) Each manufacturer shall ensure that validated processes are performed by qualified individual(s).

(2) For validated processes, the monitoring and control methods and data, the date performed, and, where appropriate, the individual(s) performing the process or the major equipment used shall be documented.

(c) When changes or process deviations occur, the manufacturer shall review and evaluate the process and perform revalidation where appropriate. These activities shall be documented.

Subpart H—Acceptance Activities

Sec. 820.80 Receiving, in-process, and finished device acceptance.

(a) General. Each manufacturer shall establish and maintain procedures for acceptance activities. Acceptance activities include inspections, tests, or other verification activities.

(b) Receiving acceptance activities. Each manufacturer shall establish and maintain procedures for acceptance of incoming product. Incoming product shall be inspected, tested, or otherwise verified as conforming to specified requirements. Acceptance or rejection shall be documented.

(c) In-process acceptance activities. Each manufacturer shall establish and maintain acceptance procedures, where appropriate, to ensure that specified requirements for in-process product are met. Such procedures shall ensure that in-process product is controlled until the required inspection and tests or other verification activities have been completed, or necessary approvals are received, and are documented.

(d) Final acceptance activities. Each manufacturer shall establish and maintain procedures for finished device acceptance to ensure that each production run, lot, or batch of finished devices meets acceptance criteria. Finished devices shall be held in quarantine or otherwise adequately controlled until released. Finished devices shall not be released for distribution until:

(1) The activities required in the DMR are completed;

(2) the associated data and documentation is reviewed;

(3) the release is authorized by the signature of a designated individual(s); and

(4) the authorization is dated.

(e) Acceptance records. Each manufacturer shall document acceptance activities required by this part. These records shall include:

(1) The acceptance activities performed;

(2) the dates acceptance activities are performed;

(3) the results;

(4) the signature of the individual(s) conducting the acceptance activities; and

(5) where appropriate the equipment used. These records shall be part of the DHR.

SEC. 820.86 ACCEPTANCE STATUS.

Each manufacturer shall identify by suitable means the acceptance status of product, to indicate the conformance or nonconformance of product with acceptance criteria. The identification of acceptance status shall be maintained throughout manufacturing, packaging, labeling, installation, and servicing of the product to ensure that only product which has passed the required acceptance activities is distributed, used, or installed.

SUBPART I—NONCONFORMING PRODUCT

SEC. 820.90 NONCONFORMING PRODUCT.

(a) Control of nonconforming product. Each manufacturer shall establish and maintain procedures to control product that does not conform to specified requirements. The procedures shall address the identification, documentation, evaluation, segregation, and disposition of nonconforming product. The evaluation of nonconformance shall include a determination of the need for an investigation and notification of the persons or organizations responsible for the nonconformance. The evaluation and any investigation shall be documented.

(b) Nonconformity review and disposition.

(1) Each manufacturer shall establish and maintain procedures that define the responsibility for review and the authority for the disposition of nonconforming product. The procedures shall set forth the review and disposition process. Disposition of nonconforming product shall be documented. Documentation shall include the justification for use of nonconforming product and the signature of the individual(s) authorizing the use.

(2) Each manufacturer shall establish and maintain procedures for rework, to include retesting and reevaluation of the nonconforming product after rework, to ensure that the product meets its current specifications. Rework and reevaluation activities, including a determination of any adverse effect from the rework upon the product, shall be documented in the DHR.

Subpart J—Corrective and Preventive Action

Sec. 820.100 Corrective and preventive action.

(a) Each manufacturer shall establish and maintain procedures for implementing corrective and preventive action. The procedures shall include requirements for:

(1) Analyzing processes, work operations, concessions, quality audit reports, quality records, service records, complaints, returned product, and other sources of quality data to identify existing and potential causes of nonconforming product, or other quality problems. Appropriate statistical methodology shall be employed where necessary to detect recurring quality problems;

(2) Investigating the cause of nonconformities relating to product, processes, and the quality system;

(3) Identifying the action(s) needed to correct and prevent recurrence of nonconforming product and other quality problems;

(4) Verifying or validating the corrective and preventive action to ensure that such action is effective and does not adversely affect the finished device;

(5) Implementing and recording changes in methods and procedures needed to correct and prevent identified quality problems;

(6) Ensuring that information related to quality problems or nonconforming product is disseminated to those directly responsible for assuring the quality of such product or the prevention of such problems; and

(7) Submitting relevant information on identified quality problems, as well as corrective and preventive actions, for management review.

(b) All activities required under this section, and their results, shall be documented.

Subpart K—Labeling and Packaging Control

Sec. 820.120 Device labeling.

Each manufacturer shall establish and maintain procedures to control labeling activities.

(a) Label integrity. Labels shall be printed and applied so as to remain legible and affixed during the customary conditions of processing, storage, handling, distribution, and where appropriate use.

(b) Labeling inspection. Labeling shall not be released for storage or use until a designated individual(s) has examined the labeling for accuracy including, where applicable, the correct unique device identifier (UDI) or universal product code (UPC), expiration date, control number, storage instructions, handling instructions, and any additional processing instructions. The release, including the date and signature of the individual(s) performing the examination, shall be documented in the DHR.

(c) Labeling storage. Each manufacturer shall store labeling in a manner that provides proper identification and is designed to prevent mixups.

(d) Labeling operations. Each manufacturer shall control labeling and packaging operations to prevent labeling mixups. The label and labeling used for each production unit, lot, or batch shall be documented in the DHR.

(e) Control number. Where a control number is required by 820.65, that control number shall be on or shall accompany the device through distribution.

[61 FR 52654, Oct. 7, 1996, as amended at 78 FR 58822, Sept. 24, 2013]

Sec. 820.130 Device packaging.

Each manufacturer shall ensure that device packaging and shipping containers are designed and constructed to protect the device from alteration or damage during the customary conditions of processing, storage, handling, and distribution.

Subpart L—Handling, Storage, Distribution, and Installation

Sec. 820.140 Handling.

Each manufacturer shall establish and maintain procedures to ensure that mixups, damage, deterioration, contamination, or other adverse effects to product do not occur during handling.

Sec. 820.150 Storage.

(a) Each manufacturer shall establish and maintain procedures for the control of storage areas and stock rooms for product to prevent mixups, damage, deterioration, contamination, or other adverse effects pending use or distribution and to ensure that no obsolete, rejected, or deteriorated product is used or distributed. When the quality of product deteriorates over time, it shall be stored in a manner to facilitate proper stock rotation, and its condition shall be assessed as appropriate.

(b) Each manufacturer shall establish and maintain procedures that describe the methods for authorizing receipt from and dispatch to storage areas and stock rooms.

Sec. 820.160 Distribution.

(a) Each manufacturer shall establish and maintain procedures for control and distribution of finished devices to ensure that only those devices approved for release are distributed and that purchase orders are reviewed to ensure that ambiguities and errors are resolved before devices are released for distribution. Where a device's fitness for use or quality deteriorates over time, the procedures shall ensure that expired devices or devices deteriorated beyond acceptable fitness for use are not distributed.

(b) Each manufacturer shall maintain distribution records which include or refer to the location of:

(1) The name and address of the initial consignee;

(2) The identification and quantity of devices shipped;

(3) The date shipped; and

(4) Any control number(s) used.

Sec. 820.170 Installation.

(a) Each manufacturer of a device requiring installation shall establish and maintain adequate installation and inspection instructions, and where appropriate test procedures. Instructions and procedures shall include directions for ensuring proper installation so that the device will perform as intended after installation. The manufacturer shall distribute the instructions and procedures with the device or otherwise make them available to the person(s) installing the device.

(b) The person installing the device shall ensure that the installation, inspection, and any required testing are performed in accordance with the manufacturer's instructions and procedures and shall document the inspection and any test results to demonstrate proper installation.

Subpart M—Records

Sec. 820.180 General requirements.

All records required by this part shall be maintained at the manufacturing establishment or other location that is reasonably accessible to responsible officials of the manufacturer and to employees of FDA designated to perform inspections. Such records, including those not stored at the inspected establishment, shall be made readily available for review and copying by FDA employee(s). Such records shall be legible and shall be stored to minimize deterioration and to prevent loss. Those records stored in automated data processing systems shall be backed up.

(a) Confidentiality. Records deemed confidential by the manufacturer may be marked to aid FDA in determining whether information may be disclosed under the public information regulation in part 20 of this chapter.

(b) Record retention period. All records required by this part shall be retained for a period of time equivalent to the design and expected life of the device, but in no case less than 2 years from the date of release for commercial distribution by the manufacturer.

(c) Exceptions. This section does not apply to the reports required by 820.20(c) Management review, 820.22 Quality audits, and supplier audit reports used to meet the requirements of 820.50(a) Evaluation of suppliers, contractors, and consultants, but does apply to procedures established under these provisions. Upon request of a designated employee of FDA, an employee in management with executive responsibility shall certify in writing that the management reviews and quality audits required under this part, and supplier audits where applicable, have been performed and documented, the dates on which they were performed, and that any required corrective action has been undertaken.

Sec. 820.181 Device master record.

Each manufacturer shall maintain device master records (DMR's). Each manufacturer shall ensure that each DMR is prepared and approved in accordance with 820.40. The DMR for each type of device shall include, or refer to the location of, the following information:

(a) Device specifications including appropriate drawings, composition, formulation, component specifications, and software specifications;

(b) Production process specifications including the appropriate equipment specifications, production methods, production procedures, and production environment specifications;

(c) Quality assurance procedures and specifications including acceptance criteria and the quality assurance equipment to be used;

(d) Packaging and labeling specifications, including methods and processes used; and

(e) Installation, maintenance, and servicing procedures and methods.

Sec. 820.184 Device history record.

Each manufacturer shall maintain device history records (DHR's). Each manufacturer shall establish and maintain procedures to ensure that DHR's for each batch, lot, or unit are maintained to demonstrate that the device is manufactured in accordance with the DMR and the requirements of this part. The DHR shall include, or refer to the location of, the following information:

(a) The dates of manufacture;

(b) The quantity manufactured;

(c) The quantity released for distribution;

(d) The acceptance records which demonstrate the device is manufactured in accordance with the DMR;

(e) The primary identification label and labeling used for each production unit; and

(f) Any unique device identifier (UDI) or universal product code (UPC), and any other device identification(s) and control number(s) used.

[61 FR 52654, Oct. 7, 1996, as amended at 78 FR 58822, Sept. 24, 2013]

Sec. 820.186 Quality system record.

Each manufacturer shall maintain a quality system record (QSR). The QSR shall include, or refer to the location of, procedures and the documentation of activities required by this part that are not specific to a particular type of device(s), including, but not limited to, the records required by 820.20. Each manufacturer shall ensure that the QSR is prepared and approved in accordance with 820.40.

Sec. 820.198 Complaint files.

(a) Each manufacturer shall maintain complaint files. Each manufacturer shall establish and maintain procedures for receiving, reviewing, and evaluating complaints by a formally designated unit. Such procedures shall ensure that:

(1) All complaints are processed in a uniform and timely manner;

(2) Oral complaints are documented upon receipt; and

(3) Complaints are evaluated to determine whether the complaint represents an event which is required to be reported to FDA under part 803 of this chapter, Medical Device Reporting.

(b) Each manufacturer shall review and evaluate all complaints to determine whether an investigation is necessary. When no investigation is made, the manufacturer shall maintain a record that includes the reason no investigation was made and the name of the individual responsible for the decision not to investigate.

(c) Any complaint involving the possible failure of a device, labeling, or packaging to meet any of its specifications shall be reviewed, evaluated, and investigated, unless such investigation has already been performed for a similar complaint and another investigation is not necessary.

(d) Any complaint that represents an event which must be reported to FDA under part 803 of this chapter shall be promptly reviewed, evaluated, and investigated by a designated individual(s) and shall be maintained in a separate portion of the complaint files or otherwise clearly identified. In addition to the information required by 820.198(e), records of investigation under this paragraph shall include a determination of:

(1) Whether the device failed to meet specifications;

(2) Whether the device was being used for treatment or diagnosis; and

(3) The relationship, if any, of the device to the reported incident or adverse event.

(e) When an investigation is made under this section, a record of the investigation shall be maintained by the formally designated unit identified in paragraph (a) of this section. The record of investigation shall include:

(1) The name of the device;

(2) The date the complaint was received;

(3) Any unique device identifier (UDI) or universal product code (UPC), and any other device identification(s) and control number(s) used;

(4) The name, address, and phone number of the complainant;

(5) The nature and details of the complaint;

(6) The dates and results of the investigation;

(7) Any corrective action taken; and

(8) Any reply to the complainant.

(f) When the manufacturer's formally designated complaint unit is located at a site separate from the manufacturing establishment, the investigated complaint(s) and the record(s) of investigation shall be reasonably accessible to the manufacturing establishment.

(g) If a manufacturer's formally designated complaint unit is located outside of the United States, records required by this section shall be reasonably accessible in the United States at either:

(1) A location in the United States where the manufacturer's records are regularly kept; or

(2) The location of the initial distributor.

[61 FR 52654, Oct. 7, 1996, as amended at 69 FR 11313, Mar. 10, 2004; 71 FR 16228, Mar. 31, 2006; 78 FR 58822, Sept. 24, 2013]

Subpart N—Servicing

Sec. 820.200 Servicing.

(a) Where servicing is a specified requirement, each manufacturer shall establish and maintain instructions and procedures for performing and verifying that the servicing meets the specified requirements.

(b) Each manufacturer shall analyze service reports with appropriate statistical methodology in accordance with 820.100.

(c) Each manufacturer who receives a service report that represents an event which must be reported to FDA under part 803 of this chapter shall automatically consider the report a complaint and shall process it in accordance with the requirements of 820.198.

(d) Service reports shall be documented and shall include:

(1) The name of the device serviced;

(2) Any unique device identifier (UDI) or universal product code (UPC), and any other device identification(s) and control number(s) used;

(3) The date of service;

(4) The individual(s) servicing the device;

(5) The service performed; and

(6) The test and inspection data.

[61 FR 52654, Oct. 7, 1996, as amended at 69 FR 11313, Mar. 10, 2004; 78 FR 58822, Sept. 24, 2013]

Subpart O—Statistical Techniques

Sec. 820.250 Statistical techniques.

(a) Where appropriate, each manufacturer shall establish and maintain procedures for identifying valid statistical techniques required for establishing, controlling, and verifying the acceptability of process capability and product characteristics.

(b) Sampling plans, when used, shall be written and based on a valid statistical rationale. Each manufacturer shall establish and maintain procedures to ensure that sampling methods are adequate for their intended use and to ensure that when changes occur the sampling plans are reviewed. These activities shall be documented.

EudraLex

Chapter 6
European Union
Annex 11: Computerised Systems

June 30, 2011
EudraLex
European Commission
Health And Consumers Directorate-General
Public Health and Risk Assessment Pharmaceuticals

The Rules Governing Medicinal Products In The European Union, Volume 4
Good Manufacturing Practice
Medicinal Products For Human And Veterinary Use

Annex 11: Computerised Systems[1]

Principle

This annex applies to all forms of computerised systems used as part of a GMP regulated activities. A computerised system is a set of software and hardware components which together fulfill certain functionalities.

The application should be validated; IT infrastructure should be qualified.

Where a computerised system replaces a manual operation, there should be no resultant decrease in product quality, process control or quality assurance. There should be no increase in the overall risk of the process.

General

1. Risk Management

Risk management should be applied throughout the lifecycle of the computerised system taking into account patient safety, data integrity and product quality. As part of a risk management system, decisions on the extent of validation and data integrity controls should be based on a justified and documented risk assessment of the computerised system.

1 Annex 11 may be accessed online at https://ec.europa.eu/health/sites/health/files/files/eudralex/vol-4/annex11_01-2011_en.pdf

2. Personnel

There should be close cooperation between all relevant personnel such as Process Owner, System Owner, Qualified Persons and IT. All personnel should have appropriate qualifications, level of access and defined responsibilities to carry out their assigned duties.

3. Suppliers and Service Providers

3.1 When third parties (e.g. suppliers, service providers) are used e.g. to provide, install, configure, integrate, validate, maintain (e.g. via remote access), modify or retain a computerised system or related service or for data processing, formal agreements must exist between the manufacturer and any third parties, and these agreements should include clear statements of the responsibilities of the third party. IT-departments should be considered analogous.

3.2 The competence and reliability of a supplier are key factors when selecting a product or service provider. The need for an audit should be based on a risk assessment.

3.3 Documentation supplied with commercial off-the-shelf products should be reviewed by regulated users to check that user requirements are fulfilled.

3.4 Quality system and audit information relating to suppliers or developers of software and implemented systems should be made available to inspectors on request.

Project Phase

4. Validation

4.1 The validation documentation and reports should cover the relevant steps of the life cycle. Manufacturers should be able to justify their standards, protocols, acceptance criteria, procedures and records based on their risk assessment.

4.2 Validation documentation should include change control records (if applicable) and reports on any deviations observed during the validation process.

4.3 An up to date listing of all relevant systems and their GMP functionality (inventory) should be available. For critical systems an up to date system description detailing the physical and logical arrangements, data flows and interfaces with other systems or processes, any hardware and software pre-requisites, and security measures should be available.

4.4 User Requirements Specifications should describe the required functions of the computerised system and be based on documented risk assessment and GMP impact. User requirements should be traceable throughout the life-cycle.

4.5 The regulated user should take all reasonable steps, to ensure that the system has been developed in accordance with an appropriate quality management system. The supplier should be assessed appropriately.

4.6 For the validation of bespoke or customised computerised systems there should be a process in place that ensures the formal assessment and reporting of quality and performance measures for all the life-cycle stages of the system.

4.7 Evidence of appropriate test methods and test scenarios should be demonstrated. Particularly, system (process) parameter limits, data limits and error handling should be considered. Automated testing tools and test environments should have documented assessments for their adequacy.

4.8 If data are transferred to another data format or system, validation should include checks that data are not altered in value and/or meaning during this migration process.

Operational Phase

5. Data

Computerised systems exchanging data electronically with other systems should include appropriate built-in checks for the correct and secure entry and processing of data, in order to minimize the risks.

6. Accuracy Checks

For critical data entered manually, there should be an additional check on the accuracy of the data. This check may be done by a second operator or by validated electronic means. The criticality and the potential consequences of erroneous or incorrectly entered data to a system should be covered by risk management.

7. Data Storage

7.1 Data should be secured by both physical and electronic means against damage. Stored data should be checked for accessibility, readability and accuracy. Access to data should be ensured throughout the retention period.

7.2 Regular back-ups of all relevant data should be done. Integrity and accuracy of backup data and the ability to restore the data should be checked during validation and monitored periodically.

8. Printouts

8.1 It should be possible to obtain clear printed copies of electronically stored data.

8.2 For records supporting batch release it should be possible to generate printouts indicating if any of the data has been changed since the original entry.

9. Audit Trails

Consideration should be given, based on a risk assessment, to building into the system the creation of a record of all GMP-relevant changes and deletions (a system generated "audit trail"). For change or deletion of GMP-relevant data the reason should be documented. Audit trails need to be available and convertible to a generally intelligible form and regularly reviewed.

10. Change and Configuration Management

Any changes to a computerised system including system configurations should only be made in a controlled manner in accordance with a defined procedure.

11. Periodic evaluation

Computerised systems should be periodically evaluated to confirm that they remain in a valid state and are compliant with GMP. Such evaluations should include, where appropriate, the current range of functionality, deviation records, incidents, problems, upgrade history, performance, reliability, security and validation status reports.

12. Security

12.1 Physical and/or logical controls should be in place to restrict access to computerized system to authorised persons. Suitable methods of preventing unauthorised entry to the system may include the use of keys, pass cards, personal codes with passwords, biometrics, restricted access to computer equipment and data storage areas.

12.2 The extent of security controls depends on the criticality of the computerised system.

12.3 Creation, change, and cancellation of access authorisations should be recorded.

12.4 Management systems for data and for documents should be designed to record the identity of operators entering, changing, confirming or deleting data including date and time.

13. Incident Management

All incidents, not only system failures and data errors, should be reported and assessed. The root cause of a critical incident should be identified and should form the basis of corrective and preventive actions.

14. Electronic Signature

Electronic records may be signed electronically. Electronic signatures are expected to:

a. have the same impact as hand-written signatures within the boundaries of the company,

b. be permanently linked to their respective record,

c. include the time and date that they were applied.

15. Batch release

When a computerised system is used for recording certification and batch release, the system should allow only Qualified Persons to certify the release of the batches and it should clearly identify and record the person releasing or certifying the batches. This should be performed using an electronic signature.

16. Business Continuity

For the availability of computerised systems supporting critical processes, provisions should be made to ensure continuity of support for those processes in the event of a system breakdown (e.g. a manual or alternative system). The time required to bring the alternative arrangements into use should be based on risk and appropriate for a particular system and the business process it supports. These arrangements should be adequately documented and tested.

17. Archiving

Data may be archived. This data should be checked for accessibility, readability and integrity. If relevant changes are to be made to the system (e.g. computer equipment or programs), then the ability to retrieve the data should be ensured and tested.

Glossary

Application: Software installed on a defined platform/hardware providing specific functionality

Bespoke/Customized computerised system: A computerised system individually designed to suit a specific business process

Commercial of the shelf software: Software commercially available, whose fitness for use is demonstrated by a broad spectrum of users.

IT Infrastructure: The hardware and software such as networking software and operation systems, which makes it possible for the application to function.

Life cycle: All phases in the life of the system from initial requirements until retirement including design, specification, programming, testing, installation, operation, and maintenance.

Process owner: The person responsible for the business process.

System owner: The person responsible for the availability, and maintenance of a computerised system and for the security of the data residing on that system.

Third Party: Parties not directly managed by the holder of the manufacturing and/or import authorisation.

EudraLex

Chapter 7
European Union
Annex 15: Qualification and Validation

March 30, 2015
European Commission
Directorate-General For Health and Food Safety
Medicinal Products – Quality, Safety and Efficacy

Eudralex, Volume 4
EU Guidelines for Good Manufacturing Practice for Medicinal Products for Human And Veterinary Use

Annex 15: Qualification and Validation[1]

Principle

This Annex describes the principles of qualification and validation which are applicable to the facilities, equipment, utilities and processes used for the manufacture of medicinal products and may also be used as supplementary optional guidance for active substances without introduction of additional requirements to EudraLex, Volume 4, Part II. It is a GMP requirement that manufacturers control the critical aspects of their particular operations through qualification and validation over the life cycle of the product and process. Any planned changes to the facilities, equipment, utilities and processes, which may affect the quality of the product, should be formally documented and the impact on the validated status or control strategy assessed. Computerised systems used for the manufacture of medicinal products should also be validated according to the requirements of Annex 11. The relevant concepts and guidance presented in ICH Q8, Q9, Q10 and Q11 should also be taken into account.

General

A quality risk management approach should be applied throughout the lifecycle of a medicinal product. As part of a quality risk management system, decisions on the scope and extent of qualification and validation should be based on a justified and documented risk assessment of the facilities, equipment, utilities and processes. Retrospective validation is no longer considered an acceptable approach. Data supporting qualification and/or validation studies which were obtained from sources outside of the manufacturers own programmes may be used provided that this approach has been justified and that there is adequate assurance that controls were in place throughout the acquisition of such data.

1 Annex 15 may be accessed at https://ec.europa.eu/health/sites/health/files/files/eudralex/vol-4/2015-10_annex15.pdf

1. Organising and Planning for Qualification and Validation

1.1. All qualification and validation activities should be planned and take the life cycle of facilities, equipment, utilities, process and product into consideration.

1.2. Qualification and validation activities should only be performed by suitably trained personnel who follow approved procedures.

1.3. Qualification/validation personnel should report as defined in the pharmaceutical quality system although this may not necessarily be to a quality management or a quality assurance function. However, there should be appropriate quality oversight over the whole validation life cycle.

1.4. The key elements of the site qualification and validation programme should be clearly defined and documented in a validation master plan (VMP) or equivalent document.

1.5. The VMP or equivalent document should define the qualification/validation system and include or reference information on at least the following:

i. Qualification and Validation policy;

ii. The organisational structure including roles and responsibilities for qualification and validation activities;

iii. Summary of the facilities, equipment, systems, processes on site and the qualification and validation status;

iv. Change control and deviation management for qualification and validation;

v. Guidance on developing acceptance criteria;

vi. References to existing documents;

vii. The qualification and validation strategy, including requalification, where applicable.

1.6. For large and complex projects, planning takes on added importance and separate validation plans may enhance clarity

1.7. A quality risk management approach should be used for qualification and validation activities. In light of increased knowledge and understanding from any changes during the project phase or during commercial production, the risk assessments should be repeated, as required. The way in which risk assessments are used to support qualification and validation activities should be clearly documented.

1.8. Appropriate checks should be incorporated into qualification and validation work to ensure the integrity of all data obtained.

2. Documentation, Including VMP

2.1. Good documentation practices are important to support knowledge management throughout the product lifecycle.

2.2. All documents generated during qualification and validation should be approved and authorised by appropriate personnel as defined in the pharmaceutical quality system.

2.3. The inter-relationship between documents in complex validation projects should be clearly defined.

2.4. Validation protocols should be prepared which defines the critical systems, attributes and parameters and the associated acceptance criteria.

2.5. Qualification documents may be combined together, where appropriate, e.g. installation qualification (IQ) and operational qualification (OQ).

2.6. Where validation protocols and other documentation are supplied by a third party providing validation services, appropriate personnel at the manufacturing site should confirm suitability and compliance with internal procedures before approval. Vendor protocols may be supplemented by additional documentation/test protocols before use.

2.7. Any significant changes to the approved protocol during execution, e.g. acceptance criteria, operating parameters etc., should be documented as a deviation and be scientifically justified.

2.8. Results which fail to meet the pre-defined acceptance criteria should be recorded as a deviation and be fully investigated according to local procedures. Any implications for the validation should be discussed in the report

2.9. The review and conclusions of the validation should be reported and the results obtained summarised against the acceptance criteria. Any subsequent changes to acceptance criteria should be scientifically justified and a final recommendation made as to the outcome of the validation.

2.10. A formal release for the next stage in the qualification and validation process should be authorised by the relevant responsible personnel either as part of the validation report approval or as a separate summary document. Conditional approval to proceed to the next qualification stage can be given where certain acceptance criteria or deviations have not been fully addressed and there is a documented assessment that there is no significant impact on the next activity.

3. Qualification Stages for Equipment, Facilities, Utilities and Systems.

3.1. Qualification activities should consider all stages from initial development of the user requirements specification through to the end of use of the equipment, facility, utility or system. The main stages and some suggested criteria (although this depends on individual project circumstances and may be different) which could be included in each stage are indicated below:

User requirements specification (URS)

3.2. The specification for equipment, facilities, utilities or systems should be defined in a URS and/or a functional specification. The essential elements of quality need to be built in at this stage and any GMP risks mitigated to an acceptable level. The URS should be a point of reference throughout the validation life cycle.

Design qualification (DQ)

3.3. The next element in the qualification of equipment, facilities, utilities, or systems is DQ where the compliance of the design with GMP should be demonstrated and documented. The requirements of the user requirements specification should be verified during the design qualification.

Factory acceptance testing (FAT) /Site acceptance testing (SAT)

3.4. Equipment, especially if incorporating novel or complex technology, may be evaluated, if applicable, at the vendor prior to delivery.

3.5. Prior to installation, equipment should be confirmed to comply with the URS/ functional specification at the vendor site, if applicable.

3.6. Where appropriate and justified, documentation review and some tests could be performed at the FAT or other stages without the need to repeat on site at IQ/OQ if it can be shown that the functionality is not affected by the transport and installation.

3.7. FAT may be supplemented by the execution of a SAT following the receipt of equipment at the manufacturing site.

Installation qualification (IQ)

3.8. IQ should be performed on equipment, facilities, utilities, or systems.

3.9. IQ should include, but is not limited to the following:

- i. Verification of the correct installation of components, instrumentation, equipment, pipe work and services against the engineering drawings and specifications;
- ii. Verification of the correct installation against pre-defined criteria;
- iii. Collection and collation of supplier operating and working instructions and maintenance requirements;
- iv. Calibration of instrumentation;
- v. Verification of the materials of construction.

Operational qualification (OQ)

3.10. OQ normally follows IQ but depending on the complexity of the equipment, it may be performed as a combined Installation/Operation Qualification (IOQ).

3.11. OQ should include but is not limited to the following:

- i. Tests that have been developed from the knowledge of processes, systems and equipment to ensure the system is operating as designed;
- ii. Tests to confirm upper and lower operating limits, and /or "worst case" conditions.

3.12. The completion of a successful OQ should allow the finalisation of standard operating and cleaning procedures, operator training and preventative maintenance requirements.

Performance qualification (PQ)

3.13. PQ should normally follow the successful completion of IQ and OQ. However, it may in some cases be appropriate to perform it in conjunction with OQ or Process Validation.

3.14. PQ should include, but is not limited to the following:

i. Tests, using production materials, qualified substitutes or simulated product proven to have equivalent behaviour under normal operating conditions with worst case batch sizes. The frequency of sampling used to confirm process control should be justified;

ii. Tests should cover the operating range of the intended process, unless documented evidence from the development phases confirming the operational ranges is available.

4. Re-Qualification

4.1. Equipment, facilities, utilities and systems should be evaluated at an appropriate frequency to confirm that they remain in a state of control.

4.2. Where re-qualification is necessary and performed at a specific time period, the period should be justified and the criteria for evaluation defined. Furthermore, the possibility of small changes over time should be assessed.

5. Process Validation

General

5.1. The requirements and principles outlined in this section are applicable to the manufacture of all pharmaceutical dosage forms. They cover the initial validation of new processes, subsequent validation of modified processes, site transfers and ongoing process verification. It is implicit in this annex that a robust product development process is in place to enable successful process validation.

5.2. Section 5 should be used in conjunction with the current EMA guideline on Process Validation.

5.2.1. The guideline on Process Validation is intended to provide guidance on the information and data t o be provided in the regulatory submission only. However GMP requirements for process validation continue throughout the lifecycle of the process

5.2.2. This approach should be applied to link product and process development. It will ensure validation of the commercial manufacturing process and maintenance of the process in a state of control during routine commercial production.

5.3. Manufacturing processes may be developed using a traditional approach or a continuous verification approach. However, irrespective of the approach used, processes must be shown to be robust and ensure consistent product quality before any product is released to the market. Manufacturing processes using the traditional approach should undergo a prospective validation programme, wherever possible, prior to certification of the product. Retrospective validation is no longer an acceptable approach.

5.4. Process validation of new products should cover all intended marketed strengths and sites of manufacture. Bracketing could be justified for new products based on extensive process knowledge from the development stage in conjunction with an appropriate ongoing verification programme.

5.5. For process validation of products which are transferred from one site to another or within the same site, the number of validation batches could be reduced by the use of a bracketing approach. However, existing product knowledge, including the content of the previous validation, should be available. Different strengths, batch sizes and pack sizes/container types may also use a bracketing approach, if justified.

5.6. For the site transfer of legacy products, the manufacturing process and controls must comply with the marketing authorisation and meet current standards for marketing authorisation for that product type. If necessary, variations to the marketing authorisation should be submitted.

5.7. Process validation should establish whether all quality attributes and process parameters, which are considered important for ensuring the validated state and acceptable product quality, can be consistently met by the process. The basis by which process parameters and quality attributes were identified as being critical or non-critical should be clearly documented, taking into account the results of any risk assessment activities.

5.8. Normally batches manufactured for process validation should be the same size as the intended commercial scale batches and the use of any other batch sizes should be justified or specified in other sections of EudraLex, Volume 4.

5.9. Equipment, facilities, utilities and systems used for process validation should be qualified. Test methods should be validated for their intended use.

5.10. For all products irrespective of the approach used, process knowledge from development studies or other sources should be accessible to the manufacturing site, unless otherwise justified, and be the basis for validation activities.

5.11. For process validation batches, production, development, or other site transfer personnel may be involved. Batches should only be manufactured by trained personnel in accordance with GMP using approved documentation. It is expected that production personnel are involved in the manufacture of validation batches to facilitate product understanding.

5.12. The suppliers of critical starting and packaging materials should be qualified prior to the manufacture of validation batches; otherwise a justification based on the application of quality risk management principles should be documented.

5.13. It is especially important that the underlying process knowledge for the design space justification (if used) and for development of any mathematical models (if used) to confirm a process control strategy should be available.

5.14. Where validation batches are released to the market, this should be pre-defined. The conditions under which they are produced should fully comply with GMP, with the validation acceptance criteria, with any continuous process verification criteria (if used) and with the marketing authorisation or clinical trial authorisation.

5.15. For the process validation of investigational medicinal products (IMP), please refer to Annex 13.

Concurrent validation

5.16. In exceptional circumstances, where there is a strong benefit-risk ratio for the patient, it may be acceptable not to complete a validation programme before routine production starts and concurrent validation could be used. However, the decision to carry out concurrent validation must be justified, documented in the VMP for visibility and approved by authorised personnel.

5.17. Where a concurrent validation approach has been adopted, there should be sufficient data to support a conclusion that any given batch of product is uniform and meets the defined acceptance criteria. The results and conclusion should be formally documented and available to the Qualified Person prior to certification of the batch.

Traditional process validation

5.18. In the traditional approach, a number of batches of the finished product are manufactured under routine conditions to confirm reproducibility.

5.19. The number of batches manufactured and the number of samples taken should be based on quality risk management principles, allow the normal range of variation and trends to be established and provide sufficient data for evaluation. Each manufacturer must determine and justify the number of batches necessary to demonstrate a high level of assurance that the process is capable of consistently delivering quality product.

5.20. Without prejudice to 5.19, it is generally considered acceptable that a minimum of three consecutive batches manufactured under routine conditions could constitute a validation of the process. An alternative number of batches may be justified taking into account whether standard methods of manufacture are used and whether similar products or processes are already used at the site. An initial validation exercise with three batches may need to be supplemented with further data obtained from subsequent batches as part of an on-going process verification exercise.

5.21. A process validation protocol should be prepared which defines the critical process parameters (CPP), critical quality attributes (CQA) and the associated acceptance criteria which should be based on development data or documented process knowledge.

5.22. Process validation protocols should include, but are not limited to the following:

i. A short description of the process and a reference to the respective Master Batch Record;

ii. Functions and responsibilities;
iii. Summary of the CQAs to be investigated;
iv. Summary of CPPs and their associated limits;
v. Summary of other (non-critical) attributes and parameters which will be investigated or monitored during the validation activity, and the reasons for their inclusion;
vi. List of the equipment/facilities to be used (including measuring/monitoring/recording equipment) together with the calibration status;
vii. List of analytical methods and method validation, as appropriate.
viii. Proposed in-process controls with acceptance criteria and the reason(s) why each in-process control is selected;
ix. Additional testing to be carried out with acceptance criteria;
x. Sampling plan and the rationale behind it;
xi. Methods for recording and evaluating results;
xii. Process for release and certification of batches (if applicable).

Continuous process verification

5.23. For products developed by a quality by design approach, where it has been scientifically established during development that the established control strategy provides a high degree of assurance of product quality, then continuous process verification can be used as an alternative to traditional process validation.

5.24. The method by which the process will be verified should be defined. There should be a science based control strategy for the required attributes for incoming materials, critical quality attributes and critical process parameters to confirm product realisation. This should also include regular evaluation of the control strategy. Process Analytical Technology and multivariate statistical process control may be used as tools. Each manufacturer must determine and justify the number of batches necessary to demonstrate a high level of assurance that the process is capable of consistently delivering quality product.

5.25. The general principles laid down in 5.1 – 5.14 above still apply.

Hybrid approach

5.26. A hybrid of the traditional approach and continuous process verification could be used where there is a substantial amount of product and process knowledge and understanding which has been gained from manufacturing experience and historical batch data.

5.27. This approach may also be used for any validation activities after changes or during ongoing process verification even though the product was initially validated using a traditional approach.

Ongoing Process Verification during Lifecycle

5.28. Paragraphs 5.28-5.32 are applicable to all three approaches to process validation mentioned above, i.e. traditional, continuous and hybrid.

5.29. Manufacturers should monitor product quality to ensure that a state of control is maintained throughout the product lifecycle with the relevant process trends evaluated.

5.30. The extent and frequency of ongoing process verification should be reviewed periodically. At any point throughout the product lifecycle, it may be appropriate to modify the requirements taking into account the current level of process understanding and process performance.

5.31. Ongoing process verification should be conducted under an approved protocol or equivalent documents and a corresponding report should be prepared to document the results obtained. Statistical tools should be used, where appropriate, to support any conclusions with regard to the variability and capability of a given process and ensure a state of control.

5.32. Ongoing process verification should be used throughout the product lifecycle to support the validated status of the product as documented in the Product Quality Review. Incremental changes over time should also be considered and the need for any additional actions, e.g. enhanced sampling, should be assessed.

6. Verification of Transportation

6.1. Finished medicinal products, investigational medicinal products, bulk product and samples should be transported from manufacturing sites in accordance with the conditions defined in the marketing authorisation, the approved label, product specification file or as justified by the manufacturer.

6.2. It is recognised that verification of transportation may be challenging due to the variable factors involved however, transportation routes should be clearly defined. Seasonal and other variations should also be considered during verification of transport

6.3. A risk assessment should be performed to consider the impact of variables in the transportation process other than those conditions which are continuously controlled or monitored, e.g. delays during transportation, failure of monitoring devices, topping up liquid nitrogen, product susceptibility and any other relevant factors.

6.4. Due to the variable conditions expected during transportation, continuous monitoring and recording of any critical environmental conditions to which the product may be subjected should be performed, unless otherwise justified.

7. Validation of Packaging

7.1. Variation in equipment processing parameters especially during primary packaging may have a significant impact on the integrity and correct functioning of the pack, e.g. blister strips, sachets and sterile components, therefore primary and secondary packaging equipment for finished and bulk products should be qualified.

7.2. Qualification of the equipment used for primary packing should be carried out at the minimum and maximum operating ranges defined for the critical process parameters such as temperature, machine speed and sealing pressure or for any other factors.

8. Qualification of Utilities

8.1. The quality of steam, water, air, other gases etc. should be confirmed following installation using the qualification steps described in section 3 above.

8.2. The period and extent of qualification should reflect any seasonal variations, if applicable, and the intended use of the utility.

8.3. A risk assessment should be carried out where there may be direct contact with the product, e.g. heating, ventilation and air-conditioning (HVAC) systems, or indirect contact such as through heat exchangers to mitigate any risks of failure.

9. Validation of Test Methods

9.1. All analytical test methods used in qualification, validation or cleaning exercises should be validated with an appropriate detection and quantification limit, where necessary, as defined in Chapter 6 of the EudraLex, Volume 4, Part I.

9.2. Where microbial testing of product is carried out, the method should be validated to confirm that the product does not influence the recovery of microorganisms.

9.3. Where microbial testing of surfaces in clean rooms is carried out, validation should be performed on the test method to confirm that sanitising agents do not influence the recovery of microorganisms.

10. Cleaning Validation

10.1. Cleaning validation should be performed in order to confirm the effectiveness of any cleaning procedure for all product contact equipment. Simulating agents may be used with appropriate scientific justification. Where similar types of equipment are grouped together, a justification of the specific equipment selected for cleaning validation is expected.

10.2. A visual check for cleanliness is an important part of the acceptance criteria for cleaning validation. It is not generally acceptable for this criterion alone to be used. Repeated cleaning and retesting until acceptable residue results are obtained is not considered an acceptable approach.

10.3. It is recognised that a cleaning validation programme may take some time to complete and validation with verification after each batch may be required for some products, e.g. investigational medicinal products. There should be sufficient data from the verification to support a conclusion that the equipment is clean and available for further use.

10.4. Validation should consider the level of automation in the cleaning process. Where an automatic process is used, the specified normal operating range of the utilities and equipment should be validated.

10.5. For all cleaning processes an assessment should be performed to determine the variable factors which influence cleaning effectiveness and performance, e.g. operators, the level of detail in procedures such as rinsing times etc. If variable factors have been identified, the worst case situations should be used as the basis for cleaning validation studies.

10.6. Limits for the carryover of product residues should be based on a toxicological evaluation[2]. The justification for the selected limits should be documented in a risk assessment which includes all the supporting references. Limits should be established for the removal of any cleaning agents used. Acceptance criteria should consider the potential cumulative effect of multiple items of equipment in the process equipment train.

10.6.1. Therapeutic macromolecules and peptides are known to degrade and denature when exposed to pH extremes and/or heat, and may become pharmacologically inactive. A toxicological evaluation may therefore not be applicable in these circumstances.

10.6.2. If it is not feasible to test for specific product residues, other representative parameters may be selected, e.g. total organic carbon (TOC) and conductivity.

10.7. The risk presented by microbial and endotoxin contamination should be considered during the development of cleaning validation protocols.

10.8. The influence of the time between manufacture and cleaning and the time between cleaning and use should be taken into account to define dirty and clean hold times for the cleaning process.

10.9. Where campaign manufacture is carried out, the impact on the ease of cleaning at the end of the campaign should be considered and the maximum length of a campaign (in time and/or number of batches) should be the basis for cleaning validation exercises.

10.10. Where a worst case product approach is used as a cleaning validation model, a scientific rationale should be provided for the selection of the worst case product and the impact of new products to the site assessed. Criteria for determining the worst case may include solubility, cleanability, toxicity and potency.

10.11. Cleaning validation protocols should specify or reference the locations to be sampled, the rationale for the selection of these locations and define the acceptance criteria.

10.12. Sampling should be carried out by swabbing and/or rinsing or by other means depending on the production equipment. The sampling materials and method should not influence the result. Recovery should be shown to be possible from all product contact materials sampled in the equipment with all the sampling methods used.

10.13. The cleaning procedure should be performed an appropriate number of times based on a risk assessment and meet the acceptance criteria in order to prove that the cleaning method is validated.

2 See EMA Guideline on setting health based exposure limits for use in risk identification in the manufacture of different medicinal products in shared facilities

10.14. Where a cleaning process is ineffective or is not appropriate for some equipment, dedicated equipment or other appropriate measures should be used for each product as indicated in chapters 3 and 5 of EudraLex, Volume 4, Part I.

10.15. Where manual cleaning of equipment is performed, it is especially important that the effectiveness of the manual process should be confirmed at a justified frequency.

11. Change Control

11.1. The control of change is an important part of knowledge management and should be handled within the pharmaceutical quality system.

11.2. Written procedures should be in place to describe the actions to be taken if a planned change is proposed to a starting material, product component, process, equipment, premises, product range, method of production or testing, batch size, design space or any other change during the lifecycle that may affect product quality or reproducibility.

11.3. Where design space is used, the impact on changes to the design space should be considered against the registered design space within the marketing authorisation and the need for any regulatory actions assessed.

11.4. Quality risk management should be used to evaluate planned changes to determine the potential impact on product quality, pharmaceutical quality systems, documentation, validation, regulatory status, calibration, maintenance and on any other system to avoid unintended consequences and to plan for any necessary process validation, verification or requalification efforts.

11.5. Changes should be authorised and approved by the responsible persons or relevant functional personnel in accordance with the pharmaceutical quality system.

11.6. Supporting data, e.g. copies of documents, should be reviewed to confirm that the impact of the change has been demonstrated prior to final approval.

11.7. Following implementation, and, where appropriate, an evaluation of the effectiveness of change should be carried out to confirm that the change has been successful.

12. Glossary

Definitions of terms relating to qualification and validation which are not given in other sections of the current EudraLex, Volume 4, are given below.

Bracketing approach. A science and risk based validation approach such that only batches on the extremes of certain predetermined and justified design factors, e.g. strength, batch size and/or pack size, are tested during process validation. The design assumes that validation of any intermediate levels is represented by validation of the extremes. Where a range of strengths is to be validated, bracketing could be applicable if the strengths are identical or very closely related in composition, e.g. for a tablet range made with different compression weights of a similar basic granulation or a capsule range made by filling different plug fill weights of the same basic composition into different size capsule shells. Bracketing can be applied to different container sizes or different fills in the same container closure system.

Change Control. A formal system by which qualified representatives of appropriate disciplines review proposed or actual changes that might affect the validated status of facilities, systems, equipment or processes. The intent is to determine the need for action to ensure and document that the system is maintained in a validated state.

Cleaning Validation. Cleaning validation is documented evidence that an approved cleaning procedure will reproducibly remove the previous product or cleaning agents used in the equipment below the scientifically set maximum allowable carryover level.

Cleaning verification. The gathering of evidence through chemical analysis after each batch/campaign to show that the residues of the previous product or cleaning agents have been reduced below the scientifically set maximum allowable carryover level.

Concurrent Validation. Validation carried out in exceptional circumstances, justified on the basis of significant patient benefit, where the validation protocol is executed concurrently with commercialisation of the validation batches.

Continuous process verification. An alternative approach to process validation in which manufacturing process performance is continuously monitored and evaluated. (ICH Q8)

Control Strategy. A planned set of controls derived from current product and process understanding that ensures process performance and product quality. The controls can include parameters and attributes related to drug substance and drug product materials and components, facility and equipment operating conditions, in-process controls, finished product specifications and the associated methods and frequency of monitoring and control. (ICH Q10)

Critical process parameter (CPP). A process parameter whose variability has an impact on a critical quality attribute and therefore should be monitored or controlled to ensure the process produces the desired quality. (ICH Q8)

Critical quality attribute (CQA). A physical, chemical, biological or microbiological property or characteristic that should be within an approved limit, range or distribution to ensure the desired product quality. (ICH Q8)

Design qualification (DQ). The documented verification that the proposed design of the facilities, systems and equipment is suitable for the intended purpose.

Design Space. The multidimensional combination and interaction of input variables, e.g. material attributes, and process parameters that have been demonstrated to provide assurance of quality. Working within the design space is not considered as a change. Movement out of the design space is considered to be a change and would normally initiate a regulatory post approval change process. Design space is proposed by the applicant and is subject to regulatory assessment and approval. (ICH Q8)

Installation Qualification (IQ). The documented verification that the facilities, systems and equipment, as installed or modified, comply with the approved design and the manufacturer's recommendations.

Knowledge management. A systematic approach to acquire, analyse, store and disseminate information. (ICH Q10)

Lifecycle. All phases in the life of a product, equipment or facility from initial development or use through to discontinuation of use.

Ongoing Process Verification (also known as continued process verification). Documented evidence that the process remains in a state of control during commercial manufacture.

Operational Qualification (OQ). The documented verification that the facilities, systems and equipment, as installed or modified, perform as intended throughout the anticipated operating ranges.

Performance Qualification (PQ). The documented verification that systems and equipment can perform effectively and reproducibly based on the approved process method and product specification.

Process Validation. The documented evidence that the process, operated within established parameters, can perform effectively and reproducibly to produce a medicinal product meeting its predetermined specifications and quality attributes.

Product realisation. Achievement of a product with the quality attributes to meet the needs of patients, health care professionals and regulatory authorities and internal customer requirements. (ICH Q10)

Prospective Validation. Validation carried out before routine production of products intended for sale.

Quality by design. A systematic approach that begins with predefined objectives and emphasises product and process understanding and process control, based on sound science and quality risk management.

Quality risk management. A systematic process for the assessment, control, communication and review of risks to quality across the lifecycle. (ICH Q9)

Simulated agents. A material that closely approximates the physical and, where practical, the chemical characteristics, e.g. viscosity, particle size, pH etc., of the product under validation.

State of control. A condition in which the set of controls consistently provides assurance of acceptable process performance and product quality.

Traditional approach. A product development approach where set points and operating ranges for process parameters are defined to ensure reproducibility.

Worst Case. A condition or set of conditions encompassing upper and lower processing limits and circumstances, within standard operating procedures, which pose the greatest chance of product or process failure when compared to ideal conditions. Such conditions do not necessarily induce product or process failure.

User requirements Specification (URS). The set of owner, user and engineering requirements necessary and sufficient to create a feasible design meeting the intended purpose of the system.

EudraLex

Chapter 8

EU Guidelines for Good Manufacturing Practice for Medicinal Products for Human and Veterinary Use

Chapter 4: Documentation

June 30, 2011
Eudralex, Volume 4
European Commission
Health and Consumers Directorate-General
Public Health and Risk Assessment
Pharmaceuticals

Principle

Good documentation constitutes an essential part of the quality assurance system and is key to operating in compliance with GMP requirements. The various types of documents and media used should be fully defined in the manufacturer's Quality Management System. Documentation may exist in a variety of forms, including paper-based, electronic or photographic media. The main objective of the system of documentation utilized must be to establish, control, monitor and record all activities which directly or indirectly impact on all aspects of the quality of medicinal products. The Quality Management System should include sufficient instructional detail to facilitate a common understanding of the requirements, in addition to providing for sufficient recording of the various processes and evaluation of any observations, so that ongoing application of the requirements may be demonstrated.

There are two primary types of documentation used to manage and record GMP compliance: instructions (directions, requirements) and records/reports. Appropriate good documentation practice should be applied with respect to the type of document.

Suitable controls should be implemented to ensure the accuracy, integrity, availability and legibility of documents. Instruction documents should be free from errors and available in writing. The term 'written' means recorded, or documented on media from which data may be rendered in a human readable form.

Required GMP documentation (by type):

Site Master File: A document describing the GMP related activities of the manufacturer.

Instructions (directions, or requirements) type:

> ***Specifications:*** Describe in detail the requirements with which the products or materials used or obtained during manufacture have to conform. They serve as a basis for quality evaluation.

---

i This document may be accessed online at https://ec.europa.eu/health/sites/health/files/files/eudralex/vol-4/chapter4_01-2011_en.pdf

Manufacturing Formulae, Processing, Packaging and Testing Instructions: Provide detail all the starting materials, equipment and computerised systems (if any) to be used and specify all processing, packaging, sampling and testing instructions. In – process controls and process analytical technologies to be employed should be specified where relevant, together with acceptance criteria.

Procedures: (Otherwise known as Standard Operating Procedures, or SOPs), give directions for performing certain operations.

Protocols: Give instructions for performing and recording certain discreet operations.

Technical Agreements: Are agreed between contract givers and acceptors for outsourced activities.

RECORD/REPORT TYPE:

Records: Provide evidence of various actions taken to demonstrate compliance with instructions, e.g. activities, events, investigations, and in the case of manufactured batches a history of each batch of product, including its distribution. Records include the raw data which is used to generate other records. For electronic records regulated users should define which data are to be used as raw data. At least, all data on which quality decisions are based should be defined as raw data

Certificates of Analysis: Provide a summary of testing results on samples of products or materials[1] together with the evaluation for compliance to a stated specification.

Reports: Document the conduct of particular exercises, projects or investigations, together with results, conclusions and recommendations.

GENERATION AND CONTROL OF DOCUMENTATION

4.1 All types of document should be defined and adhered to. The requirements apply equally to all forms of document media types. Complex systems need to be understood, well documented, validated, and adequate controls should be in place. Many documents (instructions and/or records) may exist in hybrid forms, i.e. some elements as electronic and others as paper based. Relationships and control measures for master documents, official copies, data handling and records need to be stated for both hybrid and homogenous systems. Appropriate controls for electronic documents such as templates, forms, and master documents should be implemented. Appropriate controls should be in place to ensure the integrity of the record throughout the retention period.

4.2 Documents should be designed, prepared, reviewed, and distributed with care. They

1 Alternatively the certification may be based, in-whole or in-part, on the assessment of real time data (summaries and exception reports) from batch related process analytical technology (PAT), parameters or metrics as per the approved marketing authorisation dossier.

should comply with the relevant parts of Product Specification Files, Manufacturing and Marketing Authorisation dossiers, as appropriate. The reproduction of working documents from master documents should not allow any error to be introduced through the reproduction process.

4.3 Documents containing instructions should be approved, signed and dated by appropriate and authorised persons. Documents should have unambiguous contents and be uniquely identifiable. The effective date should be defined.

4.4 Documents containing instructions should be laid out in an orderly fashion and be easy to check. The style and language of documents should fit with their intended use. Standard Operating Procedures, Work Instructions and Methods should be written in an imperative mandatory style.

4.5 Documents within the Quality Management System should be regularly reviewed and kept up-to-date.

4.6 Documents should not be hand-written; although, where documents require the entry of data, sufficient space should be provided for such entries.

Good Documentation Practices

4.7 Handwritten entries should be made in clear, legible, indelible way.

4.8 Records should be made or completed at the time each action is taken and in such a way that all significant activities concerning the manufacture of medicinal products are traceable.

4.9 Any alteration made to the entry on a document should be signed and dated; the alteration should permit the reading of the original information. Where appropriate, the reason for the alteration should be recorded.

Retention of Documents

4.10 It should be clearly defined which record is related to each manufacturing activity and where this record is located. Secure controls must be in place to ensure the integrity of the record throughout the retention period and validated where appropriate.

4.11 Specific requirements apply to batch documentation which must be kept for one year after expiry of the batch to which it relates or at least five years after certification of the batch by the Qualified Person, whichever is the longer. For investigational medicinal products, the batch documentation must be kept for at least five years after the completion or formal discontinuation of the last clinical trial in which the batch was used. Other requirements for retention of documentation may be described in legislation in relation to specific types of product (e.g. Advanced Therapy Medicinal Products) and specify that longer retention periods be applied to certain documents.

4.12 For other types of documentation, the retention period will depend on the business activity which the documentation supports. Critical documentation, including raw data (for example relating to validation or stability), which supports information in the Marketing Authorisation should be retained whilst the authorization remains in force. It may be considered acceptable to retire certain documentation (e.g. raw data supporting validation reports or stability reports) where the data has been superseded by a full set of new data. Justification for this should be documented and should take into account the requirements for retention of batch documentation; for example, in the case of process validation data, the accompanying raw data should be retained for a period at least as long as the records for all batches whose release has been supported on the basis of that validation exercise.

The following section gives some examples of required documents. The quality management system should describe all documents required to ensure product quality and patient safety.

SPECIFICATIONS

4.13 There should be appropriately authorised and dated specifications for starting and packaging materials, and finished products.

Specifications for starting and packaging materials

4.14 Specifications for starting and primary or printed packaging materials should include or provide reference to, if applicable:

a) A description of the materials, including:
   - The designated name and the internal code reference;
   - The reference, if any, to a pharmacopoeial monograph;
   - The approved suppliers and, if reasonable, the original producer of the material;
   - A specimen of printed materials;

b) Directions for sampling and testing;

c) Qualitative and quantitative requirements with acceptance limits;

d) Storage conditions and precautions;

e) The maximum period of storage before re-examination.

Specifications for intermediate and bulk products

4.15 Specifications for intermediate and bulk products should be available for critical steps or if these are purchased or dispatched. The specifications should be similar to specifications for starting materials or for finished products, as appropriate.

Specifications for finished products

4.16 Specifications for finished products should include or provide reference to:

a) The designated name of the product and the code reference where applicable;

b) The formula;

c) A description of the pharmaceutical form and package details;

d) Directions for sampling and testing
e) The qualitative and quantitative requirements, with the acceptance limits;
f) The storage conditions and any special handling precautions, where applicable;
g) The shelf-life.

MANUFACTURING FORMULA AND PROCESSING INSTRUCTIONS

Approved, written Manufacturing Formula and Processing Instructions should exist for each product and batch size to be manufactured.

4.17 The Manufacturing Formula should include:

a) The name of the product, with a product reference code relating to its specification;
b) A description of the pharmaceutical form, strength of the product and batch size;
c) A list of all starting materials to be used, with the amount of each, described; mention should be made of any substance that may disappear in the course of processing;
d) A statement of the expected final yield with the acceptable limits, and of relevant intermediate yields, where applicable

4.18 The Processing Instructions should include:

a) A statement of the processing location and the principal equipment to be used;
b) The methods, or reference to the methods, to be used for preparing the critical equipment (e.g. cleaning, assembling, calibrating, sterilising);
c) Checks that the equipment and work station are clear of previous products, documents or materials not required for the planned process, and that equipment is clean and suitable for use;
d) Detailed stepwise processing instructions [e.g. checks on materials, pre-treatments, sequence for adding materials, critical process parameters (time, temp etc)];
e) The instructions for any in-process controls with their limits;
f) Where necessary, the requirements for bulk storage of the products; including the container, labeling and special storage conditions where applicable;
g) Any special precautions to be observed.

Packaging Instructions

4.19 Approved Packaging Instructions for each product, pack size and type should exist. These should include, or have a reference to, the following:

a) Name of the product; including the batch number of bulk and finished product
b) Description of its pharmaceutical form, and strength where applicable;
c) The pack size expressed in terms of the number, weight or volume of the product in the final container;

d) A complete list of all the packaging materials required, including quantities, sizes and types, with the code or reference number relating to the specifications of each packaging material;

e) Where appropriate, an example or reproduction of the relevant printed packaging materials, and specimens indicating where to apply batch number references, and shelf life of the product;

f) Checks that the equipment and work station are clear of previous products, documents or materials not required for the planned packaging operations (line clearance), and that equipment is clean and suitable for use.

g) Special precautions to be observed, including a careful examination of the area and equipment in order to ascertain the line clearance before operations begin;

h) A description of the packaging operation, including any significant subsidiary operations, and equipment to be used;

i) Details of in-process controls with instructions for sampling and acceptance limits.

Batch Processing Record

4.20 A Batch Processing Record should be kept for each batch processed. It should be based on the relevant parts of the currently approved Manufacturing Formula and Processing Instructions, and should contain the following information:

a) The name and batch number of the product;

b) Dates and times of commencement, of significant intermediate stages and of completion of production;

c) Identification (initials) of the operator(s) who performed each significant step of the process and, where appropriate, the name of any person who checked these operations;

d) The batch number and/or analytical control number as well as the quantities of each starting material actually weighed (including the batch number and amount of any recovered or reprocessed material added);

e) Any relevant processing operation or event and major equipment used;

f) A record of the in-process controls and the initials of the person(s) carrying them out, and the results obtained;

g) The product yield obtained at different and pertinent stages of manufacture;

h) Notes on special problems including details, with signed authorisation for any deviation from the Manufacturing Formula and Processing Instructions;

i) Approval by the person responsible for the processing operations.

Note: Where a validated process is continuously monitored and controlled, then automatically generated reports may be limited to compliance summaries and exception/ out-of-specification (OOS) data reports.

Batch Packaging Record

4.21 A Batch Packaging Record should be kept for each batch or part batch processed. It should be based on the relevant parts of the Packaging Instructions.

The batch packaging record should contain the following information:

a) The name and batch number of the product,

b) The date(s) and times of the packaging operations;

c) Identification (initials) of the operator(s) who performed each significant step of the process and, where appropriate, the name of any person who checked these operations;

d) Records of checks for identity and conformity with the packaging instructions, including the results of in-process controls;

e) Details of the packaging operations carried out, including references to equipment and the packaging lines used;

f) Whenever possible, samples of printed packaging materials used, including specimens of the batch coding, expiry dating and any additional overprinting;

g) Notes on any special problems or unusual events including details, with signed authorisation for any deviation from the Packaging Instructions;

h) The quantities and reference number or identification of all printed packaging materials and bulk product issued, used, destroyed or returned to stock and the quantities of obtained product, in order to provide for an adequate reconciliation. Where there are there are robust electronic controls in place during packaging there may be justification for not including this information

i) Approval by the person responsible for the packaging operations

PROCEDURES AND RECORDS

Receipt

4.22 There should be written procedures and records for the receipt of each delivery of each starting material, (including bulk, intermediate or finished goods), primary, secondary and printed packaging materials.

4.23 The records of the receipts should include:

a) The name of the material on the delivery note and the containers;

b) The “in-house” name and/or code of material (if different from a);

c) Date of receipt;

d) Supplier’s name and, manufacturer’s name;

e) Manufacturer’s batch or reference number;

f) Total quantity and number of containers received;

g) The batch number assigned after receipt;

h) Any relevant comment.

4.24 There should be written procedures for the internal labeling, quarantine and storage of starting materials, packaging materials and other materials, as appropriate.

Sampling

4.25 There should be written procedures for sampling, which include the methods and equipment to be used, the amounts to be taken and any precautions to be observed to avoid contamination of the material or any deterioration in its quality.

Testing

4.26 There should be written procedures for testing materials and products at different stages of manufacture, describing the methods and equipment to be used. The tests performed should be recorded.

Other

4.27 Written release and rejection procedures should be available for materials and products, and in particular for the certification for sale of the finished product by the Qualified Person(s). All records should be available to the Qualified Person. A system should be in place to indicate special observations and any changes to critical data.

4.28 Records should be maintained for the distribution of each batch of a product in order to facilitate recall of any batch, if necessary.

4.29 There should be written policies, procedures, protocols, reports and the associated records of actions taken or conclusions reached, where appropriate, for the following examples:

- Validation and qualification of processes, equipment and systems;
- Equipment assembly and calibration;
- Technology transfer;
- Maintenance, cleaning and sanitation;
- Personnel matters including signature lists, training in GMP and technical matters, clothing and hygiene and verification of the effectiveness of training.
- Environmental monitoring;
- Pest control;
- Complaints;
- Recalls;
- Returns;
- Change control;
- Investigations into deviations and non-conformances;
- Internal quality/GMP compliance audits;
- Summaries of records where appropriate (e.g. product quality review);
- Supplier audits.

4.30 Clear operating procedures should be available for major items of manufacturing and test equipment.

4.31 Logbooks should be kept for major or critical analytical testing, production equipment, and areas where product has been processed. They should be used to record in chronological order, as appropriate, any use of the area, equipment/method, calibrations, maintenance, cleaning or repair operations, including the dates and identity of people who carried these operations out.

4.32 An inventory of documents within the Quality Management System should be maintained.

GUIDANCE DOCUMENTS

REGARDING GUIDANCE DOCUMENTS

The guidances reproduced in this book represent the "current thinking" of the issuing agencies on these topics. They do not establish rights for any person and are not binding on the issuing body (e.g. the US Food and Drug Administration, the European Commission, the International Medical Device Regulators Forum, etc.) or the public. Alternative approaches may be deemed satisfactory if they fulfill the requirements of the applicable laws. For more information about these guidance documents or to discuss alternative approaches, contact the office responsible for the corresponding guidance documents.[i]

Other documents that complement these guidelines are available from the relative branches of government, and the documents contained herein may be updated from time to time. It is the responsibility of the reader to ensure that the information is still valid and accurate.

FDA documents may be accessed online at https://www.fda.gov/regulatory-information.

Documents produced by the European Commission may be accessed online at https://www.ema.europa.eu/en/human-regulatory/overview/medical-devices.

Documents offered from the International Medical Device Regulators Forum (IMDRF) and the Global Harmonization Task Force for Medical Devices (GHTF) can be accessed at http://www.imdrf.org/documents/documents.asp

i "About FDA Guidance Documents" U.S. Food and Drug Administration, 2021, www.fda.gov/regulatory-information/search-fda-guidance-documents#report accessed March 1, 2021.

Chapter 9
IMDFR
Software as a Medical Device: Key Definitions

December 9, 2013
IMDRF/SaMD WG/N10FINAL:2013
Authoring Group: IMDRF SaMD Working Group
Final Document

Preface

The document herein was produced by the International Medical Device Regulators Forum (IMDRF), a voluntary group of medical device regulators from around the world. The document has been subject to consultation throughout its development.

There are no restrictions on the reproduction, distribution or use of this document; however, incorporation of this document, in part or in whole, into any other document, or its translation into languages other than English, does not convey or represent an endorsement of any kind by the International Medical Device Regulators Forum.

1.0 Introduction

Software is becoming increasingly important and pervasive in healthcare. Given the availability of a multitude of technology platforms (e.g., personal computers, smart phones, network servers, etc.), as well as increasing ease of access and distribution (e.g., internet, cloud), software created for medical purposes (software used to make clinical decisions) and non-medical purpose (e.g., administrative, financial) are being used in healthcare.

In general, existing regulations address public health risks of software when embedded in a traditional medical device. However, the current application of regulations and controls may not always translate or address the unique public health risks posed by Software as a Medical Device (SaMD) nor assure an appropriate balance between patient/consumer protection and promotion of public health by facilitating innovation.

This is the first of a collection of documents that will be developed by the International Medical Device Regulators Forum (IMDRF) to establish a common framework for regulators to incorporate converged controls into their regulatory approaches for SaMD..

This collection of IMDRF SaMD documents will provide regulators with the fundamental building blocks and a common understanding of the many kinds and importance of software for medical purposes in advancing public health. Generally medical purpose software[1] consists of:

1 Software used to make or maintain a device (testing, source code management, servicing, etc.) is not considered software with a medical purpose.

(1) software in a medical device (sometimes referred to as "embedded" or "part of");

(2) software as a medical device (SaMD).

This document IMDRF SaMD WG N10/Software as a Medical Device[2]: Key Definitions focuses on a common definition for when software is considered to be a medical device and a reminder of other key terms, some previously defined in Global Harmonization Task Force (GHTF) documents, with relevance to SaMD. The key definitions and terms developed in IMDRF SaMD WG N10 will be used to develop future documents that provide a common framework for identifying types of SaMD and associated risks and controls to minimize these risks.

Some regulators have taken individual approaches to assure safety, effectiveness, and performance of SaMD. Such approaches have common public health goals. The objective of this effort is to promote consistent expectations for SaMD and to provide an optimal level of patient safety while fostering innovation and ensuring patients and providers have continued access to advances in healthcare technology.

2.0 Scope

This document IMDRF SaMD WG N10/Software as a Medical Device: Key Definitions focuses on a common definition for when software is considered to be a medical device and a reminder of other key terms, some previously defined in Global Harmonization Task Force (GHTF) documents, with relevance to SaMD.

Software intended as an accessory to a medical device is not in the scope of this document, unless the software meets the definition of SaMD in this document.

This document focuses on the definition of the SaMD irrespective of software technology and/or platform (e.g., mobile app, cloud).

3.0 References

- GHTF/SG1/N55:2008 *Definition of the Terms Manufacturer, Authorised Representative, Distributor and Importer*
- GHTF/SG1/N70:2011 *Label and Instructions for Use for Medical Devices*
- GHTF/SG1/N71:2012 *Definition of Terms Medical Device and In Vitro Diagnostic Medical Device*
- ISO/IEC 14764:2006 *Software Engineering — Software Life Cycle Processes — Maintenance*

2 This IMDRF document converges on the term SaMD to replace the term "standalone software" or "standalone medical device software". However the concepts of standalone software are included in this converged definition of SaMD.

4.0 DEFINITIONS

This section is intentionally left blank as the definitions are contained within the body of this document.

5.0 KEY DEFINITIONS

5.1 SOFTWARE AS A MEDICAL DEVICE

The term *"Software as a Medical Device"* (SaMD) is defined as software intended to be used for one or more medical purposes that perform these purposes without being part of a hardware medical device.

Notes:

- SaMD is a medical device and includes in-vitro diagnostic (IVD) medical device.
- SaMD is capable of running on general purpose (non-medical purpose) computing platforms[3]
- "without being part of" means software not necessary for a hardware medical device to achieve its intended medical purpose;
- Software does not meet the definition of SaMD if its intended purpose is to drive a hardware medical device.
- SaMD may be used in combination (e.g., as a module) with other products including medical devices;
- SaMD may be interfaced with other medical devices, including hardware medical devices and other SaMD software, as well as general purpose software
- Mobile apps that meet the definition above are considered SaMD.

5.2 MEDICAL PURPOSE

The following two terms as defined in GHTF/SG1/N71:2012 (italicized below) identify medical purpose applicable to SaMD:

5.2.1 Medical Device

'Medical device' means any instrument, apparatus, implement, machine, appliance, implant, reagent for in vitro use, software, material or other similar or related article, intended by the manufacturer to be used, alone or in combination, for human beings, for one or more of the specific medical purpose(s) of:

- diagnosis, prevention, monitoring, treatment or alleviation of disease,
- diagnosis, monitoring, treatment, alleviation of or compensation for an injury,

3 "Computing platforms" include hardware and software resources (e.g. operating system, processing hardware, storage, software libraries, displays, input devices, programming languages etc.). "Operating systems" that SaMD require may be run on a server, a workstation, a mobile platform, or other general purpose hardware platform.

- investigation, replacement, modification, or support of the anatomy or of a physiological process,
- supporting or sustaining life,
- control of conception,
- disinfection of medical devices,
- providing information by means of in vitro examination of specimens derived from the human body;

and does not achieve its primary intended action by pharmacological, immunological or metabolic means, in or on the human body, but which may be assisted in its intended function by such means.

Note: Products which may be considered to be medical devices in some jurisdictions but not in others include:

- disinfection substances,
- aids for persons with disabilities,
- devices incorporating animal and/or human tissues,
- devices for.in-vitro fertilization or assisted reproduction technologies.

5.2.2 In Vitro Diagnostic (IVD) medical device

'In Vitro Diagnostic (IVD) medical device' means a medical device, whether used alone or in combination, intended by the manufacturer for the in-vitro examination of specimens derived from the human body solely or principally to provide information for diagnostic, monitoring or compatibility purposes.

Note 1: IVD medical devices include reagents, calibrators, control materials, specimen receptacles, software, and related instruments or apparatus or other articles and are used, for example, for the following test purposes: diagnosis, aid to diagnosis, screening, monitoring, predisposition, prognosis, prediction, determination of physiological status.

Note 2: In some jurisdictions, certain IVD medical devices may be covered by other regulations.

5.2.3 Additional considerations for SaMD

SaMD may also:

- provide means and suggestions for mitigation of a disease;
- provide information for determining compatibility, detecting, diagnosing, monitoring or treating physiological conditions, states of health, illnesses or congenital deformities;
- be an aid to diagnosis, screening, monitoring, determination of predisposition; prognosis, prediction, determination of physiological status.

5.3 SaMD Changes

SaMD Changes refer to any modifications made throughout the lifecycle of the SaMD including the maintenance phase.

Software maintenance[4] can include adaptive (e.g. keeps pace with the changing environment), perfective (e.g. recoding to improve software performance), corrective (e.g. corrects discovered problems), or preventive (e.g. corrects latent faults in the software product before they become operational faults).

Examples of SaMD changes include, but are not limited to, defect fixes; aesthetic, performance or usability enhancements; and security patches.

5.4 SaMD Manufacturer

For SaMD manufacturer the definition in GHTF/SG1/N55:2009 applies:

"Manufacturer" means any natural or legal person[5] with responsibility for design and/or manufacture of a medical device with the intention of making the medical device available for use, under his name; whether or not such a medical device is designed and/or manufactured by that person himself or on his behalf by another person(s).

Notes:

1. This 'natural or legal person' has ultimate legal responsibility for ensuring compliance with all applicable regulatory requirements for the medical device in the countries or jurisdictions where it is intended to be made available or sold, unless this responsibility is specifically imposed on another person by the Regulatory Authority (RA) within that jurisdiction.

2. The manufacturer's responsibilities are described in other GHTF guidance documents. These responsibilities include meeting both pre-market requirements and post-market requirements, such as adverse event reporting and notification of corrective actions.

3. 'Design and/or manufacture', as referred to in the above definition, may include specification development, production, fabrication, assembly, processing, packaging, repackaging, labelling, relabelling, sterilization, installation, or remanufacturing of a medical device; or putting a collection of devices, and possibly other products, together for a medical purpose.

---

4 ISO/IEC 14764:2006 Software Engineering — Software Life Cycle Processes — Maintenance
- adaptive maintenance: the modification of a software product, performed after delivery, to keep a software product usable in a changed or changing environment.
- perfective maintenance: the modification of a software product after delivery to detect and correct latent faults in the software product before they are manifested as failures
- corrective maintenance: the reactive modification of a software product performed after delivery to correct discovered problems
- preventive maintenance: the modification of a software product after delivery to detect and correct latent faults in the software product before they become operational faults

5 The term "person" that appears here and in the other definitions of this document, includes legal entities such as a corporation, a partnership or an association.

4. Any person who assembles or adapts a medical device that has already been supplied by another person for an individual patient, in accordance with the instructions for use, is not the manufacturer, provided the assembly or adaptation does not change the intended use of the medical device.
5. Any person who changes the intended use of, or modifies, a medical device without acting on behalf of the original manufacturer and who makes it available for use under his own name, should be considered the manufacturer of the modified medical device.
6. An authorised representative, distributor or importer who only adds its own address and contact details to the medical device or the packaging, without covering or changing the existing labelling, is not considered a manufacturer.
7. To the extent that an accessory is subject to the regulatory requirements of a medical device6[6], the person responsible for the design and/or manufacture of that accessory is considered to be a manufacturer.

5.5 Intended Use / Intended Purpose

For SaMD intended use, the definition in GHTF/SG1/N70:2011 "Label and Instructions for Use for Medical Devices" applies:

> The term *"intended use / intended purpose"* is the objective intent of the manufacturer regarding the use of a product, process or service as reflected in the specifications, instructions and information provided by the manufacturer.

5.5.1 Additional considerations for SaMD

Although not specifically included in the GHTF definition materials such as sales and marketing materials may be considered as "information provided by the manufacturer" and therefore reflect the objective intent of the manufacturer. Sales and marketing materials should be comprehensive and reflect the intended use of the SaMD.

6 See GHTF/SG1/N29 Information Document Concerning the Definition of the Term "Medical Device"

CSV

Chapter 10
IMDFR
SaMD: Possible Framework for Risk Categorization and Corresponding Considerations

September 18, 2014
IMDRF/SaMD WG/N12FINAL:2014
Authoring Group: Software as a Medical Device (SaMD) Working Group
Final Document

Preface

The document herein was produced by the International Medical Device Regulators Forum (IMDRF), a voluntary group of global medical device regulators from around the world. The document has been subject to consultation throughout its development.

1.0 Introduction

Software is playing an increasingly important and critical role in healthcare with many clinical and administrative purposes.

Software used in healthcare operates in a complex socio-technical environment—consisting of software, hardware, networks, and people—and frequently forms part of larger systems that must operate in a unified manner. This software frequently depends on other commercial off-the shelf (COTS) software and on other systems and data repositories for source data.

A subset of software used in healthcare meets the definition of a medical device; globally, regulatory authorities regulate such software accordingly.

Existing regulations for medical device software are largely focused on medical device software that is embedded in dedicated hardware medical devices and are focused around physical harm, transmission of energy and/or substances to or from the body, the degree of invasiveness to the body, closeness to sensitive organs, duration of use, diseases, processes and public health risk, competence of user and effect on population due to communicable diseases, etc.

Today, medical device software is often able to attain its intended medical purpose independent of hardware medical devices. It is increasingly being deployed on general-purpose hardware and delivered, in diverse care settings, on a multitude of technology platforms (e.g., personal computers, smart phones, and in the cloud) that are easily accessible. It is also being increasingly interconnected to other systems and datasets (e.g., via networks and over the Internet).

The complexity of medical device software, together with the increasing connectedness of systems, results in emergent behaviors not usually seen in hardware medical devices.

This introduces new and unique challenges. For example:

- Medical device software might behave differently when deployed to different hardware platforms.
- Often an update made available by the manufacturer is left to the user of the medical device software to install.
- Due to its non-physical nature (key differentiation), medical device software may be duplicated in numerous copies and widely spread, often outside the control of the manufacturer.

Furthermore, there are lifecycle aspects of medical device software that pose additional challenges. For instance, software manufacturers often:

- Have rapid development cycles,
- Introduce frequent changes to their software, and
- Deliver updates by mass and rapid distribution.

This document is focused on a selected subset of medical device software. This software is called *Software as a Medical Device (SaMD)* and is defined in *IMDRF SaMD WG N10 / Software as a Medical Device: Key Definitions.*

Definition: Software as a Medical Device[1]
SaMD is defined as software intended to be used for one or more medical purposes that perform these purposes without being part of a hardware medical device.

The objective of this document is to introduce a foundational approach, harmonized vocabulary and general and specific considerations for manufacturers, regulators, and users alike to address the unique challenges associated with the use of SaMD.

The approach developed in this document is intended only to establish a common understanding for SaMD and can be used as reference. This document is not intended to replace or modify existing regulatory classification schemes or requirements. Further efforts are required prior to the use of this foundational approach for possible regulatory purposes.

1 See Section 3.0 for full definition including notes.

2.0 Scope

Purpose of the document

The purpose of the document is to introduce a foundational approach, harmonized vocabulary and general and specific considerations, for manufacturers, regulators, and users alike to address the unique challenges associated with the use of SaMD by;

- Establishing common vocabulary and an approach for categorizing SaMD;
- Identifying specific information for describing SaMD in terms of the significance of the information provided by the SaMD to the healthcare decision, healthcare situation or condition, and core functionality;
- Providing criteria to categorize SaMD based on the combination of the significance of the information provided by the SaMD to the healthcare decision and the healthcare situation or condition associated with SaMD; and
- Identifying appropriate considerations, during the lifecycle process (requirements, design, development, testing, maintenance and use) of SaMD.

Field of application

- The categorization system in this document applies to SaMD defined in the related document, IMDRF SaMD WG N10 / Software as a Medical Device: Key Definitions and does not address other types of software.
- Software intended as an accessory to a medical device (i.e., software that does not in itself have a medical purpose) is not in the scope of this document.
- This document focuses on the SaMD irrespective of software technology and/or the platform (e.g., mobile app, cloud, server).
- This document does not address software that drives or controls a hardware medical device.

Relationship to other regulatory classification and standards[2]

- This document is not intended to replace or create new risk management practices rather it uses risk management principles (e.g., principles in international standards) to identify generic risks for SaMD.
- The categorization framework in this document is not a regulatory classification, nor implies a convergence of classifications rules. However, it does set a path towards common vocabulary and approach. Additional work is required to align existing classification rules with this framework.
- The categorization framework is not meant to replace or conflict with the content and/or development of technical or process standards related to software risk management activities.

2 Additional details can be found in Appendix 0.

3.0 Definitions

3.1 Software as a Medical Device

The term "Software as a Medical Device" (SaMD) is *defined as software intended to be used for one or more medical purposes that perform these purposes without being part of a hardware medical device.*

NOTES:

- *SaMD is a medical device and includes in-vitro diagnostic (IVD) medical device.*
- *SaMD is capable of running on general purpose (non-medical purpose) computing platforms.33*
- *"without being part of" means software not necessary for a hardware medical device to achieve its intended medical purpose.*
- *Software does not meet the definition of SaMD if its intended purpose is to drive a hardware medical device.*
- *SaMD may be used in combination (e.g., as a module) with other products including medical devices.*
- *SaMD may be interfaced with other medical devices, including hardware medical devices and other SaMD software, as well as general purpose software.*
- *Mobile apps that meet the definition above are considered SaMD.*

3.2 Intended Use / Intended Purpose

For SaMD intended use, the definition in GHTF/SG1/N70:2011 "Label and Instructions for Use for Medical Devices" applies:

The term "intended use / intended purpose" is the objective intent of the manufacturer regarding the use of a product, process or service as reflected in the specifications, instructions and information provided by the manufacturer.

3.3 Medical Purpose

The following two terms as defined in GHTF/SG1/N71:2012 "Definition of the Terms 'Medical Device' and 'In Vitro Diagnostic (IVD) Medical Device" (*italicized below*) identify medical purpose applicable to SaMD:

3.3.1 Medical Device

'Medical device' means any instrument, apparatus, implement, machine, appliance, implant, reagent for in vitro use, software, material or other similar or related article, intended by the

3 "Computing platforms" include hardware and software resources (e.g. operating system, processing hardware, storage, software libraries, displays, input devices, programming languages etc.).
"Operating systems" that SaMD require may be run on a server, a workstation, a mobile platform, or other general purpose hardware platform.

manufacturer to be used, alone or in combination, for human beings, for one or more of the specific medical purpose(s) of:

- *diagnosis, prevention, monitoring, treatment or alleviation of disease,*
- *diagnosis, monitoring, treatment, alleviation of or compensation for an injury,*
- *investigation, replacement, modification, or support of the anatomy or of a physiological process,*
- *supporting or sustaining life,*
- *control of conception,*
- *disinfection of medical devices,*
- *providing information by means of in vitro examination of specimens derived from the human body;*

and does not achieve its primary intended action by pharmacological, immunological or metabolic means, in or on the human body, but which may be assisted in its intended function by such means.

Note: Products which may be considered to be medical devices in some jurisdictions but not in others include:

- *disinfection substances,*
- *aids for persons with disabilities,*
- *devices incorporating animal and/or human tissues,*
- *devices for in vitro fertilization or assisted reproduction technologies.*

3.3.2 In Vitro Diagnostic (IVD) Medical Device

'In Vitro Diagnostic (IVD) medical device' means a medical device, whether used alone or in combination, intended by the manufacturer for the in-vitro examination of specimens derived from the human body solely or principally to provide information for diagnostic, monitoring or compatibility purposes.

Note 1: IVD medical devices include reagents, calibrators, control materials, specimen receptacles, software, and related instruments or apparatus or other articles and are used, for example, for the following test purposes: diagnosis, aid to diagnosis, screening, monitoring, predisposition, prognosis, prediction, determination of physiological status.

Note 2: In some jurisdictions, certain IVD medical devices may be covered by other regulations.

3.3.3 Additional considerations for SaMD

SaMD may also:

- *Provide means and suggestions for mitigation of a disease.*

- *Provide information for determining compatibility, detecting, diagnosing, monitoring or treating physiological conditions, states of health, illnesses or congenital deformities.*
- *Aid to diagnosis, screening, monitoring, determination of predisposition; prognosis, prediction, determination of physiological status.*

3.4 SaMD Changes

SaMD changes refer to any modifications made throughout the lifecycle of the SaMD including the maintenance phase.

Software maintenance[4] can include adaptive (e.g. keeps pace with the changing environment), perfective (e.g. recoding to improve software performance), corrective (e.g., corrects discovered problems), or preventive (e.g., corrects latent faults in the software product before they become operational faults).

Examples of SaMD changes include, but are not limited to, defect fixes; aesthetic, performance or usability enhancements; and security patches.

4.0 SaMD Background and Aspects Influencing Patient Safety

There are many aspects in an ever-increasing complex clinical use environment that can raise or lower the potential to create hazardous situations to patients. Some examples of these aspects include:

- The type of disease or condition
- Fragility of the patient with respect to the disease or condition
- Progression of the disease or the stage of the disease/condition
- Usability of the application
- Designed towards a specific user type
- Level of dependence or reliance by the user upon the output information
- Ability of the user to detect an erroneous output information
- Transparency of the inputs, outputs and methods to the user
- Level of clinical evidence available and the confidence on the evidence
- The type of output information and the level of influence on the clinical intervention

4 ISO/IEC 14764:2006 Software Engineering— Software Life Cycle Processes— Maintenance
- adaptive maintenance: the modification of a software product, performed after delivery, to keep a software product usable in a changed or changing environment
- perfective maintenance: the modification of a software product after delivery to detect and correct latent faults in the software product before they are manifested as failures
- corrective maintenance: the reactive modification of a software product performed after delivery to correct discovered problems
- preventive maintenance: the modification of a software product after delivery to detect and correct latent faults in the software product before they become operational faults

- Complexity of the clinical model used to derive the output information
- Known specificity of the output information
- Maturity of clinical basis of the software and confidence in the output
- Benefit of the output information vs. baseline
- Technological characteristics of the platform the software are intended to operate on
- Method of distribution of the software

Although many of these aspects may affect the importance of the output information from SaMD, only some of these aspects can be identified by the intended use of SaMD. Generally these aspects can be grouped into the following two major factors that provide adequate description of the intended use of SaMD:

A. Significance of the information provided by the SaMD to the healthcare decision, and

B. State of the healthcare situation or condition.

When these factors are included in the manufacturer's description of intended use, they can be used to categorize SaMD.

Section 6.0 provides a structured approach for a SaMD definition statement to describe the intended use. Section 7.0 provides a method for categorizing SaMD based on the major factors identified in the definition statement.

Other aspects that are not included in the two major factors (e.g., transparency of the inputs used, technological characteristics used by particular SaMD, etc.), although still important, do not influence the determination of the category of SaMD. These other aspects influence the identification of considerations that are unique to a specific approach/method used by the manufacturer of a particular category of SaMD. For example, the type of a platform, that is constantly changing, used in the implementation of SaMD may create considerations that are unique to that implementation. These considerations can also vary by the capabilities of the manufacturer or by the process rigor used to implement the SaMD. Appropriate considerations of these aspects by the manufacturers, users and other stakeholders can significantly minimize patient safety risks.

Section 8.0 provides general considerations and section 9.0 provides specific considerations that when taken into account can promote safety in the creation, implementation and use of SaMD.

5.0 Factors Important for SaMD Characterization

5.1 Significance of information provided by SaMD to healthcare decision

The intended use of the information provided by SaMD in clinical management has different significance on the action taken by the user.

5.1.1 To treat or to diagnose

Treating and diagnosing infers that the information provided by the SaMD will be used to take an immediate or near term action:

- To treat/prevent or mitigate by connecting to other medical devices, medicinal products, general purpose actuators or other means of providing therapy to a human body
- To diagnose/screen/detect a disease or condition (i.e., using sensors, data, or other information from other hardware or software devices, pertaining to a disease or condition).

5.1.2 To drive clinical management

Driving clinical management infers that the information provided by the SaMD will be used to aid in treatment, aid in diagnoses, to triage or identify early signs of a disease or condition will be used to guide next diagnostics or next treatment interventions:

- To aid in treatment by providing enhanced support to safe and effective use of medicinal products or a medical device.
- To aid in diagnosis by analyzing relevant information to help predict risk of a disease or condition or as an aid to making a definitive diagnosis.
- To triage or identify early signs of a disease or conditions.

5.1.3 To Inform clinical management

Informing clinical management infers that the information provided by the SaMD will not trigger an immediate or near term action:

- To inform of options for treating, diagnosing, preventing, or mitigating a disease or condition.
- To provide clinical information by aggregating relevant information (e.g., disease, condition, drugs, medical devices, population, etc.)

5.2 Healthcare Situation or Condition

5.2.1 Critical situation or condition

Situations or conditions where accurate and/or timely diagnosis or treatment action is vital to avoid death, long-term disability or other serious deterioration of health of an individual patient or to mitigating impact to public health. SaMD is considered to be used in a critical situation or condition where:

- The type of disease or condition is:
    - Life-threatening state of health, including incurable states,
    - Requires major therapeutic interventions,

    - Sometimes time critical, depending on the progression of the disease or condition that could affect the user's ability to reflect on the output information.
- Intended target population is fragile with respect to the disease or condition (e.g., pediatrics, high risk population, etc.)
- Intended for specialized trained users.

5.2.2 Serious situation or condition

Situations or conditions where accurate diagnosis or treatment is of vital importance to avoid unnecessary interventions (e.g., biopsy) or timely interventions are important to mitigate long term irreversible consequences on an individual patient's health condition or public health. SaMD is considered to be used in a serious situation or condition when:

- The type of disease or condition is:
    - Moderate in progression, often curable,
    - Does not require major therapeutic interventions,
    - Intervention is normally not expected to be time critical in order to avoid death, longterm disability or other serious deterioration of health, whereby providing the user an ability to detect erroneous recommendations.
- Intended target population is NOT fragile with respect to the disease or condition.
- Intended for either specialized trained users or lay users.

Note: SaMD intended to be used by lay users in a "serious situation or condition" as described here, without the support from specialized professionals, should be considered as SaMD used in a "critical situation or condition".

5.2.3 Non-Serious situation or condition

Situations or conditions where an accurate diagnosis and treatment is important but not critical for interventions to mitigate long term irreversible consequences on an individual patient's health condition or public health. SaMD is considered to be used in a non-serious situation or condition when:

- The type of disease or condition is:
    - Slow with predictable progression of disease state (may include minor chronic illnesses or states),
    - May not be curable; can be managed effectively,
    - Requires only minor therapeutic interventions, and
    - Interventions are normally noninvasive in nature, providing the user the ability to detect erroneous recommendations.

- Intended target population is individuals who may not always be patients.
- Intended for use by either specialized trained users or lay users.

6.0 SaMD Definition Statement

The intended use of SaMD is normally reflected in various sources such as the manufacturer's specifications, instructions, and other information provided by the manufacturer.

The purpose of the SaMD definition statement and the components identified below are to provide an organized factual framework. Statement "A" and "B" are to help the SaMD developer determine the SaMD category in the categorizing framework, while statement "C" is to help the manufacturer manage changes to SaMD that may result in change of the category and to address considerations specific to SaMD.

The SaMD definition statement should include a clear and strong statement about intended use, including the following:

A. The "**significance of the information provided by the SaMD to the healthcare decision**" which identifies the intended medical purpose of the SaMD. The statementshould explain how the SaMD meets one or more of the purposes described in the definition of a medical device[5], e.g. supplying information for diagnosis, prevention, monitoring, treatment etc. This statement should be structured in the following terms as defined in section 5.1.

   - Treat or diagnose
   - Drive clinical management
   - Inform clinical management

B. The "**state of the healthcare situation or condition**" that the SaMD is intended for. This statement should be structured in the following terms as defined in section 5.2.

   - Critical situation or condition
   - Serious situation or condition
   - Non-serious situation or condition

C. **Description of the SaMD's core functionality**[6] which identifies the critical features/functions of the SaMD that are essential to the intended significance of the information provided by the SaMD to the healthcare decision in the intended healthcare situation or condition. This description should include only the critical features. (See applicability of this in section 8.0, 9.0).

CH 10

5 IMDRF key definitions Final document "medical purposes" also repeated here in Section 3.3.

6 These could include specific functionality that is critical to maintain performance and safety profile, attributes identified by risk management process undertaken by the manufacturer of SaMD.

7.0 SaMD Categorization

This section provides an approach to categorize SaMD based on the factors identified in the SaMD definition statement.

7.1 Categorization Principles

The following are necessary principles important in the categorization approach of SaMD.

- The categorization relies on an accurate and complete SaMD definition statement.
- The determination of the categories is the combination of the significance of the information provided by the SaMD to the healthcare decision and the healthcare situation or condition.
- The four categories (I, II, III, IV) are based on the levels of impact on the patient or public health where accurate information provided by the SaMD to treat or diagnose, drive or inform clinical management is vital to avoid death, long-term disability or other serious deterioration of health, mitigating public health.
- The categories are in relative significance to each other. Category IV has the highest level of impact, Category I the lowest.
- When a manufacturer's SaMD definition statement states that the SaMD can be used across multiple healthcare situations or conditions it is categorized at the highest category according to the information included in the SaMD definition statement.
- When a manufacturer makes changes to SaMD[7], during the lifecycle that results in the change of the definition statement, the categorization of SaMD should be reevaluated appropriately. The SaMD is categorized according to the information included in the changed (new) SaMD definition statement.
- SaMD will have its own category according to its SaMD definition statement even when a SaMD is interfaced with other SaMD, other hardware medical devices, or used as a module in a larger system.

CH 10

7.2 SaMD Categories

State of Healthcare situation or condition	Significance of information provided by SaMD to healthcare decision		
	Treat or diagnose	Drive clinical management	Inform clinical management
Critical	IV	III	II
Serious	III	II	I
Non-serious	II	I	I

7 "SaMD changes" are defined in section 3.4

7.3 Criteria for Determining SaMD Category

Criteria for Category IV –

i. SaMD that provides information to treat or diagnose a disease or conditions in a critical situation or condition is a Category IV and is considered to be of very high impact.

Criteria for Category III –

i. SaMD that provides information to treat or diagnose a disease or conditions in a serious situation or condition is a Category III and is considered to be of high impact.

ii. SaMD that provides information to drive clinical management of a disease or conditions in a critical situation or condition is a Category III and is considered to be of high impact.

Criteria for Category II –

i. SaMD that provides information to treat or diagnose a disease or conditions in a nonserious situation or condition is a Category II and is considered to be of medium impact.

ii. SaMD that provides information to drive clinical management of a disease or conditions in a serious situation or condition is a Category II and is considered to be of medium impact.

iii. SaMD that provides information to inform clinical management for a disease or conditions in a critical situation or condition is a Category II and is considered to be of medium impact.

Criteria for Category I –

i. SaMD that provides information to drive clinical management of a disease or conditions in a non-serious situation or condition is a Category I and is considered to be of low impact.

ii. SaMD that provides information to inform clinical management for a disease or conditions in a serious situation or condition is a Category I and is considered to be of low impact.

iii. SaMD that provides information to inform clinical management for a disease or conditions in a non-serious situation or condition is a Category I and is considered to be of low impact.

7.4 EXAMPLES OF SaMD:

The examples below are intended to help illustrate the application of the framework and resulting categories.

Category IV:

- SaMD that performs diagnostic image analysis for making treatment decisions in patients with acute stroke, i.e., where fast and accurate differentiation between ischemic and hemorrhagic stroke is crucial to choose early initialization of brain-saving intravenous thrombolytic therapy or interventional revascularization.

  This example uses criteria IV.i from Section 7.3 in that the information provided by the above SaMD is used to treat a fragile patient in a critical condition that is life threatening, may require major therapeutic intervention, and is time sensitive.

- SaMD that calculates the fractal dimension of a lesion and surrounding skin and builds a structural map that reveals the different growth patterns to provide diagnosis or identify if the lesion is malignant or benign.

  This example uses criteria IV.i from Section 7.3 in that the information provided by the above SaMD is used to diagnose a disease that may be life threatening, may require major therapeutic intervention, and may be time sensitive.

- SaMD that performs analysis of cerebrospinal fluid spectroscopy data to diagnose tuberculosis meningitis or viral meningitis in children.

  This example uses criteria IV.i from Section 7.3 in that the information provided by the above SaMD is used to diagnose a disease in a fragile population with possible broader public health impact that may be life threatening, may require major therapeutic intervention, and may be time sensitive.

- SaMD that combines data from immunoassays to screen for mutable pathogens/ pandemic outbreak that can be highly communicable through direct contact or other means.

  This example uses criteria IV.i from Section 7.3 in that the information provided by the above SaMD is used to screen for a disease or condition with public health impact that may be life threatening, may require therapeutic intervention and may be time critical.

Category III:

- SaMD that uses the microphone of a smart device to detect interrupted breathing during sleep and sounds a tone to rouse the sleeper.

  This example uses criteria III.i from Section 7.3 in that the information provided by the above SaMD is used to treat a condition where intervention is normally not expected to be time critical in order to avoid death, long term disability or other serious deterioration of health.

- SaMD that is intended to provide sound therapy to treat, mitigate or reduce effects of tinnitus for which minor therapeutic intervention is useful.

This example uses criteria III.i from Section 7.3 in that the information provided by the above SaMD is used to treat a condition that may be moderate in progression, may not require therapeutic intervention and whose treatment is normally not expected to be time critical.

- SaMD that is intended as a radiation treatment planning system as an aid in treatment by using information from a patient and provides specific parameters that are tailored for a particular tumor and patient for treatment using a radiation medical device.

  This example uses criteria III.ii from Section 7.3 in that the information provided by the above SaMD is used as an aid in treatment by providing enhanced support to the safe and effective use of a medical device to a patient in a critical condition that may be life threatening and requires major therapeutic intervention.

- SaMD that uses data from individuals for predicting risk score in high-risk population for developing preventive intervention strategies for colorectal cancer.

  This example uses criteria III.ii from Section 7.3 in that the information provided by the above SaMD is used to detect early signs of a disease to treat a condition that may be life-threatening disease impacting high-risk populations, may require therapeutic intervention and may be time critical.

- SaMD that is used to provide information by taking pictures, monitoring the growth or other data to supplement other information that a healthcare provider uses to diagnose if a skin lesion is malignant or benign.

  This example uses criteria III.ii from Section 7.3 in that the information provided by the above SaMD is used as an aid to diagnosing a condition that may be life-threatening, may require therapeutic intervention and may be time critical by aggregating relevant information to detect early signs of a disease.

Category II:

- SaMD that analyzes heart rate data intended for a clinician as an aid in diagnosis of arrhythmia.

  This example uses criteria from II.ii Section 7.3 in that the information provided by the above SaMD is used to aid in the diagnosis of a disease of a condition that may be moderate in progression, may not require therapeutic intervention and whose treatment is normally not expected to be time critical.

- SaMD that interpolates data to provide 3D reconstruction of a patient's computer tomography scan image, to aid in the placement of catheters by visualization of the interior of the bronchial tree; in lung tissue; and placement of markers into soft lung tissue to guide radiosurgery and thoracic surgery.

  This example uses criteria II.ii from Section 7.3 in that the information provided by the above SaMD is used to aid in the next treatment intervention of a patient where the intervention is not normally expected to be time critical in order to avoid death, longterm disability, or other serious deterioration of health.

- SaMD that uses data from individuals for predicting risk score for developing stroke or heart disease for creating prevention or interventional strategies.

  This example uses criteria II.iii from Section 7.3 in that the information provided by the above SaMD is used to detect early signs of a disease to treat a condition that is not normally expected to be time critical in order to avoid death, long-term disability, or other serious deterioration of health.

- SaMD that integrates and analyzes multiple tests utilizing standardized rules to provide recommendations for diagnosis in certain clinical indications, e.g., kidney function, cardiac risk, iron and anemia assessment.

  This example uses criteria II.ii from Section 7.3 in that the information provided by the above SaMD is used to detect early signs of a disease to treat a condition that is not normally expected to be time critical in order to avoid death, long-term disability, or other serious deterioration of health.

  Note: This example includes both serious and potentially non-serious conditions but per the categorization principle in Section 7.1 when a manufacturer's SaMD definition statement states that the SaMD can be used across multiple healthcare situations or condition it will be categorized at the highest category according to the SaMD definition statement.

- SaMD that helps diabetic patients by calculating bolus insulin dose based on carbohydrate intake, pre-meal blood glucose, and anticipated physical activity reported to adjust carbohydrate ratio and basal insulin.

  This example uses criteria II.ii from Section 7.3 in that the information provided by the above SaMD is used to aid in treatment of a condition not normally expected to be time critical in order to avoid death, long-term disability, or other serious deterioration of health.

Category I:

- SaMD that sends ECG rate, walking speed, heart rate, elapsed distance, and location for an exercise-based cardiac rehabilitation patient to a server for monitoring by a qualified professional.

  This example uses criteria I.ii from Section 7.3 in that the information provided by the above SaMD is an aggregation of data to provide clinical information that will not trigger an immediate or near term action for the treatment of a patient condition that is not normally expected to be time critical in order to avoid death, long-term disability, or other serious deterioration of health.

- SaMD that collects data from peak-flow meter and symptom diaries to provide information to anticipate an occurrence of an asthma episode.

  This example uses criteria I.ii from Section 7.3 in that the information provided by the above SaMD is an aggregation of data to provide best option to mitigate a condition that is not normally expected to be time critical in order to avoid death, long-term disability, or other serious deterioration of health.

- SaMD that analyzes images, movement of the eye or other information to guide next diagnostic action of astigmatism.

  This example uses criteria I.i from Section 7.3 in that the information provided by the above SaMD is an aggregation of data to provide clinical information that will not trigger an immediate or near term action for the treatment of a patient condition that even if not curable can be managed effectively and whose interventions are normally noninvasive in nature.

- SaMD that uses data from individuals for predicting risk score (functionality) in healthy populations for developing the risk (medical purpose) of migraine (non-serious condition.

  This example uses criteria I.i from Section 7.3 in that the the information provided by the above SaMD is an aggregation of data to provide clinical information that will not trigger an immediate or near term action for the treatment of a patient condition that even if not curable can be managed effectively and whose interventions are normally noninvasive in nature.

- SaMD that collects output from a ventilator about a patient's carbon dioxide level and transmits the information to a central patient data repository for further consideration.

  This example uses criteria I.ii from Section 7.3 in that the the information provided by the above SaMD is an aggregation of data to provide clinical information that will not trigger an immediate or near term action for the treatment of a patient condition that is not normally expected to be time critical in order to avoid death, long-term disability, or other serious deterioration of health.

- SaMD that stores historical blood pressure information for a health care provider's later review.

  This example uses criteria I.ii from Section 7.3 in that the information provided by the above SaMD is an aggregation of data to provide clinical information that will not trigger an immediate or near term action for the treatment of a patient condition that is not normally expected to be time critical in order to avoid death, long-term disability, or other serious deterioration of health.

- SaMD intended for image analysis of body fluid preparations or digital slides to perform cell counts and morphology reviews.

  This example uses criteria I.ii from Section 7.3 in that the information provided by the above SaMD is an aggregation of data to provide clinical information that will not trigger an immediate or near term action for the treatment of a patient condition that is not normally expected to be time critical in order to avoid death, long-term disability, or other serious deterioration of health.

- SaMD intended for use by elderly patients with multiple chronic conditions that receives data from wearable health sensors, transmits data to the monitoring server, and identifies higher-level information such as tachycardia and signs of respiratory infections based on established medical knowledge and communicates this information to caregivers.

  This example uses criteria I.ii from Section 7.3 in that the information provided by the above SaMD is an aggregation of data to provide clinical information that will not trigger an immediate or near term action for the treatment of a patient condition that is not normally expected to be time critical in order to avoid death, long-term disability, or other serious deterioration of health.

- SaMD that uses hearing sensitivity, speech in noise, and answers to a questionnaire about common listening situations to self-assess for hearing loss.

  This example uses criteria from I.ii Section 7.3 in that the information provided by the above SaMD is an aggregation of data to provide clinical information that will not trigger an immediate or near term action for the treatment of a patient condition that is not normally expected to be time critical in order to avoid death, long-term disability, or other serious deterioration of health.

8.0 General Considerations for SaMD

SaMD often forms part of a clinical workflow sequence in order to improve diagnosis, treatment and patient management. However, issues with the design and/or implementation of SaMD into a workflow can lead to users making incorrect choices / decisions and can cause delays in decisions being made - this may lead to adverse consequences for patients.

Developing SaMD that are safe entails identifying risks and establishing measures that give confidence that the risks are acceptable. It is generally accepted that testing of software is not sufficient to determine that it is safe in operation. As a consequence, it is recognized that confidence should be built into software in order to assure its safety.

IEC 62304 is a standard for life-cycle development of medical device software. The standard specifies a risk-based decision model, defines some testing requirements, and highlights three major principles that promote safety relevant to SaMD:

- Risk management;
- Quality management; and
- Methodical and systematic systems engineering according to best industry practices.

The combination of these concepts allows SaMD manufacturers to follow a clearly structured and consistently repeatable decision-making process to promote safety for SaMD.

Further information on these major principles is provided below followed by discussion on some specific considerations in the areas of:

- Socio-technical environment

- Technology and system environments
- Information security with respect to safety

8.1 Design and development

Manufacturers should select and implement an adequate process for the planning, design, development, deployment, and documenting of robust and dependable software commensurate with risk—as informed by its intended purpose, reasonable foreseeable use, and the understood and defined socio-technical environment of use.

Safety needs to be addressed early in the design and development process.

Development of software in a quality-assured manner should consider the appropriate selection and implementation of system design and development methods that:

- Include a methodical and systematic development process using models, methods, architecture, and design-modelling techniques appropriate for the development language(s) and the device's intended purpose,
- Cover the various software lifecycle stages through the application of software development standards, e.g., IEC 62304, and use of software engineering guidebooks, e.g., SWEBoK guide, SEBoK guide, and
- Systematically and methodically document the design and development process (using tools as appropriate.)

8.1.1 Post Market Surveillance

Software risks can never be totally eliminated so SaMD manufacturers should continually monitor customer issues to maintain the safety level. A monitoring process should include ways to capture customer feedback, e.g., through inquiries, complaints, market studies, focus groups, servicing, etc. The inherent nature of software including SaMD allows for efficient methods to understand and capture user experiences. It is recommended that SaMD manufacturers utilize these feedback techniques to understand failure modes and perform analysis to address safety situations. It is also recommended that SaMD manufacturers extend their monitoring to automatically detect errors of the software or system, i.e., discover and recover from an error before a failure can occur.

General considerations associated with the monitoring of SaMD include:

1. Due to its non-physical nature, a SaMD may be duplicated and numerous copies and widely spread, often outside the control of the manufacturer.
2. Often an update made available by the manufacturer is left to the user of the SaMD to install. Manufacturers should make sure that appropriate mitigations address any risks that arise from the existence of different versions of the SaMD on the market.

3. Incident investigations should consider any specific case or combination of use cases that may have contributed to the failure and as appropriate manufacturers should consider accident reconstruction principles, e.g., data logging, black box recorder, etc.[8]

8.2 Changes

Manufacturers of SaMD are expected to have an appropriate level of control to manage changes. Due to the non-physical nature of software, a software change management process needs specific considerations to achieve the intended result regarding traceability and documentation.

These specific considerations include:

- Socio-technical environment considerations
- Technology and system environment considerations
- Information security with respect to safety considerations

SaMD changes *may have a significant unforeseeable effect on the healthcare situation or condition and socio-technical environment of use if not managed systematically, not only with respect to a design change in itself, but also to the impact of the changed software after it is installed and implemented.*

With any product lifecycle, change is inevitable. Failures occur and may be due to errors, ambiguities, oversights or misinterpretation of the specification that the software is intended to satisfy, carelessness or incompetence in writing code, inadequate testing, incorrect or unexpected usage of the software or other unforeseen problems. An SaMD may also fail with changes to the running environment. Changes to SaMD or its operating environment can affect its safety, quality and performance.

SaMD changes refer to any modifications made throughout the lifecycle of the SaMD including the maintenance phase. The nature of software maintenance changes can include adaptive (e.g. keeps pace with the changing environment), perfective (e.g. recoding to improve software performance), corrective (e.g. corrects discovered problems), or preventive changes (e.g. corrects latent faults in the software product before they become operational faults). These changes should be clearly identified and defined with a method of tracing the change to the specific affected software.

In order to effectively manage the changes and their impact, manufacturers must perform a risk assessment to determine if the change(s) affect the SaMD categorization and the core functionality of the SaMD as outlined in the definition statement.

Changes should undergo appropriate verification and validation before being released by the manufacturer for use.

8 Leveson, N. 2012. *Engineering a Safer World: Systems Thinking Applied to Safety*. Cambridge, MA, USA: MIT Press.

Examples of software changes (some may be considered significant and others not):

- Modification to an algorithm affecting the diagnosis or therapy delivered;
- A software change that affects the way data is read or interpreted by the user, such that the treatment or diagnosis of the patient may be altered when compared to the previous version of the software;
- Addition of a new feature to the software that may change the diagnosis or therapy delivered to the patient;
- A software change that incorporates a change to the operating system or change to the configuration on which the SaMD runs;
- A software change that affects clinical workflow.

9.0 Specific Considerations for SaMD

9.1 Socio-technical environment considerations

The term socio-technical environment concerns the SaMD's setting of use - often comprising hardware, networks, software, and people. More formally, it may be characterized into spatial (e.g., location), activity (e.g., workflow), social (e.g., responsibility), technological (e.g., devices, systems, data sources, and connections), and physical (e.g., ambient conditions) components[9].

SaMD supplies information and/or a structure for information.

The proper and safe functioning of SaMD is highly dependent on a sufficient and common understanding of the socio-technical environment that includes the manufacturer and the user.

Manufacturers should be aware of the socio-technical environment where inadequate considerations could lead to incorrect, inaccurate, and/or delayed diagnoses and treatments; and/or additional cognitive workload (which may, over time, make clinicians more susceptible to making mistakes)[10].

Similarly, users should also be aware of the socio-technical environment as presumed and designed for (limitations of the SaMD's capabilities) and by the manufacturer, as not being aware may lead to overreliance or other inaccurate use of the SaMD.

For example:

- If the user does not have sufficient skills and expertise for correct operation of the SaMD, possible inaccurate output data may not be questioned. The same may happen if the user becomes habituated and over-reliant on SaMD over time.

9 (Adapted from IEC 62366)

10 Leveson, N. 2012. *Engineering a Safer World: Systems Thinking Applied to Safety.* Cambridge, MA, USA: MIT Press.

- The introduction of SaMD sometimes changes clinical workflows in unanticipated ways; these changes may be detrimental to patient safety.
- The user may seek alternate pathways to achieve a particular functionality, otherwise called a workaround. When workarounds circumvent built-in safety features of a product, patient safety may be compromised.

Considerations for the manufacturer when identifying effects/implications and appropriate measures to safety and performance of SaMD throughout the product's design, development, and installation:

- Transparency of information on limitations with algorithms, clinical model, quality of data used to build the models, assumptions made, etc. can help users question the validity of output of the SaMD and avoid making incorrect or poor decisions;
- Integrating SaMD within real-world clinical workflows (including sufficient involvement of users from all relevant disciplines) requires attention to in situ use and tasks to ensure appropriate use of safety features;
- SaMD (and other systems connected to the SaMD) may be configured by the user in different ways than intended or foreseen by the manufacturer;
- Though not specific to SaMD, design of the user interface including: whether designs are overly complex (e.g., multiple, complicated screens), the appropriateness of designs for the target platform (e.g., smart phone screen versus desktop monitor), the dynamic nature of data (e.g., showing information at appropriate times and for an appropriate duration);
- Though not specific to SaMD, identification of appropriate means to display information such that it is understood by the intended user (e.g., usability including regionalization parameters, language translation, and selection/display of units);
- Communicating relevant information to the user (based on the activities conducted above) for the purpose of:
    - Enabling the user to decide whether or not the user can use the device in the organization in terms of available hardware, competence, network, required quality for data input. And, if he/she decides to do this, information necessary to do those measures in order to use it: inform users, establish different routines, obtain necessary hardware.
    - Enabling correct installation and configuration of SaMD for appropriate integration with clinical workflows.

9.2 Technology and System Environment Considerations

Technology and system environment refers to the ecosystem where the SaMD resides, including installed systems, interconnections, and hardware platform(s). Instructions on how to verify the appropriateness of installation of and update to SaMD as well as any changes made to the system environment (e.g., hardware and software) should be provided to the user. Reliance on hardware over which the manufacturer does not have control (operating systems not designed for a medical purpose, general-purpose hardware, networks and servers, Internet, links) should be considered and addressed by the manufacturer during design and development of SaMD (for instance, by designing robust and resilient SaMD designs).

SaMDs are always dependant on a hardware platform and often a connected environment. SaMD can be affected by cross-link interconnections – both physical connections and interoperability, i.e., the seamless communication between devices, technology and people.

Disruption in the ecosystem (e.g., resulting from service disruptions, systems maintenance or upgrades, platform failures) can result in loss of information, delayed, corrupted, or mixed patient information, or inaccurate information which may lead to incorrect or inaccurate diagnoses and/or treatments.

For example: an incorrect diagnosis is made after the connection to a clinical dataset was lost because the patient diagnosis data is not available.

Considerations for the manufacturer when identifying effects/implications to safety and performance of SaMD:

- Connections to other systems (e.g., reliability of the connection, resilience, quality of service, access, security, load capacity of connections to other systems and connection methods, system integration)
- Presenting information to the users and system integrators about the system requirements and resultant performance of the SaMD (e.g., the effect that changes to firewall rules might have on the operation of the system)
- Hardware platform(s)—such as smart phones, PC, servers—(e.g., reliability, dependencies, and interconnections with others hardware and software);
- Operating system(s) platform—such asWindows, GNU/Linux—compatibility; and
- Modifications and changes to the SaMD integration (e.g., platform updates) may have effects on SaMD that the manufacturer did not anticipate/foresee.

9.3 INFORMATION SECURITY WITH RESPECT TO SAFETY CONSIDERATIONS

Information security may be defined as the preservation of confidentiality, integrity and availability of information11[11].

Incorrect management or transmission of information by an SaMD can lead to incorrect or delayed diagnosis or treatment.

11 (From ISO/IEC 27000:2009 - Information technology— Security techniques— Information security management systems — Overview and vocabulary)

SaMD may be affected by particular factors relating to information security that may affect the integrity, availability, or accessibility of information output from the SaMD needed for correct diagnosis or treatment:

- SaMD are typically used by a variety of users with different access needs, e.g., restricted access or varying information security requirements
- Platforms where a SaMD is installed typically runs many other software applications.
- SaMD are typically connected to the Internet, networks, databases, or servers with varying information security requirements.

Considerations for the manufacturer when identifying implications for safety and performance of SaMD:

- The SaMD information security and privacy control requirements may need to be balanced with the need for timely information availability.
- Information security requires the identification and implementation of safe (and formalized) ways to store, convert and/or transmit data.
- The design should use appropriate control measures to address data integrity when common information is accessed by multiple applications and users.
- Manufacturers should make it feasible for users to safely implement information security updates.
- The protection of sensitive information requires support for sufficient access control and appropriate restriction to system settings and assets for important data.
- The design should address possible adverse system interactions with the inclusion of appropriate resilience and robustness measures.
- Instructions for users related to information security should include how to safely:
    - Install SaMD in appropriate operating environments (e.g., OS, integration of other software);
    - Manage authentication mechanisms; and
    - Update security software/spyware, operating environments, and other systems and applications, etc.

10.0 Appendix

10.1 Clarifying SaMD Definition

This Appendix provides a representative list of features and functionalities that either meet or don't meet the definition of SaMD. This list is not exhaustive; it is only intended to provide clarity and assistance in identifying when a feature or functionality is considered to be SaMD.

Examples of software that are SaMD:

- Software with a medical purpose that operates on a general purpose computing platform, i.e., a computing platform that does not have a medical purpose, is considered SaMD. For example, software that is intended for diagnosis of a condition using the tri-axial accelerometer that operates on the embedded processor on a consumer digital camera is considered a SaMD.
- Software that is connected to a hardware medical device but is not needed by that hardware medical device to achieve its intended medical purpose is SaMD and not an accessory to the hardware medical device. For example, software that allows a commercially available smartphone to view images for diagnostic purposes obtained from a magnetic resonance imaging (MRI) medical device is SaMD and not an accessory to MRI medical device.
- The SaMD definition notes states that "SaMD is capable of running on general purpose (nonmedical purpose) computing platforms." SaMD running on these general purpose computing platform could be located in a hardware medical device, For example, software that performs image post-processing for the purpose of aiding in the detection of breast cancer (CAD - computer-aided detection software) running on a general purpose computing platform located in the image-acquisition hardware medical device is SaMD.
- The SaMD definition notes states that "SaMD may be interfaced with other medical devices, including hardware medical devices and other SaMD software, as well as general purpose software." Software that provides parameters that become the input for a different hardware medical device or other SaMD is SaMD. For example, treatment planning software that supplies information used in a linear accelerator is SaMD.

Examples of software that are not SaMD:

- The SaMD definition states "SaMD is defined as software intended to be used for one or more medical purposes that perform these purposes without being part of a hardware medical device". Examples of software that are considered "part of" include software used to "drive or control" the motors and the pumping of medication in an infusion pump; or software used in closed loop control in an implantable pacemaker or other types of hardware medical devices. These types of software, sometimes referred to as "embedded software", "firmware", or "micro-code" are, not SaMD".
- Software required by a hardware medical device to perform the hardware's medical device intended use is not SaMD even if/when sold separately from the hardware medical device.
- Software that relies on data from a medical device, but does not have a medical purpose, e.g., software that encrypts data for transmission from a medical device is not SaMD.
- Software that enables clinical communication and workflow including patient registration, scheduling visits, voice calling, video calling is not SaMD.

- Software that monitors performance or proper functioning of a device for the purpose of servicing the device, e.g., software that monitors X-Ray tube performance to anticipate the need for replacement; or software that integrates and analyzes laboratory quality control data to identify increased random errors or trends in calibration on IVDs is not SaMD.
- Software that provides parameters that become the input for SaMD is not SaMD if it does not have a medical purpose. For example, a database including search and query functions by itself or when used by SaMD is not SaMD.

10.2 Analysis of SaMD Framework with Existing Classifications

This Annex is intended to clarify the following:

A — Categorization of SaMD relative to medical device classification

There are different classification schemes for different purposes.

Typically classification is based on a set of parameters/questions that assigns the object of interest into groups that suit a certain purpose.

Classifications may have the purpose to determine, for example

- Appropriate levels of regulatory oversight such as requirements for
    - Levels of third party intervention
    - Levels of conformity controls
    - Levels of quality system
- Appropriate levels of technical measures, for example
    - Technical protective means, e.g., for
        - Laser protection 1,2 or 3
        - electrical isolation, protective earth or double insulated
        - ingress of liquids, IP XX

Classification of medical devices is commonly focused on regulatory controls based on risk classes.

Categorization for SaMD, as in the case of laser protection, is only identifying different categories of SaMD by level of impact. Categorization in this document by itself does not imply regulatory controls needed to manage risks. It is only intended to provide guidance for appropriate considerations for SaMD.

B — Relationship between this document and GHTF documents.

It is important to note the following to understand the relationship between the categorization framework in this document and the classification principles for medical devices and in vitro diagnostic medical devices:

CH 10

- GHTF classification principles, unlike this document, were intended to build classification rules for regulatory control purposes. As explained earlier, this document identifies different categories of SaMD by level of impact and does not address corresponding regulatory risk classes identified in GHTF documents.
- The high-level principles used for identifying SaMD categories build substantially on the principles (rationale) underlying the classification rules established in the GHTF classification principles documents. Key factors like individual risks, public health risks, user skills, and importance of the information provided are common to both frameworks.

11.0 References

IMDRF SaMD WG N10 / Software as a Medical Device: Key Definitions

GHTF/SG1/N70:2011 “Label and Instructions for Use for Medical Devices”

GHTF/SG1/N71:2012 “Definition of the Terms ‘Medical Device’ and ‘In Vitro Diagnostic (IVD) Medical Device”

IEC 62304:2006 - Medical device software -- Software life cycle processes

ISO/IEC 14764:2006 Software Engineering— Software Life Cycle Processes — Maintenance

Guide to the Software Engineering Body of Knowledge - SWEBOK (2004), pp. 1-202 by Alain Abran, Pierre Bourque, Robert Dupuis, James W. Moore, Leonard L. Tripp edited by Alain Abran, Pierre Bourque, Robert Dupuis, James W. Moore, Leonard L. Tripp

[SEBoK] Guide to the Systems Engineering Body of Knowledge (http://www.sebokwiki.org/)

ISO/IEC 27000:2009 - Information technology— Security techniques — Information security management systems

IEC 62366:2007 Medical devices — Application of usability engineering to medical devices

Leveson, N. ‘Engineering a Safer World: Systems Thinking Applied to Safety, MIT, USA (2011)

CH 10

Chapter 11
IMDRF
SaMD: Application of Quality Management System

October 2, 2015
IMDRF/SaMD WG/N23 FINAL: 2015
Authoring Group: IMDRF SaMD Working Group
Final Document

1.0 Introduction

The International Medical Device Regulators Forum (IMDRF) seeks to establish a common and converged understanding for software intended for medical purposes and specifically for a subset of such software that is intended to function as a medical device. The IMDRF Software as a Medical Device Working Group (WG) defines this subset of software as Software as a Medical Device (SaMD) in the *IMDRF/SaMD WG/N10* document *Software as a Medical Device (SaMD): Key Definitions*; this document is the foundation for developing a common vocabulary; it defines SaMD for both manufacturers and regulators.

The SaMD WG has also provided a framework to categorize types of SaMD based on impact to patient and public health in the IMDRF/SaMD WG/N12 document *Software as A Medical Device: Possible Framework for Risk Categorization and Corresponding Considerations*. This framework establishes a common approach for categorizing SaMD, using criteria based on the combination of the significance of the information provided by the SaMD to the healthcare decision and on the healthcare situation or condition where the SaMD is used.

> ***The IMDRF/SaMD WG/N12 document also highlights the use of quality management as a general consideration towards the safety, effectiveness, and performance of SaMD and as key to ensuring the predictability and quality of SaMD.***

Quality Management System (QMS) principles, for many industrial sectors, can be found in the ISO 9000 family of standards. In addition, there are also a wide variety of current industry software development lifecycle methodologies, guidance documents, and standards that address best practices of the many aspects of software engineering quality practices. These principles are the foundation for good practices to maintain and control the quality of products in organizations of any size, ranging from a one-person enterprise to a multi-national corporation.

In the medical device sector it is generally accepted that following QMS requirements is one of the controls used to minimize and manage unintentional outcomes related to patient safety. QMS requirements for medical devices are defined by regulatory agencies in their regulations and in the international standard ISO 13485—*Medical Devices—Quality Management Systems—Requirements for Regulatory Purposes*.

In the software industry, good software quality and engineering practices are used to control the quality of software products. These practices may readily align with the general principles of medical device QMS requirements when the patient safety perspective is included.

This document highlights elements of good software quality and engineering practices and reinforces medical device quality principles that should be appropriately incorporated for an effective SaMD QMS.

This is a companion document to *IMDRF/SaMD WG/N10* and *N12* documents, further enabling convergence in vocabulary, approach, and a common thinking for regulators and industry.

2.0 Scope

The objective of the document is to provide guidance on the application of existing standardized and generally accepted QMS practices to SaMD. Furthermore, the purpose of this document is to:

- Inform the reader of SaMD specific practices. It assumes the reader is following generally accepted software lifecycle processes[1] and may not be familiar with medical device QMS;
- Provide guidance for the application of QMS for the governance of organizations responsible for delivering SaMD products and managing the SaMD lifecycle support processes (product planning; risk management; document and record control; configuration management and control; measurement, analysis, and improvement of processes and products; and managing outsourced processes, activities and products) and SaMD realization and use processes (requirements management, design, development, verification and validation, deployment, maintenance, and decommissioning);
- Highlight SaMD realization and use processes from the perspective of patient safety and clinical environment considerations as well as technology and systems environment considerations that should be addressed to ensure the safety, effectiveness, and performance of SaMD;
- Help manufacturers and regulators attain a common understanding and vocabulary for the application of medical device quality management system requirements to SaMD; and
- Complement the IMDRF SaMD framework for risk categorization and corresponding considerations found in IMDRF/SaMD WG/N12.

This document is intended for the following audience:

CH 11

---

1 These lifecycle processes are intended to include commonly referred lifecycle processes such as software development lifecycle processes (SDLC), software product lifecycle processes (SPLC) and Software System lifecycle processes (SSLC).

- Groups and/or individuals who are or want to become developers of SaMD;
- Software development organizations (large or small) that apply good software quality and engineering practices and that may not necessarily be familiar with medical device QMS requirements; and
- Organizations (divisions/departments) working within established medical device quality systems that intend to communicate the linkage between medical device quality system practice and software development practices.

Document organization and content:

- Terminology used is intended to be familiar to the software industry and illustrates how typical software-engineering activities (e.g., determining requirements) translate to equivalent activities in a medical device quality management system (e.g., identifying design inputs) used in the management, design, development, implementation, monitoring, and support of SaMD;
- Sections are organized based on processes and activities commonly found in software engineering lifecycle approaches as well as on leadership and management processes of the organization as a whole;
- SaMD lifecycle support processes (Section 7) and realization and use processes (Section 8) include considerations that are necessary to address patient safety and clinical environment as well as the technology and systems environment for SaMD;
- Examples using two fictitious companies—Magna (a large organization) and Parva (a small start-up)—are provided throughout in order to highlight some of the key points being made; and
- References ISO13485:2003, a QMS standard currently published within the medical device industry.
- Field of application:
- The guidance for the application of QMS provided in this document applies to SaMD as defined in IMDRF/SaMD WG/N10 and does not address other types of software; and
- This document focuses on SaMD irrespective of technology and/or platform (mobile app, cloud, server, etc.).

This document is not intended to:

- Provide guidance on how to undertake good software quality and engineering practices or how to implement QMSs; and
- Rewrite, repeat, or contradict QMS principles that are articulated in medical device regulations or standards.

Relationship to regulatory requirements and to technical standards:

- The document does not replace or create new QMS standards, software quality and engineering practices, or regulations; rather, it highlights certain common practices and terminology used by successful software organizations;

- This document is not intended to replace or conflict with medical device legislation, regulations, or procedures required in individual regulatory jurisdictions;
- This document is not a tutorial on risk management practices for software; rather, it highlights risk management principles throughout the software lifecycle processes and activities that are critical to the safety, effectiveness, and performance of SaMD; and
- The activities highlighted in this document are not meant to replace or conflict with the content and/or development of technical or process standards related to software risk- management activities or software-development practices but may provide input to these processes and activities.

3.0 References

- IMDRF/SaMD WG/N10 - Software as a Medical Device (SaMD): Key Definitions.
- IMDRF/SaMD WG N12 - Software as a Medical Device: Possible Framework for Risk Categorization and Corresponding Considerations.
- ISO 13485:2003 – Quality management system – Requirements for regulatory purposes.

4.0 Definitions

This document does not introduce any new definitions but rather relies on the following:

- Definition of SaMD as identified in IMDRF/SaMD WG/N10.
- Terms typically used in standards and regulations as they relate to QMS for medical devices.
- Terms and vocabulary used in software quality and engineering practices.

5.0 SaMD Quality Management Principles

Medical device QMS principles allow for scaling of activities depending on the type of medical device; risk of the product to patients; size of the organization; technology or automation used to manufacture; and other factors that are determined by the manufacturer to control quality and maintain the safe and effective performance of the medical device.

The manufacturing of SaMD, which is a software-only product, is primarily based on the development lifecycle activities often supported by the use of automated software development tools (build automation, use of source code management tools, etc.). These automated activities may in some cases replace discrete or deliberate activities (e.g., transfer of design to production) typically found in the manufacturing of hardware products. However, the principles in a QMS that provide structure and support to the lifecycle processes and activities are still applicable and important to control the quality of SaMD.

An effective QMS for SaMD should include the following principles:

- An organizational structure that provides leadership, accountability, and governance with adequate resources to assure the safety, effectiveness, and performance of SaMD (outer circle in Figure 1);
- A set of SaMD lifecycle support processes that are scalable for the size of the organization and are applied consistently across all realization and use processes (middle circle in Figure 1); and
- A set of realization and use processes that are scalable for the type of SaMD[2] and the size of the organization; and that takes into account important elements required for assuring the safety, effectiveness, and performance of SaMD (innermost circle in Figure 1).

SaMD Quality Management Principles

Figure 1: SaMD Quality Management Principles: Leadership and Organization Support, Processes, and Activities

2 2 As identified by IMDRF SaMD WG N12 document

The three principles outlined above should not be considered independently as a separate series of processes in an organization. Instead, an effective QMS establishes a distinct relationship (see *Figure 2* below) between the three principles as follows:

- The governing structure of Leadership and Organization Support should provide the foundation for SaMD lifecycle support processes; and
- The SaMD lifecycle support processes should apply across the SaMD realization and use processes.

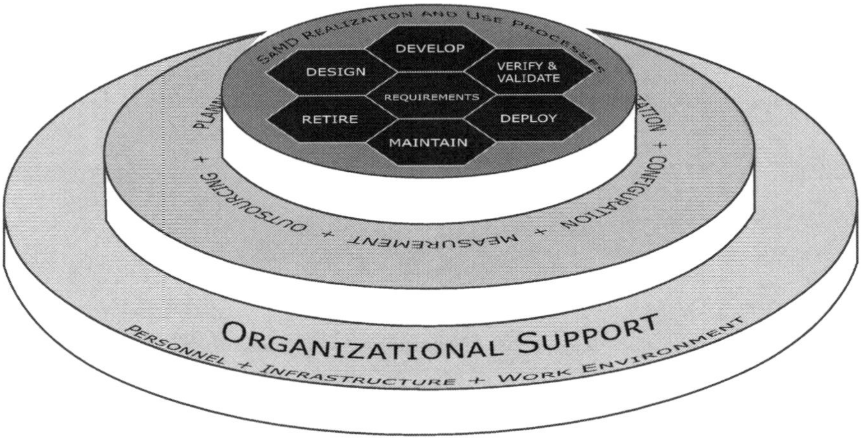

Figure 2: Relationship between Quality Management Principles

The concepts presented in this section relate to clauses 4 and 5 in ISO 13485:2003.

6.0 SaMD Leadership and Organizational Support

6.1 Leadership and Accountability in the Organization

Management of the organization provides the leadership and governance of all activities related to the lifecycle processes of SaMD including defining the strategic direction, responsibility, authority, and communication to assure the safe and effective performance of the SaMD.

The organization's leadership is also responsible for implementing the QMS, which can include developing a quality policy, quality objectives, and project-specific plans that are customer focused.

The governance structure should provide support for creating and establishing appropriate processes that are important for maintaining the quality objectives and policies[3].

In addition, the governance should include activities for systematically verifying the effectiveness of the established quality management system, such as undertaking QMS internal audits. Management review of the results of the QMS audits is a tool to ensure that the established QMS is suitable, adequate, and effective and that any necessary adjustments may be made as a result.

Example: Both Magna and Parva management have responsibilities to ensure that a QMS has been established and that the necessary patient safety considerations have been built in to the QMS and managed when entering the SaMD market. In the case of Magna, the company has an organizational structure that resulted in its Chief Medical Officer being identified as being responsible for these aspects. In the case of Parva, the company has nominated its Software Development Manager to be responsible for including necessary patient safety aspects.

CH 11

The concepts presented in this section relate to clauses 5 and 8.2.2 in ISO 13485:2003.

6.2 Resource and Infrastructure Management

The purpose of resource management is to provide the appropriate level of resources (including people, tools, environment, etc.), as needed for ensuring the effectiveness of the SaMD lifecycle processes and activities in meeting regulatory and customer requirements.

3 These processes should be tailored specifically towards the needs of the organizations and the level of documented processes, objectives, and policies should be adjusted appropriately for the type, size, and distributed nature of the organization.

The concepts presented in this section relate to clause 6 in ISO 13485:2003.

3 These processes should be tailored specifically towards the needs of the organizations and the level of documented processes, objectives, and policies should be adjusted appropriately for the type, size, and distributed nature of the organization.

6.2.1 People

It is important to ensure that people who are assigned to SaMD projects should be competent in performing their jobs. For SaMD, such a team should have competencies in technology and software engineering including an understanding of the clinical aspects of the use of the software.

Example: Both companies realize the importance of ensuring that there are competent employees to perform their assigned duties. In the case of Magna, there is a broader base of skills amongst the staff with the SaMD skills gap being addressed through an extension of already existing in-house training and education programs. For Parva, the skills gap was bridged by looking to other sources such as temporary recruits and external training programs.

The concepts presented in this section relate to clause 6.1 and 6.2 in ISO 13485:2003.

6.2.2 Infrastructure and Work Environment

Infrastructure such as equipment, information, communication networks, tools, and the physical facility, etc., should be made available throughout SaMD lifecycle processes. Such infrastructure is used to support the development, production, and maintenance of SaMD and consequently needs to be provided and maintained.

For SaMD, this may entail identifying and providing the software development and test environment that supports the SaMD realization and use processes. This may include providing a test environment that simulates the intended environment of use and tools that support managing various software configurations during the lifecycle processes, e.g., version management for source code during development.

As work environments become increasingly virtual, the reliability and dependability of the collective infrastructure environment is an important consideration (e.g., dependence on 3rd party networks and equipment).

Example: Both companies need specific environments for ensuring code and data integrity across these different infrastructure environments. In the case of Magna, existing computer networks and secure building access is leveraged directly for SaMD development. In the case of Parva, the development environment is hosted by a qualified service provider, ensuring the code and data integrity is part of the service agreement between them and the provider.

The concepts presented in this section relate to clause 6.3 and 6.4 in ISO 13485:2003.

7.0 SaMD Lifecycle Support Processes

An organization's QMS should be built and managed around processes that support the lifecycle activities of SaMD.

This section addresses important processes that are applicable across the SaMD lifecycle, regardless of the intended use of the SaMD (i.e., significance of the information provided by the SaMD to the healthcare decision and the state of the healthcare situation or condition).

There are many available methods to conduct SaMD lifecycle processes. These processes are typically scaled to address the complexity and size of the SaMD product and project (e.g., during new product introduction or for an upgrade) that needs to be created.

The elements discussed in this section are common processes and activities that should be considered throughout the SaMD lifecycle regardless of specific software product development approach or method used by the organization.

Appropriate implementation of clearly structured and consistently repeatable decision-making processes by SaMD organizations can provide confidence that efforts to minimize patient safety risk and promote patient safety have been considered.

7.1 Product Planning

The objective of planning is to provide a roadmap to be followed during the product development lifecycle. This comes from the quality principle that better results can be achieved by following a methodical and rigorous plan for managing projects such as a plan-do-check-act approach.

Product planning includes the definition of phases, activities, responsibilities, and resources needed for developing the SaMD. It is important to understand that planning is not static—it needs to be updated when new information is gathered or milestones are reached.

IMDRF/SaMD WG/N12 identifies that for SaMD, a thorough understanding of the socio-technical[4] environment (clinical perspective), and the technology and system environment (software perspective) is important in planning, as inadequate considerations could lead to incorrect, inaccurate, and/or delayed diagnoses and treatments.[5]

The implementation of SaMD lifecycle processes should adequately be informed and tailored for the type of SaMD as identified in IMDRF/SaMD WG/N12.

4 Socio-technical systems are systems that include technical systems but also operational processes and people who use and interact with the technical system. Socio-technical systems are governed by organizational policies and rules.

5 IMDRF SaMD WG N12: Section 9.1—Socio-technical environment considerations and Section 9.2—Technology and system environment considerations.

Example: Both companies carry out product planning to decide which operating systems best suited their SaMD application. The larger Magna company has chosen to build its application to work on the top five mobile phone operating systems as the company has the resources to develop on multiple platforms. While the smaller Parva has chosen to develop for the platform that is currently the market leader due to the company's constraints of resources. For both Parva and Magna, this planning phase can allow each company to take deliberate approaches to the assignment of resources.

The concepts presented in this section relate to clauses 5.4, 7.1, and 7.3.1 in ISO 13485:2003.

7.2 Risk Management: A Patient Safety Focused Process

IMDRF/SaMD WG/N12 provides a possible framework to categorize types of SaMD based on impact to patient and public health. Using the foundational categorization in *IMDRF/SaMD WG/N12*, the safety, effectiveness, and performance of SaMD can be enhanced by appropriate risk management. This risk management process should be integrated across the entire lifecycle of SaMD.

Organizations that engage in general software development continuously monitor and manage schedules and budget risks of a software project. Similarly, a SaMD organization should also monitor and manage risks to patients and users across all lifecycle processes.

For SaMD, product risk should be informed by the intended purpose; the normal use and reasonably foreseeable misuse; and the understood and defined socio-technical environment of use of the SaMD. Some general considerations associated with SaMD patient safety risk include the ease with which a SaMD may be updated, duplicated, and distributed due to its non-physical nature, and where these updates, made available by the SaMD organization, may be installed by others.

Risk management in the context of this document, outlines a risk-based approach to patient safety.[6] Specifically, related to QMS, some points that should be considered include:

- Identification of hazards;
- Estimation and evaluation of associated risks;
- Actions to control risks; and
- Methods to monitor effectiveness of the actions implemented to control risks.

For example, it is helpful to chart sources of hazards along multiple dimensions, such as:

User-Based

Is the SaMD product appropriate for all intended users? For instance, are there hazards posed by visual acuity for an elderly user, or for patients with peripheral neuropathy? Is the device being used in a clinical or home environment?

6 ISO 14971:2007 is one commonly used standard that can be used to guide an appropriate medical device risk management process.

Application-Based

Should a SaMD application be available on any device, or should it be restricted to certain devices in such a way that it could help to mitigate user risk?

Device-Based

Is a device with a smaller screen, such as a smartphone, adequate for the intended application? Can a smaller screen display a large set of information without losing the information or making it cumbersome to the users in a way that could affect patient safety?

Environment-Based

Is continuity of use (and therefore, safety) of the SaMD product compromised when there are environmental disruptions (e.g., interruptions in use, background noise, loss of network connectivity)?

Security-Based

Is analysis being performed that includes evaluating the security threats to SaMD product software code during manufacturing, maintenance and in-service use? Does this analysis also include, for example, intrusion detection, penetration testing, vulnerability scanning, and data integrity testing to minimize system and patient risks?

Software risk management requires a balanced evaluation of both safety and security. Security risks may affect the confidentiality, integrity, and availability of data handled by the SaMD. When considering mitigations to protect device security, the manufacturer should ensure that security risk controls do not take precedence over safety considerations.

Example: Both Magna and Parva know the importance of carrying out systematic risk management activities throughout their SaMD lifecycles. Magna has a dedicated department whose members ensure that the risk of the product is within acceptable limits, including considerations of patient harm. Parva has chosen to train its SaMD developers in risk-management activities and, with this knowledge, they collectively ensure that the risk of the product is within acceptable limits, including considerations of patient harm. Both of the above approaches ensure that the necessary risk management activities are carried out.

The concepts presented in this section relate to clause 7.1 in ISO 13485:2003.

7.3 Document and Record Control

Records are used to provide evidence of results achieved or activities performed as a part of the QMS or SaMD lifecycle processes as well as justifications for any QMS or SaMD lifecycle processes not performed. Records can be in paper or electronic form.

For SaMD lifecycle processes, document control and records management makes it easier for the users of those documents and records, both within and outside (outsourced contractors, customers, etc.) the organization, to share and collaborate in the many activities related to the SaMD lifecycle processes. Document control and records management also serves to help communicate and preserve the rationale for why certain decisions were made, such as those related to patient safety or risk management.

Records generated to demonstrate QMS conformity should be appropriately identified, stored, protected, and retained for an established period of time. The following activities are examples of ways to manage and maintain appropriate documentation in the QMS system:

- Reviewing and approving documents before use;
- Ensuring current versions of applicable documents are available at points of use to help prevent the use of obsolete documents;
- Retaining obsolete documentation for an established period;
- Controlling documents against unauthorized or unintended changes; and
- Maintaining and updating documents across all SaMD lifecycle processes.

Example: In the cases of Magna and Parva, it is important to manage and control documentation throughout the SaMD lifecycle processes. Documentation does not mean bureaucracy; rather, it is the foundation to drive traceability, repeatability, scalability, and reliability in SaMD projects. Magna uses established documentation processes and techniques that include the use of a commercially available requirements management tool throughout the SaMD lifecycle processes. Parva has re-purposed its source-code control software to enable the company to manage its documentation in a controlled way.

The concepts presented in this section relate to clause 4.2 in ISO 13485:2003.

7.4 Configuration Management and Control

Control of configurable items, including source code, releases, documents, software tools, etc., is important in order to maintain the integrity and traceability of the configuration throughout the SaMD lifecycle.

A systematic documentation of the SaMD and its supporting design and development, including a robust and documented configuration and change management process, is necessary to identify its constituent parts, to provide a history of changes made to it, and to enable recovery/recreation of past versions of the software, i.e., traceability of the SaMD.

For SaMD, configuration is also an important consideration to enable the correct installation and integration of the SaMD into the clinical environment. This information enables users to decide, for example, whether or not the SaMD can be used with available hardware and networks, whether it is necessary to establish different routines and training, or whether it is necessary to obtain new or reconfigure existing hardware.

In the management of SaMD configuration, software tools are generally used to manage source code, releases, documents, deployment, maintenance, etc. In SaMD, the notion of configuration management and its complexity is amplified by the heterogeneity of the environment in which the SaMD will operate; using the right tools and techniques is important.

Example: For Magna and Parva the importance of configuration management is well understood. In both cases the companies' patients can access the SaMD products through multiple devices (e.g., smartphone, PC, and tablet) each of which require specific configurations and optimization of user experiences. The need for multi-device access enforces the importance of a robust and documented configuration management process to ensure the integrity and traceability of the various configurations across product lines.

The concepts presented in this section relate to clauses 4.2.3, 4.2.4, 7.3.7, 7.5.1, and 7.5.3 in ISO 13485:2003.

7.5 Measurement, Analysis, and Improvement of Processes and Products

Measurement of quality characteristics of software products and processes is used to manage and improve product realization and use. An effective measurement of key factors, often associated with issues related to risk, can help identify the capabilities needed to deliver safe and effective SaMD. Opportunities to monitor, measure, and analyze for improvement exist before, during, and after SaMD lifecycle processes, activities and tasks, and are completed with the intent to objectively demonstrate the quality of the SaMD. Post market surveillance including monitoring, measurement and analysis of quality data can include logging and tracking of complaints, clearing technical issues, determining problem causes and actions to address, identify, collect, analyze, and report on critical quality characteristics of products developed. For SaMD, monitoring to demonstrate through objective measurement that processes are being followed does not itself guarantee good software, just as monitoring software quality alone does not guarantee that the objectives for a process are being achieved. Aspects important for the measurement, analysis, and improvement of SaMD processes and products include:

- Evaluation of the SaMD and its lifecycle processes should be based on defined responsibilities and predetermined activities including using leading and lagging safety indicators and collecting and analyzing appropriate quality data. The analysis of this data, such as analysis of customer complaints, problem reports, bug reports, nonconformity to product requirements, service reports, and trends of processes and products should be used to evaluate the quality of the SaMD and the quality of the SaMD lifecycle processes and where/if improvement of these processes can be made. For SaMD, customer complaints may be the major source of the quality data that the organization should analyze.
- Corrections and corrective actions may be required when a process is not correctly followed or the SaMD does not meet its specified requirements (i.e., when a nonconforming process or product exists).
- Nonconforming SaMD should be contained to prevent unintended use or delivery. The detected nonconformity should be analyzed and actions taken to eliminate the detected nonconformity (i.e., correction); and to identify and eliminate the cause(s) of the detected nonconformity (i.e., corrective action) to prevent recurrence of the detected nonconformity in the future. In some cases a potential nonconformity may be

CH 11

identified, and actions such as safeguards and process changes can be taken, to prevent nonconformities from occurring (i.e., preventive action).

- Actions taken to address the cause of SaMD nonconformities, as well as actions taken to eliminate potential SaMD nonconformities, should be verified/validated before SaMD release and should be evaluated for effectiveness.
- Lessons learned from the analysis of past projects, including the results from internal or external audits of the SaMD lifecycle processes, can be used to improve the safety, effectiveness, and performance of SaMD. The manufacturer should also have processes in place for the collection of active and passive post market surveillance information in order to make appropriate decisions relating to future releases.
- After the product is in the market, it is important to maintain vigilance for vulnerability to intentional and unintentional security threats as part of post market surveillance.

Example: Customer feedback is an important part of monitoring the performance to improve the product over time. Both Magna and Parva are in the process of developing a new and improved version of their SaMD. Magna has a dedicated department that works independently but in conjunction with sales, marketing, and product development to formally survey its large customer base to gain insights into product performance. In the case of Parva, the company invites some of its early adopters and customers into an office to conduct a round-table discussion to get to the same kind of feedback. Both companies also use embedded analytical tools to gain insights into customer behavior with respect to their use of their respective products. They also routinely review and evaluate customer complaints to identify trends and potential areas for improvement. Based on the review of various sources of data, both Magna and Parva redesigned their SaMD to address common issues identified by customer feedback, complaints, and any new/updated clinical evidence.

The concepts presented in this section relate to clauses 7.2.3, 7.3.7, 7.5.1.1, 8.1, 8.2, 8.3, 8.4, and 8.5 in ISO 13485:2003.

7.6 Managing Outsourced Processes, Activities, and Products

An effective QMS system takes into account and ensures quality of SaMD when processes, activities, or products are outsourced (i.e., are not completely conducted/made in-house). An organization may choose to outsource different parts of its SaMD process, activities, or product based on its in-house strengths and competencies. Similarly, an organization may procure a commercial-off-the-shelf (COTS) product or another SaMD for integration into its SaMD. In both of these instances, understanding, maintaining control, and managing the effect of such outsourced processes, activities, or products is important and necessary to deliver safe and effective SaMD.

A SaMD organization may, for example, outsource customer service as a process, or outsource the development activity for a particular module of the SaMD. As with any outsourcing strategy, the following are considerations that are commonly achieved through the use of contractual terms in order to provide confidence in the services and products delivered to manage or mitigate patient safety risk of SaMD:

- Understand the capabilities and competencies of potential outsourcing suppliers;
- Clearly communicate the roles and responsibilities of the outsourcing supplier;
- Extensively define the quality requirements for the outsourced process, activity, or product;
- Clearly establish upfront the criteria for and review of deliverables, frequency of intermediate inspections, and relevant audits of the supplier; and
- Select and qualify the appropriate outsourcing supplier to deliver safe and effective SaMD.

When a SaMD organization plans to procure a COTS product, such as a third-party database for integration in its SaMD, or procure another SaMD to be integrated as a module, the following are examples that may enhance the understanding of the effect of these decisions and help manage the resultant effect on the SaMD:

- Understanding the capabilities and limitations of the COTS product can inform the management of the risks, design choices, and extent of verification and validation needed for the SaMD; and
- Understanding the processes/methods/frequency that the COTS manufacturer employs to update, enhance, or make corrections to its products should be used to inform the selection of the COTS product and the potential effect on the SaMD manufacturer's QMS processes and activities.

Example: Magna and Parva have historically used open-source code or other COTS code as part of product development. In the development of SaMD, it is critical for both Magna and Parva to properly verify and validate the integration of open source code or COTS code. When appropriate, it is also critical to formally evaluate, document, and periodically audit suppliers to ensure compliance with QMS requirements. Both companies are also responsible for monitoring and managing the potential for defects in the COTS, as these defects can contribute to the overall risks of the SaMD and may introduce threats to the larger system within which the SaMD resides. Regardless of the type of code that is used and who is supplying the code, Magna and Parva are ultimately responsible for the safety and performance of the SaMD.

The concepts presented in this section relate to clauses 7.4, 7.4.1, 7.4.2, 7.4.3, and 8.5.1 in ISO 13485:2003.

8.0 SaMD Realization and Use Processes

This section identifies key lifecycle processes[7] that should be identified in the methodologies used in an organization that manufactures SaMD.

The following are important perspectives that should be considered for each of the activities in this section.

- SaMD lifecycle support processes in Section 0 (product planning; risk management: a patient safety focused approach; document and record control; configuration management and control; measurement, analysis and improvement of processes and product; managing outsourced processes and products) should be applied throughout the SaMD realization and use processes.
- This section highlights those activities commonly found in software engineering lifecycle approaches (process, activities, tasks, etc.) that are important for an effective SaMD QMS.
- The activities presented in this section should be included irrespective of methodology used. The presentation of the material does not imply executing the activities in a serial fashion or as discrete phases in the SaMD project; rather, these activities should be looked upon as elements to be addressed as part of any development methodology employed.

The concepts presented in this section relate to clause 7 in ISO 13485:2003.

8.1 Requirements Management

Developing appropriate requirements helps to ensure that SaMD will satisfy the needs across the socio-technical environment including those of users and patients. These clinical needs should be clearly articulated and the requirements captured in line with the intended use of SaMD as characterized by the "state of the healthcare situation or condition" and the "significance of information provided by SaMD to the healthcare decision" and the resulting impact to patient and public health as identified in *IMDRF SaMD WG N12.*

This is a customer-driven process that requires clear, and often repeated, customer interaction to understand the user needs. These user needs are then translated into requirements. Well-documented requirements can then inform the testing activities later in the design cycle. There are other sources of requirements that can include regulatory or non-customer specified performance requirements.

7 IEC 62304:2006 is one commonly used software development lifecycle standard that can be used to develop a medical device software lifecycle process.

Patient Safety and Clinical Environment Considerations

- SaMD is used in various clinical and home use environments and, consequently, in addition to functional requirements, there are requirements that include considerations of patient/user safety. Some requirements originate from the risk-management process that evaluates risks to patients and users, and which may identify mitigations that become part of the requirements.
- Further considerations need to be given to the integrity of data used in the SaMD which may result in specific requirements to ensure that data is secure and to mitigate against the loss or corruption of sensitive data.[8]
- Requirements for SaMD often need to include additional and specific requirements for performing upgrades that consider potential effects on peripheral components of the system as well as appropriate notification and coordination with customers.[9]

Technology and Systems Environment Considerations

- SaMD runs on an underlying platform and operating system, often from a third party, the functionality of which should be considered as part of the requirements, as the platforms and operating systems can be potential sources of harm.
- Requirements may also need to define non-functional aspects of a system such as service or performance related requirements for the hardware platforms that may host the SaMD or means of connecting/networking to the wider environment.
- Requirements should be captured in concert with stakeholders (patients, clinicians, end users, etc.) in the process of use of the SaMD.

Note: Requirements may change as the developer better understands how the SaMD functions in the clinical environment and how a customer uses it. Consequently, it is important to apply usability engineering principles to the formative development and testing of the software to ensure that the requirements were appropriately translated into design inputs.

Example: The definition and maintenance of requirements are important in ensuring that the product meets its intended use. For Magna and Parva, requirements serve the purpose of clearly defining what is to be developed in their respective SaMD products. In the case of Magna, a cross-functional product team leverages existing document templates to capture requirements and an existing document-review process to approve the requirements for use. In the case of Parva, screen shots, sketches, and rapid prototypes are used to refine and capture the product requirements for the SaMD features. In both cases, the requirements are captured in a way that ensures that user, patient, and regulatory requirements are satisfied/met.

The concepts presented in this section relate to clauses 7.2.1, 7.2.2, 7.2.3, 4.2, and 7.1d in ISO 13485:2003.

8 *IMDRF SaMD WG N12*: Section 9.3—Information security with respect to safety considerations
9 *IMDRF SaMD WG N12*: Section 8.2—Changes

8.2 Design

The purpose of the design activity is to define the architecture, components, and interfaces of the software system based on user requirements, and any other performance requirements, in line with the intended use of the SaMD and the various clinical and home use environments it is intended to operate in.

The requirements are analyzed in order to produce a description of the software's internal structure that will serve as the basis for its implementation. When complete, the SaMD design activity should describe the software architecture, i.e., how the software is decomposed and organized into its components, including considerations for safety critical elements, the interfaces between those components (and any external elements), and a sufficiently detailed description of each component.

One of the key aspects of the design process is to arrive at a clear and concise design solution that is an effective, well described (e.g., captured in software requirements specifications) logical architecture that best meets the user needs and that enables other lifecycle processes and activities such as development, verification, validation, safe deployment, and maintenance of the SaMD.

Building quality into SaMD requires that safety and security should be evaluated within each phase of the product lifecycle and at key milestones. Security threats and their potential effect on patient safety should be considered as possible actors on the system in all SaMD lifecycle activities.

The goal is to engineer a system that: a) maintains patient safety and the confidentiality, availability, and integrity of critical functions and data; b) is resilient against intentional and unintentional threats; and c) is fault-tolerant and recoverable to a safe state in the presence of an attack.

Patient Safety and Clinical Environment Considerations

- Where a SaMD will be used—in the home, at the hospital bedside, in a physician's office or clinic—the users (e.g., patients, clinicians, and others who may interact or use the SaMD) should be considered in the design activities.
- Clinical hazards already identified should be an input in the design phase.

Technology and Systems Environment Considerations

- Architectural design may be driven by the safety critical nature of SaMD and by the risk- mitigation solutions. Risk mitigation solutions may include segregation of specific functions into particular modules that are isolated from other areas/modules of the software.
- SaMD design should have appropriate controls in place to ensure robustness in the event of unanticipated upgrades of the underlying platform.
- SaMD design should include consideration and the taking of appropriate measures when integrating or using software components or infrastructure with limited or uncontrollable knowledge of capabilities and limitations, such as legacy software,

undocumented application programing interfaces (API), and wireless network infrastructure. Such measures should identify the risks that could be introduced to the SaMD product and the extent of implications to the design of the SaMD.

- External resources, sensors, and services used by high-risk aspects of the application should be abstracted such that automated testing can be performed based on consistently simulated values and that operational health considerations can be enforced as a separated concern through mitigated access and mutually understood error conditions.

Example: Magna has a structure within its software department that enables it to distribute the design of different software modules amongst different teams. These teams work in parallel to each other with the interface considerations of the modules being discussed as a specific activity at pre-defined points in the design phase. Parva use uses one multi-disciplined team to develop the design. The company develops its design in an iterative way and considers the internal interfaces as each design effort is complete. Both companies complete their design activity in a controlled and effective manner.

The concepts presented in this section relate to clauses 7.3, 7.3.2, 7.3.3, 7.3.4, 7.3.7 and 7.3.1b in ISO 13485:2003.

8.3 Development

The development activity transforms the requirements, architecture, design (including interface definition), recognized coding practices (secure), and architecture patterns into software items and the integration of those software items into a SaMD.

The result is a software item/system/product that satisfies specified requirements, architecture, and design. Good development practice incorporates appropriate review activities, (e.g. code review, peer review, creator self-review) and follows a defined implementation strategy (e.g., build new, acquire new, re-use of existing elements). Design changes resulting from the review activity or development activity should be adequately captured and communicated to ensure that other development and QMS activities remain current.

Use of appropriately qualified automated tools and supporting infrastructure is important for managing configuration and having traceability to other lifecycle activities.

Patient Safety and Clinical Environment Considerations

- The implementation of clinical algorithms adopted should be transparent to the user in order to avoid misuse or unintended use.
- The implementation of proper access controls and audit trail mechanisms should be balanced with the usability of SaMD as intended.
- Technology and Systems Environment Considerations

- Development activity should leverage the inherent nature of SaMD that allows for efficient methods to understand the user's environment and prevent and manage failures.
- Attention to detail is critical in areas of underlying implementation of the algorithm—a simple data overwrite can potentially lead to an adverse event. Some examples of these critical areas include: memory usage and allocation, dependency on communication, speed of operation, and prioritization of tasks.
- Many SaMD deal with data entry, and the methods through which data is validated and the effect on the downstream data consumer is an important SaMD consideration.
- As SaMD runs on an underlying platform, rigorous and strict adherence to development guidance as set forth by the platform developer should be followed to ensure backward compatibility.

Example: For both Magna and Parva, coding is central to the delivery of the companies' SaMD product. Magna conducts peer code reviews for SaMD by scheduling periodic peer-review sessions with multiple coders who are not directly involved with the code under review. In the case of Parva, the company does not have a large coding team, and has only one developer who is an expert in his or her chosen operating system. The company uses a technique of "design for code readability", thereby allowing the code review activity to be conducted with a member of the team who is not an expert. Both achieve what is required by good software code review guidelines including the need for independence in the review activity.

CH 11

The concepts presented in this section relate to clauses 7.3, 7.3.2, 7.3.3, 7.3.4, 7.3.7 and 7.3.1b in ISO 13485:2003.

8.4 Verification and Validation

The verification and validation (V&V) activities should be targeted towards the criticality and impact to patient safety of the SaMD, as discussed in *IMDRF/SaMD WG/N12*.

Typically, verification (providing assurance that the design and development activity at each development stage conforms to the requirements) and validation (providing reasonable confidence that the software meets its intended use/user needs and operational requirements) activities ensure that all elements from the SaMD design and development—including any changes made during maintenance/upgrades—have been implemented correctly and that objective evidence of this implementation is recorded.

A defined set of V&V activities should focus on the interface of the SaMD to the operating system, outsourced components, and other dependencies related to the computing platform.

Patient Safety and Clinical Environment Considerations

- These V&V activities should include scenarios that cover the clinical user/use environment (usability, instructions for use, etc.). This can be accomplished, in part, through structured human factors testing using a subset of patients/clinicians.

- These activities should confirm that software safety elements work properly (i.e., patient safety / clinical use risk elements, etc.). These activities are also commonly included as part of user acceptance testing (UAT).
- Confirmation of acceptable failure behavior in the clinical environment should be established. This may include confirmation of the ability of the software to continue to operate in the specified degraded modes (e.g., fail-safe, fail-secure, or fail-soft).
- Consideration of a variety of user groups to ensure software can be used by persons of different demographics.

Technology and Systems Environment Considerations

- The extent of test coverage should be driven by the risk profile of the device determined by the intended use and SaMD definition statement.[10]
- Interoperability of components and compatibility to other platforms/devices/interfaces, etc. with which SaMD works should be considered.
- Adequate coverage and traceability to the known hazard-related functions of SaMD should be provided.
- The coverage of boundary conditions and exceptions (robustness, stress testing, data security, integrity, and continuity of SaMD availability) should be included.
- Companies should employ rigorous impact analysis of changes made to SaMD (i.e., regression testing) to ensure updates do not compromise the safety, effectiveness, and performance of SaMD.

Example: In both Magna and Parva, testing coverage and regression testing are important. Magna has a number of test engineers that execute the test plans and regression testing while monitoring coverage. Parva invested in a test automation tool that allows continuous test/build cycle which monitors coverage and regression testing on each checked-in build. Where automation is not possible an independent software developer runs the manual test suite prior to each release. Both companies achieve the appropriate level of test coverage with the necessary levels of independence.

The concepts presented in this section relate to clauses 7.3.5, 7.3.6 and 7.4.3 in ISO 13485:2003.

8.5 Deployment

Deployment activities include aspects of delivery, installation, setup, and configuration that support a controlled and effective distribution of SaMD to the customer, including any planned risk mitigation for hazards identified throughout the SaMD lifecycle support processes and SaMD realization and use processes.

10 *IMDRF SaMD WG N12:* Section 6—SaMD Definition Statement.

Some aspects of deployment activities may need to be performed every time a SaMD is distributed to the user (e.g., distributing an upgrade or fix as a result of maintenance activity). In some cases, especially when SaMD is a large system or is part of a large system, the deployment activities may depend on an extensive collaborative effort with the user (which can include training the users) for an effective use of SaMD or the system.

Patient Safety and Clinical Environment Considerations

- Deploying SaMD into a clinical environment can require considerations of peripheral components if it is intended to be part of a clinical IT network, such as establishing platform and OS requirements as well as responsibility agreements. The deployment activity should be clearly defined for the customer as the cooperation of hospital IT, integration engineers, clinical engineers, hospital risk managers and others who often may not be part of a typical deployment of other products may often be required.
- Deployment needs to consider the end user and use environment(s) of SaMD. This would be particularly true if used in the home. The deployment activity needs to be tailored to the user's abilities and background. Appropriate human factors engineering practices can aid in understanding this aspect and would affect the user requirements capture activity.
- Where possible, user documentation and user training materials should identify any limitations with SaMD. These may include limitations of the algorithm, provenance of data used, assumptions made, etc., that should be considered during deployment.
- There should be communication of relevant information to enable correct installation and configuration of the SaMD for appropriate integration with clinical workflows. This can include instructions on how to verify the appropriateness of the installation and update to SaMD as well as any changes made to the system environment.

Technology and Systems Environment Considerations

- Deployment should also include the collection of the settings and the environment of each installation for configuration management. This information should be maintained throughout the life of SaMD at each installation.
- Deployment of SaMD when installed on specific platforms should be according to the intended use that was verified and validated.
- Processes should be in place to ensure the appropriate and correct version is delivered to the user.
- The choice of deployment method should consider the integrity of the SaMD to ensure that the software can be delivered in a secure and reliable manner.
- Deployment methods and procedures should ensure repeatability of SaMD delivery, installation, setup, configuration, intended operation, and maintenance.
- Methods that confirm that the software is delivered consistently and comprehensively and that it is used in a defined environment are also important. Non-technical measures may have to be implemented as part of the software product package for deployment.

- When deploying an update to SaMD, updating user manual(s), anomaly lists, or providing training may be necessary.

Note: Non-technical measures can include warning/confirmation dialogs, warning displays, usage notes, and user training requirements.

Example: *For Both Magna and Parva, when a SaMD is deployed on 'the cloud' or a mobile platform, it is critical to ensure integrity of the deployment activity with an extended network of stakeholders. For instance, a SaMD application that is designed for use on a smart phone should be supported with proper processes and documentation that include parties such as app stores and private app clouds, as well as third-party hosting service providers, etc. Unlike the deployment of general consumer software, for example, these extended deployment stakeholders should be qualified and integrated per the QMS requirements for outsourcing and third-party supplier management.*

The concepts presented in this section relate to clauses 7.2.3, 7.5, 7.5.1.2.1, 7.5.1.2.2, 7.5.1.2.3[11] and 7.5.5 in ISO 13485:2003.

8.6 Maintenance

Maintenance includes activities and tasks to modify a previously deployed SaMD. Maintenance activities can be adaptive, perfective, preventive, and corrective activities originating from software lifecycle processes and activities including in-service monitoring, customer feedback, in-house testing or other information, or changes to user requirements or changes in the socio-technical environment.

When a previously deployed SaMD requires maintenance, all appropriate SaMD lifecycle support processes, and SaMD realization and use processes should be considered. Maintenance activities should preserve the integrity of the SaMD without introducing new safety, effectiveness, performance, and security hazards.

To effectively manage the maintenance activities and any resulting changes and their effect on SaMD, a risk assessment should be performed to determine if the change(s) affect SaMD categorization and the core functionality of SaMD as outlined in the SaMD definition statement.[12]

Patient Safety and Clinical Environment Considerations

- Within the context of SaMD it is important to understand how systems, software, context of use, usability, data, and documentation might be affected by changes, particularly with regards to safety, effectiveness, and performance.

CH 11

11 For software products, capabilities like performance, security and safety heavily depend on the computing environment and platforms put in place. The use context and the processes used with the software product will generally influence the above capabilities. Though at the time of deployment or runtime the SaMD organization may have little or no technical control over such factors, the SaMD organization's hazards or mitigations analysis should consider the socio-technical aspects of the intended use and the intended/foreseeable use context of the SaMD

12 *IMDRF SaMD WG N12* - Section 8.2 Changes

- The SaMD manufacturer should take into account implications and introduction of patient safety risk as a result of changes to architecture and code.
- As highlighted in other SaMD lifecycle processes and SaMD lifecycle activities, people, technology, infrastructure, and new hazards resulting from implementation and use activities should be considered.
- It is important to understand the effect of the change on patient safety and the need for addressing the change in a timely manner when appropriate.

Technology and Systems Environment Considerations

- There should be processes that manage risk arising from changes to system, environment, and data.
- SaMD manufacturers should make it feasible for users to safely implement information security updates.
- Instructions for users related to information security should include how to safely update security software/spyware, operating environment, and other systems and applications, etc.

Example: *Magna has a process that controls change of its SaMD through a change-control board. This is a multi-disciplined team that meets at regular intervals to review the change requests and recommend (or reject) them for incorporation in the next version of software. Parva has assigned its project manager to act as a customer representative; as part of this role, she reviews the feedback items received and adds any relevant issue to the backlog of the next release. Both companies prioritize the change requests to ensure that any significant issues are dealt with in a timely manner.*

The concepts presented in this section relate to clauses 7.2.3, 7.5, 7.5.1.2.3, 7.5.4, 7.6 and 8.2.1 in ISO 13485:2003.

8.7 Decommissioning (Retirement or End-of-Life Activity)

The purpose of decommissioning activities is to terminate maintenance, support, and distribution of SaMD in a controlled and a managed fashion. Although not specifically mentioned in ISO 13485 as a clause, the standard does require planning of product realization in the design which would include decommissioning.

Decommissioning activities are important to minimize the impact to patient and public health safety as a result of retiring the SaMD. These activities may include aspects of configuration management that apply to the document; source code or the delivered SaMD; and communicating a plan to the user for gracefully terminating maintenance and support of SaMD.

This process indicates an end to active support, and may entail deactivation and/or removal of SaMD and its supporting data. The decommissioning of SaMD data is of special importance.

While the product and/or access may be terminated, there may be country specific requirements for managing the data.

Patient Safety and Clinical Environment Considerations

- Provide clarity to users which services (e.g., bug fixes, updates, patches, technical support, etc.) will be available once end-of-life (EOL) is signed-off.
- Appropriately safeguard patient data and any other confidential data. This may include removal, migrating patients to a new SaMD or another product, safe archival of user information, etc.

Technology and Systems Environment Considerations

- Inform customers of important EOL milestones, with sufficient lead-time for users to find, evaluate, and qualify possible alternatives.
- Archive a user's environment in an agreed-upon state, which may include steps to protect the security and integrity of information and/or systems.

Example*: For both Magna and Parva, it is necessary to have procedures that ensure effective decommissioning, documentation, and data archival for SaMD products. Both have a process that asks for a decommissioning plan to be created. This plan takes consideration of the following points to arrive at an effective solution for decommissioning a SaMD:*

- *What minimum retention time periods are defined by each territory in which the devices are marketed;*
- *Will any data be migrated onto new/replacement devices/software systems and, if so, will any data conversion be needed and how will this be validated;*
- *Will the SaMD be withdrawn or will it be only a withdrawal of support for the device;*
- *How sensitive legacy data (patient information, etc.) will be securely stored; and*
- *How the users of the device that is to be decommissioned will be informed and supported.*

In this way both companies can make the appropriate decisions to effectively and gracefully plan the decommissioning of their devices.

The concepts presented in this section relate to clauses 4.2, 7, and 7.5.1.1 in ISO 13485:2003.

Appendix A: Mapping Medical Device Regulations to IMDRF/SaMD WG/N23

The following table provides a mapping of applicable clauses, articles, and subsections of the regulations for a QMS for SaMD for the jurisdictions represented in the current IMDRF SaMD WG members. It is important to note that not all jurisdictions may require demonstration of compliance to a QMS for all types of medical devices. Regulatory requirements may also permit exclusions or provide alternative arrangements to be addressed in a QMS. It is the responsibility of the organization to ensure conformity with appropriate jurisdictional regulatory requirements. The objective of this table is to share how QMS requirements map to the elements presented in the IMDRF/SaMD WG/N23 when compliance to a QMS is required in the specified jurisdictions.

Applicability to Health Canada regulations:

- The Medical Devices Regulations require class II, III and IV medical devices to be manufactured (class II) or designed and manufactured (class III & IV) under CAN/CSA ISO 13485:2003.

Applicability to Europe Union regulations:

- EU legislation foresees the QMS to be assessed by third parties only for certain classes of products.
- EN ISO 13485:2012 Annexes ZA, ZB, ZC specify in detail which parts of the relevant Annexes to Directive 90/385 (Active Implantable Medical Devices (AIMD) Directives 93/42 (Medical Device Directive (MDD) and 98/79 (In Vitro Diagnostic Directive (IVDD) align to clauses of ISO 13485:2012.
- Note: MEDDEV Guidance 2.1/6 Guidelines On The Qualification And Classification Of Stand Alone Software Used In Healthcare Within The Regulatory Framework Of Medical Devices", while not binding, constitutes a significant additional reference.

CH 11

Applicability to Australian regulations:

- The Therapeutic Goods (Medical Devices) Regulations 2002 require manufacturers to demonstrate compliance with appropriate conformity assessment procedures as specified in Division 3.2, three of which require implementation of a QMS.
- The Conformity assessment standards order (standard for quality management systems and quality assurance techniques) 2008 enables the use of ISO13485 to demonstrate compliance with applicable clauses of those procedures. Mapping is as per the following table key: [Code]—Procedure name (legislative reference):
    - [P5]—Product Quality Assurance procedures (Schedule 3, Part 5, Clause 5.4)
    - [P4]—Production Quality Assurance procedures (Schedule 3, Part 4, Clause 4.4)
    - [P1]—Full Quality Assurance procedures (Schedule 3, Clause Part 1, 1.4)
    - [All]—required for all (Product, Production, and Full Quality Assurance) conformity assessment procedures
- The # symbol is used to indicate clauses of ISO 13485 considered to additionally be applicable to software medical devices under Australian legislation.

N23	TOPIC	ISO 13485:2003	Australia	Brazil RDC 16/2013	China MD GMP ([2014]64)	Japan MHLW QMS Ordinance	US 21 CFR
5.0--SAMD QUALITY MANAGEMENT PRINCIPLES	Quality management strategy	4	A11	2.1	3,24	5	820.5
	Management responsibility	5	A11		5-7,78		
6.0--SAMD LEADERSHIP AND ORGANIZATIONAL SUPPORT							
6.1--LEADERSHIP AND ACCOUNTABILITY IN THE ORGANIZATION	Management responsibility	5	A11				
	Management commitment	5.1	A11	2.2.5 2.2.6	6	10	820.20b
	Customer focus	5.2	A11			11	
	Quality policy	5.3	A11	2.2.1	6	12	820.20a
	Quality planning	5.4	A11		6	13, 14	820.20d
	Responsibility and authority	5.5	A11	2.2.3	5	15	820.20b1
	Management representative	5.5.2	A11	2.2.5	7	16	820.20b3
	Internal communication	5.5.3	A11	2.2.1		17	
	Management review	5.6	A11	2.2.6	78	18, 19, 20	820.20
	Internal audit	8.2.2	A11				
6.2--RESOURCE AND INFRASTRUCTURE MANAGEMENT	Resource Management	6	A11				
6.2.1--PEOPLE	Provision of resources	6.1	A11	2.3	6	21	820.20b2
	Skill management	6.2	A11	2.3	8-10	22, 23	820.25
6.2.2--INFRASTRUCTURE AND WORK ENVIRONMENT	Infrastructure	6.3	A11	5.1	12-23	24	820.70f,g
	Work environment	6.4	A11	5.1	11	25	820.70c
7.0--MANAGING SaMD LIFECYCLE SUPPORT PROCESSES							
7.1--PRODUCT PLANNING	Quality planning	5.4	A11		6	13	820.20d
	Planning of product realization	7.1	A11	4.1	28, 29	26	820.30a, 70a
	Design planning	7.3.1	P1	4.1	28,29	30	820.30a,b
7.2--RISK MANAGEMENT: A PATIENT SAFETY FOCUSED PROCESS	Planning of product realization	7.1	ALL	2.4	4,38	26-5, 26-6	820.3g

CH 11

N23	TOPIC	ISO 13485:2003	Australia	Brazil RDC 16/2013	China MD GMP ([2014]64)	Japan MHLW QMS Ordinance	US 21 CFR
7.3--DOCUMENT CONTROL AND RECORDS	Quality system record		A11	3.1.6	24		820.186
	Documentation requirements - General	4.2.1	A11		24	6	820.20e
	Quality manual	4.2.2	A11	2.2.1	24	7	820.20e
	Document control	4.2.3	A11	3.1	25,26	8	820.4
	Control of records	4.2.4	A11	3.1.6.2	27	9	820.18
	Device master record		A11	4.2	50	6-2	820.181
7.4--CONFIGURATION MANAGEMENT AND CONTROL	Document control	4.2.3	A11	3.1	25,26	8	820.4
	Control of records	4.2.4	A11	3.1.6.2	27	9	820.18
	Control of design and development changes	7.3.7	P1	4.1.10	37	36	820.30i
	Production and service provision - General requirements	7.5.1.1	A11	5.1	45,46	40	820.70a, g,l,h
	Identification	7.5.3.1	A11	6.4	51	47	820.6
	Traceability	7.5.3.2	A11	6.4	53	48	820.65
	Status identification	7.5.3.3	A11		52	50	820.86
7.5--MEASUREMENT, ANALYSIS AND IMPROVEMENT OF PROCESSES, ACTIVITIES AND PRODUCT	Measurement, analysis, and improvement	8	A11				
	Conformity assurance	8.1	A11	2.2.5.1, 2.2.6	78	54	820.8
	Feedback	8.2.1	A11		66	55	
			A11	7.2	71		820.198
			A11	7.2.1.4, 7.2.1.5	75,76		822
	Internal audits	8.2.2	A11	7.3	77	56	820.22
	Process monitoring	8.2.3	A11	7.3, 2.2.6		57	820.70a
	Product monitoring	8.2.4	A11	7.3, 2.2.6	59,60	58	820.8
	Nonconforming product	8.3	A11	6.5	67-70	60	820.9
	Data analysis	8.4	A11	2.2.6, 9	73	61	820.25
	Improvement	8.5	A11				

N23	TOPIC	ISO 13485:2003	Australia	Brazil RDC 16/2013	China MD GMP ([2014]64)	Japan MHLW QMS Ordinance	US 21 CFR
7.5--MEASUREMENT, ANALYSIS AND IMPROVEMENT OF PROCESSES, ACTIVITIES AND PRODUCT (cont'd)	Improvement - General	8.5.1	A11	2.2.1	71,76	62	
	Improvement - General	8.5.1	A11	7.2	72,75	62	803
	Corrective action	8.5.2	A11	7.1	74	63	820.1
	Preventive action	8.5.3	A11	7.1	74	64	820.1
	Customer communication	7.2.3		7.2	66,71	29	
	Control of design and development changes	7.3.7	P1	4.1.10			820.70b
	Production and service provision - General requirements	7.5.1.1	A11	4.1.11	62		820.184
7.6--MANAGING OUTSOURCED PROCESSES, ACTIVITIES AND PRODUCTS	Purchasing process	7.4	A11	2.5	39,40	37	820.5
	Vendor evaluation	7.4.1	A11	2.5.2	41,42	37	820.50a
	Purchasing information	7.4.2	A11	2.5.1	43	38	820.50b
	Verification of purchased product	7.4.3	A11	2.5.4	44		820.8
	Improvement - General	8.5.1	A11	2.2.1	71,76	62	
	Improvement - General	8.5.1	A11	7.2	72 ,75	62	803
8.0--SAMD REALIZATION AND USE PROCESSES							
8.1--REQUIREMENTS MANAGEMENT	Customer requirements capture	7.2.1	A11	A11		27	27
	Contract review	7.2.2	A11	A11		28	
	Customer communication	7.2.3	A11	A11	66,71	29	
	Quality system record		A11	A11	24		820.186
	Documentation requirements - General	4.2.1	A11	A11	24	6	820.20e
	Quality manual	4.2.2	A11	A11	24	7	820.20e
	Document control	4.2.3	A11	A11	25,26	8	820.4
	Control of records	4.2.4	A11	A11	27	9	820.18
	Documentation requirements - General	4.2.1	A11	A11	50	6-2	820.181
	Requirements records	7.1d	A11	A11	24		

CH 11

N23	Topic	ISO 13485:2003	Australia	Brazil RDC 16/2013	China MD GMP ([2014]64)	Japan MHLW QMS Ordinance	US 21 CFR
8.2--DESIGN + 8.3--DEVELOPMENT	Design and development	7.3	P1				
	Design inputs	7.3.2		4.1.3	30	31	820.30c
	Design and development outputs	7.3.3	P1	4.1.5	31	32	820.30d
	Design and development outputs	7.3.3	P1	4.1.11			820.30j
	Design review	7.3.4	P1	4.1.6	33	33	820.30e
	Design transfer	7.3.1b	P1	4.1.7	32	30-3-2	820.30h
	Control of design and development changes	7.3.7	P1		37	36	
8.4--VERIFICATION AND VALIDATION	Design verification	7.3.5	P1	4.1.4	34	34	820.30f
	Design validation	7.3.6	P1	4.1.8	35,36	35	820.30g
	Verification of purchased product	7.4.3	A11	2.5.6	44	39	820.80b
8.5—DEPLOYMENT	Customer communication	7.2.3	A11	7.2	66,71	29	
	Production and service provision		A11				
	Contamination control	7.5.1.2.1	A11	6.2.1	48	41	820.70e
	Installation	7.5.1.2.2	A11	8.1	65	42	820.17
	Distribution	7.5.5	A11	6.3	62		820.16
	Servicing	7.5.1.2.3	A11	8.2	64	43	820.2
8.6--MAINTENANCE	Customer communication	7.2.3	A11	7.2	66,71	29	
	Production and service provision		A11				
	Servicing	7.5.1.2.3	A11	8.2	64	43	820.2
	Customer property (confidential health information)	7.5.4	A11			51	
	Monitoring & measuring devices	7.6	A11	5.4	56-58	53	820.72
	Feedback	8.2.1	A11		66	55	

CH 11

N23	TOPIC	ISO 13485:2003	Australia	Brazil RDC 16/2013	China MD GMP ([2014]64)	Japan MHLW QMS Ordinance	US 21 CFR
8.7-- DECOMMISSIONING	Control of records	4.2.4	A11	3.1.6	24		820.186
	Documentation requirements - General	4.2.1	A11		24	6	820.20e
	Quality manual	4.2.2	A11	2.2.1	24	7	820.20e
	Document control	4.2.3	A11	3.1	25,26	8	820.4
	Control of records	4.2.4	A11	3.1.6.2	27	9	820.18
	Production and service provision -General requirements	7.5.1.1	A11	4.2	50	6-2	820.181
	Product realization	7	A11				

The following clauses are not specifically addressed in this document:

N23	TOPIC	ISO 13485:2003	Australia	Brazil RDC 16/2013	China MD GMP ([2014]64)	Japan MHLW QMS Ordinance	US 21 CFR
These clauses are not specifically addressed by N23	Control of production and service provisions	7.5.1.2	A11		47	41	
	Process validation	7.5.2	P1, P4		49	45	820.75
	Traceability documentation	7.5.3.2.1	A11			48	
	Requirements for active implantable	7.5.3.2.2				49	
	Status identification	7.5.3.3	A11			50	
	Device packaging	7.5.5	A11		55	52	820.13
	Handling	7.5.5	A11		55	52	820.14
	Storage	7.5.5	A11		55	52	820.15
	Monitoring and measurement	8.2.4.1	A11			58	
	Monitoring and measurement of active implantable	8.2.4.2				59	
	Sterilization records	7.5.1.3				44	820.184
	Production personnel						820.70d
	Production and service provision - General requirements	7.5.1.1	P1, P4				820.12
	Issue and implementation of advisory notices		A11				806
	Medical device tracking						821
	Device classification						860
	Label design						801

CH 11

CSV

Chapter 12
IMDFR
Software as a Medical Device (SaMD): Clinical Evaluation

Issued by IMDRF: June 22, 2017
Issued by FDA: December 8, 2017
IMDRF/SaMD WG/N41FINAL:2017
Authorizing Group: Software as a Medical Device Working Group
USDHHS/FDA/CDRH
Final Document

FDA Preface

IMDRF is a voluntary group of medical device regulators from around the world who have come together to accelerate international medical device regulatory harmonization and convergence. The IMDRF Management Committee (IMDRF MC) chartered the SaMD Working Group (WG) to develop a regulatory framework for SaMD and to develop converged principles for global regulators to adopt in their respective jurisdictions. This IMDRF document has been unanimously approved by the IMDRF MC. For more information on IMDRF activities, please see http://www.imdrf.org/index.asp.

This guidance adopts the internationally converged principles agreed upon by the IMDRF. FDA adoption of these principles provides FDA with an initial framework when further developing FDA's specific regulatory approaches and expectations for regulatory oversight. This guidance does not provide recommendations for FDA Staff and Industry to apply to specific regulatory situations, nor does it modify current regulatory expectations, including those for regulatory submissions, at this time. The words require or requirements used in this document do not reflect FDA regulatory requirements and are intended only to be considerations for Industry and FDA staff. FDA intends to consider the principles of this guidance in the development of regulatory approaches for SaMD and digital health technologies. In developing regulatory approaches based on the principles of this guidance, the agency intends to follow a public process, including providing opportunities for public input. For more information on FDA adoption of IMDRF documents as an FDA guidance document, please see https://www.fda.gov/MedicalDevices/InternationalPrograms/IMDRF/default.htm.

IMDRF Preface

The document herein was produced by the International Medical Device Regulators Forum (IMDRF), a voluntary group of medical device regulators from around the world. The document has been subject to consultation throughout its development.

1.0 Executive Summary

This document is the fourth issued by the International Medical Device Regulatory Forum (IMDRF) that provides a path for global regulators to converge on terminology, a risk-based framework, an understanding of quality management system principles, and in this document, an approach to making Software as a Medical Device (SaMD) clinically meaningful to users.[1] This document focuses on the activities needed to clinically evaluate SaMD — and relies on the reader to gain knowledge from the previous documents as a pre-requisite to this document.

This document, and previous documents, provides harmonized principles for individual jurisdictions to adopt based on their own regulatory framework. They are not regulations.

This document describes a converged approach for planning the process for clinical evaluation of a SaMD (software with a medical purpose as defined in ***SaMD N10***[[1]2]), as illustrated in Figure 1, to establish that:

- There is a valid clinical association between the output of a SaMD and the targeted clinical condition (to include pathological process or state); and
- That the SaMD provides the expected technical and clinical data.

Clinical Evaluation		
Valid Clinical Association	Analytical Validation	Clinical Validation
Is there a valid clinical association between your SaMD output and your SaMD's targeted clinical condition?	Does your SaMD correctly process input data to generate accurate, reliable, and precise output data?	Does use of your SaMD's accurate, reliable, and precise output data achieve your intended purpose in your target population in the context of clinical care?

Figure 1 - Clinical Evaluation Process

The knowledge gained from previous documents is critical to the understanding of information in this document. This document builds on previously introduced vocabulary, risk-based considerations, and SaMD lifecycle processes and activities to help emphasize the clinical considerations essential to the success and adoption of SaMD as illustrated in Figure 2.

1 Users include patients, healthcare providers, specialized professionals, lay users, consumers.
2 Internet addresses (URLs) can be found in the References section.

CH 12

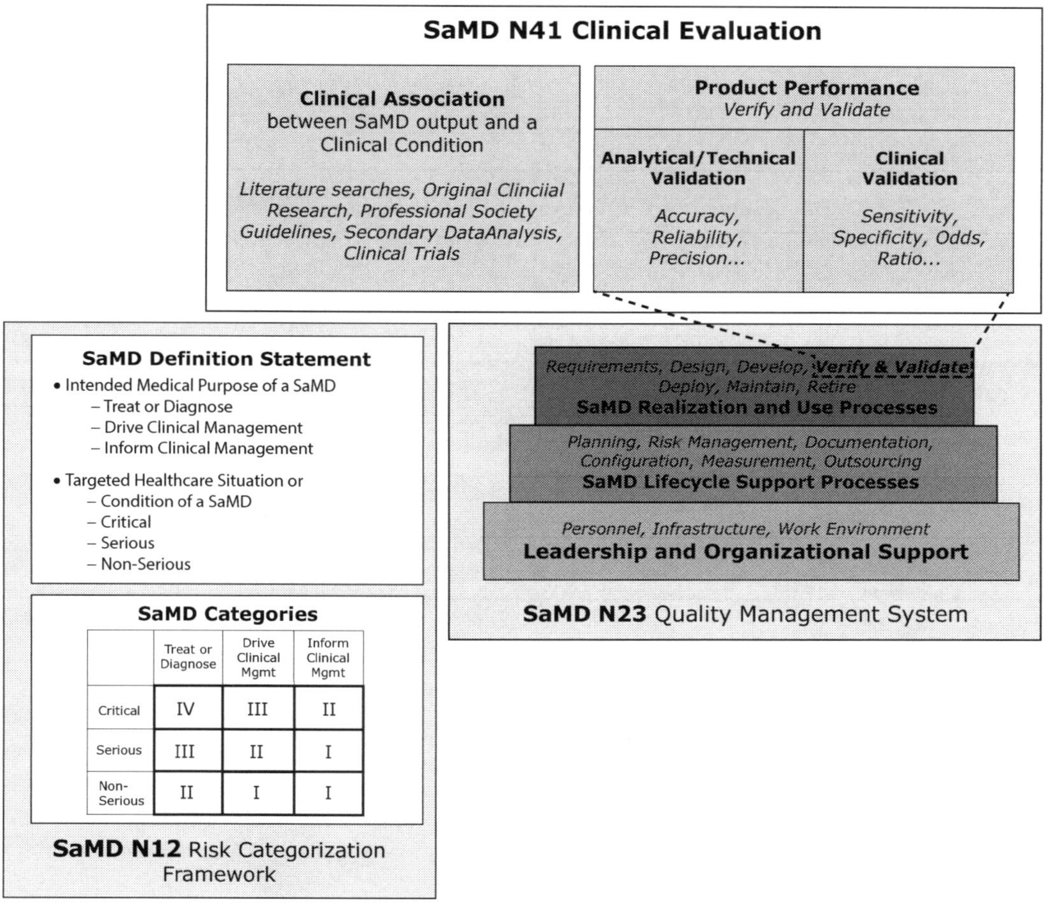

Figure 2- SaMD Landscape

2.0 Background

The IMDRF has acknowledged that software is an increasingly critical area of healthcare product development and has developed a series of documents concerning the definition, the categorization, and the application of quality systems principles of SaMD.

In 2013, IMDRF's SaMD Working Group released SaMD N10[1] *Software as a Medical Device (SaMD): Key Definitions to create a standard terminology for SaMD.* The following year, IMDRF adopted SaMD N12[2] *Software as a Medical Device: Possible Framework for Risk Categorization and Corresponding Considerations* which proposes a method for categorizing SaMD based on the seriousness of the condition the SaMD is intended to address. In 2015, the SaMD Working Group published SaMD N23[3] *Software as a Medical Device (SaMD): Application of Quality Management System*, outlining how manufacturers should follow Quality Management System (QMS) Principles for medical devices as well as good software engineering practices.

Knowledge of the previous three IMDRF SaMD documents is a prerequisite for readers of this document.

This document, and previous documents, provides harmonized principles for individual jurisdictions to adopt based on their own regulatory framework. They are not regulations.

The goal, strategy, principles and concepts, and implementation pathway for a harmonized SaMD framework are illustrated below in Figure 3.

CH 12

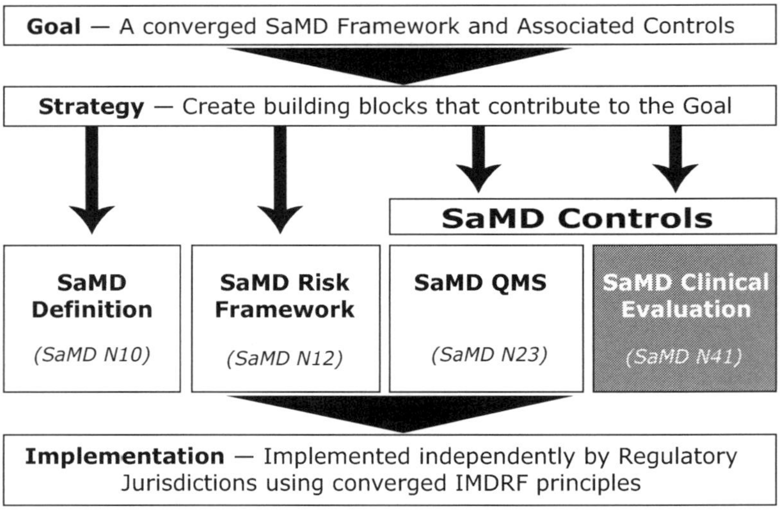

Figure 3 — SaMD Regulatory Pathway

3.0 INTRODUCTION

The International Medical Device Regulators Forum (IMDRF) seeks to establish a common and converged understanding of clinical evaluation and principles for demonstrating the safety, effectiveness and performance of SaMD.

As illustrated in Figure 4, this document represents a global harmonization effort to articulate this process.

Clinical Evaluation		
Valid Clinical Association	Analytical Validation	Clinical Validation
Is there a valid clinical association between your SaMD output and your SaMD's targeted clinical condition?	Does your SaMD correctly process input data to generate accurate, reliable, and precise output data?	Does use of your SaMD's accurate, reliable, and precise output data achieve your intended purpose in your target population in the context of clinical care?

Figure 4 - Clinical Evaluation Process

The document further explains that:

- Clinical evaluation should be an iterative and continuous process as part of the quality management system for medical devices (*See SaMD N23*[3] *for more information*);
- Certain SaMD may require independent review of the results of the clinical evaluation, akin to peer review or design review, to ensure that the SaMD is clinically meaningful to users. The level of evaluation and independent review should be commensurate with the risk posed by the specific SaMD (*See SaMD N12*[2] *for more information*); and
- Software is unique in its level of connectivity, which may allow the continuous monitoring of the safety, effectiveness, and performance of SaMD. This document encourages manufacturers to use this feature to understand and modify software based on real-world performance. (*See 9.0 Pathway for Continuous Learning Leveraging Real World Performance Data for more information*).

Healthcare decisions increasingly rely on information provided by the output of SaMD where these decisions can impact clinical outcomes and patient care. As such, global regulators expect that performance metrics for a SaMD have a scientific level of rigor that is commensurate with the risk and impact of the SaMD to demonstrate assurance of safety, effectiveness, and performance.

4.0 SCOPE

This document focuses on the activities needed to clinically evaluate SaMD — and relies on the reader to gain knowledge from the previous documents as a pre-requisite to this document. Specifically, this document:

- Expects readers to have knowledge of the vocabulary, approach, and common thinking of previous IMDRF SaMD documents;
- Expects readers to understand that the concepts are limited to SaMD, as defined in *SaMD N10*[1], which focuses on software with a medical purpose; and
- Refers to – and paraphrases as needed — previous Global Harmonization Task Force (GHTF[3]) and IMDRF documents that provide a common understanding and application of terminology, concepts and principles for a clinical evaluation that demonstrates the performance metrics of a SaMD.

This document does NOT exhaustively address all regulatory requirements relevant to SaMD, which may vary by jurisdiction (e.g., informed consent, pre-market regulatory review). In addition, this document does not repeat the following concepts from previous SaMD documents:

- The definition of a SaMD (*SaMD N10*[1]);
- Examples of SaMD (*SaMD N12*[2]);
- Where a SaMD fits in the risk categorization and the descriptions of the risk categories (*SaMD N12*[2]); and
- Which Quality Management principles are appropriate for SaMD (*SaMD N23*[3]).

5.0 Definitions

5.1 Clinical Evaluation of a SaMD

Clinical Evaluation
The assessment and analysis of clinical data pertaining to a medical device to verify the clinical safety, performance and effectiveness of the device when used as intended by the manufacturer.

Figure 5—Clinical Evaluation

For purposes of this document "Clinical evaluation of a SaMD" is defined as a set of ongoing activities conducted in the assessment and analysis of a SaMD's clinical safety, effectiveness and performance as intended by the manufacturer in the SaMD's definition statement.

This definition is consistent with prior SaMD documents and is adapted from *GHTF SG5 N2R8:2007*[8].

Clinical Evaluation see *GHTF SG5 N2R8:2007*[8]

5.2 Valid Clinical Association of a SaMD

Valid Clinical Association
Is there a valid clinical association between your SaMD output and your SaMD's targeted clinical condition?

Figure 6—Valid Clinical Association

For purposes of this document, valid clinical association, also known as scientific validity, is used to refer to the extent to which the SaMD's output (concept, conclusion, measurements) is clinically accepted or well-founded (based on an established scientific framework or body of

3 GHTF was a voluntary group of representatives from national medical device regulatory authorities and industry representatives. GHTF was disbanded in 2012 and its mission has been taken over by the IMDRF.

evidence[4]), and corresponds accurately in the real world to the healthcare situation and condition identified in the SaMD definition statement.

A valid clinical association is an indicator of the level of clinical acceptance and how much meaning and confidence can be assigned to the clinical significance of the SaMD's output in the intended healthcare situation and the clinical condition/physiological state.[5]

SaMD Definition Statement see Section 6.0 in *SaMD N12*[2]
SaMD Clinical Considerations see Section 9.1 in *SaMD N12*[2

5.3 Analytical/Technical Validation of a SaMD

Analytical Validation
Does your SaMD correctly process input data to generate accurate, reliable, and precise output data?

Figure 7—Analytical Validation

Analytical validation measures the ability of a SaMD to accurately, reliably and precisely generate the intended technical output from the input data. Said differently, analytical validation:

- Confirms and provides objective evidence that the software was correctly constructed – namely, correctly and reliably processes input data and generates output data with the appropriate level of accuracy, and repeatability and reproducibility (i.e., precision); and
- Demonstrates that (a) the software meets its specifications and (b) the software specifications conform to user needs and intended uses.

The analytical validation is generally evaluated and determined by the manufacturer during the verification and validation phase of the software development lifecycle using a QMS.

Analytical validation is necessary for any SaMD.

SaMD Verification and Validation see Section 8.4 in *SaMD N23*[3]

CH 12

5.4 Clinical Validation of a SaMD

Clinical Validation
Does use of your SaMD's accurate, reliable, and precise output data achieve your intended purpose in your target population in the context of clinical care?

Figure 8-Clinical Validation

Clinical validation measures the ability of a SaMD to yield a clinically meaningful output associated to the target use of SaMD output in the target health care situation or condition identified in the SaMD definition statement. Clinically meaningful means the positive impact of a SaMD on the health of an individual or population, to be specified as meaningful, measurable, patient-relevant clinical outcome(s), including outcome(s) related to the function of the SaMD (e.g., diagnosis, treatment, prediction of risk, prediction of treatment response), or a positive impact on individual or public health.

4 https://www.ncbi.nlm.nih.gov/pmc/articles/PMC3261486/
5 https://www.ncbi.nlm.nih.gov/pmc/articles/PMC2993536/

Clinical validity is evaluated and determined by the manufacturer during the development of a SaMD before it is distributed for use (pre-market) and after distribution while the SaMD is in use (post-market).

Clinical validation of a SaMD can also be viewed as the relationship between the verification and validation results of the SaMD algorithm and the clinical conditions of interest. Clinical validation is a necessary component of clinical evaluation for all SaMD and can be demonstrated by either:

- Referencing existing data from studies conducted for the same intended use;
- Referencing existing data from studies conducted for a different intended use, where extrapolation of such data can be justified; or
- Generating new clinical data for a specific intended use.

Clinical validation is necessary for any SaMD.

SaMD Verification and Validation see Section 8.4 in *SaMD N23*[3]

6.0 General Principles and Context of SaMD Clinical Evaluation Process

A SaMD can best be described as software that utilizes an algorithm (logic, set of rules, or model) that operates on data input (digitized content) to produce an output that is intended for medical purposes as defined by the SaMD manufacturer (Figure 9). The risks and benefits posed by SaMD outputs are largely related to the risk of inaccurate or incorrect output of the SaMD, which may impact the clinical management of a patient.

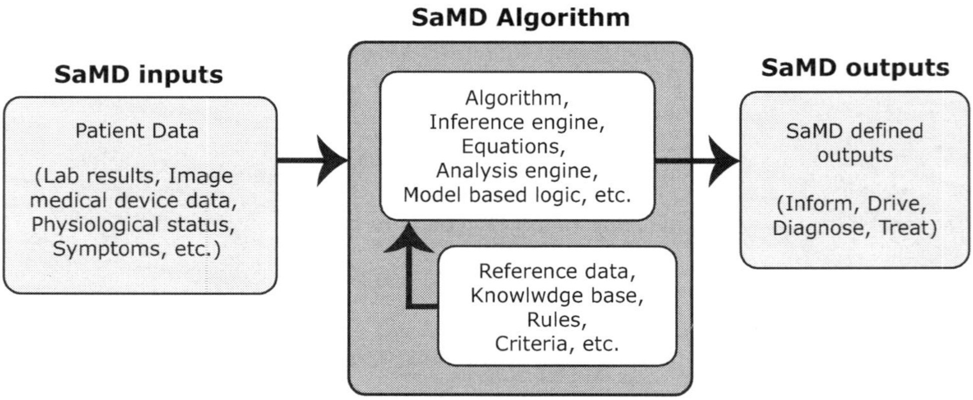

Figure 9—SaMD Basic Programming Model

6.1 SaMD Definition Statement and SaMD Category

The SaMD definition statement, as defined in *SaMD N12*[2], is used by the SaMD manufacturer to identify the intended medical purpose of the SaMD (treat, diagnose, drive clinical management, inform clinical management), to state the healthcare situation or condition that the SaMD is intended for (critical, serious, non-serious), and to describe the core functionality of the SaMD.

The SaMD manufacturer will use the factors identified in the SaMD definition statement to determine the category of a SaMD in the SaMD categorization framework as illustrated in Figure 10.

ⓘ SaMD Definition Statement see Section 6.0 in *SaMD N12*[2]
ⓘ SaMD Categorization Framework see Section 7.0 in *SaMD N12*[2]

State of Healthcare Situation or Condition	Significance of information provided by SaMD to the healthcare decision		
	Treat or Diagnose	Drive Clinical Management	Inform Clinical Management
Critical	IV	III	II
Serious	III	II	I
Non-Serious	II	I	I

Figure 10—SaMD N12*[2] *Framework

6.2 Clinical Evaluation Processes

A SaMD manufacturer is expected to implement on-going lifecycle processes to thoroughly evaluate the product's performance in its intended market. As part of normal new product introduction processes, prior to product launch (pre-market) the manufacturer generates evidence of the product's accuracy, specificity, sensitivity, reliability, limitations, and scope of use in the intended use environment with the intended user, and generates a SaMD definition statement. Once the product is on the market (post-market), as part of normal lifecycle management processes, the manufacturer continues to collect real world performance data (e.g., complaints, safety data), to further understand the customer's needs to ensure the product is meeting those needs, and to monitor the product's continued safety, effectiveness and performance in real-world use. This real world performance data allows the manufacturer to identify and correct any problems, support future expansions in functionality, meet anticipated user demands, or improve the effectiveness of the device.

Product lifecycle activities, which include clinical evaluation activities as illustrated in Figure 11, should follow appropriate planning processes as part of an organization's lifecycle activities and processes, as described in *SaMD N23*[3].

Risk assessment done as part of the SaMD's lifecycle activities and processes should also be considered when conducting clinical evaluation.

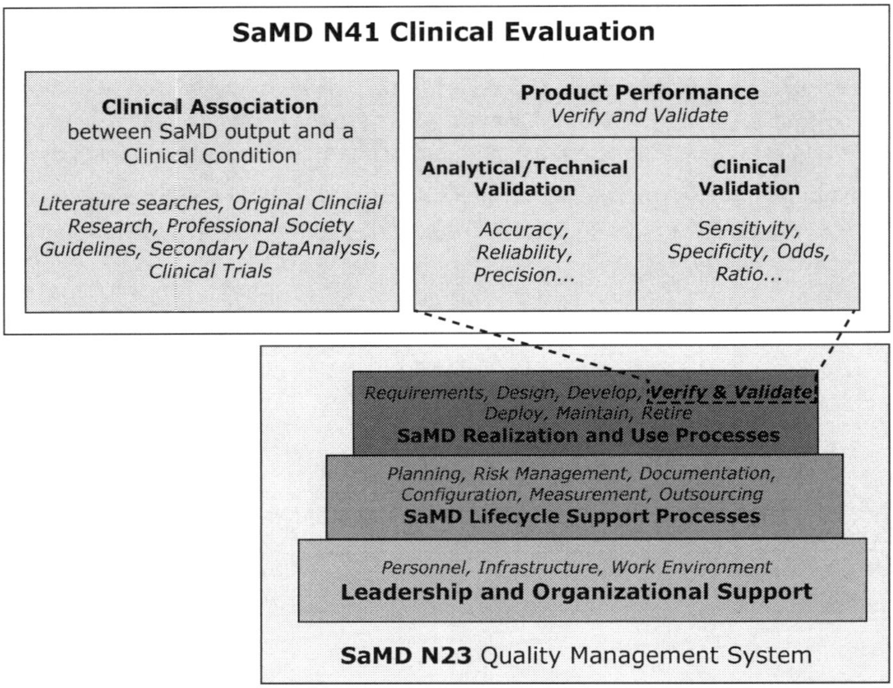

Figure 11 - SaMD Clinical Evaluation Landscape

ⓘ Pre-market see *GHTF Study Group 1 documents*[4]

ⓘ Post-market see *GHTF Study Group 2 documents*[5]

ⓘ SaMD Considerations for Risk Management see Section 7.2 in *SaMD N23*[3]

ⓘ SaMD User Needs Intended Use see Section 8.3 of *SaMD N23*[3]

ⓘ SaMD Clinical Evidence see Section 8.4 in *SaMD N23*[3]

7.0 SaMD Clinical Evaluation Process Flow Chart

Clinical evaluation is a systematic and planned process to continuously generate, collect, analyze, and assess the clinical data[6] pertaining to a SaMD in order to generate clinical evidence verifying the clinical association and the performance metrics of a SaMD when used as intended by the manufacturer. The quality and breadth of the clinical evaluation is determined by the role of the SaMD for the target clinical condition, and assures that the output of the SaMD is clinically valid and can be used reliably and predictably.

This section uses simple steps to help SaMD manufacturers through the approach to generating evidence for the clinical evaluation of a SaMD and provides links to techniques, definitions and sources that are available to help a SaMD manufacturer generate appropriate evidence.

Note: The examples used are not intended to be comprehensive. All data sources and statistical methods should be tailored to the specific SaMD and its intended use.

Clinical Evaluation		
① Valid Clinical Association	② Analytical Validation	③ Clinical Validation
Is there a valid clinical association between your SaMD output and your SaMD's targeted clinical condition?	Does your SaMD correctly process input data to generate accurate, reliable, and precise output data?	Does use of your SaMD's accurate, reliable, and precise output data achieve your intended purpose in your target population in the context of clinical care?

Figure 12 - Clinical Evaluation

① Valid Clinical Association:

Is there a valid clinical association between your SaMD output, based on the inputs and algorithms selected, and your SaMD's targeted clinical condition?

Step 1: Verify that the association between the SaMD output and the targeted clinical condition is supported by evidence.

Note: All SaMD should demonstrate a valid clinical association.

Question: How do I "generate evidence"?

You can verify by using existing evidence or you can verify by generating new evidence.

Examples of existing evidence

- ❑ Literature searches
- ❑ Original clinical research
- ❑ Professional society guidelines

6 Clinical data is defined as safety and/or performance information that are generated from the clinical use of a medical device. Source: GHTF SG5 N1R8:2007[7]

Examples of generating new evidence

- ❑ Secondary data analysis
- ❑ Perform clinical trials

② Analytical Validation:

Does your SaMD meet technical requirements?

Step 1: Generate evidence that shows that the output of your SaMD is technically what you expected.

Note: All SaMD should demonstrate analytical validation.

Question: How do I "generate evidence"?

You can generate evidence during verification and validation activities as part of your quality management system or as part of your good software engineering practices, or by generating new evidence through use of curated databases or use of previously collected patient data.

Verification: confirmation through provision of objective evidence that specified requirements have been fulfilled. Source: *GHTF SG3 N18:2010*[6] Section 2.7

Validation: confirmation through provision of objective evidence that the requirements for a specific intended use or application have been fulfilled. Source: *GHTF SG3 N18:2010*[6] Section 2.8

③ Clinical Validation:

Does your SaMD generate clinically relevant outputs?

Step 1: Generate evidence that shows your:

- SaMD has been tested in your target population and for your intended use; and that
- Users can achieve clinically meaningful outcomes through predictable and reliable use.

Note: All SaMD should demonstrate clinical validation.

Question: How do I "generate evidence"?

You can generate evidence to validate clinical significance during verification and validation activities as part of your quality management system or as part of your good software engineering practices, referencing existing data sources from studies conducted for the same intended use. Where available data references studies conducted for a different intended use, extrapolation or generation of new clinical data may be required.

Examples of measures of clinical validation

- ❑ Sensitivity
- ❑ Specificity
- ❑ Positive predictive value (PPV)
- ❑ Negative predictive value (NPV)
- ❑ Number needed to treat (NNT)
- ❑ Number needed to harm (NNH)
- ❑ Likelihood ratio negative (LR-)
- ❑ Likelihood ratio positive (LR+)
- ❑ Odds ratio (OR)
- ❑ Clinical usability / User Interface
- ❑ Confidence interval

7.1 Considerations for Generating and Assessing Evidence

Being able to generate evidence to demonstrate the valid clinical association, analytical validation and clinical validation of a SaMD is essential to establishing the SaMD's value for users. The degree of evidence generation needed for a given SaMD will depend on parameters including but not necessarily limited to the:

- Maturity of evidence underlying the clinical association; and
- Confidence in the evidence, as applied to a specific SaMD.

The purpose of the assessment of the evidence is to select information based on its merits and limitations to demonstrate that the clinical evaluation evidence is high-quality, relevant, and supportive of the SaMD intended use.

For example, an assessment of clinical association would classify a SaMD as having either a:

a) Well-established clinical association: These SaMD have outputs with well-documented association as identified in sources such as clinical guidelines, clinical studies in peer reviewed journals, consensus for the use of the SaMD, international reference materials or other similar well-established comparators in terms of previously marketed devices / SaMD; or a

b) Novel clinical association: These SaMD may involve new inputs, algorithms or outputs, new intended target population, or new intended use. An example may include the combination of non-standard inputs such as mood or pollen count, with standard inputs such as gait, blood pressure or other physiological and environmental signals using novel algorithms to detect early onset of a deterioration of health or diagnosis of a disease.

What if I can't generate evidence to demonstrate ①, ②, or ③?

- Perform ongoing data analysis
- Modify your intended use to one that can be supported by available evidence
- Modify the target clinical association
- Make changes to the software

8.0 Importance of Independent Review of a SaMD's Clinical Evaluation

SaMD categories are based on the levels of impact on the patient or public health where accurate information provided by the SaMD is important to treat or diagnose, drive clinical management or inform clinical management. For additional information on SaMD categorization, please see Section 7.0 in *SaMD N12*[2]. As part of the risk-based approach, and subject to individual jurisdiction's laws, independent review of clinical evidence of certain low-risk SaMD may be less important and the manufacturer may 'self-declare' the appropriateness of the evidence. Again, subject to individual jurisdiction's laws, independent review of clinical evidence of more high-risk SaMD is more important in providing users the confidence in the SaMD's performance metrics, including but not limited to, identification of design errors or limitation, broadening technical competence, testing the appropriateness of assumptions, and management of bias.

The recommendation for independent review highlights where the evidence generated from the clinical evaluation of the SaMD should be reviewed by someone who has not been significantly involved in the development of the SaMD, and who does not have anything to gain from the SaMD, and who can objectively assess the SaMD's intended purpose and the conformity with the overall clinical evaluation evidence. The level of clinical evaluation and importance of independent review should be commensurate with the risk posed by the SaMD. This document recommends where independent review is more or less important.

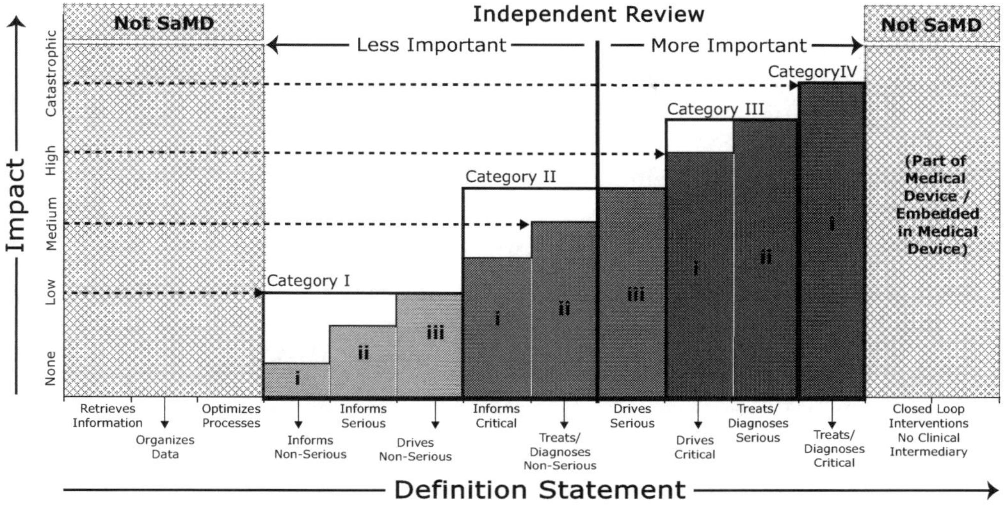

Figure 13 - Risk Based Approach to Importance of Independent Review

Figure 13 illustrates where independent review is more or less important. In the figure, the red, vertical dividing line differentiates where independent review is less important and where independent review is more important for different SaMD categories. Independent review is more important for SaMD that 'Treats/Diagnoses Serious and Critical' health care situations and conditions and SaMD that 'Drives Critical' health care situations and conditions. Independent review in this document does not necessarily imply regulatory review but instead demonstrates the concept where independence in review of the results is important.

For purposes of this document 'less important' independent review is analogous to the concept of design review performed in the QMS system. Less important independent reviews can be conducted by individuals within the company or by utilizing outside experts.

For purposes of this document 'more important' independent review may be conducted by outside experts such as formal consultation with regulators, third parties on behalf of regulators, or the editorial board of a peer-reviewed journal, but may also be conducted by "non-conflicted" internal expert reviewers without significant involvement in the development of the SaMD.

9.0 Pathway for Continuous Learning Leveraging Real World Performance Data

SaMD may leverage connectivity between devices, and people to continuously monitor the safety, effectiveness and performance of the SaMD.

A SaMD manufacturer may have a hypothesis about future functionality and intended use of a SaMD that may be informed by continuously collecting and analyzing data on use of the SaMD in a post-market setting. Monitoring real world performance data can help the SaMD functionality and intended use evolve after initial introduction into the market. Such data may include post-market information such as safety data, results from performance studies, on-going clinical evidence generation for medical devices, new research publications / results that support or strengthen the clinical association of the SaMD output to a clinical condition, or direct end-user feedback, that can help the SaMD manufacturer understand the real world performance of the SaMD. This may lead to a change to the SaMD definition statement if supported by the clinical evidence generated through clinical evaluation leveraging real world performance data from the continuous monitoring as illustrated in Figure 14.

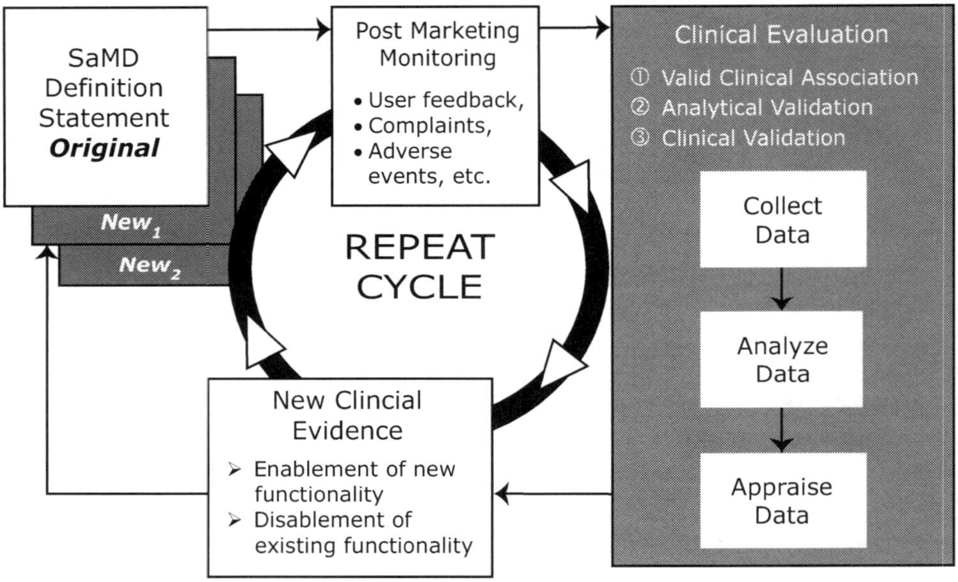

Figure 14 - Pathway for Continuous Learning - Use of Real World SaMD Performance Data in Ongoing SaMD Clinical Evaluation

Learning may impact the original category of a SaMD in the following ways:

- Real world performance data may provide evidence that the analytical or clinical validity of a SaMD is superior to the performance measures initially evaluated by the SaMD manufacturer, or
- Real world performance data may provide evidence that analytical or clinical validity of a SaMD is inferior to the performance measures initially evaluated by the SaMD manufacturer.

CH
12

As additional clinical evidence is gathered to confirm the hypothesis and create and support new intended use, the SaMD manufacturer will update the clinical evaluation and generate a new definition statement. Then the cycle repeats.

This document encourages SaMD manufacturers to leverage SaMD's capability to capture real-world performance data to understand user interactions with the SaMD, and conduct ongoing monitoring of analytical and technical performance to support future intended uses.

9.1 Considerations for Continuous Learning Leveraging Real World Performance Data

- SaMD should facilitate post-market information gathering to allow for disablement of existing or enablement of new functionality within the SaMD.
- It is not necessary for the collection of real world performance data by the SaMD manufacturer to rely on the active involvement of the end user. The SaMD manufacturer should aim to impose the least burdensome approach possible in its data collection and leverage the capability of SaMD to collect clinical evidence.
- With ongoing clinical evaluation the risk categorisation may potentially change, necessitating a change in the SaMD definition statement.
- Real world performance data including post-market information may not be sufficient to generate complete clinical evidence necessary for a change to the SaMD definition statement; as such the SaMD manufacturer should appropriately take into account other clinical evaluation steps required to support the change in SaMD definition statement.
- During the continuous learning across the life cycle, SaMD manufacturers should consider the recommendations in the previous section on independent review when new information changes the category of the SaMD as illustrated in Figure 15.
- The "continuous learning" referred to here is not "machine learning software" (i.e., where software device keeps learning automatically after it has been released into the market); rather it refers to collecting post-market information.
- Manufacturers should appropriately review the post-market information collected to determine if there are any changes to the safety, effectiveness or performance, or possible impact on benefits and risks of the SaMD that would indicate a need for a design change or a labeling change regarding contraindications, warnings, precautions or instructions for use. The labeling should identify limitations of the SaMD relevant to its clinical performance and interpretation of its output in a way that is understood by end users. The assessment of post-market information may also lead to a change of intended use (e.g., expansion, modification, or restriction).

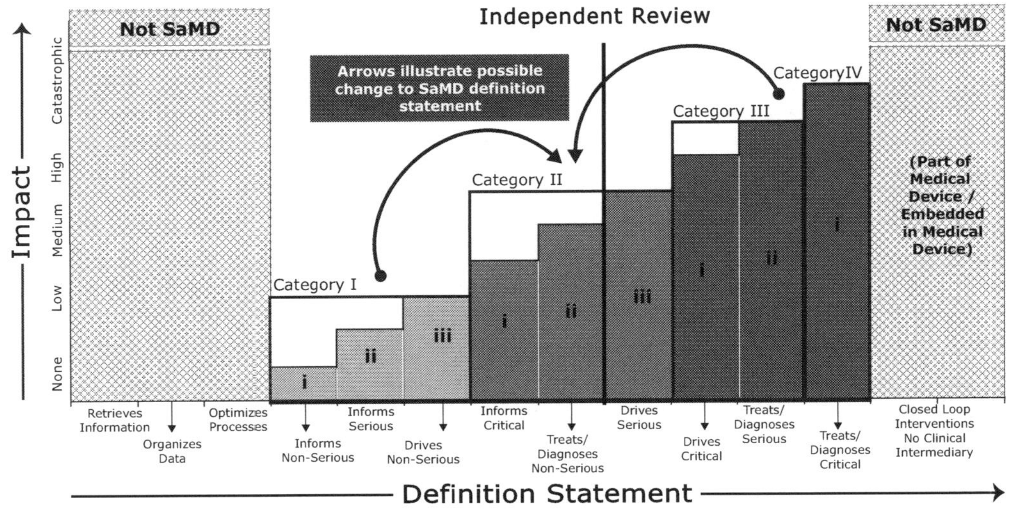

Figure 15 — Change to SaMD category from continuous learning

NOTE: A change to the SaMD definition statement may be subject to regulatory requirements in the individual jurisdiction and a SaMD manufacturer should consult with the regulatory authorities in their jurisdiction.

ⓘ SaMD Software Changes see *Section 7.5 in SaMD N23*[3]

ⓘ SaMD Continuous Improvement see *Section 7.5 in SaMD N23*[3]

ⓘ Medical Devices Post Market see *GHTF SG3 N79R11:2009*[15]

ⓘ Medical Devices Observation Studies see *Section 6.1 in GHTF SG5 N8:2012*[16]

APPENDIX – COMPARISON OF SAMD CLINICAL EVALUATION PROCESS TO PROCESS FOR *GENERATING CLINICAL EVIDENCE FOR IVD MEDICAL DEVICES IN GHTF/SG5/N7:2012*[13]

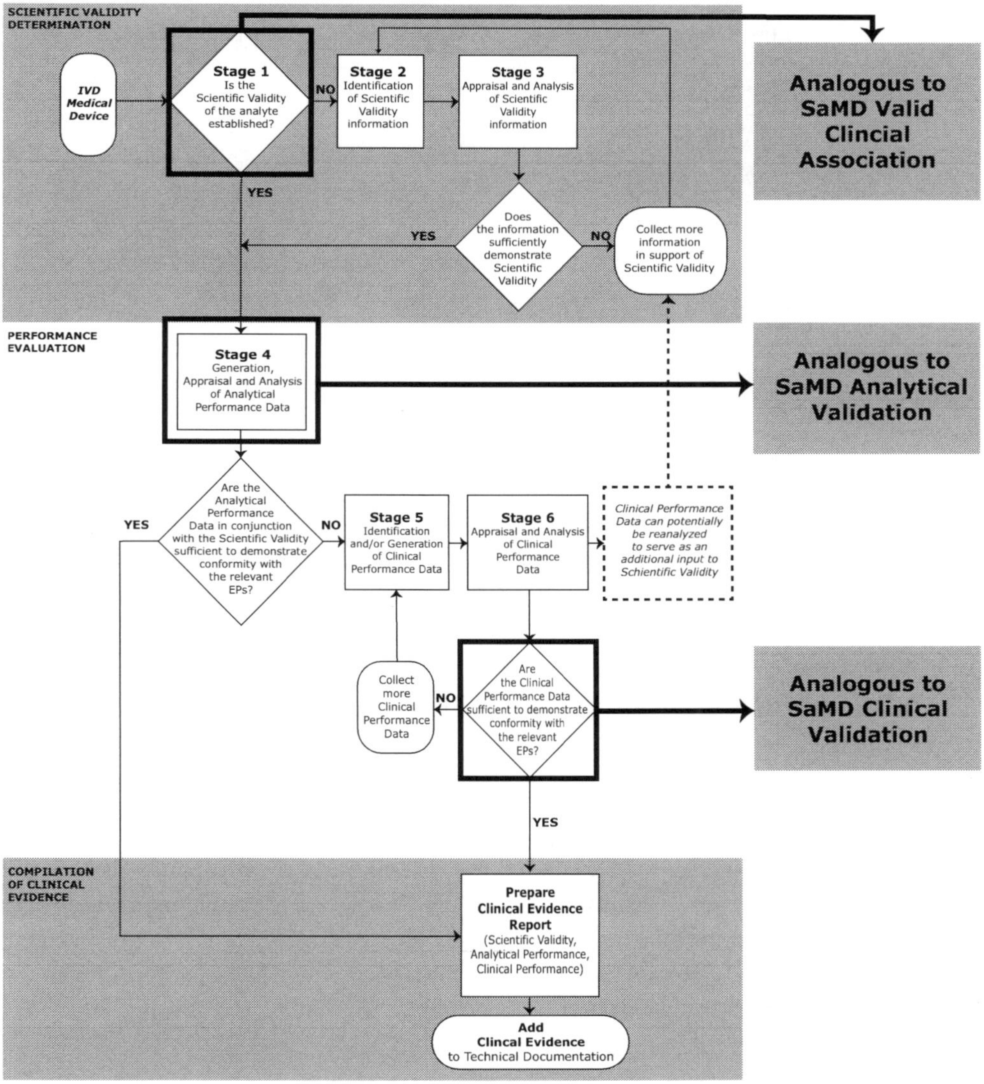

CH 12

References

IMDRF Documents:

1. SaMD N10: Software as a Medical Device (SaMD): Key Definitions — http://www.imdrf.org/docs/imdrf/final/technical/imdrf-tech-131209-samd-key-definitions-140901.pdf
2. SaMD N12: Software as a Medical Device (SaMD): Possible Framework for Risk Categorization and Corresponding Considerations — http://www.imdrf.org/docs/imdrf/final/technical/imdrf-tech-140918-samd-framework-risk-categorization-141013.pdf
3. SaMD N23: Software as a Medical Device (SaMD): Application of Quality Management System — http://www.imdrf.org/docs/imdrf/final/technical/imdrf-tech-151002-samd-qms.pdf

GHTF Documents:

4. GHTF Pre-market: GHTF Study Group 1 documents — http://www.imdrf.org/documents/doc-ghtf-sg1.asp
5. GHTF Post-market: GHTF Study Group 2 documents—http://www.imdrf.org/documents/doc-ghtf-sg2.asp
6. GHTF SG3 N18:2010: Quality management system –Medical Devices – Guidance on corrective action and preventive action and related QMS processes — http://www.imdrf.org/docs/ghtf/final/sg3/technical-docs/ghtf-sg3-n18-2010-qms-guidance-on-corrective-preventative-action-101104.pdf
7. GHTF SG5 N1R8:2007: Clinical Evidence – Key Definitions and Concepts— http://www.imdrf.org/docs/ghtf/final/sg5/technical-docs/ghtf-sg5-n1r8-clinical-evaluation-key-definitions-070501.pdf
8. GHTF SG5 N2R8:2007: Clinical Evaluation — http://www.imdrf.org/docs/ghtf/final/sg5/technical-docs/ghtf-sg5-n2r8-2007-clinical-evaluation-070501.pdf
9. GHTF SG5 N3:2010: Clinical Investigations — http://www.imdrf.org/docs/ghtf/final/sg5/technical-docs/ghtf-sg5-n3-clinical-investigations-100212.pdf
10. GHTF SG5 N4: Post-Market Clinical Follow-up Studies — http://www.imdrf.org/docs/ghtf/final/sg5/technical-docs/ghtf-sg5-n4-post-market-clinical-studies-100218.pdf
11. GHTF SG5 N6:2012: Clinical Evidence for IVD medical devices – Key Definitions and Concepts — http://www.imdrf.org/docs/ghtf/final/sg5/technical-docs/ghtf-sg5-n6-2012-clinical-evidence-ivd-medical-devices-121102.pdf
12. GHTF SG1 N68:2012: Essential Principles of Safety and Performance of Medical Devices — http://www.imdrf.org/docs/ghtf/final/sg1/technical-docs/ghtf-sg1-n68-2012-safety-performance-medical-devices-121102.pdf
13. GHTF SG5 N7:2012: Clinical Evidence for IVD medical devices - Scientific Validity Determination and Performance Evaluation— http://www.imdrf.org/docs/ghtf/final/sg5/technical-docs/ghtf-sg5-n7-2012-scientific-validity-determination-evaluation-121102.pdf

14. GHTF SG1 N70:2011: Label and Instructions for Use for Medical Devices— http://www.imdrf.org/docs/ghtf/final/sg1/technical-docs/ghtf-sg1-n70-2011-label-instruction-use-medical-devices-110916.pdf

15. GHTF SG2 N79R11:2009: Medical Devices: Post Market Surveillance: National Competent Authority Report Exchange Criteria and Report Form — http://www.imdrf.org/docs/ghtf/final/sg2/technical-docs/ghtf-sg2-n79r11-medical-devices-post-market-surveillance-090217.pdf

16. GHTF SG5 N8:2012: Clinical Evidence for IVD Medical Devices - Clinical Performance Studies for In Vitro Diagnostic Medical Devices — http://www.imdrf.org/docs/ghtf/final/sg5/technical-docs/ghtf-sg5-n8-2012-clinical-performance-studies-ivd-medical-devices-121102.pdf

International Standards:

17. ISO 14155:2011: Clinical investigation of medical devices for human subjects — Good clinical practice — http://www.iso.org/iso/home/store/catalogue_ics/catalogue_detail_ics.htm?csnumber=45557

18. ISO 14971:2007: Application of risk management to medical devices — http://www.iso.org/iso/en/CatalogueDetailPage.CatalogueDetail?CSNUMBER=31550&ICS1=11&ICS2=40&ICS3=1

19. ISO 62304/A1: 2015: Medical device software – Software life-cycle processes — https://www.iso.org/standard/64686.html

20. IEC 62366-1:2015: Medical Devices – Part 1: Application of usability engineering to medical devices — https://www.iso.org/standard/63179.html

21. IEC 80002-1:2009: Medical device software — Part 1: Guidance on the application of ISO 14971 to medical device software — http://www.iso.org/iso/iso_catalogue/catalogue_tc/catalogue_detail.htm?csnumber=54146

22. ISO 82304-1:2016: Health software – Part 1: General requirements for product safety — https://www.iso.org/standard/59543.html

GLOSSARY

Algorithm — a finite set of instructions (or rules) that defines a sequence of operations for solving a particular computational problem for all problem instances for a problem set.

Analytical Validation — measures the ability of a SaMD to accurately and reliably generate the intended technical output, from the input data.

Basic Programming — problem-solving process used to create a computer program.

Claim — the objective intent of the manufacturer regarding the use of a product, process or service as reflected in the specifications, instructions and information provided by the manufacturer. (Also see Intended Use / Purpose) Additional resources: see *Section 4.0 in GHTF SG1 N68:2012[*[12]

Clinical Association — refers to the extent to which the SaMD's output (concept, conclusion, measurements) is clinically accepted or well founded (existence of an established scientific framework or body of evidence) that corresponds accurately in the real world to the healthcare situation and condition identified in the SaMD definition statement. (Also see ***Scientific Validity***)

Clinical Considerations — aspects that can raise or lower the potential to create hazardous situations to patients. Additional resources: see *Sections 4.0 and 9.1 in SaMD N12*[2]

Clinical Data — defined as safety and/or performance information that is generated from the clinical use of a medical device. Additional resources: see *GHTF SG5 N1R8:2007*[7]

Clinical Evaluation — the assessment and analysis of clinical data pertaining to a medical device to verify the clinical safety, performance and effectiveness of the device when used as intended by the manufacturer. Additional resources: see *GHTF N2R8:2007*[8]

CH 12

Clinical Evidence — an important component of the technical documentation of a medical device, which along with other design verification and validation documentation, device description, labelling, risk analysis and manufacturing information, is needed to allow a manufacturer to demonstrate conformity with the Essential Principles. Additional resources: see *Section 7.5 in SaMD N23*[3] , and *GHTF SG5 N8:2012*[16], *GHTF SG5 N6:2012*[11], *GHTF SG5 N1R8:2007*[7]

Clinical Performance — the ability of a device to yield results that are correlated with a particular clinical condition/physiological state in accordance with target population and intended user. (Also see ***Clinical Validation***) Additional resources: see *Section 4.0 in GHTF SG1 N68:2012*[12]

Clinical Research — use of clinical data generated through clinical use. Additional resources: see *Section 6.2 in GHTF G5 N2R8:2007*[8]

Clinical Trials — A properly conducted clinical investigation, including compliance to the clinical investigation plan and local laws and regulations, ensures the protection of human subjects, the integrity of the data and that the data obtained is acceptable for the purpose of demonstrating conformity to the Essential Principles. Additional resources: see *Section 6 in GHTF SG5 N3:2010*[9]

Clinical Usability — the means by which the user and a computer system interact, in particular the use of input devices and software and the evaluation of safety considerations for device users, use environments and user interfaces. Additional resources see *ISO/IEC 62366-1:2015*[20], *SaMD N12*[2]*Section 4.0, SaMD N23*[3] *Section 7.2 and 8.4* (Also see ***Usability, User Interface***)

Clinical Validation — measures the ability of a SaMD to yield a clinically meaningful output associated to the target use of SaMD output in with the target health care situation or condition identified in the SaMD definition statement. (Also see ***Clinical Performance***)

Continuous Monitoring — collecting post-market information. Additional resources: see *Section 7.5 in SaMD N23*[3]

Confidence Interval — An interval about a point estimate that quantifies the statistical uncertainty in the true value being estimated (e.g. an accuracy metric) due to variability in the subject/sample selection process. A $1 - \alpha$ level confidence interval contains the true value in $100(1 - \alpha)$ % of applications, but in any given application either contains it or does not. Additional resources: see *Section 7.4 in GHTF SG5 N8:2012*[16]

Critical (situation or condition) — situations or conditions where accurate and/or timely diagnosis or treatment action is vital to avoid death, long-term disability or other serious deterioration of health of an individual patient or to mitigating impact to public health. Additional resources: see *Section 5.2.1 in in SaMD N12*[2]

Definition Statement — clear and strong statement about intended use that explains how the SaMD meets one or more of the purposes described in the definition of a medical device and describes the SaMD's core functionality. Additional resources: see *Section 6.0 in in SaMD N12*[2]

Diagnose (SaMD output to) — information provided by the SaMD will be used to take an immediate or near term action. Additional resources: see *Section 5.1.1 in in SaMD N12*[2] (Also see ***Treat (SaMD output to)***)

Drive Clinical Management (SaMD output to) — the information provided by the SaMD will be used to aid in treatment, aid in diagnoses, to triage or identify early signs of a disease or condition will be used to guide next diagnostics or next treatment interventions. Additional resources: see *Section 5.1.2 in SaMD N12*[2]

Effectiveness — when it can be determined that a device, based upon valid scientific evidence, that in a significant portion of the target population, the use of the device for its intended uses and conditions of use, when accompanied by adequate directions for use and warnings against unsafe use, will provide clinically significant results. (Also see ***Safety, Performance***)

Functionality — identifies the critical features/functions of the SaMD that are essential to the intended significance of the information provided by the SaMD to the healthcare decision in the intended healthcare situation or condition. Additional resources: see *Sections 6.0, 7.3, 8.2, 9.1, and 10.1 in SaMD N12*[2]

Global Harmonization Task Force — was a voluntary group of representatives from national medical device regulatory authorities and industry representatives. GHTF was disbanded in 2012 and its mission has been taken over by the IMDRF.

Hypothesis — a supposition or proposed explanation made as a starting point for further investigation. Evidence is not necessary to form a hypothesis.

Independent Review — the process of subjecting a work, research, or ideas to the scrutiny of others who are experts in the same field.

Inform Clinical Management (SaMD output to) — Informing clinical management infers that the information provided by the SaMD will not trigger an immediate or near term action. Additional resources: see *Section 5.1.3 in in SaMD N12*[2]

Input (SaMD) — one or several defined numeric tables or models accepted by an algorithm. (Also see ***Basic Programming Model, Outputs***)

Intended (Medical, Purpose, Use) — the objective intent of the manufacturer regarding the use of a product, process or service as reflected in the specifications, instructions and information provided by the manufacturer. (Also see ***Claim***)

CH 12

International Medical Device Regulatory Forum — a voluntary group of medical device regulators from around the world who have come together to build on the strong foundational work of the Global Harmonization Task Force on Medical Devices (GHTF), and to accelerate international medical device regulatory harmonization and convergence.

Labeling — the label, instructions for use, and any other information that is related to identification, technical description, intended purpose and proper use of the medical device, but excluding shipping documents. Additional resources: see *Section 4.0 in GHTF SG1 N70:2011*[14]

Least Burdensome — addressing a premarket issue that involves the most appropriate investment of time, effort, and resources.

Likelihood Ratio Negative (LR-) — (1 – sensitivity) / specificity = ratio of the probabilities of testing negative in patients with and without disease or clinical condition. It can be interpreted as the increase in the odds of disease given a test negative result relative to the pretest odds. Additional resources: see *Section 7.2 in GHTF SG5 N7:2012*[13]

Likelihood Ratio Positive (LR+) — sensitivity / (1 – specificity) = ratio of the probabilities of testing positive in patients with and without disease or clinical condition. It can be interpreted as the increase in the odds of disease given a test positive result relative to the pretest odds. Additional resources: see *Section 7.2 in GHTF SG5 N7:2012*[13]

Literature Search — use of published clinical data that establishes a valid clinical association. Additional resources: see *Section 6.1 in GHTF SG5 N2R8:2007*[8]

Machine Learning Software (Incremental) — software device for which input data is continuously used to automatically extend the existing device's knowledge i.e. to further train the device after it has been released into the market.

Negative Predictive Value (NPV) — proportion of test negative patients who do not have the disease or clinical condition. Additional resources: see *Section 7.2 in GHTF SG5 N7:2012*[13]

Non-Serious (situation or condition) — situations or conditions where an accurate diagnosis and treatment is important but not critical for interventions to mitigate long term irreversible consequences on an individual patient's health condition or public health. Additional resources: see *Section 5.2.3 in SaMD N12*[2]

Number Needed To Harm (NNH) — number of patients that need to be treated in order have an adverse effect on one patient.

Number Needed To Treat (NNT) — average number of patients that need to be treated in order to have an impact on one person.

Odds Ratio (OR) — ratio of the odds of disease or clinical condition given the SaMD test result is S to the odds of disease given the SaMD test result is not S. OR is equivalent to ratio of likelihood ratio positive to likelihood ratio negative.

CH 12

Output — results obtained from an algorithm.

Performance (Essential Principles) — a product's behavior must not cause harm to a person, place or thing if something goes wrong. (Also see ***Effectiveness, Safety***)

Performance (Metrics) — measures behaviors, activities and performance.

Performance (Real World) — information on real-world device use and performance from a wider patient population than a more controlled study or pertinent literature, and thus provide information that cannot be obtained through such studies. (Also see ***Real World Performance***)

Performance (Studies) — establish or confirm aspects of device performance which cannot be determined by analytical validation, literature and/or previous experience gained by routine testing. Additional resources: see *Section 5.0 in GHTF SG5 N8:2012*[16]

Positive Predictive Value (PPV) — proportion of test positive patients who have the disease or clinical condition. Additional resources: see *Section 7.2 in GHTF SG5 N7:2012*[13]

Post-market Surveillance — the practice of monitoring the safety of a medical device after it has been released on the market. Additional resources: see *GHTF Study Group 2*[5] *documents; GHTF SG2 N79R11:2009*[15]

Pre-market — the period prior to a product being available for purchase. Additional resources: see *GHTF Study Group 1*[4] *documents*

Professional Society Guidelines — practices and documents recommended by leading authorities; use of existing, well-established standards and/or clinical data. Additional resources: see *Section 9 in GHTF SG5 N2R8:2007*[8]

Real World (SaMD) Evidence — evidence derived from aggregation and analysis of real world data elements.

Real World Data — product information generated after a product has been released to the market that can provide insight into the performance of the product used in actual clinical settings, in routine medical practice, and by regular use by consumers.

Real World Performance — information on real-world device use and performance from a wider patient population than a more controlled study or pertinent literature, and thus provide information that cannot be obtained through such studies. (Also see ***Performance (Real World)***)

Risk Categorization Framework (SaMD) — a framework to determine the category of a SaMD based on the significance of the information provided to the healthcare decision and on the state of the healthcare situation or condition that the SaMD is intended for. Additional resources: see *Section 7.0 in in SaMD N12*[2]

Safety — a product should be designed and manufactured in such a way that, when used under the conditions and for the purposes intended and, where applicable, by virtue of the technical knowledge, experience, education or training, and the medical and physical conditions of intended users, they will perform as intended. (Also see ***Effectiveness, Performance***)

Safety Data — adverse events and other problems with medical devices that impact the health and safety of patients; safety data may be collected in the same activity as performance data; absence of safety issues during clinical performance testing is an indicator of safety.

Scientific Validity — refers to the extent to which the SaMD's output (concept, conclusion, measurements) is clinically accepted or well founded (existence of an established scientific framework or body of evidence) that corresponds accurately in the real world to the healthcare situation and condition identified in the SaMD definition statement. (Also see ***Clinical Association***)

Secondary Data Analysis — use of analyzed data collected for another purpose.

Sensitivity — effectiveness of a SaMD to correctly identifies patients with the intended clinical disease or condition. Additional resources: see *Section 4.0 in GHTF SG5 N7:2012*[13]

Serious (situation or condition) — situations or conditions where accurate diagnosis or treatment is of vital importance to avoid unnecessary interventions (e.g., biopsy) or timely interventions are important to mitigate long term irreversible consequences on an individual patient's health condition or public health. Additional resources: see *Section 5.2.2 in SaMD N12*[2]

Specificity — correctly identifies across a range of available measurements patients that do not have the intended disease or condition. Additional resources: see *Section 4.0 in GHTF SG5 N7:2012*[13]

Treat (SaMD output to) — information provided by the SaMD will be used to take an immediate or near term action. Additional resources: see *Section 5.1.1 in in SaMD N12*[2]

Usability — the means by which the user and a computer system interact, in particular the use of input devices and software and the evaluation of safety considerations for device users, use environments and user interfaces. Additional resources see *ISO/IEC 62366-1:2015* [20], *SaMD N12*[2] *Section 4.0, SaMD N23*[3] *Section 7.2 and 8.4* (Also see ***Clinical Usability, User Interface***)

User Interface — the means by which the user and a computer system interact, in particular the use of input devices and software and the evaluation of safety considerations for device users, use environments and user interfaces. Additional resources see *ISO/IEC 62366-1:2015*[20], *SaMD N12*[2] *Section 4.0, SaMD N23*[3] *Section 7.2 and 8.4* (Also see ***Clinical Usability, Usability***)

User(s) — includes patients, healthcare providers, specialized professionals, lay users, consumers.

Validation — confirmation through provision of objective evidence that the requirements for a specific intended use or application have been fulfilled. Additional resources: see *Section 2.8 in GHTF SG3 N18:2010*[6]

Verification — confirmation through provision of objective evidence that specified requirements have been fulfilled. Additional resources: see *Section 2.7 in GHTF SG3 N18:2010*[6]

CSV

Chapter 13
General Principles of Software Validation; Final Guidance for Industry and FDA Staff

January 11, 2002
U.S. Department Of Health and Human Services
Food and Drug Administration
Center for Devices and Radiological Health
Center for Biologics Evaluation and Research

SECTION 1. PURPOSE

This guidance outlines general validation principles that the Food and Drug Administration (FDA) considers to be applicable to the validation of medical device software or the validation of software used to design, develop, or manufacture medical devices. This final guidance document, Version 2.0, supersedes the draft document, *General Principles of Software Validation, Version 1.1*, dated June 9, 1997.

SECTION 2. SCOPE

This guidance describes how certain provisions of the medical device Quality System regulation apply to software and the agency's current approach to evaluating a software validation system. For example, this document lists elements that are acceptable to the FDA for the validation of software; however, it does not list all of the activities and tasks that must, in all instances, be used to comply with the law.

The scope of this guidance is somewhat broader than the scope of validation in the strictest definition of that term. Planning, verification, testing, traceability, configuration management, and many other aspects of good software engineering discussed in this guidance are important activities that together help to support a final conclusion that software is validated.

This guidance recommends an integration of software life cycle management and risk management activities. Based on the intended use and the safety risk associated with the software to be developed, the software developer should determine the specific approach, the combination of techniques to be used, and the level of effort to be applied. While this guidance does not recommend any specific life cycle model or any specific technique or method, it does recommend that software validation and verification activities be conducted throughout the entire software life cycle.

Where the software is developed by someone other than the device manufacturer (e.g., off-the-shelf software) the software developer may not be directly responsible for compliance with FDA regulations.

In that case, the party with regulatory responsibility (i.e., the device manufacturer) needs to assess the adequacy of the off-the-shelf software developer's activities and determine what additional efforts are needed to establish that the software is validated for the device manufacturer's intended use.

2.1. Applicability

This guidance applies to:

- Software used as a component, part, or accessory of a medical device;
- Software that is itself a medical device (e.g., blood establishment software);
- Software used in the production of a device (e.g., programmable logic controllers in manufacturing equipment); and
- Software used in implementation of the device manufacturer's quality system (e.g., software that records and maintains the device history record).

This document is based on generally recognized software validation principles and, therefore, can be applied to any software. For FDA purposes, this guidance applies to any software related to a regulated medical device, as defined by Section 201(h) of the Federal Food, Drug, and Cosmetic Act (the Act) and by current FDA software and regulatory policy. This document does not specifically identify which software is or is not regulated.

2.2. Audience

This guidance provides useful information and recommendations to the following individuals:

- Persons subject to the medical device Quality System regulation
- Persons responsible for the design, development, or production of medical device software
- Persons responsible for the design, development, production, or procurement of automated tools used for the design, development, or manufacture of medical devices or software tools used to implement the quality system itself
- FDA Investigators
- FDA Compliance Officers
- FDA Scientific Reviewers

2.3. The Least Burdensome Approach

We believe we should consider the least burdensome approach in all areas of medical device regulation. This guidance reflects our careful review of the relevant scientific and legal requirements and what we believe is the least burdensome way for you to comply with those requirements. However, if you believe that an alternative approach would be less burdensome, please contact us so we can consider your point of view. You may send your written comments to the contact person listed in the preface to this guidance or to the CDRH Ombudsman.

Comprehensive information on CDRH's Ombudsman, including ways to contact him, can be found on the Internet at: http://www.fda.gov/cdrh/resolvingdisputes/ombudsman.html.

2.4. Regulatory Requirements for Software Validation

The FDA's analysis of 3140 medical device recalls conducted between 1992 and 1998 reveals that 242 of them (7.7%) are attributable to software failures. Of those software related recalls, 192 (or 79%) were caused by software defects that were introduced when changes were made to the software after its initial production and distribution. Software validation and other related good software engineering practices discussed in this guidance are a principal means of avoiding such defects and resultant recalls.

Software validation is a requirement of the Quality System regulation, which was published in the Federal Register on October 7, 1996 and took effect on June 1, 1997. (See Title 21 Code of Federal Regulations (CFR) Part 820, and 61 Federal Register (FR) 52602, respectively.) Validation requirements apply to software used as components in medical devices, to software that is itself a medical device, and to software used in production of the device or in implementation of the device manufacturer's quality system.

Unless specifically exempted in a classification regulation, any medical device software product developed after June 1, 1997, regardless of its device class, is subject to applicable design control provisions. (See of 21 CFR §820.30.) This requirement includes the completion of current development projects, all new development projects, and all changes made to existing medical device software. Specific requirements for validation of device software are found in 21 CFR §820.30(g). Other design controls, such as planning, input, verification, and reviews, are required for medical device software. (See 21 CFR §820.30.) The corresponding documented results from these activities can provide additional support for a conclusion that medical device software is validated.

Any software used to automate any part of the device production process or any part of the quality system must be validated for its intended use, as required by 21 CFR §820.70(i). This requirement applies to any software used to automate device design, testing, component acceptance, manufacturing, labeling, packaging, distribution, complaint handling, or to automate any other aspect of the quality system.

In addition, computer systems used to create, modify, and maintain electronic records and to manage electronic signatures are also subject to the validation requirements. (See 21 CFR §11.10(a).) Such computer systems must be validated to ensure accuracy, reliability, consistent intended performance, and the ability to discern invalid or altered records.

Software for the above applications may be developed in-house or under contract. However, software is frequently purchased off-the-shelf for a particular intended use. All production and/or quality system software, even if purchased off-the-shelf, should have documented requirements that fully define its intended use, and information against which testing results and other evidence can be compared, to show that the software is validated for its intended use.

The use of off-the-shelf software in automated medical devices and in automated manufacturing and quality system operations is increasing. Off-the-shelf software may have many capabilities, only a few of which are needed by the device manufacturer. Device manufacturers are responsible for the adequacy of the software used in their devices, and used to produce devices. When device manufacturers purchase "off-the-shelf'' software, they must ensure that it will perform as intended in their chosen application. For off-the-shelf software used in manufacturing or in the quality system, additional guidance is included in Section 6.3 of this document. For device software, additional useful information may be found in FDA's *Guidance for Industry, FDA Reviewers, and Compliance on Off-The-Shelf Software Use in Medical Devices*.

2.4. *[SIC]* QUALITY SYSTEM REGULATION VS PRE-MARKET SUBMISSIONS

This document addresses Quality System regulation issues that involve the implementation of software validation. It provides guidance for the management and control of the software validation process. The management and control of the software validation process should not be confused with any other validation requirements, such as process validation for an automated manufacturing process.

Device manufacturers may use the same procedures and records for compliance with quality system and design control requirements, as well as for pre-market submissions to FDA. This document does not cover any specific safety or efficacy issues related to software validation. Design issues and documentation requirements for pre-market submissions of regulated software are not addressed by this document. Specific issues related to safety and efficacy, and the documentation required in pre-market submissions, should be addressed to the Office of Device Evaluation (ODE), Center for Devices and Radiological Health (CDRH) or to the Office of Blood Research and Review, Center for Biologics Evaluation and Research (CBER). See the references in Appendix A for applicable FDA guidance documents for pre-market submissions.

SECTION 3. CONTEXT FOR SOFTWARE VALIDATION

Many people have asked for specific guidance on what FDA expects them to do to ensure compliance with the Quality System regulation with regard to software validation. Information on software validation presented in this document is not new. Validation of software, using the principles and tasks listed in Sections 4 and 5, has been conducted in many segments of the software industry for well over 20 years.

Due to the great variety of medical devices, processes, and manufacturing facilities, it is not possible to state in one document all of the specific validation elements that are applicable. However, a general application of several broad concepts can be used successfully as guidance for software validation. These broad concepts provide an acceptable framework for building a comprehensive approach to software validation. Additional specific information is available from many of the references listed in Appendix A.

3.1. DEFINITIONS AND TERMINOLOGY

Unless defined in the Quality System regulation, or otherwise specified below, all other terms used in this guidance are as defined in the current edition of the FDA *Glossary of Computerized System and Software Development Terminology.*

The medical device Quality System regulation (21 CFR 820.3(k)) defines "establish" to mean "define, document, and implement." Where it appears in this guidance, the words "establish" and "established" should be interpreted to have this same meaning.

Some definitions found in the medical device Quality System regulation can be confusing when compared to commonly used terminology in the software industry. Examples are requirements, specification, verification, and validation.

3.1.1 Requirements and Specifications

While the Quality System regulation states that design input requirements must be documented, and that specified requirements must be verified, the regulation does not further clarify the distinction between the terms "requirement" and "specification." A requirement can be any need or expectation for a system or for its software. Requirements reflect the stated or implied needs of the customer, and may be market-based, contractual, or statutory, as well as an organization's internal requirements. There can be many different kinds of requirements (e.g., design, functional, implementation, interface, performance, or physical requirements). Software requirements are typically derived from the system requirements for those aspects of system functionality that have been allocated to software. Software requirements are typically stated in functional terms and are defined, refined, and updated as a development project progresses. Success in accurately and completely documenting software requirements is a crucial factor in successful validation of the resulting software.

A specification is defined as "a document that states requirements." (See 21 CFR §820.3(y).) It may refer to or include drawings, patterns, or other relevant documents and usually indicates the means and the criteria whereby conformity with the requirement can be checked. There are many different kinds of written specifications, e.g., system requirements specification, software requirements specification, software design specification, software test specification, software integration specification, etc. All of these documents establish "specified requirements" and are design outputs for which various forms of verification are necessary.

3.1.2 Verification and Validation

CH 13

The Quality System regulation is harmonized with ISO 8402:1994, which treats "verification" and "validation" as separate and distinct terms. On the other hand, many software engineering journal articles and textbooks use the terms "verification" and "validation" interchangeably, or in some cases refer to software "verification, validation, and testing (VV&T)" as if it is a single concept, with no distinction among the three terms.

Software verification provides objective evidence that the design outputs of a particular phase of the software development life cycle meet all of the specified requirements for that phase. Software verification looks for consistency, completeness, and correctness of the software and its supporting documentation, as it is being developed, and provides support for a subsequent conclusion that software is validated. Software testing is one of many verification activities intended to confirm that software development output meets its input requirements. Other verification activities include various static and dynamic analyses, code and document inspections, walkthroughs, and other techniques.

Software validation is a part of the design validation for a finished device, but is not separately defined in the Quality System regulation. For purposes of this guidance, FDA considers software validation to be "**confirmation by examination and provision of objective evidence that software specifications conform to user needs and intended uses, and that the particular requirements implemented through software can be consistently fulfilled.**" In practice, software validation activities may occur both during, as well as at the end of the software development life cycle to ensure that all requirements have been fulfilled. Since software is usually part of a larger hardware system, the validation of software typically includes evidence that all software requirements have been implemented correctly and completely and are traceable to system requirements. A conclusion that software is validated is highly dependent upon comprehensive software testing, inspections, analyses, and other verification tasks performed at each stage of the software development life cycle. Testing of device software functionality in a simulated use environment, and user site testing are typically included as components of an overall design validation program for a software automated device.

Software verification and validation are difficult because a developer cannot test forever, and it is hard to know how much evidence is enough. In large measure, software validation is a matter of developing a "level of confidence" that the device meets all requirements and user expectations for the software automated functions and features of the device. Measures such as defects found in specifications documents, estimates of defects remaining, testing coverage, and other techniques are all used to develop an acceptable level of confidence before shipping the product. The level of confidence, and therefore the level of software validation, verification, and testing effort needed, will vary depending upon the safety risk (hazard) posed by the automated functions of the device. Additional guidance regarding safety risk management for software may be found in Section 4 of FDA's *Guidance for the Content of Pre-market Submissions for Software Contained in Medical Devices*, and in the international standards *ISO/IEC 14971-1 and IEC 60601-1-4* referenced in Appendix A.

3.1.3 IQ/OQ/PQ

CH 13

For many years, both FDA and regulated industry have attempted to understand and define software validation within the context of process validation terminology. For example, industry documents and other FDA validation guidance sometimes describe user site software validation in terms of installation qualification (IQ), operational qualification (OQ) and performance qualification (PQ). Definitions of these terms and additional information regarding IQ/OQ/PQ may be found in FDA's Guideline on General Principles of Process Validation, dated May 11, 1987, and in FDA's Glossary of Computerized System and Software Development Terminology, dated August 1995.

While IQ/OQ/PQ terminology has served its purpose well and is one of many legitimate ways to organize software validation tasks at the user site, this terminology may not be well understood among many software professionals, and it is not used elsewhere in this document. However, both FDA personnel and device manufacturers need to be aware of these differences in terminology as they ask for and provide information regarding software validation.

3.2. Software Development as Part of System Design

The decision to implement system functionality using software is one that is typically made during system design. Software requirements are typically derived from the overall system requirements and design for those aspects in the system that are to be implemented using software. There are user needs and intended uses for a finished device, but users typically do not specify whether those requirements are to be met by hardware, software, or some combination of both. Therefore, software validation must be considered within the context of the overall design validation for the system.

A documented requirements specification represents the user's needs and intended uses from which the product is developed. A primary goal of software validation is to then demonstrate that all completed software products comply with all documented software and system requirements. The correctness and completeness of both the system requirements and the software requirements should be addressed as part of the design validation process for the device. Software validation includes confirmation of conformance to all software specifications and confirmation that all software requirements are traceable to the system specifications. Confirmation is an important part of the overall design validation to ensure that all aspects of the medical device conform to user needs and intended uses.

3.3. Software is Different from Hardware

While software shares many of the same engineering tasks as hardware, it has some very important differences. For example:

- The vast majority of software problems are traceable to errors made during the design and development process. While the quality of a hardware product is highly dependent on design, development and manufacture, the quality of a software product is dependent primarily on design and development with a minimum concern for software manufacture. Software manufacturing consists of reproduction that can be easily verified. It is not difficult to manufacture thousands of program copies that function exactly the same as the original; the difficulty comes in getting the original program to meet all specifications.
- One of the most significant features of software is branching, i.e., the ability to execute alternative series of commands, based on differing inputs. This feature is a major contributing factor for another characteristic of software – its complexity. Even short programs can be very complex and difficult to fully understand.
- Typically, testing alone cannot fully verify that software is complete and correct. In addition to testing, other verification techniques and a structured and documented development process should be combined to ensure a comprehensive validation approach.
- Unlike hardware, software is not a physical entity and does not wear out. In fact, software may improve with age, as latent defects are discovered and removed. However, as software is constantly updated and changed, such improvements are sometimes countered by new defects introduced into the software during the change.

- Unlike some hardware failures, software failures occur without advanced warning. The software's branching that allows it to follow differing paths during execution, may hide some latent defects until long after a software product has been introduced into the marketplace.
- Another related characteristic of software is the speed and ease with which it can be changed. This factor can cause both software and non-software professionals to believe that software problems can be corrected easily. Combined with a lack of understanding of software, it can lead managers to believe that tightly controlled engineering is not needed as much for software as it is for hardware. In fact, the opposite is true. **Because of its complexity, the development process for software should be even more tightly controlled than for hardware, in order to prevent problems that cannot be easily detected later in the development process.**
- Seemingly insignificant changes in software code can create unexpected and very significant problems elsewhere in the software program. The software development process should be sufficiently well planned, controlled, and documented to detect and correct unexpected results from software changes.
- Given the high demand for software professionals and the highly mobile workforce, the software personnel who make maintenance changes to software may not have been involved in the original software development. Therefore, accurate and thorough documentation is essential.
- Historically, software components have not been as frequently standardized and interchangeable as hardware components. However, medical device software developers are beginning to use component-based development tools and techniques. Object-oriented methodologies and the use of off-the-shelf software components hold promise for faster and less expensive software development. However, component-based approaches require very careful attention during integration. Prior to integration, time is needed to fully define and develop reusable software code and to fully understand the behavior of off-the-shelf components.

For these and other reasons, software engineering needs an even greater level of managerial scrutiny and control than does hardware engineering.

3.4. Benefits of Software Validation

Software validation is a critical tool used to assure the quality of device software and software automated operations. Software validation can increase the usability and reliability of the device, resulting in decreased failure rates, fewer recalls and corrective actions, less risk to patients and users, and reduced liability to device manufacturers. Software validation can also reduce long term costs by making it easier and less costly to reliably modify software and revalidate software changes. Software maintenance can represent a very large percentage of the total cost of software over its entire life cycle. An established comprehensive software validation process helps to reduce the long-term cost of software by reducing the cost of validation for each subsequent release of the software.

3.5 Design Review

Design reviews are documented, comprehensive, and systematic examinations of a design to evaluate the adequacy of the design requirements, to evaluate the capability of the design to meet these requirements, and to identify problems. While there may be many informal technical reviews that occur within the development team during a software project, a formal design review is more structured and includes participation from others outside the development team. Formal design reviews may reference or include results from other formal and informal reviews. Design reviews may be conducted separately for the software, after the software is integrated with the hardware into the system, or both. Design reviews should include examination of development plans, requirements specifications, design specifications, testing plans and procedures, all other documents and activities associated with the project, verification results from each stage of the defined life cycle, and validation results for the overall device.

Design review is a primary tool for managing and evaluating development projects. For example, formal design reviews allow management to confirm that all goals defined in the software validation plan have been achieved. The Quality System regulation requires that at least one formal design review be conducted during the device design process. However, it is recommended that multiple design reviews be conducted (e.g., at the end of each software life cycle activity, in preparation for proceeding to the next activity). Formal design review is especially important at or near the end of the requirements activity, before major resources have been committed to specific design solutions. Problems found at this point can be resolved more easily, save time and money, and reduce the likelihood of missing a critical issue.

Answers to some key questions should be documented during formal design reviews. These include:

- Have the appropriate tasks and expected results, outputs, or products been established for each software life cycle activity?
- Do the tasks and expected results, outputs, or products of each software life cycle activity:
    - ✓ Comply with the requirements of other software life cycle activities in terms of correctness, completeness, consistency, and accuracy?
    - ✓ Satisfy the standards, practices, and conventions of that activity?
    - ✓ Establish a proper basis for initiating tasks for the next software life cycle activity?

CH 13

Section 4. Principles of Software Validation

This section lists the general principles that should be considered for the validation of software.

4.1. Requirements

A documented software requirements specification provides a baseline for both validation and verification. The software validation process cannot be completed without an established software requirements specification (Ref: 21 CFR 820.3(z) and (aa) and 820.30(f) and (g)).

4.2. Defect Prevention

Software quality assurance needs to focus on preventing the introduction of defects into the software development process and not on trying to "test quality into" the software code after it is written. Software testing is very limited in its ability to surface all latent defects in software code. For example, the complexity of most software prevents it from being exhaustively tested. **Software testing is a necessary activity. However, in most cases software testing by itself is not sufficient to establish confidence that the software is fit for its intended use.** In order to establish that confidence, software developers should use a mixture of methods and techniques to prevent software errors and to detect software errors that do occur. The "best mix" of methods depends on many factors including the development environment, application, size of project, language, and risk.

4.3. Time and Effort

To build a case that the software is validated requires time and effort. Preparation for software validation should begin early, i.e., during design and development planning and design input. The final conclusion that the software is validated should be based on evidence collected from planned efforts conducted throughout the software lifecycle.

4.4. Software Life Cycle

Software validation takes place within the environment of an established software life cycle. The software life cycle contains software engineering tasks and documentation necessary to support the software validation effort. In addition, the software life cycle contains specific verification and validation tasks that are appropriate for the intended use of the software. This guidance does not recommend any particular life cycle models – only that they should be selected and used for a software development project.

4.5. Plans

The software validation process is defined and controlled through the use of a plan. The software validation plan defines "what" is to be accomplished through the software validation effort. Software validation plans are a significant quality system tool. Software validation plans specify areas such as scope, approach, resources, schedules and the types and extent of activities, tasks, and work items.

4.6. Procedures

The software validation process is executed through the use of procedures. These procedures establish "how" to conduct the software validation effort. The procedures should identify the specific actions or sequence of actions that must be taken to complete individual validation activities, tasks, and work items.

4.7. Software Validation after a Change

Due to the complexity of software, a seemingly small local change may have a significant global system impact. When any change (even a small change) is made to the software, the validation status of the software needs to be re-established. **Whenever software is changed, a validation analysis should be conducted not just for validation of the individual change, but also to determine the extent and impact of that change on the entire software system.** Based on this analysis, the software developer should then conduct an appropriate level of software regression testing to show that unchanged but vulnerable portions of the system have not been adversely affected. Design controls and appropriate regression testing provide the confidence that the software is validated after a software change.

4.8. Validation Coverage

Validation coverage should be based on the software's complexity and safety risk – not on firm size or resource constraints. The selection of validation activities, tasks, and work items should be commensurate with the complexity of the software design and the risk associated with the use of the software for the specified intended use. For lower risk devices, only baseline validation activities may be conducted. As the risk increases additional validation activities should be added to cover the additional risk. Validation documentation should be sufficient to demonstrate that all software validation plans and procedures have been completed successfully.

4.9. Independence of Review

Validation activities should be conducted using the basic quality assurance precept of "independence of review." Self-validation is extremely difficult. When possible, an independent evaluation is always better, especially for higher risk applications. Some firms contract out for a third-party independent verification and validation, but this solution may not always be feasible. Another approach is to assign internal staff members that are not involved in a particular design or its implementation, but who have sufficient knowledge to evaluate the project and conduct the verification and validation activities. Smaller firms may need to be creative in how tasks are organized and assigned in order to maintain internal independence of review.

4.10. Flexibility and Responsibility

Specific implementation of these software validation principles may be quite different from one application to another. The device manufacturer has flexibility in choosing how to apply these validation principles, but retains ultimate responsibility for demonstrating that the software has been validated.

Software is designed, developed, validated, and regulated in a wide spectrum of environments, and for a wide variety of devices with varying levels of risk. FDA regulated medical device applications include software that:

- Is a component, part, or accessory of a medical device;
- Is itself a medical device; or
- Is used in manufacturing, design and development, or other parts of the quality system.

In each environment, software components from many sources may be used to create the application (e.g., in-house developed software, off-the-shelf software, contract software, shareware). In addition, software components come in many different forms (e.g., application software, operating systems, compilers, debuggers, configuration management tools, and many more). The validation of software in these environments can be a complex undertaking; therefore, it is appropriate that all of these software validation principles be considered when designing the software validation process. The resultant software validation process should be commensurate with the safety risk associated with the system, device, or process.

Software validation activities and tasks may be dispersed, occurring at different locations and being conducted by different organizations. However, regardless of the distribution of tasks, contractual relations, source of components, or the development environment, the device manufacturer or specification developer retains ultimate responsibility for ensuring that the software is validated.

SECTION 5. ACTIVITIES AND TASKS

Software validation is accomplished through a series of activities and tasks that are planned and executed at various stages of the software development life cycle. These tasks may be one time occurrences or may be iterated many times, depending on the life cycle model used and the scope of changes made as the software project progresses.

5.1. SOFTWARE LIFE CYCLE ACTIVITIES

This guidance does not recommend the use of any specific software life cycle model. Software developers should establish a software life cycle model that is appropriate for their product and organization. The software life cycle model that is selected should cover the software from its birth to its retirement. Activities in a typical software life cycle model include the following:

- Quality Planning
- System Requirements Definition
- Detailed Software Requirements Specification
- Software Design Specification
- Construction or Coding
- Testing
- Installation
- Operation and Support
- Maintenance
- Retirement

Verification, testing, and other tasks that support software validation occur during each of these activities. A life cycle model organizes these software development activities in various ways and provides a framework for monitoring and controlling the software development project. Several software life cycle models (e.g., waterfall, spiral, rapid prototyping, incremental development, etc.) are defined in FDA's *Glossary of Computerized System and Software Development*

Terminology, dated August 1995. These and many other life cycle models are described in various references listed in Appendix A.

5.2. Typical Tasks Supporting Validation

For each of the software life cycle activities, there are certain "typical" tasks that support a conclusion that the software is validated. However, the specific tasks to be performed, their order of performance, and the iteration and timing of their performance will be dictated by the specific software life cycle model that is selected and the safety risk associated with the software application. For very low risk applications, certain tasks may not be needed at all. However, the software developer should at least consider each of these tasks and should define and document which tasks are or are not appropriate for their specific application. The following discussion is generic and is not intended to prescribe any particular software life cycle model or any particular order in which tasks are to be performed.

5.2.1. Quality Planning

Design and development planning should culminate in a plan that identifies necessary tasks, procedures for anomaly reporting and resolution, necessary resources, and management review requirements, including formal design reviews. A software life cycle model and associated activities should be identified, as well as those tasks necessary for each software life cycle activity. The plan should include:

- The specific tasks for each life cycle activity;
- Enumeration of important quality factors (e.g., reliability, maintainability, and usability);
- Methods and procedures for each task;
- Task acceptance criteria;
- Criteria for defining and documenting outputs in terms that will allow evaluation of their conformance to input requirements;
- Inputs for each task;
- Outputs from each task;
- Roles, resources, and responsibilities for each task;
- Risks and assumptions; and
- Documentation of user needs.

Management must identify and provide the appropriate software development environment and resources. (See 21 CFR §820.20(b)(1) and (2).) Typically, each task requires personnel as well as physical resources. The plan should identify the personnel, the facility and equipment resources for each task, and the role that risk (hazard) management will play. A configuration management plan should be developed that will guide and control multiple parallel development activities and ensure proper communications and documentation. Controls are necessary to ensure positive and correct correspondence among all approved versions of the specifications documents, source code, object code, and test suites that comprise a software system. The controls also should ensure accurate identification of, and access to, the currently approved versions.

Procedures should be created for reporting and resolving software anomalies found through validation or other activities. Management should identify the reports and specify the contents, format, and responsible organizational elements for each report. Procedures also are necessary for the review and approval of software development results, including the responsible organizational elements for such reviews and approvals.

Typical Tasks – Quality Planning

- Risk (Hazard) Management Plan
- Configuration Management Plan
- Software Quality Assurance Plan
  - Software Verification and Validation Plan
    - ❑ Verification and Validation Tasks, and Acceptance Criteria
    - ❑ Schedule and Resource Allocation (for software verification and validation activities)
    - ❑ Reporting Requirements
  - Formal Design Review Requirements
  - Other Technical Review Requirements
- Problem Reporting and Resolution Procedures
- Other Support Activities

5.2.2. Requirements

Requirements development includes the identification, analysis, and documentation of information about the device and its intended use. Areas of special importance include allocation of system functions to hardware/software, operating conditions, user characteristics, potential hazards, and anticipated tasks. In addition, the requirements should state clearly the intended use of the software.

The software requirements specification document should contain a written definition of the software functions. It is not possible to validate software without predetermined and documented software requirements. Typical software requirements specify the following:

- All software system inputs;
- All software system outputs;
- All functions that the software system will perform;
- All performance requirements that the software will meet, (e.g., data throughput, reliability, and timing);

- The definition of all external and user interfaces, as well as any internal software-to-system interfaces;
- How users will interact with the system;
- What constitutes an error and how errors should be handled;
- Required response times;
- The intended operating environment for the software, if this is a design constraint (e.g., hardware platform, operating system);
- All ranges, limits, defaults, and specific values that the software will accept; and
- All safety related requirements, specifications, features, or functions that will be implemented in software.

Software safety requirements are derived from a technical risk management process that is closely integrated with the system requirements development process. Software requirement specifications should identify clearly the potential hazards that can result from a software failure in the system as well as any safety requirements to be implemented in software. The consequences of software failure should be evaluated, along with means of mitigating such failures (e.g., hardware mitigation, defensive programming, etc.). From this analysis, it should be possible to identify the most appropriate measures necessary to prevent harm.

The Quality System regulation requires a mechanism for addressing incomplete, ambiguous, or conflicting requirements. (See 21 CFR 820.30(c).) Each requirement (e.g., hardware, software, user, operator interface, and safety) identified in the software requirements specification should be evaluated for accuracy, completeness, consistency, testability, correctness, and clarity. For example, software requirements should be evaluated to verify that:

- There are no internal inconsistencies among requirements;
- All of the performance requirements for the system have been spelled out;
- Fault tolerance, safety, and security requirements are complete and correct;
- Allocation of software functions is accurate and complete;
- Software requirements are appropriate for the system hazards; and
- All requirements are expressed in terms that are measurable or objectively verifiable.

A software requirements traceability analysis should be conducted to trace software requirements to (and from) system requirements and to risk analysis results. In addition to any other analyses and documentation used to verify software requirements, a formal design review is recommended to confirm that requirements are fully specified and appropriate before extensive software design efforts begin. Requirements can be approved and released incrementally, but care should be taken that interactions and interfaces among software (and hardware) requirements are properly reviewed, analyzed, and controlled.

<u>Typical Tasks – Requirements</u>

- Preliminary Risk Analysis

- Traceability Analysis
  - Software Requirements to System Requirements (and vice versa)
  - Software Requirements to Risk Analysis
- Description of User Characteristics
- Listing of Characteristics and Limitations of Primary and Secondary Memory
- Software Requirements Evaluation
- Software User Interface Requirements Analysis
- System Test Plan Generation
- Acceptance Test Plan Generation
- Ambiguity Review or Analysis

5.2.3. Design

In the design process, the software requirements specification is translated into a logical and physical representation of the software to be implemented. The software design specification is a description of what the software should do and how it should do it. Due to complexity of the project or to enable persons with varying levels of technical responsibilities to clearly understand design information, the design specification may contain both a high level summary of the design and detailed design information. The completed software design specification constrains the programmer/coder to stay within the intent of the agreed upon requirements and design. A complete software design specification will relieve the programmer from the need to make ad hoc design decisions.

The software design needs to address human factors. Use error caused by designs that are either overly complex or contrary to users' intuitive expectations for operation is one of the most persistent and critical problems encountered by FDA. Frequently, the design of the software is a factor in such use errors. Human factors engineering should be woven into the entire design and development process, including the device design requirements, analyses, and tests. Device safety and usability issues should be considered when developing flowcharts, state diagrams, prototyping tools, and test plans. Also, task and function analyses, risk analyses, prototype tests and reviews, and full usability tests should be performed. Participants from the user population should be included when applying these methodologies.

The software design specification should include:

- Software requirements specification, including predetermined criteria for acceptance of the software;
- Software risk analysis;
- Development procedures and coding guidelines (or other programming procedures);
- Systems documentation (e.g., a narrative or a context diagram) that describes the systems context in which the program is intended to function, including the relationship of hardware, software, and the physical environment;

- Hardware to be used;
- Parameters to be measured or recorded;
- Logical structure (including control logic) and logical processing steps (e.g., algorithms);
- Data structures and data flow diagrams;
- Definitions of variables (control and data) and description of where they are used;
- Error, alarm, and warning messages;
- Supporting software (e.g., operating systems, drivers, other application software);
- Communication links (links among internal modules of the software, links with the supporting software, links with the hardware, and links with the user);
- Security measures (both physical and logical security); and
- Any additional constraints not identified in the above elements.

The first four of the elements noted above usually are separate pre-existing documents that are included by reference in the software design specification. Software requirements specification was discussed in the preceding section, as was software risk analysis. Written development procedures serve as a guide to the organization, and written programming procedures serve as a guide to individual programmers. As software cannot be validated without knowledge of the context in which it is intended to function, systems documentation is referenced. If some of the above elements are not included in the software, it may be helpful to future reviewers and maintainers of the software if that is clearly stated (e.g., There are no error messages in this program).

The activities that occur during software design have several purposes. Software design evaluations are conducted to determine if the design is complete, correct, consistent, unambiguous, feasible, and maintainable. Appropriate consideration of software architecture (e.g., modular structure) during design can reduce the magnitude of future validation efforts when software changes are needed. Software design evaluations may include analyses of control flow, data flow, complexity, timing, sizing, memory allocation, criticality analysis, and many other aspects of the design. A traceability analysis should be conducted to verify that the software design implements all of the software requirements. As a technique for identifying where requirements are not sufficient, the traceability analysis should also verify that all aspects of the design are traceable to software requirements. An analysis of communication links should be conducted to evaluate the proposed design with respect to hardware, user, and related software requirements. The software risk analysis should be re-examined to determine whether any additional hazards have been identified and whether any new hazards have been introduced by the design.

At the end of the software design activity, a Formal Design Review should be conducted to verify that the design is correct, consistent, complete, accurate, and testable, before moving to implement the design. Portions of the design can be approved and released incrementally for implementation; but care should be taken that interactions and communication links among various elements are properly reviewed, analyzed, and controlled.

Most software development models will be iterative. This is likely to result in several versions of both the software requirement specification and the software design specification. All approved versions should be archived and controlled in accordance with established configuration management procedures.

Typical Tasks – Design

- Updated Software Risk Analysis
- Traceability Analysis - Design Specification to Software Requirements (and vice versa)
- Software Design Evaluation
- Design Communication Link Analysis
- Module Test Plan Generation
- Integration Test Plan Generation
- Test Design Generation (module, integration, system, and acceptance)

5.2.4. Construction or Coding

Software may be constructed either by coding (i.e., programming) or by assembling together previously coded software components (e.g., from code libraries, off-the-shelf software, etc.) for use in a new application. Coding is the software activity where the detailed design specification is implemented as source code. Coding is the lowest level of abstraction for the software development process. It is the last stage in decomposition of the software requirements where module specifications are translated into a programming language.

Coding usually involves the use of a high-level programming language, but may also entail the use of assembly language (or microcode) for time-critical operations. The source code may be either compiled or interpreted for use on a target hardware platform. Decisions on the selection of programming languages and software build tools (assemblers, linkers, and compilers) should include consideration of the impact on subsequent quality evaluation tasks (e.g., availability of debugging and testing tools for the chosen language). Some compilers offer optional levels and commands for error checking to assist in debugging the code. Different levels of error checking may be used throughout the coding process, and warnings or other messages from the compiler may or may not be recorded. However, at the end of the coding and debugging process, the most rigorous level of error checking is normally used to document what compilation errors still remain in the software. If the most rigorous level of error checking is not used for final translation of the source code, then justification for use of the less rigorous translation error checking should be documented. Also, for the final compilation, there should be documentation of the compilation process and its outcome, including any warnings or other messages from the compiler and their resolution, or justification for the decision to leave issues unresolved.

Firms frequently adopt specific coding guidelines that establish quality policies and procedures related to the software coding process. Source code should be evaluated to verify its compliance with specified coding guidelines. Such guidelines should include coding conventions regarding clarity, style, complexity management, and commenting. Code comments should provide useful and descriptive information for a module, including expected inputs and outputs, variables referenced, expected data types, and operations to be performed. Source code should also be evaluated to verify its compliance with the corresponding detailed design specification. Modules ready for integration and test should have documentation of compliance with coding guidelines and any other applicable quality policies and procedures.

Source code evaluations are often implemented as code inspections and code walkthroughs. Such static analyses provide a very effective means to detect errors before execution of the code. They allow for examination of each error in isolation and can also help in focusing later dynamic testing of the software. Firms may use manual (desk) checking with appropriate controls to ensure consistency and independence. Source code evaluations should be extended to verification of internal linkages between modules and layers (horizontal and vertical interfaces), and compliance with their design specifications. Documentation of the procedures used and the results of source code evaluations should be maintained as part of design verification.

A source code traceability analysis is an important tool to verify that all code is linked to established specifications and established test procedures. A source code traceability analysis should be conducted and documented to verify that:

- Each element of the software design specification has been implemented in code;
- Modules and functions implemented in code can be traced back to an element in the software design specification and to the risk analysis;
- Tests for modules and functions can be traced back to an element in the software design specification and to the risk analysis; and
- Tests for modules and functions can be traced to source code for the same modules and functions.

Typical Tasks – Construction or Coding

- Traceability Analyses
  - Source Code to Design Specification (and vice versa)
  - Test Cases to Source Code and to Design Specification
- Source Code and Source Code Documentation Evaluation
- Source Code Interface Analysis
- Test Procedure and Test Case Generation (module, integration, system, and acceptance)

5.2.5. Testing by the Software Developer

Software testing entails running software products under known conditions with defined inputs and documented outcomes that can be compared to their predefined expectations. It is a time consuming, difficult, and imperfect activity. As such, it requires early planning in order to be effective and efficient.

Test plans and test cases should be created as early in the software development process as feasible. They should identify the schedules, environments, resources (personnel, tools, etc.), methodologies, cases (inputs, procedures, outputs, expected results), documentation, and reporting criteria. The magnitude of effort to be applied throughout the testing process can be linked to complexity, criticality, reliability, and/or safety issues (e.g., requiring functions or modules that produce critical outcomes to be challenged with intensive testing of their fault tolerance features). Descriptions of categories of software and software testing effort appear in the literature, for example:

- NIST Special Publication 500-235, *Structured Testing: A Testing Methodology Using the Cyclomatic Complexity Metric*;
- NUREG/CR-6293, *Verification and Validation Guidelines for High Integrity Systems*; and
- IEEE Computer Society Press, *Handbook of Software Reliability Engineering*.

Software test plans should identify the particular tasks to be conducted at each stage of development and include justification of the level of effort represented by their corresponding completion criteria.

Software testing has limitations that must be recognized and considered when planning the testing of a particular software product. Except for the simplest of programs, software cannot be exhaustively tested. Generally it is not feasible to test a software product with all possible inputs, nor is it possible to test all possible data processing paths that can occur during program execution. There is no one type of testing or testing methodology that can ensure a particular software product has been thoroughly tested. Testing of all program functionality does not mean all of the program has been tested. Testing of all of a program's code does not mean all necessary functionality is present in the program. Testing of all program functionality and all program code does not mean the program is 100% correct! Software testing that finds no errors should not be interpreted to mean that errors do not exist in the software product; it may mean the testing was superficial.

An essential element of a software test case is the expected result. It is the key detail that permits objective evaluation of the actual test result. This necessary testing information is obtained from the corresponding, predefined definition or specification. A software specification document must identify what, when, how, why, etc., is to be achieved with an engineering (i.e., measurable or objectively verifiable) level of detail in order for it to be confirmed through testing. The real effort of effective software testing lies in the definition of what is to be tested rather than in the performance of the test.

A software testing process should be based on principles that foster effective examinations of a software product. Applicable software testing tenets include:

- The expected test outcome is predefined;
- A good test case has a high probability of exposing an error;
- A successful test is one that finds an error;
- There is independence from coding;
- Both application (user) and software (programming) expertise are employed;
- Testers use different tools from coders;

- Examining only the usual case is insufficient;
- Test documentation permits its reuse and an independent confirmation of the pass/fail status of a test outcome during subsequent review.

Once the prerequisite tasks (e.g., code inspection) have been successfully completed, software testing begins. It starts with unit level testing and concludes with system level testing. There may be a distinct integration level of testing. A software product should be challenged with test cases based on its internal structure and with test cases based on its external specification. These tests should provide a thorough and rigorous examination of the software product's compliance with its functional, performance, and interface definitions and requirements.

Code-based testing is also known as structural testing or "white-box" testing. It identifies test cases based on knowledge obtained from the source code, detailed design specification, and other development documents. These test cases challenge the control decisions made by the program; and the program's data structures including configuration tables. Structural testing can identify "dead" code that is never executed when the program is run. Structural testing is accomplished primarily with unit (module) level testing, but can be extended to other levels of software testing.

The level of structural testing can be evaluated using metrics that are designed to show what percentage of the software structure has been evaluated during structural testing. These metrics are typically referred to as "coverage" and are a measure of completeness with respect to test selection criteria. The amount of structural coverage should be commensurate with the level of risk posed by the software. Use of the term "coverage" usually means 100% coverage. For example, if a testing program has achieved "statement coverage," it means that 100% of the statements in the software have been executed at least once. Common structural coverage metrics include:

- **Statement Coverage** – This criteria requires sufficient test cases for each program statement to be executed at least once; however, its achievement is insufficient to provide confidence in a software product's behavior.
- **Decision (Branch) Coverage** – This criteria requires sufficient test cases for each program decision or branch to be executed so that each possible outcome occurs at least once. It is considered to be a minimum level of coverage for most software products, but decision coverage alone is insufficient for high-integrity applications.
- **Condition Coverage** – This criteria requires sufficient test cases for each condition in a program decision to take on all possible outcomes at least once. It differs from branch coverage only when multiple conditions must be evaluated to reach a decision.
- **Multi-Condition Coverage** – This criteria requires sufficient test cases to exercise all possible combinations of conditions in a program decision.
- **Loop Coverage** – This criteria requires sufficient test cases for all program loops to be executed for zero, one, two, and many iterations covering initialization, typical running and termination (boundary) conditions.

- **Path Coverage** – This criteria requires sufficient test cases for each feasible path, basis path, etc., from start to exit of a defined program segment, to be executed at least once. Because of the very large number of possible paths through a software program, path coverage is generally not achievable. The amount of path coverage is normally established based on the risk or criticality of the software under test.
- **Data Flow Coverage** – This criteria requires sufficient test cases for each feasible data flow to be executed at least once. A number of data flow testing strategies are available.

Definition-based or specification-based testing is also known as functional testing or "black-box" testing. It identifies test cases based on the definition of what the software product (whether it be a unit (module) or a complete program) is intended to do. These test cases challenge the intended use or functionality of a program, and the program's internal and external interfaces. Functional testing can be applied at all levels of software testing, from unit to system level testing.

The following types of functional software testing involve generally increasing levels of effort:

- **Normal Case** – Testing with usual inputs is necessary. However, testing a software product only with expected, valid inputs does not thoroughly test that software product. By itself, normal case testing cannot provide sufficient confidence in the dependability of the software product.
- **Output Forcing** – Choosing test inputs to ensure that selected (or all) software outputs are generated by testing.
- **Robustness** – Software testing should demonstrate that a software product behaves correctly when given unexpected, invalid inputs. Methods for identifying a sufficient set of such test cases include Equivalence Class Partitioning, Boundary Value Analysis, and Special Case Identification (Error Guessing). While important and necessary, these techniques do not ensure that all of the most appropriate challenges to a software product have been identified for testing.
- **Combinations of Inputs** – The functional testing methods identified above all emphasize individual or single test inputs. Most software products operate with multiple inputs under their conditions of use. Thorough software product testing should consider the combinations of inputs a software unit or system may encounter during operation. Error guessing can be extended to identify combinations of inputs, but it is an ad hoc technique. Cause-effect graphing is one functional software testing technique that systematically identifies combinations of inputs to a software product for inclusion in test cases.

Functional and structural software test case identification techniques provide specific inputs for testing, rather than random test inputs. One weakness of these techniques is the difficulty in linking structural and functional test completion criteria to a software product's reliability. Advanced software testing methods, such as statistical testing, can be employed to provide further assurance that a software product is dependable. Statistical testing uses randomly generated test data from defined distributions based on an operational profile (e.g., expected use, hazardous use, or malicious use of the software product). Large amounts of test data are generated and can be targeted to cover particular areas or concerns, providing an increased possibility of identifying individual and multiple rare operating conditions that were not anticipated by either the software product's designers or its testers. Statistical testing also provides high structural coverage. It does require a stable software product. Thus, structural and functional testing are prerequisites for statistical testing of a software product.

Another aspect of software testing is the testing of software changes. Changes occur frequently during software development. These changes are the result of 1) debugging that finds an error and it is corrected, 2) new or changed requirements ("requirements creep"), and 3) modified designs as more effective or efficient implementations are found. Once a software product has been baselined approved), any change to that product should have its own "mini life cycle," including testing. Testing of a changed software product requires additional effort. Not only should it demonstrate that the change was implemented correctly, testing should also demonstrate that the change did not adversely impact other parts of the software product. Regression analysis and testing are employed to provide assurance that a change has not created problems elsewhere in the software product. Regression analysis is the determination of the impact of a change based on review of the relevant documentation (e.g., software requirements specification, software design specification, source code, test plans, test cases, test scripts, etc.) in order to identify the necessary regression tests to be run. Regression testing is the rerunning of test cases that a program has previously executed correctly and comparing the current result to the previous result in order to detect unintended effects of a software change. Regression analysis and regression testing should also be employed when using integration methods to build a software product to ensure that newly integrated modules do not adversely impact the operation of previously integrated modules.

In order to provide a thorough and rigorous examination of a software product, development testing is typically organized into levels. As an example, a software product's testing can be organized into unit, integration, and system levels of testing.

1) Unit (module or component) level testing focuses on the early examination of sub-program functionality and ensures that functionality not visible at the system level is examined by testing. Unit testing ensures that quality software units are furnished for integration into the finished software product.

2) Integration level testing focuses on the transfer of data and control across a program's internal and external interfaces. External interfaces are those with other software (including operating system software), system hardware, and the users and can be described as communications links.

3) System level testing demonstrates that all specified functionality exists and that the software product is trustworthy. This testing verifies the as-built program's functionality and performance with respect to the requirements for the software product as exhibited on the specified operating platform(s). System level software testing addresses functional concerns and the following elements of a device's software that are related to the intended use(s):

- Performance issues (e.g., response times, reliability measurements);
- Responses to stress conditions, e.g., behavior under maximum load, continuous use;
- Operation of internal and external security features;
- Effectiveness of recovery procedures, including disaster recovery;
- Usability;
- Compatibility with other software products;
- Behavior in each of the defined hardware configurations; and
- Accuracy of documentation.

Control measures (e.g., a traceability analysis) should be used to ensure that the intended coverage is achieved.

System level testing also exhibits the software product's behavior in the intended operating environment. The location of such testing is dependent upon the software developer's ability to produce the target operating environment(s). Depending upon the circumstances, simulation and/or testing at (potential) customer locations may be utilized. Test plans should identify the controls needed to ensure that the intended coverage is achieved and that proper documentation is prepared when planned system level testing is conducted at sites not directly controlled by the software developer. Also, for a software product that is a medical device or a component of a medical device that is to be used on humans prior to FDA clearance, testing involving human subjects may require an Investigational Device Exemption (IDE) or Institutional Review Board (IRB) approval.

Test procedures, test data, and test results should be documented in a manner permitting objective pass/fail decisions to be reached. They should also be suitable for review and objective decision making subsequent to running the test, and they should be suitable for use in any subsequent regression testing. Errors detected during testing should be logged, classified, reviewed, and resolved prior to release of the software. Software error data that is collected and analyzed during a development life cycle may be used to determine the suitability of the software product for release for commercial distribution. Test reports should comply with the requirements of the corresponding test plans.

Software products that perform useful functions in medical devices or their production are often complex. Software testing tools are frequently used to ensure consistency, thoroughness, and efficiency in the testing of such software products and to fulfill the requirements of the planned testing activities. These tools may include supporting software built in-house to facilitate unit (module) testing and subsequent integration testing (e.g., drivers and stubs) as well as commercial software testing tools. Such tools should have a degree of quality no less than the software product they are used to develop. Appropriate documentation providing evidence of the validation of these software tools for their intended use should be maintained (see section 6 of this guidance).

Typical Tasks – Testing by the Software Developer

- Test Planning
- Structural Test Case Identification
- Functional Test Case Identification
- Traceability Analysis - Testing
  - Unit (Module) Tests to Detailed Design
  - Integration Tests to High Level Design
  - System Tests to Software Requirements
- Unit (Module) Test Execution
- Integration Test Execution
- Functional Test Execution
- System Test Execution
- Acceptance Test Execution
- Test Results Evaluation
- Error Evaluation/Resolution
- Final Test Report

5.2.6. User Site Testing

Testing at the user site is an essential part of software validation. The Quality System regulation requires installation and inspection procedures (including testing where appropriate) as well as documentation of inspection and testing to demonstrate proper installation. (See 21 CFR §820.170.) Likewise, manufacturing equipment must meet specified requirements, and automated systems must be validated for their intended use. (See 21 CFR §820.70(g) and 21 CFR §820.70(i) respectively.)

Terminology regarding user site testing can be confusing. Terms such as beta test, site validation, user acceptance test, installation verification, and installation testing have all been used to describe user site testing. For purposes of this guidance, the term "user site testing" encompasses all of these and any other testing that takes place outside of the developer's controlled environment. This testing should take place at a user's site with the actual hardware and software that will be part of the installed system configuration. The testing is accomplished through either actual or simulated use of the software being tested within the context in which it is intended to function.

Guidance contained here is general in nature and is applicable to any user site testing. However, in some areas (e.g., blood establishment systems) there may be specific site validation issues that need to be considered in the planning of user site testing. Test planners should check with the FDA Center(s) with the corresponding product jurisdiction to determine whether there are any additional regulatory requirements for user site testing.

User site testing should follow a pre-defined written plan with a formal summary of testing and a record of formal acceptance. Documented evidence of all testing procedures, test input data, and test results should be retained.

There should be evidence that hardware and software are installed and configured as specified. Measures should ensure that all system components are exercised during the testing and that the versions of these components are those specified. The testing plan should specify testing throughout the full range of operating conditions and should specify continuation for a sufficient time to allow the system to encounter a wide spectrum of conditions and events in an effort to detect any latent faults that are not apparent during more normal activities.

Some of the evaluations that have been performed earlier by the software developer at the developer's site should be repeated at the site of actual use. These may include tests for a high volume of data, heavy loads or stresses, security, fault testing (avoidance, detection, tolerance, and recovery), error messages, and implementation of safety requirements. The developer may be able to furnish the user with some of the test data sets to be used for this purpose.

In addition to an evaluation of the system's ability to properly perform its intended functions, there should be an evaluation of the ability of the users of the system to understand and correctly interface with it. Operators should be able to perform the intended functions and respond in an appropriate and timely manner to all alarms, warnings, and error messages.

During user site testing, records should be maintained of both proper system performance and any system failures that are encountered. The revision of the system to compensate for faults detected during this user site testing should follow the same procedures and controls as for any other software change.

The developers of the software may or may not be involved in the user site testing. If the developers are involved, they may seamlessly carry over to the user's site the last portions of design-level systems testing. If the developers are not involved, it is all the more important that the user have persons who understand the importance of careful test planning, the definition of expected test results, and the recording of all test outputs.

Typical Tasks – User Site Testing

- Acceptance Test Execution
- Test Results Evaluation
- Error Evaluation/Resolution
- Final Test Report

5.2.7. Maintenance and Software Changes

As applied to software, the term maintenance does not mean the same as when applied to hardware. The operational maintenance of hardware and software are different because their failure/error mechanisms are different. Hardware maintenance typically includes preventive hardware maintenance actions, component replacement, and corrective changes. Software maintenance includes corrective, perfective, and adaptive maintenance but does not include preventive maintenance actions or software component replacement.

Changes made to correct errors and faults in the software are corrective maintenance. Changes made to the software to improve the performance, maintainability, or other attributes of the software system are perfective maintenance. Software changes to make the software system usable in a changed environment are adaptive maintenance.

When changes are made to a software system, either during initial development or during post release maintenance, sufficient regression analysis and testing should be conducted to demonstrate that portions of the software not involved in the change were not adversely impacted. This is in addition to testing that evaluates the correctness of the implemented change(s).

The specific validation effort necessary for each software change is determined by the type of change, the development products affected, and the impact of those products on the operation of the software. Careful and complete documentation of the design structure and interrelationships of various modules, interfaces, etc., can limit the validation effort needed when a change is made. The level of effort needed to fully validate a change is also dependent upon the degree to which validation of the original software was documented and archived. For example, test documentation, test cases, and results of previous verification and validation testing need to be archived if they are to be available for performing subsequent regression testing. Failure to archive this information for later use can significantly increase the level of effort and expense of revalidating the software after a change is made.

In addition to software verification and validation tasks that are part of the standard software development process, the following additional maintenance tasks should be addressed:

- **Software Validation Plan Revision** - For software that was previously validated, the existing software validation plan should be revised to support the validation of the revised software. If no previous software validation plan exists, such a plan should be established to support the validation of the revised software.
- **Anomaly Evaluation** – Software organizations frequently maintain documentation, such as software problem reports that describe software anomalies discovered and the specific corrective action taken to fix each anomaly. Too often, however, mistakes are repeated because software developers do not take the next step to determine the root causes of problems and make the process and procedural changes needed to avoid recurrence of the problem. Software anomalies should be evaluated in terms of their severity and their effects on system operation and safety, but they should also be treated as symptoms of process deficiencies in the quality system. A root cause analysis of anomalies can identify specific quality system deficiencies. Where trends are identified (e.g., recurrence of similar software anomalies), appropriate corrective and preventive actions must be implemented and documented to avoid further recurrence of similar quality problems. (See 21 CFR 820.100.)
- **Problem Identification and Resolution Tracking** - All problems discovered during maintenance of the software should be documented. The resolution of each problem should be tracked to ensure it is fixed, for historical reference, and for trending.

- **Proposed Change Assessment** - All proposed modifications, enhancements, or additions should be assessed to determine the effect each change would have on the system. This information should determine the extent to which verification and/or validation tasks need to be iterated.
- **Task Iteration** - For approved software changes, all necessary verification and validation tasks should be performed to ensure that planned changes are implemented correctly, all documentation is complete and up to date, and no unacceptable changes have occurred in software performance.
- **Documentation Updating** – Documentation should be carefully reviewed to determine which documents have been impacted by a change. All approved documents (e.g., specifications, test procedures, user manuals, etc.) that have been affected should be updated in accordance with configuration management procedures. Specifications should be updated before any maintenance and software changes are made.

SECTION 6. VALIDATION OF AUTOMATED PROCESS EQUIPMENT AND QUALITY SYSTEM SOFTWARE

The Quality System regulation requires that "when computers or automated data processing systems are used as part of production or the quality system, the [device] manufacturer shall validate computer software for its intended use according to an established protocol." (See 21 CFR §820.70(i)). This has been a regulatory requirement of FDA's medical device Good Manufacturing Practice (GMP) regulations since 1978.

In addition to the above validation requirement, computer systems that implement part of a device manufacturer's production processes or quality system (or that are used to create and maintain records required by any other FDA regulation) are subject to the Electronic Records; Electronic Signatures regulation. (See 21 CFR Part 11.) This regulation establishes additional security, data integrity, and validation requirements when records are created or maintained electronically. These additional Part 11 requirements should be carefully considered and included in system requirements and software requirements for any automated record-keeping systems. System validation and software validation should demonstrate that all Part 11 requirements have been met.

Computers and automated equipment are used extensively throughout all aspects of medical device design, laboratory testing and analysis, product inspection and acceptance, production and process control, environmental controls, packaging, labeling, traceability, document control, complaint management, and many other aspects of the quality system. Increasingly, automated plant floor operations can involve extensive use of embedded systems in:

- programmable logic controllers;
- digital function controllers;
- statistical process control;
- supervisory control and data acquisition;

- robotics;
- human-machine interfaces;
- input/output devices; and
- computer operating systems.

Software tools are frequently used to design, build, and test the software that goes into an automated medical device. Many other commercial software applications, such as word processors, spreadsheets, databases, and flowcharting software are used to implement the quality system. All of these applications are subject to the requirement for software validation, but the validation approach used for each application can vary widely.

Whether production or quality system software is developed in-house by the device manufacturer, developed by a contractor, or purchased off-the-shelf, it should be developed using the basic principles outlined elsewhere in this guidance. The device manufacturer has latitude and flexibility in defining how validation of that software will be accomplished, but validation should be a key consideration in deciding how and by whom the software will be developed or from whom it will be purchased. The software developer defines a life cycle model. Validation is typically supported by:

- verifications of the outputs from each stage of that software development life cycle; and
- checking for proper operation of the finished software in the device manufacturer's intended use environment.

6.1. How Much Validation Evidence is Needed?

The level of validation effort should be commensurate with the risk posed by the automated operation. In addition to risk other factors, such as the complexity of the process software and the degree to which the device manufacturer is dependent upon that automated process to produce a safe and effective device, determine the nature and extent of testing needed as part of the validation effort. Documented requirements and risk analysis of the automated process help to define the scope of the evidence needed to show that the software is validated for its intended use. For example, an automated milling machine may require very little testing if the device manufacturer can show that the output of the operation is subsequently fully verified against the specification before release. On the other hand, extensive testing may be needed for:

- a plant-wide electronic record and electronic signature system;
- an automated controller for a sterilization cycle; or
- automated test equipment used for inspection and acceptance of finished circuit boards in a life-sustaining / life-supporting device.

Numerous commercial software applications may be used as part of the quality system (e.g., a spreadsheet or statistical package used for quality system calculations, a graphics package used for trend analysis, or a commercial database used for recording device history records or for complaint management). The extent of validation evidence needed for such software depends on the device manufacturer's documented intended use of that software. For example, a device manufacturer who chooses not to use all the vendor-supplied capabilities of the software only needs to validate those functions that will be used and for which the device manufacturer is dependent upon the software results as part of production or the quality system. However, high risk applications should not be running in the same operating environment with non-validated software functions, even if those software functions are not used. Risk mitigation techniques such as memory partitioning or other approaches to resource protection may need to be considered when high risk applications and lower risk applications are to be used in the same operating environment. When software is upgraded or any changes are made to the software, the device manufacturer should consider how those changes may impact the "used portions" of the software and must reconfirm the validation of those portions of the software that are used. (See 21 CFR §820.70(i).)

6.2. Defined User Requirements

A very important key to software validation is a documented user requirements specification that defines:

- the "intended use" of the software or automated equipment; and
- the extent to which the device manufacturer is dependent upon that software or equipment for production of a quality medical device.

The device manufacturer (user) needs to define the expected operating environment including any required hardware and software configurations, software versions, utilities, etc. The user also needs to:

- document requirements for system performance, quality, error handling, startup, shutdown, security, etc.;
- identify any safety related functions or features, such as sensors, alarms, interlocks, logical processing steps, or command sequences; and
- define objective criteria for determining acceptable performance.

The validation must be conducted in accordance with a documented protocol, and the validation results must also be documented. (See 21 CFR §820.70(i).) Test cases should be documented that will exercise the system to challenge its performance against the pre-determined criteria, especially for its most critical parameters. Test cases should address error and alarm conditions, startup, shutdown, all applicable user functions and operator controls, potential operator errors, maximum and minimum ranges of allowed values, and stress conditions applicable to the intended use of the equipment. The test cases should be executed and the results should be recorded and evaluated to determine whether the results support a conclusion that the software is validated for its intended use.

A device manufacturer may conduct a validation using their own personnel or may depend on a third party such as the equipment/software vendor or a consultant. In any case, the device manufacturer retains the ultimate responsibility for ensuring that the production and quality system software:

- is validated according to a written procedure for the particular intended use; and

- will perform as intended in the chosen application.

The device manufacturer should have documentation including:

- defined user requirements;
- validation protocol used;
- acceptance criteria;
- test cases and results; and
- a validation summary

that objectively confirms that the software is validated for its intended use.

6.3. Validation of Off-The-Shelf Software and Automated Equipment

Most of the automated equipment and systems used by device manufacturers are supplied by third-party vendors and are purchased off-the-shelf (OTS). The device manufacturer is responsible for ensuring that the product development methodologies used by the OTS software developer are appropriate and sufficient for the device manufacturer's intended use of that OTS software. For OTS software and equipment, the device manufacturer may or may not have access to the vendor's software validation documentation. If the vendor can provide information about their system requirements, software requirements, validation process, and the results of their validation, the medical device manufacturer can use that information as a beginning point for their required validation documentation. The vendor's life cycle documentation, such as testing protocols and results, source code, design specification, and requirements specification, can be useful in establishing that the software has been validated. However, such documentation is frequently not available from commercial equipment vendors, or the vendor may refuse to share their proprietary information.

Where possible and depending upon the device risk involved, the device manufacturer should consider auditing the vendor's design and development methodologies used in the construction of the OTS software and should assess the development and validation documentation generated for the OTS software. Such audits can be conducted by the device manufacturer or by a qualified third party. The audit should demonstrate that the vendor's procedures for and results of the verification and validation activities performed the OTS software are appropriate and sufficient for the safety and effectiveness requirements of the medical device to be produced using that software.

Some vendors who are not accustomed to operating in a regulated environment may not have a documented life cycle process that can support the device manufacturer's validation requirement. Other vendors may not permit an audit. Where necessary validation information is not available from the vendor, the device manufacturer will need to perform sufficient system level "black box" testing to establish that the software meets their "user needs and intended uses." For many applications black box testing alone is not sufficient. Depending upon the risk of the device produced, the role of the OTS software in the process, the ability to audit the vendor, and the sufficiency of vendor-supplied information, the use of OTS software or equipment may or may not be appropriate, especially if there are suitable alternatives available. The device manufacturer should also consider the implications (if any) for continued maintenance and support of the OTS software should the vendor terminate their support.

For some off-the-shelf software development tools, such as software compilers, linkers, editors, and operating systems, exhaustive black-box testing by the device manufacturer may be impractical. Without such testing – a key element of the validation effort – it may not be possible to validate these software tools. However, their proper operation may be satisfactorily inferred by other means. For example, compilers are frequently certified by independent third-party testing, and commercial software products may have "bug lists", system requirements and other operational information available from the vendor that can be compared to the device manufacturer's intended use to help focus the "black-box" testing effort. Off-the-shelf operating systems need not be validated as a separate program. However, system-level validation testing of the application software should address all the operating system services used, including maximum loading conditions, file operations, handling of system error conditions, and memory constraints that may be applicable to the intended use of the application program.

For more detailed information, see the production and process software references in Appendix A.

Appendix A — References

Food and Drug Administration References

Design Control Guidance for Medical Device Manufacturers, Center for Devices and Radiological Health, Food and Drug Administration, March 1997.

Do It by Design, An Introduction to Human Factors in Medical Devices, Center for Devices and Radiological Health, Food and Drug Administration, March 1997.

Electronic Records; Electronic Signatures Final Rule, 62 Federal Register 13430 (March 20, 1997).

Glossary of Computerized System and Software Development Terminology, Division of Field Investigations, Office of Regional Operations, Office of Regulatory Affairs, Food and Drug Administration, August 1995.

Guidance for the Content of Pre-market Submissions for Software Contained in Medical Devices, Office of Device Evaluation, Center for Devices and Radiological Health, Food and Drug Administration, May 1998.

Guidance for Industry, FDA Reviewers and Compliance on Off-the-Shelf Software Use in Medical Devices, Office of Device Evaluation, Center for Devices and Radiological Health, Food and Drug Administration, September 1999.

Guideline on General Principles of Process Validation, Center for Drugs and Biologics, & Center For Devices and Radiological Health, Food and Drug Administration, May 1987.

Medical Devices; Current Good Manufacturing Practice (CGMP) Final Rule; Quality System Regulation , 61 Federal Register 52602 (October 7, 1996).

Reviewer Guidance for a Pre-Market Notification Submission for Blood Establishment Computer Software, Center for Biologics Evaluation and Research, Food and Drug Administration, January 1997

Student Manual 1, Course INV545, Computer System Validation, Division of Human Resource Development, Office of Regulatory Affairs, Food and Drug Administration, 1997.

Technical Report, Software Development Activities, Division of Field Investigations, Office of Regional Operations, Office of Regulatory Affairs, Food and Drug Administration, July 1987.

Other Government References

W. Richards Adrion, Martha A. Branstad, John C. Cherniavsky. *NBS Special Publication 500-75, Validation, Verification, and Testing of Computer Software*, Center for Programming Science and Technology, Institute for Computer Sciences and Technology, National Bureau of Standards, U.S. Department of Commerce, February 1981.

Martha A. Branstad, John C Cherniavsky, W. Richards Adrion, *NBS Special Publication 500-56, Validation, Verification, and Testing for the Individual Programmer*, Center for Programming Science and Technology, Institute for Computer Sciences and Technology, National Bureau of Standards, U.S. Department of Commerce, February 1980.

J.L. Bryant, N.P. Wilburn, *Handbook of Software Quality Assurance Techniques Applicable to the Nuclear Industry*, NUREG/CR-4640, U.S. Nuclear Regulatory Commission, 1987.

H. Hecht, et.al., *Verification and Validation Guidelines for High Integrity Systems*. NUREG/CR-6293. Prepared for U.S. Nuclear Regulatory Commission, 1995.

H. Hecht, et.al., *Review Guidelines on Software Languages for Use in Nuclear Power Plant Safety Systems, Final Report*. NUREG/CR-6463. Prepared for U.S. Nuclear Regulatory Commission, 1996.

J.D. Lawrence, W.L. *Persons, Survey of Industry Methods for Producing Highly Reliable Software*, NUREG/CR-6278, U.S. Nuclear Regulatory Commission, 1994.

J.D. Lawrence, G.G. Preckshot, *Design Factors for Safety-Critical Software, NUREG/CR-6294*, U.S. Nuclear Regulatory Commission, 1994.

Patricia B. Powell, Editor. *NBS Special Publication 500-98, Planning for Software Validation, Verification, and Testing*, Center for Programming Science and Technology, Institute for Computer Sciences and Technology, National Bureau of Standards, U.S. Department of Commerce, November 1982.

Patricia B. Powell, Editor. *NBS Special Publication 500-93, Software Validation, Verification, and Testing Technique and Tool Reference Guide*, Center for Programming Science and Technology, Institute for Computer Sciences and Technology, National Bureau of Standards, U.S. Department of Commerce, September 1982.

Delores R. Wallace, Roger U. Fujii, *NIST Special Publication 500-165, Software Verification and Validation: Its Role in Computer Assurance and Its Relationship with Software Project Management Standards*, National Computer Systems Laboratory, National Institute of Standards and Technology, U.S. Department of Commerce, September 1995.

Delores R. Wallace, Laura M. Ippolito, D. Richard Kuhn, *NIST Special Publication 500-204, High Integrity Software, Standards and Guidelines*, Computer Systems Laboratory, National Institute of Standards and Technology, U.S. Department of Commerce, September 1992.

Delores R. Wallace, et.al. *NIST Special Publication 500-234, Reference Information for the Software Verification and Validation Process*. Computer Systems Laboratory, National Institute of Standards and Technology, U.S. Department of Commerce, March 1996.

Delores R. Wallace, Editor. *NIST Special Publication 500-235, Structured Testing: A Testing Methodology Using the Cyclomatic Complexity Metric*. Computer Systems Laboratory, National Institute of Standards and Technology, U.S. Department of Commerce, August 1996.

International and National Consensus Standards

ANSI / ANS-10.4-1987, *Guidelines for the Verification and Validation of Scientific and Engineering Computer Programs for the Nuclear Industry*, American National Standards Institute, 1987.

ANSI / ASQC Standard D1160-1995, *Formal Design Reviews*, American Society for Quality Control, 1995.

ANSI / UL 1998:1998, *Standard for Safety for Software in Programmable Components*, Underwriters Laboratories, Inc., 1998.

AS 3563.1-1991, *Software Quality Management System, Part 1: Requirements*. Published by Standards Australia [Standards Association of Australia], 1 The Crescent, Homebush, NSW 2140.

AS 3563.2-1991, *Software Quality Management System, Part 2: Implementation Guide*. Published by Standards Australia [Standards Association of Australia], 1 The Crescent, Homebush, NSW 2140.

IEC 60601-1-4:1996, *Medical electrical equipment, Part 1: General requirements for safety, 4. Collateral Standard: Programmable electrical medical systems*. International Electrotechnical Commission, 1996.

IEC 61506:1997, *Industrial process measurement and control – Documentation of application software*. International Electrotechnical Commission, 1997.

IEC 61508:1998, *Functional safety of electrical/electronic/programmable electronic safety-related systems*. International Electrotechnical Commission, 1998.

IEEE Std 1012-1986, *Software Verification and Validation Plans*, Institute for Electrical and Electronics Engineers, 1986.

IEEE Standards Collection, *Software Engineering, Institute of Electrical and Electronics Engineers*, Inc., 1994. ISBN 1-55937-442-X.

ISO 8402:1994, *Quality management and quality assurance – Vocabulary*. International Organization for Standardization, 1994.

ISO 9000-3:1997, *Quality management and quality assurance standards - Part 3: Guidelines for the application of ISO 9001:1994 to the development, supply, installation and maintenance of computer software*. International Organization for Standardization, 1997.

ISO 9001:1994, *Quality systems – Model for quality assurance in design, development, production, installation, and servicing*. International Organization for Standardization, 1994.

ISO 13485:1996, *Quality systems – Medical devices – Particular requirements for the application of ISO 9001*. International Organization for Standardization, 1996.

ISO/IEC 12119:1994, *Information technology – Software packages – Quality requirements and testing*, Joint Technical Committee ISO/IEC JTC 1, International Organization for Standardization and International Electrotechnical Commission, 1994.

ISO/IEC 12207:1995, *Information technology – Software life cycle processes*, Joint Technical Committee ISO/IEC JTC 1, Subcommittee SC 7, International Organization for Standardization and International Electrotechnical Commission, 1995.

ISO/IEC 14598:1999, *Information technology – Software product evaluation*, Joint Technical Committee ISO/IEC JTC 1, Subcommittee SC 7, International Organization for Standardization and International Electrotechnical Commission, 1999.

ISO 14971-1:1998, *Medical Devices – Risk Management – Part 1: Application of Risk Analysis.* International Organization for Standardization, 1998.

Software Considerations in Airborne Systems and Equipment Certification. Special Committee 167 of RTCA. RTCA Inc., Washington, D.C. Tel: 202-833-9339. Document No. RTCA/DO-178B, December 1992.

Production Process Software References

The Application of the Principles of GLP to Computerized Systems, Environmental Monograph #116, Organization for Economic Cooperation and Development (OECD), 1995.

George J. Grigonis, Jr., Edward J. Subak, Jr., and Michael Wyrick, "Validation Key Practices for Computer Systems Used in Regulated Operations," *Pharmaceutical Technology*, June 1997.

Guide to Inspection of Computerized Systems in Drug Processing, Reference Materials and Training Aids for Investigators, Division of Drug Quality Compliance, Associate Director for Compliance, Office of Drugs, National Center for Drugs and Biologics, & Division of Field Investigations, Associate Director for Field Support, Executive Director of Regional Operations, Food and Drug Administration, February 1983.

Daniel P. Olivier, "Validating Process Software", *FDA Investigator Course: Medical Device Process Validation*, Food and Drug Administration.

GAMP Guide For Validation of Automated Systems in Pharmaceutical Manufacture,Version V3.0, Good Automated Manufacturing Practice (GAMP) Forum, March 1998:

Volume 1, Part 1: User Guide

Part 2: Supplier Guide

Volume 2: Best Practice for User and Suppliers.

Technical Report No. 18, Validation of Computer-Related Systems. PDA Committee on Validation of Computer-Related Systems. PDA Journal of Pharmaceutical Science and Technology, Volume 49, Number 1, January-February 1995 Supplement.

Validation Compliance Annual 1995, International Validation Forum, Inc.

General Software Quality References

Boris Beizer, *Black Box Testing, Techniques for Functional Testing of Software and Systems*, John Wiley & Sons, 1995. ISBN 0-471-12094-4.

Boris Beizer, *Software System Testing and Quality Assurance*, International Thomson Computer Press, 1996. ISBN 1-85032-821-8.

Boris Beizer, *Software Testing Techniques, Second Edition*, Van Nostrand Reinhold, 1990. ISBN 0-442-20672-0.

Richard Bender, *Writing Testable Requirements, Version 1.0*, Bender & Associates, Inc., Larkspur, CA 94777, 1996.

Frederick P. Brooks, Jr., *The Mythical Man-Month, Essays on Software Engineering*, Addison-Wesley Longman, Anniversary Edition, 1995. ISBN 0-201-83595-9.

Silvana Castano, et.al., *Database Security*, ACM Press, Addison-Wesley Publishing Company, 1995. ISBN 0-201-59375-0.

Computerized Data Systems for Nonclinical Safety Assessment, Current Concepts and Quality Assurance, Drug Information Association, Maple Glen, PA, September 1988.

M. S. Deutsch, *Software Verification and Validation, Realistic Project Approaches*, Prentice Hall, 1982.

Robert H. Dunn and Richard S. Ullman, *TQM for Computer Software, Second Edition*, McGraw-Hill, Inc., 1994. ISBN 0-07-018314-7.

Elfriede Dustin, Jeff Rashka, and John Paul, *Automated Software Testing – Introduction, Management and Performance*, Addison Wesley Longman, Inc., 1999. ISBN 0-201-43287-0.

Robert G. Ebenau and Susan H. Strauss, *Software Inspection Process*, McGraw-Hill, 1994. ISBN 0-07-062166-7.

Richard E. Fairley, *Software Engineering Concepts*, McGraw-Hill Publishing Company, 1985. ISBN 0-07-019902-7.

Michael A. Friedman and Jeffrey M. Voas, S*oftware Assessment - Reliability, Safety, Testability*, Wiley-Interscience, John Wiley & Sons Inc., 1995. ISBN 0-471-01009-X.

Tom Gilb, Dorothy Graham, *Software Inspection*, Addison-Wesley Publishing Company, 1993. ISBN 0-201-63181-4.

Robert B. Grady, *Practical Software Metrics for Project Management and Process Improvement*, PTR Prentice-Hall Inc., 1992. ISBN 0-13-720384-5.

Les Hatton, Safer C: *Developing Software for High-integrity and Safety-critical Systems*, McGraw-Hill Book Company, 1994. ISBN 0-07-707640-0.

Janis V. Halvorsen, *A Software Requirements Specification Document Model for the Medical Device Industry*, Proceedings IEEE SOUTHEASTCON '93, Banking on Technology, April 4th -7th, 1993, Charlotte, North Carolina.

Debra S. Herrmann, *Software Safety and Reliability: Techniques, Approaches and Standards of Key Industrial Sectors*, IEEE Computer Society, 1999. ISBN 0-7695-0299-7.

Bill Hetzel, *The Complete Guide to Software Testing, Second Edition*, A Wiley-QED Publication, John Wiley & Sons, Inc., 1988. ISBN 0-471-56567-9.

Watts S. Humphrey, *A Discipline for Software Engineering*. Addison-Wesley Longman, 1995. ISBN 0-201-54610-8.

Watts S. Humphrey, *Managing the Software Process*, Addison-Wesley Publishing Company, 1989. ISBN 0-201-18095-2.

Capers Jones, *Software Quality, Analysis and Guidelines for Success*, International Thomson Computer Press, 1997. ISBN 1-85032-867-6.

J.M. Juran, Frank M. *Gryna, Quality Planning and Analysis, Third Edition*, McGraw-Hill, 1993. ISBN 0-07-033183-9.

Stephen H. Kan, *Metrics and Models in Software Quality Engineering*, Addison-Wesley Publishing Company, 1995. ISBN 0-201-63339-6.

Cem Kaner, Jack Falk, Hung Quoc Nguyen, *Testing Computer Software, Second Edition*, Vsn Nostrand Reinhold, 1993. ISBN 0-442-01361-2.

Craig Kaplan, Ralph Clark, Victor Tang, *Secrets of Software Quality, 40 Innovations from IBM*, McGraw-Hill, 1995. ISBN 0-07-911795-3.

Edward Kit, *Software Testing in the Real World*, Addison-Wesley Longman, 1995. ISBN 0-201-87756-2.

Alan Kusinitz, "Software Validation", *Current Issues in Medical Device Quality Systems*, Association for the Advancement of Medical Instrumentation, 1997. ISBN 1-57020-075-0.

Nancy G. Leveson, *Safeware, System Safety and Computers*, Addison-Wesley Publishing Company, 1995. ISBN 0-201-11972-2.

Michael R. Lyu, Editor, *Handbook of Software Reliability Engineering*, IEEE Computer Society Press, McGraw-Hill, 1996. ISBN 0-07-039400-8.

Steven R. Mallory, *Software Development and Quality Assurance for the Healthcare Manufacturing Industries*, Interpharm Press,Inc., 1994. ISBN 0-935184-58-9.

Brian Marick, *The Craft of Software Testing*, Prentice Hall PTR, 1995. ISBN 0-13-177411-5.
Steve McConnell, Rapid Development, Microsoft Press, 1996. ISBN 1-55615-900-5.

Glenford J. Myers, *The Art of Software Testing*, John Wiley & Sons, 1979. ISBN 0-471-04328-1.

Peter G. Neumann, *Computer Related Risks*, ACM Press/Addison-Wesley Publishing Co., 1995. ISBN 0-201-55805-X.

Daniel Olivier, *Conducting Software Audits, Auditing Software for Conformance to FDA Requirements*, Computer Application Specialists, San Diego, CA, 1994.

William Perry, *Effective Methods for Software Testing*, John Wiley & Sons, Inc. 1995. ISBN 0-471-06097-6.

William E. Perry, Randall W. Rice, *Surviving the Top Ten Challenges of Software Testing*, Dorset House Publishing, 1997. ISBN 0-932633-38-2.

Roger S. Pressman, *Software Engineering, A Practitioner's Approach, Third Edition*, McGraw-Hill Inc., 1992. ISBN 0-07-050814-3.

Roger S. Pressman, *A Manager's Guide to Software Engineering*, McGraw-Hill Inc., 1993 ISBN 0-07-050820-8.

A. P. Sage, J. D. Palmer, *Software Systems Engineering*, John Wiley & Sons, 1990.

Joc Sanders, Eugene Curran, *Software Quality*, Addison-Wesley Publishing Co., 1994. ISBN 0-201-63198-9.

Ken Shumate, Marilyn Keller, Software Specification and Design, *A Disciplined Approach for Real-Time Systems*, John Wiley & Sons, 1992. ISBN 0-471-53296-7.

Dennis D. Smith, *Designing Maintainable Software*, Springer-Verlag, 1999.ISBN 0-387-98783-5.

Ian Sommerville, Software Engineering, Third Edition, Addison Wesley Publishing Co., 1989. ISBN 0-201-17568-1.

Karl E. Wiegers, *Creating a Software Engineering Culture*, Dorset House Publishing, 1996. ISBN 0-932633-33-1.

Karl E. Wiegers, *Software Inspection, Improving Quality with Software Inspections, Software Development*, April 1995, pages 55-64.

Karl E. Wiegers, *Software Requirements*, Microsoft Press, 1999. ISBN 0-7356-0631-5.

Appendix B — Development Team

<u>Center for Devices and Radiological Health</u>

Office of Compliance	Stewart Crumpler
Office of Device Evaluation	James Cheng
	Donna-Bea Tillman
Office of Health and Industry Programs	Bryan Benesch
	Dick Sawyer
Office of Science and Technology	John Murray
Office of Surveillance and Biometrics	Howard Press

<u>Center for Drug Evaluation and Research</u>

Office of Medical Policy	Charles Snipes

<u>Center for Biologics Evaluation and Research</u>

Office of Compliance and Biologics Quality	Alice Godziemski

<u>Office of Regulatory Affairs</u>

Office of Regional Operations	David Bergeson
	Joan Loreng

CSV

Chapter 14

Changes to Existing Medical Software Policies Resulting from Section 3060 of the 21st Century Cures Act

Guidance for Industry and FDA Staff

September 27, 2019.
U.S. Department of Health and Human Services
Food and Drug Administration
Center for Devices and Radiological Health
Center for Biologics Evaluation and Research

I. Introduction

Section 3060(a) of the 21st Century Cures Act (Cures Act) amended section 520 of the Federal Food, Drug, and Cosmetic Act (FD&C Act) on December 13, 2016, removing certain software functions from the definition of device in section 201(h) of the FD&C Act. This guidance provides FDA's current thinking regarding the amended device definition and the resulting effect the amended definition has on FDA's guidances related to medical device software. The concepts detailed in this guidance are also reflected in the following guidance documents through Level 2 updates:[1]

- General Wellness: Policy for Low Risk Devices[2]
- Mobile Medical Applications[3]
- Off-The-Shelf Software Use in Medical Devices[4]
- Medical Device Data Systems, Medical Image Storage Devices, and Medical Image Communications Devices[5]

The following guidance document has been withdrawn, for the reasons described in Section IV.D:

- Guidance for the Submission of Premarket Notifications for Medical Image Management Devices

---

1 A Level 2 guidance document sets forth "existing practices or minor changes in interpretation or policy. Level 2 guidance documents include all guidance documents that are not classified as Level 1" (21 CFR 10.115(c)(2)). Because this final guidance sets forth the initial interpretations of FDA's statutory and regulatory requirements relating to software functions, it is a Level 1 guidance (21 CFR 10.115(c)(1)). FDA is making Level 2 updates to the listed guidance documents to make them consistent with existing practices as expressed in this final guidance.

2 Available at https://www.fda.gov/regulatory-information/search-fda-guidance-documents/general-wellness-policy-low-risk-devices.

3 Available at https://www.fda.gov/regulatory-information/search-fda-guidance-documents/policy-device-software-functions-and-mobile-medical-applications.

4 Available at https://www.fda.gov/regulatory-information/search-fda-guidance-documents/shelf-software-use-medical-devices.

5 Available at https://www.fda.gov/regulatory-information/search-fda-guidance-documents/medical-device-data-systems-medical-image-storage-devices-and-medical-image-communications-devices.

FDA's guidance documents, including this guidance, do not establish legally enforceable responsibilities. Instead, guidances describe the Agency's current thinking on a topic and should be viewed only as recommendations, unless specific regulatory or statutory requirements are cited. The use of the word *should* in Agency guidance means that something is suggested or recommended, but not required.

II. Background

On December 13, 2016, the Cures Act was enacted. Section 3060(a) of this legislation, titled "Clarifying Medical Software Regulation," amended the FD&C Act to add section 520(o), which describes software functions that are excluded from the definition of device in 201(h) of the FD&C Act. Section 3060(d) of the Cures Act amended section 201(h) of the FD&C Act to state that the term device does not include the software functions excluded pursuant to section 520(o). This guidance focuses on section 520(o)(1)(A) – (D) of the FD&C Act, reproduced below.

Section 520 of the Federal Food, Drug, and Cosmetic Act (21 U.S.C. 360j)

(o) REGULATION OF MEDICAL AND CERTAIN DECISIONS SUPPORT SOFTWARE.—

(1) The term device, as defined in section 201(h), shall not include a software function that is intended—

(A) for administrative support of a health care facility, including the processing and maintenance of financial records, claims or billing information, appointment schedules, business analytics, information about patient populations, admissions, practice and inventory management, analysis of historical claims data to predict future utilization or cost-effectiveness, determination of health benefit eligibility, population health management, and laboratory workflow;

(B) for maintaining or encouraging a healthy lifestyle and is unrelated to the diagnosis, cure, mitigation, prevention, or treatment of a disease or condition;

(C) to serve as electronic patient records, including patient-provided information, to the extent that such records are intended to transfer, store, convert formats, or display the equivalent of a paper medical chart, so long as—

(i) such records were created, stored, transferred, or reviewed by health care professionals, or by individuals working under supervision of such professionals;

(ii) such records are part of health information technology that is certified under section 3001(c)(5) of the Public Health Service Act; and

(iii) such function is not intended to interpret or analyze patient records, including medical image data, for the purpose of the diagnosis, cure, mitigation, prevention, or treatment of a disease or condition;

(D) for transferring, storing, converting formats, or displaying clinical laboratory test or other device data and results, findings by a health care professional with respect to such data and results, general information about such findings, and general background information about such laboratory test or other device, unless such function is intended to interpret or analyze clinical laboratory test or other device data, results, and findings...

III. Scope

This guidance details the changes to existing guidance documents that relate to the regulation of the software functions described in section 520(o)(1)(A) – (D) of the FD&C Act. These sections describe software functions that do not meet the device definition in 201(h) of the FD&C Act. Section 3060 also describes limited circumstances when software functions described in 520(o)(1)(A) – (D) would remain devices.[6,7]

FDA provides clarification of its proposed interpretation of section 520(o)(1)(E) of the FD&C Act, which is for software functions intended to provide decision support for the diagnosis, treatment, prevention, cure, or mitigation of disease or other conditions (often referred to as clinical decision support software), in a separate guidance document. Section 520(o)(2) of the FD&C Act describes the regulation of a product with multiple functions, including at least one device function and at least one software function that is not a device. FDA also provides its proposed recommendations on the regulation of such products with multifunctionality in a separate guidance document.

IV. Interpretation of the Cures Act and Modifications to Existing Guidance Documents

FDA's interpretation of each provision of section 520(o)(1)(A) – 520(o)(1)(D) of the FD&C Act, described in Sections A – D below has been added to the Background sections of the indicated guidances that have been revised, after consideration of timely filed comments, through Level 2 updates to incorporate the changes detailed in this guidance. Similarly, FDA has made changes to the examples in the guidances, after consideration of comments, through Level 2 updates, as described below.

Section 3060 of the Cures Act created a function-specific definition, and as such, the functions excluded from the device definition under section 520(o) of the FD&C Act are independent of the platform on which they might run. In order to clarify this, we have made changes to the relevant guidances, through Level 2 updates. Additionally, where appropriate, we are clarifying that the policies in the guidance documents are function-specific and apply across platforms. For example, as appropriate, instances of "mobile application" in the Mobile Medical Applications (MMA)

6 The Cures Act also provides that a software function described in section 520(o)(1)(A) – (D) of the FD&C Act will not be excluded from the device definition under section 201(h) of the FD&C Act if FDA makes a finding that the software function would be reasonably likely to have serious adverse health consequences and certain substantive and procedural criteria are met. (Section 520(o)(3) of the FD&C Act).

7 The Cures Act further provides that a software function described in section 520(o)(1)(A) – (D) of the FD&C Act will not be excluded from the device definition under section 201(h) of the FD&C Act if the software meets the criteria for class III classification under section 513(a)(1)(C) of the FD&C Act. (Section 520(o)(4)(C) of the FD&C Act). The Cures Act also states that this statutory provision shall not be construed to limit FDA's authority to regulate software used in the manufacture and transfusion of blood and blood components to assist in the prevention of disease in humans. (Section 520(o)(4)(B) of the FD&C Act).

guidance has been changed to "software function," and the title of the guidance has been revised to "Policy for Device Software Functions and Mobile Medical Applications."

A. Software Function Intended for Administrative Support of a Health Care Facility

Section 520(o)(1)(A) of the FD&C Act states that the term "device" does not include a software function that is intended "for administrative support of a health care facility, including the processing and maintenance of financial records, claims or billing information, appointment schedules, business analytics, information about patient populations, admissions, practice and inventory management, analysis of historical claims data to predict future utilization or cost-effectiveness, determination of health benefit eligibility, population health management, and laboratory workflow." FDA has not historically considered most of these software functions to be devices; however, we propose the following modification in order to provide additional clarity.

Section 3.2.2. of the Guidance for Off-the-Shelf Software Use in Medical Devices,[8] titled "Exemption of Laboratory Information Management Systems," has been removed from the guidance. Laboratory Information Systems (LIS) and Laboratory Information Management Systems (LIMS) functions intended for administrative support of laboratories and/or for transferring, storing, converting formats, or displaying clinical laboratory test data and results are not considered to be within the definition of the term device, according to section 201(h) of the FD&C Act, as amended by the Cures Act (see section 520(o)(1)(A) and (D) of the FD&C Act). Therefore, these software functions are not subject to requirements under the FD&C Act. However, some LIS and LIMS include software functions that remain device functions, including software functions that analyze medical device data in order to provide a notification or flag (e.g., that a parameter is out of range) and such functions will continue to be regulated as devices as specified in Section IV.D.

B. Software Function Intended for Maintaining or Encouraging a Healthy Lifestyle

FDA considers a product with an intended use for maintaining or encouraging a "healthy lifestyle" to mean a product with an intended use that encourages or maintains a "general state of health or healthy activity," as defined in the FDA guidance General Wellness: Policy for Low Risk Devices ("General Wellness Guidance").[9] In that guidance, CDRH defines a general wellness product as products that (1) are intended for only general wellness use, as defined in that guidance, and (2) present a low risk to the safety of users and other persons. That guidance defines two categories of general wellness intended uses:

(1) an intended use that relates to maintaining or encouraging a general state of health or a healthy activity, or

(2) an intended use that relates the role of healthy lifestyle with helping to reduce the risk or impact of certain chronic diseases or conditions and where it is well understood

8 Available at https://www.fda.gov/regulatory-information/search-fda-guidance-documents/shelf-software-use-medical-devices.

9 Available at https://www.fda.gov/regulatory-information/search-fda-guidance-documents/general-wellness-policy-low-risk-devices.

and accepted that healthy lifestyle choices may play an important role in health outcomes for the disease or condition.

Section 520(o)(1)(B) of the FD&C Act states that the term device does not include a software function that is intended "for maintaining or encouraging a healthy lifestyle and is unrelated to the diagnosis, cure, mitigation, prevention, or treatment of a disease or condition." This provision affects the two categories of general wellness intended uses differently, as described below:

1. General Wellness Intended Use That Relates to Maintaining or Encouraging a General State of Health or a Healthy Activity

According to section 520(o)(1)(B) of the FD&C Act, a software function with a healthy lifestyle claim (e.g., products that fall within the first category of general wellness intended uses as defined by the General Wellness Guidance) is not a device as long as its claims are unrelated to the diagnosis, cure, mitigation, prevention, or treatment of a disease or condition. For example, software with healthy lifestyle claims, such as weight management, physical fitness, relaxation or stress management, mental acuity, self-esteem, sleep management, or sexual function, are not devices when not related to the diagnosis, cure, mitigation, prevention, or treatment of a disease or condition.

Section 520(o)(1) of the FD&C Act describes software functions, not hardware products, that do not meet the definition of a device under section 201(h) of the FD&C Act as amended. Therefore, hardware with general wellness intended uses that relate to maintaining or encouraging a general state of health or healthy activity that otherwise meet the definition of device in section 201(h) will continue to be regulated as devices. FDA notes that many such functions do not otherwise meet the definition of a device under section 201(h) of the FD&C Act; however, for those hardware products that do otherwise meet the definition of device, FDA intends to apply the considerations in the General Wellness Guidance.

2. General Wellness Product Use That Relates the Role of Healthy Lifestyle with Helping to Reduce the Risk or Impact of Certain Chronic Diseases or Conditions and Where it is Well Understood and Accepted That Healthy Lifestyle Choices May Play an Important Role in Health Outcomes for the Disease or Condition

If the intended use of the software function is related to the diagnosis, cure, mitigation, prevention, or treatment of a disease or condition, then the product is not excluded from the definition of the term "device" under section 520(o)(1)(B) of the FD&C Act. Since the second category of a general wellness intended uses, as defined in the General Wellness Guidance, relates to the mitigation or prevention of a disease or condition, these products are not excluded from the definition of device as modified by this new provision of the FD&C Act. This second category of general wellness intended uses relates to sustaining or offering general improvement to functions associated with a general state of health while making reference to help reduce the risk of or help living well with certain chronic diseases or conditions. FDA's policy for general wellness products in the second category can be found in the General Wellness Guidance.[10]

10 Available at https://www.fda.gov/regulatory-information/search-fda-guidance-documents/general-well-

The following examples in Section V of the General Wellness Guidance are not devices:

- A mobile application that plays music to "soothe and relax" an individual and to "manage stress." Such a software function is not a device function (Illustrative Example 1).
- A mobile application that solely monitors and records daily energy expenditure and cardiovascular workout activities to "allow awareness of one's exercise activities to improve or maintain good cardiovascular health." Such a software function is not a device function (Illustrative Example 2).
- A mobile application that monitors and records food consumption to "manage dietary activity for weight management and alert the user, health care provider, or family member of unhealthy dietary activity." Such a software function is not a device function (Illustrative Example 3).

These examples remain in the General Wellness Guidance, because they continue to meet the definition of general wellness products; however, the title of Section V has been changed to "Examples of General Wellness Products that Are Not Medical Devices and Examples of General Wellness Products that Are Medical Devices for which FDA Does Not Intend to Enforce Requirements" to reflect the bullets above that indicate that some of these examples are not medical devices under section 201(h) of the FD&C Act.

For the MMA guidance,[11] the following examples in Appendix B (Examples of mobile apps for which FDA intends to exercise enforcement discretion) have been moved to Appendix A (Examples of mobile apps that are NOT medical devices) of the MMA Guidance, because they no longer meet the definition of the term "device" pursuant to section 520(o)(1)(B) of the FD&C Act:

- Mobile apps that are intended for individuals to log, record, track, evaluate, or make decisions or behavioral suggestions related to developing or maintaining general fitness, health or wellness, such as those that:
  - Provide tools to promote or encourage healthy eating, exercise, weight loss, or other activities generally related to a healthy lifestyle or wellness;
  - Provide dietary logs, calorie counters, or make dietary suggestions;
  - Provide meal planners and recipes;
  - Track general daily activities or make exercise or posture suggestions;
  - Track a normal baby's sleeping and feeding habits;
  - Actively monitor and trend exercise activity;
  - Help healthy people track the quantity or quality of their normal sleep patterns;
  - Provide and track scores from mind-challenging games or generic "brain age" tests;

ness-policy-low-risk-devices.

11 Available at https://www.fda.gov/regulatory-information/search-fda-guidance-documents/policy-device-software-functions-and-mobile-medical-applications.

- Provide daily motivational tips (e.g., via text or other types of messaging) to reduce stress and promote a positive mental outlook;
- Use social gaming to encourage healthy lifestyle habits;
- Calculate calories burned in a workout.

C. Software Function Intended to Serve as Electronic Patient Records

Under section 520(o)(1)(C) of the FD&C Act, the term device does not include certain software functions that are intended to serve as electronic patient records. Specifically, software functions that are intended to transfer, store, convert formats, or display electronic patient records that are the equivalent of a paper medical chart are not devices, if all the following three criteria outlined in section 520(o)(1)(C)(i) – (iii) are met:

1. Such records were created, stored, transferred, or reviewed by health care professionals (HCPs), or by individuals working under supervision of such professionals, (section 520(o)(1)(C)(i) of the FD&C Act);
2. Such records are part of information technology certified under a program of voluntary certification kept or recognized by the Office of the National Coordinator for Health Information Technology (ONC) under section 3001(c)(5) of the Public Health Service Act ("ONC Health IT Certification Program")[12](section 520(o)(1)(C)(ii) of the FD&C Act); and
3. Such software functions are not intended for interpretation or analysis of patient records, including medical image data, for the purpose of the diagnosis, cure, mitigation, prevention, or treatment of a disease or condition (section 520(o)(1)(C)(iii) of the FD&C Act).

1. Records created, stored, transferred, or reviewed by HCPs, patients, or other individuals

Section 520(o)(1)(C)(i) of the FD&C Act describes software functions that are intended to transfer, store, convert formats, or display electronic patient records that are not devices, if those functions are performed by HCPs or individuals working under HCP supervision.

Software functions that enable patients, individuals, or non-HCPs to create, store, or transfer health records are considered personal health records (PHRs). These software functions in PHR systems that are not intended for use in the diagnosis, cure, mitigation, prevention, or treatment of a disease or condition are not devices under section 201(h) of the FD&C Act.

2. Certified under ONC Health IT Certification Program

Under section 520(o)(1)(C) of the FD&C Act, the term device does not include software functions that meet the other criteria in section 520(o)(1)(C)(i) and (iii) of the FD&C Act and that are certified under the ONC Health IT Certification Program.

12 "About the ONC Health IT Certification Program," available at https://www.healthit.gov/policy-researchers-implementers/about-onc-health-it-certification-program. A comprehensive listing of all health information technology, which has been certified under the ONC Health IT Certification program, is available at the Certified Health IT Product List at https://chpl.healthit.gov/#/resources/overview.

Based on our current understanding of the risks of these devices, FDA does not intend at this time to enforce compliance to the requirements of the FD&C Act for software functions that are not certified under the ONC Health IT Certification Program if they meet the other criteria in section 520(o)(1)(C)(i) and (iii) of the FD&C Act.[13]

As described above, software functions in PHR systems that are intended for use by patients, individuals, or non-HCPs are not devices under section 201(h) of the FD&C Act (not by operation of section 520(o) of the FD&C Act). As such, there is no requirement for ONC certification of these PHR software functions.

3. Not intended for interpretation or analysis of patient records

Software functions excluded from the device definition by section 520(o)(1)(C) of the FD&C Act may be contained in electronic health record (EHR) systems, PHR systems, and other health information technology (IT). Such EHR or PHR systems may also contain other software functions that could meet the definition of a device. FDA's approach to oversight of software functions that meet the definition of a device in a system with software functions that do not meet the definition of device (products with multiple functions) will be addressed in a separate guidance document. Similarly, FDA's approach to oversight of software functions that provide interpretation or analysis of records will be addressed in a separate guidance document on section 520(o)(1)(E) of the FD&C Act.

Therefore, in the MMA Guidance,[14] the following examples in Section V.B (Examples of mobile apps for which FDA intends to exercise enforcement discretion) are not devices (pursuant to section 520(o)(1)(C) of the FD&C Act), and have been moved to Appendix A (Examples of mobile apps that are NOT medical devices) of that guidance:

- **Software functions that enable individuals to interact with EHR software certified under the ONC Health IT Certification Program** – These are software functions that provide individuals with access to health record systems or enable them to gain electronic access to health information stored within an EHR system. Software functions that only allow individuals to view, transfer, or download EHR data are also included in this category. These software functions are generally meant to facilitate general patient health information management and health record-keeping activities.
    - Note: This example has been changed to clarify that only EHR software functions certified under the ONC Health IT Certification Program are not devices according to the FD&C Act, as amended by the Cures Act. This example has also been changed where it previously described "mobile apps" to the term "software function." As described above, similar changes are made throughout the MMA guidance, but not detailed in this guidance.
    - For clarity, this example and other types of electronic patient record functions must meet the full description of section 520(o)(1)(C) in the FD&C Act, in that

CH 14

13 "Nothing in this subsection shall be construed as limiting the authority of the [FDA] to— (A) exercise enforcement discretion as to any device subject to regulation under this Act . . ." (section 520(o)(4) of the FD&C Act).
14 "Nothing in this subsection shall be construed as limiting the authority of the [FDA] to— (A) exercise enforcement discretion as to any device subject to regulation under this Act . . ." (section 520(o)(4) of the FD&C Act).

they are not devices only if they are reviewed by HCPs, certified under the ONC Health IT Certification Program, and are not intended for interpretation or analysis for the purpose of the diagnosis, cure, mitigation, prevention, or treatment of a disease or condition. However, FDA does not intend, at this time and based on our current understanding of the risks of these devices, to enforce compliance with requirements of the FD&C Act that apply to these software functions if the only requirement of 520(o)(1)(C) that they fail to meet is certification under the ONC Health IT Certification Program.

- Provide patients with simple tools to organize and track their health information;
- Provide easy access to information related to patients' health conditions or treatments;
- Help patients document, show, or communicate potential medical conditions to health care providers;
- **Mobile apps that provide patients with simple tools to organize and track their health information** – These are apps that provide patients with tools to organize and track health information without providing recommendations to alter or change a previously prescribed treatment or therapy. Examples include:
  - Apps that provide simple tools for patients with specific conditions or chronic disease (e.g., obesity, anorexia, arthritis, diabetes, heart disease) to record their events or measurements (e.g., blood pressure measurements, drug intake times, diet, daily routine or emotional state) and share this information with their health care provider as part of a disease-management plan.
    - Note this example has been modified to replace "log, track, or trend" with "record" to align with the language in the Cures Act.
- **Mobile apps that are specifically marketed to help patients document, show, or communicate to providers potential medical conditions** – These products either pose little or no risk, or are the sole responsibility of the health care providers who have used them in medical applications. Examples include:
  - Apps that serve as videoconferencing portals specifically intended for medical use and to enhance communications between patients, health care providers, and caregivers;
  - Note this example has been modified to remove the sentence: These are apps that in their labeling or promotional materials are not promoted for medical uses but which, by virtue of other circumstances surrounding their distribution, may meet the definition of a medical device.
  - The second example included as a sub-bullet remains a device function under enforcement discretion, because its functions extend beyond functions intended to transfer, store, convert formats, or display the equivalent of a paper medical chart. This example remains in Section V.B (Examples of mobile apps for which FDA intends to exercise enforcement discretion) of the MMA guidance: Apps specifically intended for medical uses that utilize the mobile device's built-in camera or a

connected camera for purposes of documenting or transmitting pictures (e.g., photos of a patient's skin lesions or wounds) to supplement or augment what would otherwise be a verbal description in a consultation between health care providers or between health care providers and patients/caregivers.

And in the MMA Guidance,[15] the following examples have been moved from Appendix B (Examples of mobile apps for which FDA intends to exercise enforcement discretion) to Appendix A (Examples of mobile apps that are NOT medical devices). The phrase "that is [or are] certified under the ONC Health IT Certification Program" was added to these examples, as appropriate, to clarify that EHR software functions are not devices only if they are certified under the ONC Health IT Certification Program.

- Mobile apps that enable, during an encounter, a health care provider to access their patient's personal health record (health information) that is hosted on a web-based or other platform;
- Software functions for HCPs certified under the ONC Health IT Certification Program, such as those that help track or manage patient immunizations by documenting the need for immunization, consent form, and immunization lot number.
    - This example has been changed from "assessing the need for immunization" to "documenting the need..." because the example is intended to serve as an example of an electronic patient record, and not clinical decision support software. FDA intends to provide clarification of section 520(o)(1)(E) of the FD&C Act and clinical decision support software in a separate guidance document.
- Mobile apps that help asthmatics record (i.e., collect and log) inhaler usage, asthma episodes experienced, location of user at the time of an attack, or environmental triggers of asthma attacks.
    - Note this example has been changed to replace the word "track" with "record (i.e., collect and log)".
- Software functions certified under the ONC Health IT Certification Program that prompt the HCP to manually enter symptomatic, behavioral or environmental information, the specifics of which are pre-defined by a HCP, and store the information for later review;
- Mobile apps that record the clinical conversation a clinician has with a patient and sends it (or a link) to the patient to access after the visit;
- Mobile apps that allow a user to record (i.e., collect and log) data, such as blood glucose, blood pressure, heart rate, weight, or other data from a device to eventually share with a health care provider, or upload it to an online (cloud) database, personal health record, or electronic health record that is certified under the ONC Health IT Certification Program.
    - Note this example has been modified to replace "collect, log, track and trend" with "record (i.e., collect and log)".

15 Available at https://www.fda.gov/regulatory-information/search-fda-guidance-documents/policy-device-software-functions-and-mobile-medical-applications.

- Enable patients or providers to interact with PHR systems or EHR systems that are certified under the ONC Health IT Certification Program.
  - Note, this example is considered not a medical device because interacting with PHR or EHR systems is an example of transferring, storing, converting formats, or displaying EHR or PHR data.

D. Software Function Intended for Transferring, Storing, Converting Formats, Displaying Data and Results

Under section 520(o)(1)(D) of the FD&C Act, the term "device" does not include a software function that is intended "for transferring, storing, converting formats, or displaying clinical laboratory test or other device data and results unless such function is intended to interpret or analyze clinical laboratory test or other device data, results, and findings" (section 520(o)(1)(D) of the FD&C Act).

Medical Device Data Systems, medical image storage devices, and medical image communications devices are defined as:

1. Medical Device Data System (MDDS), defined as a software, electronic, or electrical hardware that is intended to provide one or more of the following uses, whether or not it is intended for immediate clinical action (i.e., active patient monitoring), without controlling or altering the functions or parameters of any connected medical devices:
   a. The electronic transfer of medical device data;
   b. The electronic storage of medical device data;
   c. The electronic conversion of medical device data from one format to another format in accordance with a preset specification; or
   d. The electronic display of medical device data. Examples of MDDS include physical communications medium (including wireless hardware), modems, interfaces, and a communications protocol.
2. Medical image storage device, defined as a device that provides electronic storage and retrieval functions for medical images. Examples include devices employing magnetic and optical discs, magnetic tape, and digital memory.
3. Medical image communications device, defined as a device that provides electronic transfer of medical image data between medical devices. It may include a physical communications medium, modems, interfaces, and a communications protocol.

The software functions that meet the definitions of Medical Device Data Systems (MDDS), medical image storage devices, or medical image communications devices provided in the Medical Device Data Systems, Medical Image Storage Devices, and Medical Image Communications Devices Guidance (or MDDS Guidance,[16] and the Guidance for the Submission of Premarket Notifications for Medical Image Management Devices, are now not devices under section 201(h) of the FD&C Act, pursuant to section 520(o)(1)(D) of the FD&C

16 Available at https://www.fda.gov/regulatory-information/search-fda-guidance-documents/medical-device-data-systems-medical-image-storage-devices-and-medical-image-communications-devices.

Act. As such, software functions that are solely intended to transfer, store, convert formats, and display medical device data and results, including medical images, waveforms, signals, or other clinical information are not devices and thus are not subject to FDA regulatory requirements. However, software functions that analyze or interpret medical device data in addition to transferring, storing, converting formats, or displaying clinical laboratory test or other device data and results remain subject to FDA's regulatory oversight, unless they meet the criteria outlined in section 520(o)(1)(E) of the FD&C Act.

Section 520(o)(1) of the FD&C Act describes software functions, not hardware products, that do not meet the definition of a device under section 201(h) of the FD&C Act. Therefore, the hardware included in the identification above (such as electrical hardware, magnetic and optical discs, physical communications medium, etc.) that are intended to transfer, store, convert formats, and display medical device data and results remain devices. FDA's existing policy, described in the MDDS Guidance,[17] applies to such devices, provided that the hardware function is limited to assisting the following software functions: electronic transfer, storage, conversion of formats, or display of medical device data. Specialized medical display hardware devices for digital mammography, radiology, pathology, and ophthalmology (see, for example, 21 CFR 892.2050) and other specialized medical display hardware integral to the safe and effective use of a medical device hardware product (such as integral 3D displays in robotic surgery systems and displays built into ICU bedside monitors) have not been considered MDDS, medical image storage, or medical image communications devices. Such medical display hardware devices and other specialized medical display hardware integral to a medical device are not excluded from the device definition by the Cures Act.

There may be MDDS products that are considered multiple function products in that they may have a software function that is not a device and another function that is a device. Consistent with section 520(o)(2) of the FD&C Act, FDA does not regulate the MDDS software functions that meet the definition of 520(o)(1)(D) of the FD&C Act in a MDDS multiple function product. If a multiple function product contains MDDS hardware functions, FDA does not, at this time and based on our current understanding of the risks of these devices, intend to enforce the requirements under the FD&C Act. However, FDA may assess the impact that such software and hardware MDDS functions have on the safety and effectiveness of the device function(s) in a multiple function device product. As noted above, FDA intends to provide recommendations on the regulation of such products with multifunctionality in a separate guidance document.

In some cases, software functions that transfer, store, convert formats, or display medical device data and results are utilized on hardware that is not intended by the hardware manufacturer for a device function under section 201(h) of the FD&C Act. For example, general-purpose hardware IT infrastructure intended for data transfer (e.g., network router), data storage (e.g., network attached storage (NAS)), conversion of data (e.g., PDF software), and display of data (computer monitor) are not device functions. Such products do not

17 Available at https://www.fda.gov/regulatory-information/search-fda-guidance-documents/medical-device-data-systems-medical-image-storage-devices-and-medical-image-communications-devices.

meet the definition of a device in section 201(h) of the FD&C Act for either the software or hardware function and are therefore not regulated as devices.

Section 520(o)(1)(D) of the FD&C Act does not capture software functions intended to generate alarms or alerts or prioritize patient-related information on multi-patient displays, because these functions involve analysis or interpretation of laboratory test or other device data and results. For example, if a software function is intended to prioritize patients in an Intensive Care Unit based on their clinical status, then this function is intended to interpret or analyze device data, results, and findings and is, therefore, not excluded from the definition of device under section 520(o)(1)(D) of the FD&C Act. Similarly, software functions that analyze medical device data in order to provide a notification or flag (e.g., that a parameter is out of range) are not excluded from the definition of device under subsection (D)). The examples included in the draft of this guidance that described alarms, alerts, or flags have been removed from this guidance, because they are not excluded from the definition of device under subsection (D). These functions are addressed in section 520(o)(1)(E) of the FD&C Act, the regulation of which will be described in a separate guidance document.

The MDDS Guidance[18] has been revised to clarify that software functions that are solely intended to transfer, store, convert formats, and display medical device data and results, including medical images, waveforms, signals, or other clinical information are not devices and thus are not subject to FDA regulatory requirements, whether or not the use is for immediate clinical action. Accordingly, the definition of MDDS has been revised in that guidance to describe hardware that transfers, stores, converts formats, and displays medical device data as "Device-MDDS" whereas the software functions that transfer, store, convert formats, and display data have been defined as "Non-Device-MDDS." Additional updates to the MDDS guidance include:

- In the Background section, the following list of examples has been labeled as Non-Device-MDDS, because they are examples of MDDS software functions:
    - The electronic transfer or exchange of medical device data. For example, this would include software that collects output from a ventilator about a patient's CO2 level and transmits the information to a central patient data repository.
    - The electronic storage and retrieval of medical device data. For example, software that stores historical blood pressure information for later review by a health care provider.
    - The electronic conversion of medical device data from one format to another in accordance with a preset specification. For example, software that converts digital data generated by a pulse oximeter into a digital format that can be printed.
    - The electronic display of medical device data. For example, software that displays a previously stored electrocardiogram for a particular patient.

18 Available at https://www.fda.gov/regulatory-information/search-fda-guidance-documents/medical-device-data-systems-medical-image-storage-devices-and-medical-image-communications-devices.

- In the Background section, the following examples of MDDS have been revised to clarify that only the software functions are Non-Device-MDDS:
  - Any assemblage or arrangement of network components that includes specialized software expressly created for a purpose consistent with the intended for use in the MDDS regulation.
    - Note "or hardware" has been removed from this example.
  - Software functions specifically labeled (per 21 CFR Part 801) by the manufacturer as a MDDS, provided such software functions do not provide additional functionality.
    - Note "products" has been replaced with "software functions."
  - Custom software that is written by entities other than the original medical device manufacturer (for example, hospitals, third party vendors) that directly connects to a medical device, to obtain medical device information.
  - Modified portions of software that are part of an IT infrastructure created and/or modified (writing and compiling software) for specific MDDS functionality. For example, when modifying software for MDDS functionality, only the modified portion is considered MDDS; the original software is not.
    - Note "or hardware" has been removed from this example.
- In the Background section, the section title "Examples of devices that perform monitoring but are not considered to perform 'active patient monitoring'" has been revised to "Examples of products that transfer, store, convert formats, or display medical device data and are Non-Device-MDDS."
- In the Policy section of the MDDS guidance, FDA describes its compliance policy with respect to the following devices:
  - MDDS subject to 21 CFR 880.6310,
  - Medical image storage devices subject to 21 CFR 892.2010, and
  - Medical image communications devices subject to 21 CFR 892.2020.

  As described above, FDA intends to continue this policy for hardware products considered MDDS, medical image storage, or medical image communications devices, provided that the hardware function is limited to the excluded software functions of electronic transfer, storage, conversion of formats, or display of medical device data. FDA intends to amend the regulations so that they describe the hardware functions that remain device functions, and to remove reference to software functions that are not device functions pursuant to section 520(o)(1)(D) of the FD&C Act. Accordingly, the Policy section has been amended to include the following:

  - Software functions that meet the definitions of MDDS, medical image storage devices, or medical image communications devices are not devices under section 201(h) of the FD&C Act. Hardware that are intended to transfer, store, convert formats, and display medical device data and results remain devices. FDA does not intend to enforce the requirements under the FD&C Act for hardware products considered MDDS, medical image storage, or medical image communications devices.

In the MMA Guidance,[19] the following example has been revised and moved from Section V.A (Subset of mobile apps that are the focus of FDA's regulatory oversight) to Appendix A (Examples of mobile apps that are NOT medical devices):

- *Examples of displays of patient-specific medical device data include*: software function to display medical images directly from a Picture Archiving and Communication System (PACS) server.
    - Note: The remote display of data from bedside monitors has been removed from this example, because such non-device display functions are covered in other examples, while this example is not likely to be a real-world example of a product, since such product would likely include other software functions that analyze or interpret medical device data that may continue to be subject to FDA's regulatory oversight.

In the MMA Guidance, the following examples have been moved from Appendix B (Examples of mobile apps for which FDA intends to exercise enforcement discretion) to Appendix A (Examples of mobile apps that are NOT medical devices):

- Software functions that are intended for transferring, storing, converting formats, or displaying clinical laboratory test or other device data and results, findings by a health care professional with respect to such data and results, general information about such findings, and general background information about such laboratory test or other device, unless such function is intended to interpret or analyze clinical laboratory test or other device data, results and findings.
    - Software functions that transfer, store, convert formats, and display medical device data without modifying the data and do not control or alter the functions or parameters of any connected medical device (i.e., mobile apps that meet the definition of MDDS).
    - Software functions that meet the definition of MDDS and connect to a nursing central station and display (but do not analyze or interpret) medical device data to a physician's mobile platform for review.
    - Software functions that are not intended for diagnostic image review such as image display for multidisciplinary patient management meetings (e.g., rounds) or patient consultation (and include a persistent on-screen notice, such as "for informational purposes only and not intended for diagnostic use").
    - Note that in these examples, "mobile apps" has been replaced with "software functions" to clarify that the software functions are Non-Device-MDDS.

19 Available at https://www.fda.gov/regulatory-information/search-fda-guidance-documents/policy-device-software-functions-and-mobile-medical-applications.

In the MMA Guidance, the following examples in Appendix C (Examples of mobile apps that are the focus of FDA's regulatory oversight) have been revised as described below:

- Mobile apps that are used in active patient monitoring or analyzing patient-specific medical device data and therefore are the focus of FDA's regulatory oversight:
    - Mobile apps that connect to bedside (or cardiac) monitors and transfer the data to a central viewing station for display and active patient monitoring. Possible product code(s): DSI, MHX, MLD (21 CFR 870.1025), DRT, MWI, MSX (21 CFR 870.2300).
        - This sub-bullet has been revised to say: Software functions that acquire or process physiological signals. Possible product code(s): DSI, MHX, MLD (21 CFR 870.1025), DRT, MWI, MSX (21 CFR 870.2300).
    - Mobile apps that connect to a perinatal monitoring system and transfer uterine contraction and fetal heart rate data to another display to allow for remote monitoring of labor progress. Possible product code(s): HGM (21 CFR 884.2740).
        - This sub-bullet has been revised to say: Software functions that process uterine contraction and fetal heart rate data for remote monitoring of labor progress. Possible product code(s): HGM (21 CFR 884.2740).
    - Mobile apps that are intended to display images for diagnostic review may be regulated as a picture archiving and communications system. Possible product code(s): LLZ (21 CFR 892.2050).
        - This sub-bullet has been revised to say: Software functions that are intended to process images for diagnostic review may be regulated as a picture archiving and communications system. Possible product code(s): LLZ (21 CFR 892.2050).

And the following example of a software function and its associated text in Section V.B of the MMA Guidance is no a longer device pursuant to section 520(o)(1)(D) of the FD&C Act and has been moved to Appendix A (Examples of mobile apps that are NOT medical devices) of that guidance:

- Software functions that meet the definition of Medical Device Data Systems – These are software functions that are intended to transfer, store, convert formats, and display medical device data, without controlling or altering the functions or parameters of any connected medical device. These include those software functions for a secondary display to a regulated medical device when these apps are not intended to provide primary diagnosis, to be used to make treatment decisions, or to be used in connection with active patient monitoring.
    - Note the text of this example has been modified to clarify that only the software functions intended to transfer, store, convert formats, and display medical device data are not medical devices (i.e., Non-Device-MDDS).

The Guidance for the Submission of Premarket Notifications for Medical Image Management Devices has been withdrawn, because some software functions described in that guidance no longer meet the definition of a device, as amended. For the limited subset of Medical

Image Management Devices that continue to meet the definition of a device and continue to require a 510(k) submission, the information provided in that document, which was written in 2000, is out of date. CDRH encourages manufacturers to reference the most recent FDA-recognized versions of relevant voluntary consensus standards instead.

CSV

Chapter 15
Guidance for Industry
Computerized Systems Used in Clinical Investigations

May 2007
U.S. Department of Health and Human Services
Food and Drug Administration (FDA)
Office of the Commissioner (OC)

I. Introduction

This document provides to sponsors, contract research organizations (CROs), data management centers, clinical investigators, and institutional review boards (IRBs), recommendations regarding the use of computerized systems in clinical investigations. The computerized system applies to records in electronic form that are used to create, modify, maintain, archive, retrieve, or transmit clinical data required to be maintained, or submitted to the FDA. Because the source data[1] are necessary for the reconstruction and evaluation of the study to determine the safety of food and color additives and safety and effectiveness of new human and animal drugs,[2] and medical devices, this guidance is intended to assist in ensuring confidence in the reliability, quality, and integrity of electronic source data and source documentation (i.e., electronic records).

This guidance supersedes the guidance of the same name dated April 1999; and supplements the guidance for industry on *Part 11, Electronic Records; Electronic Signatures — Scope and Application* and the Agency's international harmonization efforts[3] when applying these guidances to source data generated at clinical study sites.

FDA's guidance documents, including this guidance, do not establish legally enforceable responsibilities. Instead, guidances describe the Agency's current thinking on a topic and should be viewed only as recommendations, unless specific regulatory or statutory requirements are cited. The use of the word *should* in Agency guidances means that something is suggested or recommended, but not required.

---

1 Under 21 CFR 312.62(b), reference is made to records that are part of case histories as "supporting data"; the *ICH E6 Good Clinical Practice* consolidated guidance uses the term "source documents." For the purpose of this guidance, these terms describe the same information and have been used interchangeably.

2 Human drugs include biological drugs.

3 In August 2003, FDA issued the guidance for industry entitled *Part 11, Electronic Records; Electronic Signatures-Scope and Application* clarifying that the Agency intends to interpret the scope of part 11 narrowly and to exercise enforcement discretion with regard to part 11 requirements for validation, audit trails, record retention, and record copying. In 1996, the International Conference on Harmonisation of TechnicalRequirements for Registration of Pharmaceuticals for Human Use (ICH) issued *E6 Good Clinical Practice: Consolidated Guidance.*

II. Background

There is an increasing use of computerized systems in clinical trials to generate and maintain source data and source documentation on each clinical trial subject. Such electronic source data and source documentation must meet the same fundamental elements of data quality (e.g., attributable, legible, contemporaneous, original,[4] and accurate) that are expected of paper records and must comply with all applicable statutory and regulatory requirements. FDA's acceptance of data from clinical trials for decision-making purposes depends on FDA's ability to verify the quality and integrity of the data during FDA on-site inspections and audits. (21 CFR 312, 511.1(b), and 812).

In March 1997, FDA issued 21 CFR part 11, which provides criteria for acceptance by FDA, under certain circumstances, of electronic records, electronic signatures, and handwritten signatures executed to electronic records as equivalent to paper records and handwritten signatures executed on paper. After the effective date of 21 CFR part 11, significant concerns regarding the interpretation and implementation of part 11 were raised by both FDA and industry. As a result, we decided to reexamine 21 CFR part 11 with the possibility of proposing additional rulemaking, and exercising enforcement discretion regarding enforcement of certain part 11 requirements in the interim.

This guidance finalizes the draft guidance for industry entitled *Computerized Systems Used in Clinical Trials*, dated September 2004 and supplements the guidance for industry entitled *Part 11, Electronic Records; Electronic Signatures – Scope and Application* (Scope and Application Guidance), dated August 2003. The Scope and Application Guidance clarified that the Agency intends to interpret the scope of part 11 narrowly and to exercise enforcement discretion with regard to part 11 requirements for validation, audit trails, record retention, and record copying. However, other Part 11 provisions remain in effect.

The approach outlined in the Scope and Application Guidance, which applies to electronic records generated as part of a clinical trial, should be followed until such time as Part 11 is amended.

III. Scope

The principles outlined in this guidance should be used for computerized systems that contain any data that are relied on by an applicant in support of a marketing application, including computerized laboratory information management systems that capture analytical results of tests conducted during a clinical trial. For example, the recommendations in this guidance would apply to computerized systems that create source documents (electronic records) that satisfy the requirements in 21 CFR 312.62(b) and 812.140(b), such as case histories. This guidance also applies to recorded source data transmitted from automated instruments directly to a computerized system (e.g., data from a chemistry autoanalyser or a Holter monitor to a laboratory information system). This guidance also applies when source documentation is created in hardcopy and later entered into a computerized system, recorded by direct entry into a

4 FDA is allowing original documents to be replaced by copies provided the copies are identical and have been verified as such (See, e.g., FDA Compliance Policy Guide # 7150.13). See Definitions section for a definition of original data.

computerized system, or automatically recorded by a computerized system (e.g., an ECG reading). The guidance does not apply to computerized medical devices that generate such data and that are otherwise regulated by FDA.

IV. Recommendations

This guidance provides the following recommendations regarding the use of computerized systems in clinical investigations.

A. Study Protocols

Each specific study protocol should identify each step at which a computerized system will be used to create, modify, maintain, archive, retrieve, or transmit source data. This information can be included in the protocol at the time the investigational new drug application (IND), Investigational Device Exemption (IDE), or Notice of Claimed Investigational Exemption for a New Animal Drug containing the protocols is submitted or at any time after the initial submission.

The computerized systems should be designed: (1) to satisfy the processes assigned to these systems for use in the specific study protocol (e.g., record data in metric units, blind the study), and (2) to prevent errors in data creation, modification, maintenance, archiving, retrieval, or transmission (e.g., inadvertently unblinding a study).

B. Standard Operating Procedures

There should be specific procedures and controls in place when using computerized systems to create, modify, maintain, or transmit electronic records, including when collecting source data at clinical trial sites. A list of recommended standard operating procedures (SOPs) is provided in Appendix A. Such SOPs should be maintained either on-site or be remotely accessible through electronic files as part of the specific study records, and the SOPs should be made available for use by personnel and for inspection by FDA.

C. Source Documentation and Retention

When original observations are entered directly into a computerized system, the electronic record is the source document. Under 21 CFR 312.62, 511.1(b)(7)(ii) and 812.140, the clinical investigator must retain records required to be maintained under part 312, § 511.1(b), and part 812, for a period of time specified in these regulations. This requirement applies to the retention of the original source document, or a copy of the source document.

When source data are transmitted from one system to another (e.g., from a personal data assistant to a sponsor's server), or entered directly into a remote computerized system (e.g., data are entered into a remote server via a computer terminal that is located at the clinical site), or an electrocardiogram at the clinical site is transmitted to the sponsor's computerized system, a copy of the data should be maintained at another location, typically at the clinical site but possibly at some other designated site. Copies should be made contemporaneously with data entry and should be preserved in an appropriate format, such as XML, PDF or paper formats.

D. Internal Security Safeguards

1. Limited Access

Access must be limited to authorized individuals (21 CFR 11.10(d). This requirement can be accomplished by the following recommendations. We recommend that each user of the system have an individual account. The user should log into that account at the beginning of a data entry session, input information (including changes) on the electronic record, and log out at the completion of data entry session. The system should be designed to limit the number of log-in attempts and to record unauthorized access log-in attempts.

Individuals should work only under their own password or other access key and not share these with others. The system should not allow an individual to log onto the system to provide another person access to the system. We also recommend that passwords or other access keys be changed at established intervals commensurate with a documented risk assessment. When someone leaves a workstation, the person should log off the system. Alternatively, an automatic log off may be appropriate for long idle periods. For short periods of inactivity, we recommend that a type of automatic protection be installed against unauthorized data entry (e.g., an automatic screen saver can prevent data entry until a password is entered).

2. Audit Trails

It is important to keep track of all changes made to information in the electronic records that document activities related to the conduct of the trial (audit trails). The use of audit trails or other security measures helps to ensure that only authorized additions, deletions, or alterations of information in the electronic record have occurred and allows a means to reconstruct significant details about study conduct and source data collection necessary to verify the quality and integrity of data. Computer-generated, time-stamped audit trails or other security measures can also capture information related to the creation, modification, or deletion of electronic records and may be useful to ensure compliance with the appropriate regulation.

The need for audit trails should be determined based on a justified and documented risk assessment that takes into consideration circumstances surrounding system use, the likelihood that information might be compromised, and any system vulnerabilities. Should it be decided that audit trails or other appropriate security measures are needed to ensure electronic record integrity, personnel who create, modify, or delete electronic records should not be able to modify the documents or security measures used to track electronic record changes. Computer-generated, time-stamped electronic audits trails are the preferred method for tracking changes to electronic source documentation.

Audit trails or other security methods used to capture electronic record activities should describe when, by whom, and the reason changes were made to the electronic record. Original information should not be obscured though the use of audit trails or other security measures used to capture electronic record activities.

3. Date/Time Stamps

Controls should be established to ensure that the system's date and time are correct. The ability to change the date or time should be limited to authorized personnel, and such personnel should be notified if a system date or time discrepancy is detected. Any changes to date or time should always be documented. We do not expect documentation of time changes that systems make automatically to adjust to daylight savings time conventions.

We recommend that dates and times include the year, month, day, hour, and minute and encourage synchronization of systems to the date and time provided by international standardsetting agencies (e.g., U.S. National Institute of Standards and Technology provides information about universal time, coordinated (UTC)).

Computerized systems are likely to be used in multi-center clinical trials and may be located in different time zones. For systems that span different time zones, it is better to implement time stamps with a clear understanding of the time zone reference used. We recommend that system documentation explain time zone references as well as zone acronyms or other naming conventions.

E. External Security Safeguards

In addition to internal safeguards built into a computerized system, external safeguards should be put in place to ensure that access to the computerized system and to the data is restricted to authorized personnel. Staff should be kept thoroughly aware of system security measures and the importance of limiting access to authorized personnel.

Procedures and controls should be put in place to prevent the altering, browsing, querying, or reporting of data via external software applications that do not enter through the protective system software.

You should maintain a cumulative record that indicates, for any point in time, the names of authorized personnel, their titles, and a description of their access privileges. That record should be kept in the study documentation, accessible for use by appropriate study personnel and for inspection by FDA investigators.

We also recommend that controls be implemented to prevent, detect, and mitigate effects of computer viruses, worms, or other potentially harmful software code on study data and software.

F. Other System Features

1. Direct Entry of Data

We recommend that you incorporate prompts, flags, or other help features into your computerized system to encourage consistent use of clinical terminology and to alert the user to data that are out of acceptable range. You should not use programming features that automatically enter data into a field when the field is bypassed (default entries). However, you can use programming features that permit repopulation of information specific to the subject. To avoid falsification of data, you should perform a careful analysis in deciding whether and when to use software programming instructions that permit data fields to be automatically populated.

2. Retrieving Data

The computerized system should be designed in such a way that retrieved data regarding each individual subject in a study is attributable to that subject. Reconstruction of the source documentation is essential to FDA's review of the clinical study submitted to the Agency. Therefore, the information provided to FDA should fully describe and explain how source data were obtained and managed, and how electronic records were used to capture data.

It is not necessary to reprocess data from a study that can be fully reconstructed from available documentation. Therefore, the actual application software, operating systems, and software development tools involved in the processing of data or records need not be retained.

3. Dependability System Documentation

For each study, documentation should identify what software and hardware will be used to create, modify, maintain, archive, retrieve, or transmit clinical data. Although it need not be submitted to FDA, this documentation should be retained as part of the study records and be available for inspection by FDA (either on-site or remotely accessible).

4. System Controls

When electronic formats are the only ones used to create and preserve electronic records, sufficient backup and recovery procedures should be designed to protect against data loss. Records should regularly be backed up in a procedure that would prevent a catastrophic loss and ensure the quality and integrity of the data. Records should be stored at a secure location specified in the SOP. Storage should typically be offsite or in a building separate from the original records.

We recommend that you maintain backup and recovery logs to facilitate an assessment of the nature and scope of data loss resulting from a system failure.

5. Change Controls

The integrity of the data and the integrity of the protocols should be maintained when making changes to the computerized system, such as software upgrades, including security and performance patches, equipment, or component replacement, or new instrumentation. The effects of any changes to the system should be evaluated and some should be validated depending on risk. Changes that exceed previously established operational limits or design specifications should be validated. Finally, all changes to the system should be documented.

G. Training of Personnel

Those who use computerized systems must determine that individuals (e.g., employees, contractors) who develop, maintain, or use computerized systems have the education, training and experience necessary to perform their assigned tasks (21 CFR 11.10(i)). Training should be provided to individuals in the specific operations with regard to computerized systems that they are to perform.

Training should be conducted by qualified individuals on a continuing basis, as needed, to ensure familiarity with the computerized system and with any changes to the system during the course of the study.

We recommend that computer education, training, and experience be documented.

DEFINITIONS

The following is a list of definitions for terms used in, and for the purposes of, this guidance document.

Audit Trail: For the purpose of this guidance, an *audit trail* is a process that captures details such as additions, deletions, or alterations of information in an electronic record without obliterating the original record. An audit trail facilitates the reconstruction of the course of such details relating to the electronic record.

Certified Copy: A *certified copy* is a copy of original information that has been verified, as indicated by a dated signature, as an exact copy having all of the same attributes and information as the original.

Computerized System: A *computerized system* includes computer hardware, software, and associated documents (e.g., user manual) that create, modify, maintain, archive, retrieve, or transmit in digital form information related to the conduct of a clinical trial.

Direct Entry: *Direct entry* is recording data where an electronic record is the original means of capturing the data. Examples are the keying by an individual of original observations into a system, or automatic recording by the system of the output of a balance that measures subject's body weight.

Electronic Record: An *electronic record* is any combination of text, graphics, data, audio,pictorial, or other information representation in digital form that is created, modified, maintained, archived, retrieved, or distributed by a computer system.

Original data: For the purpose of this guidance, *original data* are those values that represent the first recording of study data. FDA is allowing original documents and the original data recorded on those documents to be replaced by copies provided the copies are identical and have been verified as such (see FDA Compliance Policy Guide # 7150.13).

Source Documents: Original documents and records including, but not limited to, hospital records, clinical and office charts, laboratory notes, memoranda, subjects' diaries or evaluation checklists, pharmacy dispensing records, recorded data from automated instruments, copies or transcriptions certified after verification as being accurate and complete, microfiches, photographic negatives, microfilm or magnetic media, x-rays, subject files, and records kept at the pharmacy, at the laboratories, and at medico-technical departments involved in a clinical trial.

Transmit: *Transmit* is to transfer data within or among clinical study sites, contract research organizations, data management centers, sponsors, or to FDA.

Appendix A

Standard Operating Procedures

Standard operating procedures (SOPs) and documentation pertinent to the use of a computerized system should be made available for use by appropriate study personnel at the clinical site or remotely and for inspection by FDA. The SOPs should include, but are not limited to, the following processes.

- System setup/installation (including the description and specific use of software, hardware, and physical environment and the relationship)
- System operating manual
- Validation and functionality testing
- Data collection and handling (including data archiving, audit trails, and risk assessment)
- System maintenance (including system decommissioning)
- System security measures
- Change control
- Data backup, recovery, and contingency plans
- Alternative recording methods (in the case of system unavailability)
- Computer user training
- Roles and responsibilities of sponsors, clinical sites and other parties with respect to the use of computerized systems in the clinical trials

References

FDA, *21 CFR Part 11*, "Electronic Records; Electronic Signatures; Final Rule." *Federal Register* Vol. 62, No. 54, 13429, March 20, 1997.

FDA, *Compliance Program Guidance Manual*, "Compliance Program 7348.810 – Bioresearch Monitoring - Sponsors, Contract Research Organizations and Monitors," February 21, 2001.

FDA, *Compliance Program Guidance Manual*, "Compliance Program 7348.811 – Bioresearch Monitoring - Clinical Investigators," September 30, 2000.

FDA, *Good Clinical Practice VICH* GL9.

FDA, *Guideline for the Monitoring of Clinical Investigations*.

FDA, *Information Sheets for Institutional Review Boards and Clinical Investigators*. http://www.fda.gov/ic/ohrt/irbs/default.htm

FDA, *E6 Good Clinical Practice: Consolidated Guidance*. http://www.fda.gov/cder/guidance/959fnl.pdf.

FDA, *Part 11, Electronic Records; Electronic Signatures — Scope and Application*, 2003.

FDA, *General Principles of Software Validation; Guidance for Industry and FDA Staff*.

CSV

Chapter 16
Guidance for Industry
Computerized Systems Used in Clinical Trials

April 1999
U.S. Department of Health and Human Services
Food and Drug Administration
Center for Biologic Evaluation and Research (CBER)
Center for Drug Evaluation and Research (CDER)
Center for Devices and Radiological Health (CDRH)
Center for Food Safety and Nutrition (CFSAN)
Center for Veterinary Medicine (CVM)
Office of Regulatory Affairs (ORA)

I. Introduction

This document addresses issues pertaining to computerized systems used to create, modify, maintain, archive, retrieve, or transmit clinical data intended for submission to the Food and Drug Administration (FDA). These data form the basis for the Agency's decisions regarding the safety and efficacy of new human and animal drugs, biologics, medical devices, and certain food and color additives. As such, these data have broad public health significance and must be of the highest quality and integrity.

FDA established the Bioresearch Monitoring (BIMO) Program of inspections and audits to monitor the conduct and reporting of clinical trials to ensure that data from these trials meet the highest standards of quality and integrity and conform to FDA's regulations. FDA's acceptance of data from clinical trials for decision-making purposes is dependent upon its ability to verify the quality and integrity of such data during its onsite inspections and audits. To be acceptable the data should meet certain fundamental elements of quality whether collected or recorded electronically or on paper. Data should be attributable, original, accurate, contemporaneous, and legible. For example, attributable data can be traced to individuals responsible for observing and recording the data. In an automated system, attributability could be achieved by a computer system designed to identify individuals responsible for any input.

This guidance addresses how these elements of data quality might be satisfied where computerized systems are being used to create, modify, maintain, archive, retrieve, or transmit clinical data. Although the primary focus of this guidance is on computerized systems used at clinical sites to collect data, the principles set forth may also be appropriate for computerized systems at contract research organizations, data management centers, and sponsors. Persons using the data from computerized systems should have confidence that the data are no less reliable than data in paper form.

Computerized medical devices, diagnostic laboratory instruments and instruments in analytical laboratories that are used in clinical trials are not the focus of this guidance. This guidance does not address electronic submissions or methods of their transmission to the Agency.

This guidance document reflects long-standing regulations covering clinical trial records. It also addresses requirements of the Electronic Records/Electronic Signatures rule (21 CFR part 11).

The principles in this guidance may be applied where source documents are created (1) in hardcopy and later entered into a computerized system, (2) by direct entry by a human into a computerized system, and (3) automatically by a computerized system.

II. Definitions

Audit Trail means, for the purposes of this guidance, a secure, computer generated, time-stamped electronic record that allows reconstruction of the course of events relating to the creation, modification, and deletion of an electronic record.

Certified Copy means a copy of original information that has been verified, as indicated by dated signature, as an exact copy having all of the same attributes and information as the original.

Commit means a saving action, which creates or modifies, or an action which deletes, an electronic record or portion of an electronic record. An example is pressing the key of a key-board that causes information to be saved to durable medium.

Computerized System means, for the purpose of this guidance, computer hardware, soft-ware, and associated documents (e.g., user manual) that create, modify, maintain, archive, retrieve, or transmit in digital form information related to the conduct of a clinical trial.

Direct Entry means recording data where an electronic record is the original capture of the data. Examples are the keying by an individual of original observations into the system, or automatic recording by the system of the output of a balance that measures subjectÂ's body weight.

Electronic Case Report Form (e-CRF) means an auditable electronic record designed to record information required by the clinical trial protocol to be reported to the sponsor on each trial subject.

Electronic Patient Diary means an electronic record into which a subject participating in a clinical trial directly enters observations or directly responds to an evaluation checklist.

Electronic Record means any combination of text, graphics, data, audio, pictorial, or any oth-er information representation in digital form that is created, modified, maintained, archived, retrieved, or distributed by a computer system.

Electronic Signature means a computer data compilation of any symbol or series of symbols, executed, adopted, or authorized by an individual to be the legally binding equivalent of the individual's handwritten signature.

Software Validation means confirmation by examination and provision of objective evidence that software specifications conform to user needs and intended uses, and that the particular requirements implemented through the software can be consistently fulfilled. For the purposes of this document, design level validation is that portion of the software validation that takes place in parts of the software life cycle before the software is delivered to the end user.

Source Documents means original documents and records including, but not limited to, hospital records, clinical and office charts, laboratory notes, memoranda, subjects' diaries or evaluation checklists, pharmacy dispensing records, recorded data from automated instruments, copies or transcriptions certified after verification as being accurate and complete, microfiches, photographic negatives, microfilm or magnetic media, x-rays, subject files, and records kept at the pharmacy, at the laboratories, and at medico-technical departments involved in the clinical trial.

Transmit means, for the purposes of this guidance, to transfer data within or among clinical study sites, contract research organizations, data management centers, or sponsors. Other Agency guidance covers transmission from sponsors to the Agency.

III. General Principles

A. Each study protocol should identify at which steps a computerized system will be used to create, modify, maintain, archive, retrieve, or transmit data.

B. For each study, documentation should identify what software and, if known, what hardware is to be used in computerized systems that create, modify, maintain, archive, retrieve, or transmit data. This documentation should be retained as part of study records.

C. Source documents should be retained to enable a reconstruction and evaluation of the trial.

D. When original observations are entered directly into a computerized system, the electronic record is the source document.

E. The design of a computerized system should ensure that all applicable regulatory requirements for recordkeeping and record retention in clinical trials are met with the same degree of confidence as is provided with paper systems.

F. Clinical investigators should retain either the original or a certified copy of all source documents sent to a sponsor or contract research organization, including query resolution correspondence.

G. Any change to a record required to be maintained should not obscure the original information. The record should clearly indicate that a change was made and clearly provide a means to locate and read the prior information.

H. Changes to data that are stored on electronic media will always require an audit trail, in accordance with 21 CFR 11.10(e). Documentation should include who made the changes, when, and why they were made.

I. The FDA may inspect all records that are intended to support submissions to the Agency, regardless of how they were created or maintained.

J. Data should be retrievable in such a fashion that all information regarding each individual subject in a study is attributable to that subject.

K. Computerized systems should be designed: (1) So that all requirements assigned to these systems in a study protocol are satisfied (e.g., data are recorded in metric units, requirements that the study be blinded); and, (2) to preclude errors in data creation, modification, maintenance, archiving, retrieval, or transmission.

Security measures should be in place to prevent unauthorized access to the data and to the computerized system.

IV. Standard Operating Procedures

Standard Operating Procedures (SOPs) pertinent to the use of the computerized system should be available on site.

SOPs should be established for, but not limited to:

- System Setup/Installation
- Data Collection and Handling
- System Maintenance
- Data Backup, Recovery, and Contingency Plans
- Security
- Change Control

Data Entry

A. Electronic Signatures

1. To ensure that individuals have the authority to proceed with data entry, the data entry system should be designed so that individuals need to enter electronic signatures, such as combined identification codes/passwords or biometric-based electronic signatures, at the start of a data entry session.
2. The data entry system should also be designed to ensure attributability. Therefore, each entry to an electronic record, including any change, should be made under the electronic signature of the individual making that entry. However, this does not necessarily mean a separate electronic signature for each entry or change. For example, a single electronic signature may cover multiple entries or changes.
   a. The printed name of the individual who enters data should be displayed by the data entry screen throughout the data entry session. This is intended to preclude the possibility of a different individual inadvertently entering data under someone else's name.

If the name displayed by the screen during a data entry session is not that of the person entering the data, then that individual should log on under his or her own name before continuing.

3. Individuals should only work under their own passwords or other access keys and should not share these with others. Individuals should not log on to the system in order to provide another person access to the system.
4. Passwords or other access keys should be changed at established intervals.
5. When someone leaves a workstation, the person should log off the system. Failing this, an automatic log off may be appropriate for long idle periods. For short periods of inactivity, there should be some kind of automatic protection against unauthorized data entry. An example could be an automatic screen saver that prevents data entry until a password is entered.

B. Audit Trails

1. Section 21 CFR 11.10(e) requires persons who use electronic record systems to maintain an audit trail as one of the procedures to protect the authenticity, integrity, and, when appropriate, the confidentiality of electronic records.
    a. Persons must use secure, computer-generated, time-stamped audit trails to independently record the date and time of operator entries and actions that create, modify, or delete electronic records. A record is created when it is saved to durable media, as described under "commit" in Section II, Definitions.
    b. Audit trails must be retained for a period at least as long as that required for the subject electronic records (e.g., the study data and records to which they pertain) and must be available for agency review and copying.
2. Personnel who create, modify, or delete electronic records should not be able to modify the audit trails.
3. Clinical investigators should retain either the original or a certified copy of audit trails.
4. FDA personnel should be able to read audit trails both at the study site and at any other location where associated electronic study records are maintained.
5. Audit trails should be created incrementally, in chronological order, and in a manner that does not allow new audit trail information to overwrite existing data in violation of §11.10(e).

C. Date/Time Stamps

Controls should be in place to ensure that the system's date and time are correct.

The ability to change the date or time should be limited to authorized personnel and such personnel should be notified if a system date or time discrepancy is detected. Changes to date or time should be documented.

Dates and times are to be local to the activity being documented and should include the year, month, day, hour, and minute. The Agency encourages establishments to synchronize systems to the date and time provided by trusted third parties.

Clinical study computerized systems will likely be used in multi-center trials, perhaps located in different time zones. Calculation of the local time stamp may be derived in such cases from a remote server located in a different time zone.

VI. System Features

A. Systems used for direct entry of data should include features that will facilitate the collection of quality data.

Prompts, flags, or other help features within the computerized system should be used to encourage consistent use of clinical terminology and to alert the user to data that are out of acceptable range. Features that automatically enter data into a field when that field is bypassed should not be used.

Electronic patient diaries and e-CRFs should be designed to allow users to make annotations. Annotations add to data quality by allowing ad hoc information to be captured. This information may be valuable in the event of an adverse reaction or unexpected result. The record should clearly indicate who recorded the annotations and when (date and time).

B. Systems used for direct entry of data should be designed to include features that will facilitate the inspection and review of data. Data tags (e.g., different color, different font, flags) should be used to indicate which data have been changed or deleted, as documented in the audit trail.

C. Retrieval of Data

Recognizing that computer products may be discontinued or supplanted by newer (possibly incompatible) systems, it is nonetheless vital that sponsors retain the ability to retrieve and review the data recorded by the older systems. This may be achieved by maintaining support for the older systems or transcribing data to the newer systems.

When migrating to newer systems, it is important to generate accurate and complete copies of study data and collateral information relevant to data integrity. This information would include, for example, audit trails and computational methods used to derive the data. Any data retrieval software, script, or query logic used for the purpose of manipulating, querying, or extracting data for report generating purposes should be documented and maintained for the life of the report. The transcription process needs to be validated.

D. Reconstruction of Study

FDA expects to be able to reconstruct a study. This applies not only to the data, but also how the data were obtained or managed. Therefore, all versions of application software, operating systems, and software development tools involved in processing of data or records should be available as long as data or records associated with these versions are required to be retained. Sponsors may retain these themselves or may contract for the vendors to retain the ability to run (but not necessarily support) the software. Although FDA expects sponsors or vendors to retain the ability to run older versions of software, the agency acknowledges that, in some cases, it will be difficult for sponsors and vendors to run older computerized systems.

VII. Security

A. Physical Security

In addition to internal safeguards built into the system, external safeguards should be in place to ensure that access to the computerized system and to the data is restricted to authorized personnel.

Staff should be thoroughly aware of system security measures and the importance of limiting access to authorized personnel.

SOPs should be in place for handling and storing the system to prevent unauthorized access.

B. Logical Security

Access to the data at the clinical site should be restricted and monitored through the system's software with its required log-on, security procedures, and audit trail. The data should not be altered, browsed, queried, or reported via external software applications that do not enter through the protective system software.

There should be a cumulative record that indicates, for any point in time, the names of authorized personnel, their titles, and a description of their access privileges. The record should be in the study documentation accessible at the site.

If a sponsor supplies computerized systems exclusively for clinical trials, the systems should remain dedicated to the purpose for which they were intended and validated.

If a computerized system being used for the clinical study is part of a system normally used for other purposes, efforts should be made to ensure that the study software is logically and physically isolated as necessary to preclude unintended interaction with non-study software. If any of the software programs are changed the system should be evaluated to determine the effect of the changes on logical security.

Controls should be in place to prevent, detect, and mitigate effects of computer viruses on study data and software.

VIII. System Dependability

The sponsor should ensure and document that computerized systems conform to the sponsor's established requirements for completeness, accuracy, reliability, and consistent intended performance.

A. Systems documentation should be readily available at the site where clinical trials are conducted. Such documentation should provide an overall description of computerized systems and the relationship of hardware, software, and physical environment.

B. FDA may inspect documentation, possessed by a regulated company, that demonstrates validation of software. The study sponsor is responsible, if requested, for making such documentation available at the time of inspection at the site where software is used. Clinical investigators are not generally responsible for validation unless they originated or modified software.

1. For software purchased off-the-shelf, most of the validation should have been done by the company that wrote the software. The sponsor or contract research organization should have documentation (either original validation documents or on-site vendor audit documents) of this design level validation by the vendor, and should have itself performed functional testing (e.g., by use of test data sets) and researched known software limitations, problems, and defect corrections.

In the special case of database and spreadsheet software that is (1) purchased off-the-shelf, (2) designed for and widely used for general purposes, (3) unmodified, and (4) not being used for direct entry of data, the sponsor or contract research organization may not have documentation of design level validation. However, the sponsor or contract research organization should have itself performed functional testing (e.g., by use of test data sets) and researched known software limitations, problems, and defect corrections.

2. Documentation important to demonstrate software validation includes:

Written design specification that describes what the software is intended to do and how it is intended to do it;

A written test plan based on the design specification, including both structural and functional analysis; and,

Test results and an evaluation of how these results demonstrate that the predetermined design specification has been met.

C. Change Control

Written procedures should be in place to ensure that changes to the computerized system such as software upgrades, equipment or component replacement, or new instrumentation will maintain the integrity of the data or the integrity of protocols.

The impact of any change to the system should be evaluated and a decision made regarding the need to revalidate. Revalidation should be performed for changes that exceed operational limits or design specifications.

All changes to the system should be documented.

IX. System Controls

A. Software Version Control

Measures should be in place to ensure that versions of software used to generate, collect, maintain, and transmit data are the versions that are stated in the systems documentation.

B. Contingency Plans

Written procedures should describe contingency plans for continuing the study by alternate means in the event of failure of the computerized system.

C. Backup and Recovery of Electronic Records

Backup and recovery procedures should be clearly outlined in the SOPs and be sufficient to protect against data loss. Records should be backed up regularly in a way that would prevent a catastrophic loss and ensure the quality and integrity of the data.

Backup records should be stored at a secure location specified in the SOPs. Storage is typically offsite or in a building separate from the original records.

Backup and recovery logs should be maintained to facilitate an assessment of the nature and scope of data loss resulting from a system failure.

X. Training of Personnel

A. Qualifications

Each person who enters or processes data should have the education, training, and experience or any combination thereof necessary to perform the assigned functions.

Individuals responsible for monitoring the trial should have education, training, and experience in the use of the computerized system necessary to adequately monitor the trial.

B. Training

Training should be provided to individuals in the specific operations that they are to perform.

Training should be conducted by qualified individuals on a continuing basis, as needed, to ensure familiarity with the computerized system and with any changes to the system during the course of the study.

C. Documentation

Employee education, training, and experience should be documented.

XI. Records Inspection

A. FDA may inspect all records that are intended to support submissions to the Agency, regardless of how they were created or maintained. Therefore, systems should be able to generate accurate and complete copies of records in both human readable and electronic form suitable for inspection, review, and copying by the Agency. Persons should contact the Agency if there is any doubt about what file formats and media the Agency can read and copy.

B. The sponsor should be able to provide hardware and software as necessary for FDA personnel to inspect the electronic documents and audit trail at the site where an FDA inspection is taking place.

XII. Certification of Electronic Signatures

As required by 21 CFR 11.100(c), persons using electronic signatures to meet an FDA signature requirement shall, prior to or at the time of such use, certify to the agency that the electronic signatures in their system, used on or after August 20, 1997, are intended to be the legally binding equivalent of traditional handwritten signatures.

As set forth in 21 CFR 11.100(c), the certification shall be submitted in paper form signed with a traditional handwritten signature to the Office of Regional Operations (HFC-100), 5600 Fishers Lane, Rockville Maryland 20857. The certification is to be submitted prior to or at the time electronic signatures are used. However, a single certification may cover all electronic signatures used by persons in a given organization. This certification is a legal document created by persons to acknowledge that their electronic signatures have the same legal significance as their traditional handwritten signatures. An acceptable certification may take the following form:

"Pursuant to Section 11.100 of Title 21 of the Code of Federal Regulations, this is to certify that [name of organization] intends that all electronic signatures executed by our employees, agents, or representatives, located anywhere in the world, are the legally binding equivalent of traditional handwritten signatures."

XIII. References

FDA, *Software Development Activities*, 1987.

FDA, *Guideline for the Monitoring of Clinical Investigations*, 1988.

FDA, *Guidance for Industry: Good Target Animal Practices: Clinical Investigators and Monitors*, 1997.

FDA, *Compliance Program Guidance Manual*, "Compliance Program 7348.810 - Sponsors, Contract Research Organizations and Monitors," October 30, 1998.

FDA, *Compliance Program Guidance Manual*, "Compliance Program 7348.811 - Bioresearch Monitoring - Clinical Investigators," September 2, 1998.

FDA, Information Sheets for Institutional Review Boards and Clinical Investigators, 1998.

FDA, Glossary of Computerized System and Software Development Terminology, 1995.

FDA, *21 CFR Part 11, Electronic Records; Electronic Signatures*; Final Rule. *Federal Register* Vol. 62, No. 54, 13429, March 20, 1997.

FDA, [draft] Guidance for Industry: General Principles of Software Validation, draft 1997.

International Conference on Harmonisation, Good Clinical Practice: *Consolidated Guideline, Federal Register* Vol 62, No. 90, 25711, May 9, 1997.

Chapter 17
Deciding When to Submit a 510(k) for a Software Change to an Existing Device
Guidance for Industry and FDA Staff

October 25, 2017.
U.S. Department of Health and Human Services
Food and Drug Administration
Center for Devices and Radiological Health
Center for Biologics Evaluation and Research

I. Introduction

This guidance will assist industry and Agency staff in determining when a software (including firmware) change to a medical device may require a manufacturer to submit and obtain FDA clearance of a new premarket notification (510(k)). This guidance is not intended to implement significant policy changes to FDA's current thinking on when submission of a new 510(k) is required for a software change to a 510(k)-cleared device (or group of devices) or other device subject to 510(k) requirements, such as a preamendments device or a device that was granted marketing authorization via the De Novo classification process under section 513(f)(2) of the Food, Drug, and Cosmetic Act (FD&C Act) (also referred to together as "existing devices").

Rather, the intent of this guidance is to enhance the predictability, consistency, and transparency of the "when to submit" decision-making process by providing a least burdensome approach, and describing in greater detail the regulatory framework, policies, and practices underlying such a decision, specifically as it relates to software changes.

For the current edition of the FDA-recognized standards referenced in this document, see the FDA Recognized Consensus Standards Database at http://www.accessdata.fda.gov/scripts/cdrh/cfdocs/cfStandards/search.cfm.

FDA's guidance documents, including this guidance, do not establish legally enforceable responsibilities. Instead, guidances describe the Agency's current thinking on a topic and should be viewed only as recommendations, unless specific regulatory or statutory requirements are cited. The use of the word should in Agency guidance means that something is suggested or recommended, but not required.

II. Background

The regulatory criteria in 21 CFR 807.81(a)(3) state that a premarket notification must be submitted when:

> *(3) The device is one that the person currently has in commercial distribution or is reintroducing into commercial distribution, but that is about to be significantly changed or modified in design, components, method of manufacture, or intended use. The following constitute significant changes or modifications that require a premarket notification:*
>
> *(i) A change or modification in the device that could significantly affect the safety or effectiveness of the device, e.g., a significant change or modification in design, material, chemical composition, energy source, or manufacturing process.*
>
> *(ii) A major change or modification in the intended use of the device.*

FDA issued the original guidance *Deciding When to Submit a 510(k) for a Change to an Existing Device (K97-1)* on January 10, 1997 to provide guidance on this regulatory language. As stated in that guidance, the key issue in the interpretation of 21 CFR 807.81(a)(3) is that the phrase "could significantly affect the safety or effectiveness of the device" and the use of the adjectives "major" and "significant" sometimes lead FDA and device manufacturers to different interpretations. The original guidance provided the Agency's interpretation of these terms, with principles and points for manufacturers to consider in analyzing how changes in devices may affect safety or effectiveness and determining whether a new 510(k) must be submitted for a particular type of change. The current guidance preserves the basic format and content of the original, with updates to add clarity. The added clarity is intended to increase consistent interpretations of the guidance by FDA staff and manufacturers and provide a more transparent framework for determining when submission of a new 510(k) is required.

The 510(k) Process and the Quality System Regulation

Any guidance on 510(k)s for changes to a legally marketed device should consider the role the Quality System (QS) regulation, 21 CFR Part 820, plays in changes to devices. For some types of changes to a device, the Agency believes that submission of a new 510(k) is not required and that reliance on existing QS requirements is the least burdensome approach to reasonably assure the safety and effectiveness of the changed device.

Regardless of whether a change requires premarket review, the QS regulation requires manufacturers of finished medical devices to review and approve changes to device design and production (21 CFR 820.30 and 820.70) and document changes and approvals in the device master record (21 CFR 820.181). Any process whose results cannot be fully verified by subsequent inspection and testing must be validated (21 CFR 820.75), and changes to the process require review, evaluation, and revalidation of the process where appropriate (21 CFR 820.75(c)).

The net effect of the QS regulation is to require that, when manufacturers of a finished medical device make a change in the design of a device, there is a process in place to demonstrate that the manufactured device meets the change in design specifications (or the original specifications, if no change was intended). They must keep records, and these records must be made available to an FDA investigator upon request (see Section 704(e) of the FD&C Act). For many changes to a device, submission of a new 510(k) may not be required. In these cases, including many software design changes, compliance with the QS regulation can reasonably assure the safety and effectiveness of the changed device.

Least Burdensome Principles

The least burdensome provision concerning 510(k)s states that FDA "shall only request information that is necessary..." and "shall consider the least burdensome means of demonstrating substantial equivalence..." (see section 513(i)(1)(D)(i) of the FD&C Act). While not changing the standard for substantial equivalence, this provision states that FDA shall only request the "minimum required information" necessary to support a determination of substantial equivalence (see sections 513(i)(1)(D)(ii)-(iii) of the FD&C Act). The recommendations discussed in this guidance for evaluating when a change in a medical device would trigger the requirement that a manufacturer submit a new 510(k) to the Agency are consistent with least burdensome principles, and applies them in discussing the considerations that may affect the decision-making about when to submit a new 510(k) for a device change or modification.

III. Scope

As used in this guidance, "software" is the set of electronic instructions used to control the actions or output of a medical device, to provide input to or output from a medical device, or to provide the actions of a medical device. This definition includes software that is embedded within or a component of a medical device, software that is an accessory to another medical device, or software that is intended to be used for one or more medical purposes that performs these purposes without being part of a hardware medical device.[1]

This guidance will aid manufacturers of medical devices subject to premarket notification requirements who intend to modify a 510(k)-cleared device (or group of devices) or other device subject to 510(k) requirements, such as a preamendments device or a device that was granted marketing authorization via the De Novo classification process[2] under section 513(f)(2) of the FD&C Act (also referred to together as "existing devices"), during the process of deciding whether the change exceeds the regulatory threshold of 21 CFR 807.81(a)(3) for submission and clearance of a new 510(k). Note that any person required to register under 21 CFR 807.20 who plans to introduce a device into commercial distribution for the first time must, per 21 CFR 807.81(a)(2), submit a 510(k) if that device is not exempt from premarket notification requirements. Also note that devices with changes requiring submission of a new 510(k) may not be legally commercially distributed before FDA clears the changed device (21 CFR 807.100(a) and sections 513(f)(1) and 513(i) of the FD&C Act). Private label distributors and repackagers are exempt from submitting

1 IMDRF/SaMD WG/N10: Software as a Medical Device (SaMD): Key Definitions (http://www.imdrf.org/docs/imdrf/final/technical/imdrf-tech-131209-samd-key-definitions-140901.pdf).

2 This guidance applies to devices granted marketing authorization via the De Novo classification process and that are not exempt from premarket notification requirements.

a 510(k) if they satisfy the requirements of 21 CFR 807.85(b). This guidance is not intended to address changes to devices that are 510(k)-exempt or that require premarket approval (PMA).

This guidance specifically addresses software modifications and is intended as a companion to Deciding When to Submit a 510(k) for a Change to an Existing Device (http://www.fda.gov/downloads/MedicalDevices/DeviceRegulationandGuidance/GuidanceDocu ments/ucm080243.pdf). Any modifications that are not modifications to software are not within the scope of this guidance; such changes (e.g., labeling changes) should be evaluated using *Deciding When to Submit a 510(k) for a Change to an Existing Device*. Both guidance documents explain FDA's current thinking on 21 CFR 807.81(a)(3), and as such, the threshold for submission of a new 510(k) in response to a change to an existing device is not different between the two guidances; however the terminology used may differ due to the nature of the technology and the assessment of the risks associated with the change. In addition, it may be necessary to refer to other relevant FDA guidance documents that aid in the evaluation of non- software device modifications. It is the manufacturer's responsibility to collectively evaluate the combination of both software and non-software changes to evaluate the impact of a change to a device. For those circumstances where the proposed change is not addressed in this guidance, in *Deciding When to Submit a 510(k) for a Change to an Existing Device*, or in a device-specific guidance, manufacturers are encouraged to contact the appropriate office in CDRH or CBER.

When there are multiple changes that affect labeling or hardware in addition to software, the manufacturer should assess the changes using both the general and software-specific modifications guidances. If use of either guidance leads to a "New 510(k)" conclusion, submission of a new 510(k) is likely required.

This guidance does not apply to software for which the Agency has stated in guidance that it does not intend to enforce compliance with applicable regulatory controls (see, e.g., *Mobile Medical Applications Guidance for Industry and FDA Staff* https://www.fda.gov/downloads/medicaldevices/deviceregulationandguidance/guidancedocumen ts/ucm263366.pdf. Further, this guidance does not address the software lifecycle (covered in AAMI/ANSI/IEC 62304: *Medical device software - software life cycle processes*), what documentation should be included in a 510(k) for a software modification (covered in *Guidance for the Content of Premarket Submissions for Software Contained in Medical Devices* (http://www.fda.gov/downloads/MedicalDevices/DeviceRegulationandGuidance/GuidanceDocu ments/ucm089593.pdf)) or the principles that are applicable to the validation of medical device software (covered in *General Principles of Software Validation; Final Guidance for Industry and FDA Staff* (http://www.fda.gov/downloads/MedicalDevices/DeviceRegulationandGuidance/GuidanceDocu ments/ucm085371.pdf)).

This guidance is also intended to apply to situations when a legally marketed existing device is the subject of a recall, correction, or removal, and a change in the device or its labeling is necessary. For more information on recommended procedures in a recall situation, please see *Blue Book Memorandum K95-1, 510(k) Requirements During Firm-Initiated Recalls* (http://www.fda.gov/MedicalDevices/DeviceRegulationandGuidance/GuidanceDocuments/ucm0 80297.htm). As stated in that guidance, if a correction alters a device rather than simply restoring it to its original specifications, submission of a new 510(k) may be required. FDA may use this guidance in determining whether submission of a new 510(k) is warranted in cases where the correction does alter the device.

This guidance does not specifically address combination products, such as drug/device or biologic/device combinations; however, the general principles and concepts described herein may be helpful to manufacturers in determining whether submission of a 510(k) is required for changes to software-containing device constituent parts of combination products.

Software modifications may be identified by many names, including, but not limited to: bug fix, hot fix, patch, software change, code change, or tweak. Regardless of name or form, these are considered design changes under the Quality System regulation, 21 CFR Part 820.

This guidance is not intended to supersede final device-specific guidance (such as the *Infusion Pumps Total Product Life Cycle* https://www.fda.gov/downloads/medicaldevices/deviceregulationandguidance/guidancedocumen ts/ucm209337.pdf), but may cover areas not addressed in any final device-specific guidance.

IV. Guiding Principles

In using this guidance for deciding whether to submit a new 510(k) for a change to an existing device, a number of guiding principles should be followed. Some derive from existing FDA 510(k) policy and are widely known, and others are necessary for using the logic scheme contained in this guidance. Thus, anyone using this guidance should bear in mind the following Guiding Principles:

1. **Changes made with intent to significantly affect safety or effectiveness of a device** – If a manufacturer modifies their device with the intent to significantly affect the safety or effectiveness of the device (for example, to significantly improve clinical outcomes, to mitigate a known risk, in response to adverse events, etc.), submission of a new 510(k) is likely required. A change intended to significantly affect the safety or effectiveness of the device is considered to be a change that "could significantly affect the safety or effectiveness of the device" and thus requires submission of a new 510(k) regardless of the considerations outlined below. Changes that are not intended to significantly affect the safety or effectiveness of a device, however, should still be evaluated to determine whether the change could significantly affect device safety or effectiveness.

   If a manufacturer modifies their device to address a violation or recall, they should refer to FDA guidances *Blue Book Memorandum K95-1, 510(k) Requirements During Firm-Initiated Recalls* (http://www.fda.gov/MedicalDevices/DeviceRegulationandGuidance/GuidanceDocument s/ucm080297.htm) and *Distinguishing Medical Device Recalls from Medical Device Enhancements* (https://www.fda.gov/downloads/medicaldevices/deviceregulationandguidance/guidanced ocuments/ucm418469.pdf).

2. **Initial risk-based assessment** – To determine whether a change or modification could significantly affect the safety or effectiveness of a device, the manufacturer should first conduct a risk-based assessment, using the guidance below, of whether the change could significantly affect the device's safety or effectiveness, either positively or negatively. This

risk-based assessment should identify and analyze all new risks and changes in existing risks resulting from the device change, and lead to an initial decision whether or not submission of a new 510(k) is required.

For the purposes of this guidance, we have chosen the term "risk-based assessment" to describe the analysis that should be completed to assist in the determination of whether or not a change could significantly affect safety or effectiveness of the device. Although common risk analysis methods define risk in terms of device harms and their effects on safety, it is important to note that whether submission of a new 510(k) is required depends on whether the change could significantly affect the safety or effectiveness of the device. Therefore, manufacturers should also consider the possible effects a device change may have on device effectiveness. As such, we have chosen to use the distinct terminology of "risk-based assessment."

3. **Unintended consequences of changes** – After a manufacturer considers whether the change was made with the intent to significantly affect safety or effectiveness, the manufacturer should also consider whether the change could have unintended consequences. Software modifications may trigger additional unintended or unplanned consequences which should be assessed using the flowchart (and its companion text) to determine if submission of a new 510(k) is needed. For example, an intended operating system (OS) upgrade may trigger unintended effects in device drivers and software code embedded in the device and/or may require an update to other components for compatibility purposes. Manufacturers should consider all consequences of changes to fully assess whether submission of a new 510(k) is required.
4. **Use of risk management** – A risk-based assessment as referred to throughout this document is based on the combination of multiple risk concepts that are important for managing the risks of medical devices. Hazards and hazardous situations, risk estimation, risk acceptability, risk control, risk/benefit analysis and overall risk evaluation are all concepts that can be applied during the design and development of a medical device. The concept of risk, as defined in ISO 14971: *Medical devices – Application of risk management to medical devices*, is the combination of the probability of occurrence of harm and the severity of that harm. Although the risk terminology used in this document is primarily derived from ISO 14971, we recognize that an individual manufacturer's terminology may differ. Because 21 CFR 807.81(a)(3)(i) requires submission of a new 510(k) when a change "could significantly affect safety or effectiveness," both safety and effectiveness should be considered in evaluating a device's risk profile and performing a risk-based assessment. The risk terminology from the currently FDA-recognized version of IEC TR 80002-1: *Medical device software – Part 1: Guidance on the application of ISO 14971* to medical device software is also used in this guidance. For software, failures tend to be systematic in nature and therefore the probability of occurrence of a software failure cannot be determined using traditional statistical methods. While it may be possible to estimate the probability for other events in the sequence, if the overall probability of occurrence of harm cannot be estimated, the estimation of risk should be based on the severity of harm alone.

5. **The role of testing (i.e., verification and validation activities) in evaluating whether a change could significantly affect safety and effectiveness** – If the initial decision following the risk-based assessment is that submission of a new 510(k) is not required, this decision should be confirmed by successful, routine verification and validation activities. If routine verification and validation activities produce any unexpected results, any prior decision that submission of a new 510(k) is not required should be reconsidered in light of these issues (i.e., go through the flowchart again). Because 21 CFR 807.81(a)(3) requires submission of a new 510(k) for a change that "could significantly affect safety or effectiveness," if the result of a risk-based assessment is that a change could significantly affect safety or effectiveness, submission of a new 510(k) is required even if routine verification and validation activities are conducted successfully without any unexpected results. Note that verification and validation requirements apply for all devices subject to 21 CFR 820.30, and must be conducted regardless of whether submission of a new 510(k) is required.
6. **Evaluating simultaneous changes to determine whether submission of a new 510(k) is required** – Because many simultaneous changes may be considered at once, each change should be assessed separately, as well as in aggregate. Note that, for software, each individual line change in the code may not constitute an individual change in the device.
7. **Appropriate comparative device and cumulative effect of changes** – In using this guidance to help determine whether a particular change requires submission of a new 510(k), a manufacturer should conduct a risk-based assessment that compares the changed device to their device as previously found to be substantially equivalent in their most recently cleared 510(k), to their preamendments device (if the device was in commercial distribution before May 28, 1976 and there have not been changes to it subsequently cleared in a 510(k)), or to their device that FDA granted marketing authorization via the De Novo classification process (if there have not been changes to it subsequently cleared in a 510(k)). The appropriate comparative device is referred to as the "original device" throughout this guidance document. Of note, this comparison is different from a substantial equivalence comparison between the modified device and a legally marketed predicate device. Manufacturers may make a number of changes without having to submit a new 510(k), but each time they make a change, the modified device should be compared to the original device (i.e., the device described in their most recently cleared 510(k) for the device, to their legally marketed preamendments device, or to their device that was granted marketing authorization via the De Novo classification process). When the cumulative effect of individual changes triggers the regulatory threshold for submission, the manufacturer should submit a new 510(k). When it does not, the manufacturer must document the change(s) (see 21 CFR Part 820.30).
8. **Documentation requirement** – Whenever manufacturers change their device, they must take certain actions to comply with the QS regulation, 21 CFR Part 820, unless the device in question is exempt by regulation from the QS regulation. The QS regulation requires, among other things, that device changes be documented. The scope and type of

documentation may vary, but the process of documenting the decisions described in this guidance should be established as part of the manufacturer's own quality system.

9. **510(k) submissions for modified devices** – When a new 510(k) is submitted for a device with multiple changes, that 510(k) should describe all changes that trigger the requirement for submission of a new 510(k). To help ensure that FDA has a complete understanding of the device under review, that 510(k) should also describe other changes since the most recently cleared 510(k) (i.e., those that did not require submission of a new 510(k)) that would have been documented as part of the first 510(k) for that device. For instance, 510(k)s typically include a listing of device warnings in the labeling, so if a warning in the device's labeling had been changed, that change should be described in the new 510(k) for the software modification even if that labeling change did not itself trigger the requirement for submission of a new 510(k) and the 510(k) is being triggered by a software modification only. A 510(k) would not typically identify or describe individual components of a circuit board, such as resistors, or identify the specific version of a printer driver, and therefore FDA would not expect changes to the resistors or the printer driver to be listed in the new 510(k) for a modified device because the first 510(k) would have not included information about the resistors or printer drivers. Please note that manufacturers should know which versions of off-the-shelf software and/or firmware are included in their device even if that level of detail is not included in a 510(k).

   If a manufacturer makes multiple changes to a device, but only one change triggers the requirement for submission of a new 510(k), the changes that do not require submission of a new 510(k) may be immediately implemented, so long as those changes can be implemented independently of changes that do require submission of a new 510(k). Any immediately implemented change should still be documented in accordance with applicable QS regulations and the manufacturer's documentation procedures. Those changes should, however, also be described in the new 510(k) for the change that does require submission.

10. **Substantial equivalence determinations** – Manufacturers should understand that, even though they may follow this guidance and submit a new 510(k), a substantially equivalent determination is not assured. See FDA's guidance *The 510(k) Program: Evaluating Substantial Equivalence in Premarket Notifications (510(k))* (https://www.fda.gov/downloads/medicaldevices/deviceregulationandguidance/guidanced ocuments/ucm284443.pdf) for more information on the decision-making process FDA uses to determine substantial equivalence.

IV. How to Use This Guidance

This guidance uses a flowchart and text with considerations and examples to guide manufacturers through the logic scheme we recommend to arrive at a decision on whether to submit a new 510(k) for a software change to an existing device. A single logic scheme covering all the intricacies in software modifications and their impact on the decision to submit a new 510(k) would be impractical to develop. Rather, for ease of use, a flowchart and text expected to cover the most common software modifications has been created.

Manufacturers should use the flowchart in concert with the Guiding Principles above, the text below, and additional factors in section VI. Manufacturers should answer the questions posed for each individual type of change (e.g., performance specification change, OS driver change) until a decision is made either to submit a new 510(k) or to document the basis for concluding that submission of a new 510(k) is not required. As mentioned above, when making the decision on whether to submit a new 510(k) for changes, the manufacturer's basis for comparison of any changed device should be the original device. Manufacturers are required to submit a new 510(k) when a change (or changes) exceeds the 21 CFR 807.81(a)(3) threshold, "could significantly affect the safety or effectiveness of the device," or constitutes a "major change or modification in the intended use of the device." This significant effect could be positive or negative. One must keep in mind that what may on the surface appear to be one discrete change to a device may involve multiple changes of various types. Appendix A provides a number of examples with rationale that can be helpful in working through this guidance.

In cases with multiple changes, manufacturers should use all applicable parts of the flowchart and companion text, including the Guiding Principles in Section IV of this guidance.

Note that the flowchart entries, "new 510(k)" and "document," are written in this way only for conciseness. The reader should interpret "new 510(k)" as submission of **a new 510(k) is likely required and "document" as a new 510(k) is likely not required, document your analysis, and file it for future reference.** The goal of the flowchart is to provide guidance in answering a manufacturer's questions on whether submission of a new 510(k) is likely required for a software change and to minimize the number of instances where the answer would be uncertain.

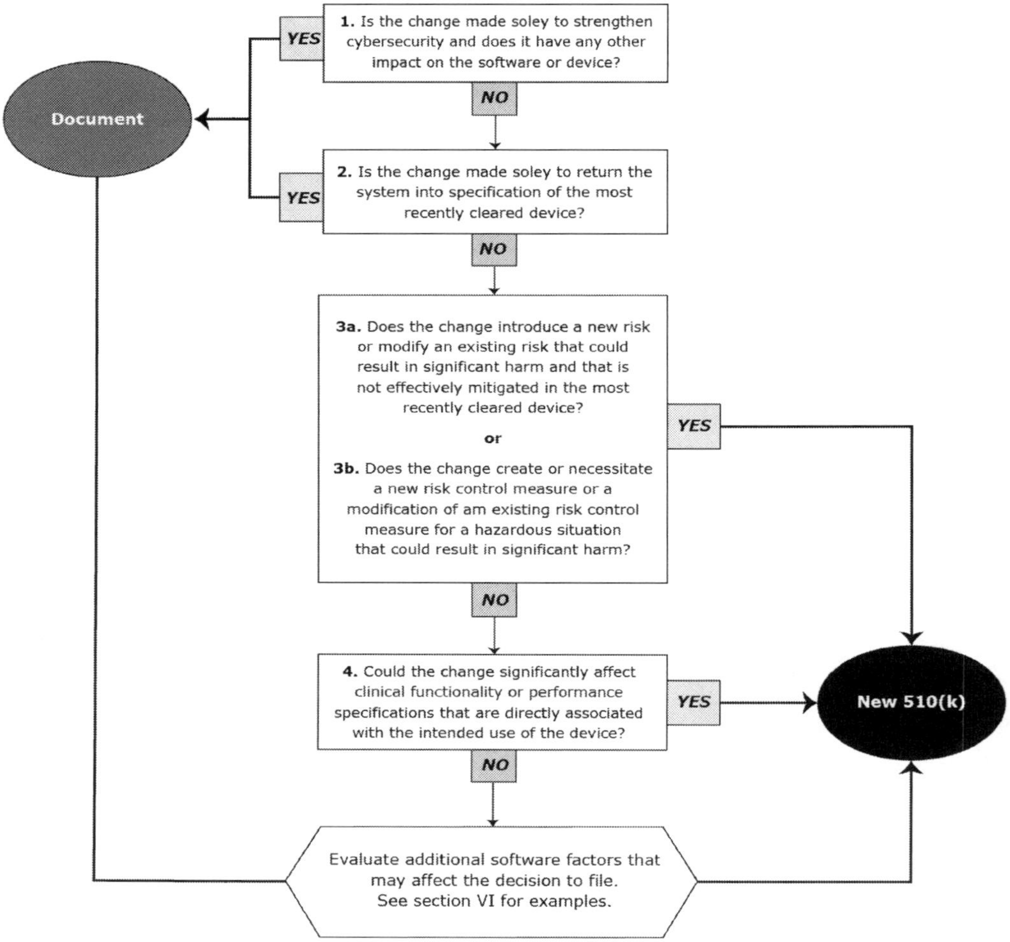

This flowchart is not intended to be used as a 'stand-alone' document and should only be considered in conjunction with the accompanying text in this guidance.

Figure 1. When to Submit a New 510(k) For a Software Change to an Existing Device.

1. Is the change made solely to strengthen cybersecurity and does not have any other impact on the software or device?

In many cases, a change made solely to strengthen cybersecurity is not likely to require submission of a new 510(k). Cybersecurity updates are considered a subset of software changes that are implemented to strengthen the security of a system, protect information, and reduce disruption in service. FDA expects manufacturers to ensure that such changes do not impact the safety or effectiveness of the device by performing necessary analysis, verification, and/or validation. If a manufacturer becomes aware of any incidental or unintended impacts of the change on other aspects of the software or device, the manufacturer should continue through the remaining questions in this guidance. The manufacturer should also refer to FDA's guidance *Content of Premarket Submissions for Management of Cybersecurity in Medical Devices* (http://www.fda.gov/downloads/medicaldevices/deviceregulationandguidance/guidancedocumen ts/ucm356190.pdf) and *Postmarket Management of Cybersecurity in Medical Devices* (https://www.fda.gov/downloads/medicaldevices/deviceregulationandguidance/guidancedocume nts/ucm482022.pdf).

2. Is the change made solely to return the system into specification of the most recently cleared device?

When a change to the software only restores the device to the specifications of the most recently cleared device, then submission of a new 510(k) is likely not required. Generally, it is unlikely that modifications to software solely to restore the device to the most recently cleared device's specifications could significantly impact safety, effectiveness, or intended use of the device; however, manufacturers should evaluate the impact of the software changes. Manufacturers should conduct an analysis that involves determining the overall impact of the change to the device in terms of risk assessment and performance. The concepts expressed in Questions 3 and 4 below could be helpful in this analysis. In addition, this analysis is important for evaluating any modification that adds new features that appeared in the specification of the most recently cleared device but were not yet implemented.

Missing, incomplete, ambiguous, or conflicting software requirements may lead to a software modification that involves updating specifications, resulting in additional software code changes. In these situations, the answer to this question is likely "no" and the manufacturer should proceed to Question 3.

Generally, manufacturers are not required to submit a new 510(k) for changes to a specification document to clarify to an existing software requirement or to capture a missing software requirement, provided that this does not necessitate any changes to software code or product performance specifications. However, manufacturers should still assess the impact of the changes on other software documentation when applying appropriate design controls.

3. What are the impacts of any changes to risks associated with use of the device and the impacts of any changes to the risk controls for the device?

a) Does the change introduce a new risk or modify an existing risk that could result in significant harm and that is not effectively mitigated in the most recently cleared device?

The purpose of this question is to determine whether a new risk is created or has been identified, or if an existing risk is modified, as a result of the software change. The term "risk" is meant to broadly include hazard, hazardous situation, or cause of an existing hazard or hazardous situation. A "hazardous situation" exists when there is exposure to a hazard (i.e., a potential source of harm) that can lead to physical injury or damage to the health of people. The term "cause" refers to one possible component in the "sequence of events," that can lead to a hazardous situation and possible harm, as described in ISO 14971. These are identified and defined by the manufacturer in the risk management file for the device. Significant harm refers to situations where the risk level is serious or more severe, e.g., the risk could result in injury or impairment requiring professional medical intervention, permanent impairment, or death.

Submission of a new 510(k) is likely required if <u>**all**</u> of the following criteria are met:

1. The change creates a new or modifies a hazard, hazardous situation, or cause in the risk management file.
2. The level of harm associated with the new or modified hazard, hazardous situation, or cause is considered serious or more severe, e.g., the hazard, hazardous situation, or cause of the hazardous situation could result in injury or impairment requiring professional medical intervention, permanent impairment, or death. The pre-mitigation risk score should be assessed in order to focus on the effects of the change.
3. The hazard, hazardous situation, or cause is not already effectively mitigated in the most recently cleared device.
    - Note: This criterion is met if there are no existing risk control measures in the most recently cleared device that reduce the risk associated with this hazard, hazardous situation, or cause to an acceptable level.
    - Note: New hazards, hazardous situations, or causes of hazardous situations may be effectively mitigated by risk controls that were already included in the device for other hazards, hazardous situations, or causes.

If all of the above criteria are not met, proceed to Question 3b.

b) Does the change create or necessitate a new risk control measure or a modification of an existing risk control measure for a hazardous situation that could result in significant harm?

It is possible that introducing new risk control measures or implementing changes to existing risk control measures could significantly affect the safety or effectiveness of the product, and thus such changes should be evaluated. It may be that the change is directly tied to the risk control measures or the software change may necessitate a new or modified risk control measure. Changes to or additions of risk control measures may be necessary due to new, modified, or previously unknown hazardous situations or causes thereof. If the changes to risk controls are necessary to prevent significant harm, submission of a new 510(k) is likely required. Conversely, submission of a new 510(k) is likely not required when implementing redundant risk control measures or enhancing existing risk control measures if the risk control measures in the most recently cleared device effectively mitigated the hazardous situation.

If the answer to this question is no, proceed to Question 4.

4. Could the change significantly affect clinical functionality or performance specifications that are directly associated with the intended use of the device?

Changes in performance specifications encompass everything from routine specification changes necessary to improve device performance to significant product redesigns. For the purpose of this question, specifications include elements that could influence the device's ability to clinically perform as intended. These specifications may address attributes such as speed, strength, response times, throughput, limits of operation, reliability, delivery rate, or assay performance.

If the software change could significantly affect clinical functionality or performance specifications that are directly associated with the intended use of the device, then submission of a new 510(k) is likely required. For *in vitro* diagnostic devices (IVDs), this includes a change that could have clinically significant impact in terms of clinical decision-making. This question does not address direct changes to the indications for use and/or intended use of the device. If there is a change in the indications for use and/or intended use of the device, refer to FDA's guidance, *Deciding When to Submit a 510(k) for a Change to an Existing Device* (http://www.fda.gov/downloads/MedicalDevices/DeviceRegulationandGuidance/GuidanceDocu ments/ucm080243.pdf).

For IVDs, performance generally refers to the analytical and clinical specifications established as part of the most recent 510(k) clearance. Analytical performance refers to the documented ability of an IVD test or test system to measure or detect a target analyte or substance that the IVD test or test system is represented or purported to identify or measure. Clinical performance refers to the documented ability of an IVD test or test system to identify, measure, monitor, or predict the presence or absence of, or the future development of, a clinical condition or predisposition, for which the device is intended.

Depending on the assay, analytical performance specifications may be defined by:

- Analytical Sensitivity: limit of detection, reactivity (inclusivity);
- Analytical Specificity: exclusivity, cross-reactivity, interference;
- Cut-off and equivocal zone; and/or
- Precision: site-to-site reproducibility, within-laboratory precision/repeatability.

There are also times when IVD functionality or performance specifications could be changed but the change is not related to the IVD's intended use and the performance of the modified device could not be significantly affected when compared to previously cleared performance claims, and thus submission of a new 510(k) would not be required.

V. Additional Factors to Consider When Determining When to Submit a New 510(k) for a Software Change to an Existing Device

In addition to the questions above, the common issues below should also be considered when determining if submission of a new 510(k) is required.

Medical device software is used in a wide variety of applications and is subject to a wide variety of changes. This guidance, therefore, cannot address every type of software change. Nonetheless, the questions in the flowchart and the associated recommendations in the text provide a guide for manufacturers' decision-making and associated documentation. The goal of the guidance is to provide examples of software changes that clearly could have a significant impact on the safety or effectiveness of the device based on functional changes to the device's operation (Note: modifications in the intended use of the device are covered in *Deciding When to Submit a 510(k) for a Change to an Existing Device* (http://www.fda.gov/downloads/MedicalDevices/DeviceRegulationandGuidance/GuidanceDocu ments/ucm080243.pdf)). The impact of software changes on safety and effectiveness may not always be clear. This is often the case when making general code changes to software that are not necessarily intended to change function, but rather to perform what could be described as "code maintenance" or "infrastructure" modifications. These types of changes can, if not controlled properly, create unexpected changes to how the device functions. These types of changes, as well as others described in this section, should therefore involve a careful evaluation of their potential impact on device safety and effectiveness.

In addition to change management, these types of changes should also involve careful consideration of the overall architecture of the software. If the software architecture was developed in a planned, modular format, the likelihood of unintended impact to other areas of the code may be significantly reduced. On the other hand, if the software code was developed in a looser construct, without a clear architectural plan, the ability to clearly delineate between functional modules in the code may be reduced. The potential impact to device safety and effectiveness increases in code with looser construct, due to the inherent risk of unintended changes in code without clear boundaries in the functional modules.

The purpose of this section is to provide guidance regarding evaluation of certain types of software changes, such as "code maintenance" and "infrastructure" changes. Manufacturers are encouraged to discuss these "gray areas" with the relevant CDRH or CBER Office and Division if there are questions about whether to submit a new 510(k) for these or other types of software changes. In most cases, this will be the Division under which the device was originally cleared.

Common Software Change Types

The following list of common change types are intended to help manufacturers consider additional factors that may affect a decision to submit a new 510(k). Note that this list is not exhaustive. Any questions should be discussed with the respective CDRH Offices and/or CBER Offices and/or Divisions responsible for the device being modified.

Some of the common software change types include:

- **"Infrastructure"** changes are modifications made to the software support system. Examples include but are not limited to: switching compilers, changing programming languages (C to C++, C++ to Java), or changing software drivers or libraries.

  The complexity of the change should be taken into consideration while determining whether the change requires submission of a new 510(k). For example, when changing programming languages, the similarity of the programming syntax between the two languages, as well as other factors (such as the coding paradigm associated with the old and new code), should be considered. A change from C to C++ may not entail significant code writing if the syntax is similar. On the other hand, moving from a functional or logical coding paradigm to an Object Oriented Programming paradigm, in conjunction with the change from C to C++, could involve significant software re-write, and submission of a new 510(k) is likely required.

  Similar analysis generally applies to software driver changes, OS changes, etc. It should be noted that significant changes to verification and validation scripts might be a signal that significant infrastructure changes have taken place and should be examined. Updates to scripts alone do not indicate that submission of a new 510(k) is required; however, it is important to understand why the scripts are being updated.

- **"Architecture"** changes are modifications to the overall structure of the software. Examples include but are not limited to: porting to a new OS, software changes to support a new hardware platform, and new middleware.

  These changes may impact the overall performance of the device or extend the environment in which the device can operate. The extent of the changes and the impact that they have on the device should be considered in determining whether submission of a new 510(k) is required.

- **"Core algorithm"** changes are modifications made to an algorithm that directly impact or contribute to the device's intended use. Examples include: alarm algorithms on a monitor, a motor control algorithm for an infusion pump, and a detection module and measurement engine algorithm for an IVD.

  Changes to the core algorithm that impact performance are addressed by the preceding section and flowchart. However, it is important to understand that a complete rewrite of the algorithm, even with the same performance claims and risk profile, may be significant enough to require submission of a new 510(k) because the rewrite may impact performance indirectly.

- **"Clarification of Requirements – No Change to Functionality"** are changes made to clarify software requirements after a product has received premarket clearance. This clarification may be revised phrasing of an existing requirement or creation of a new requirement altogether, without changing or adding functionality. Changes made to clarify the requirements as discussed here likely do not require submission of a new 510(k).
- **"Cosmetic Changes – No Change to Functionality"** are changes made to the appearance of the device that do not impact the clinical use of the device. For example, changing the company logo that is displayed on the background of every screen could involve modifying multiple software modules; while the number of modules impacted may be large, it is unlikely that the intended change could significantly impact the device's safety and effectiveness or intended use, and submission of a new 510(k) is likely not required.
- **"Reengineering"** and **"refactoring"** are two common software maintenance techniques. **"Reengineering"** is defined as the examination and alteration of software to reconstitute it in a new form, and includes the subsequent implementation of the new form. It is often undertaken to replace aging legacy software. **"Refactoring"** is a disciplined technique for restructuring a software program's internal structure without changing its clinical performance specification. Refactoring seeks to improve a program structure and its maintainability. In general, reengineering often results in broader and more complex changes, while refactoring is often narrower in scope and less complex. The complexity of the change and the impact on risk controls or performance should be considered to determine whether the change requires submission of a new 510(k). Changes that are minor modifications to enhance the maintainability of the device within its specification context are unlikely to require submission of a new 510(k). Changes involving significant software re-write likely require submission of a new 510(k) because of the impact on the performance and on the risk controls.

Appendix A. Software Modification Examples

The following are hypothetical examples of software changes with explanations as to why they likely would or would not require submission of a new 510(k). Note that these generalized examples do not necessarily account for every possible detail, risk, or consideration a manufacturer should evaluate, and should not be taken to mean that the changes described definitely do or do not require submission of a new 510(k). Real-world device modification decisions will depend on the particular details of the change and the specific device in question.

The examples below are only intended to illustrate the principles and recommendations discussed above with regard to a particular question. As such, the examples each contain only the response to the question that is being highlighted; this does not necessarily mean that an earlier question would not have appropriately led to a decision to submit a new 510(k).

1. Flowchart Question 1 Examples

1.1. Proactive software security patch

Description: A device manufacturer finds a security vulnerability as part of an ongoing security evaluation of their device. The manufacturer modifies the software solely to remove this vulnerability. The manufacturer's analysis determined that the change does not have any other impact on the software or the device.

#	*Question*	*Yes/No*	*Rationale*
1	Is the change made solely to strengthen cybersecurity and does not have any other impact on the software or device?	Yes	The change is made solely to address cybersecurity vulnerabilities or to strengthen cybersecurity. The manufacturer's analysis determined that the change does not impact any other aspects of the software or device.

Outcome: Document the change to file.

1.2. Adding encryption and additional access control for remote users

Description: A manufacturer makes a software modification to add encryption to the configuration file of the device, and add passcode requirements for remote users, in addition to the password needed to access the device. A timeout is also added for remote users. The manufacturer's analysis determined that the change does not have any other impact on the software or the device.

#	*Question*	*Yes/No*	*Rationale*
1	Is the change made solely to strengthen cybersecurity and does not have any other impact on the software or device?	Yes	The change is made to restrict user/ customer access to appropriate levels and provide protection to the device configuration information, in order to strengthen the cybersecurity of the device. The manufacturer's analysis determined that the change does not have any other impact on the software or the device.

Outcome: Document the change to file.

2. Flowchart Question 2 Examples

2.1. Modify system to meet specification

Description: A manufacturer makes a software modification to prevent system software from truncating Specimen Identification (ID) barcode information. Without the change, the software system would truncate the Specimen ID from the point of an inserted invalid character. For instance, if the invalid character was "%" and the Specimen ID barcode was "12345%678," the system software would read and assign a Specimen ID of "12345." This defect could lead to mis-association of patient data. Incorrect software collation of patient information with patient results could lead to incorrect reports. The specification of the most recently cleared device indicated what constituted an invalid character and how invalid characters were to be handled. However, the software did not handle this one particular invalid character in line with the specification. A change is made to the software to prevent the truncation of Specimen ID barcode information where an invalid character has been inserted.

#	*Question*	*Yes/No*	*Rationale*
2	Is the change made solely to return the system into specification of the most recently cleared device?	Yes	The software change disallowed use of the specific invalid character in Specimen IDs as defined in the instrument host interface specification. The original specification indicated how all illegal characters were to be handled. The existing device handled all but one as indicated in the specification. The change is made solely to ensure the software meets the original specification.

Outcome: Document the change to file.

2.2. Correcting DICOM retrieve parameter error

Description: A PACS (Picture Archiving and Communication System) is able to automatically retrieve prior studies from a radiology information system to allow comparison with the current study. A software error resulted in a non DICOM-compliant (Digital Imaging and Communications in Medicine standard; http://dicom.nema.org/) sending of query parameters that prevented the automatic fetching of prior studies. A manual workaround existed, allowing the user to open these prior studies as needed. The manufacturer implements a software change to bring the product back to specification regarding DICOM conformance (send and retrieve).

#	Question	Yes/No	Rationale
2	Is the change made solely to return the system into specification of the most recently cleared device?	Yes	The software change is implemented solely to return the system into specification of the most recently cleared device regarding DICOM conformance (send and retrieve) by automatically opening prior studies as expected in a routing reading workflow.

Outcome: Document the change to file.

2.3. Error during maintenance procedure

Description: A manufacturer makes a software modification to fix an automated scheduled daily maintenance procedure. The defect concerned the cleaning solution bottle size parameter used in a maintenance procedure. The defect impacted the system's ability to detect fluid on the bottle septum and caused intermittent fluid detection errors during the maintenance procedure. The user may need to repeat the procedure 2-3 times to complete the procedure without error. A software change is made to update the size parameter as was originally documented in the software specifications.

#	Question	Yes/No	Rationale
2	Is the change made solely to return the system into specification of the most recently cleared device?	Yes	The change is to correct the software error to change the bottle size parameter back to the specified bottle size to bring system back into specification.

Outcome: Document the change to file.

2.4. Data error

Description: An issue was observed in IVD analyzer software that collects reagent administrative records (e.g., material number, lot number, expiration date). The records are to be written by the software into a database table. After enough records are collected to fill the table, newly-collected records are then to be written in the first row of the table, overwriting previous records. Because of a software bug, the system mistakenly merges the new data with the existing data in the first row of the table. The cause of the anomaly was determined to be a coding error that did not affect any of the software requirements. A change was made to correct the software code in the control unit of the analyzer to ensure that data written to a row in the table is not merged with any existing data. The change to the software involved modification of a table within the analyzer software to add new columns to track the administrative data stored for reagents to prevent data from being merged.

#	*Question*	*Yes/No*	*Rationale*
2	Is the change made solely to return the system into specification of the most recently cleared device?	Yes	The change was only to address a software anomaly and was not a change in specification or functionality of the most recently cleared device.

Outcome: Document the change to file.

2.5. Database error

Description: An issue was observed for an IVD analyzer in the field. The IVD analyzer software collects reagent administrative records (e.g., material number, lot number, expiration date). The records are to be written by the software into a database table. After enough records are collected to fill the table, newly-collected records are then to be written in the first row of the table, overwriting previous records. Under certain conditions, the software system mistakenly merges the new data with the existing data in the first row of the table in the database, which may lead to an incorrect result. The cause of the bug was found to be an incorrectly worded software requirement that led to an error in the software code. The requirement was rewritten. An additional software change was made to correct the software code in the control unit of the analyzer. Code was modified to ensure that data written to a database is not merged with any existing data.

The change to the software involved creating an entirely separate database within the instrument software, specifically for the administrative records stored for reagents to prevent records from being merged. This change required a specification change at the unit level to describe the new database.

#	*Question*	*Yes/No*	*Rationale*
2	Is the change made solely to return the system into specification of the most recently cleared device?	No	A change was made to correct a coding error by adding a new database. This caused a change to the design specifications of the software.

Outcome: Continue to question 3.

3. Flowchart Question 3a Examples

3.1. Adding a new diagnostic parameter

Description: An electroencephalogram (EEG) diagnostic monitor was cleared with spectral edge frequency (SEF) and peak power (PP) as quantitative parameters. The device's intended use is to monitor brain electrical activity through electrodes placed on the surface of the head. A software modification is made to add Amplitude Integrated EEG (aEEG) as an additional quantitative parameter that was not included in the original premarket notification.

#	*Question*	*Yes/No*	*Rationale*
3a	Does the change introduce a new risk or modify an existing risk that could result in significant harm and that is not effectively mitigated in the most recently cleared device?	Yes	The hazardous situation most commonly associated with quantitative diagnostic parameters is the risk of incorrect or confusing information to the physician leading to a misdiagnosis, which could result in significant harm. While the causes of incorrect information for SEF and PP would be included in the original risk files, aEEG introduces a new cause related to an error in the aEEG calculation. Submission of a new 510(k) is required because the new cause is not effectively mitigated in the most recently cleared device and the hazardous situation, as discussed above, could result in significant harm.

Outcome: Submit the change in a new 510(k).

3.2. Removing a diagnostic parameter

Description: An electroencephalogram (EEG) diagnostic monitor was cleared with Spectral Edge Frequency (SEF) and Peak Power (PP). SEF and PP are used by neurologists as quantitative parameters along with the raw EEG trace and other clinical metrics to arrive at a clinical decision. The device's intended use is to monitor brain electrical activity through electrodes placed on the surface of the head. A modification is made to remove PP from the displayed quantitative parameters based on a marketing- conducted survey that indicated customers did not use PP in their clinical decisions.

#	Question	Yes/No	Rationale
3a	Does the change introduce a new risk or modify an existing risk that could result in significant harm and that is not effectively mitigated in the most recently cleared device?	No	Removal of PP does not introduce a new risk or modify any of the existing risks for the device.

Outcome: Continue to question 3b.

3.3. Customer maintenance procedure

Description: The manufacturer makes a software modification to prevent a patient sample probe motor from overheating during a customer maintenance procedure. Power is applied to the sample probe motor to keep the sample probe assembly in a locked position during the user maintenance procedure. In the field, it was reported that applying power to the sample probe motor for more than 20 minutes causes the motor to overheat and creates a potential minor burn hazard (i.e., it becomes too hot to touch safely). The software change applies a timeout to power being applied to the sample probe motor during the maintenance procedure; after ten minutes, power to the sample probe motor is turned off. An additional software change adds a message window at the beginning of the procedure to alert the user that the procedure must be completed within a ten-minute window or the system will cut power to the motor. A limit of ten minutes was determined to keep the motor from overheating to the point of creating a potential minor burn hazard.

#	Question	Yes/No	Rationale
3a	Does the change introduce a new risk or modify an existing risk that could result in significant harm and that is not effectively mitigated in the most recently cleared device?	No	The change provides a mitigation to an existing hazardous situation that was not appropriately mitigated in the cleared device. However, the hazardous situation could not cause significant harm.

Outcome: Continue to question 3b.

3.4. Adding new programming mode to a cardiac monitor

Description: The device is an implantable, automatically activated monitoring system that records subcutaneous electrocardiograms designed to record the arrhythmias in a patient. The manufacturer has made a software modification to add an alternative programming mode to change the way the device interacts with the programmer. This new programming mode provided different capabilities for data programming, interrogating, and managing the device data and function. The mode introduces new technology that impacts the safety profile of the device as a result of the energy transfer that occurs during programming.

#	Question	Yes/No	Rationale
3a	Does the change introduce a new risk or modify an existing risk that could result in significant harm and that is not effectively mitigated in the most recently cleared device?	Yes	This feature introduces new risks based on the new programming mode that could cause significant harm as a result of energy transfer to the patient.

Outcome: Submit the change in a new 510(k).

3.5. Imaging catheters – new optical module and new laser

Description: The device is an imaging catheter for coronary arteries that includes lasers and optical components. The manufacturer modifies the device software to integrate new optical modules and a new advanced laser method. The integration of the new components and function pose new risks to patients as a result of the new control parameters for the laser which could result in patient injury if not integrated appropriately.

#	Question	Yes/No	Rationale
3a	Does the change introduce a new risk or modify an existing risk that could result in significant harm and that is not effectively mitigated in the most recently cleared device?	Yes	The change introduces new hazardous situations associated with interoperability. This change introduces a new hazardous situation as a result of the optical module not recognizing the new catheter and therefore not providing the correct laser settings, which could result in significant harm.

Outcome: Submit the change in a new 510(k).

4. Flowchart Question 3b Examples

4.1. Modification of a risk control

Description: The device is a robotically assisted surgical system that utilizes position sensors. The system incorporates primary and secondary sensors to monitor the movement of actuators to prevent uncontrolled motion of the instrument in the event of a component failure. The system goes into a fault state and halts motion if the position information between the sensors does not match within a certain threshold. The threshold for each actuator is programmed in the software and there is a specification for how much overall movement is acceptable at the tip of the instrument before movement stops. The manufacturer makes a software change to the threshold settings for the position sensors; specifically, the software specification that defines the tip movement was widened and the software was changed to allow the wider tolerance. The change was made to minimize false assertion of the safety system, and the change in the specification for movement at the tip of the instrument was still within an appropriate safety tolerance for the device, as determined by analysis done by the manufacturer. However, the change modified an existing risk control (distance that can be traveled under fault conditions) that could significantly affect safety or effectiveness.

#	Question	Yes/No	Rationale
3b	Does the change create or necessitate a new risk control measure or a modification of an existing risk control measure for a hazardous situation that could result in significant harm?	Yes	The modified threshold values do not meet the specification for overall tip movement, which was required in the most recently cleared device to effectively mitigate the hazardous situation that could result in significant harm. Thus, the change necessitated modification of an existing risk control in the most recently cleared device and submission of a new 510(k) is required.

Outcome: Submit the change in a new 510(k).

4.2. Modification of threshold settings

Description: The device is a robotically assisted surgical system that utilizes position sensors. The system incorporates primary and secondary sensors to monitor the movement of actuators to prevent uncontrolled motion of the instrument in the event of a component failure. The system goes into a fault state and halts motion if the position information between the sensors does not match within a certain threshold. The threshold for each actuator is programmed in the software and there is a specification for how much overall movement is acceptable at the tip of the instrument before movement stops. The manufacturer makes a software change to the threshold settings for the position sensors; specifically, the software was modified to better calculate overall movement. The change was made to minimize false assertion of the safety system, which required the surgeon to hit an override button to continue. This requirement can be a nuisance and distract from surgery. The modified software continued to meet the specification for movement at the tip of the instrument after a component failure.

#	Question	Yes/No	Rationale
3b	Does the change create or necessitate a new risk control measure or a modification of an existing risk control measure for a hazardous situation that could result in significant harm?	No	This change modifies sensor threshold parameters so that transient conditions that can be present during normal operation do not cause unnecessary activation of the risk control measure. The change makes the system more noise-tolerant without impacting true positive detection for the risk control measure. The overall movement criteria are met under all fault conditions.

Outcome: Continue to Question 4.

4.3. Adding user interface alerts and controls

Description: An IVD analyzer manufacturer makes software modifications to replace existing modes of controls for handling samples having invalid characters in specimen IDs (specimen identification mis-association) received from Laboratory Information System or middleware vendors. Existing manual modes of control were adequate, but required operator interaction to evaluate whether a result record for a sample had an invalid specimen ID. The new modes of control include additional automation through a design improvement that will not generate results for a sample having an invalid specimen ID. Instead, the system software will: (1) generate a warning message to the operator that an invalid specimen ID was detected; (2) not generate or report results for a sample having an invalid specimen ID; and (3) create a system log entry.

#	Question	Yes/No	Rationale
3b	Does the change create or necessitate a new risk control measure or a modification of an existing risk control measure for a hazardous situation that could result in significant harm?	Yes	This software change modifies the risk control that identifies invalid characters by automating a previously manual process. If the invalid characters are not identified appropriately, then patient laboratory test results could be lost or replaced by incorrect results. Loss or replacement of results could influence treatment decisions, which could cause significant harm.

Outcome: Submit the change in a new 510(k).

4.4. Print patient information on PACS report

Description: A PACS provides the option to print images along with a copy of the diagnostic findings from the radiologist. There is data on each page allowing the user to match each page to the corresponding information (e.g., patient ID, Study Identifier). This data helps to address the known risk of pages being mixed-up after printout. Based on customer preference, the manufacturer decided to enhance this existing risk control and have actual patient information and demographics printed on each page. This is intended to be easier for the user to identify which pages belong together and, as a result, further decrease the risk of mixing up printed pages.

#	Question	Yes/No	Rationale
3b	Does the change create or necessitate a new risk control measure or a modification of an existing risk control measure for a hazardous situation that could result in significant harm?	No	The risk is already sufficiently mitigated with the original risk controls (that is, to have patient identification related information on each printed page). This software modification is a redundant risk control that was not made in response to a new, modified, or previously unknown hazardous situation or cause thereof.

Outcome: Continue to Question 4.

4.5. Infusion pump alarm

Description: A general purpose infusion pump has one alarm to alert the user when an occlusion has been detected. The software change modifies the existing alarm to provide two alarms related to occlusion: occlusion downstream and occlusion upstream. These alarms provide specific information to help resolve the occlusion.

#	Question	Yes/No	Rationale
3b	Does the change create or necessitate a new risk control measure or a modification of an existing risk control measure for a hazardous situation that could result in significant harm?	Yes	The change modifies the risk control, i.e., the alarm, which is already present for occlusion. This risk control is necessary to improve safety by effectively mitigating specific occlusion events that could result in significant harm if not resolved correctly.

Outcome: Submit the change in a new 510(k).

5. Flowchart Question 4 Examples

5.1. Improve sample throughput 1

Description: A manufacturer makes a software performance enhancement to improve sample throughput time by 20%. Software modifications include changes to decrease assay cycle times by allowing for shorter sample reaction incubation times. Decreasing sample assay times could have an impact on run performance and/or assay performance in a manner that could have a negative impact on diagnosis or therapy delivered to patients.

#	Question	Yes/No	Rationale
4	Could the change significantly affect clinical functionality or performance specifications that are directly associated with the intended use of the device?	Yes	The change is to increase the throughput performance specification, but has a significant impact on the performance of the device. There is a shorter reaction incubation time and therefore a potential significant impact on diagnostic utility and effectiveness.

Outcome: Submit the change in a new 510(k).

5.2. Improve sample throughput 2

Description: A manufacturer makes a software modification to improve sample throughput by 5% by decreasing pre-analytic processing time. Software modifications include a change to decrease sample delivery time from the sample load area to the sample aspiration area. As described here, decreasing sample delivery times do not have an impact on assay performance.

#	Question	Yes/No	Rationale
4	Could the change significantly affect clinical functionality or performance specifications that are directly associated with the intended use of the device?	No	The modifications do not impact assay performance as it relates to intended use. Improvement resulted from technical analysis of the sample delivery algorithm to optimize timing and remove unnecessary timing delays.

Outcome: If the factors identified in Section VI are not relevant for this change, document the change to file.

5.3. Software change to modify summary window

Description: A manufacturer makes a software modification to increase the number of images that can be viewed in a summary view for an ingestible telemetric gastrointestinal capsule imaging system. The new software allows for four images to be viewed simultaneously instead of two while a user reviews the images. The specifications for the image quality are not impacted by this change.

#	Question	Yes/No	Rationale
4	Could the change significantly affect clinical functionality or performance specifications that are directly associated with the intended use of the device?	No	The change does not significantly impact functionality or performance specifications that are directly associated with the intended use of the device. Having more images in the window allows for the physician to review more images without increasing software loading time.

Outcome: If the factors identified in Section VI are not relevant for this change, document the change to file.

5.4. OEM module

Description: A multi-parameter monitor device was originally cleared with version A of an original equipment manufacturer (OEM) module for blood oxygen saturation (SpO2). The OEM makes a change to version A of the SpO2 sensor. The change to the SpO2 sensor did not require submission of a new 510(k) and the change did not impact the specifications for the SpO2 in terms of data acquisition or processing. However, the SpO2 does identify itself to the multi-parameter monitor using a new version number. This requires a software change on the multi-parameter monitor to allow for successful interoperability with the new version of the sensor.

#	Question	Yes/No	Rationale
4	Could the change significantly affect clinical functionality or performance specifications that are directly associated with the intended use of the device?	No	The clinical functionality is not affected. The software modification allows for successful integration of this version of the sensor.

Outcome: If the factors identified in Section VI are not relevant for this change, document the change to file.

5.5. Sterilizer user interface change

Description: A sterilizer display provides vital information on the temperature, the pressure, and the remaining cycle time. Software changes are made to increase the font size of these parameters on the display due to customer feedback (not related to any adverse events). The items are all in the same location and the appearance is unchanged aside from the larger font size.

#	Question	Yes/No	Rationale
4	Could the change significantly affect clinical functionality or performance specifications that are directly associated with the intended use of the device?	No	Since the information was previously displayed, the change has no significant effect on the functionality or the performance of the device.

Outcome: If the factors identified in Section VI are not relevant for this change, document the change to file.

5.6. Modify device algorithms

Description: A manufacturer makes a software modification to enhance an arrhythmia detection algorithm. The device is intended to provide detection alarms for life- threatening arrhythmias in an intensive care unit (ICU) environment. The change impacts sensitivity and specificity and therefore the detection of arrhythmias, which are critical to the clinical performance of the device.

#	Question	Yes/No	Rationale
4	Could the change significantly affect clinical functionality or performance specifications that are directly associated with the intended use of the device?	Yes	The modification has direct impact on diagnostic performance of the device in that the performance of the arrhythmia detection was changed.

Outcome: Submit the change in a new 510(k).

5.7. Modification to alarm duration

Description: A manufacturer makes a software modification to allow users to silence a low-risk alarm on a dialysis system. The change consists of a "snooze" button that silences the alarm for a set amount of time before resounding.

#	Question	Yes/No	Rationale
4	Could the change significantly affect clinical functionality or performance specifications that are directly associated with the intended use of the device?	No	The silencing of a non-critical alarm does not impact the clinical functionality. The criteria for the alarm are unchanged from the most recently cleared device.

Outcome: If the factors identified in section VI are not relevant for this change, document the change to file.

CSV

Chapter 18

Guidance for Industry and FDA Staff[1]

Guidance for the Content of Premarket Submissions for Software Contained in Medical Devices

May 11, 2005
U.S. Department of Health and Human Services
Food and Drug Administration
Center for Devices and Radiological Health
Office of Device Evaluation
Office of In Vitro Diagnostics
Center for Biologics Evaluation and Research Office of Blood Research and Review

Introduction

This guidance document is intended to provide information to industry regarding the documentation that we recommend you include in premarket submissions for software devices, including stand alone software applications and hardware-based devices that incorporate software. This document is a result of ongoing efforts to state our recommendations more clearly and ensure they remain current as technology advances. This document also combines into one guidance recommendations previously included in two guidance documents.i

The Least Burdensome Approach

The issues identified in this guidance document represent those that we believe should be addressed before your device can be marketed. In developing the guidance, we carefully considered the relevant statutory criteria for Agency decision-making. We also considered the burden that may be incurred in your attempt to follow the guidance and address the issues we have identified. We believe that we have considered the least burdensome approach to resolving the issues presented in the guidance document. If, however, you believe that there is a less burdensome way to address the issues, you should follow the procedures outlined in the guidance, **A Suggested Approach to Resolving Least Burdensome Issues**, http://www.fda.gov/cdrh/modact/leastburdensome.html.

FDA's guidance documents, including this guidance, do not establish legally enforceable responsibilities. Instead, guidances describe the Agency's current thinking on a topic and should be viewed only as recommendations, unless specific regulatory or statutory requirements are cited. The use of the word *should* in Agency guidances means that something is suggested or recommended, but not required.

1 This document supersedes Guidance for the Content of Premarket Submissions for Software Contained in Medical Devices, issued May 29, 1998, and Reviewer Guidance for a Premarket Notification Submission for Blood Establishment Computer Software, issued January 13, 1997

Scope

For the purposes of this document, we refer to devices that contain one or more software components, parts, or accessories, or are composed solely of software as "software devices," including:

- firmware and other means for software-based control of medical devices
- stand-alone software applications
- software intended for installation in general-purpose computers
- dedicated hardware/software medical devices.
- accessories to medical devices when those accessories contain or are composed of software.

This guidance applies to software devices regardless of the means by which the software is delivered to the end user, whether factory-installed, installed by a third-party vendor, or field-installed or -upgraded.

Software not covered by this guidance includes software designed for manufacturing or other process-control functions but not intended for use as a device. For further information or to clarify the requirements for your device, please contact the responsible FDA review division.

This guidance document applies to all types of premarket submissions for software devices, including:

- Premarket Notification (510(k)) including Traditional, Special, and Abbreviated submissions
- Premarket Approval Application (PMA)
- Investigational Device Exemption (IDE)
- Humanitarian Device Exemption (HDE), including amendments and supplements.

Relationship to Other Documents

FDA Guidance Documents

We intend this document to complement other existing guidance documents that provide recommendations related to software. For example, we recommend that you also refer to the guidance "General Principles of Software Validation"ii for recommendations on software related to a device (including software that is a stand-alone device or that is a component, part, or accessory of a device). We recommend that you refer to the "Guidance for Off-the-Shelf Software Use in Medical Devices"[iii] in cases where your device uses off-the-shelf software.

Manufacturers of Software Devices should create and maintain software-related documentation in accordance with the requirements of the Quality System Regulationiv (QS regulation) (21 CFR part 820). As with other FDA guidance documents that provide recommendations, please note that following the recommendations of this guidance is not a substitute for compliance with the QS regulation.

Software-Related Consensus Standards

The emergence of consensus standards related to software has helped to improve the consistency and quality of software development and documentation, particularly with respect to critical activities such as risk assessment and management. When possible, we harmonized the terminology and recommendations in this guidance with software-related consensus standards such as ISO 14971[v] and AAMI SW68.[vi]

TERMINOLOGY

Verification and Validation

This document uses the terms "verification" and "validation" (also referred to as "V&V") as they are defined in the QS regulation.[iv]

Verification "means confirmation by examination and provision of objective evidence that specified requirements have been fulfilled." 21 CFR 820.3(aa). In a software development environment, software verification is confirmation that the output of a particular phase of development meets all of the input requirements for that phase. Software testing is one of several verification activities intended to confirm that the software development output meets its input requirements. Other verification activities include:

- walk-throughs
- various static and dynamic analyses
- code and document inspections
- module level testing
- integration testing.

Design validation "means establishing by objective evidence that device specifications conform with user needs and intended use(s)." 21 CFR 820.3(z)(2). Use of the term validation in this document is limited to design validation and does not include process validation as defined in 21 CFR 820.3(z)(1).

One component of design validation is software validation. Software validation refers to establishing, by objective evidence, that the software conforms with the user needs and intended uses of the device. Software validation is a part of design validation of the finished device. It involves checking for proper operation of the software in its actual or simulated use environment, including integration into the final device where appropriate. Software validation is highly dependent upon comprehensive software testing and other verification tasks previously completed at each stage of the software development life cycle. Planning, verification, traceability, configuration management, and many other aspects of good software engineering are important activities that together help to support a conclusion that software is validated.

Minor and Serious Injuries

For the purposes of this document, we use the term minor injury to mean any injury that does not meet the definition of a serious injury as defined in 21 CFR 803.3(bb)(1)*[sic]*[2].This regulation defines serious injury as an injury or illness that:

i. is life threatening;

ii. results in permanent impairment of a body function or permanent damage to a body structure; or

iii. necessitates medical or surgical intervention to preclude permanent impairment of a body function or permanent damage to a body structure.

For the purposes of this document, the term permanent is defined as "irreversible impairment or damage to a body structure or function, excluding trivial impairment or damage." 21 CFR 803.3(bb)(2)*[sic]*.

Level of Concern

Introduction

The documentation that we recommend you include in a premarket submission generally depends on the device's Level of Concern. For the purposes of this guidance document, Level of Concern refers to an estimate of the severity of injury that a device could permit or inflict, either directly or indirectly, on a patient or operator as a result of device failures, design flaws, or simply by virtue of employing the device for its intended use. We recommend that you describe the role of the software in causing, controlling, and/or mitigating hazards that could result in injury to the patient or the operator, because this is also a factor in determining the appropriate Level of Concern for your device.

The extent of documentation that we recommend you submit for your Software Device is proportional to the Level of Concern associated with the device. Level of Concern is defined only for use in this context and is not related to device classification (Class I, II or III) or to hazard or risk analysis *per se.*

Major, Moderate, or Minor Level of Concern

The following sections provide recommendations for determining the Level of Concern that may be appropriate for your Software Device and recommendations for documentation that you should submit for each Level of Concern. We recommend that you determine the Level of Concern before any mitigation of relevant hazards. In other words, the Level of Concern should be driven by the hazard analysis in the absence of mitigations, regardless of the effects of the mitigations on the individual hazards.

FDA recommends that you state in your submission the Level of Concern you have determined for your Software Device. It may be Major, Moderate or Minor as defined below. We also recommend that you describe how you arrived at that Level of Concern. The Level of Concern is

2 The correct citation for the definition of "serious injury" as utilized in this document is 21CFR§803.3(w)

based on how the operation of the software associated with device function affects the patient or operator. The effect may be direct or indirect.

Major

We believe the level of concern is Major if a failure or latent flaw could directly result in death or serious injury to the patient or operator. The level of concern is also Major if a failure or latent flaw could indirectly result in death or serious injury of the patient or operator through incorrect or delayed information or through the action of a care provider.

Moderate

We believe the level of concern is Moderate if a failure or latent design flaw could directly result in minor injury to the patient or operator. The level of concern is also Moderate if a failure or latent flaw could indirectly result in minor injury to the patient or operator through incorrect or delayed information or through the action of a care provider.

Minor

We believe the level of concern is Minor if failures or latent design flaws are unlikely to cause any injury to the patient or operator.

Determining Level of Concern

We have provided the following key questions to assist you in determining the Level of Concern. We recommend that you assess the Level of Concern before mitigating any hazard; that is, you should assess your software device against these questions as though you have not implemented hazard mitigations.

If the answer to any question is No, continue on to the next question. As discussed in more detail later, we recommend that you include the basis for your conclusion as to the Level of Concern in your submission. In all cases, we recommend that you assess the Level of Concern within the context of the worst possible, reasonably foreseeable, clinical consequences of failure of the Software Device.

Table 1 Major Level of Concern

If the answer to any <u>**one**</u> question below is **Yes**, the Level of Concern for the Software Device is likely to be **Major**.
1. Does the Software Device qualify as Blood Establishment Computer Software? (Blood Establishment Computer Software is defined as software products intended for use in the manufacture of blood and blood components or for the maintenance of data that blood establishment personnel use in making decisions regarding the suitability of donors and the release of blood or blood components for transfusion or further manufacture.)
2. Is the Software Device intended to be used in combination with a drug or biologic?
3. Is the Software Device an accessory to a medical device that has a Major Level of Concern?
4. Prior to mitigation of hazards, could a failure of the Software Device result in death or serious injury, either to a patient or to a user of the device? Examples of this include the following:
a. Does the Software Device control a life supporting or life sustaining function?
b. Does the Software Device control the delivery of potentially harmful energy that could result in death or serious injury, such as radiation treatment systems, defibrillators, and ablation generators?
c. Does the Software Device control the delivery of treatment or therapy such that an error or malfunction could result in death or serious injury?
d. Does the Software Device provide diagnostic information that directly drives a decision regarding treatment or therapy, such that if misapplied it could result in serious injury or death?
e. Does the Software Device provide vital signs monitoring and alarms for potentially life threatening situations in which medical intervention is necessary?

Table 2 Moderate Level of Concern

If the Software Device **is not Major** Level of Concern and the answer to any <u>**one**</u> question below is **Yes,** the Level of Concern is likely to be **Moderate.**
1. Is the Software Device an accessory to a medical device that has a Moderate Level of Concern?
2. Prior to mitigation of hazards, could a failure of the Software Device result in Minor Injury, either to a patient or to a user of the device?
3. Could a malfunction of, or a latent design flaw in, the Software Device lead to an erroneous diagnosis or a delay in delivery of appropriate medical care that would likely lead to Minor Injury?

If the answers to all of the questions in Tables 1 and 2 above are **No**, the Level of Concern is **Minor**.

The review divisions at FDA are available to discuss any questions you may have about the Level of Concern for your Software Device. If you believe the Level of Concern for your device is Major and you have not previously filed a premarket submission for this type of Software Device, we recommend that you contact the appropriate division at FDA to discuss your Software Device before filing your submission.

Software-related Documentation

Software-related documentation that you provide in your premarket submission should be consistent with the intended use of the Software Device, the Level of Concern, and the type of submission. This section describes the documentation that we recommend you include in your premarket submission based on the Level of Concern (see Table 3). However, you should follow the recommendations in device-specific guidance, if available for your device. In general, the documentation provided in your submission should:

- describe the design of your device
- document how your design was implemented
- demonstrate how the device produced by your design implementation was tested
- show that you identified hazards appropriately and managed risks effectively
- provide traceability to link together design, implementation, testing, and risk management.

The type and extent of documentation that we recommend you submit is summarized in Table 3. Our recommendations are keyed to the Level of Concern of your device. These recommendations are predicated on your effective implementation and management of the QSR, including Design Controls.[iv]

We believe the documents that we recommend submitting will generally be the same documents that you would normally generate during the development of a Software Device. Therefore, in a properly managed and documented medical device software development environment, the documents that you submit in response to the recommendations in this guidance may be copies of your product development documents.

We explain the documents that we recommend submitting in the sections following Table 3. In some instances, the recommended documentation for the Level of Concern may take the form of statements in the body of the submission; other documents, such as the Software Requirements Specification, will likely be stand-alone documents copied into the submission.

Table 3. Documentation Based on Level of Concern

SOFTWARE DOCUMENTATION	MINOR CONCERN	MODERATE CONCERN	MAJOR CONCERN
Level of Concern	A statement indicating the Level of Concern and a description of the rationale for that level.		
Software Description	A summary overview of the features and software operating environment.		
Device Hazard Analysis	Tabular description of identified hardware and software hazards, including severity assessment and mitigations.		
Software Requirements Specification (SRS)	Summary of functional requirements from SRS.	The complete SRS document.	
Architecture Design Chart	No documentation is necessary in the submission.	Detailed depiction of functional units and software modules. May include state diagrams as well as flow charts.	
Software Design Specification (SDS)	No documentation is necessary in the submission.	Software design specification document.	
Traceability Analysis	Traceability among requirements, specifications, identified hazards and mitigations, and Verification and Validation testing.		
Software Development Environment Description	No documentation is necessary in the submission.	Summary of software life cycle development plan, including a summary of the configuration management and maintenance activities.	Summary of software life cycle development plan. Annotated list of control documents generated during development process. Include the configuration management and maintenance plan documents.
Verification and Validation Documentation	Software functional test plan, pass/fail criteria, and results.	Description of V&V activities at the unit, integration, and system level. System level test protocol, including pass/fail criteria, and tests results.	Description of V&V activities at the unit, integration, and system level Unit, integration and system level test protocols, including pass/fail criteria, test report, summary, and tests results.
Revision Level History	Revision history log, including release version number and date.		
Unresolved Anomalies (Bugs or Defects)	No documentation is necessary in the submission.	List of remaining software anomalies, annotated with an explanation of the impact on safety or effectiveness, including operator usage and human factors.	

Level of Concern

We recommend that you indicate the Level of Concern for your Software Device, determined before the effects of any mitigations. We recommend that you clearly state which one of the three levels of concern is appropriate for your device and include documentation of the rationale for your decision. We also recommend that your documentation make your decision-making process apparent to FDA.

Software Description

We recommend that you provide a comprehensive overview of the device features that are controlled by software, and describe the intended operational environment. Generally, we recommend that you provide the information in paragraph format and highlight major or operationally significant software features. The software description should include information on the following:

- programming language
- hardware platform
- operating system (if applicable)
- use of Off-the-Shelf software (if applicable).

If your device uses Off-the Shelf software, please refer to the FDA guidance document "Guidance for Off-the-Shelf Software Use in Medical Devices."[iii]

If this information is included in another document, such as the Software Requirements Specification, your submission should contain an annotation and a reference to the document in the submission where this information is located.

Device Hazard Analysis

We recommend that you submit a Device Hazard Analysis for all Software Devices. The Device Hazard Analysis should take into account all device hazards associated with the device's intended use, including both hardware and software hazards. We recommend that you present the information in tabular form with a line item for each identified hazard. This document can be in the form of an extract of the software-related items from a comprehensive risk management document, such as the Risk Management Summary described in ISO 14971.[v] In this format, each line item should include:

- identification of the hazardous event
- severity of the hazard
- cause(s) of the hazard
- method of control (e.g., alarm, hardware design)
- corrective measures taken, including an explanation of the aspects of the device design/ requirements, that eliminate, reduce, or warn of a hazardous event; and
- verification that the method of control was implemented correctly.

When performing a hazard analysis, we recommend that you address all foreseeable hazards, including those resulting from intentional or inadvertent misuse of the device.

Software Requirements Specification

The Software Requirements Specification (SRS) documents the requirements for the software. This typically includes functional, performance, interface, design, developmental, and other requirements for the software. In effect, this document describes what the Software Device is supposed to do. Examples of some typical requirements that would be included in a SRS are described below. For Software Devices that are identified as Minor Level of Concern, we recommend that you provide only the summary functional requirements section from the SRS, including identification of off-the-shelf software. For Software Devices that are identified as Major or Moderate Level of Concern, we recommend that you provide the complete SRS document.

Hardware Requirements

Hardware requirements generally include:

- microprocessors
- memory devices
- sensors
- energy sources
- safety features
- communications.

Programming Language Requirements

Programming language requirements include program size requirements or restrictions, and information on management of memory leaks.

Interface Requirements

Interface requirements generally include both communication between system components and communication with the user such as:

- printers
- monitors
- keyboard
- mouse.

Software Performance and Functional Requirements

Software performance and functional requirements include algorithms or control characteristics for therapy, diagnosis, monitoring, alarms, analysis, and interpretation with full text references or supporting clinical data, if necessary. Software performance and functional requirements may also include:

- device limitations due to software
- internal software tests and checks
- error and interrupt handling
- fault detection, tolerance, and recovery characteristics
- safety requirements
- timing and memory requirements
- identification of off-the-shelf software, if appropriate.

Architecture Design Chart

This document is typically a flowchart or similar depiction of the relationships among the major functional units in the Software Device, including relationships to hardware and to data flows such as networking. It is usually not necessary to include every function call and module in this document; however, there should be sufficient information to allow for review of the organization of the software relative to the functionality and to the intended use of the Software Device. For Moderate and Major Level of Concern devices, detailed information such as state diagrams may be useful to clearly depict the relationships among the software functional units. If the Architecture Design Chart is included in another document such as the SRS then you should include in your submission a statement to that effect and a reference to the location of the Architecture Design Chart in the submission.

Software Design Specification

The Software Design Specification (SDS) describes the implementation of the requirements for the Software Device. In terms of the relationship between the SRS and the SDS, the SRS describes what the Software Device will do and the SDS describes how the requirements in the SRS are implemented. The information presented in the SDS should be sufficient to ensure that the work performed by the software engineers who created the Software Device was clear and unambiguous, with minimal ad hoc design decisions. The SDS may contain references to other documents, such as detailed software specifications. However, the document you submit should, in and of itself, provide adequate information to allow for review of the implementation plan for the software requirements in terms of intended use, functionality, safety, and effectiveness.

Traceability Analysis

A Traceability Analysis links together your product design requirements, design specifications, and testing requirements. It also provides a means of tying together identified hazards with the implementation and testing of the mitigations. We recommend that you submit for review explicit traceability among these activities and associated documentation because they are essential to effective product development and to our understanding of product design, development and testing, and hazard mitigations. The Traceability Analysis commonly consists of a matrix with line items for requirements, specifications and tests, and pointers to hazard mitigations. It is possible to document traceability simply through a shared organizational structure with a common numbering scheme; however, we recommend that you include some mechanism, such as a matrix for guiding the reviewer through the information you submit.

Software Development Environment Description

For Moderate and Major Level of Concern Software Devices, the submission should include a summary of the software development life cycle plan. This summary should describe the sponsor's software development life cycle and the processes that are in place to manage the various life cycle activities. For Major Level of Concern Software Devices, this document should also include an annotated list of the control/baseline documents generated during the software development process and a list or description of software coding standards.

As mentioned elsewhere, configuration or change management is a crucial aspect of software development. Changes to the Software Device after initial market release should be subject to positive control, with definitive specification and test plans including well-defined regression testing where appropriate. The description of the development environment should provide information on your configuration management and maintenance plan that addresses these aspects of the software development life cycle. For a Major Level of Concern device, we recommend that you provide sufficient detail to allow for a thorough understanding of the configuration management and maintenance plan. For a Moderate Level of Concern device, we recommend that you provide only a summary of the configuration management and maintenance plans.

Verification and Validation Documentation

The terms "verification" and "validation" described earlier in this document refer to two phases of Software Device testing. This section recommends the type of testing documentation you should include in a premarket submission for a Software Device, based on the Level of Concern.

Minor Level of Concern Devices

For Minor Level of Concern devices, we recommend that you submit documentation of system or device level testing, and, where appropriate, integration testing. The documentation submitted should include system or device level test pass/fail criteria and a summary of the test results.

Moderate Level of Concern Devices

For Moderate Level of Concern devices, we recommend that you submit a summary list of validation and verification activities and the results of these activities. We also recommend that you submit your pass/fail criteria. You should ensure that the Traceability Analysis effectively links these activities and results to your design requirements and specifications.

Major Level of Concern Devices

For Major Level of Concern devices, we recommend that you submit the information recommended above for Moderate Level of Concern devices and a description of any tests that were not passed. We also recommend that you include any modifications made in response to failed tests and documentation of results demonstrating that the modifications were effective. Documentation provided in your submission should include examples of unit integration testing and a summary of the results.

Revision Level History

Your submission should include the history of software revisions generated during the course of product development. This typically takes the form of a line-item tabulation of the major changes to the software during the development cycle, including date, version number, and a brief description of the changes in the version relative to the previous version. The last entry in the list should be the final version to be incorporated in the released device. This entry should also include any differences between the tested version of software and the released version, along with an assessment of the potential effect of the differences on the safety and effectiveness of the device.

Unresolved Anomalies (Bugs or Defects)

For Moderate and Major Level of Concern Software Devices, the submission should include a list of all unresolved software anomalies. For each anomaly, we recommend that you indicate the:

- problem
- impact on device performance
- any plans or timeframes for correcting the problem (where appropriate).

We recommend that you annotate each item with an explanation of the impact of the anomaly on device safety or effectiveness, including operator usage and human factors issues. Typically, this list can be generated as an output of a change control board or similar mechanism for evaluation and disposition of unresolved software anomalies. We recommend that you communicate this list to the end user as appropriate to assist in the proper operation of the device. In all instances where it is practical to do so, you should include any mitigations or possible work-arounds for unresolved anomalies; this recommendation applies to Blood Establishment Computer Software in particular.

The Special 510(k) Program

For a premarket submission to qualify for review under the Special 510(k) Program, the device should be a modification of your 510(k) cleared device that you own, where the modification does not alter the intended use or the fundamental scientific technology of the devicevii. In a Special 510(k), you should follow the recommendations in this guidance on the documentation to submit, but submit only the documentation related to the modification that prompted the submission. For example, when submitting the documentation of requirements and specifications in a Special 510(k), the documentation should focus on the modifications and may not necessarily include all of the requirements and specifications of the entire device.

We recommend that you submit the regression testing performed to verify and validate the modifications. We recommend that you submit your test plans, pass/fail criteria, and summary results rather than test data. In all cases, the type of software-related documentation and the level of detail you provide should be appropriate to the Level of Concern associated with your device in the context of the modifications. Since a Special 510(k) submission relies on your declaration of conformance to design controls, we believe you cannot properly submit a Special 510(k) until you have completed testing or other activities relied on by your declaration (see section 514(c)(1)(B) of the Federal Food, Drug, and Cosmetic Act (Act) (21 U.S.C. 360d(c)(1)(B)).

The Abbreviated 510(k) Program

An Abbreviated 510(k) submission must include the required elements identified in 21 CFR 807.87. In an Abbreviated 510(k), FDA may consider the contents of the documentation recommended in this guidance to be appropriate supporting data within the meaning of 21 CFR 807.87(f) or (g).

Therefore, we recommend that you submit the documentation described in this guidance.[viii]

If you choose to rely on an FDA-recognized standard for any part of the device design or testing, you may include either a:

- statement that testing will be conducted and meet specified acceptance criteria before the product is marketed; or
- declaration of conformity to the standard.[ix]

Because a declaration of conformity is based on results from testing, we believe you cannot properly submit a declaration of conformity until you have completed the testing the standard describes. For more information, please refer to section 514(c)(1)(B) of the Act and the FDA guidance, "Use of Standards in Substantial Equivalence Determinations."[x]

If you declare conformance to a standard that recommends specific tests or testing methods for your Software Device, we recommend that you submit documentation of pass/fail criteria and associated test results along with your declaration of conformance. We also recommend that you list deviations from the tests and test methods specified in the standard and explain these deviations in terms of the impact on the safety and effectiveness of the Software Device. A list of FDA recognized consensus standards is available on the CDRH web site.[xi]

Additional Topics

Risk Assessment and Management

Background

Inadequate or inappropriate software development life cycle and risk management activities, inappropriate use of a Software Device, or operational errors can result in a variety of potential failures or design flaws. Among these are unsafe or ineffective delivery of energy, drugs, and life-supporting or life-sustaining functions. The delivery of incorrect or incomplete information causing a misdiagnosis or selection of the wrong treatment or therapy is also a potential failure associated with certain Software Devices. Therefore, the risks associated with potential failures or design flaws are a concern during the review of Software Devices.

Risk Assessment and Level of Concern

As mentioned earlier, your assessment of the risks associated with your Software Device should assist you in determining an appropriate Level of Concern. We also recommend that you consider the Level of Concern for other devices of the same generic type or intended use. If you believe a different Level of Concern is appropriate for your device, we recommend that you submit a detailed explanation of your rationale.

Risk Management

The risk associated with Software Devices varies over a continuum from negligible to very severe. In general, FDA considers risk as the product of the severity of injury and the probability of its occurrence. However, software failures are systemic in nature and therefore the probability of occurrence cannot be determined using traditional statistical methods. Therefore, we recommend that you base your estimation of risk for your Software Device on the severity of the hazard resulting from failure, assuming that the failure will occur. We also recommend that you use risk identification and control techniques described in consensus standards such as ISO 14971.[v]

Software Change Management

Design, development, testing, and version control of revisions to the software are as important as development and testing of the software that was reviewed in the premarket submission. We believe the majority of software-related device problems that occur in the field, including software- related device recalls, happen to devices that are running software that has been revised since premarket review. In some instances, revisions that did not require FDA review were implicated in adverse events and recalls.xii We believe this indicates the need for careful control of software revisions.

Blood Establishment Computer Software

In premarket submissions for Blood Establishment Computer Software, you should submit a complete copy of the User's Manual as it will be provided to the user, including, but not limited to, a description of all limitations. Additionally, you should submit the documentation you will provide to the user to describe all outstanding anomalies or software defects with corresponding workarounds, where applicable, if these issues are not addressed in the User's Manual.

Software of Unknown Pedigree (SOUP)

Some or all of the software contained in a Software Device may have been obtained by the submitter from a third party. The type and quality of documentation that accompanies this software can vary considerably. Software for which adequate documentation may be difficult to obtain is referred to as Software of Unknown Pedigree or "SOUP."

It may be difficult for you to obtain, generate, or reconstruct appropriate design documentation as described in this guidance for SOUP. Therefore, we recommend that you explain the origin of the software and the circumstances surrounding the software documentation. Additionally, your Hazard Analysis should encompass the risks associated with the SOUP regarding missing or incomplete documentation or lack of documentation of prior testing. Nonetheless, the responsibility for adequate testing of the device and for providing appropriate documentation of software test plans and results remains with you.

Virus Protection Software

Software applications designed to protect information systems, including Software Devices, from harmful or malicious code ("viruses," "worms," etc.) are becoming more commonplace as devices become increasingly interconnected and therefore exposed to the external information environment. Issues related to installation and testing of virus protection software are beyond the scope of this document. You may contact the CDRH Office of Compliance for more information on this topic.

Interfaces, Networking, and Network Infrastructure

As mentioned above, Software Devices are increasingly interconnected, both through point-to-point interfaces for exchange of specific data with specific devices and by connection to local and wide area networks and the Internet. While data exchange and communication infrastructure such as telephone lines, local area networks, and broadband connections are not regulated as medical devices, connection to these carriers affects the operation of Software Devices, sometimes adversely. An example is a Software Device that is connected to a local area network and ceases to operate properly when a problem occurs with the network interface. We recommend that your software design should take into account both the capabilities and liabilities of the interfaces provided with your device, and in particular that your hazard analysis and mitigations encompass these issues.

Combination Products

Generally, the recommendations of this guidance will apply to the device component of combination products (such as drug-device and biologics-device combinations) when the device component meets the definition of a Software Device. For more information, you may contact the Office of Combination Products or the FDA review division that will have the lead review for your combination product.

References

i This document combines the recommendations in "Guidance for FDA Reviewers and Industry: Guidance for the Content of Premarket Submissions for Software Contained in Medical Devices" issued on May 29, 1998, and "Reviewer Guidance for a Premarket Notification Submission for Blood Establishment Computer Software" issued on January 13, 1997.

ii "General Principles of Software Validation," http://www.fda.gov/cdrh/comp/guidance/938.html.

iii "Guidance for Off-the-Shelf Software Use in Medical Devices" http://www.fda.gov/cdrh/ode/guidance/585.pdf.

iv 21 CFR 820.30 Subpart C – Design Controls of the Quality System Regulation.

v ISO 14971-1; Medical devices - Risk management - Part 1: Application of risk analysis.

vi AAMI SW68:2001; Medical device software - Software life cycle processes.

vii See "The New 510(k) Paradigm – Alternate Approaches to Demonstrating Substantial Equivalence in Premarket Notifications – Final Guidance," available on the FDA Web site at http://www.fda.gov/cdrh/ode/parad510.html.

viii For more information see Device Advice, "How to Prepare an Abbreviated 510(k)," http://www.fda.gov/cdrh/devadvice/3145.html, in particular the section titled "Information Required in an Abbreviated 510(k)."

ix See "Required Elements for a Declaration of Conformity to a Recognized Standard (Screening Checklist for All Premarket Notification [510(K)] Submissions)," http://www.fda.gov/cdrh/ode/reqrecstand.html.

x See "Use of Standards in Substantial Equivalence Determinations," http://www.fda.gov/cdrh/ode/guidance/1131.html.

xi http://www.accessdata.fda.gov/scripts/cdrh/cfdocs/cfStandards/search.cfm.

xii For information on determining when revisions to software should result in a new premarket submission, you should consult the relevant FDA guidances such as "Deciding When to Submit a 510(k) for a Change to an Existing Device," http://www.fda.gov/cdrh/ode/510kmod.html. See also 21 CFR 807.81(a)(3).

Chapter 19
Guidance for Industry
Cybersecurity for Networked Medical Devices Containing Off-the-Shelf (OTS) Software

January 14, 2005
U.S. Department of Health and Human Services
Food and Drug Administration Center for Devices and Radiological Health
Office of Compliance Office of Device Evaluation

Introduction

A growing number of medical devices are designed to be connected to computer networks. Many of these networked medical devices incorporate off-the-shelf software that is vulnerable to cybersecurity threats such as viruses and worms. These vulnerabilities may represent a risk to the safe and effective operation of networked medical devices and typically require an ongoing maintenance effort throughout the product life cycle to assure an adequate degree of protection. FDA is issuing this guidance to clarify how existing regulations, including the Quality System (QS) Regulation, apply to such cybersecurity maintenance activities.

FDA's guidance documents, including this guidance, do not establish legally enforceable responsibilities. Instead, guidances describe the Agency's current thinking on a topic and should be viewed only as recommendations, unless specific regulatory or statutory requirements are cited. The use of the word should in Agency guidances means that something is suggested or recommended, but not required.

The Least Burdensome Approach

We believe we should consider the least burdensome approach in all areas of medical device regulation. This guidance reflects our careful review of the relevant scientific and legal requirements and what we believe is the least burdensome way for you to comply with those requirements. However, if you believe that an alternative approach would be less burdensome, please contact us so we can consider your point of view. You may send your written comments to the contact persons listed on the coversheet to this guidance or to the CDRH Ombudsman. Comprehensive information on CDRH's Ombudsman, including ways to contact him, can be found on the Internet at http://www.fda.gov/cdrh/ombudsman/.

Background

This guidance outlines general principles that we consider to be applicable to software maintenance actions required to address cybersecurity vulnerabilities for networked medical devices—specifically, those that incorporate off-the-shelf (OTS) software. The guidance is organized in question-and-answer format, providing responses to questions that have frequently been posed to FDA staff. The "I" in the questions and the "you" in the answers are intended to apply to device manufacturers who incorporate OTS software in their medical devices.

The QS regulation, 21 CFR Part 820, applies to software maintenance actions. In addition, FDA has issued several guidance documents on software, including:

General Principles of Software Validation; Final Guidance for Industry and FDA Staff, January 11, 2002, http://www.fda.gov/cdrh/comp/guidance/938.html.

Guidance for Industry, FDA Reviewers and Compliance on Off-the-Shelf Software Use in Medical Devices, September 9, 1999, http://www.fda.gov/cdrh/ode/guidance/585.html.

Guidance for FDA Reviewers and Industry, Guidance for the Content of Premarket Submissions for Software Contained in Medical Devices, May 29, 1998, http://www.fda.gov/cdrh/ode/57.html.

Questions and Answers

1. Which medical devices are covered by this guidance?

This guidance provides recommendations for medical devices that incorporate off-the-shelf (OTS) software and that can be connected to a private intranet or the public Internet. This guidance is addressed to device manufacturers who incorporate OTS software in their medical devices. However, this information also may be useful to network administrators in health care organizations and information technology vendors.

2. What is a cybersecurity vulnerability?

For purposes of this guidance, a cybersecurity vulnerability exists whenever the OTS software provides the opportunity for unauthorized access to the network or the medical device. Cybersecurity vulnerabilities open the door to unwanted software changes that may have an effect on the safety and effectiveness of the medical device.

3. What is it about "network-connected medical devices" that causes so much concern?

Vulnerabilities in cybersecurity may represent a risk to the safe and effective operation of networked medical devices using OTS software. Failure to properly address these vulnerabilities could result in an adverse effect on public health. A major concern with OTS software is the need for timely software patches to correct newly discovered vulnerabilities in the software.

4. Who is responsible for ensuring the safety and effectiveness of medical devices that incorporate OTS software?

You (the device manufacturer who uses OTS software in your medical device) bear the responsibility for the continued safe and effective performance of the medical device, including the performance of OTS software that is part of the device.[1]

1 For more information, you should refer to "Guidance for Industry, FDA Reviewers and Compliance on Off- The-Shelf Software Use in Medical Devices," Sept. 9, 1999 (see Background section of this guidance).

5. How should purchasers and users of these medical devices respond to information about a cybersecurity vulnerability?

FDA recommends that purchasers and users of medical devices that may be subject to a cybersecurity vulnerability contact you with their concerns. As **Question 4** explains, you are responsible for the performance of OTS software that is part of your device. Although there may be times when it is appropriate for the user to become involved (see **Question 9** below), the user should not attempt to make changes without seeking your advice and recommendations.

6. What regulations apply to software patches that address cybersecurity vulnerabilities?

The need to be vigilant and responsive to cybersecurity vulnerabilities is part of your obligation under 21 CFR 820.100 to systematically analyze sources of information and implement actions needed to correct and prevent problems. The preamble to the QS regulation explains that actions taken should "be appropriate to the magnitude of the problem and commensurate with the risks encountered" (61 Fed. Reg. 52633; Oct. 7, 1996). Information in this guidance will remind you of some of the actions that ordinarily will be necessary to address this particular type of software concern.

Under 21 CFR 820.30(g), design validation requires that devices conform to defined user needs and intended uses, including an obligation to perform software validation and risk analysis, where appropriate. Software changes to address cybersecurity vulnerabilities are design changes and must be validated before approval and issuance. 21 CFR 820.30(i).

7. Is FDA premarket review required prior to implementation of a software patch to address a cybersecurity vulnerability?

Usually not. In general, FDA review is necessary when a change or modification could significantly affect the safety or effectiveness of the medical device. 21 CFR 807.81(a)(3), 814.39.

a. *510(k)*. For medical devices cleared for market under the 510(k) program, you may refer to our guidance entitled, "Deciding When to Submit a 510(k) for a Change to an Existing Device."[2] That guidance explains that a new 510(k) submission to FDA is necessary for a change or modification to an existing medical device if:

- The medical device has a new or changed indication for use (e.g., the diseases or conditions the medical device is intended to treat); or
- The proposed change (e.g, modification in design, energy source, chemical composition, or material) could significantly affect the safety or effectiveness of the medical device.

It is possible, but unlikely, that a software patch will need a new 510(k) submission.[3] As with all changes made to devices, you should document the basis of your decisions in the design history file. See 21 CFR 820.3(e), 820.30(j).

2 "Deciding When to Submit a 510(k) for a Change to an Existing Device," Jan. 10, 1997, http://www.fda.gov/cdrh/ode/510kmod.html.

3 If a submission is necessary, you should refer to "Guidance for FDA Reviewers and Industry, Guidance for the Content of Premarket Submissions for Software Contained in Medical Devices," May 29, 1998 (see Background section of this guidance).

b. *Premarket Approval Application (PMA)*. For medical devices approved under PMAs (21 CFR Part 814), a PMA supplement is required for a software patch if the patch results in a change to the approved indications for use or is deemed by the manufacturer to have an adverse effect on the safety and effectiveness of the approved medical device. 21 CFR 814.39. Otherwise, you should report your decision to apply a software patch to your PMA device to FDA in your annual reports. See 21 CFR 814.39(b), 814.84.

8. Should I validate the software changes made to address cybersecurity vulnerabilities?

Yes. See answer to **Question 4**. You should validate all software design changes, including computer software changes to address cybersecurity vulnerabilities, according to an established protocol before approval and issuance. 21 CFR 820.30(i). You may refer to the "General Principles of Software Validation; Final Guidance for Industry and FDA Staff" (see **Background** section) for more information about how to validate software changes. For most software changes intended to address cybersecurity vulnerabilities, analysis, inspection, and testing should be adequate and clinical validation should not be necessary.

9. What else should I do to ensure cybersecurity for networked medical devices?

You should maintain formal business relationships with your OTS software vendors to ensure timely receipt of information concerning quality problems and recommended corrective and preventive actions. Because of the frequency of cybersecurity patches, we recommend that you develop a single cybersecurity maintenance plan to address compliance with the QS regulation and the issues discussed in this guidance document.

While it is customary for the medical device manufacturer to perform these software maintenance activities, there may be situations in which it is appropriate for the user facility, OTS vendor, or a third party to be involved. Your software maintenance plan should provide a mechanism for you to exercise overall responsibility while delegating specific tasks to other parties. The vast majority of healthcare organizations will lack detailed design information and technical resources to assume primary maintenance responsibility for medical device software and, therefore, will rely on you to assume the primary maintenance responsibility.

10. Do I need to report a cybersecurity patch?

Not usually, because most software patches are installed to reduce the risk of developing a problem associated with a cybersecurity vulnerability and not to address a risk to health posed by the device. In most cases, therefore, you would not need to report a cybersecurity patch under 21 CFR Part 806 so long as you have evaluated the change and recorded the correction in your records. However, if the software patch affects the safety or effectiveness of the medical device, you should report the correction to FDA, even if a software maintenance plan is in effect.

CSV

Chapter 20
Policy for Device Software Functions and Mobile Medical Applications
Guidance for Industry and FDA Staff

September 27, 2019.
U.S. Department of Health and Human Services
Food and Drug Administration
Center for Devices and Radiological Health
Center for Biologics Evaluation and Research

I. Introduction

The Food and Drug Administration (FDA) recognizes the extensive variety of actual and potential functions of software applications (apps) and mobile apps, the rapid pace of innovation, and their potential benefits and risks to public health. The FDA is issuing this guidance document to inform manufacturers, distributors, and other entities about how the FDA intends to apply its regulatory authorities to select software applications intended for use on mobile platforms (mobile applications or "mobile apps") or on general-purpose computing platforms. Given the rapid expansion and broad applicability of software functions deployed on mobile or other general-purpose computing platforms, the FDA is issuing this guidance document to clarify the subset of software functions to which the FDA intends to apply its authority.

FDA refers to software functions that are device functions as "device software functions." Device software functions may include "Software as a Medical Device (SaMD)" and "Software in a Medical Device (SiMD).[1,2]" Software functions that meet the definition of a device may be deployed on mobile platforms, other general-purpose computing platforms, or in the function or control of a hardware device. If a software function that meets the definition of a device is deployed on a mobile platform, it may be referred to as a "mobile medical app." The policies described in this guidance are independent of the platform on which they might run, are function-specific, and apply across platforms. Therefore, the policies described using terms such as "mobile medical apps," "mobile medical app manufacturers," "device software functions," and "device software function manufacturers" are not specific to whether the the function is deployed on a mobile platform or other general purpose-computing platform.

Many software functions are not medical devices (meaning such software functions do not meet the definition of a device under section 201(h) of the Federal Food, Drug, and Cosmetic Act (FD&C Act)), and FDA does not regulate them as devices. Some software functions may meet the

1 See FDA website on "Software as a Medical Device (SaMD)," available at https://www.fda.gov/medical-devices/digital-health/software-medical-device-samd.

2 See the International Medical Device Regulators Forum final document, "Software as a Medical Device (SaMD): Key Definitions," available at http://www.imdrf.org/docs/imdrf/final/technical/imdrf-tech-131209-samd-key-definitions-140901.pdf.

definition of a medical device, but because they pose a lower risk to the public, FDA intends to exercise enforcement discretion over these devices (meaning it will not enforce requirements under the FD&C Act).

Consistent with the FDA's existing oversight approach that considers functionality of the software rather than platform, the FDA intends to apply its regulatory oversight to only those software functions that are medical devices and whose functionality could pose a risk to a patient's safety if the device were to not function as intended.

FDA is issuing this guidance to provide clarity and predictability for software manufacturers. This document has been updated to be consistent with section 3060(a) of the 21st Century Cures Act, which amended section 520 of the FD&C Act, removing certain software functions from the definition of device in section 201(h) of the FD&C Act, and the guidance document entitled "Medical Device Data Systems, Medical Image Storage Devices, and Medical Image Communications Devices," originally issued on February 9, 2015.[3] Examples of mobile apps and software on the FDA web site[4] (that were added after September 25, 2013) were incorporated into the appropriate appendices of this document for consistency.

For the current edition of the FDA-recognized standard(s) referenced in this document, see the FDA Recognized Consensus Standards Database.[5] For more information regarding use of consensus standards in regulatory submissions, please refer to the FDA guidance titled Appropriate Use of Voluntary Consensus Standards in Premarket Submissions for Medical Devices[6] and "Standards Development and the Use of Standards in Regulatory Submissions Reviewed in the Center for Biologics Evaluation and Research."[7]

FDA's guidance documents, including this guidance, do not establish legally enforceable responsibilities. Instead, guidances describe the Agency's current thinking on a topic and should be viewed only as recommendations, unless specific regulatory or statutory requirements are cited. The use of the word should in Agency guidance means that something is suggested or recommended, but not required.

---

3 Available at https://www.fda.gov/regulatory-information/search-fda-guidance-documents/medical-device-data-systems-medical-image-storage-devices-and-medical-image-communications-devices.

4 Available at https://www.fda.gov/medical-devices/digital-health/device-software-functions-and-mobile-medical-applications.

5 Available at https://www.accessdata.fda.gov/scripts/cdrh/cfdocs/cfStandards/search.cfm.

6 Available at https://www.fda.gov/regulatory-information/search-fda-guidance-documents/appropriate-use-voluntary-consensus-standards-premarket-submissions-medical-devices.

7 Available at https://www.fda.gov/regulatory-information/search-fda-guidance-documents/standards-development-and-use-standards-regulatory-submissions-reviewed-center-biologics-evaluation

II. Background

As mobile platforms become more user friendly, computationally powerful, and readily available, innovators have begun to develop mobile apps of increasing complexity to leverage the portability mobile platforms can offer. Some of these new software functions are specifically targeted to assisting individuals in their own health and wellness management. Other software functions are targeted to health care providers as tools to improve and facilitate the delivery of patient care.

In 1989, FDA prepared a general policy statement on how it planned to determine whether a computer-based product and/or software-based product is a device, and, if so, how the FDA intended to regulate it. The document, "FDA Policy for the Regulation of Computer Products," became known as the "Draft Software Policy." After 1989, however, the use of computer and software products as medical devices grew exponentially and the types of products diversified and grew more complex (and that trend has continued). As a result, the FDA determined that the draft policy did not adequately address all of the issues related to the regulation of all medical devices containing software. Therefore, in 2005, the Draft Software Policy was withdrawn.[8]

Although the FDA has not issued an overarching software policy, the Agency has formally classified certain types of software applications that meet the definition of a device and, through classification, identified specific regulatory requirements that apply to these devices and their manufacturers. These software devices include products that feature one or more software components, parts, or accessories, as well as devices that are composed solely of software.

The FDA has previously clarified that when a software application is used to analyze medical device data, it has traditionally been regulated as an accessory to a medical device[9] or as medical device software. In 2014, the International Medical Device Regulators Forum established globally harmonized vocabulary for such software applications and defined the term "Software as a Medical Device (SaMD).[10]"

As is the case with traditional medical devices, certain software functions that are device functions (referred to in this document as 'device software functions') can pose potential risks to public health. Moreover, certain device software functions may pose risks that are unique to the characteristics of the platform on which the software function is run. For example, the interpretation of radiological images on a mobile device could be adversely affected by the smaller screen size, lower contrast ratio, and uncontrolled ambient light of the mobile platform. FDA intends to take these risks into account in assessing the appropriate regulatory oversight for these products.

---

8 Annual Comprehensive List of Guidance Documents at the Food and Drug Administration (70 FR 824 at 890) (January 5, 2005).

9 See "Medical Device Accessories - Describing Accessories and Classification Pathways" Guidance, available at https://www.fda.gov/regulatory-information/search-fda-guidance-documents/medical-device-accessories-describing-accessories-and-classification-pathways.

10 See the International Medical Device Regulators Forum final document, "Software as a Medical Device (SaMD): Key Definitions," available at http://www.imdrf.org/docs/imdrf/final/technical/imdrf-tech-131209-samd-key-definitions-140901.pdf.

This guidance clarifies and outlines the FDA's current thinking. The Agency will continue to evaluate the potential impact these technologies might have on improving health care, reducing potential medical mistakes, and protecting patients.

III. Definitions

A. Mobile Platform

For purposes of this guidance, "mobile platforms" are defined as commercial off-the-shelf (COTS) computing platforms, with or without wireless connectivity, that are handheld in nature. Examples of these mobile platforms include mobile computers such as smart phones, tablet computers, or other portable computers.

B. Mobile Application (Mobile App)

For purposes of this guidance, a mobile application or "mobile app" is defined as a software application that can be executed (run) on a mobile platform (i.e., a handheld commercial off-the-shelf computing platform, with or without wireless connectivity), or a web-based software application that is tailored to a mobile platform but is executed on a server.

C. Mobile Medical Application (Mobile Medical App)

For purposes of this guidance, a "mobile medical app" is a mobile app that incorporates device software functionality that meets the definition of device in section 201(h) of the FD&C Act[11]; and either is intended:

- to be used as an accessory to a regulated medical device; or
- to transform a mobile platform into a regulated medical device.

11 Products that are built with or consist of computer and/or software components or applications are subject to regulation as devices when they meet the definition of a device in section 201(h) of the FD&C Act. That provision defines a device as "...an instrument, apparatus, implement, machine, contrivance, implant, in vitro reagent, or other similar or related article, including any component, part, or accessory", that is "... intended for use in the diagnosis of disease or other conditions, or in the cure, mitigation, treatment, or prevention of disease, in man ..." or "... intended to affect the structure or any function of the body of man or other animals..." and "does not include software functions excluded pursuant to section 520(o) of the FD&C Act." Thus, software applications that run on a desktop computer, laptop computer, remotely on a website or "cloud," or on a handheld computer may be subject to device regulation if they are intended for use in the diagnosis or the cure, mitigation, treatment, or prevention of disease, or to affect the structure or any function of the body of man. The level of regulatory control necessary to assure safety and effectiveness varies based upon the risk the device presents to public health. (See Appendix D for examples).

The intended use of a mobile app determines whether it meets the definition of a "device." As stated in 21 CFR 801.4,[12] intended use may be shown by labeling[13] claims, advertising materials, or oral or written statements by manufacturers or their representatives. When the intended use of a mobile app is for the diagnosis of disease or other conditions, or the cure, mitigation, treatment, or prevention of disease, or is intended to affect the structure or any function of the body of man, the mobile app is a device under section 201(h) of the FD&C Act if it is not a software function excluded from the device definition by section 520(o) of the FD&C Act.

One example is a mobile app that makes a light emitting diode (LED) operate. If the manufacturer intends the system to illuminate objects generally (i.e., without a specific medical device intended use), the mobile app would not be considered a medical device. If, however, through marketing, labeling, and the circumstances surrounding the distribution, the mobile app is promoted by the manufacturer for use as a light source for doctors to examine patients, then the intended use of the light source would be similar to a conventional device such as an ophthalmoscope.

In general, if a software function is intended for use in performing a medical device function (i.e. for diagnosis of disease or other conditions, or the cure, mitigation, treatment, or prevention of disease) it is a medical device, regardless of the platform on which it is run. For example, mobile apps intended to run on smart phones to analyze and interpret EKG waveforms to detect heart function irregularities would be considered similar to software running on a desktop computer that serves the same function, which is regulated under 21 CFR 870.2340 ("Electrocardiograph"). FDA's oversight approach to software functions is focused on their functionality, just as we focus on the functionality of conventional devices. Our oversight is not determined by the platform. Under this guidance, FDA would not regulate the sale or general/conventional consumer use of smartphones or tablets. FDA's oversight applies to software functions performing medical device functions, such as when a mobile medical app or software application transforms a mobile platform or a general purpose computing platform into a medical device. However, as previously noted, we intend to apply this oversight authority only to those software applications whose functionality could pose a risk to a patient's safety if the software applications were to not function as intended.

12 12 "The words 'intended uses' or words of similar import ... refer to the objective intent of the persons legally responsible for the labeling of devices. The intent is determined by such persons' expressions or may be shown by the circumstances surrounding the distribution of the article. This objective intent may, for example, be shown by labeling claims, advertising matter, or oral or written statements by such persons or their representatives. It may be shown by the circumstances that the article is, with the knowledge of such persons or their representatives, offered and used for a purpose for which it is neither labeled nor advertised. The intended uses of an article may change after it has been introduced into interstate commerce by its manufacturer. If, for example, a packer, distributor, or seller intends an article for different uses than those intended by the person from whom he received the devices, such packer, distributor, or seller is required to supply adequate labeling in accordance with the new intended uses. But if a manufacturer knows, or has knowledge of facts that would give him notice that a device introduced into interstate commerce by him is to be used for conditions, purposes, or uses other than the ones for which he offers it, he is required to provide adequate labeling for such a device which accords with such other uses to which the article is to be put." 21 CFR 801.4.

13 "The term 'labeling' means all labels and other written, printed, or graphic matter (1) upon any article or any of its containers or wrappers, or (2) accompanying such article." Section 201(m) of the FD&C Act, 21 U.S.C. 321(m).

D. Regulated Medical Device

For purposes of this guidance, a "regulated medical device" is defined as a product that meets the definition of device in section 201(h) of the FD&C Act and that has been cleared or approved by the FDA review of a premarket submission or otherwise classified by the FDA.

This definition can include novel devices, whether or not on a mobile platform, that the FDA will clear or approve by the review of a premarket submission or otherwise classify. Examples of regulated medical devices are identified in Appendix D.

E. Mobile Medical App Manufacturer

For purposes of this guidance, a "mobile medical app manufacturer" is any person or entity that manufactures mobile medical apps in accordance with the definitions of manufacturer in 21 CFR Parts 803, 806, 807, and 820.[14] A mobile medical app manufacturer may include anyone who initiates specifications, designs, labels, or creates a software system or application for a regulated medical device in whole or from multiple software components. This term does not include persons who exclusively distribute mobile medical apps without engaging in manufacturing functions; examples of such distributors may include owners and operators of "Google Play," "iTunes App Store," and "BlackBerry App World." Examples of mobile medical app manufacturers include any person or entity that:

- Creates, designs, develops, labels, re-labels, remanufactures, modifies, or creates a mobile medical app software system from multiple components. This could include a person or entity that creates a mobile medical app by COTS software components and markets the product to perform as a mobile medical app;
- Initiates specifications or requirements for mobile medical apps or procures product development/manufacturing services from other individuals or entities (second party) for subsequent commercial distribution. For example, when a "developer" (i.e., an entity that provides engineering, design, and development services) creates a mobile medical app from the specifications that were initiated by the "author," the "author" who initiated and developed specifications for the mobile medical app is considered a "manufacturer" of the mobile medical app under 21 CFR 803.3. For purposes of this guidance, manufacturers of a mobile medical app would include persons or entities who are the creators of the original idea (initial specifications) for a mobile medical app, unless another entity assumes all responsibility for manufacturing and distributing the mobile medical app, in which case that other entity would be the "manufacturer.[15]"

14 Regulatory definitions of the term "manufacturer" or "manufacture" appear in 21 CFR Parts 803, 806, 807, and 820. For example – under FDA's 21 CFR 807.3(d) – establishment registration and device listing for manufacturers and initial importers of devices – *"Manufacture, preparation, propagation, compounding, assembly, or processing of a device means the making by chemical, physical, biological, or other procedures of any article that meets the definition of device in section 201(h) of the act. These terms include the following activities: (1) Repackaging or otherwise changing the container, wrapper, or labeling of any device package in furtherance of the distribution of the device from the original place of manufacture to the person who makes final delivery or sale to the ultimate consumer; (2) Initial importation of devices manufactured in foreign establishments; or (3) Initiation of specifications for devices that are manufactured by a second party for subsequent commercial distribution by the person initiating specifications."*

15 See 21 CFR 803.3 (definition of manufacturer) and 21 CFR 807.20(a)(2).

Software "developers" of a mobile medical app that are only responsible for performing design and development activities to transform the author's specifications into a mobile medical app would not constitute manufacturers, and instead the author would be considered the manufacturer;

- Creates a mobile medical app and hardware attachments for a mobile platform that are intended to be used as a medical device by any combination of the mobile medical app, hardware attachments, and the mobile platform;
- Creates a mobile medical app or a software system that provides users access to the medical device function through a website subscription, software as a service,[16] or other similar means.

In contrast, the following are examples of persons or entities that are NOT considered to be mobile medical app manufacturers (i.e., persons not within the definition of manufacturer in 21 CFR Parts 803, 806, 807, and 820). Because they are not manufacturers, none of the persons or entities in these examples would have to register their establishments, list their products with the FDA,[17] or submit a premarket application:

- Manufacturers or distributors of mobile platforms who solely distribute or market their platform and do not intend (by marketing claims – e.g., labeling claims or advertising material) the platform to be used for medical device functions. When mobile medical apps are run on a mobile platform, the mobile platform is treated as a component of the mobile medical app's intended use.[18] Therefore the mobile platform manufacturer is exempt from the Quality System regulation and registration and listing requirements.[19] For example, if it is possible to run mobile medical apps on BrandNamePhone but BrandNamePhone is not marketed by BrandNameCompany as intended for use as a medical device, then BrandNameCompany would not be considered a mobile medical app manufacturer or a medical device manufacturer. Also, in this example, the BrandName Phone sold to consumers would not be regulated by FDA as a medical device. FDA does not consider entities that exclusively distribute mobile medical apps, such as the owners and operators of the "iTunes App Store" or the "Android Market," to be medical device manufacturers. FDA also does not consider mobile platform manufacturers to be medical device manufacturer just because their mobile platform could be used to run a mobile medical app regulated by FDA.
- Third parties who solely provide market access to mobile medical apps (i.e. solely distribute mobile apps), but do not engage in any manufacturing functions as defined in 21 CFR Parts 803, 806, 807, and 820. Examples of such third parties may include owners and operators that are only engaged in providing an online market place that allow

16 By this we mean to include any "server software application" that provides a service to a client software application on a mobile platform.

17 See 21 CFR 807.65 and 21 CFR 807.85.

18 See 21 CFR 820.3(c), which defines a component as "any raw material, substance, piece, part, software, firmware, labeling, or assembly which is intended to be included as part of the finished, packaged, and labeled device."

19 See 21 CFR 807.65(a) and 21 CFR 820.1(a).

mobile medical app manufacturers to commercially distribute their mobile medical apps. Specific examples of such online market places include "Google Play," "iTunes Store," and "BlackBerry App World";

- Providers of tools, services, or infrastructure used in the development, distribution, or use of a mobile medical app. Examples include providers of internet connectivity (i.e., internet service), providers of general-purpose computer or information technology, providers that host the web service for content or software application. Other examples of providers of tools, services, or infrastructure include customer support services, data center hosting services, cloud hosting services, application hosting services, wireless carriers, or providers of software development kits. However, a creator of a mobile medical app or a software system that provides users access to the medical device function through a website subscription, software as a service,[20] or other similar means is considered a mobile medical app manufacturer;
- Licensed practitioners, including physicians, dentists, and optometrists, who manufacture a mobile medical app or alter a mobile medical app solely for use in their professional practice and do not label or promote their mobile medical apps to be generally used by other licensed practitioners or other individuals.[21,22] For example, if Dr. XYZ, a licensed practitioner, creates a mobile medical app called the "XYZ-recorder" that enables attaching an ECG electrode to a smartphone, and provides the "XYZ-recorder" to his/her patient to use it to record the patient's electrocardiographic readings for 24 hours, Dr. XYZ is not considered a mobile medical app manufacturer. If Dr. XYZ is in a group practice (including a telehealth network) and permits other physicians in the practice to provide the XYZ-recorder to their patients, Dr. XYZ is not considered a mobile medical apps manufacturer. However, if Dr. XYZ, the licensed practitioner, distributes the "XYZ-recorder" and, through labeling or promotion intends to make it generally available to or to be generally used by other physicians (or other specially qualified persons), Dr. XYZ would be considered a mobile medical app manufacturer;
- Persons who manufacture mobile medical apps solely for use in research, teaching, or analysis and do not introduce such devices into commercial distribution. We note that while persons conducting research using mobile medical apps involving human subjects are exempt from registration and listing, they may instead be subject to investigational device exemption regulations.[23,24]

---

20 As identified in footnote 15, we mean to include any "server software application" that provides a service to a client software application on a mobile platform.

21 21 Section 510(g)(2) of the FD&C Act: – *Registration of producers of drugs or devices – Exclusions from application of section:* "practitioners licensed by law to prescribe or administer drugs or devices and who manufacture, prepare, propagate, compound, or process drugs or devices solely for use in the course of their professional practice."

22 See 21 CFR 807.65(d).

23 See 21 CFR 807.65(f).

24 See 21 CFR 812.1.

IV. Scope

This guidance explains the FDA's intentions to focus its oversight on a subset of software functions. Mobile medical apps, as defined in Section III, include only those mobile apps that meet the definition of a device and either are intended:

- to be used as an accessory to a regulated medical device; or
- to transform a mobile platform into a regulated medical device.

Appendix A provides examples of software functions, some of which are mobile apps, that FDA does NOT consider to meet the definition of a device and, therefore, are NOT device software functions or mobile medical apps for the purposes of this guidance.

Section V.B and Appendix B provide examples of software functions, some of which are mobile apps, that MAY meet the definition of a device but for which the FDA intends to exercise enforcement discretion because they pose a low risk to patients.[25]

This guidance does not address the approach for software that performs patient-specific analysis to aid or support clinical decision-making.

FDA's policies regarding accessories to medical devices are not unique to device software functions and go beyond the scope of this guidance. Specifically this guidance does not address FDA's general approach for accessories to medical devices.

If you are developing a software function that meets the definition of a device (such as a mobile medical app) with an entirely new intended use, we encourage you to contact FDA to discuss what regulatory requirements may apply.

V. Regulatory Approach for Device Software Functions

As described in this guidance, FDA intends to apply its regulatory oversight to only those software functions that are medical devices and whose functionality could pose a risk to a patient's safety if the device were to not function as intended. This approach to overseeing device software functions is consistent with our existing approach to overseeing medical device functionality of a product and the risks it poses to patients regardless of the shape, size, or the platform. The FDA believes that this subset of device software functions poses the same or similar potential risks to the public health as currently regulated devices if they fail to function as intended.

The FDA strongly recommends that manufacturers of all software and mobile apps that may meet the definition of a device follow the Quality System[26] regulation (that includes good manufacturing practices) in the design and development of their device software functions, and initiate prompt corrections to their devices, when appropriate, to prevent patient and user harm.

25 This indicates that for certain device software functions, such as those in Appendix B, the FDA intends not to pursue enforcement action for violations of the FD&C Act and applicable regulations by a manufacturer of a software function that meets the definition of a device in section 201(h) of the FD&C Act as specified in this guidance. This does not constitute a change in the requirements of the FD&C Act or any applicable regulation.

26 See 21 CFR Part 820.

For device software functions, manufacturers must meet the requirements associated with the applicable device classification. If the device, on its own, falls within a medical device classification, its manufacturer is subject to the requirements associated with that classification. A device software function, like other devices, may be classified as class I (general controls), class II (special controls in addition to general controls), or class III (premarket approval).[27]

A. Device software functions: Subset of software functions that are the focus of FDA's regulatory oversight

Software functions may take a number of forms, but it is important to note that the FDA intends to apply its regulatory oversight to only the subset of software functions identified below and in Appendix C. These software functions can transform a general-purpose computing platform or mobile platform into a regulated medical device by using attachments, display screens, sensors, or other such methods. Regardless of the mechanism behind the transformation, FDA considers such software to be device software functions.

The following are software functions that FDA considers to be device software functions subject to regulatory oversight:

1. **Software functions that are an extension of one or more medical devices by connecting28 to such device(s) for purposes of controlling29 the device(s) or analyzing medical device data.**

    - *Examples of software functions that control medical devices include*: software that provides the ability to control inflation and deflation of a blood pressure cuff through a mobile platform and mobile apps that control the delivery of insulin on an insulin pump by transmitting control signals to the pumps from the mobile platform.

      Device software functions of these types are considered accessories to the connected device and are required to comply with the controls applicable to that connected device. The FDA considers such device software functions to extend the intended use and functionality of the connected medical device. As a result, the device software function would be required to comply with the regulations applicable to the connected medical device in order to address any associated risks.

2. **Software functions (typically, mobile apps) that transform the mobile platform into a regulated medical device by using attachments, display screens, or sensors or by including functionalities similar to those of currently regulated medical devices. Software functions that use attachments, display screens, sensors or other such similar components to transform a mobile platform into a regulated medical device are required to comply with the device classification associated with the transformed platform.**

27 See footnotes 8 and 10.

28 To meet this criterion, the device software functions or mobile medical apps need not be physically connected to the regulated medical device (i.e. the connection can be wired or wireless).

29 Controlling the intended use, function, modes, or energy source of the connected medical device.

- *Examples of these types of software functions include*: a software function that uses a mobile platform for medical device functions, such as attachment of a blood glucose strip reader to a mobile platform to function as a glucose meter; or attachment of electrocardiograph (ECG) electrodes to a mobile platform to measure, store, and display ECG signals; a software function that uses the built-in accelerometer on a mobile platform to collect motion information for monitoring sleep apnea; a software function that uses sensors (internal or external) on a mobile platform for creating electronic stethoscope function is considered to transform the mobile platform into an electronic stethoscope; manufacturers of such a mobile app are required to follow the requirements of 21 CFR 870.1875(b) (Electronic Stethoscope); and similarly a software function that displays radiological images for diagnosis transforms the mobile platform into a class II Picture Archiving and Communications System (PACS) under 21 CFR 892.2050.

  The FDA has cleared several mobile medical apps with attachments to a mobile platform. Specifically, patient monitoring mobile apps that monitor a patient for heart rate variability from a signal produced by an electrocardiograph, vectorcardiograph, or blood pressure monitor are classified as cardiac monitoring software under 21 CFR 870.2300 (Cardiac monitor). Other mobile medical apps that use a hardware attachment or interface to a monitoring system that have been cleared include an automatic electronic blood pressure monitor under 21 CFR 870.1130 and a perinatal monitoring system under 21 CFR 884.2740.

3. **Software functions that become a regulated medical device by performing patient-specific analysis and providing patient-specific diagnosis, or treatment recommendations. These types of functions are similar to or perform the same function as those types of software devices that have been previously cleared or approved.**

   - *Examples of software functions that perform sophisticated analysis or interpret data (electronically collected or manually entered) from another medical device include*: software functions that use patient-specific parameters and calculate dosage or create a dosage plan for radiation therapy; Computer Aided Detection software (CAD) image processing software[30]; and radiation therapy treatment planning software[31]. We believe that these types of software present the same level of risk to patients regardless of the platform on which they run.

   The FDA encourages manufacturers of such device software functions that perform patient-specific analysis to contact FDA to discuss what, if any, regulatory requirements may apply. For additional examples see Appendix C.

30 21 CFR 892.2050.
31 21 CFR 892.2050.

B. Software functions for which FDA intends to exercise enforcement discretion (meaning that FDA does not intend to enforce requirements under the FD&C Act)

FDA intends to exercise enforcement discretion for software functions that:

1. Help patients (i.e., users) self-manage their disease or conditions without providing specific treatment or treatment suggestions; or
2. Automate simple tasks for health care providers.

Some software functions in the above categories and listed below may be considered device software functions, and others might not. For these examples listed below that are devices, FDA intends to exercise enforcement discretion because they pose a low risk to patients.

The following examples represent software functions for which the FDA intends to exercise enforcement discretion:

3. **Software functions that provide or facilitate supplemental clinical care, by coaching or prompting, to help patients manage their health in their daily environment** – These are software functions that supplement[32] professional clinical care by facilitating behavioral change or coaching patients with specific diseases or identifiable health conditions in their daily environment. Examples include:
   - Software functions that coach patients with conditions such as cardiovascular disease, hypertension, diabetes, or obesity, and promote strategies for maintaining a healthy weight, getting optimal nutrition, exercising and staying fit, managing salt intake, or adhering to pre-determined medication dosing schedules[33] by simple prompting.

4. **Software functions that provide easy access to information related to patients' health conditions or treatments (beyond providing an electronic "copy" of a medical reference)** – This includes software that provides contextually-relevant information to users by matching patient-specific information (e.g., diagnosis, treatments, allergies, signs, or symptoms) to reference information routinely used in clinical practice[34] (e.g., practice guidelines) to facilitate a user's assessment of a specific patient. Examples include:

---

32 By this we mean that the app can be safely used by a patient without active oversight by a medical professional and, when used for serious conditions necessitating professional medical care, use of the app is not intended to replace or discourage seeking treatment from a health care provider.

33 We consider these device software functions to be "medication reminders - Product code NXQ" currently defined as "*A medication reminder is a device intended for medical purposes to provide alerts to patients or health care providers for pre-determined medication dosing schedules. The device may incorporate wireless communication.*" The FDA intends to not enforce applicable regulatory requirements for this specific product code (NXQ) identified under 21 CFR 890.5050 - Daily activity assist device.

34 The type of information provided is from authoritative medical sources, as recognized by the field or discipline that is the subject of the software.

- Software functions that use a patient's diagnosis to provide a clinician with best practice treatment guidelines for common illnesses or conditions such as influenza; or
- Software functions that are drug-drug interaction or drug-allergy look-up tools.

5. **Software functions that are specifically marketed to help patients communicate with healthcare providers by supplementing or augmenting the data or information by capturing an image for patients to convey to their healthcare providers about potential medical conditions** – These products either pose little or no risk, or are the sole responsibility of the health care providers who have experience with them in medical applications. Examples include:
   - Apps specifically intended for medical uses that utilize the mobile device's built-in camera or a connected camera for purposes of documenting or transmitting pictures (e.g., photos of a patient's skin lesions or wounds) to supplement or augment what would otherwise be a verbal description in a consultation between health care providers or between health care providers and patients/caregivers.
6. **Software functions that perform simple calculations routinely used in clinical practice** – These are software functions that are intended to provide a convenient way for clinicians to perform various simple medical calculations taught in medical schools[35] and are routinely used in clinical practice. This software is generally tailored for clinical use, but retains functionality that is similar to simple general-purpose tools such as paper charts, spread sheets, timers, or generic mathematical calculators. Examples of such general-purpose tools include medical calculators for:
   - Body Mass Index (BMI);
   - Total Body Water / Urea Volume of Distribution;
   - Mean arterial pressure;
   - Glascow Coma Scale score;
   - APGAR score;
   - NIH Stroke Scale; or
   - Delivery date estimator.

See Appendix B for additional examples for the above categories.

35 The types of information in these calculators are available in medical sources, which includes medical text-books used in the curriculum of accredited medical schools.

VI. Regulatory Requirements

This guidance, including Appendix C and existing medical device regulatory classifications in Appendix D, is intended to assist manufacturers in determining if the software functionality meets the definition of a device and FDA's expectations for that product. Additional information can be found in "Device Advice: Classify Your Medical Device.[36]" This section describes in greater detail the regulatory requirements applicable to device software functions under this guidance (as described in Section V).

Manufacturers of device software functions are subject to the requirements described in the applicable device classification regulation below. Depending on the classification and the associated regulation for the device software function, manufacturers are required to follow associated controls established by the regulation.

In general, the associated controls for each class of device are outlined below.

Class I devices: General Controls, including:

- Establishment registration, and Medical Device listing (21 CFR Part 807);
- Quality System (QS) regulation (21 CFR Part 820);
- Labeling Requirements (21 CFR Part 801);
- Medical Device Reporting (21 CFR Part 803);
- Premarket Notification (21 CFR Part 807);
- Reporting Corrections and Removals (21 CFR Part 806); and
- Investigational Device Exemption (IDE) requirements for clinical studies of investigational devices (21 CFR Part 812).

Class II devices: General Controls (as described for Class I), Special Controls, and (for most Class II devices) Premarket Notification.

Class III devices: General Controls (as described for Class I), and Premarket Approval (21 CFR Part 814).

Appendix E provides a brief summary of the above requirements. Additional information is available at https://www.fda.gov/medical-devices/device-advice-comprehensive-regulatory-assistance, under "Overview of Medical Device Regulation[37]" and "How to Study and Market Your Device.[38]" If you need further assistance, you may contact the Division of Industry and Consumer Education (DICE): Email: DICE@fda.hhs.gov; phone: 301-796-7100 or 800-638-2041.

---

36 Available at https://www.fda.gov/medical-devices/overview-device-regulation/classify-your-medical-device.

37 Available at https://www.fda.gov/medical-devices/device-advice-comprehensive-regulatory-assistance/overview-device-regulation.

38 Available at https://www.fda.gov/medical-devices/device-advice-comprehensive-regulatory-assistance/how-study-and-market-your-device.

Appendix A: Examples of Software Functions that are NOT Medical Devices

This Appendix provides a representative list of software functionalities to illustrate the types of software that could be used in a health care environment, in clinical care, or patient management, but are not considered medical devices. Because these software functions are not considered medical devices, FDA does not regulate them. The FDA understands that there may be other unique and innovative software functions that may not be covered in this list that may also constitute health care related software. This list is not exhaustive; it is only intended to provide clarity and assistance in identifying when a software function is not considered to be a medical device.

Specific examples of software functions that FDA does not consider to be devices and with no regulatory requirements under the current laws administered by FDA include:

1. **Software functions that are intended to provide access to electronic "copies" (e.g., e-books, audio books) of medical textbooks or other reference materials with generic text search capabilities** – These are not devices because the software is intended to be used as reference material and is not intended for use in the diagnosis of disease or other conditions, or in the cure, mitigation, treatment, or prevention of disease by facilitating a health professional's assessment of a specific patient, replacing the judgment of clinical personnel, or performing any clinical assessment. Examples of these types of software functions include:
    - Medical dictionaries;
    - Electronic copies of medical textbooks or literature articles such as the Physician's Desk Reference or Diagnostic and Statistical Manual of Mental Disorders (DSM);
    - Library of clinical descriptions for diseases and conditions;
    - Encyclopedia of first-aid or emergency care information;
    - Medical abbreviations and definitions;
    - Translations of medical terms across multiple languages.
2. **Software functions that are intended for health care providers to use as educational tools for medical training or to reinforce training previously received** – These may have more functionality than providing an electronic copy of text (e.g., videos, interactive diagrams), but are not devices because they are intended generally for user education and are not intended for use in the diagnosis of disease or other conditions, or in the cure, mitigation, treatment, or prevention of disease by facilitating a health professional's assessment of a specific patient, replacing the judgment of clinical personnel, or performing any clinical assessment. Examples of these types of software functions include:
    - Medical flash cards with medical images, pictures, graphs, etc.;
    - Question/Answer quiz apps;

- Interactive anatomy diagrams or videos;
- Surgical training videos;
- Medical board certification or recertification preparation apps;
- Games that simulate various cardiac arrest scenarios to train health professionals in advanced CPR skills.

3. **Software functions that are intended for general patient education and facilitate patient access to commonly used reference information** – This software can be patient-specific (i.e., filters information to patient-specific characteristics), but is intended for increased patient awareness, education, and empowerment, and ultimately supports patient-centered health care. These functions are not devices because they are intended generally for patient education, and are not intended for use in the diagnosis of disease or other conditions, or in the cure, mitigation, treatment, or prevention of disease by aiding clinical decision-making (i.e., to facilitate a health professional's assessment of a specific patient, replace the judgment of a health professional, or perform any clinical assessment). Examples include software functions that:
    - Provide a portal for health care providers to distribute educational information (e.g., interactive diagrams, useful links, and resources) to their patients regarding their disease, condition, treatment, or up-coming procedure;
    - Help guide patients to ask appropriate questions to their physician relevant to their particular disease, condition, or concern;
    - Provide information about gluten-free food products or restaurants;
    - Help match patients with potentially appropriate clinical trials and facilitate communication between the patient and clinical trial investigators;
    - Provide tutorials or training videos on how to administer first-aid or CPR;
    - Allow users to input pill shape, color, or imprint and displays pictures and names of pills that match this description;
    - Find the closest medical facilities and doctors to the user's location;
    - Provide lists of emergency hotlines and physician/nurse advice lines;
    - Provide and compare costs of drugs and medical products at pharmacies in the user's location.
4. **Software functions that automate general office operations in a health care setting** and are not intended for use in the diagnosis of disease or other conditions, or in the cure, mitigation, treatment, or prevention of disease. Examples include software functions that:
    - Determine billing codes like ICD-9 (international statistical classification of diseases);
    - Enable insurance claims data collection and processing and other apps that are similarly administrative in nature;
    - Analyze insurance claims for fraud or abuse;

- Perform medical business accounting functions or track and trend billable hours and procedures;
- Generate reminders for scheduled medical appointments or blood donation appointments;
- Help patients track, review, and pay medical claims and bills online;
- Manage shifts for doctors;
- Manage or schedule hospital rooms or bed spaces;
- Provide wait times and electronic check-in for hospital emergency rooms and urgent care facilities;
- Allow health care providers or staff in health care settings to process payments (for example, using a HIPAA compliant app to process payments);
- Track or perform patient satisfaction survey after an encounter or a clinical visit.

5. **Software functions that are generic aids or general-purpose products** – This software is not considered a device because it is not intended for use in the diagnosis of disease or other conditions, or in the cure, mitigation, treatment, or prevention of disease. Examples include software functions that:
    - Use the mobile platform as a magnifying glass (but are not specifically intended for medical purposes39[39]);
    - Use the mobile platform for recording audio, note-taking, replaying audio with amplification, or other similar functionalities;
    - Allow patients or health care providers to interact through email, web-based platforms, video, or other communication mechanisms (but are not specifically intended for medical purposes);
    - Provide maps and turn-by-turn directions to medical facilities;
    - Allow health care providers to communicate in a secure and protected method (for example using a HIPAA compliant app to send messages between health care providers in a hospital).
6. **Software functions that are intended for individuals to log, record, track, evaluate, or make decisions or behavioral suggestions related to developing or maintaining general fitness, health or wellness**, such as those that:
    - Provide tools to promote or encourage healthy eating, exercise, weight loss, or other activities generally related to a healthy lifestyle or wellness;
    - Provide dietary logs, calorie counters or make dietary suggestions;

39 Medical purpose magnifiers are regulated either under 21 CFR 886.5840 – Magnifying spectacles ("devices that consist of spectacle frames with convex lenses intended to be worn by a patient who has impaired vision to enlarge images"), or under 21 CFR 886.5540 – Low-vision magnifiers ("a device that consists of a magnifying lens intended for use by a patient who has impaired vision. The device may be held in the hand or attached to spectacles").

- Provide meal planners and recipes;
- Track general daily activities or make exercise or posture suggestions;
- Track a normal baby's sleeping and feeding habits;
- Actively monitor and trend exercise activity;
- Help healthy people track the quantity or quality of their normal sleep patterns;
- Provide and track scores from mind-challenging games or generic "brain age" tests;
- Provide daily motivational tips (e.g., via text or other types of messaging) to reduce stress and promote a positive mental outlook;
- Use social gaming to encourage healthy lifestyle habits;
- Calculate calories burned in a workout.

7. **Software functions that enable individuals to interact with EHR software certified under the ONC Health IT Certification Program** – These are software functions that provide individuals with access to health record systems or enable them to gain electronic access to health information stored within an EHR system. Software functions that only allow individuals to view, transfer, or download EHR data are also included in this category. These software functions are generally meant to facilitate general patient health information management and health record-keeping activities.
8. Software functions that provide patients with simple tools to organize and track their health information;
9. Software functions that provide easy access to information related to patients' health conditions or treatments;
10. **Software functions that provide patients with simple tools to organize and record their health information** – These are software functions that provide patients with tools to organize and record health information without providing recommendations to alter or change a previously prescribed treatment or therapy. Examples include:
    - Software functions that provide simple tools for patients with specific conditions or chronic disease (e.g., obesity, anorexia, arthritis, diabetes, heart disease) to record their events or measurements (e.g., blood pressure measurements, drug intake times, diet, daily routine, or emotional state) and share this information with their health care provider as part of a disease-management plan.
11. **Software functions that are specifically marketed to help patients document, show, or communicate to providers regarding potential medical conditions** – These products either pose little or no risk, or are the sole responsibility of the health care providers who have used them in medical applications. Examples include:
    - Software that serves as a videoconferencing portal specifically intended for medical use and to enhance communications between patients, health care providers, and caregivers.

12. Software functions that enable, during an encounter, a health care provider to access their patient's personal health record (health information) that is hosted on a web-based or other platform;

13. Software functions for health care providers certified under the ONC Health IT Certification Program, such as those that help track or manage patient immunizations by documenting the need for immunization, consent form, and immunization lot number;

14. Software functions that help asthmatics record (i.e., collect and log) inhaler usage, asthma episodes experienced, location of user at the time of an attack, or environmental triggers of asthma attacks;

15. Software functions certified under the ONC Health IT Certification Program that prompt the health care provider to manually enter symptomatic, behavioral, or environmental information, the specifics of which are pre-defined by a health care provider, and store the information for later review;

16. Software functions that record the clinical conversation a clinician has with a patient and sends it (or a link) to the patient to access after the visit;

17. Software functions that allow a user to record (i.e., collect and log) data, such as blood glucose, blood pressure, heart rate, weight, or other data from a device to eventually share with a heath care provider, or upload it to an online (cloud) database, or personal or electronic health record (PHR or EHR, respectively) that is certified under the ONC Health IT Certification Program;

18. Software functions that enable patients or health care providers to interact with PHR systems or EHR systems that are certified under the ONC Health IT Certification Program;

19. **Software functions that meet the definition of Non-Device-MDDS**[40]– These are software functions that are solely intended to transfer, store, convert formats, and display medical device data or results, without controlling or altering the functions or parameters of any connected medical device. These include those software functions that are used as a secondary display to a regulated medical device when these apps are not intended to provide primary diagnosis or to be used to make treatment decisions, or software functions that are used in connection with active patient monitoring;

20. **Software functions that display patient-specific medical device data** – These include software functions that display medical images directly from a Picture Archiving and Communication System (PACS) server;

21. **Software functions that are intended for transferring, storing, converting formats or displaying** clinical laboratory test or other device data and results, findings by a health

40 Non-Device-MDDS is considered to be software functions that are solely intended to transfer, store, convert formats, and display medical device data or results, in accordance with the "Medical Device Data Systems, Medical Image Storage Devices, and Medical Image Communications Devices" Guidance, available at https://www.fda.gov/regulatory-information/search-fda-guidance-documents/medical-device-data-systems-medical-image-storage-devices-and-medical-image-communications-devices.

care professional with respect to such data and results, general information about such findings, and general background information about such laboratory test or other device, unless such function is intended to interpret or analyze clinical laboratory test or other device data, results and findings.

- o Software functions that transfer, store, convert formats, and display medical device data without modifying the data and do not control or alter the functions or parameters of any connected medical device (i.e., software functions that meet the definition of Non-Device-MDDS);
- o Software functions that meet the definition of Non-Device-MDDS and connect to a nursing central station and display (but do not analyze or interpret) medical device data to a physician's mobile platform for review;
- o Software functions that are not intended for diagnostic image review such as image display for multidisciplinary patient management meetings (e.g., rounds) or patient consultation (and include a persistent on-screen notice, such as "for informational purposes only and not intended for diagnostic use").

Appendix B: Examples of Software Functions for which FDA intends to exercise enforcement discretion

This Appendix provides examples of software functions that MAY meet the definition of medical device but for which FDA intends to exercise enforcement discretion. These software functions may be intended for use in the diagnosis of disease or other conditions, or in the cure, mitigation, treatment, or prevention of disease. Even though this software MAY meet the definition of medical device, FDA intends to exercise enforcement discretion for these types of software functions because they pose lower risk to the public.

The FDA understands that there may be other unique and innovative software functions that may not be covered in this list that may also constitute health care related software. This list is not exhaustive; it is only intended to provide clarity and assistance in identifying the software functions that will not be subject to regulatory requirements at this time.

1. Software functions that help patients with diagnosed psychiatric conditions (e.g., post-traumatic stress disorder (PTSD), depression, anxiety, obsessive compulsive disorder) maintain their behavioral coping skills by providing a "Skill of the Day" behavioral technique or audio messages that the user can access when experiencing increased anxiety;
2. Software functions that provide periodic educational information, reminders, or motivational guidance to smokers trying to quit, patients recovering from addiction, or pregnant women;
3. Mobile apps that use GPS location information to alert asthmatics of environmental conditions that may cause asthma symptoms or alert an addiction patient (substance abusers) when near a pre-identified, high-risk location;

4. Software functions that use video and video games to motivate patients to do their physical therapy exercises at home;
5. Software functions that prompt a user to enter which herb and drug they would like to take concurrently and provide information about whether interactions have been seen in the literature and a summary of what type of interaction was reported;
6. Software functions that use patient characteristics such as age, sex, and behavioral risk factors to provide patient-specific screening, counseling, and preventive recommendations from well-known and established authorities;
7. Software functions that use a checklist of common signs and symptoms to provide a list of possible medical conditions and advice on when to consult a health care provider;
8. Software functions that guide a user through a questionnaire of signs and symptoms to provide a recommendation for the type of health care facility most appropriate to their needs;
9. Software functions that are intended to allow a user to initiate a pre-specified nurse call or emergency call using broadband or cellular phone technology;
10. Software functions that enable a patient or caregiver to create and send an alert or general emergency notification to first responders;
11. Software functions that keep track of medications and provide user-configured reminders for improved medication adherence;
12. Software functions that provide patients a portal into their own health information, such as access to information captured during a previous clinical visit or historical trending and comparison of vital signs (e.g., body temperature, heart rate, blood pressure, or respiratory rate);
13. Software functions that aggregate and display trends in personal health incidents (e.g., hospitalization rates or alert notification rates);
14. Software functions allow a user to collect (electronically or manually entered) blood pressure data and share this data through e-mail, track and trend it, or upload it to a personal or electronic health record;
15. Software functions that provide oral health reminders or tracking tools for users with gum disease;
16. Software functions that provide prediabetes patients with guidance or tools to help them develop better eating habits or increase physical activity;
17. Software functions that display, at opportune times, images or other messages for a substance abuser who wants to stop addictive behavior;
18. Software functions that provide drug-drug interactions and relevant safety information (side effects, drug interactions, active ingredient) as a report based on demographic data (age, gender), clinical information (current diagnosis), and current medications.

Appendix C: Examples of Software Functions that are the focus of FDA's regulatory oversight (Device Software Functions and Mobile Medical Apps)

This Appendix provides examples of software functions that are considered medical devices (i.e., device software functions), and on which FDA will focus its regulatory oversight. This software meets the definition of a device under section 201(h) of the FD&C Act and its functionality poses a risk to a patient's safety if the software were to not function as intended. Each example below provides a list of possible relevant product code(s) and/or regulation number.

FDA also encourages device software manufacturers to search FDA's public databases, such as the "Product Classification[41]" database and the "510(k) Premarket Notification[42]" database, to determine the level of regulation for a given device and for the most up-to-date information about the relevant regulatory requirements.

Software functions (typically mobile apps) that transform a mobile platform into a regulated medical device and therefore are the focus of FDA's regulatory oversight: These mobile apps use a mobile platform's built-in features such as light, vibrations, camera, or other similar sources to perform medical device functions (e.g., mobile medical apps that are used by a licensed practitioner to diagnose or treat a disease). Possible product codes: Varies depending on the intended use and software function; see additional examples below.

- Software functions that use a sensor or lead that is connected to a mobile platform to measure and display the electrical signal produced by the heart (electrocardiograph or ECG). Possible product code(s): DPS, MLC, OEY (21 CFR 870.2340), MLO, MWJ (21 CFR 870.2800).
- Software functions that use a sensor or electrode attached to the mobile platform or tools within the mobile platform itself (e.g., microphone and speaker) to electronically amplify and "project sounds associated with the heart, arteries and veins and other internal organs" (i.e., an electronic stethoscope). Possible product code: DQD (21 CFR 870.1875(b)).
- Software functions that use a sensor or electrode attached to the mobile platform or tools within the mobile platform itself (e.g., accelerometer) to measure physiological parameters during cardiopulmonary resuscitation (CPR) and give feedback about the quality of CPR being delivered. Possible product code: LIX (21 CFR 870.5200).
- Software functions that use a sensor attached to the mobile platform or tools within the mobile platform itself to record, view, or analyze eye movements for use in the diagnosis of balance disorders (i.e., nystagmograph). Possible product code: GWN (21 CFR 882.1460).
- Software functions that use tools within the mobile platform (e.g., speaker) to produce controlled levels of test tones and signals intended for use in conducting diagnostic

41 Available at https://www.accessdata.fda.gov/scripts/cdrh/cfdocs/cfPCD/classification.cfm.
42 Available at https://www.accessdata.fda.gov/scripts/cdrh/cfdocs/cfPMN/pmn.cfm.

hearing evaluations and assisting in the diagnosis of possible otologic disorders (i.e., an audiometer). Possible product code: EWO (21 CFR 874.1050).

- Software functions that use a sensor attached to the mobile platform or tools within the mobile platform itself (e.g., accelerometer) to measure the degree of tremor caused by certain diseases (i.e., a tremor transducer). Possible product code: GYD (21 CFR 882.1950).
- Software functions that use a sensor attached to the mobile platform or tools within the mobile platform itself (e.g., accelerometer, microphone) to measure physiological parameters (e.g., limb movement, electrical activity of the brain (EEG)) during sleep and are intended for use in diagnosis of specific diseases or conditions such as sleep apnea. Possible product code(s): OLV (21 CFR 882.1400), LEL, MNR (21 CFR 868.2375), FLS, NPF (21 CFR 868.2377).
- Software functions that use an attachment to the mobile platform to measure blood oxygen saturation for diagnosis of specific disease or condition. Possible product code(s): DQA, NLF, MUD, NMD (21 CFR 870.2700) or DPZ (21 CFR 870.2710).
- Software functions that present donor history questions to a potential blood donor and record and/or transmit the responses to those questions for a blood collection facility to use in determining blood donor eligibility prior to collection of blood or blood components. Possible product code: MMH (21 CFR 864.9165).
- Software functions that use an attachment to the mobile platform to measure blood glucose levels. Possible product code: NBW (21 CFR 862.1345).
- Software functions that use that use an attachment to the mobile platform (e.g., light source, laser) to treat acne, reduce wrinkles, or remove hair. Possible product code: OLP, OHT, OHS (21 CFR 878.4810), OZC (21 CFR 890.5740).
- Software functions that use a microphone or speaker within a mobile platform to serve as a audiometer to allow health care providers to determine hearing loss at different frequencies. Possible product code: EWO (21 CFR 874.1050).
- Software functions that analyze an image of a skin lesion using mathematical algorithms, such as fractal analysis, and provide the user with an assessment of the risk of the lesion.

Software functions that connect to an existing device type for purposes of controlling its operation, function, or energy source and therefore are the focus of FDA's regulatory oversight: These software functions are those that control the operation or function (e.g., changes settings) of an implantable or body worn medical device. Possible product codes: Varies depending on the intended use and function of the parent medical device; see additional examples below.

- Software functions that alter the function or settings of an infusion pump. Possible product codes: MEB, FRN, LZH, LZG, OPP, MEA (21 CFR 880.5725), FIH (21 CFR 876.5820), LKK.

- Software functions that act as wireless remote controls or synchronization devices for computed tomography (CT) or X-Ray machines. Possible product code: JAK (21 CFR 892.1750), IZL (21 CFR 892.1720), KPR (21 CFR 892.1680).
- Software functions that control or change settings of an implantable neuromuscular stimulator. Possible product code(s): GZC (21 CFR 882.5860).
- Software functions that calibrate, control, or change settings of a cochlear implant. Possible product code(s): MCM.
- Software functions that control the inflation or deflation of a blood-pressure cuff. Possible product code: DSJ (21 CFR 870.1100), DSK (21 CFR 870.1110), DXN (21 CFR 870.1130).
- Software functions that are used to calibrate hearing aids and assess the electroacoustic frequency and sound intensity characteristics emanating from a hearing aid, master hearing aid, group hearing aid or group auditory trainer. Possible product code ETW (21 CFR 874.3310).

Software functions that are used in active patient monitoring to analyze patient-specific medical device data and therefore are the focus of FDA's regulatory oversight:

- Software functions that acquire or process physiological signals that connect to bedside (or cardiac) monitors for active patient monitoring. Possible product code(s): DSI, MHX, MLD (21 CFR 870.1025), DRT, MWI, MSX (21 CFR 870.2300).
- Software functions that process uterine contraction and fetal heart rate data for remote monitoring of labor progress. Possible product code(s): HGM (21 CFR 884.2740).
- Software functions that are intended to process images for diagnostic review may be regulated as a picture archiving and communications system. Possible product code(s): LLZ (21 CFR 892.2050).

Appendix D: Examples of current regulations

This Appendix provides additional examples of classifications for regulated medical devices, the Class according to which they are regulated, and their regulation numbers as listed in Title 21 of the Code of Federal Regulations (CFR). This list is intended as a starting point for software manufacturers to assist them in identifying regulated medical devices.

In the table below -- Regulation Number 8xx.yyyy refers to regulation 21 CFR 8xx.yyyy; Device Class 1, 2, 3 – indicates the classification that applies to the device; Submission Type "510(k) exempt," – means that the manufacturer is not required to submit a premarket notification (i.e., 510(k)) prior to marketing the device. However, the 510(k) exemption may be subject to certain limitations. Submission type "510(k)," – means that the manufacturer is typically required to submit a premarket notification.

Regulation number	Regulation Description	Example Device(s) within the Regulation (and current product code)	Device Class	Submission Type
862.1345	Glucose test system	System, Test, Blood Glucose, Over The Counter (NBW)	2	510(k)
862.2100	Calculator/data processing module for clinical use	Digital Image, Storage And Communications, Non-Diagnostic, Laboratory Information System (NVV)	1	510(k) exempt
864.9165	Blood Establishment Computer Software and Accessories	Blood Establishment Computer Software (BECS), Blood Transfusion Management, Blood Donation Management	2	510(k)
868.1850	Monitoring spirometer	Spirometer, Monitoring (W/Wo Alarm) (BZK)	2	510(k)
868.1920	Esophageal stethoscope with electrical conductors	Stethoscope, Esophageal, With Electrical Conductors (BZT)	2	510(k)
868.2375	Breathing Frequency Monitor	Ventilatory Effort Recorder (MNR)	2	510(k)
868.2377	Apnea Monitor	Monitor, Apnea, Home Use (NPF)	2	510(k)
870.1025	Arrhythmia detector and alarm (including ST-segment measurement and alarm)	Detector and Alarm, Arrhythmia (DSI)	2	510(k)
870.1110	Blood-Pressure Computer	Computer, Blood-Pressure (DSK)	2	510(k)
870.1130	Noninvasive blood pressure measurement system	System, Measurement, Blood-Pressure, Non-Invasive (DXN)	2	510(k)
870.1875(b)	Stethoscope	Lung Sound Monitor (OCR) Stethoscope, Electronic (DQD)	2 2	510(k) exempt 510(k)
870.2300	Cardiac Monitor (including cardiotachometer and rate alarm)	Monitor, Cardiac (Incl. Cardiotachometer & Rate Alarm) (DRT) Monitor, Physiological, Patient (Without Arrhythmia Detection Or Alarms) (MWI) System, Network And Communication, Physiological Monitors (MSX)	2 2 2	510(k) 510(k) 510(k)
870.2340	Electrocardiograph	Monitor, St Segment (MLC) Single Lead Over-the-Counter Electrocardiograph (OEY)	2 2	510(k) 510(k)
870.2700	Oximeter	Oximeter (DQA)	2	510(k)
870.2770	Impedance plethysmograph	Analyzer, Body Composition (MNW)	2	510(k)

Regulation number	*Regulation Description*	*Example Device(s) within the Regulation (and current product code)*	*Device Class*	*Submission Type*
870.2800	Medical magnetic tape recorder	Electrocardiograph, Ambulatory, With Analysis Algorithm (MLO) Recorder, Event, Implantable Cardiac, (Without Arrhythmia Detection) (MXC)	2 2	510(k) 510(k)
874.1050	Audiometer	Audiometer (EWO)	2	510(k) exempt
874.3400	Tinnitus masker	Masker, Tinnitus (KLW)	2	510(k)
874.4770	Otoscope	Otoscope (ERA)	1	510(k) exempt
876.1500	Endoscope and accessories	Endoscopic Video Imaging System/Component, Gastroenterology-Urology (FET)	2	510(k)
876.1725	Gastrointestinal motility monitoring system	Recorder, External, Pressure, Amplifier & Transducer (FES)	2	510(k)
878.4160	Surgical camera and accessories	Camera, Cine, Microsurgical, With Audio (FWK) Camera, Still, Microsurgical (FTH) Camera, Television, Endoscopic, With Audio (FWG)	1 1 1	510(k) exempt 510(k) exempt 510(k) exempt
878.4810	Laser surgical instrument for use in general and plastic surgery and in dermatology	Light Based Over The Counter Wrinkle Reduction (OHS) Over-The-Counter Powered Light Based Laser For Acne (OLP)	2 2	510(k) 510(k)
880.2400	Bed-patient monitor	Monitor, Bed Patient (KMI)	1	510(k) exempt
880.2700	Stand-on patient scale	Scale, Stand-On, Patient (FRI)	1	510(k) exempt
880.2910	Clinical electronic thermometer	Thermometer, Electronic, Clinical (FLL)	2	510(k)
880.5580	Acupuncture needle	Locator, Acupuncture Point (BWJ)	2	510(k) exempt
880.6350	Battery-powered medical examination light	Light, Examination, Medical, Battery Powered (KYT)	1	510(k) exempt
882.1400	Electroencephalograph	Full-montage electroencephalograph (GWQ) Standard polysomnograph with electroencephalograph (OLV)	2 2	510(k) 510(k)
882.1550	Nerve conduction velocity measurement device	Device, Nerve conduction velocity measurement (JXE)	2	510(k)
882.1620	Intracranial pressure monitoring device	Device, Monitoring, Intracranial pressure (GWM)	2	510(k)
882.1890	Evoked response photic stimulator	Stimulator, Photic, Evoked response (GWE)	2	510(k)

Regulation number	Regulation Description	Example Device(s) within the Regulation (and current product code)	Device Class	Submission Type
882.1900	Evoked response auditory stimulator	Stimulator, Auditory, Evoked response (GWJ)	2	510(k)
882.1950	Tremor transducer	Transducer, Tremor (GYD)	2	510(k)
884.2730	Home uterine activity monitor	Monitor, Heart Rate, Fetal, Non-Stress Test (Home Use) (MOH)	2	510(k)
884.2740	Perinatal monitoring system and accessories	System, Monitoring, Perinatal (HGM)	2	510(k)
884.2800	Computerized labor monitoring system	System, Monitoring, For Progress Of Labor (NPB)	2	510(k)
884.2900	Fetal stethoscope	Stethoscope, Fetal (HGN)	1	510(k) exempt
884.6120	Assisted reproductive accessories	Accessories, Assisted Reproduction (MQG)	2	510(k)
884.6190	Assisted reproductive microscopes and microscope accessories	Microscope And Microscope Accessories, Reproduction, Assisted (MTX)	1	510(k) exempt
886.1510	Eye movement monitor	Monitor, Eye Movement, Diagnostic (HMC)	2	510(k)
886.1570	Ophthalmoscope	Ophthalmoscope, Battery-powered (HLJ)	2	510(k) exempt
886.1930	Tonometer and accessories	Tonograph (HPK)	2	510(k)
886.5540	Low-vision magnifier	Magnifier, Hand-Held, Low-Vision (HJF) Spectacle Microscope, Low-Vision (HKC)	1 1	510(k) exempt 510(k) exempt
892.1560	Ultrasonic pulsed echo imaging system	System, Imaging, Optical Coherence Tomography (Oct) (NQQ)	2	510(k)
892.2030	Medical image digitizer	Digitizer, Image, Radiological (LMA) Digitizer, Images, Ophthalmic (NFH)	2 2	510(k) exempt 510(k) exempt
892.2050	Picture archiving and communications system	System, Image Processing, Radiological (LLZ) System, Image Management, Opthalmic (NFJ)	2 2	510(k) 510(k)

Appendix E: Brief description of certain device regulatory requirements

This Appendix provides a high level description of certain regulatory requirements for medical devices, including device software functions. The FDA has additional resources and publications online that describe these and other requirements in detail.

1. Establishment Registration and Medical Device Listing

Under 21 CFR Part 807, manufacturers of medical devices are required to annually register their establishments[43] with FDA and provide a list of the devices they market. The registration and listing requirement is a means of keeping FDA advised of who is manufacturing devices, and of the types of devices an establishment is manufacturing. Medical device manufacturers are required to register their establishments with FDA and to list[44] by identifying to FDA the devices they are marketing.

Additional information can be found in "Device Advice: Device Registration and Listing.[45]" If you need further assistance, you may contact the Division of Risk Management Operations, Regulatory Policy and Systems Branch: Email: reglist@fda.hhs.gov, phone: 301-796-7400. Assistance is also available from, Division of Industry and Consumer Education (DICE): Email: DICE@fda.hhs.gov, phone: 301-796-7100 or 800-638-2041.

2. Investigational Device Exemption (IDE) requirements

An IDE allows an investigational device to be used in a clinical study in order to collect safety and effectiveness data required to support a Premarket Approval (PMA) application or a Premarket Notification 510(k) submission to FDA. Clinical studies with devices of significant risk must be approved by FDA and by an Institutional Review Board (IRB) before the study can begin. Studies with devices of non-significant risk must be approved by the IRB only before the study can begin.

Medical device manufacturers who are creating software with novel technologies are encouraged to engage in early collaboration meetings with the FDA to receive recommendations for testing and development of those devices requiring clinical investigations to support marketing.

Additional information about these meetings is described in guidance issued on February 28, 2001: "Early Collaboration Meetings Under the FDA Modernization Act (FDAMA); Final Guidance for Industry and for CDRH Staff.[46]"

---

43 Under 21 CFR 807.3(c), "Establishment" is defined as "a place of business under one management at one general physical location at which a device is manufactured, assembled, or otherwise processed."

44 See 21 CFR Part 807.

45 Available at https://www.fda.gov/medical-devices/how-study-and-market-your-device/device-registration-and-listing.

46 Available at https://www.fda.gov/regulatory-information/search-fda-guidance-documents/early-collaboration-meetings-under-fda-modernization-act-fdama-final-guidance-industry-and-cdrh.

Further information regarding the investigational device exemption can be found in "Device Advice: Investigational Device Exemption.[47]"

3. Labeling requirements

Medical device manufacturers are required to comply with applicable labeling regulations found in 21 CFR Part 801 for medical devices and 21 CFR Part 809 for in vitro diagnostic products.

4. Premarket submission for approval or clearance

Medical device manufacturers should identify the current classification covering their device. Manufacturers are required to prepare and submit to the FDA an appropriate premarket submission, as required for their device classification.

Additional information can be found in "Device Advice: Device Registration and Listing.[48]"

5. Quality System Regulation (QS Regulation)

Medical device manufacturers are required to comply with the QS regulation.[49] The QS regulation does not prescribe in detail how a manufacturer must produce a specific device, but provides a framework for all manufacturers to develop and follow to help ensure that their products consistently meet applicable requirements and specifications. As part of this framework, manufacturers are required to develop requirements for their products that will result in devices that are safe and effective, and to establish methods and procedures to design, produce, and distribute their devices.

Furthermore, manufacturers are required, as part of the QS regulation (21 CFR 820.30), to appropriately verify and validate their device software functions along with the computing platform to ensure safe and effective operation of the device.

Manufacturers are required to ensure that adequate controls and processes are in place through purchasing controls to ensure safe distribution, installation, and operation of the device software function.

Additional information regarding the QS regulation and can be found at "Quality System (QS) Regulation/Medical Device Good Manufacturing Practices.[50]"

6. Medical Device Reporting (MDR) (Adverse event reporting)

The Medical Device Reporting (MDR) regulation requires manufacturers and importers of medical devices to submit reports to the FDA whenever they receive or otherwise become aware of information, from any source, that reasonably suggests that a device they market

47 Available at https://www.fda.gov/medical-devices/how-study-and-market-your-device/device-advice-investigational-device-exemption-ide.

48 Available at https://www.fda.gov/medical-devices/how-study-and-market-your-device/device-registration-and-listing.

49 See 21 CFR Part 820.

50 Available at https://www.fda.gov/medical-devices/postmarket-requirements-devices/quality-system-qs-regulationmedical-device-good-manufacturing-practices.

may have caused or contributed to a death or serious injury, or has malfunctioned and the device or a similar device that they market would be likely to cause or contribute to a reportable death or serious injury if the malfunction were to recur.[51] MDR requires medical device manufacturers to:

- Submit MDR reportable events involving their medical devices as described in 21 CFR 803.10(c) and 803.50;
- Submit 5-day reports as described in 21 CFR 803.53;
- Submit supplemental reports as described in 21 CFR 803.56;
- Develop, maintain, and implement written procedures for the identification and evaluation of all medical device events to determine whether the event is MDR reportable as described in 21 CFR 803.17;
- Conduct an investigation of each event and evaluate the cause of the event as described in 21 CFR 803.50(b)(3); and
- Establish and maintain complete files for all complaints concerning adverse medical device events as described in 21 CFR 803.18.

The MDR report (FDA Form 3500A) must contain all the information described in 21 CFR 803.52 that is reasonably known to the manufacturer. Information reasonably known includes any information that:

- Can be obtained by contacting a user facility, importer, or other initial reporter;
- Is in the possession of the manufacturer; or
- Can be obtained by analysis, testing, or other evaluation of the device.

For additional instructions on how to complete the 3500A form, refer to the document titled "Instructions for Completing Form FDA 3500A.[52]"

For additional guidance on the MDR regulation and the reporting requirements, refer to the document titled "Medical Device Reporting for Manufacturers.[53]"

For Questions about Medical Device Reporting, including interpretation of MDR policy:

- Call: (301) 796-6670 (voice)
- Email: RSMB@fda.hhs.gov
- Mail: Food and Drug Administration, Center for Devices and Radiological Health, Reporting Systems Monitoring Branch, 10903 New Hampshire Avenue, WO Bldg. 66, Room 3217, Silver Spring, MD 20993-0002

51 See 21 CFR Part 803.
52 Available at https://www.fda.gov/safety/forms-reporting-fda/instructions-completing-form-fda-3500.
53 Available at https://www.fda.gov/regulatory-information/search-fda-guidance-documents/medical-device-reporting-manufacturers.

7. Correcting Problems

A medical device manufacturer may voluntarily take action at any time or may be requested to take action by the FDA to correct problems. Voluntary action is usually taken by device manufacturers. Examples of the types of actions that a device manufacturer may be requested to take include, but are not limited to:

- Inspecting the device for problems;
- Repairing the device;
- Adjusting settings on the device; and
- Upgrading software to reduce risk from a "bug" or unintended response.

Under certain circumstances, FDA may initiate a request that a manufacturer address a problem with a device through other means, including by removal of the product from the market. When recommending corrective action, the FDA intends to take into account the essential role that certain device software functions take as an integral part of a larger patient care system.

Reporting Corrections to FDA:

In accordance with 21 CFR 806.10, medical device manufacturers are required to promptly report, within 10 working days from the time the correction is initiated, to the FDA certain actions concerning device corrections and removals. Specifically, medical device manufacturers are required to report to FDA any corrections made to a device to reduce a risk to health posed by the device or to remedy a violation of the FD&C Act caused by the device that may present a risk to health.

The reporting requirement does not extend to all modifications to devices. For example, certain actions that would improve the quality of a mobile medical app but that would not reduce a risk to health posed by the mobile medical app or remedy a violation of the FD&C Act are not required to be reported under 21 CFR 806.1(b).[54] If there is not a "risk to health" involved, a report to FDA is not required, but the device manufacturer must keep a record of the correction. An example of such action taken by the manufacturer could be changes made to correct a defect that creates a nuisance for the user but does not present a risk to the health of the user or patient.

More information about reporting requirements under 21 CFR Part 806 is available in "Device Advice: Recalls, Corrections, and Removals.[55]"

54 Under 21 CFR 806.1(b), the following actions are exempt from the reporting requirements of Part 806: (1) Actions taken by device manufacturers or importers to improve the performance or quality of a device but that do not reduce a risk to health posed by the device or remedy a violation of the act caused by the device. (2) Market withdrawals as defined in 21 CFR 806.2(h). (3) Routine servicing as defined in 21 CFR 806.2(k). (4) Stock recoveries as defined in 21 CFR 806.2(l).

55 Available at https://www.fda.gov/medical-devices/postmarket-requirements-devices/recalls-corrections-and-removals-devices.

Appendix F: Frequently Asked Questions (FAQs)

1) I have a software function that is not identified in this guidance. What is the best way to get additional information from the FDA about my product?

Answer: FDA recognizes that this guidance does not describe all types of software used in health care. Some manufacturers may be unsure whether their software function is considered a medical device that is subject to regulatory oversight, or whether their medical device could be under FDA's intent to exercise enforcement discretion. If the device is subject to regulatory oversight, manufacturers may have questions about which regulatory requirements are applicable to their software function.

After reviewing this guidance, FDA encourages software manufacturers to contact the Agency to obtain more information using one of the following ways:

- Phone or e-mail – For information about regulatory requirements, contact the Division of Industry and Consumer Education (DICE). Email: DICE@fda.hhs.gov; phone: 301-796-7100 or 800-638-2041. For information about whether your software or mobile app is considered a medical device, contact digitalhealth@fda.hhs.gov.

  If your question relates to apps used in blood establishments or another area of CBER regulation, contact the Office of Communication, Outreach and Development, Center for Biologics Evaluation and Research, 10903 New Hampshire Ave., Bldg. 71, Room 3128, Silver Spring; e-mail: ocod@fda.hhs.gov; phone: 1-800-835-4709 or 240-402-7800.
- Online – The FDA has several resources and publications online that describe various regulatory requirements in detail. FDA's "Device Advice[56]" website and online courses at "CDRH Learn[57]" are a good place to start. Other sections in this guidance provide links to more detailed information related to more specific topics.
- Letter – For written feedback about the classification and the regulatory requirements that may be applicable to a device software function, manufacturers should use the 513(g) process. Specifically, a manufacturer should submit the following for a 513(g) submission:
  - User fee;
  - Cover letter;
  - Description of the software;
  - Description of what the software is to be used for; and
  - Any proposed labeling or promotional material for the software and, as applicable, any labeling or promotional material of a similar, legally marketed device, if available.

56 Available at https://www.fda.gov/medical-devices/device-advice-comprehensive-regulatory-assistance.
57 Available at https://www.fda.gov/training-and-continuing-education/cdrh-learn.

FDA will generally issue a response to the 513(g), in the form of a confidential letter to the manufacturer, within 60 days of receipt of the request for information. For more specific information about what to include in a 513(g) and where to send it, refer to FDA's guidance document titled "FDA and Industry Procedures for Section 513(g) Requests for Information Contains Nonbinding Recommendations Under the Federal Food, Drug, and Cosmetic Act.[58]" For more information about 513(g) user fees, refer to FDA's guidance document titled "User Fees for 513(g) Requests for Information.[59]"

2) Why does FDA recommend that manufacturers follow the Quality System (QS) regulation for those software that MAY be devices and could be device software functions but for which FDA intends to exercise enforcement discretion?

Answer: FDA believes all manufacturers of medical device software should have in place an adequate quality management system that helps ensure that their products consistently meet applicable requirements and specifications and can support the software throughout its total life cycle. Adequate quality management systems incorporate appropriate risk management strategies, good design practices, adequate verification and validation, and appropriate methods to correct and prevent risks to patients and adverse events that may arise from the use of the product. All of these elements are part of FDA's QS regulation.

3) Is FDA's QS regulation similar to software development practices I already use?

Answer: Most likely. Though not all of the principles in the QS regulation are applicable to the development and manufacture of quality device software functions,[60] the majority of them are applicable and are consistent with commonly used and accepted good software development practices, such as those from the Institute of Electrical and Electronics Engineers' (IEEE), Software Engineering Body of Knowledge (SWEBOK), and Carnegie Mellon Software Engineering Institute's Capability Maturity Model Integration (CMMI) methods.

The FDA's approach to QS regulation is also harmonized with certain international standards such as ISO 9001 and ISO 13485.[61] Similar to these international standards, the QS regulation does not prescribe in detail how a manufacturer must produce a specific device, but provides a framework for all manufacturers to develop and follow to help ensure that their products consistently meet applicable requirements and specifications. The QS regulation can apply to and be scaled for any size manufacturer and any type of product. It also allows for a manufacturer to choose those requirements most appropriate for its given device and manufacturing process.[62]

---

58 Available at https://www.fda.gov/regulatory-information/search-fda-guidance-documents/fda-and-industry-procedures-section-513g-requests-information-under-federal-food-drug-and-cosmetic.

59 Available at https://www.fda.gov/regulatory-information/search-fda-guidance-documents/user-fees-513g-requests-information.

60 Certain portions of the QS regulation that apply to medical device hardware (such as the production and process controls outlined in 21 CFR 820.70) may not clearly apply to device software functions.

61 ISO 9001 Quality management systems – Requirements and ISO 13485 Medical devices – Quality management systems – Requirements for regulatory purposes.

62 See 21 CFR 820.1 (stating "if a manufacturer engages in only some operations subject to the requirements in this part, and not in others, that manufacturer need only comply with those requirements applicable to the operations in which it is engaged.").

4) What are some examples of parts of the QS regulation that are of particular importance to device software functions and where can I find more information about them?

Answer: Though not a complete list, some examples of principles within the QS regulation that are relevant to all device manufacturers include risk assessment and management, design controls, and corrective and preventive actions. Risk assessment and management is a critical part of good quality management systems. Good design practices are important to the development and manufacture of safe medical devices. It is also important for manufacturers to have procedures in place to identify, analyze, correct, and prevent software-related causes of patient or user harm. References related to these examples are provided in Appendix E of this guidance. Additional references about these principles that manufacturers may find useful include the following:

FDA's "Design Control Guidance for Medical Device Manufacturers," available at https://www.fda.gov/regulatory-information/search-fda-guidance-documents/design-control-guidance-medical-device-manufacturers.

FDA's "General Principles of Software Validation" guidance, available at

https://www.fda.gov/regulatory-information/search-fda-guidance-documents/general-principles-software-validation.

5) Do all the device software function manufacturers have to submit a premarket submission and receive FDA clearance or approval before marketing?

Answer: No, not all manufacturers have to submit a premarket submission (i.e., a 510(k) or PMA) prior to marketing their device software function. This determination depends on the classification of the device. Manufacturers of devices that are exempt from 510(k) or PMA requirements do not have to file a submission with FDA prior to marketing their device. For example, the majority of class I devices are exempt from the premarket submission requirements and are subject to the least regulatory control.

Regardless of whether medical devices are subject to the premarket submission requirements, most medical devices (including Class I devices) have to comply with other basic regulatory requirements that are called "General Controls." More information about what "General Controls" are and what a medical device manufacturer should do to comply with these requirements, can be found in "Device Advice: General Controls for Medical Devices" and "Regulatory Controls.[63]"

6) Some FDA classifications state they are "510(k) exempt." What does 510(k) exempt mean and how do I know if it applies to my product?

Answer: If a classification states the device type is "510(k) exempt," this means that the manufacturer is not required to submit a premarket notification (i.e., a 510(k)) prior to marketing the device. However, the 510(k) exemption may be subject to certain limitations. Manufacturers are encouraged to confirm the device's exempt status and any limitations to

63 Available at https://www.fda.gov/medical-devices/regulatory-controls/general-controls-medical-devices and at https://www.fda.gov/medical-devices/overview-device-regulation/regulatory-controls.

that status that may apply in accordance with 21 CFR Parts 862-892. Additional information about 510(k) exempt devices can be found at: https://www.accessdata.fda.gov/scripts/cdrh/cfdocs/cfpcd/315.cfm.

7) If a 510(k) is required for my device software function, what type of software documentation does FDA recommend I include in the submission?

Answer: FDA's recommendations for the software-related documentation that you provide in your premarket submission are addressed in detail in the FDA's "Guidance for the Content of Premarket Submissions for Software Contained in Medical Devices.[64]"

If the device software function uses off-the-shelf software, manufacturers should also refer to FDA's "Guidance for Industry, FDA Reviewers, and Compliance on Off-the-Shelf Software Use in Medical Devices.[65]"

8) I am a medical device manufacturer and making my product labeling available electronically using a mobile app. Is my app considered a mobile medical app?

Answer: Mobile apps that provide electronic access and are intended for use as a digital version of medical device labeling or instructions for use are not considered a medical device on their own and therefore are not considered mobile medical apps. These are apps from a device manufacturer that provide information to support the company's own device. Examples include apps that provide an electronic copy of cleared or approved medical device labeling or apps that provide video instruction for how to use a medical device. These types of apps are not considered devices within themselves, but instead are considered part of the medical device labeling and are subject to the regulatory labeling requirements relevant to that particular product.

9) Is an electronic method of collecting clinical investigations, for example through a mobile app, considered a device software function, and if so, what requirements apply?

Answer: Software used for data collection in clinical studies (such as electronic Patient Reported Outcomes (ePRO) apps) is not considered on its own to be a device software function. However, manufacturers and users of this type of software should see FDA's guidance related to use of computers in clinical trials, "Electronic Source Data in Clinical Investigations,[66]" issued on September 17, 2013.

10) I am a medical device manufacturer. Is an electronic method of collecting and storing quality systems information in my manufacturing process considered a medical device?

Answer: Software used in the production process for medical devices, or for collecting, storing and maintaining quality system data collection for medical devices (including complaint submissions) is not considered a medical device on its own. This software does not

64 Available at https://www.fda.gov/regulatory-information/search-fda-guidance-documents/guidance-content-premarket-submissions-software-contained-medical-devices.

65 Available at https://www.fda.gov/regulatory-information/search-fda-guidance-documents/shelf-software-use-medical-devices.

66 Available at https://www.fda.gov/regulatory-information/search-fda-guidance-documents/electronic-source-data-clinical-investigations.

meet the definition of medical device but is part of the quality system. However this software is required to comply with the appropriate good manufacturing practices (GMP) regulations (see 21 CFR Part 820).

Appendix G: Additional Resources

A. Guidance Documents

1. Guidance for Industry – Cybersecurity for Networked Medical Devices Containing Off-the-Shelf (OTS) Software, available at https://www.fda.gov/regulatory-information/search-fda-guidance-documents/cybersecurity-networked-medical-devices-containing-shelf-ots-software.
2. Information for Healthcare Organizations about FDA's "Guidance for Industry: Cybersecurity for Networked Medical Devices Containing Off-The-Shelf (OTS) Software," available at https://www.fda.gov/regulatory-information/search-fda-guidance-documents/information-healthcare-organizations-about-fdas-guidance-industry-cybersecurity-networked-medical.

B. Standards

AAMI = Association for the Advancement of Medical Instrumentation

ANSI = American National Standards Institute

IEC = International Electrotechnical Commission

IEEE = Institute of Electrical and Electronics Engineers

ISO = International Organization for Standardization

1. ISO/IEC/IEEE 90003 Software engineering – Guidelines for the application of ISO 9001:2015 to computer software.
2. ISO 9001 Quality management systems – Requirements.
3. ISO 13485 Medical devices – Quality management systems – Requirements for regulatory purposes.
4. ISO 9000 Quality management systems – Fundamentals and vocabulary.
5. ISO 14971 Medical devices — Application of risk management to medical devices.
6. IEC 62304 Medical device software – Software life cycle processes.
7. IEEE Std 1012 IEEE Standard for System, Software, and Hardware Verification and Validation.
8. ISO/IEC 25051 Software engineering – Systems and software product Quality Requirements and Evaluation (SQuaRE) – Requirements for quality of Ready to Use

Software Product (RUSP) and instructions for testing.

9. ISO/IEC/IEEE 12207 Systems and software engineering – Software life cycle processes.
10. AAMI TIR36 Validation of software for regulated processes.
11. IEC/TR 80002-1 Medical device software – Part 1: Guidance on the application of ISO 14971 to medical device software.
12. ANSI/AAMI ES60601-1 Medical electrical equipment – Part 1: General requirements for basic safety and essential performance (particularly clause 14).
13. IEC 61508-2 Functional safety of electrical/electronic/programmable electronic safety-related systems – Part 2: Requirements for electrical/electronic/programmable electronic safety-related systems.

CSV

Chapter 21
Use of Electronic Records and Electronic Signatures in Clinical Investigations Under 21 CFR Part 11 – Questions and Answers
Guidance for Industry and FDA Staff

June 2017
Draft Guidance/Guidance for Industry[1]
U.S. Department of Health and Human Services Food and Drug Administration
Center for Drug Evaluation and Research (CDER)
Center for Biologics Evaluation and Research (CBER)
Center for Devices and Radiological Health (CDRH)

I. INTRODUCTION

This document provides guidance to sponsors, clinical investigators, institutional review boards (IRBs), contract research organizations (CROs), and other interested parties on the use of electronic records and electronic signatures in clinical investigations of medical products[2] under 21 CFR part 11, Electronic Records; Electronic Signatures.[3]

This guidance clarifies, updates, and expands upon recommendations in the guidance for industry Part 11, Electronic Records; Electronic Signatures – Scope and Application (referred to as the 2003 part 11 guidance)[4] that pertain to clinical investigations conducted under 21 CFR parts 312 and 812.[5] Thus, this guidance is limited to outlining the scope and application of part 11 requirements for clinical investigations of medical products.

This guidance discusses the following:

- Procedures that may be followed to help ensure that ***electronic records*** and ***electronic signatures*** meet FDA requirements and that the records and signatures are considered trustworthy, reliable, and generally equivalent to paper records and handwritten signatures executed on paper

---

1 This guidance has been prepared by the Office of Medical Policy in the Center for Drug Evaluation and Research in coordination with the Center for Biologics Evaluation and Research, the Center for Devices and Radiological Health, and the Office of Regulatory Affairs at the Food and Drug Administration.

2 2 For the purposes of this guidance, unless otherwise noted, the term clinical investigations refers to FDA-regulated clinical investigations of medical products conducted under an investigational new drug application (IND) according to 21 CFR part 312 or under an investigational device exemption according to 21 CFR part 812. In this guidance, medical products include human drugs and biological products, medical devices, and combination products.

3 In this guidance, 21 CFR part 11 is referred to as part 11 regulations.

4 For more information, see the guidance for industry *Part 11, Electronic Records; Electronic Signatures – Scope and Application*. We update guidances periodically. To make sure you have the most recent version of a guidance, check the FDA guidance web page at https://www.fda.gov/Drugs/GuidanceComplianceRegulatoryInformation/Guidances/default.htm. Also, see the *Federal Register* of September 5, 2003 (68 FR 52779).

5 See Appendix I of this guidance for a list of other guidances that contain applicable recommendations.

- The use of a risk-based approach when deciding to validate ***electronic systems***, implement ***audit trails*** for electronic records, and archive records that are pertinent to clinical investigations conducted under parts 312 and 812

The goals of this guidance are as follows:

- Update recommendations for applying and implementing part 11 requirements in the current environment of electronic systems used in clinical investigations
- Clarify and further expand on the risk-based approach described in the 2003 part 11 guidance to validation, audit trails, and archiving of records
- Encourage and facilitate the use of electronic records and systems to improve the quality and efficiency of clinical investigations

The Glossary in Appendix II defines many of the terms used in this guidance. Words or phrases found in the Glossary appear in ***bold italics*** at first mention.

In general, FDA's guidance documents do not establish legally enforceable responsibilities. Instead, guidances describe the Agency's current thinking on a topic and should be viewed only as recommendations, unless specific regulatory or statutory requirements are cited. The use of the word *should* in Agency guidances means that something is suggested or recommended, but not required.

II. Background

In March 1997, FDA published a final rule to establish criteria that must be met when a record required by a predicate rule[6] is created, modified, maintained, archived, retrieved, or transmitted in electronic form in place of a paper record and when electronic signatures are used in place of traditional handwritten signatures.[7] The part 11 regulations, which apply to all FDA program areas, were intended to permit the widest possible use of electronic technology. These regulations are compatible with FDA's responsibility for protecting the public health, while also ensuring the authenticity, the reliability, and, when appropriate, the confidentiality of electronic records, and ensuring that the signer cannot readily repudiate the signed record as not being genuine.[8]

The 2003 part 11 guidance represented FDA's interpretation of the regulations and was tailored to the technological environment that prevailed. Since 2003, advances in technology have expanded the uses and capabilities of electronic systems in clinical investigations. In addition, electronic systems and technologies are used and managed in novel ways, services are shared or contracted between organizations in new ways, and electronic data flow between parties is more efficient and more prevalent. The standards and capabilities of electronic systems have improved, and features— such as audit trails, automated date-and-time stamps, appropriate validation, and

6 The underlying requirements set forth in the Federal Food, Drug, and Cosmetic Act (FD&C Act), the Public Health Service Act, and FDA regulations (other than part 11) are referred to in this guidance as *predicate rules*.

7 See 21 CFR part 11.

8 See 62 FR 13430 (March 20, 1997).

the ability to generate copies and retain records — are standard components of many electronic systems.

FDA's overall approach to the 2003 part 11 guidance was to provide a narrow and practical interpretation of part 11 requirements. FDA continues to support and promote such a narrow and practical interpretation in this guidance, including the Agency's continuing intent to exercise enforcement discretion regarding certain part 11 requirements for validation, audit trails, record retention, and record copying.[9] FDA reminds sponsors, however, that records must still be maintained or submitted in accordance with the underlying predicate rules, and the Agency can take regulatory action for noncompliance with such predicate rules. In addition, FDA continues to encourage sponsors and other regulated entities to use a risk-based approach, as introduced in the 2003 part 11 guidance and further described in this guidance, when deciding to validate electronic systems, implement audit trails, or archive required records for clinical investigations.

Acknowledging the technological advances and remaining consistent with FDA's overall approach to the part 11 requirements, FDA clarifies in this guidance the part 11 controls that sponsors and other regulated entities must implement, as appropriate,[10] in the current technological environment. Furthermore, FDA regards the validation of electronic systems, the ability to generate complete and accurate copies of records, the ability to archive records, and the use of audit trails as powerful tools for ensuring the quality and reliability of electronic records.

Therefore, in this guidance, FDA encourages and further clarifies the risk-based approach to validation of electronic systems, implementation of electronic audit trails, and archiving of electronic records to continue to ensure the quality, authenticity, and reliability of electronic records from their point of creation to their modification, maintenance, archiving, retrieval, or transmission.[11]

III. Scope

In general, part 11 requirements apply to electronic records and electronic signatures and to the electronic systems used to create, modify, maintain, archive, retrieve, or transmit them (also, see section IV.A.Q5).[12]

This guidance applies to the following electronic records and electronic signatures:

- Records required for clinical investigations of medical products that are maintained in electronic format in place of paper format, including all records that are necessary for FDA to reconstruct a study
- Records required for clinical investigations of medical products that are maintained in electronic format and where the electronic record is relied on to perform regulated activities

9 For more information about the part 11 requirements for validation, audit trails, record retention, and record copying, see § 11.10(a) through (c) and (e) and the corresponding requirements in § 11.30.

10 For more information, see § 11.10(d) and (f) through (k) and § 11.30.

11 See footnote 4.

12 See footnote 4.

- Records for clinical investigations submitted to FDA in electronic format under predicate rules, even if such records are not specifically identified in FDA regulations (see 122 § 11.1(b))
- Electronic signatures required for clinical investigations intended to be the equivalent of handwritten signatures, initials, and other general signings

This guidance addresses the applicability of part 11 requirements for the following electronic systems used to create, modify, maintain, archive, retrieve, or transmit an electronic record referenced in the bulleted list above for clinical investigations:

- Electronic systems, including ***commercial off-the-shelf (COTS)*** and ***customized electronic systems*** owned or managed by sponsors and other regulated entities
- Electronic services, outsourced by the sponsor or other regulated entities
- Electronic systems primarily used in the provision of medical care
- ***Mobile technology***
- Telecommunication systems

For electronic systems that fall under the scope of part 11 regulations, the regulations distinguish the systems as closed or open (see §§ 11.10 and 11.30, respectively).[13] This distinction is seldom relevant because of the pervasive use of the internet and web-based systems. By permitting access to electronic systems through use of the internet, the security that results from restricting physical access may be lost. Therefore, it would be prudent to implement additional security measures for such systems above and beyond those controls for closed systems described in § 11.10, such as document encryption and the use of appropriate electronic signature standards to ensure the authenticity, integrity, and confidentiality of records (see § 11.30).

IV. Questions and Answers: Scope and Application of Part 11 Requirements in Clinical Investigations

A. Electronic Systems Owned or Managed by Sponsors and Other Regulated Entities

Examples of electronic systems used in clinical investigations that are owned or managed by sponsors and other regulated entities (e.g., CROs, IRBs) include ***electronic case report forms (eCRFs)***; ***electronic data capture (EDC) systems***, electronic trial master files (eTMFs), electronic Clinical Data Management System (eCDMS), electronic Clinical Trial Management System (eCTMS), Interactive Voice Response System (IVRS), Interactive Web Response System (IWRS), centralized, web-based electronic patient-reported outcomes (ePRO) portals, and electronic IRB human subject application systems (eIRBs). Requirements and recommendations for these systems are described in this section.

13 For the regulatory definition of a closed system, see 21 CFR 11.3(b)(4). For the regulatory definition of an open system, see 21 CFR 11.3(b)(9).

Q1. What should sponsors and other regulated entities consider when using a risk-based approach for validation of electronic systems used in clinical investigations?

Consistent with the policy announced in the 2003 part 11 guidance, sponsors and other regulated entities should use a risk-based approach[14] for validating electronic systems owned or managed by sponsors and other regulated entities.15[15] Validation is critical to ensure that the electronic system is correctly performing its intended function. Validation may include, but is not limited to, demonstrating correct installation of the electronic system and testing of the system to ensure that it functions in the manner intended.

Electronic records for FDA-regulated clinical investigations of medical products are used in a broad range of settings, which vary in importance and complexity. Similarly, the reliability and complexity of electronic systems that are used are variable. When using a risk-based approach for validating electronic systems, sponsors and other regulated entities should consider (1) the purpose and significance of the record, including the extent of error that can be tolerated without compromising the reliability and utility of the record for its regulatory purpose and (2) the attributes and intended use of the electronic system used to produce the record.

In general, sponsors and other regulated entities should have electronic systems validated if those systems *process*[16] critical records (e.g., records containing laboratory and study endpoint data, information on serious adverse events and study participant deaths, information on drug and device accountability and administration) that are submitted to FDA. The extent of validation should be tailored to the nature of the system and its intended use.

For COTS office utilities software in general use, such as word processing, spreadsheets, and portable document format (PDF) tools or for electronic systems that process non-critical procedural records, the extent of validation should be guided by the organization's internal business practices and needs.

For COTS systems that perform functions beyond office utilities, such as COTS EDC systems, validation should include a description of standard operating procedures and documentation from the ***vendor*** that includes, but is not limited to, results of their testing and validation to establish that the electronic system functions in the manner intended.

For COTS systems that are integrated with other systems or for customized systems that are developed to meet a unique business need of a user,[17] sponsors and other regulated entities

14 This guidance does not provide comprehensive detail on how to perform a risk assessment. There are many risk-assessment methodologies and tools from a variety of industries that can be applied. For more information, see the International Council for Harmonisation (ICH) guidance for industry *Q9 Quality Risk Management*. Also, see the International Organization for Standardization's (ISO) standard *ISO 31010:2009 Risk Management – Risk Assessment Techniques.*

15 See the guidance for industry *Computerized Systems Used in Clinical Investigations.*

16 For the purposes of this guidance, to process records includes actions such as creating, modifying, maintaining, archiving, retrieving, or transmitting.

17 An example of a user's unique business need may include customization in order to integrate with other soft-

should develop and document a validation plan, conduct the validation in accordance with the plan, and document the validation results. Such documentation may be reviewed and copied during an FDA inspection. Validation for these systems may include, but is not limited to, user acceptance testing, dynamic testing, and stress testing. Sponsors and other regulated entities should perform the validation before the use of these systems, in addition to initial testing of the electronic system, to ensure that the system functions in the manner intended.

In addition, processes should be in place to control changes to the electronic system and evaluate the extent of revalidation that the changes may necessitate. When changes are made to the electronic system (e.g., system and software upgrades, including security and performance patches, equipment or component replacement, or new instrumentation), sponsors and other regulated entities should evaluate the effect of the changes and validate the changes using a risk-based approach.[18] For example, some changes may be minor (e.g., bug fixes or security patches); other changes may be major or particularly significant (e.g., that cause the system to operate outside of previously validated operating limits). If the risk assessment determines that the change is minor or does not affect the system requirements, the extent of validation should be guided by the organization's internal business practices and needs. Major changes may require additional re-validation and critical changes could trigger a re-validation of the entire system.

Q2. For electronic systems owned or managed by sponsors and other regulated entities that fall under the scope of 21 CFR part 11, what will be FDA's focus during inspections?

For these electronic systems that fall under the scope of part 11, an FDA inspection will focus on the implementation of the electronic system, including changes made to the system once in use and documentation of validation to test system functionality after implementation, where applicable. During inspection, FDA will focus on any ***source data*** that are transferred to another data format or system to ensure that checks are in place and that ***critical data***[19] are not altered in value or meaning during the migration process. FDA will also review standard operating procedures and support mechanisms in place, such as training, technical support, and auditing to ensure that the system is functioning and is being used in the manner intended.

Q3. Should sponsors and other regulated entities perform audits of the vendor's electronic systems and products?

Sponsors and other regulated entities often perform audits of the vendor's electronic systems and products to assess the vendor's design and development methodologies used in the construction of the electronic system or the product, as well as the vendor's validation

ware systems or to address internal processes.

18 See footnote 15.

19 Examples of critical data may include documentation of informed consent, drug accountability and administration information, or study endpoints and protocol-required safety assessments. For more information, see section IV.A of the guidance for industry *Oversight of Clinical Investigations – A Risk-Based Approach to Monitoring.*

documentation. To reduce the time and cost burden, sponsors and other regulated entities should consider periodic, but shared audits conducted by trusted third parties.

Sponsors and other regulated entities should base their decision to perform vendor audits on a risk-based approach as described in this guidance (see section IV.A.Q1). For example, vendor audits may be important when using customized electronic systems or when integrating COTS systems with other systems.

Q4. Under 21 CFR 11.10(d), what are FDA's expectations regarding the use of internal and external security safeguards?

Sponsors and other regulated entities must ensure that procedures and processes are in place to safeguard the authenticity, integrity, and, when appropriate, the confidentiality of electronic records (see §§ 11.10 and 11.30). Therefore, logical and physical access controls must be employed for electronic systems that are used in clinical investigations, particularly for systems that provide access to multiple users or that reside on networks (see §§ 11.10(d) and 11.30). Sponsors and other regulated entities must ensure that procedures and processes are in place to limit access to their electronic system to authorized users (see §§ 11.10(d) and 11.30). There should also be external security safeguards in place to prevent, detect, and mitigate effects of computer viruses, worms, and other potentially harmful software code on study data and software (e.g., firewalls, antivirus and anti-spy software).[20]

Q5. Under what circumstances are part 11 requirements not applicable for electroniccopies of paper records?

Part 11 requirements are not intended to apply to electronic systems that are merely incidental to creating paper records that are subsequently maintained in traditional paper-based systems. In such cases, the electronic systems would function essentially the same way that manual typewriters or pens would function, and any signatures would be traditional handwritten signatures. Storage and retrieval of records would be of the traditional file cabinet variety. More importantly, the overall reliability and trustworthiness of the records and FDA's ability to access the records would primarily derive from generally accepted procedures and controls for paper records. Therefore, when sponsors or other regulated entities use electronic systems to generate paper printouts of electronic records and those paper records meet all the requirements of the applicable regulations, and persons rely on the paper records to perform regulated activities, FDA generally would not consider sponsors or other regulated entities to be using electronic records in place of paper records (see § 11.1(b)). In these instances, part 11 regulations would not apply to the electronic systems used to generate paper records.

However, if simple screenshots or paper printouts are used to produce a report and that report fails to capture important metadata (e.g., the ***data originator*** and the audit trail of the data) that are recorded in the electronic system, such paper records would be regarded as incomplete unless the accompanying metadata are included. FDA would require access to

20 20 For more information on internal and external security controls, see the guidance for industry *Computerized Systems Used in Clinical Investigations.*

the electronic system used to produce those data to review the complete record (see 21 CFR 312.58, 312.68, 812.140, and 812.145).

Q6. Can sponsors and other regulated entities use and retain electronic copies of source documents in place of the original paper source documents?

Yes. FDA permits the interchangeable use of electronic records and paper records for the archiving and protection of records provided that recordkeeping and retention requirements are met (see 21 CFR 56.115, 312.57, 312.62, and 812.140). If the sponsor or other regulated entity intends to use an electronic copy in place of the paper source data (i.e., intends to destroy the paper source data), then part 11 regulations would apply to the electronic system used to create the copy (see §§ 11.10 and 11.30)). A process should be in place to certify that the electronic copy is an accurate representation of the original paper document. The copy of the original record should be verified as having all of the same attributes and information as the original record and certified as indicated by a dated signature. Sponsors and other regulated entities should have written procedures to ensure consistency in the certification process.

In addition, some electronic copies vary in terms of their ability to be modified. For electronic copies in which the records are modifiable, it would be important to have audit trails in place to ensure the trustworthiness and reliability of the electronic copy. Also, as noted earlier, 21 CFR 11.10 and 11.30 require physical, logical, and procedural controls designed to ensure the authenticity and integrity of electronic records.

Q7. Can electronic copies be used as accurate reproductions of electronic records?

Yes. True copies of electronic records may be made and maintained in the format of theoriginal records or in a compatible format if the content and meaning of the original records are preserved and if a suitable reader and copying equipment (e.g., software and hardware, including media readers) are readily available. Sponsors and other regulated entities should designate which electronic document is the original and should certify the electronic copies by generating the copies through a validated process. This process should ensure that electronic copies of electronic originals have the same information, including data that describe the context, content, and structure of the data as the original.

Q8. Can sponsors and other regulated entities use durable electronic storage devices to archive required records from a clinical investigation?

Yes. Using an electronic means, such as a durable electronic storage device is an acceptable method to archive study-related records at the end of the study. Sponsors and other regulated entities should ensure that the integrity of the original data and the content and meaning of the record are preserved. In addition, if the electronic records are archived in such a way that the records can be searched, sorted, or analyzed, sponsors and other regulated entities should provide electronic copies with the same capability to FDA during inspection if it is reasonable and technically feasible. During inspection, FDA may request to review and copy records in a human readable form using electronic system hardware.

Q9. Does FDA provide preliminary audit service to inspect an electronic system used in a clinical investigation to ensure compliance with part 11 controls?

No. FDA does not perform preliminary audits to evaluate electronic systems (e.g., EDC system, CTMS) to ensure compliance with part 11 requirements. These systems would be evaluated during a regulatory inspection.

Q10. If a non-U.S. site is conducting a clinical investigation, are records required by FDA regulations subject to part 11 requirements?

If a non-U.S. site is conducting a clinical investigation under an investigational new drug application (IND), the clinical investigator and the sponsor must follow FDA regulations, including part 11. If required records (e.g., drug disposition, case report forms, case 350 histories)[21] are kept in electronic format, part 11 requirements will apply (see section III). Device clinical investigations conducted at non-U.S sites generally are not conducted under an investigational device exemption (IDE). However, in the event where non-U.S. clinical investigation sites agree to comply with 21 CFR part 812, for example, per the requirements outlined in the study protocol or in the investigator agreement, then the clinical investigator and the sponsor should follow FDA regulations, including part 11.

For foreign clinical studies not conducted under an IND or an IDE that are submitted to FDA in support of a research or marketing application, good clinical practice standard for electronic records and electronic systems would apply.[22]

B. Outsourced Electronic Services

FDA recognizes that sponsors and other regulated entities may choose to outsource electronic services. Examples of these types of electronic services are data management services, including ***cloud computing*** services. According to the National Institute of Standards and Technology, cloud computing is defined as "a model for enabling ubiquitous, convenient, on-demand network access to a shared pool of configurable computing resources (e.g., networks, servers, storage, applications, services) that can be rapidly provisioned and released with minimal management effort or service provider interaction."[23]

When these electronic services are used to process data for FDA-regulated clinical investigations, sponsors and other regulated entities should consider whether there are adequate controls

---

21 See § 312.62.

22 For more information about foreign clinical studies not conducted under an IND, see 21 CFR 312.120 and the ICH guidance *E6(R2) Good Clinical Practice — Integrated Addendum to ICH E6(R1): Guideline for Good Clinical Practice E6(R2)* (available at http://www.ich.org/products/guidelines/efficacy/article/efficacy-guidelines.html). For information about devices, see the draft guidance for industry and Food and Drug Administration staff *Acceptance of Medical Device Data From Studies Conducted Outside the United States.* When final, this guidance will represent FDA's current thinking on this topic.

23 See the National Institute of Standards and Technology's definition of *cloud computing* (available at http://csrc.nist.gov/publications/PubsSPs.html#800-145).

in place to ensure the reliability and confidentiality of the data. Sponsors and other regulated entities should consider the factors in the following bulleted list when determining the suitability of the outsourced electronic services. If the outsourced electronic service does not provide the data security safeguards described in the following bulleted list, sponsors and other regulated entities should consider the risks of using such service (e.g., infringement of patient privacy rights, lack of reliability of the data in the clinical investigation and its regulatory implications).

- Validation documentation (see sections IV.A.Q1 and IV.B.Q15)
- Ability to generate accurate and complete copies of records
- Availability and retention of records for FDA inspection for as long as the records are required by applicable regulations
- Archiving capabilities
- Access controls (see section IV.A.Q4) and authorization checks for users' actions
- Secure, computer-generated, time-stamped audit trails of users' actions and changes to data
- Encryption of data at rest and in transit 395
- Electronic signature controls (see section V) 397
- Performance record of the electronic service vendor and the electronic service provided
- Ability to monitor the electronic service vendor's compliance with electronic service security and the data integrity controls

Q11. If sponsors and other regulated entities outsource electronic services, who is responsible for meeting the regulatory requirements?

Sponsors and other regulated entities are responsible for meeting the regulatory requirements. Moreover, sponsors are responsible for assessing the authenticity and reliability of any data used to support a marketing application for a medical product. Thus, the sponsor is ultimately responsible for the clinical investigation and for ensuring that all records and data required to adequately perform and document the clinical investigation are obtained and available to FDA upon request and in a timely and reasonable manner (21 CFR 312.57, 312.58, 312.62, 312.68, 812.140, and 812.145).

Q12. Should sponsors or other regulated entities establish service agreements with the electronic service vendor?

Yes, sponsors and other regulated entities should obtain service agreements with the electronic service vendor. Before entering into an agreement, the sponsor or other regulated entity should evaluate and select electronic services based on the electronic service vendor's ability to meet the part 11 requirements and data security safeguards described in the previous bulleted list (see section IV.B). Service agreements should include a clear description of these specified requirements and the roles and responsibilities of the electronic service vendor.

Q13. Does FDA consider it acceptable for data to be distributed across a cloud computing service's hardware at several different geographic locations at the same time without being able to identify the exact location of the data at any given time?

If appropriate controls are in place, there are no limitations regarding the geographic location of cloud computing services. However, it is critical for sponsors and other regulated entities to understand the data flow and know the location of the cloud computing service's hardware in order to conduct a meaningful risk assessment regarding data access, integrity, and security. Data privacy laws may differ from country to country. Therefore, sponsors and other regulated entities should perform appropriate risk assessments to ensure that data residing on storage devices outside their country can be retrieved and accessed during FDA inspections.

Q14. What should sponsors and other regulated entities have available on site to demonstrate that their electronic service vendor is providing services in accordance with FDA's regulatory requirements?

Sponsors and other regulated entities should have the following information available to FDA upon request at each of their regulated facilities that use the outsourced electronic services:

- Specified requirements of the outsourced electronic service
- A service agreement defining what is expected from the electronic service vendor (see section IV.B.Q12)
- Procedures for the electronic service vendor to notify the sponsor or other regulated entity of changes and incidents with the service

Q15. What should sponsors and other regulated entities consider when deciding to validate outsourced electronic services that are used in clinical investigations?

A risk-based approach to validation similar to that described in section IV.A.Q1 should be taken for outsourced electronic services.

It is ultimately the responsibility of the sponsor or other regulated entity to ensure that the outsourced electronic service is validated as appropriate. Sponsors and other regulated entities should obtain documentation from the electronic service vendor that includes, but is not limited to, a description of standard operating procedures and results of testing and validation to establish that the outsourced electronic service functions in the manner intended.

Q16. Under what circumstances would FDA choose to inspect the electronic service vendor?

Under certain circumstances, FDA may choose to inspect the electronic service vendors, such as when they are or were engaged in providing services and functions that fall under areas regulated by FDA. For example, if the criticality of the investigation requires inspection and the required records are not available from the sponsor or the clinical investigation site, FDA may choose to inspect records specific to the clinical investigation at the vendor's facilities to ensure that FDA requirements are met. The sponsor or other regulated entity is ultimately responsible for ensuring that regulated records and data are available to FDA during an investigation or an inspection.

C. Electronic Systems Primarily Used in the Provision of Medical Care

For the purposes of this guidance, electronic systems used in the provision of medical care (e.g., electronic health records (EHRs)) generally are systems that are (1) designed for medical care of patients not enrolled in a clinical investigation and (2) owned and managed by the institutions providing medical care. These electronic systems may produce additional electronic records during the course of patients' care (e.g., hospital admission records, electronic health records, pharmacy records, laboratory records, imaging records, electronic consultation records) that may be useful for providing data in clinical investigations. As provided in the guidance for industry *Electronic Source Data in Clinical Investigations*, FDA does not intend to assess compliance of these systems with part 11.[24] For more information on best practices for using data from EHRs in FDA-regulated clinical investigations, see the draft guidance for industry *Use of Electronic Health Records Data in Clinical Investigations*."[25]

D. Mobile Technology

Sponsors and other regulated entities may use mobile technology during the course of a clinical investigation to capture, record, or transmit data directly from study participants. The recommendations in this section apply to mobile technology used in a clinical investigation whether that technology is provided by the sponsor or owned by the study participant (i.e., ***bring your own device (BYOD)***). For the purposes of this guidance, mobile technology refers to portable electronic technology used in clinical investigations that allows for off-site and remote data capture directly from study participants and includes ***mobile platforms, mobile applications (mobile apps),***[26] ***wearable biosensors*** and other remote and ingestible sensors, and other portable and implantable electronic devices.

Q17. What access controls should sponsors implement for mobile technology accessed by study participants for use in clinical investigations?

Where possible, sponsors should ensure that basic user access controls (e.g., identification (ID) code, username and password combination, or electronic thumbprints and other

24 For more information, see the guidance for industry *Electronic Source Data in Clinical Investigations*.

25 When final, this guidance will represent FDA's current thinking on this topic.

26 For the purposes of this guidance, we do not distinguish between a *mobile app* and a "mobile medical app." A "mobile medical app" is a *mobile app* that meets the definition of device in section 201(h) of the FD&C Act and either is intended to be used as an accessory to a regulated medical device or to transform a mobile platform into a regulated medical device. For more information, see the guidance for industry and Food and Drug Administration staff *Mobile Medical Applications*.

biometrics) are implemented, as appropriate, for mobile technology used by study participants in clinical investigations.

Specifically, for mobile apps that rely on study participants' user entry, access controls must be in place to ensure that entries come from the study participant (see 21 CFR 11.10(d)). For wearable biosensors and other portable electronic devices intended for a single study participant to wear or use (e.g., small physiologic sensors with no display screen), basic user access controls may be difficult to implement. In cases where access controls are impractical, sponsors should consider obtaining a signed declaration from the study participant confirming that the device will only be used by the study participant. Basic user access controls are not necessary when using ingestible sensors and implantable electronic devices.

Q18. When using mobile technology to capture data directly from study participants in clinical investigations, how do sponsors identify the data originator?

For the purposes of recordkeeping, audit trail, and inspection, each electronic data element should be associated with an authorized data originator. The data originator may be a person, a computer system, a device, or an instrument that is authorized to enter, change, or transmit data elements via a secure protocol into the sponsor's EDC system or into the electronic system of a trusted proxy agent such as a contract research organization.[27]

If a study participant who is using the mobile technology actively participates in the performance measure by entering and submitting data to the sponsor's EDC system (e.g., when using an ePRO app or when performing visual acuity testing), the study participant should be identified as the data originator.

If the mobile technology, such as an activity tracker or a glucose sensor, transmits data automatically to the sponsor's EDC system without any human intervention, the mobile technology should be identified as the data originator. In these cases, a ***data element identifier*** should be created that automatically identifies the particular mobile technology (e.g., name and type) as the originator of the data element. Information associated with a data element includes the origin of the data element, the date and time of entry, and the ID number of the study participant to whom the data element applies. Once set by the electronic system, this value should not be alterable in any way.[28]

In some cases, data from the mobile technology may be obtained in the course of medical care and may be entered manually or automatically into an EHR. The EHR data may, in turn, be used in a clinical investigation and entered into the sponsor's EDC system. In this situation, identifying the EHR as the data originator is sufficient because sponsors are not expected to know the details about all of the users and mobile health technologies that contribute information to the patient's EHR (see section IV.C).

The sponsor should develop, maintain, and make available a list of authorized data originators. When identification of data originators relies on usernames and unique

27 See footnote 24.
28 See footnote 24.

passwords, controls must be employed to ensure the security and the integrity of the authorized usernames and passwords (see 21 CFR 11.10(d)). When electronic thumbprints or other biometrics are used in place of username and password combinations, controls must be designed to ensure that the biometric identifier cannot be used by anyone other than the identifier's owner (see § 11.200(b) and section V.Q27).[29]

Q19. Does FDA consider the mobile technology to contain the source data?

When mobile technology is used in a clinical investigation to capture, record, and transmit study-related data directly from study participants, the data are collected and stored, perhaps for very short periods of time on the mobile technology before being transmitted to the sponsor's EDC system. In some cases, the data may pass temporarily through various electronic hubs or gateways before reaching the sponsor's EDC system. This could make the location of the source data difficult to determine.

FDA considers source data as data that are first recorded in a permanent manner. In general, for data collected directly from study participants through mobile technology, the first permanent record is located in the sponsor's EDC system or the EHR, and not in the mobile technology. FDA does not intend to inspect each individual mobile technology used in a clinical investigation to capture, record, and transmit data directly from study participants because access controls (see section IV.D.Q17), audit trails (see section IV.D.Q20), and validation (see section IV.D.Q21) that would be applied would help ensure the reliability of the data.

Q20. What should sponsors consider when implementing audit trails on data obtained directly from study participants using the mobile technology in the clinical investigation?

When data are copied or transmitted directly from the mobile technology to the sponsor's EDC system or from the mobile technology to the EHR and then to the sponsor's EDC system, the audit trail begins at the time the data enter the sponsor's EDC system. The sponsor's EDC system should capture the date and time that the data enter the EDC system and identification of the data originator (i.e., study participant, mobile technology, or EHR). In addition, the date and time that the measurement was made should be recorded and available to FDA at the time of inspection if it differs from the date and time the data enter the EDC system.

In cases where the study participant actively participates in the performance measure and manually enters the data into the mobile platform (e.g., tablet computers, smart phones) or other portable device, the mobile technology should be designed to prevent unauthorized modifications to the data before those data are transmitted to the sponsor's EDC system.

After the data are transmitted to the sponsor's EDC system, only clinical investigators or delegated study personnel who are authorized to make changes should perform modifications or corrections to the data. Modified and corrected data elements should

29 See footnote 24.

have data element identifiers that reflect the date, time, and data originator and the reason for the change. Modified and corrected data should not obscure previous entries. Clinical investigators should review and electronically sign the completed eCRF for each study participant before the data are archived or submitted to FDA. Use of electronic signatures must comply with part 11 (see section V).[30]

Q21. What should sponsors consider when using a risk-based approach to validation of mobile technology used in clinical investigations?

For mobile technology, validation ensures that the mobile technology is reliably capturing, transmitting, and recording data to produce accurate, reliable, and complete records. For example, if a wearable biosensor detects a blood glucose level of 87 milligrams per deciliter, the validation should ensure that the value is correctly and reliably captured, transmitted, and recorded in the sponsor's EDC system. Sponsors should validate the mobile technology before use in the clinical investigation. In addition, sponsors should ensure that device and software updates do not affect the reliability of the data that enter the sponsor's EDC system.

Part 11 regulations do not address the performance of wearable biosensors, mobile apps, or portable devices (i.e., the ability to measure what they are designed to measure). For example, validation does not apply to the ability of an activity tracker to accurately and reliably measure the number of steps walked. Although performance of the mobile technology is critical to the clinical investigation, recommendations for the performance of specific mobile technology designed to measure specific biomarkers or physical activity are beyond the scope of this guidance. For mobile technology that meets the definition of device as defined in section 201(h) of the Federal Food, Drug, and Cosmetic Act (21 U.S.C. 321(h)), other regulations and policies may apply.

Q22. What security safeguards should sponsors implement to ensure security and confidentiality of data when mobile technology is used to capture, record, and transmit data directly from study participants in clinical investigations?

The mobile technology must ensure the security and confidentiality of the data when the technology is used in clinical investigations (see 21 CFR 11.10 and 11.30). If the data are transmitted wirelessly from the mobile technology to the sponsor's EDC system in a clinical investigation, the data must be encrypted at rest and in transit to prevent access by intervening or malicious parties (see § 11.30).

For wearable biosensors and other portable or electronic implantable devices, data encryption may be sufficient to ensure the security and confidentiality of the data. On the other hand, additional controls may be important when using mobile apps and mobile platforms. In addition to having encryption and basic user access controls in place (see 44 section IV.D.Q17), sponsors should consider implementing additional security safeguards as follows:

- Remote wiping and remote disabling

30 See footnote 24.

- Disable function for installing and using file-sharing applications
- Firewalls
- Procedures and processes to delete all stored health information before discarding or reusing the mobile device

Q23. Does FDA expect sponsors, clinical investigators, study personnel, and study participants to be trained on the use of a specific mobile technology if the technology is used in a clinical investigation?

Yes. Sponsors, clinical investigators, study personnel, and study participants must be adequately trained on the use of any mobile technology they will use in a clinical investigation (see 21 CFR 11.10(i)). Training should occur before the use of the mobile technology and whenever changes are made (e.g., software or system upgrades) to the mobile technology during the course of the clinical investigation. In addition, clinical investigators and study personnel should periodically reassess and retrain study participants, as necessary, on systems that are more complex or that pose a higher risk to the conduct of the study.

E. Telecommunication Systems

Clinical investigators and study personnel may use many different types of telecommunication systems, such as telephones, email, live chat, and ***telemedicine*** or video conferencing systems to communicate with study participants during the conduct of clinical investigations. Clinical investigators and study personnel may record study-related data obtained during the course of the communications in the study participant's health record or in the case report form.

When these telecommunication systems are interactive and used for real-time communication, the interactions are regarded as similar to face-to-face interactions (i.e., the clinical investigator or study personnel and the study participant actively participate in real-time communication through audio, video, and other live chat communication), and part 11 regulations do not apply to the telecommunication system. In these interactions, there is an opportunity to hear or see the study participant or to query the source of the text to confirm that the study participant who is interacting with the investigator is the study participant participating in the study.

When these interactive telecommunication systems are used to record source data in a permanent manner, allowing the interactive communication and data to be reviewed at a later date by the sponsor, clinical investigator, study personnel, and FDA, sponsors and other regulated entities should consider whether there are adequate controls in place to ensure that the reliability, confidentiality, and privacy of records are preserved. Sponsors should also consider the processes that are in place to ensure user authentication and to prevent alteration of source data.

V. Electronic Signatures

An electronic signature is a computer data compilation of any symbol or series of symbols executed, adopted, or authorized by an individual to be the legally binding equivalent of the individual's handwritten signature (§ 11.3(b)(7)). In general, a signature may not be denied legal effect or validity solely because it is in electronic format, and a contract or other record relating to a transaction may not be denied legal effect, validity, or enforceability solely because an electronic signature or electronic record was used in its formation.[31]

FDA regulations found in part 11 set forth the criteria under which FDA considers electronic records, electronic signatures, and handwritten signatures executed to electronic records to be trustworthy, reliable, and generally equivalent to a handwritten signature executed on paper (see 21 CFR 11.1(a)). To be considered equivalent to full handwritten signatures, electronic signatures must comply with all applicable requirements under part 11. Electronic records that are electronically signed must contain information associated with the signing that clearly indicates the printed name of the signer, the date and time when the signature was executed, and the meaning associated with the signature (see § 11.50). The name, date and time, and meaning are subject to the same controls as electronic records and must be included as part of any human readable form of the electronic record (see § 11.50(b)). In addition, electronic signatures and handwritten signatures executed to electronic records must be linked to the respective electronic records to ensure that the signatures cannot be excised, copied, or otherwise transferred to falsify an electronic record by ordinary means (§ 11.70).

Q24. What methods may be used to create valid electronic signatures?

FDA does not mandate or specify any particular methods for electronic signatures, including any particular biometric method upon which an electronic signature may be based. Part 11 regulations permit a wide variety of methods to create electronic signatures, including the use of computer-readable ID cards, biometrics, ***digital signatures***, and username and password combinations.

When a document is electronically signed, the electronic signature must be accompanied by a computer-generated, time-stamped audit trail (see §§ 11.10(e) and 11.50(b)). When study participants provide an electronic signature, clinical investigators should ensure that the participants understand the legal significance of the signature.

Q25. How should sponsors and regulated entities verify the identity of the individual who will be electronically signing records as required in 21 CFR 11.100(b)?

Electronic signatures should be instituted in a manner that is reasonably likely to prevent fraudulent use. Therefore, the part 11 regulations require that an organization verify the identity of an individual before the organization establishes, assigns, or otherwise sanctions an individual's electronic signature or any element of such electronic signature (see

31 See the Electronic Signatures in Global and National Commerce Act, which was enacted on June 30, 2000 (Public Law 106-229;114 Stat. 464) (15 U.S.C. 7001-7006).

§11.100(b)). The electronic signature should also be implemented in a manner that prevents repudiation by the signatory and includes safeguards to confirm the identity of the individual and safeguards to prevent alteration of the electronic signature.

FDA does not specify any particular method for verifying the identity of an individual and accepts many different methods. For example, verifying someone's identity can be done by using information from some form of official identification, such as a birth certificate, a government-issued passport, or a driver's license. In addition, use of security questions to confirm an individual's identity may also be considered.

Q26. When an individual executes a series of signings during a single, continuous period of controlled system access, could the initial logging into an electronic system using a unique username and password be used to perform the first signing and satisfy the requirements found in 21 CFR 11.200(a)?

When an individual logs into an electronic system using a username and password, it is not necessary to re-enter the username when an individual executes a series of signings during a single, continuous period of controlled system access. After a user has logged into a system using a unique username and password, all signatures during the period of controlled system access can be performed using the password alone (see § 11.200(a)).[32] The signed document must contain information that clearly indicates the printed name of the signer, the date and time the signature was executed, and the meaning associated with the signature (see § 11.50).

In addition, in such cases, the signing should be done under controlled conditions that prevent another person from impersonating the legitimate signer. Such controlled conditions may include (1) requiring an individual to remain in close proximity to the workstation throughout the signing session (2) using measures for automatic inactivity disconnect that would de-log the first individual if no entries or actions were taken within a fixed, short time frame and (3) requiring that the single component needed for subsequent signings be known to and usable only by the authorized individual.[33]

To make it impractical to falsify records, the electronic signature component executed for initial signing must be used only by its genuine owner (see § 11.200(a)(2)). The electronic signatures must be administered and executed to ensure that attempted use by anyone other than the genuine owners requires collaboration of two or more individuals (see § 11.200(a)(3)).

32 See 62 FR 13430 at 13457 (March 20, 1997).
33 See footnote 32.

Q27. What requirements must electronic signatures based on biometrics meet to be considered an accepted biometric method?

Biometrics means "a method of verifying an individual's identity based on measurements of the individual's physical features or repeatable actions where those features and/or actions are both unique to that individual and measurable."[34] Examples of biometric methods may include fingerprints, hand geometry (i.e., finger lengths and palm size), iris patterns, retinal patterns, or voice prints.

Electronic signatures based on biometrics must be designed to ensure that they cannot be used by anyone other than their genuine owners (§ 11.200(b)). Therefore, suitable biometrics should be uniquely identified with the individual and should not change over time.

FDA does not specify any particular biometric method upon which an electronic signature may be based. Electronic signatures based on biometrics are accepted if they meet the requirements found in the part 11 regulations, as stated earlier in this section (i.e., the signed electronic record must contain pertinent information associated with the signing (see § 11.50), the electronic signatures are subject to the same controls as the electronic records and must be included as part of any human readable form of the electronic record (see § 11.50(b), and the electronic signature must be linked to its respective electronic records (§ 11.70)). In addition, biometrics should be performed based on government and industry standards. For example, the various government agencies and standards development organizations that develop biometric standards include the following:

- National Institute of Standards and Technology
- International Committee for Information Technology Standards
- International Organization for Standardization/International Electrotechnical Commission (ISO/IEC) Joint Technical Committee 1/Subcommittee 37
- Organization for the Advancement of Structured Information Standards
- American National Standards Institute

Q28. Does FDA certify electronic systems and methods used to obtain electronic signatures?

No. FDA does not certify individual electronic systems and methods used to obtain electronic signatures. Compliance with the provisions of part 11 is the basis for FDA's acceptance of any electronic signature system, regardless of the particular technology or brand used. This approach is consistent with FDA's policy in a variety of program areas. For example, FDA does not certify manufacturing equipment used to make drugs or medical devices.

34 See 21 CFR 11.3(b)(3).

APPENDIX I: OTHER GUIDANCES WITH APPLICABLE RECOMMENDATIONS[35]

Guidance for Industry *Part 11, Electronic Records; Electronic Signatures – Scope and Application*

ICH Guidance for Industry *Q9 Quality Risk Management*

Guidance for Industry *Computerized Systems Used in Clinical Investigations*

Guidance for Industry *Electronic Source Data in Clinical Investigations*

Draft Guidance for Industry *Use of Electronic Health Records Data in Clinical Investigations*

Guidance for Industry and Food and Drug Administration Staff *Mobile Medical Applications*

ICH Guidance *E6(R2) Good Clinical Practice—Integrated Addendum to ICH E6(R1): Guideline for Good Clinical Practice E6(R2)*

Guidance for Institutional Review Boards, Investigators, and Sponsors *Use of Electronic Informed Consent, Questions and Answers*

APPENDIX II: GLOSSARY OF TERMS

The following is a list of terms and definitions used in this guidance and their definitions:

Audit Trail is a process that captures details of information, such as additions, deletions, or alterations, in an electronic record without obscuring the original record. An audit trail facilitates the reconstruction of the course of such details relating to the electronic record.

Biometrics means a method of verifying an individual's identity based on measurements of the individual's physical features or repeatable actions where those features and/or actions are both unique to that individual and measurable (21 CFR 11.3(b)(3)).

Bring Your Own Device (BYOD) refers to the policy of permitting study participants to use their personally owned mobile devices to capture, record, and transmit data in clinical investigations.

Certified Copy is a copy (paper or electronic) of original information that has been verified, as indicated by a dated signature, as an exact copy, having all of the same attributes and information as the original.

Cloud Computing is a model for enabling ubiquitous, convenient, on-demand network access to a shared pool of configurable computing resources (e.g., networks, servers, storage, applications, and services) that can be rapidly provisioned and released with minimal management effort or service provider interaction.

Commercial Off-The-Shelf (COTS) Systems refer to commercially available electronic systems (including hardware or software) that can be purchased from third-party vendors.

35 Draft guidances have been included for completeness only. As draft documents, they are not intended to be implemented until published in final form.

Critical Data may include documentation of informed consent, drug accountability and administration information, or study endpoints and protocol-required safety assessments.

Customized Electronic Systems refer to systems and software that are specially developed for a specific user, an organization, or a business to meet specific business needs.

Data Element is a single observation associated with a subject in a clinical study. Examples include birth date, white blood cell count, pain severity measure, and other clinical observations made and documented during a study.

Data Element Identifier is the information associated with a data element that includes the origin of the data element, the date and time of entry, and the identification number of the study subject to whom the data element applies. Once set by the electronic system, this value should not be alterable in any way.

Data Originator is an origination type associated with each data element that identifies the source of the data element's capture in the eCRF. This could be a person, a computer system, a device, or an instrument that is authorized to enter, change, or transmit data elements into the eCRF (also, sometimes known as an author).

Digital Signature means an electronic signature based upon cryptographic methods of originator authentication, computed by using a set of rules and a set of parameters such that the identity of the signer and the integrity of the data can be verified (21 CFR 11.3(5)).

Electronic Case Report Form (eCRF) is an auditable electronic record of information that generally is reported to the sponsor on each trial subject, according to a clinical investigation protocol. The eCRF enables clinical investigation data to be systematically captured, reviewed, managed, stored, analyzed, and reported.

Electronic Data Capture (EDC) Systems refer to electronic systems designed to collect and manage clinical trial data in an electronic format.

Electronic Record means any combination of text, graphics, data, audio, pictorial, or other information representation in digital form that is created, modified, maintained, archived, retrieved, or distributed by a computer system (21 CFR 11.3(b)(6)).

Electronic Signature means a computer data compilation of any symbol or series of symbols executed, adopted, or authorized by an individual to be the legally binding equivalent of the individual's handwritten signature (21 CFR 11.3(b)(7)).

Electronic Systems refer to systems, including hardware and software, that produce electronic records.

Mobile Applications (Mobile Apps) are software applications that can be executed (run) on a mobile platform (i.e., a handheld commercial off-the-shelf computing platform, with or without wireless connectivity) or a web-based software application that is tailored to a mobile platform but is executed on a server.[36] An example includes electronic patient-reported outcomes (ePRO)applications on smart phones.

Mobile Platforms are commercial off-the-shelf (COTS) computing platform, with or without wireless connectivity, that are handheld in nature. Examples include tablet computers, smart phones, or other portable computers.[37]

Mobile Technology refers to portable electronic technology used in clinical investigations that allows for off-site and remote data capture directly from study participants and includes mobile platforms, mobile apps, wearable biosensors and other remote and ingestible sensors, and other portable and implantable electronic devices.

Source Data are all information in original records and certified copies of original records of clinical findings, observations, or other activities (in a clinical investigation) used for the reconstruction and evaluation of the trial. Source data are contained in source documents (original records or certified copies).

Telemedicine refers to the use of electronic applications, devices, and services, including two-way video, email, smart phones, wireless tools and other forms of telecommunications systems in the provision of health care.

Vendor refers to a third-party supplier not regulated by FDA that sells electronic goods and services to sponsors and other regulated entities.

Wearable Biosensors comprise miniaturized sensors worn as on- or in-body accessories (e.g., watches, bracelets, clothing) that allow for continuous monitoring of physiological, biochemical, and motion signals for both diagnostic and monitoring applications. These wearable biosensors may be paired with mobile platforms (e.g., smart phones). Examples of wearable biosensors include accelerometers, activity trackers, wireless heart rate monitors, pulse oximetry sensors, and glucose sensors.

---

36 36 For more information, see the guidance for industry and Food and Drug Administration staff Mobile Medical Applications.
37 See footnote 36.

CSV

Chapter 22
Guidance for Industry
Part 11, Electronic Records; Electronic Signatures — Scope and Application

August 2003

Guidance for Industry[1]

U.S. Department of Health and Human Services Food and Drug Administration

Center for Drug Evaluation and Research (CDER) Center for Biologics Evaluation and Research (CBER)

Center for Devices and Radiological Health (CDRH)

Center for Food Safety and Applied Nutrition (CFSAN) Center for Veterinary Medicine (CVM)

Office of Regulatory Affairs (ORA)

I. Introduction

This guidance is intended to describe the Food and Drug Administration's (FDA's) current thinking regarding the scope and application of part 11 of Title 21 of the Code of Federal Regulations; Electronic Records; Electronic Signatures (21 CFR Part 11).[2]

This document provides guidance to persons who, in fulfillment of a requirement in a statute or another part of FDA's regulations to maintain records or submit information to FDA,[3] have chosen to maintain the records or submit designated information electronically and, as a result, have become subject to part 11. Part 11 applies to records in electronic form that are created, modified, maintained, archived, retrieved, or transmitted under any records requirements set forth in Agency regulations. Part 11 also applies to electronic records submitted to the Agency under the Federal Food, Drug, and Cosmetic Act (the Act) and the Public Health Service Act (the PHS Act), even if such records are not specifically identified in Agency regulations (§ 11.1). The underlying requirements set forth in the Act, PHS Act, and FDA regulations (other than part 11) are referred to in this guidance document as *predicate rules*.

As an outgrowth of its current good manufacturing practice (CGMP) initiative for human and animal drugs and biologics,[4] FDA is re-examining part 11 as it applies to all FDA regulated products. We anticipate initiating rulemaking to change part 11 as a result of that re-examination. This guidance explains that we will narrowly interpret the scope of part 11. While the re-

1 This guidance has been prepared by the Office of Compliance in the Center for Drug Evaluation and Research (CDER) in consultation with the other Agency centers and the Office of Regulatory Affairs at the Food and Drug Administration.

2 62 FR 13430

3 These requirements include, for example, certain provisions of the Current Good Manufacturing Practice regulations (21 CFR Part 211), the Quality System regulation (21 CFR Part 820), and the Good Laboratory Practice for Nonclinical Laboratory Studies regulations (21 CFR Part 58).

4 See *Pharmaceutical CGMPs for the 21st Century: A Risk-Based Approach; A Science and Risk -Based Approach to Product Quality Regulation Incorporating an Integrated Quality Systems Approach* at www.fda.gov/oc/guidance/gmp.html.

examination of part 11 is under way, we intend to exercise enforcement discretion with respect to certain part 11 requirements. That is, we do not intend to take enforcement action to enforce compliance with the validation, audit trail, record retention, and record copying requirements of part 11 as explained in this guidance. However, records must still be maintained or submitted in accordance with the underlying predicate rules, and the Agency can take regulatory action for noncompliance with such predicate rules.

In addition, we intend to exercise enforcement discretion and do not intend to take (or recommend) action to enforce any part 11 requirements with regard to systems that were operational before August 20, 1997, the effective date of part 11 (commonly known as legacy systems) under the circumstances described in section III.C.3 of this guidance.

Note that part 11 remains in effect and that this exercise of enforcement discretion applies only as identified in this guidance.

FDA's guidance documents, including this guidance, do not establish legally enforceable responsibilities. Instead, guidances describe the Agency's current thinking on a topic and should be viewed only as recommendations, unless specific regulatory or statutory requirements are cited. The use of the word should in Agency guidances means that something is suggested or recommended, but not required.

II. Background

In March of 1997, FDA issued final part 11 regulations that provide criteria for acceptance by FDA, under certain circumstances, of electronic records, electronic signatures, and handwritten signatures executed to electronic records as equivalent to paper records and handwritten signatures executed on paper. These regulations, which apply to all FDA program areas, were intended to permit the widest possible use of electronic technology, compatible with FDA's responsibility to protect the public health.

After part 11 became effective in August 1997, significant discussions ensued among industry, contractors, and the Agency concerning the interpretation and implementation of the regulations. FDA has (1) spoken about part 11 at many conferences and met numerous times with an industry coalition and other interested parties in an effort to hear more about potential part 11 issues; (2) published a compliance policy guide, CPG 7153.17: Enforcement Policy: 21 CFR Part 11; Electronic Records; Electronic Signatures; and (3) published numerous draft guidance documents including the following:

- *21 CFR Part 11; Electronic Records; Electronic Signatures, Validation*
- *21 CFR Part 11; Electronic Records; Electronic Signatures, Glossary of Terms*
- *21 CFR Part 11; Electronic Records; Electronic Signatures, Time Stamps*
- *21 CFR Part 11; Electronic Records; Electronic Signatures, Maintenance of Electronic Records*
- *21 CFR Part 11; Electronic Records; Electronic Signatures, Electronic Copies of Electronic Records*

Throughout all of these communications, concerns have been raised that some interpretations of the part 11 requirements would (1) unnecessarily restrict the use of electronic technology in a manner that is inconsistent with FDA's stated intent in issuing the rule, (2) significantly increase the costs of compliance to an extent that was not contemplated at the time the rule was drafted, and (3) discourage innovation and technological advances without providing a significant public health benefit. These concerns have been raised particularly in the areas of part 11 requirements for validation, audit trails, record retention, record copying, and legacy systems.

As a result of these concerns, we decided to review the part 11 documents and related issues, particularly in light of the Agency's CGMP initiative. In the Federal Register of February 4, 2003 (68 FR 5645), we announced the withdrawal of the draft guidance for industry, *21 CFR Part 11; Electronic Records; Electronic Signatures, Electronic Copies of Electronic Records*. We had decided we wanted to minimize industry time spent reviewing and commenting on the draft guidance when that draft guidance may no longer represent our approach under the CGMP initiative. Then, in the *Federal Register* of February 25, 2003 (68 FR 8775), we announced the withdrawal of the part 11 draft guidance documents on validation, glossary of terms, time stamps,[5] maintenance of electronic records, and CPG 7153.17. We received valuable public comments on these draft guidances, and we plan to use that information to help with future decision- making with respect to part 11. We do not intend to re- issue these draft guidancedocuments or the CPG.

We are now re-examining part 11, and we anticipate initiating rulemaking to revise provisions of that regulation. To avoid unnecessary resource expenditures to comply with part 11 requirements, we are issuing this guidance to describe how we intend to exercise enforcement discretion with regard to certain part 11 requirements during the re-examination of part 11. As mentioned previously, part 11 remains in effect during this re-examinatio n period. 110

III. Discussion

A. Overall Approach to Part 11 Requirements

As described in more detail below, the approach outlined in this guidance is based on three main elements:

- Part 11 will be interpreted narrowly; we are now clarifying that fewer records will be considered subject to part 11.
- For those records that remain subject to part 11, we intend to exercise enforcement discretion with regard to part 11 requirements for validation, audit trails, record retention, and record copying in the manner described in this guidance and with regard to all part 11 requirements for systems that were operational before the effective date of part 11 (also known as legacy systems).

5 Although we withdrew the draft guidance on time stamps, our current thinking has not changed in that when using time stamps for systems that span different time zones, we do not expect you to record the signer's local time. When using time stamps, they should be implemented with a clear understanding of the time zone reference used. In such instances, system documentation should explain time zone references as well as zone acronyms or other naming conventions.

- We will enforce all predicate rule requirements, including predicate rule record and recordkeeping requirements.

It is important to note that FDA's exercise of enforcement discretion as described in this guidance is limited to specified part 11 requirements (setting aside legacy systems, as to which the extent of enforcement discretion, under certain circumstances, will be more broad). We intend to enforce all other provisions of part 11 including, but not limited to, certain controls for closed systems in § 11.10. For example, we intend to enforce provisions related to the following controls and requirements:

- limiting system access to authorized individuals
- use of operational system checks
- use of authority checks
- use of device checks
- determination that persons who develop, maintain, or use electronic systems have the education, training, and experience to perform their assigned tasks
- establishment of and adherence to written policies that hold individuals accountable for actions initiated under their electronic signatures
- appropriate controls over systems documentation
- controls for open systems corresponding to controls for closed systems bulleted above (§11.30)
- requirements related to electronic signatures (e.g., §§ 11.50, 11.70, 11.100, 11.200, and 11.300)

We expect continued compliance with these provisions, and we will continue to enforce them. urthermore, persons must comply with applicable predicate rules, and records that are required to be maintained or submitted must remain secure and reliable in accordance with the predicate rules.

B. Details of Approach – Scope of Part 11

1. Narrow Interpretation of Scope

We understand that there is some confusion about the scope of part 11. Some have understood the scope of part 11 to be very broad. We believe that some of those broad interpretations could lead to unnecessary controls and costs and could discourage innovation and technological advances without providing added benefit to the public health. As a result, we want to clarify that the Agency intends to interpret the scope of part 11 narrowly.

Under the narrow interpretation of the scope of part 11, with respect to records required to be maintained under predicate rules or submitted to FDA, when persons choose to use records in electronic format in place of paper format, part 11 would apply. On the other hand, when persons use computers to generate paper printouts of electronic records, and those paper records meet all the requirements of the applicable predicate rules and persons rely on the paper records to perform their regulated activities, FDA would generally not consider persons to be "using electronic records in lieu of paper records" under §§ 11.2(a) and 11.2(b). In these instances, the use of computer systems in the generation of paper records would not trigger part 11.

2. Definition of Part 11 Records

Under this narrow interpretation, FDA considers part 11 to be applicable to the following records or signatures in electronic format (part 11 records or signatures): 177

- Records that are required to be maintained under predicate rule requirements and that are maintained in electronic format in place of paper format. On the other hand, records (and any associated signatures) that are not required to be retained under predicate rules, but that are nonetheless maintained in electronic format, are not part 11 records.

  We recommend that you determine, based on the predicate rules, whether specific records are part 11 records. We recommend that you document such decisions.

- Records that are required to be maintained under predicate rules, that are maintained in electronic format in addition to paper format, and that are relied on to perform regulated activities.

  In some cases, actual business practices may dictate whether you are using electronic records instead of paper records under § 11.2(a). For example, if a record is required to be maintained under a predicate rule and you use a computer to generate a paper printout of the electronic records, but you nonetheless rely on the electronic record to perform regulated activities, the Agency may consider you to be using the electronic record instead of the paper record. That is, the Agency may take your business practices into account in determining whether part 11 applies.

  Accordingly, we recommend that, for each record required to be maintained under predicate rules, you determine in advance whether you plan to rely on the electronic record or paper record to perform regulated activities. We recommend that you document this decision (e.g., in a Standard Operating Procedure (SOP), or specification document).

- Records submitted to FDA, under predicate rules (even if such records are not specifically identified in Agency regulations) in electronic format (assuming the records have been identified in docket number 92S-0251 as the types of submissions the Agency accepts in electronic format). However, a record that is not itself submitted, but is used in generating a submission, is not a part 11 record unless it is otherwise required to be maintained under a predicate rule and it is maintained in electronic format.

- Electronic signatures that are intended to be the equivalent of handwritten signatures, initials, and other general signings required by predicate rules. Part 11 signatures include electronic signatures that are used, for example, to document the fact that certain events or actions occurred in accordance with the predicate rule (e.g. approved, reviewed, and verified).

C. Approach to Specific Part 11 Requirements

1. Validation

The Agency intends to exercise enforcement discretion regarding specific part 11 requirements for validation of computerized systems (§ 11.10(a) and corresponding requirements in § 11.30). Although persons must still comply with all applicable predicate rule requirements for validation (e.g., 21 CFR 820.70(i)), this guidance should not be read to impose any additional requirements for validation.

We suggest that your decision to validate computerized systems, and the extent of the validation, take into account the impact the systems have on your ability to meet predicate rule requirements. You should also consider the impact those systems might have on the accuracy, reliability, integrity, availability, and authenticity of required records and signatures. Even if there is no predicate rule requirement to validate a system, in some instances it may still be important to validate the system. 228

We recommend that you base your approach on a justified and documented risk assessment and a determination of the potential of the system to affect product quality and safety, and record integrity. For instance, validation would not be important for a word processor used only to generate SOPs.

For further guidance on validation of computerized systems, see FDA's guidance for industry and FDA staff *General Principles of Software Validation* and also industry guidance such as the *GAMP 4 Guide* (See References).

2. Audit Trail

The Agency intends to exercise enforcement discretion regarding specific part 11 requirements related to computer- generated, time-stamped audit trails (§ 11.10 (e), (k)(2) and any corresponding requirement in §11.30). Persons must still comply with all applicable predicate rule requirements related to documentation of, for example, date (e.g., § 58.130(e)), time, or sequencing of events, as well as any requirements for ensuring that changes to records do not obscure previous entries.

Even if there are no predicate rule requirements to document, for example, date, time, or sequence of events in a particular instance, it may nonetheless be important to have audit trails or other physical, logical, or procedural security measures in place to ensure the trustworthiness and reliability of the records.[6] We recommend that you base your decision on whether to apply audit trails, or other appropriate measures, on the need to comply with predicate rule requirements, a justified and documented risk assessment, and a determination of the potential effect on product quality and safety and record integrity. We suggest that you apply appropriate controls based on such an assessment. Audit trails can be particularly appropriate when users are expected to create, modify, or delete regulated records during normal operation.

6 Various guidance documents on information security are available (see References).

3. Legacy Systems[7]

The Agency intends to exercise enforcement discretion with respect to all part 11 requirements for systems that otherwise were operational prior to August 20, 1997, the effective date of part 11, under the circumstances specified below.

This means that the Agency does not intend to take enforcement action to enforce compliance with any part 11 requirements if all the following criteria are met for a specific system:

- The system was operational before the effective date.
- The system met all applicable predicate rule requirements before the effective date.
- The system currently meets all applicable predicate rule requirements.
- You have documented evidence and justification that the system is fit for its intended use (including having an acceptable level of record security and integrity, if applicable).

If a system has been changed since August 20, 1997, and if the changes would prevent the system from meeting predicate rule requirements, Part 11 controls should be applied to Part 11 records and signatures pursuant to the enforcement policy expressed in this guidance.

4. Copies of Records

The Agency intends to exercise enforcement discretion with regard to specific part 11 requirements for generating copies of records (§ 11.10 (b) and any corresponding requirement in

280 §11.30). You should provide an investigator with reasonable and useful access to records during an inspection. All records held by you are subject to inspection in accordance with predicate rules (e.g., §§ 211.180(c), (d), and 108.35(c)(3)(ii)).

We recommend that you supply copies of electronic records by:

- Producing copies of records held in common portable formats when records are maintained in these formats
- Using established automated conversion or export methods, where available, to make copies in a more common format (examples of such formats include, but are not limited to, PDF, XML, or SGML)

In each case, we recommend that the copying process used produces copies that preserve the content and meaning of the record. If you have the ability to search, sort, or trend part 11 records, copies given to the Agency should provide the same capability if it is reasonable and technically feasible. You should allow inspection, review, and copying of records in a human readable form at your site using your hardware and following your established procedures and techniques for accessing records.

---

7 In this guidance document, we use the term legacy system to describe systems already in operation before the effective date of part 11.

CH 22

5. Record Retention

The Agency intends to exercise enforcement discretion with regard to the part 11 requirements for the protection of records to enable their accurate and ready retrieval throughout the records retention period (§ 11.10 (c) and any corresponding requirement in §11.30). Persons must still comply with all applicable predicate rule requirements for record retention and availability (e.g., §§ 211.180(c),(d), 108.25(g), and 108.35(h)).

We suggest that your decision on how to maintain records be based on predicate rule requirements and that you base your decision on a justified and documented risk assessment and a determination of the value of the records over time.

FDA does not intend to object if you decide to archive required records in electronic format to nonelectronic media such as microfilm, microfiche, and paper, or to a standard electronic file format (examples of such formats include, but are not limited to, PDF, XML, or SGML). Persons must still comply with all predicate rule requirements, and the records themselves and any copies of the required records should preserve their content and meaning. As long as predicate rule requirements are fully satisfied and the content and meaning of the records are preserved and archived, you can delete the electronic version of the records. In addition, paper and electronic record and signature components can co-exist (i.e., a hybrid[8] situation) as long as predicate rule requirements are met and the content and meaning of those records are preserved.

8 Examples of hybrid situations include combinations of paper records (or other nonelectronic media) and electronic records, paper records and electronic signatures, or handwritten signatures executed to electronic records.

IV. References

Food and Drug Administration References

1. *Glossary of Computerized System and Software Development Terminology* (Division of Field Investigations, Office of Regional Operations, Office of Regulatory Affairs, FDA 1995) (http://www. fda.gov/ora/inspect_ref/igs/gloss.html)
2. *General Principles of Software Validation; Final Guidance for Industry and FDA Staff* (FDA, Center for Devices and Radiological Health, Center for Biologics Evaluation and Research, 2002) (http://www.fda.gov/cdrh/comp/guidance/938.html)
3. *Guidance for Industry, FDA Reviewers, and Compliance on Off-The-Shelf Software Use in Medical Devices* (FDA, Center for Devices and Radiological Health, 1999) (http://www. fda.gov/cdrh/ode/guidance/585.html)
4. *Pharmaceutical CGMPs for the 21st Century: A Risk-Based Approach; A Science and Risk-Based Approach to Product Quality Regulation Incorporating an Integrated Quality Systems Approach* (FDA 2002) (http://www.fda.gov/oc/guidance/gmp.html)

Industry References

1. *The Good Automated Manufacturing Practice (GAMP) Guide for Validation of Automated Systems*, GAMP 4 (ISPE/GAMP Forum, 2001) (http://www.ispe.org/gamp/)
2. ISO/IEC 17799:2000 (BS 7799:2000) Information technology – Code of practice for information security management (ISO/IEC, 2000)
3. ISO 14971:2002 Medical Devices- Application of risk management to medical devices (ISO, 2001)

CH 22

Chapter 23
General Wellness: Policy for Low Risk Devices
Guidance for Industry and FDA Staff

September 27, 2019.
U.S. Department of Health and Human Services
Food and Drug Administration
Center for Devices and Radiological Health

I. Introduction

The Food and Drug Administration (FDA) is issuing this guidance document to provide clarity to industry and FDA staff on the Center for Devices and Radiological Health's (CDRH's) compliance policy for low risk products that promote a healthy lifestyle (general wellness products).[1] This guidance does not apply to products (e.g., drugs, biologics, dietary supplements, foods, or cosmetics) regulated by other FDA Centers or to combination products.[2]

Section 3060(a) of the 21st Century Cures Act (Cures Act) amended section 520 of the Federal Food, Drug, and Cosmetic Act (FD&C Act) on December 13, 2016, removing certain software functions, including those intended for maintaining or encouraging a healthy lifestyle that are unrelated to the diagnosis, cure, mitigation, prevention, or treatment of a disease or condition, from the definition of device in section 201(h) of the FD&C Act.

Section 520(o)(1)(B) of the FD&C Act, states that software that is intended "for maintaining or encouraging a healthy lifestyle and is unrelated to the diagnosis, cure, mitigation, prevention, or treatment of a disease or condition" is not a device under section 201(h) of the FD&C Act.

This guidance clarifies FDA's interpretation of this provision and its application to general wellness products.

FDA's guidance documents, including this guidance, do not establish legally enforceable responsibilities. Instead, guidances describe the Agency's current thinking on a topic and should be viewed only as recommendations, unless specific regulatory or statutory requirements are cited. The use of the word should in Agency guidance means that something is suggested or recommended, but not required.

---

1 This guidance does not change or rescind any requirements of the Federal Food, Drug, and Cosmetic Act (FD&C Act) or any applicable regulations. This guidance also does not preclude FDA from consulting with the Consumer Product Safety Commission (CPSC) as to whether a general wellness product is a consumer product under CPSC's authority or a device. FDA may coordinate with other agencies and authorities, such as the CPSC, to determine jurisdiction over products. If a product is a device under section 201(h) of the FD&C Act, it is generally excluded from CPSC's authority over "consumer products" under the Consumer Product Safety Act (15 U.S.C. § 2052(a)(5)(ii)(H)). However, CPSC and FDA may both have jurisdiction over certain medical devices under other statutory authorities the CPSC administers.

2 For determinations on combination products, contact the Office of Combination Products at combination@fda.gov. See 21 CFR 3.2(e) for the definition of a combination product.

II. Policy on Low Risk General Wellness Products

CDRH does not intend to examine low risk general wellness products to determine whether they are devices[3] within the meaning of the FD&C Act or, if they are devices, whether they comply with the premarket review and post-market regulatory requirements for devices under the FD&C Act and implementing regulations, including, but not limited to: registration and listing and premarket notification requirements (21 CFR Part 807); labeling requirements (21 CFR Part 801 and 21 CFR 809.10); good manufacturing practice requirements as set forth in the Quality System regulation (21 CFR Part 820); and Medical Device Reporting (MDR) requirements (21 CFR Part 803).

For purposes of this guidance, CDRH defines **general wellness products** as products that meet the following two factors: (1) are intended for only general wellness use, as defined in this guidance, and (2) present a low risk to the safety of users and other persons. General wellness products may include exercise equipment, audio recordings, video games, software programs[4] and other products that are commonly, though not exclusively, available from retail establishments (including online retailers and distributors that offer software to be directly downloaded), when consistent with the two factors above.

CDRH regularly receives inquiries about whether particular products are devices as defined by the FD&C Act. There are instances where certain general wellness products, as discussed in this guidance, do not meet the definition of a device under section 201(h) of the FD&C Act and therefore are not subject to the FD&C Act's regulatory requirements for devices.

Additionally, section 520(o)(1)(B) of the FD&C Act excludes software functions that are intended for maintaining or encouraging a healthy lifestyle and are unrelated to the diagnosis, cure, mitigation, prevention, or treatment of a disease or condition from the definition of device in section 201(h) of the FD&C Act.[5] We have included examples of products below that meet the definition of general wellness products to help illustrate the concepts in the guidance.

A product's inclusion under the general wellness policy in this guidance does not establish that it has been shown to be safe and/or effective for its intended use.

---

3 The term "device" is defined in 201(h) of the FD&C Act to include an "instrument, apparatus, implement, machine, contrivance, implant, in vitro reagent, or other similar or related article, including any component, part, or accessory, which is ...intended for use in the diagnosis of disease or other conditions, or in the cure, mitigation, treatment, or prevention of disease, in man ... or intended to affect the structure or any function of the body of man..." and "does not include software functions excluded pursuant to section 520(o) of the FD&C Act."

4 For more discussion regarding FDA's regulatory approach towards certain device software functions and mobile medical applications, see the FDA Guidance: Policy for Device Software Functions and Mobile Medical Applications, available at https://www.fda.gov/regulatory-information/search-fda-guidance-documents/policy- device-software-functions-and-mobile-medical-applications.

5 "Nothing in this subsection shall be construed as limiting the authority of the [FDA] to— (A) exercise enforcement discretion as to any device subject to regulation under this Act . . ." (section 520(o)(4) of the FD&C Act).

III. General Wellness Products

A **general wellness product**, for the purposes of this guidance, has (1) an intended use that relates to maintaining or encouraging a general state of health or a healthy activity, or (2) an intended use that relates the role of healthy lifestyle with helping to reduce the risk or impact of certain chronic diseases or conditions and where it is well understood and accepted that healthy lifestyle choices may play an important role in health outcomes for the disease or condition.

If the product's intended uses are not limited to the above general wellness intended uses, this guidance does not apply.

The first category of general wellness intended uses involve claims about sustaining or offering general improvement to functions associated with a general state of health that **do not make any reference to diseases or conditions**. For the purposes of this guidance, this first category of general wellness claims relate to:

- weight management,
- physical fitness, including products intended for recreational use,
- relaxation or stress management,
- mental acuity,
- self-esteem (e.g., devices with a cosmetic function that make claims related only to self-esteem),
- sleep management, or
- sexual function.

The following are examples of this category of general wellness claims:

- Claims to promote or maintain a healthy weight, encourage healthy eating, or assist with weight loss goals;
- Claims to promote relaxation or manage stress;
- Claims to increase, improve, or enhance the flow of qi "energy";
- Claims to improve mental acuity, instruction following, concentration, problem- solving, multitasking, resource management, decision-making, logic, pattern recognition, or eye-hand coordination;
- Claims to enhance learning capacity;
- Claims to promote physical fitness, such as to help log, track, or trend exercise activity, measure aerobic fitness, improve physical fitness, develop or improve endurance, strength or coordination, or improve energy (e.g., "fitness" or "activity" trackers);
- Claims to promote sleep management, such as to track sleep trends;
- Claims to promote self-esteem, such as to boost self-esteem;

- Claims that address a specific body structure or function, such as to increase or improve muscle size or body tone, tone or firm the body or muscle, or enhance or improve sexual performance;
- Claims to improve general mobility or to assist individuals who are mobility impaired in a recreational activity (e.g., sport wheelchairs, beach access wheelchairs); and
- Claims to enhance an individual's participation in recreational activities by monitoring the consequences of participating in such activities, such as to monitor heart rate or monitor frequency or impact of collisions.

The following are examples of claims that **do not** fall into this category of general wellness claims:

- A claim that a product will treat or diagnose obesity;
- A claim that a product will treat an eating disorder, such as anorexia;
- A claim that a product helps treat an anxiety disorder;
- A claim that a computer game will diagnose or treat autism;
- A claim that a product will treat muscle atrophy or erectile dysfunction; and
- A claim to restore a structure or function impaired due to a disease or condition, e.g., a claim that a prosthetic device enables amputees to walk.[6]

The second category of general wellness intended uses relate to sustaining or offering general improvement to functions associated with a general state of health while **making reference to diseases or conditions**. For the purposes of this guidance, this second category of general wellness claims is comprised of two subcategories:

1) intended uses to promote, track, and/or encourage choice(s), which, as part of a healthy lifestyle, **may help to reduce the risk of** certain chronic diseases or conditions; and
2) intended uses to promote, track, and/or encourage choice(s) which, as part of a healthy lifestyle, **may help living well** with certain chronic diseases or conditions.

Both subcategories of disease-related general wellness claims should only be based on references where it is well understood that healthy lifestyle choices may reduce the risk or impact of a chronic disease or medical condition. That is, the claim that the healthy lifestyle choice(s) may play an important role in health outcomes should be generally accepted; such associations are described in peer-reviewed scientific publications or official statements made by healthcare professional organizations.[7] Examples of chronic diseases for which a healthy lifestyle is associated with risk reduction or help in living well with that disease include heart disease, high blood pressure, and type 2 diabetes.

6 Products intended to restore a structure or function impaired due to a disease might be regulated by FDA as devices. For example, an artificial limb prosthesis intended to provide disabled persons the ability to walk might be regulated under 21 CFR 890.3420 or 21 CFR 890.3500.

7 By organizations we mean associations and colleges such as American Medical Association (AMA), American Heart Association (AHA), American Association of Clinical Endocrinologists (AACE), American College of Rheumatology, etc.

The following are examples of this category of disease-related general wellness claims:

- Software Product U coaches breathing techniques and relaxation skills, which, as part of a healthy lifestyle, may help living well with migraine headaches.
- Software Product V tracks and records your sleep, work and exercise routine which, as part of a healthy lifestyle, may help living well with anxiety.
- Product W promotes making healthy lifestyle choices such as getting enough sleep, eating a balanced diet, and maintaining a healthy weight, which may help living well with type 2 diabetes.
- Product X promotes physical activity, which, as part of a healthy lifestyle, may help reduce the risk of high blood pressure.
- Software Product Y tracks your caloric intake and helps you manage a healthy eating plan to maintain a healthy weight and balanced diet. Healthy weight and balanced diet may help living well with high blood pressure and type 2 diabetes.
- Product Z tracks activity sleep patterns and promotes healthy sleep habits, which, as part of a healthy lifestyle, may help reduce the risk for developing type 2 diabetes.

IV. Determining Risk for General Wellness Products

CDRH's general wellness policy applies only to general wellness products that are low risk.[8] If the answer to any of the following questions is YES, the product is not low risk and is not covered by this guidance.

1) Is the product invasive[9]?
2) Is the product implanted?
3) Does the product involve an intervention or technology that may pose a risk to the safety of users and other persons if specific regulatory controls are not applied, such as risks from lasers or radiation exposure?

In assessing whether a product is low risk for purposes of this guidance, FDA recommends that you also consider whether CDRH actively regulates products of the same type as the product in question. For example, CDRH actively regulates external penile rigidity devices, which are devices intended to create or maintain sufficient penile rigidity for sexual intercourse, under 21 CFR 876.5020 as class II devices exempt from premarket notification with special controls. The special controls for these devices address risks to health that are associated with the use of these devices, including, without limitation, tissue injury, trauma or infection.[10] Therefore, these types of devices would not be considered low risk general wellness products.

8 Whether a device is classified as class I under section 513(a)(1) of the FD&C Act does not necessarily mean that it is "low risk" for purposes of this guidance.

9 For purposes of this guidance, "invasive" means penetrates or pierces the skin or mucous membranes of the body.

10 See the FDA Guidance: Class II Special Controls Guidance Document: External Penile Rigidity Devices, issued on December 28, 2004, available at https://www.fda.gov/regulatory-information/search-fda-guidance- documents/class-ii-special-controls-guidance-document-external-penile-rigidity-devices-guidance-industry-and.

The following are examples of products that would **not** be considered "low risk" as described in this guidance:

- Sunlamp products promoted for tanning purposes, due to risks to a user's safety from the ultraviolet radiation, including, without limitation, an increased risk of skin cancer.[11]
- Implants promoted for improved self-image or enhanced sexual function. Implants pose risks to users such as rupture or adverse reaction to implant materials and risks associated with the implantation procedure.
- A laser product that claims to improve confidence in user's appearance by rejuvenating the skin. Although the claims of rejuvenating the skin and improving confidence in user's appearance are general wellness claims, laser technology presents risks of skin and eye burns.
- A neurostimulation product that claims to improve memory, due to the risks to a user's safety from electrical stimulation.
- A product that claims to enhance a user's athletic performance by providing suggestions based on the results of relative lactic acid testing, when the product uses venipuncture to obtain the blood samples needed for testing. Such a product is not low risk because it is invasive (e.g., obtains blood samples by piercing the skin) and also because the product involves an intervention that may pose a risk to the safety of the user and other persons if specific regulatory controls are not applied (e.g., venipuncture may pose a risk of infection transmission).

V. Examples of General Wellness Products That are Not Medical Devices and Examples of General Wellness Products that Are Medical Devices for which FDA Does Not Intend to Enforce Requirements

Illustrative Example 1: A software function plays music to "soothe and relax" an individual and to "manage stress." Such a software function is not a device function.

This software function has claims that relate only to relaxation or stress management, not to any disease or medical condition, and thus are general wellness claims. In addition, the technology to play music does not pose a risk to the safety of users and other persons if specific regulatory controls are not applied. Therefore, this product meets both factors for a low risk general wellness product.

11 See Final Order reclassifying UV lamps intended to tan the skin from class I exempt from premarket notification to class II (special controls): General and Plastic Surgery Devices: Reclassification of Ultraviolet Lamps for Tanning, Henceforth To Be Known as Sunlamp Products and Ultraviolet Lamps Intended for Use in Sunlamp Products, available at https://www.federalregister.gov/articles/2014/06/02/2014-12546/general-and- plastic-surgery-devices-reclassification-of-ultraviolet-lamps-for-tanning-henceforth-to.

Illustrative Example 2: A software function that solely monitors and records daily energy expenditure and cardiovascular workout activities to "allow awareness of one's exercise activities to improve or maintain good cardiovascular health." Such a software function is not a device function.

This software function has a claim that relates to a specific organ only in the context of general health and does not refer to a disease or medical condition. In addition, although the monitoring or recording of exercise activities present risks (such as inaccuracy), when made in the absence of disease or medical condition claims, the technology does not pose a risk to the safety of users and other persons if specific regulatory controls are not applied. Therefore, this product meets both factors for a low risk general wellness product.

Illustrative Example 3: A software function monitors and records food consumption to "manage dietary activity for weight management and alert the user, healthcare provider, or family member of unhealthy dietary activity." Such a software function is not a device function.

This software function has a claim that relates to dietary choices and weight management, and thus is a general wellness claim. In addition, the technology for monitoring or recording food consumption does not pose a risk to the safety of users and other persons if specific regulatory controls are not applied. Therefore, this product meets both factors for a low risk general wellness product.

Illustrative Example 4: A software function that reminds users to keep exposed skin out of direct sunlight when the UV index is high, which, as part of a healthy lifestyle, may help reduce the risk of skin cancer.

This claim relates to tracking preventive measures which, as part of a healthy lifestyle, may help reduce the risk of a medical condition. The claim is for a healthy lifestyle choice and it is generally accepted that the choice may play an important role in health outcomes. Thus, it is a general wellness claim. In addition, the technology reminding users to keep exposed skin out of direct sunlight does not pose a risk to the safety of users and other persons if specific regulatory controls are not applied. Therefore, this product meets both factors for a low risk general wellness product.

Illustrative Example 5: A portable product that is intended to monitor the pulse rate of users during exercise and hiking.

This claim relates only to exercise and hiking and does not refer to a disease or medical condition. Thus, it is a general wellness claim. In addition, the technology for monitoring pulse rate does not pose a risk to the safety of users and other persons if specific regulatory controls are not applied. Therefore, this product meets both factors for a low risk general wellness product.

Illustrative Example 6: A product is intended to mechanically exfoliate the face, hands and feet to make the skin smoother and softer. The product cannot be used in a manner that penetrates or pierces the skin.

This claim relates to self-esteem and does not refer to a specific disease or medical condition, and thus is a general wellness claim. In addition, the product is noninvasive as it does not penetrate the stratum corneum and the technology for exfoliating the face does not pose a risk to the safety of users and other persons if specific regulatory controls are not applied. Therefore, this product meets both factors for a low risk general wellness product.

Note: However, if the product is intended to exfoliate the skin in order to enhance the delivery of a topically applied product containing one or more active pharmaceutical ingredients through the stratum corneum, the product would be invasive. Therefore, the product would **not** be a low risk general wellness product.

VI. Determining whether General Wellness Products are within Scope of the Guidance

The following questions reflect the framework described in this guidance to determine whether general wellness products are within the scope of the guidance. Please note that these questions are intended to be addressed in the context of the full text of the guidance.

A1. Does the product have an intended use that relates to maintaining or encouraging a general state of health or a healthy activity?

Does the product only involve claims about sustaining or offering general improvement to functions associated with a general state of health that do not make any reference to diseases or conditions? Claims in this category include: weight management, physical fitness, relaxation or stress management, mental acuity, self-esteem, sleep management, or sexual function.

YES ⟹	**Go to A3.**
NO ⟹	**Go to A2.**

A2. Does the product have an intended use that relates the role of healthy lifestyle with helping to reduce the risk or impact of certain chronic diseases or conditions? *(In answering this question, the following two questions must be considered together.)*

a) Does the product have an intended use that relates to sustaining or offering general improvement to functions associated with a general state of health while making reference to diseases or conditions, and where it is well understood and accepted that healthy lifestyle choices may play an important role in health outcomes for the disease or condition?

AND

b) Is the relation between healthy lifestyle and disease specifically expressed as "**may help to reduce the risk of,**" or "**may help living well with**," a chronic disease or condition?

YES ⟹	**Go to A3.** *Both questions A2(a) and A2(b) must be answered "Yes" in order to proceed to question A3.*
NO ⟹	Product is **NOT** a low risk general wellness product, and is **outside the scope of this guidance.**

A3. Is the product low risk?

Is the product not invasive, and not implanted, and does not involve a technology that may pose a risk to the safety of users or other persons if specific regulatory controls are not applied, such as risks from lasers or radiation exposure? In answering this question, consider whether CDRH actively regulates products of the same type as the product in question.

YES ⟹	The product **is likely a general wellness product within the scope of this guidance**, but the factors and examples in the guidance should be reviewed to confirm the status of the product.
NO ⟹	Product is **NOT** a low risk general wellness product, and is **outside the scope of this guidance.**

CSV

Chapter 24
Guidance for Industry
Blood Establishment Computer System Validation in the User's Facility

April 2013
U.S. Department of Health and Human Services
Food and Drug Administration
Center for Biologics Evaluation and Research

I. Introduction

We, FDA, are issuing this guidance to assist you, blood establishments, in developing a blood establishment computer system validation program, consistent with recognized principles of software validation, quality assurance, and current good software engineering practices. This guidance addresses a blood establishment's validation of its Blood Establishment Computer *System* (system) which incorporates Blood Establishment Computer *Software* (BECS). In the context of this guidance, the term "user's facility" means the blood establishment.

This guidance describes the following:

- Requirements in Title 21 Code of Federal Regulations (21 CFR) (e.g., 21 CFR 211.68, 606.100(b), and 606.160) that apply to blood establishment validation of systems; and
- FDA's recommendations for the validation of systems.

While this guidance may provide manufacturers of BECS with information about validation of computer systems in the user's facility, this guidance does not address the software manufacturer's validation responsibilities, or the submission of a 510(k) premarket notification for BECS. For guidance on validation applicable to the manufacturer of medical device software, including BECS, see the FDA guidance document entitled, "General Principles of Software Validation: Final Guidance for Industry and FDA Staff" dated January 2002 (Ref. 1). For guidance on the submission of a 510(k) for BECS, see the FDA guidance document entitled "Guidance for Industry and FDA Staff: Guidance for the Content of Premarket Submissions for Software Contained in Medical Devices" dated May 2005 (Ref. 2).

This guidance finalizes the draft guidance entitled "Guidance for Industry: Blood Establishment Computer System Validation in the User's Facility" dated October 2007.

FDA's guidance documents, including this guidance, do not establish legally enforceable responsibilities. Instead, guidances describe the FDA's current thinking on a topic and should be viewed only as recommendations, unless specific regulatory or statutory requirements are cited.

The use of the word *should* in FDA guidances means that something is suggested or recommended, but not required.

II. Background

A. Description of Blood Establishment Computer System

A Blood Establishment Computer System (system) includes: computer hardware; computer software; peripheral devices; networks; personnel; and documentation, e.g., User's Manuals and Standard Operating Procedures (SOPs). The computer software used in a system includes BECS, which is a medical device. Systems also are regulated as equipment under 21 CFR Part 606 (Current Good Manufacturing Practice for Blood and Blood Components), specifically 21 CFR 606.60, and as automated or electronic equipment under 21 CFR Part 211, Subpart D (Equipment), specifically 21 CFR 211.68.

B. Description of Blood Establishment Computer Software

BECS is software designed to be used in a blood establishment and is intended for use in the diagnosis of disease or other conditions in donors, or in the prevention of disease in humans by preventing the release of unsuitable blood and blood components. Some of the intended uses of BECS include:

- Use during the manufacturing process for determining donor eligibility and release of the blood or blood component as suitable for transfusion or further manufacture;
- Use in transfusion services to perform compatibility testing and other related functions;
- Use to establish positive patient identification prior to transfusion by scanning machine readable information such as barcodes on patient wristbands (or other electronic data storage items), specimen containers, and blood product labels; and
- • Use to perform other functions associated with transfusion, such as recording patient vital signs and tracking blood products.

C. Definitions and Terminology

In addition to the following definitions used in this guidance, you may find other terms relating to systems and BECS in the FDA Glossary of Computer Systems Software Development Terminology (Ref. 3). The use of some terms in this guidance or in FDA regulations may vary somewhat from some uses in industry. For example, both FDA and the International Organization for Standardization (ISO 8402:1994) regard "verification" and "validation" as separate and distinct terms. However, many software engineering journals and textbooks use the terms "verification" and "validation" interchangeably, or in some cases, refer to software "verification, validation, and testing (VV&T)" as a single concept, with no distinction among the three terms. We provide the following definitions in an effort to clarify our meaning of specific terms where our usage may vary somewhat from some uses in industry.

Qualification operational means establishing confidence that process equipment and sub-systems are capable of consistently operating within established limits and tolerances (Ref. 3).

Risk assessment means a comprehensive evaluation of the risk and its associated impact (Ref. 3).

Software regression testing means re-running test cases which a program has previously executed correctly to detect errors caused by changes or corrections made during software development (Ref. 1).

Software validation means confirmation by examination and provision of objective evidence that the particular requirements for the software's intended uses can be consistently fulfilled (Ref. 1).

Software verification means confirmation by examination and provision of objective evidence that specified requirements have been fulfilled (Ref. 1). In a software development or manufacturing environment, software verification provides objective evidence that the design outputs of a particular phase of the software development life cycle meet all of the specified requirements for that phase.

User validation means testing new equipment or a new process in the environment where it will be used to ensure that it will reliably produce a product that meets pre-determined qualifications and quality standards (Ref. 4).

III. Discussion

A. Vendor Selection for BECS

While not strictly part of system validation, we recommend that you evaluate and compare the available BECS with the needs of your blood establishment and select a BECS that meets your requirements. We further recommend that you monitor reports of adverse events and recalls applicable to your BECS (Refs. 5 through 9).

We provide a list of 510(k) cleared BECS on our web site (Ref. 9). You should note that the version number listed is the version that received clearance; however, the manufacturer may have released an upgrade that did not require a new 510(k) clearance. You also should note that the list on our website is cumulative and may include BECS that may no longer be available or supported by the original manufacturer.

B. System Documentation

You must maintain documentation for your system (21 CFR 211.68, 211.100(a), 606.100(b)(15), 606.160(b)(5)). You should ensure that the documentation is current, accurate, and as detailed as necessary to ensure proper use and operation of the system. We recommend you include, but not necessarily limit, the documentation you maintain to the following, as applicable to your blood establishment:

- Information available from the software developer, such as:
  - Hardware specifications and hardware requirements;
  - Instruction manuals, e.g., User's Manual, Operations Manual, Installation Manual, System Administration Manual, etc.;
  - Environmental requirements;
  - Network diagram;

- System description;
- List and location of peripheral devices such as printers and terminals;
- Processor type(s);
- Operating system and version number;
- System memory;
- Disk configuration;
- Type and location of backup media;
- List of interfaces; and
- List of environments on system, e.g., test, training, production, etc.

- Information available from the system administrator, such as:
  - Validation records;
  - Record of hardware and software maintenance, including date performed;
  - Record of changes made to the system hardware, software and peripheral devices, including date;
  - User training records;
  - SOPs; and
  - Problem reports and their resolution.

Note: Although a remote access log is not part of validation records, you may consider keeping a log of remote access to any part of your system, such as the BECS or laboratory instruments. We recommend this log include the date, time, reason for the access and the name of the person connecting to your system.

C. Validation Plan

Before you start user validation, you must define and control how you will validate the system through the use of a written plan designed to assure proper performance

(21 CFR 211.68(a)). A written plan is not "designed to assure proper performance" unless it requires user validation prior to routine use, on a routine basis, and any time a change is made that has the potential to affect the functions of the system. In addition, input to and output from the system must be checked for accuracy (21 CFR 211.68(b)). Therefore, before you start validation, you must develop a validation protocol and acceptance criteria to ensure the system is performing properly (21 CFR 211.68(a)).

The validation plan defines "what" the validation effort should cover. Validation plans specify areas such as scope, approach, resources, schedules, training, the types and extent of activities, tasks, and work items, identification and resolution of software defects/bugs or anomalies, responsibility and the approval process (Ref. 1).

D. Scope of Validation

Your activities should assure that the system components have been validated and are suitable for your specific operations and workload and can accurately and repeatedly meet your needs (as defined in your requirements documents). You should validate your system at your location using the same software, hardware, SOPs, and personnel who will use the system after it is formally implemented. Thus, in cases where a central server is used by multiple locations, not only the main server but also each individual location should have a validation plan that is specific to the functions and configurations at each location. Equipment vendors may provide assistance for equipment qualification and consultants may provide assistance with the validation project. However, you are ultimately responsible for validation of your system in your facility.

Validation of your BECS falls under your Current Good Manufacturing Practice (cGMP) requirements and should reflect and anticipate the BECS' actual use in your establishment. We recognize that it is a common practice for software manufacturers to provide test cases to blood establishments for use in system validation. We recommend that you carefully assess the software manufacturer's test cases, consider your own intended use of the software, your internal policies and procedures, and add or change test plans as appropriate to ensure that the software will accurately and repeatedly meet your requirements. The test cases should include those that represent "worst case scenarios," e.g., maximum numbers of users working simultaneously, all possible activities occurring simultaneously, etc.

We recognize that BECS validation is difficult because you cannot test indefinitely, and it is hard to determine how much evidence is sufficient. Generally, software validation is a matter of developing a "level of confidence" (Ref. 1) that the software device meets all requirements and user expectations for the automated functions and features of the software.

E. Risk Assessment

The level of confidence and, therefore, the level of validation effort needed, varies depending upon the potential hazards posed by the automated functions of the system. Your test plan and test cases should be developed based on a risk assessment. We, therefore, recommend that you perform a risk assessment early in the validation process. After performing that assessment, you should determine the degree of validation necessary based on the identified risks, and then develop your test plan and test cases accordingly. The highest risk functions of the system should be tested more comprehensively. For example, because of the potentially fatal consequences of a transfusion based on an improper crossmatch between donor and recipient, the validation of the electronic or computer crossmatch would require more extensive testing.

Because of the complexity of software, especially BECS, it is difficult to predict the probability of a hazard occurrence. Therefore, when you conduct your risk assessment, we recommend you consider most hazards to have a high probability of occurrence.

F. Validation Procedures

You must develop SOPs for your validation activities as required by 21 CFR 211.68(a), 211.100(a), and 606.100(b)(15). We recommend that your validation SOPs include, but not necessarily be limited to, the following:

- Writing a validation plan;
- Performing system maintenance;
- Performing a risk assessment;
- Writing a validation report;
- Addressing change control;
- Writing test cases;
- Amending test cases;
- Handling validation deviations; and
- Validating after a change.

G. Validation Activities

Consider the following points as you prepare to perform validation activities:

- We recommend that you perform validation in the "test environment" or "test partition" of your system. After successful validation, you or your software manufacturer should copy or move the file configuration on which you performed your validation into the production environment.
- Each executed test case in your pre-defined written test plan should include the input, expected output, actual output, acceptance criteria, whether the test passed or failed, the name or initials of the person performing the test, and the date the test was performed. Test cases should include normal results (results within the"normal" range), abnormal results (unacceptable results or those outside the "normal" range) and boundary results or values. Boundary testing is testing at the boundary of a specification, in other words, at the limit, just below the limit, and just over the limit. Boundary values are "off-by-one errors." An example of boundary testing is testing for a hematocrit of 37%, 38% and 39% if the cutoff (or boundary value) for hematocrit is 38%. You should also test for "absurd" results (invalid or nonsense results). Examples of absurd or unexpected values might be an alpha result in a numeric field, a hematocrit of 110% or a blank (or leading blank) in a result field.
- You must retain validation records (21 CFR 211.68(b), 211.100(b), 606.160(b)(5)(ii)). Your records should include documented evidence of all test cases, test input data and test results. Test results should include screen prints. For traceability purposes and to facilitate quality assurance review and follow-up, we recommend that any supporting documentation, such as screen-prints, where appropriate, be identified to link them to the specific test case.

- We recommend that you test at simulated peak production times in an appropriately sized test environment and with the maximum number of concurrent users to assure proper system performance.
- We recommend that you test to assure you have correctly defined system security and that all users can log on with the correct security privileges.
- We recommend that you qualify equipment, validate all interfaces, including those to a Hospital Information System (HIS) (e.g., admissions, discharges and transfers (ADT)); a Laboratory Information System (LIS) (e.g., order entry/results return (OE/RR)); and all instrument interfaces, as applicable. Monitoring of interface error files should continue subsequent to implementation as unforeseen transaction types or data elements may cause disastrous results (for instance, orders not being received, results posting to the incorrect donor/patient record, etc.).
- You must train personnel in the use of the system procedures (21 CFR 211.25(a), 600.10(b), 606.20(b)). Training should include assessing an individual's ability to understand and correctly use the system. You should evaluate your personnel's ability to perform system maintenance procedures, such as backups, and their ability to respond in an appropriate and timely manner to all alarms, warnings and error messages.
- We recommend that you verify the output of system reports. We recommend you include any reports containing donor or recipient history information, product quarantine reports, donor or patient merge reports, and patient chart reports (as applicable) in this effort. It is particularly important to ensure that reports print in lower and upper case if the system keeps records of red blood cell phenotype or antibodies.
- We recommend that you closely monitor the system for a period of time after installation of the new or upgraded software in the production environment to detect any discrepancies that were not identified by the test cases.
- If your system includes the use of wireless radio frequency (RF) technology, we recommend that you evaluate the device for wireless coexistence, performance, data integrity, security, electromagnetic compatibility (EMC), and electromagnetic interference (EMI) in the setting in which you will use it. For further information, see the FDA draft guidance document entitled, "Draft Guidance for Industry and FDA Staff, Radio-Frequency Wireless Technology in Medical Devices" (Ref. 10). When finalized, this draft guidance will represent FDA's current thinking on this topic.
- Although not a function of your system, we recommend that you validate the data conversion from your legacy system to your new system to avoid problems such as duplicate donor records and deferral codes.

H. Validation Report

You must document your validation activities pursuant to 21 CFR 211.68, 211.100(b), and 606.160(b)(5). Your validation report should include a summary of the test results, including any variances or failed tests, any amendments made to the test cases or the validation plan, an evaluation of the outcome of your testing, and approvals or sign-offs by management, including dates.

I. Validation after a Change

When the BECS manufacturer modifies the software, the manufacturer should inform you of other functions that might be affected. We recommend that your contract with a software manufacturer specifically address this issue. However, you are ultimately responsible for assuring that the system used in your establishment has been validated for use in your establishment.

Due to the complexity of systems and BECS, a seemingly small local change (e.g., software, hardware, peripherals, or infrastructure) may have a significant global system effect. When any change (even a small change) is made to the software on the system, a software regression analysis should be conducted, not just for validation of the individual change, but also to determine the extent and impact of that change on the entire system. Based on the analysis, you should then conduct an appropriate level of software regression testing to show that unchanged but vulnerable portions of the system have not been adversely affected. Appropriate regression analysis and testing provide the confidence that the system is validated after a software change (Ref. 2). We recommend that you perform regression testing, when indicated by your analysis, by re-running test cases that previously passed.

J. Integrated Package vs. Stand-Alone

If your system or BECS is part of an integrated package on a Laboratory Information System (LIS) or Hospital Information System (HIS) rather than a stand-alone system, you should also consider how changes made to functionality shared by the LIS or HIS and BECS (such as ADT, orders, etc.) might affect your system or BECS. You should determine what functions or files your LIS or HIS and your BECS share by discussing this with your BECS manufacturer.

IV. REFERENCES

1. General Principles of Software Validation: Final Guidance for Industry and FDA Staff (January 11, 2002), http://www.fda.gov/MedicalDevices/DeviceRegulationandGuidance/GuidanceDocuments/ucm085281.htm.

2. Guidance for Industry and FDA Staff: Guidance for the Content of Premarket Submissions for Software Contained in Medical Devices (May 11, 2005), http://www.fda.gov/MedicalDevices/DeviceRegulationandGuidance/GuidanceDocuments/ucm089543.htm.

3. FDA Glossary of Computer Systems Software Development Terminology, (8/95) http://www.fda.gov/ICECI/Inspections/InspectionGuides/ucm074875.htm.

4. Guidance for Industry: "Computer Crossmatch" (Computerized Analysis of the Compatibility between the Donor's Cell Type and the Recipient's Serum or Plasma Type) (April 2011) http://www.fda.gov/downloads/BiologicsBloodVaccines/GuidanceComplianceRegulatoryInformation/Guidances/Blood/UCM252894.pdf.

5. Warning Letters http://www.fda.gov/ICECI/EnforcementActions/WarningLetters/default.htm.

6. Adverse Event Reports (Maude Database), http://www.accessdata.fda.gov/scripts/cdrh/cfdocs/cfmaude/textsearch.cfm.

7. FDA Enforcement Reports Index, http://www.fda.gov/safety/recalls/enforcementreports/default.htm.

8. Recalls, Market Withdrawals and Safety Alerts, http://www.fda.gov/Safety/Recalls/default.htm.

9. 510(k) Blood Establishment Computer Software, http://www.fda.gov/BiologicsBloodVaccines/BloodBloodProducts/ApprovedProducts/SubstantiallyEquivalent510kDeviceInformation/ucm134987.htm.

10. Draft Guidance for Industry and FDA Staff, Radio-Frequency Wireless Technology in Medical Devices (draft released for comment on January 3, 2007), http://www.fda.gov/MedicalDevices/DeviceRegulationandGuidance/GuidanceDocuments/ucm077210.htm.

CSV

Chapter 25
Medical Device Data Systems, Medical Image Storage Devices, and Medical Image Communications Devices
Guidance for Industry and FDA Staff

September 27, 2019
U.S. Department of Health and Human Services
Food and Drug Administration
Center for Devices and Radiological Health
Center for Biologics Evaluation and Research

I. Introduction

The Food and Drug Administration (FDA) recognizes that the progression to digital health offers the potential for better, more efficient patient care and improved health outcomes. To achieve this goal requires that many medical devices be interoperable with other types of medical devices and with various types of health information technology. The foundation for such inter-communication is hardware and software, typically referred to as medical device data systems (MDDS) that transfer, store, convert formats, and display medical device data or medical imaging data.

On February 15, 2011, the FDA issued a regulation down-classifying MDDS from Class III (high-risk) to Class I (low-risk) ("MDDS regulation").[1] Since down-classifying MDDS, the FDA has gained additional experience with these types of technologies, and has determined that these devices pose a low risk to the public. On February 9, 2015, the FDA issued a guidance document to inform manufacturers, distributors, and other entities that the Agency does not intend to enforce compliance with the regulatory controls that apply to MDDS, medical image storage devices, and medical image communications devices, due to the low risk they pose to patients and the importance they play in advancing digital health.

Since the issuance of the guidance document in 2015, section 3060(a) of the 21st Century Cures Act (Cures Act) amended section 520 of the Federal Food, Drug, and Cosmetic Act (FD&C Act) on December 13, 2016, removing certain software functions from the definition of device in section 201(h) of the FD&C Act. Pursuant to section 520(o)(1)(D) of the FD&C Act, *software functions* that are *solely intended* to transfer, store, convert formats, and display medical device data or medical imaging data, unless the software function is intended to interpret or analyze clinical laboratory test or other device data, results, and findings, are not devices and are not subject to FDA laws and regulations applicable to devices. The definition of MDDS in 21 CFR 880.6310 is currently inconsistent with the definition of device as amended pursuant to the Cures Act. FDA intends to amend the regulation to be consistent with the amended device definition. FDA's current thinking on the definition of MDDS is reflected in this guidance.

---

1 See Medical Devices; Medical Device Data Systems Final Rule (76 FR 8637) (Feb. 15, 2011).

Hardware products that are intended to transfer, store, convert formats, and display medical device data and results remain devices under section 201(h) of the FD&C Act. FDA does not intend to enforce compliance with the regulatory controls for such devices, provided that the hardware function is limited to assisting the following software functions: electronic transfer, storage, conversion of formats, or display of medical device data.

The policy described in this guidance document is also consistent with the Agency's updated guidance entitled "Policy for Device Software Functions and Mobile Medical Applications," originally issued on February 9, 2015, with the title "Mobile Medical Applications.[2]"

FDA's guidance documents, including this guidance, do not establish legally enforceable responsibilities. Instead, guidances describe the Agency's current thinking on a topic and should be viewed only as recommendations, unless specific regulatory or statutory requirements are cited. The use of the word *should* in Agency guidance means that something is suggested or recommended, but not required.

II. Background

FDA uses the following terms in this guidance:

Non-Device-MDDS: *Software functions* that are *solely intended* to transfer, store, convert formats, and display medical device data or results.

Device-MDDS: *Hardware functions* that are *solely intended* to transfer, store, convert formats, and display medical device data or results.

FDA further defines Non-Device-MDDS and Device-MDDS through the following examples:

A Non-Device-MDDS is a software function solely intended to provide one or more of the following uses, without controlling or altering the functions or parameters of any connected medical devices, which may or may not be intended for active patient monitoring[3]:

- The electronic transfer or exchange of medical device data. For example, this would include software that collects output from a ventilator about a patient's CO2 level and transmits the information to a central patient data repository.
- The electronic storage and retrieval of medical device data. For example, software that stores historical blood pressure information for later review by a health care provider.
- The electronic conversion of medical device data from one format to another in accordance with a preset specification. For example, software that converts digital data generated by a pulse oximeter into a digital format that can be printed.

2 Available at https://www.fda.gov/regulatory-information/search-fda-guidance-documents/policy-device- software-functions-and-mobile-medical-applications.

3 As noted in the preamble of the MDDS regulation, the word "active" represents "any d*evice that is intended to be relied upon in deciding to take immediate clinical action*" (21 CFR 8637 at 8644). FDA further noted that there are existing classifications for patient monitoring devices (See, e.g., 21 CFR Part 880, Subpart C (general hospital and personal use monitoring devices); 21 CFR Part 868, Subpart C (anesthesiology monitoring devices); 21 CFR Part 884, Subpart C (obstetrical and gynecological monitoring devices); and 21 CFR Part 870, Subpart C (cardiovascular monitoring devices)).

- The electronic display of medical device data. For example, software that displays a previously stored electrocardiogram for a particular patient.

Other examples of Non-Device-MDDS include:

- Any assemblage or arrangement of network components that includes specialized software expressly created for a purpose consistent with the intended use in the MDDS regulation.
- Software functions specifically labeled (per 21 CFR Part 801) by the manufacturer as a MDDS, provided such products do not provide additional functionality.
- Custom software that is written by entities other than the original medical device manufacturer (for example, hospitals, third party vendors) that directly connects to a medical device, to obtain medical device information.
- Modified portions of software that are part of an Information Technology (IT) infrastructure created and/or modified (writing and compiling software) for specific MDDS functionality. For example, when modifying software for MDDS functionality, only the modified portion is considered MDDS; the original software is not.

A MDDS does not modify the data, and it does not control the functions or parameters of any connected medical device. Software functions intended to generate alarms or alerts or prioritize patient-related information on multi-patient displays, which are typically used for active patient monitoring, are considered device software functions because these functions involve analysis or interpretation of laboratory test or other device data and results. As noted above, a Non-Device-MDDS may include software functions that transfer, store, convert formats, or display medical device data that may or may not be intended for active patient monitoring.

Software functions that are device functions intended for active patient monitoring include the following characteristics:

- The clinical context requires a timely response (e.g. in-hospital patient monitoring).
- The clinical condition (disease or diagnosis) requires a timely response (e.g., a monitor that is intended to detect life-threatening arrhythmias, such as ventricular fibrillation, or a device used to actively monitor diabetes for time-sensitive intervention).

Examples of devices that provide active patient monitoring include:

  - A nurse telemetry station that receives and displays information from a bedside hospital monitor in an ICU.
  - A device that receives and/or displays information, alarms, or alerts from a monitoring device in a home setting and is intended to alert a caregiver to take an immediate clinical action.

Examples of products that transfer, store, convert formats, or display medical device data and are Non-Device-MDDS:

  - An application that transmits a child's temperature to a parent/guardian while the child is in the nurse/health room of a school.

- An application that facilitates the remote display of information from a blood glucose meter, where the user of the meter can independently review their glucose and glucose levels, and which is not intended to be used for taking immediate clinical action. In these cases, remotely displaying information such as the most recent blood glucose value or time-lapse between blood glucose measurements is not considered active patient monitoring.

This guidance also provides the policy for medical image storage and medical image communications devices. These devices are defined as follows:

- A medical image storage device, defined under 21 CFR 892.2010, is a device that provides electronic storage and retrieval functions for medical images.
- A medical image communications device, defined under 21 CFR 892.2020, is a device that provides electronic transfer of medical image data between medical devices.

III. Policy for Medical Device Data Systems, Medical Image Storage Devices, and Medical Image Communications Devices

A. Policy for Non-Device-MDDS

Software functions that meet the definition of Non-Device-MDDS, medical image storage devices, or medical image communications devices are not devices under section 201(h) of the FD&C Act. As such, software functions that are *solely intended* to transfer, store, convert formats, and display medical device data and results, including medical images, waveforms, signals, or other clinical information, are not devices and thus are not subject to FDA regulatory requirements applicable to devices. However, software functions that analyze or interpret medical device data in addition to transferring, storing, converting formats, or displaying clinical laboratory test or other device data and results remain subject to FDA's regulatory oversight, unless they meet the criteria outlined in section 520(o)(1)(E) of the FD&C Act.

B. Policy for DeviceMDDS

Hardware functions that are intended to transfer, store, convert formats, and display medical device data and results remain devices under section 201(h) of the FD&C Act. FDA does not intend to enforce the requirements under the FD&C Act for hardware products that are considered to be Device-MDDS, medical image storage, or medical image communications devices, provided that the hardware function is limited to assisting the following software functions: electronic transfer, storage, conversion of formats, or display of medical device data. These hardware functions may include the following regulations:

a) MDDS subject to 21 CFR 880.6310,

b) Medical image storage devices subject to 21 CFR 892.2010, and

c) Medical image communications devices subject to 21 CFR 892.2020.

This means that for hardware functions that meet the definitions in the regulations listed above, the FDA does not intend to enforce compliance with the regulatory controls, including registration and listing, premarket review, postmarket reporting, and quality system regulation for manufacturers of these types of devices.

Each Device-MDDS regulation listed above contains an exemption from premarket notification; however, limitations to this exemption identified under 21 CFR 880.9 and 21 CFR 892.9 require a premarket notification in the listed circumstances. Even when exceeding these limitations, FDA does not intend to enforce compliance with the regulatory controls for for hardware functions that meet the definitions identified by the above regulations. For example, to the extent that these limitations apply, FDA does not intend to enforce compliance with regulatory controls for a Device-MDDS that is an in vitro device that is intended for assessing the risk of cardiovascular diseases (21 CFR 880.9(c)(4)) or for use in diabetes management (21 CFR 880.9(c)(5)).

Specialized medical display hardware devices for digital mammography, radiology, pathology, and ophthalmology (see, for example, 21 CFR 892.2050) and other specialized medical display hardware integral to the safe and effective use of a medical device hardware product (such as integral 3D displays in robotic surgery systems and displays built into ICU bedside monitors) have not been considered MDDS, medical image storage, or medical image communications devices. Such medical display hardware devices and other specialized medical display hardware integral to a medical device are not excluded from the device definition by the Cures Act and are not considered to be Device-MDDS.

In some cases, software functions that transfer, store, convert formats, or display medical device data and results are utilized on hardware that is not intended by the hardware manufacturer for a device function under section 201(h) of the FD&C Act. For example, general-purpose hardware IT infrastructure intended for data transfer (e.g., network router), data storage (e.g., network attached storage (NAS)), conversion of data (e.g., PDF software), and display of data (computer monitor) are not device functions. Such products do not meet the definition of a device in section 201(h) of the FD&C Act for either the software or hardware function and are therefore not regulated as devices.

C. Multiple Function Device Products that contain Non-Device-MDDS or Device-MDDS

Consistent with section 520(o)(2) of the FD&C Act, which describes the regulation of a product with multiple functions, including at least one device function and at least one software function that is not a device, FDA does not regulate the Non-Device-MDDS functions contained in a multiple function device product. If a multiple function device product contains Device-MDDS functions, FDA does not, at this time and based our current understanding of the risks of these devices, intend to enforce the requirements under the FD&C Act. However, FDA may assess the impact that such Non-Device-MDDS and Device- MDDS functions have on the safety and effectiveness of the device function(s) in the multiple function device product. FDA intends to provide recommendations on the regulation of such products with multifunctionality in a separate guidance document.

Chapter 26
Off-The-Shelf Software Use in Medical Devices
Guidance for Industry and FDA Staff

September 27, 2019
U.S. Department of Health and Human Services
Food and Drug Administration
Center for Devices and Radiological Health

I. Introduction

Off-the-shelf (OTS) Software is commonly being considered for incorporation into medical devices as the use of general-purpose computer hardware becomes more prevalent. The use of OTS Software in a medical device allows the manufacturer to concentrate on the application software needed to run device-specific functions. However, OTS Software intended for general-purpose computing may not be appropriate for a given specific use in a medical device. The medical device manufacturer using OTS Software generally gives up software life cycle control, but still bears the responsibility for the continued safe and effective performance of the medical device.

This guidance document was developed to address the many questions asked by medical device manufacturers regarding what they need to provide in a premarket submission to the FDA when they use OTS Software. The specific response to these questions depends on the medical device in question and the impact on patient, operator, or bystander safety if the OTS Software fails. Thus, the answer to the question, "What do I need to document?" may differ and is based on the risk analysis that is an integral part of designing a medical device. The detail of documentation to be provided to FDA and the level of life cycle control necessary for the medical device manufacturer increase as severity of the hazards to patients, operators, or bystanders from OTS Software failure increases.

This document lays out in broad terms how the medical device manufacturer can consider what is necessary to document for submission to the Agency. A basic set of need-to-document items is recommended for all OTS Software, and a detailed discussion is provided on additional (special) needs and responsibilities of the manufacturer when the severity of the hazards from OTS Software failure become more significant.

For the current edition of the FDA-recognized standard(s) referenced in this document, see the FDA Recognized Consensus Standards Database.[1] For more information regarding use of consensus standards in regulatory submissions, please refer to the FDA guidance titled Appropriate Use of Voluntary Consensus Standards in Premarket Submissions for Medical Devices.[2]"

---

1 Available at https://www.accessdata.fda.gov/scripts/cdrh/cfdocs/cfStandards/search.cfm.
2 Available at https://www.fda.gov/regulatory-information/search-fda-guidance-documents/appropri-

FDA's guidance documents, including this guidance, do not establish legally enforceable responsibilities. Instead, guidances describe the Agency's current thinking on a topic and should be viewed only as recommendations, unless specific regulatory or statutory requirements are cited. The use of the word *should* in Agency guidance means that something is suggested or recommended, but not required.

II. Scope

The purpose of this document is to describe the information that generally should be provided in a medical device application involving OTS Software. This information is in addition to the documentation described in the Guidance for the Content of Premarket Submissions for Software Contained in Medical Devices.[3] Many of the principles outlined herein may also be helpful to device manufacturers in establishing design controls and validation plans for use of OTS Software in their devices. This guidance discusses key elements reviewers should look for in the submission, thereby providing a common baseline from which both manufacturers and reviewers can operate. This should improve predictability of Agency interaction with sponsors regarding applications involving OTS Software.

The guidance provided in this document reflects a safety-based approach to risk management and is designed to be consistent with international standards on risk management. Existing international standards indicate that the estimation of risk should be considered as the product of the severity of harm and the probability of occurrence of harm. Probabilities of occurrence are calculated based on clinical and engineering considerations. On the clinical side, manufacturers use patient populations, user skill sets, labeling, and risk benefit analysis to calculate risk and acceptable risk levels. On the software engineering side, probabilities of occurrence would normally be based on software failure rates. However, software failures are systematic in nature and therefore their probability of occurrence can not be determined using traditional statistical methods.

Because the risk estimates for hazards related to software cannot easily be estimated based on software failure rates, CDRH has concluded that engineering risk management for medical device software should focus on the severity of the harm that could result from the software failure. 'Hazard Analysis' is defined as the identification of hazards and their initiating causes. Based on the definition of 'Risk Analysis,[4]' hazard analysis is actually a subset of risk analysis; because risk analysis for software cannot be based on probability of occurrence, the actual function of risk analysis for software can then be reduced to a hazard analysis function. Technically speaking, the use of either term risk or hazard analysis is appropriate. However, CDRH has chosen to use the term hazard analysis to reinforce the concept that calculating risk based on software failure rates is generally not justified, and that it is more appropriate to manage software safety risk based on the severity of harm rather then the software failure rates.

ate-use-voluntary-consensus-standards-premarket-submissions-medical-devices.

3 Available at https://www.fda.gov/regulatory-information/search-fda-guidance-documents/guidance-content-premarket-submissions-software-contained-medical-devices.

4 ISO 14971 Medical devices — Application of risk management to medical devices.

III. Definitions

Following a safety-based approach to risk analysis, we define:

Hazard – A possible source of danger or a condition that could result in human injury.

Hazard Analysis – Identification of hazards and their initiating causes.

Hazard Mitigation – Reduction in the severity of the hazard, the likelihood of the occurrence, or both.

Major Level of Concern – The Level of Concern is major if operation of the software associated with device function directly affects the patient, operator, and/or bystander so that failures or latent flaws could result in death or serious injury to the patient, operator, and/or bystander, or if it indirectly affects the patient, operator, and/or bystander (e.g., through the action of care provider) such that incorrect or delayed information could result in death or serious injury to the patient, operator, and/or bystander.

Minor Level of Concern – The Level of Concern is minor if failures or latent design flaws would not be expected to result in any injury to the patient, operator, and/or bystander.

Moderate Level of Concern – The Level of Concern is moderate if the operation of the software associated with device function directly affects the patient, operator, and/or bystander so that failures or latent design flaws could result in non-serious injury to the patient, operator, and/or bystander, or if it indirectly affects the patient, operator, and/or bystander (e.g., through the action of the care provider) where incorrect or delayed information could result in non-serious injury of the patient, operator, and/or bystander.

Off-the-Shelf Software (OTS Software) – A generally available software component, used by a medical device manufacturer for which the manufacturer cannot claim complete software life cycle control.

Risk Analysis – Investigation of available information to identify hazards and to estimate risks.[5]

Risk Control – The process through which decisions are reached and implemented for reducing risks to, or maintaining risks within, specified limits.[6]

Safety – In the regulation of medical devices, safety means that the probable benefits to health for its intended use when accompanied by adequate directions and warnings against unsafe use, outweigh any probable risks. In this guidance we will use the words "safety and effectiveness" to remind ourselves that safety is only meaningful in the context of the benefit-risk considerations and the labeling.

5 ISO 14971 Medical devices — Application of risk management to medical devices.

6 ISO 14971 Medical devices – Application of risk management to medical devices.

Serious Injury – As adopted from the Medical Device Reporting (MDR) regulation in 21 CFR 803.3(w), means an injury or illness that:

1. Is life threatening,
2. Results in permanent impairment of a body function or permanent damage to a body structure, or
3. Necessitates medical or surgical intervention to preclude permanent impairment of a body function or permanent damage to a body structure.

Permanent – For the purpose of this subpart, permanent means irreversible impairment or damage to a body structure or function excluding trivial impairment or damage.

Other software terminology used in this document is defined in FDA's Glossary of Computer System Software Development Terminology.[7]

IV. OTS Software Decision Schematic

The content of the application supporting use of OTS Software in a medical device depends on the results of the hazard analysis. Figure 1 provides a schematic of the decision process and a table of contents for Section V of this guidance document.

Table 1 summarizes the recommended contents for an OTS Software submission based on Figure 1.

CH 26

Minor Level of Concern Before Mitigations	*Minor Level of Concern After Mitgations*	*Moderate Level of Concern*	*Major Level of Concern After Mitigations*
Hazard Analysis	Hazard Analysis	Hazard Analysis	Hazard Analysis
Basic Documentation	Basic Documentation	Basic Documentation	Basic Documentation
	Hazard Mitigations	Hazard Mitigations	Hazard Mitigations
		Describe and Justify Residual Risk	Describe and Justify Residual Risk
			Special Documentation

Table 1. Documentation Summary from Figure 1.

7 Available at https://www.fda.gov/inspections-compliance-enforcement-and-criminal-investigations/inspection-guides/glossary-computer-system-software-development-terminology-895.

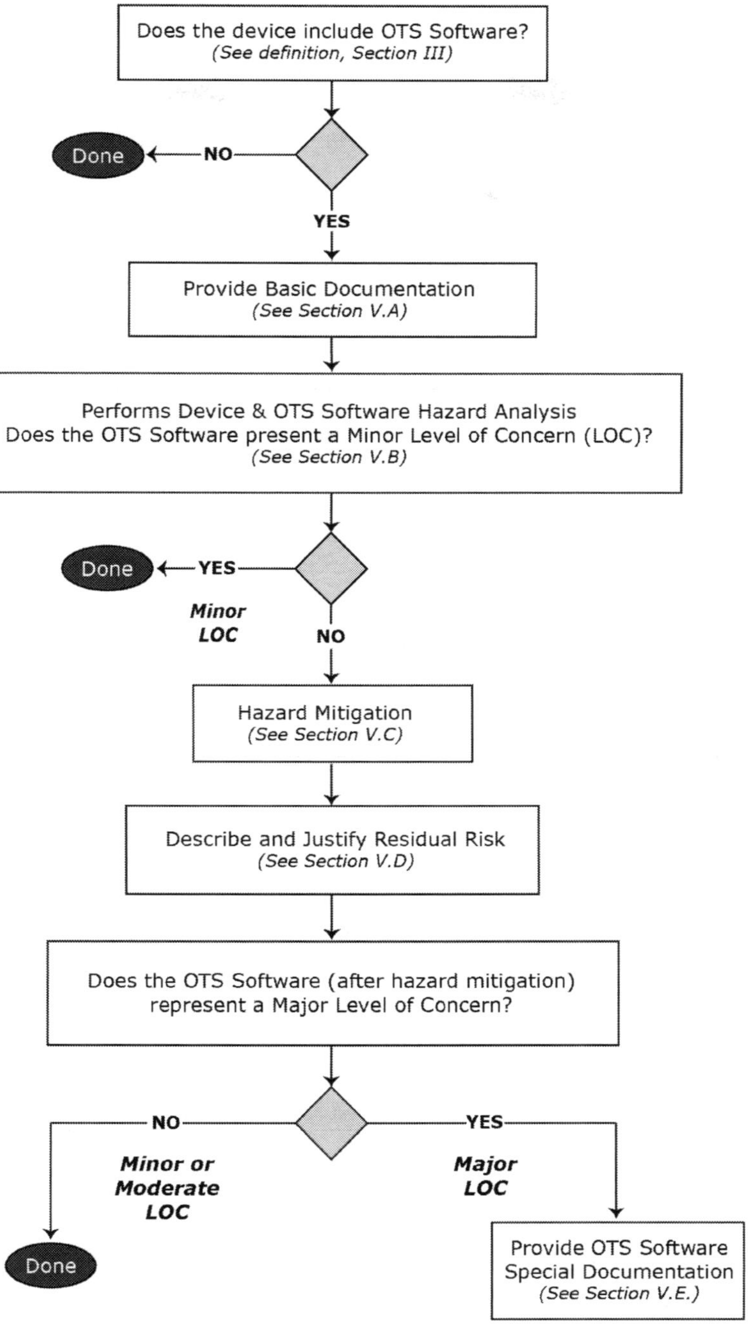

Figure 1. OTS Software Decision Schematic

V. OTS Software Use

A. Basic Documentation for OTS Software

The OTS Software Basic Documentation is intended to answer the following questions:

1. What is it?

For each component of OTS Software used, the following should be specified:

- Title and Manufacturer of the OTS Software.
- Version Level, Release Date, Patch Number, and Upgrade Designation, as appropriate.
- Any OTS Software documentation that will be provided to the end user.
- Why is this OTS Software appropriate for this medical device?
- What are the expected design limitations of the OTS Software?

Note: The medical device manufacturer should only use the OTS Software as specified in an appropriate document, i.e., design record. If the version of the OTS Software changes, the appropriate document should be updated to reflect the change.

2. What are the Computer System Specifications for the OTS Software?

For what configuration will the OTS Software be validated? The following should be specified:

- Hardware specifications: processor (manufacturer, speed, and features), RAM (memory size), hard disk size, other storage, communications, display, etc.
- Software specifications: operating system, drivers, utilities, etc. The software requirements specification (SRS) listing for each item should contain the name (e.g., Windows 10, Excel, Sun OS, etc.), specific version levels (e.g., 4.1, 5.0, etc.) and a complete list of any patches that have been provided by the OTS Software manufacturer.

3. How will you assure appropriate actions are taken by the End User?

- What aspects of the OTS Software and system can (and/or must) be installed/configured?
- What steps are permitted (or must be taken) to install and/or configure the product?
- How often will the configuration need to be changed?
- What education and training are suggested or required for the user of the OTS Software?
- What measures have been designed into the medical device to prevent the operation of any non-specified OTS Software, e.g., word processors, games? Operation of non-specified OTS Software may be prevented by system design, preventive measures, or labeling. Introduction may be prevented by disabling input (USB, CD, modems).

4. What does the OTS Software do?

What function does the OTS Software provide in this device? This is equivalent to the software requirements in the Guidance for the Content of Premarket Submissions for

Software Contained in Medical Devices[8] for this OTS Software. The following should be specified:

- What is the OTS Software intended to do? The sponsor's design documentation should specify exactly which OTS components will be included in the design of the medical device and to what extent OTS Software is involved in error control and messaging in device error control.
- What are the links with other software including software outside the medical device (not reviewed as part of this or another application)? The links to outside software should be completely defined for each medical device/module. The design documentation should include a complete description of the linkage between the medical device software and any outside software (e.g., networks).

5. How do you know it works?

Based on the Level of Concern:

- Describe testing, verification, and validation of the OTS Software and ensure it is appropriate for the device hazards associated with the OTS Software. (See Note 1.)
- Provide the results of the testing. (See Note 2.)
- Is there a current list of OTS Software problems (bugs) and access to updates?

Note 1: FDA recommends that software test, verification, and validation plans identify the exact OTS Software (title and version) that is to be used. When the software is tested it should be integrated and tested using the specific OTS Software that will be delivered to the user.

Note 2: If the manufacturer allows the use of the medical device with different versions of OTS Software, then the manufacturer should validate the medical device for each OTS Software version.

6. How will you keep track of (control) the OTS Software?

An appropriate plan should answer the following questions:

- What measures have been designed into the medical device to prevent the introduction of incorrect versions? On startup, ideally, the medical device should check to verify that all software is the correct title, version level, and configuration. If the correct software is not loaded, the medical device should warn the operator and shut down to a safe state.
- How will you maintain the OTS Software configuration?
- Where and how will you store the OTS Software?
- How will you ensure proper installation of the OTS Software?
- How will you ensure proper maintenance and life cycle support for the OTS Software?

8 8 Available at https://www.fda.gov/regulatory-information/search-fda-guidance-documents/guidance-content-premarket-submissions-software-contained-medical-devices.

B. OTS Software Hazard Analysis

A comprehensive risk management approach includes hazard analysis and mitigation that continues iteratively throughout the life of the product. The manufacturer is expected to perform an **OTS Software hazard analysis** as a part of a **medical device (system) hazard analysis**.

OTS Software failure, malfunction, or misuse may present a hazard to the patient, operators, or bystanders. Figure 2 summarizes the typical hazard management and mitigation process that would include a hazard analysis of the OTS Software component.

The submission should include the following information to document the OTS Software hazard analysis:

- A list of all potential hazards identified.
- The estimated severity of each identified hazard.
- A list of all potential causes of each identified hazard.

> ***Note:*** A tabular format of the OTS Software hazard analysis or a tabular summary will facilitate review. The hazard analysis for OTS Software may be included in the overall device hazard analysis provided adequate documentation is provided.

If the device with the OTS Software represents a Minor Level of Concern, then the Level of Concern for the OTS Software can be no greater. The hazard analysis for the OTS Software in such a device may simply document the Minor Level of Concern of the device.

Where failure, malfunction, or misuse of the OTS Software poses no possibility of injury to the patient, operators, or bystanders, then the OTS Software is said to present a Minor Level of Concern, and the fulfillment of the Basic Documentation (see Section V.A) will be considered sufficient.

C. OTS Software Hazard Mitigation

Hazard mitigation activities may seek to reduce the severity of the hazard, the likelihood of the occurrence, or both. Hazard mitigation interventions may be considered in three categories with the following order of precedence:

- Design (or redesign)
- Protective measures (passive measures)
- Warning the user (labeling)

These approaches may involve hardware and/or software. These three mitigation approaches are by no means mutually exclusive and may be used concurrently. The most desirable approach is to design in effective controls, i.e., eliminate the need for a hazardous operation or component. Protective measures are considered passive (from the user's standpoint) since they do not require any action on the part of the user. The least effective approaches depend on some action (or lack of action) on the part of the medical device user.

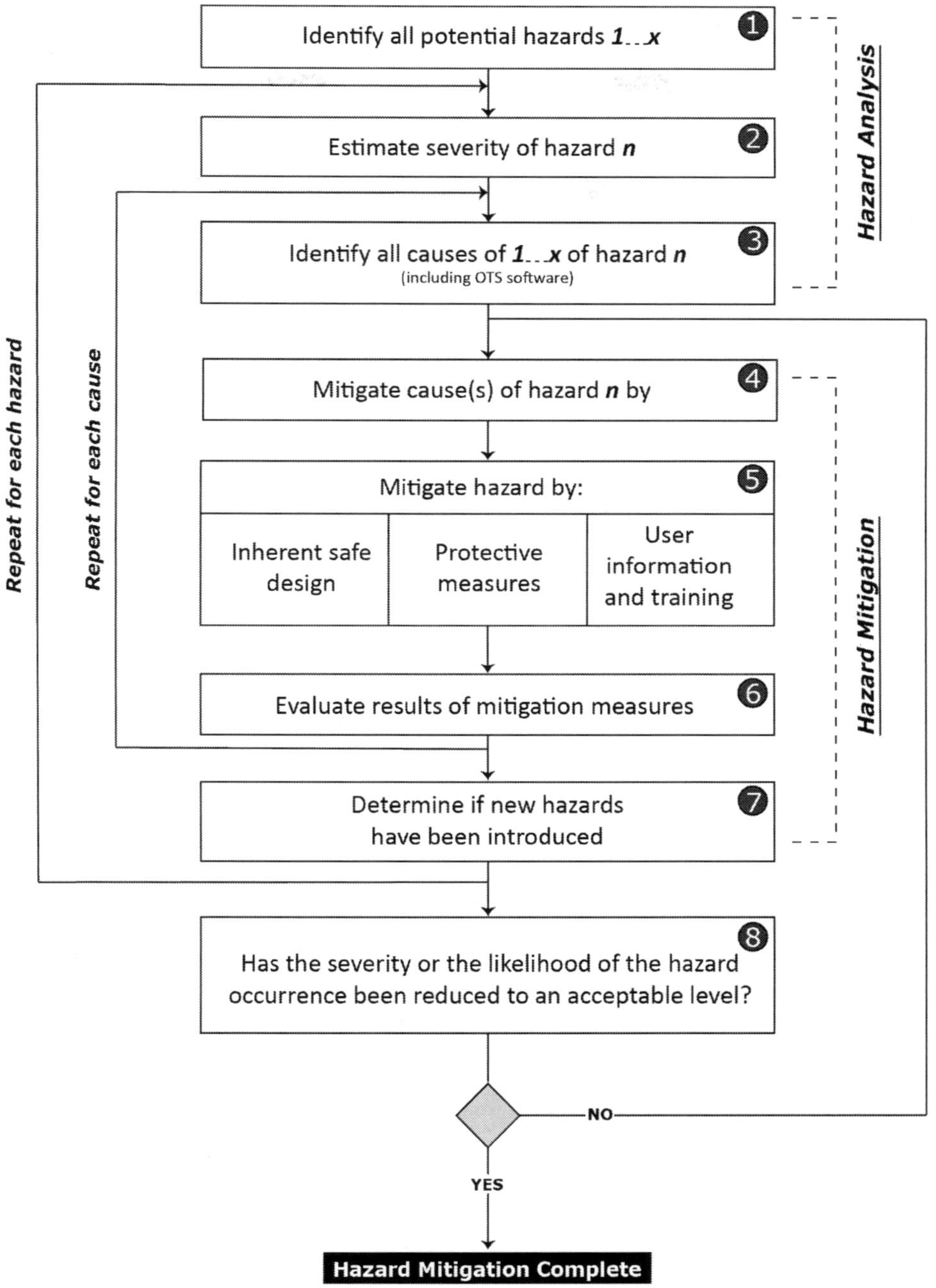

Figure 2. Typical Hazard Analysis and Mitigation

The submission should include the following information to document the OTS Software hazard mitigation:

1. A list of all identified medical device hazards associated with the OTS Software;
2. The steps taken to mitigate each hazard; and
3. The residual risk.

Note: A tabular format of the risk management or a tabular summary will facilitate review. These results will typically be included as a part of the overall medical device hazard analysis and mitigation plan.

One example of a comprehensive approach to injury prevention in public health was developed around ten "countermeasures.[9]" Table 2 illustrates a generic approach to the hazard mitigation, in this case, to preventing injury-related energy release to patients, operators, or bystanders.

With implementation of each hazard mitigation, the residual risk is assessed as well as assessment of any new hazards that may be introduced.

Acceptable levels of residual risk, based on the severity or the likelihood of the residual risk occurring, will depend on the intended use of the medical device and the function performed by the software. In the case of diagnostic tests, injury includes results that can lead to unnecessary invasive diagnostic testing (e.g., biopsy) or withholding or delaying important diagnostic or therapeutic procedures.

The sponsor will need to describe and justify the residual risk (Section V.D) for Moderate or Major Levels of Concern. Where failure, malfunction, or misuse of the OTS Software is likely to result in death or serious injury to the patient, operators, or bystanders, then the OTS Software is said to present a Major Level of Concern. If the residual risk from the OTS Software presents a Major Level of Concern, the sponsor will need to fulfill Special Documentation (Section V.E).

1. Prevent accumulation of the energy.
2. Reduce the amount of the energy delivered.
3. Prevent inappropriate release of the energy.
4. Modify the release of the energy.
5. Separate the patient from the energy in time and space.
6. Provide physical barriers between the energy and the patient.
7. Change the surfaces or basic structures at the interface.
8. Reduce likelihood of misapplication or Increase resistance of the patient.
9. Provide rapid emergency response to injury.
10. Improve medical care and rehabilitation after the injury.

Table 2. Injury Reduction Countermeasures

9 Haddon W, Baker SP. "Injury Control." Preventative and Community Medicine. Eds. Clark D, MacMahon B. New York: Little Brown & Company, 1981. 109-140. Abs: A readable discussion of basic injury reduction strategies from some of the most experienced in the field.

D. Describe and Justify Residual Risk

The sponsor should provide a detailed (complete) discussion of the risk that remains.

The risk related to the use of OTS Software should be considered in relation to the risk of the alternatives, e.g., custom developed software. Any experience (data) with the use of the OTS Software in this or a related application should be presented by the sponsor and will be considered by the reviewers. Whether the residual risk is acceptable depends on the specific medical device application.

E. Special Documentation for OTS Software

To fulfill Special Documentation for OTS Software of a Major Level of Concern, the medical device manufacturer is expected to:

1. Provide assurance to FDA that the product development methodologies used by the OTS Software developer are appropriate and sufficient for the intended use of the OTS Software within the specific medical device. FDA recommends this include an audit of the OTS Software developer's design and development methodologies used in the construction of the OTS Software. This audit should thoroughly assess the development and qualification documentation generated for the OTS Software (see Note below).

   Note: If such an audit is not possible and after hazard mitigation, the OTS Software still represents a Major Level of Concern, the use of such OTS Software may not be appropriate for the intended medical device application.
2. Demonstrate that the procedures and results of the verification and validation activities performed for the OTS Software are appropriate and sufficient for the safety and effectiveness requirements of the medical device. Verification and validation activities include not only those performed by the OTS Software developer, but also include those performed by the medical device manufacturer when qualifying the OTS Software for its use in the specific medical device.
3. Demonstrate the existence of appropriate mechanisms for assuring the continued maintenance and support of the OTS Software should the original OTS Software developer terminate their support.

VI. OTS Software Used in Marketing Applications

A. Examples

Examples of medical devices using OTS Software are described in this section. These examples illustrate the reasoning that leads to defining the Level of Concern for a medical device and thus the kinds of development processes that should be used and the information to be provided in a regulatory submission.

(1) Corneal Topographer

Minor Level of Concern medical device (see Section V.A).

Intended Use: A corneal topographer provides images of the abnormalities in the curvature of the cornea, the simplest being astigmatism.

Description: A corneal topographer consists of a hollow cone that the patient looks into from the base looking towards the interior of the point (like looking into the big end of a megaphone with one eye). The inside of the cone is white with black concentric circles. The concentric circles reflect off the eye and are imaged by a camera with a computer controlled lens situated at the point of the cone looking at the patient's eye. The shapes of the reflections of the concentric circles are used to develop a topographic map of the cornea curvature that is printed out.

OTS Software: An OTS operating system such as Windows is commonly used to interface the user, the microcomputer hardware platform, the corneal topographer, data storage, and output devices.

OTS Software Level of Concern: A corneal topographer represents no threat of direct harm to the patient. The risk of indirect harm from a misdiagnosis relating to medical device malfunction is small since the worst case is an incorrect image that is considered correct. The OTS Software in this medical device thus represents a Minor Level of Concern (see Section V.B) and should satisfy Basic Documentation (see Section V.A).

(2) Perineometer

Minor Level of Concern medical device (see Section V.A).

Intended Use: Perineometers are used to provide feedback to a patient performing muscle strengthening exercises (Kegel exercises) for the treatment of certain types of urinary incontinence.

Description: There are two types of perineometers: those that measure pressure, and those that measure electrical activity (EMG) from muscles. Each device consists of a probe that is placed into either the vagina or the rectum, and a monitoring unit. The pressure devices use an air-filled probe connected to the monitoring unit by a piece of plastic tubing. When the patient performs the exercise, the probe is compressed, and the monitoring unit reports the change in pressure. The electrical devices use an electrode to measure the electrical activity of the target muscles during the exercises, and this information is reported by the monitoring unit.

OTS Software: An OTS operating system, such as DOS or Windows, may be used to record and display the data collected by the monitoring unit.

OTS Software Level of Concern: Perineometers represent no threat of direct injury to the patient, since no energy is applied by the medical device to the patient. The risk of indirect injury due to inaccurate feedback during the exercise session is expected to be small, as these medical devices are only used as an adjunct to exercise therapy, and they are used under clinical supervision. The OTS Software in this medical device thus represents a Minor

Level of Concern (see Section V.B) and should satisfy the Basic Documentation (see Section V.A).

(3) Implantable Medical Device Programmers

Describe and Justify Residual Risk (see Section V.E).

Intended Use: An implantable medical device programmer provides interface and two-way communication with an implantable cardioverter-defibrillator (ICD) or cardiac pacemaker.

Description: An implantable medical device programmer consists of an electromagnetic programming head that is placed over the implanted device and provides through-the-skin communication with the implanted device, the personal computer (PC) interface, and the PC hardware and software. The programmer permits the physician-user to:

- Query the implant for performance history (device and patient), and, in some systems, for print-out of the recorded electrograms;
- Set the adjustable (programmable) characteristics of the implant;
- Provide the induced shock for system initialization and diagnostic purposes; and
- Verify implant operating characteristics and status (including battery) via signals from the implant.

OTS Software: An OTS operating system such as DOS or Windows is used to provide a user interface (sometimes graphical), interface to the PC (hardware platform), and interface with data storage, and output devices.

OTS Software Level of Concern: The on-board software for the implant satisfies the definition of Major Level of Concern software (life supporting/life sustaining) and would need to satisfy the Special Documentation (see Section V.E). Whether the device programmer can be considered of lesser Level of Concern depends primarily on the protection designed into the implant or the programmer. Steps taken to mitigate the risk might include:

- Design of the implant to minimize the possibility of misprogramming to inappropriate operational states;
- Design of the programmer interface to minimize the chance of miscommunication, including hardening of the hardware against electromagnetic interference (EMI);
- Limiting the part of the OTS Software that is utilized in the programming application;
- Protecting the PC from use for other applications, including consideration of the following:
    - Software design features to protect against adding unwanted software, modification, or system use; and
    - Hardware design features to protect against unwanted system use.

Other points that might be offered to support use of OTS Software in the programmer might include:

1. Documented experience (data) with use of the OTS Software in this application.
    - What was the system in place to detect and report problems?
    - What is the rate of problems reported compared to other (perhaps non-OTS Software) systems?
2. Documented experience with the OTS Software in other relevant applications.
    - What are the reported problems (bug list) and how many are relevant to this application?
    - Has there been difficulty in developing work-arounds for the problems relevant to this application?

The review team must decide whether the overall programmer system as implemented satisfies the necessary system safety and effectiveness (see Section V.E).

B. 510(k) Issues with OTS Software

The conditions under which a new or changed medical device including OTS Software will require a new 510(k) are the same as for a device not involving OTS Software. These conditions are given in the CDRH's guidances, "Deciding When to Submit a 510(k) for a Change to an Existing Device,[10]" and "Deciding When to Submit a 510(k) for a Software Change to an Existing Device.[11]"

(1) OTS Software Changes Requiring a 510(k)

For medical devices where the OTS Software represents a Minor Level of Concern, OTS Software changes would not typically require a new 510(k). However, the manufacturer is responsible for validating the change.

For other medical devices, the decision as to whether a new 510(k) is required depends on the intended use of the device; the function of the OTS Software; and to what extent the risks due to OTS Software have been mitigated (see guidances on when to submit a 510(k) for a modification[12,13]).

C. Investigational Device Exemption Issues with OTS Software

The requirements for an investigational device exemption (IDE) are the same whether or not the medical device contains OTS Software. The OTS Software may be a component of a medical

10 Available at https://www.fda.gov/regulatory-information/search-fda-guidance-documents/deciding-when-submit-510k-change-existing-device.

11 Available at https://www.fda.gov/regulatory-information/search-fda-guidance-documents/deciding-when-submit-510k-software-change-existing-device.

12 Available at https://www.fda.gov/regulatory-information/search-fda-guidance-documents/deciding-when-submit-510k-change-existing-device.

13 Available at https://www.fda.gov/regulatory-information/search-fda-guidance-documents/deciding-when-submit-510k-software-change-existing-device.

device or the OTS Software may be the entire medical device, e.g., diagnostic software. The conditions that would require submission of an IDE are specified in section 21 CFR 812 and generally include changes that would affect the patient population for which the medical device is intended; conditions of use of the device (including those recommended or suggested in the labeling or advertising; the probable benefit from the use of the device weighed against any probable injury or illness from such use); or the reliability of the medical device.

Some specific issues related to OTS Software might include initial (beta) testing of an OTS Software medical device in clinical studies. Such a study must comply with applicable IDE requirements.[14] For non-significant risk medical devices, that includes approval by an institutional review board (IRB) and patient informed consent. For significant risk studies, the initial user testing (beta testing) protocol would be included in an IDE submission. For example, beta testing of radiation treatment planning software, including any OTS Software modules, would be conducted under a full IDE with FDA approval as a prerequisite. See the guidance on "Significant Risk and Nonsignificant Risk Medical Device Studies[15]" for more information.

D. Exemption of Certain Diagnostic Devices

If the product incorporating the OTS Software is a diagnostic medical device, it may be exempted from IDE requirements, if it meets the criteria in section 21 CFR 812.2(c)(3). For example, clinical (beta) testing of a noninvasive diagnostic device that does not require significant risk invasive sampling procedure and that does not introduce energy into the body, is exempted from IRB approval, patient informed consent, and other IDE requirements, if a medically established diagnostic product or procedure is used to confirm the diagnosis.

E. Premarket Approval Issues with OTS Software

The criteria and requirements for premarket approval (PMA) applications are in section 21 CFR 814. When a manufacturer submits a PMA submission for a medical device, there must be valid scientific evidence (including clinical evidence, if needed) to support a reasonable assurance of safety and effectiveness of the device.[16]

The OTS Software used in a medical device is evaluated in the context of the overall medical device. The extent to which the medical device manufacturer ensures that the OTS Software was developed using appropriate life cycle control depends upon the overall risk of the medical device, the role of the OTS Software, and the Level of Concern associated with possible failures of the OTS Software component.

For example, a commercially available neural network, used by a medical device manufacturer for pattern recognition, would require extensive validation if used in a Pap smear screening device, in computer-assisted radiology, or for computer-assisted analysis of ECG waveforms. The same neural network, used for less critical computer-assisted analysis of EEG waveforms, might require less rigorous software documentation. Likewise, a commercially available personal

CH 26

14 See 21 CFR 812.

15 Available at https://www.fda.gov/regulatory-information/search-fda-guidance-documents/significant-risk-and-nonsignificant-risk-medical-device-studies.

16 See 21 CFR 860.7.

computer operating system with graphical user interface, would require extensive documentation and evidence of validation when intended for use in a cardiac pacemaker programmer. Less documentation and verification of the OTS operating system would be required for programming an artificial ear.

F. Artificial Intelligence

OTS knowledge-based software (for example, artificial intelligence, expert systems, and neural net software) are being developed for a number of medical applications. A typical system accepts clinical findings (sometimes including imaging data) and generates probabilities of disease states and/or recommendations for subsequent data gathering or treatment. The clinician may order a surgical biopsy or other invasive tests or initiate therapy based on the system output. Such systems should be tested and reviewed in a manner consistent with both their safety and effectiveness of their direct effects (recommendations) and indirect effects (missed appropriate diagnostic testing and treatment).

G. Product Labeling

FDA recommends that the user's manual specify the version(s) of the OTS Software that can be used with the medical device. Such specification would not be needed for embedded software (i.e., the user does not select the OTS Software and cannot change the software provided by the medical device manufacturer).

The user's manual should contain appropriate warnings to the user indicating that the use of any software other than those specified will violate the safety, effectiveness, and design controls of this medical device and that such use may result in an increased risk to users and patients. Further description of what comprises a warning and how to write it are included in the Device Labeling Guidance[17] and the guidance on Labeling – Regulatory Requirements for Medical Devices.[18]

When OTS medical device software is delivered on a magnetic / user installable medium, the package should include labeling that indicates the minimum hardware platforms on which the software is validated to run (processor, memory, disk, interface, etc.). The appropriate testing for the user to assure proper installation should also be described in the labeling.

If the hardware on which the OTS Software runs is a stand-alone computer and the user is not "locked out" by hardware or software system features, then the user should be warned against installing any other software (utilities or applications programs) on the computer.

17 Available at https://www.fda.gov/regulatory-information/search-fda-guidance-documents/device-labeling-guidance-g91-1-blue-book-memo.

18 Available at https://www.fda.gov/regulatory-information/search-fda-guidance-documents/labeling-regulatory-requirements-medical-devices-fda-89-4203.

VII. Appendix

The purpose of these Appendices is to provide background and comment on various OTS Software. Based on the Level of Concern, device manufacturers should either use or not use Commercial Off-the-shelf Software (COTS).

A. Operating Systems

The operating system software is the primary software program that manages the basic functions of the computer and its associated hardware, including peripherals. The operating system provides a basic user interface, is responsible for managing applications programs and tasks, controlling memory allocation and data storage devices, and providing input/output for the computer, as well as any additional peripheral devices that are present.

"Open" hardware (mass market) architecture computers vary widely in architectural and organizational characteristics such as timing, addressing, and processing. Operating systems and application software executing on these platforms should be "robust" enough to perform appropriately in this environment.

OTS driver software packages provide interface functions between the CPU, operating system, and the input/output peripheral. However, the performance and functionality of the OTS driver software may be affected by the overall system configuration and the OTS hardware. In general, OTS driver software packages can be classified into the following input/output interface types: serial, parallel, video signal, telemetry, LAN, and internal bus.

In most cases, a particular software driver derives from a particular interface protocol and contains the data signals, control signals, and timing signals for proper operation.

Since tests for most input/output interface/bus configurations require the particular bus analysis or logic analysis, scope, and knowledge of the particular interface protocol, the validation process for the OTS driver software package should be part of the system interface validation process for higher levels of concern. This includes the verification of the data values in both directions for the data signals; various mode settings for the control signals in both directions (if applicable); and the input/output interrupt and timing functions of the driver with the CPU and operating system.

B. Utilities and Drivers

The purpose of this Appendix is to provide general recommendations and background for the use of OTS utility and driver software packages in the medical device validation process.

Utility software is generally designed to work with a specific operating system. Unlike applications software, utility software is intended to supplant or enhance functions typically performed by the operating system. Examples of utility programs are memory managers, file managers, and virus checkers. Networking software can also be considered as utility software in that it allows multiple computers to access the same resources. Operating systems can also be designed to support or enable network operations without any additional utility software.

OTS operating systems are commonly considered for incorporation into medical devices as the use of general-purpose computer hardware becomes more prevalent. The use of OTS operating system software allows device manufacturers to concentrate on the application software needed to run device-specific functions. However, an OTS operating system software is intended for general-purpose computing and may not be appropriate for a given specific use in a medical device. Developers of OTS operating systems typically design their systems for general-purpose business or consumer computing environments and tasks where software failures and errors are more accepted. This acceptability of errors in the general-purpose computing environment may make the OTS operating system software inappropriate for less error-tolerant environments or applications.

The incorporation of OTS operating system software may also introduce unnecessary functions and complexity into a medical device. General-purpose functional requirements typically result in the OTS operating system software being large and unwieldy in the attempt to incorporate more functionality into the operating system. This excess functionality is typically never used for specific medical device applications and increases the likelihood that errors may be introduced into the operating system. The basic functions of an OTS operating systems used for medical device applications are typically the graphical user interface environment and the hardware interface functions. There are a number of operating systems used for timing- or resource-critical applications that provide the basic functionality needed to support user and hardware interfaces, but do not have many of the disadvantages of general-purpose business or consumer operating systems.

OTS utility software packages can perform the following functions: math functions (fast Fourier transform, sin, cos); display functions (graphic); management functions (copy, delete, store various computer data/files); and the data manipulation function (transfer from one Boolean type or both). The validation for these types of the software should be appropriate to the Level of Concern.

C. Local Area Networks (LANs)

The purpose of this Appendix is to provide general recommendations and background for the network aspects of OTS Software use. Medical devices, particularly multi-parameter patient monitors and imaging systems, are increasingly networked for clinical work groups, centralized monitoring, and storage of patient medical data and records. LANs and other networks support more and more communication and sharing of images, measurement data, audio, video, graphics, text, etc. This heterogeneous media environment comes at a cost of more processing power, higher bandwidth or network speed, sophisticated object-relational databases, and security and access considerations.

The evaluation of networked medical devices begins with a definition of the technical requirements of the network application and the understanding of those requirements.

(1) Requirements Analysis

1. Speed – The response time required for safe and effective operation determines the LAN data rate (bandwidth) for the medical device system. The CPU processing power and clock speed required at device monitors, workstations, and client machines should be appropriate so that bottlenecks do not occur.

2. LAN Architecture – The size of the LAN (the number of user nodes) and the topology of the LAN should be specified.
    - Discuss to what extent the LAN needs to be fault tolerant, e.g., when a workstation fails?
    - Discuss to what extent the LAN needs to be scaleable, i.e., can new user nodes be added without degrading system performance?
    - Discuss to what extent the main device software needs to be computationally self-sufficient or distributed.
3. Network Operating System (NOS) – Whether OTS or proprietary, this selection should consider the trade-off between robustness and flexibility.
4. Data Integrity – One of the most important issues for any medical device operating in a network is data integrity. The manufacturer should ensure that the network system software and hardware incorporate error checking, handling, and correction measures commensurate with the Level of Concern of the device.
    - Transmission of data packets and files should include error detection and correction. Error detection methods include parity, checksum, and cyclic redundancy check (CRC).
    - Transaction rollback after non-committed changes or network failure, supports data integrity in medical device LANs.
    - Critical data and files may be stored in duplicate at separate locations.
5. Network Management and Security – User authorization and authentication should precede accesses to sensitive patient information.

The above five items are not independent. Decisions made in one item area may affect the performance of the LAN in another area.

(2) Implementation

The speed required by the medical device system dictates the hardware selection, the network interface cards and transmissions protocols. For example, if the conventional Ethernet protocol (maximum transmission speed of 10 Mbps) is too slow for the intended application, then a different transmission protocol will be needed.

Simplicity of the LAN architecture versus fault tolerance is a trade-off that may arise in the implementation of the networked medical device systems. The LAN could be implemented as a linear bus network (perhaps the simplest scheme), but if any connecting link on the bus fails, the whole network can fail. A star topology with redundant centralized hub is an example of a more complex but more robust network structure.

Segmentation of high bandwidth applications may be employed to improve LAN performance. Limiting the data traffic to data intensive clusters reduces traffic throughout the overall LAN.

D. Device Master Files

Much of the information regarding development and validation of OTS Software may not be readily available to the medical device manufacturer who wishes to use the OTS Software as a device component. Commercial OTS Software vendors who wish to make their OTS Software available for use in medical devices, but do not want to share the confidential and/or proprietary details of their software development and validation with customers (medical device manufacturers), may direct the information in a device master file to the FDA. Additional information on Device Master Files can be found on the FDA website: https://www.fda.gov/medical-devices/premarket-approval-pma/master-files.

E. Maintenance and Obsolescence

This Appendix addresses relevant maintainability issues with regard to OTS Software in medical devices.

Maintenance activities are generally considered to begin subsequent to the establishment and distribution of a medical device product baseline. The distinction between maintenance and product development is an important one. Product development design activities generally lead to a system structure of highly integrated components and logic. Maintenance activities introduce changes into this structure that may lead to a loss in the integrity of the structure. Structure integrity may be affected through changes due to new design requirements, corrections, or environmental adaptations. These types of changes may impact the integrity of the structure organization, architecture, logic, integration, or any combination of these characteristics. Maintenance of products with OTS Software components may be particularly problematic for reasons discussed in the main body of this document, i.e., the sponsor does not have control of the OTS Software component life cycle process.

In particular, this section identifies general safety and effectiveness, design, verification / validation, change, installation, and decommissioning concerns. These concerns may be applied to all regulated medical device software and stand-alone medical software devices. The appropriate evaluation will depend on the Level of Concern.

Assumptions for this Section include:

- Manufacturer Good Software Development Practices (GSDP) and Good Corrective Action Practices (GCAP) are in place.
- A product baseline exists.
- A new product baseline based on a prior product baseline is under CDRH review.

Each concern below corresponds to a product development life cycle phase. The concerns identify fundamental maintenance concerns relevant to medical devices that include software. Guidance in the main body of this document provides the procedural foundation for concerns in this Section.

(1) Safety

Introduction of new or modified OTS components to a product baseline may impact the safety of the product. Therefore a safety impact assessment of the medical device should be performed and associated hazards documented in a Failure Modes and Effects Analysis (FMEA) table. Each hazard's consequence should be provided and expressed qualitatively; e.g. major, moderate, or minor. Traceability between these identified hazards, their design requirements, and test reports should be provided.

Analysis should include the review of release bulletins (known error reports), user manuals, specifications, patches, and literature and internet searches for other user's experience with this OTS Software.

The submission should answer the following questions:

- Has a FMEA with traceability to requirements and test reports been provided?
- Are safety functions isolated from new OTS component(s)?
- Does the new OTS component affect system safety integrity?
- What new human factors conditions are introduced with new OTS components?

(2) Design

Introduction of new or modified OTS Software components to a product baseline may impact the original design of the product. This impact may result from necessary changes to the product structure organization, architecture, logic, integration, or a combination of these characteristics.

Problems attributable to structural changes include:

- New system resource requirements, such as shared and/or fixed memory;
- New timing considerations;
- New memory organization (e.g., 16 bit to 32 bit to 64 bit words), partitioning;
- New human factor issues;
- New data integrity issues; and
- New software required to create the final code (build tools).

Consequently the submission should answer the following questions:

- How will the new OTS Software component(s) change the performance characteristics?
- How will the new OTS Software component(s) change the operational environment?
- Is data integrity preserved?

(3) Verification and Validation

As in the establishment of a product baseline, verification and validation (V&V) activities should occur when maintenance changes are made to a product baseline. Analysis of these changes directs necessary V&V activities. New OTS Software components in a product baseline introduce unknown logic paths and complexities into the product. "Black-box" testing of OTS Software components may allow some validation claims to be made. However, the unknown logic paths and complexities of OTS Software components make it important to know that design structure or logic elsewhere in the system is not impacted. This means a full system regression test should be performed. Results of these validation activities should be documented.

The submission should answer the following questions:

- Do test reports provide objective evidence that identified OTS Software component hazards have been addressed?
- Do test reports provide objective evidence that all identified system hazards have been addressed?
- Has a system regression test been performed?

(4) Installation

Changes in a product baseline structure resulting from the integration of new OTS Software components may impact installation requirements. This impact can range from minor documentation changes to field upgrades. The reviewer should ascertain the impact of OTS Software component changes on fielded products.

The submission should answer the following question: What is the impact of new OTS Software components on fielded medical device products?

For example: Do new OTS Software components correctly operate within the specifications of medical devices currently fielded?

(5) Obsolescence

Rapid technology changes, economics, and market demand are shrinking product life spans. A direct consequence of these phenomena is that an OTS Software component today may not exist two years from now. Short life spans are a particular characteristic of software because it is relatively easy to change. Obsolescence of OTS Software components can have significant impact on regulated products because the device manufacturer may lose the ability to properly support fielded products. The sponsor needs to support fielded medical device products with OTS Software components.

The submission should answer the following questions:

- Will the old OTS Software component still be available for fielded medical devices?
- Is there a retirement plan for OTS Software components to be replaced/eliminated?
- Do new OTS Software component(s) replace fielded components?

(6) Change Control

The submission must identify the product to be considered. Therefore, the product configuration provided should specify:

- Hardware platform (e.g. microprocessor, minimum memory required, addressable word size);
- Software platform (e.g. operating system, communications, databases, necessary utilities, etc.);
- OTS component(s) other than (B) above (see basic requirements in the main body of this document); and
- Internally developed application(s).

CSV

Chapter 27
Data Integrity and Compliance with Drug CGMP Questions and Answers
Guidance for Industry

December 2018
U.S. Department of Health and Human Services
Food and Drug Administration
Center for Drug Evaluation and Research (CDER)
Center for Biologics Evaluation and Research (CBER)
Center for Veterinary Medicine (CVM)

I. Introduction

The purpose of this guidance is to clarify the role of data integrity in current good manufacturing practice (CGMP) for drugs, as required in 21 CFR parts 210, 211, and 212. Unless otherwise noted, the term *CGMP* in this guidance refers to CGMPs for drugs (including biologics). FDA's authority for CGMP comes from section 501(a)(2)(B) of the Federal Food, Drug, and Cosmetic Act (FD&C Act). Part 210 covers Current Good Manufacturing Practice in Manufacturing, Processing, Packing, or Holding of Drugs; General; part 211 covers Current Good Manufacturing Practice for Finished Pharmaceuticals; and part 212 covers Current Good Manufacturing Practice for Positron Emission Tomography (PET) Drugs. All citations to parts 211 and 212 in this document pertain to finished pharmaceuticals and PET drugs, but these requirements are also consistent with Agency guidance on CGMP for active pharmaceutical ingredients with respect to data integrity.[1] This guidance provides the Agency's current thinking on the creation and handling of data in accordance with CGMP requirements.

FDA expects that all data be reliable and accurate (see the "Background" section). CGMP regulations and guidance allow for flexible and risk-based strategies to prevent and detect data integrity issues. Firms should implement meaningful and effective strategies to manage their data integrity risks based on their process understanding and knowledge management of technologies and business models.[2]

Meaningful and effective strategies should consider the design, operation, and monitoring of systems and controls based on risk to patient, process, and product. Management's involvement in and influence on these strategies is essential in preventing and correcting conditions that can lead to data integrity problems. It is the role of management with executive responsibility to create a quality culture where employees understand that data integrity is an organizational core

---

1 See the International Council for Harmonisation (ICH) guidance for industry *Q7 Good Manufacturing Practice Guide for Active Pharmaceutical Ingredients*. We update guidances periodically. To make sure you have the most recent version of a guidance, check the FDA Drugs guidance web page at https://www.fda.gov/Drugs/Guidance-ComplianceRegulatoryInformation/Guidances/default.htm.

2 See ICH guidance for industry Q9 Quality Risk Management.

value and employees are encouraged to identify and promptly report data integrity issues. In the absence of management support of a quality culture, quality systems can break down and lead to CGMP noncompliance.

In general, FDA's guidance documents do not establish legally enforceable responsibilities. Instead, guidances describe the Agency's current thinking on a topic and should be viewed only as recommendations, unless specific regulatory or statutory requirements are cited. The use of the word should in Agency guidances means that something is suggested or recommended, but not required.

II. Background

In recent years, FDA has increasingly observed CGMP violations involving data integrity during CGMP inspections. This is troubling because ensuring data integrity is an important component of industry's responsibility to ensure the safety, efficacy, and quality of drugs, and of FDA's ability to protect the public health. These data integrity-related CGMP violations have led to numerous regulatory actions, including warning letters, import alerts, and consent decrees. The underlying premise in §§ 210.1 and 212.2 is that CGMP sets forth minimum requirements to assure that drugs meet the standards of the FD&C Act regarding safety, identity, strength, quality, and purity.[3] Requirements with respect to data integrity in parts 211 and 212 include, among other things:

- § 211.68 (requiring that "backup data are exact and complete" and "secure from alteration, inadvertent erasures, or loss" and that "output from the computer ... be checked for accuracy").
- § 212.110(b) (requiring that data be "stored to prevent deterioration or loss").
- §§ 211.100 and 211.160 (requiring that certain activities be "documented at the time of performance" and that laboratory controls be "scientifically sound").
- § 211.180 (requiring that records be retained as "original records," or "true copies," or other "accurate reproductions of the original records").
- §§ 211.188, 211.194, and 212.60(g) (requiring "complete information," "complete data derived from all tests," "complete record of all data," and "complete records of all tests performed").
- §§ 211.22, 211.192, and 211.194(a) (requiring that production and control records be "reviewed" and that laboratory records be "reviewed for accuracy, completeness, and compliance with established standards").
- §§ 211.182, 211.186(a), 211.188(b)(11), and 211.194(a)(8) (requiring that records be "checked," "verified," or "reviewed").

CH 27

3 According to section 501(a)(2)(B) of the FD&C Act, a drug shall be deemed adulterated if "the methods used in, or the facilities or controls used for, its manufacture, processing, packing, or holding do not conform to or are not operated or administered in conformity with current good manufacturing practice to assure that such drug meets the requirement of the act as to safety and has the identity and strength, and meets the quality and purity characteristics, which it purports or is represented to possess."

When considering how to meet many of these regulatory requirements, it may be useful to ask the following questions:

- Are controls in place to ensure that data is complete?
- Are activities documented at the time of performance?
- Are activities attributable to a specific individual?
- Can only authorized individuals make changes to records?
- Is there a record of changes to data?
- Are records reviewed for accuracy, completeness, and compliance with established standards?
- Are data maintained securely from data creation through disposition after the record's retention period?

This guidance helps answer these questions and enables an understanding of key concepts behind the regulatory requirements.

While not in the scope of this guidance, data integrity-related CGMP violations can also impact or be directly linked to application filing, review, and regulatory actions.

Electronic signature and record-keeping requirements are laid out in 21 CFR part 11 and apply to certain records subject to records requirements set forth in Agency regulations, including parts 210, 211, and 212. For more information, see guidance for industry *Part 11, Electronic Records; Electronic Signatures—Scope and Application*, which outlines FDA's current thinking regarding the scope and application of part 11 pending FDA's reexamination of part 11 as it applies to all FDA-regulated products.

III. Questions and Answers

1. Please clarify the following terms as they relate to CGMP records:

a. What is "data integrity"?

For the purposes of this guidance, data integrity refers to the completeness, consistency, and accuracy of data. Complete, consistent, and accurate data should be attributable, legible, contemporaneously recorded, original or a true copy, and accurate (ALCOA).[4]

Data integrity is critical throughout the CGMP data life cycle, including in the creation, modification, processing, maintenance, archival, retrieval, transmission, and disposition of

4 These characteristics are important to ensuring data integrity and are addressed throughout the CGMP regulations for drugs. For *attributable*, see §§ 211.101(d), 211.122, 211.186, 211.188(b)(11), and 212.50(c)(10); for *legible*, see §§ 211.180(e) and 212.110(b); for *contemporaneously recorded* (at the time of performance), see §§ 211.100(b) and 211.160(a); for *original or a true copy*, see §§ 211.180 and 211.194(a); and for *accurate*, see §§ 211.22(a), 211.68, 211.188, and 212.60(g).

data after the record's retention period ends.[5] System design and controls should enable easy detection of errors, omissions, and aberrant results throughout the data's life cycle.

b. What is "metadata"?

Metadata is the contextual information required to understand data. A data value is by itself meaningless without additional information about the data. Metadata is often described as data about data. Metadata is structured information that describes, explains, or otherwise makes it easier to retrieve, use, or manage data. For example, the number "23" is meaningless without metadata, such as an indication of the unit "mg." Among other things, metadata for a particular piece of data could include a date/time stamp documenting when the data were acquired, a user ID of the person who conducted the test or analysis that generated the data, the instrument ID used to acquire the data, material status data, the material identification number, and audit trails.

Data should be maintained throughout the record's retention period with all associated metadata required to reconstruct the CGMP activity (e.g., §§ 211.188 and 211.194). The relationships between data and their metadata should be preserved in a secure and traceable manner.

c. What is an "audit trail"?

For purposes of this guidance, audit trail means a secure, computer-generated, time-stamped electronic record that allows for reconstruction of the course of events relating to the creation, modification, or deletion of an electronic record. For example, the audit trail for a high performance liquid chromatography (HPLC) run should include the user name, date/time of the run, the integration parameters used, and details of a reprocessing, if any. Documentation should include change justification for the reprocessing.

Audit trails include those that track creation, modification, or deletion of data (such as processing parameters and results) and those that track actions at the record or system level (such as attempts to access the system or rename or delete a file).

CGMP-compliant record-keeping practices prevent data from being lost or obscured and ensure that activities are documented at the time of performance (see §§ 211.68, 211.100, 211.160(a), 211.188, and 211.194). Electronic record-keeping systems, which include audit trails, can support these CGMP requirements.

d. How does FDA use the terms "static" and "dynamic" as they relate to record formats?

For the purposes of this guidance, static is used to indicate a fixed-data record such as a paper record or an electronic image, and dynamic means that the record format allows interaction between the user and the record content. For example, a dynamic chromatographic record may allow the user to change the baseline and reprocess chromatographic data so that the resulting peaks may appear smaller or larger. It also may

5 For examples of record retention periods, see §§ 211.180 and 212.110(c).

allow the user to modify formulas or entries in a spreadsheet used to compute test results or other information such as calculated yield.

e. How does FDA use the term "backup" in § 211.68(b)?

FDA uses the term backup in § 211.68(b) to refer to a true copy of the original record that is maintained securely throughout the record retention period (e.g., § 211.180). Backup data must be exact, complete, and secure from alteration, inadvertent erasures, or loss (§ 211.68(b)). The backup file should contain the data (which includes associated metadata) and should be in the original format or in a format compatible with the original format.

FDA's use of the term backup is consistent with the term archive as used in guidance for industry and FDA staff General Principles of Software Validation.

Temporary backup copies (e.g., in case of a computer crash or other interruption) would not satisfy the requirement in § 211.68(b) to maintain a backup file of data.

f. What are the "systems" in "computer or related systems" in § 211.68?

The American National Standards Institute (ANSI) defines systems as people, machines, and methods organized to accomplish a set of specific functions.[6] Computer or related systems can refer to computer hardware, software, peripheral devices, networks, cloud infrastructure, personnel, and associated documents (e.g., user manuals and standard operating procedures).[7]

2. When is it permissible to invalidate a CGMP result and exclude it from the determination of batch conformance?

Data created as part of a CGMP record must be evaluated by the quality unit as part of release criteria (see §§ 211.22 and 212.70) and maintained for CGMP purposes (e.g., § 211.180).[8] Electronic data generated to fulfill CGMP requirements include relevant metadata required to reconstruct the CGMP activity captured in the record. Invalidating test results to exclude them from quality unit decisions about conformance to a specification requires a valid, documented, scientifically sound justification. See, for example, §§ 211.160(b), 211.188, 211.192, and 212.71(b) and the guidance for industry Investigating Out-of-Specification (OOS) Test Results for Pharmaceutical Production. Even if test results are legitimately invalidated on the basis of a scientifically sound investigation, the full CGMP batch record provided to the quality unit would include the original (invalidated) data, along with the investigation report that justifies invalidating the result. The requirements for record retention and review do not differ depending on the data format; paper-based and electronic data record-keeping systems are subject to the same requirements.

6 American National Standard for Information Systems, *Dictionary for Information Systems*, American National Standards Institute, 1991.

7 See guidance for industry and FDA staff *General Principles of Software Validation.*

8 For purposes of this guidance, the term quality unit is synonymous with the term quality control unit. For the definition of quality control unit, see § 210.3(b)(15).

3. Does each CGMP workflow on a computer system need to be validated?

Yes, a CGMP workflow, such as creation of an electronic master production and control record (MPCR), is an intended use of a computer system to be checked through validation (see

§§ 211.63, 211.68(b), and 211.110(a)). The extent of validation studies should be commensurate with the risk posed by the automated system. When the same system is used to perform both CGMP and non-CGMP functions, the potential for non-CGMP functions to affect CGMP operations should be assessed and mitigated appropriately.[9]

If you validate the computer system but you do not validate it for its intended use, you cannot know if your workflow runs correctly.[10] For example, qualifying the Manufacturing Execution System (MES) platform, a computer system, ensures that it meets its relevant requirements and specifications; however, it does not demonstrate that a given MPCR generated by the MES contains the correct calculations. In this example, validating the workflow ensures that the intended steps, requirements, and calculations in the MPCR are accurate and perform properly. This is similar to reviewing a paper MPCR and ensuring all supporting procedures are in place before the MPCR is implemented in production (see §§ 211.100, 211.186, and 212.50(b) and the guidance for industry PET Drugs—Current Good Manufacturing Practice (CGMP)).

FDA recommends you implement appropriate controls to manage risks associated with each element of the system. Controls that are appropriately designed to validate a system for its intended use address software, hardware, personnel, and documentation.

4. How should access to CGMP computer systems be restricted?

You must exercise appropriate controls to assure that changes to computerized MPCRs or other CGMP records or input of laboratory data into computerized records can be made only by authorized personnel (§ 211.68(b)). Other examples of records for which control should be restricted to authorized personnel include automated visual inspection records, electronic materials management system records, and automated dispensing system weighing records. FDA recommends that you restrict the ability to alter specifications, process parameters, data, or manufacturing or testing methods by technical means where possible (e.g., by limiting permissions to change settings or data).

The system administrator role, including any rights to alter files and settings, should be assigned to personnel independent from those responsible for the record content. To assist in controlling access, it is important that manufacturers establish and implement a method for documenting authorized personnel's access privileges for each CGMP computer system in use (e.g., by maintaining a list of authorized individuals) (see § 211.68(b)).

9 See note 8.

10 In computer science, validation refers to ensuring that software meets its requirements. However, this may not meet the definition of process validation as found in guidance for industry Process Validation: General Principles and Practices: "The collection and evaluation of data ... which establishes scientific evidence that a process is capable of consistently delivering quality products." See also ICH guidance for industry Q7 Good Manufacturing Practice Guide for Active Pharmaceutical Ingredients, which defines validation as providing assurance that a specific process, method, or system will consistently produce a result meeting predetermined acceptance criteria. For purposes of this guidance, validation is being used in a manner consistent with the above guidance documents.

5. Why is FDA concerned with the use of shared login accounts for computer systems?

When login credentials are shared, a unique individual cannot be identified through the login and the system would not conform to the CGMP requirements in parts 211 and 212. FDA requires that system controls, including documentation controls, be designed in accordance with CGMP to assure product quality (e.g., §§ 211.100 and 212.50). For example, you must implement documentation controls that ensure that the actions as described in question 4 are attributable to a specific individual (see §§ 211.68(b), 211.188(b)(11), 211.194(a)(7) and (8), and 212.50(c)(10)).

Shared, read-only user accounts that do not allow the user to modify data or settings are acceptable for viewing data, but they do not conform with the part 211 and 212 requirements for actions, such as second person review, to be attributable to a specific individual.

6. How should blank forms be controlled?

There must be document controls in place to assure product quality (see §§ 211.100, 211.160(a), 211.186, 212.20(d), and 212.60(g)). For example, bound paginated notebooks, stamped for official use by a document control group, provide good document control because they allow easy detection of unofficial notebooks as well as any gaps in notebook pages. If used, blank forms (e.g., electronic worksheets, laboratory notebooks, and MPCRs) should be controlled by the quality unit or by another document control method. As appropriate, numbered sets of blank forms may be issued and should be reconciled upon completion of all issued forms. Incomplete or erroneous forms should be kept as part of the permanent record along with written justification for their replacement (see, e.g., §§ 211.192, 211.194, 212.50(a), and 212.70(f)(1)(vi)). All data required to recreate a CGMP activity should be maintained as part of the complete record.

7. Who should review audit trails?

Audit trail review is similar to assessing cross-outs on paper when reviewing data. Personnel responsible for record review under CGMP should review the audit trails that capture changes to data associated with the record as they review the rest of the record (e.g., §§ 211.22(a), 211.101(c) and (d), 211.103, 211.182, 211.186(a), 211.192, 211.194(a)(8), and 212.20(d)). For example, all production and control records, which includes audit trails, must be reviewed and approved by the quality unit (§ 211.192). The regulations provide flexibility to have some activities reviewed by a person directly supervising or checking information (e.g., § 211.188). FDA recommends a quality system approach to implementing oversight and review of CGMP records.[11]

8. How often should audit trails be reviewed?

If the review frequency for the data is specified in CGMP regulations, adhere to that frequency for the audit trail review. For example, § 211.188(b) requires review after each significant step in manufacture, processing, packing, or holding, and § 211.22 requires data review before batch release. In these cases, you would apply the same review frequency for the audit trail.

11 See guidance for industry Quality Systems Approach to Pharmaceutical CGMP Regulations. See also guidance for industry Contract Manufacturing Arrangements for Drugs: Quality Agreements for information about auditing as it relates to contract facilities.

If the review frequency for the data is not specified in CGMP regulations, you should determine the review frequency for the audit trail using knowledge of your processes and risk assessment tools. The risk assessment should include evaluation of data criticality, control mechanisms, and impact on product quality.[12]

Your approach to audit trail review and the frequency with which you conduct it should ensure that CGMP requirements are met, appropriate controls are implemented, and the reliability of the review is proven.

See the audit trail definition in 1.c. above for further information on audit trails.

9. Can electronic copies be used as accurate reproductions of paper or electronic records?

Yes. Electronic copies can be used as true copies of paper or electronic records, provided the copies preserve the content and meaning of the original record, which includes all metadata required to reconstruct the CGMP activity and the static or dynamic nature of the original records.

True copies of dynamic electronic records may be made and maintained in the format of the original records or in a format that allows for the content and meaning of the original records to be preserved if a suitable reader and copying equipment (e.g., software and hardware, including media readers) are readily available (§§ 211.180(d) and 212.110).

10. Is it acceptable to retain paper printouts or static records instead of original electronic records from stand-alone computerized laboratory instruments, such as an FT-IR instrument?

A paper printout or static record may satisfy retention requirements if it is the original record or a true copy of the original record (see §§ 211.68(b), 211.188, 211.194, and 212.60). During data acquisition, for example, pH meters and balances may create a paper printout or static record as the original record. In this case, the paper printout or static record, or a true copy, must be retained (§ 211.180).

However, electronic records from certain types of laboratory instruments—whether stand-alone or networked—are dynamic, and a printout or a static record does not preserve the dynamic record format that is part of the complete original record. For example, the spectral file created by FT-IR (Fourier transform infrared spectroscopy) is dynamic and can be reprocessed.

However, a static record or printout is fixed and would not satisfy CGMP requirements to retain original records or true copies (§ 211.180(d)). Also, if the full spectrum is not displayed in the printout, contaminants may be excluded.

You must ensure that original laboratory records, including paper and electronic records, are subject to second-person review (§ 211.194(a)(8)) to make certain that all test results and

12 Risks to data include, but are not limited to, the potential to be deleted, amended, or excluded without authorization or without detection. Examples of audit trails that may be appropriate to review on a risk-based frequency include audit trails that capture instrument operational status, instrument communication logs, and alert records.

associated information are appropriately reported. Similarly, in microbiology, a contemporaneous written record is maintained of the colony counts of a petri dish, and the record is then subject to second-person review.

Document control requirements in § 211.180 pertain only to CGMP records.

For more information on static and dynamic records, see 1.d. in this guidance. For PET drugs, see the guidance for industry *PET Drugs—Current Good Manufacturing Practice (CGMP)* for discussion of equipment and laboratory controls, including regulatory requirements for records.

11. Can electronic signatures be used instead of handwritten signatures for master production and control records?

Yes, electronic signatures with the appropriate controls can be used instead of handwritten signatures or initials in any CGMP required record. Although § 211.186(a) specifies a "full signature, handwritten," an electronic signature with the appropriate controls to securely link the signature with the associated record fulfills this requirement (21 CFR 11.2(a)). See part 11, which establishes criteria for when electronic signatures are considered the legally binding equivalent of handwritten signatures. Firms using electronic signatures should document the controls used to ensure that they are able to identify the specific person who signed the records electronically.

There is no requirement for a handwritten signature for the MPCR in the PET CGMP regulations (21 CFR part 212).

12. When does electronic data become a CGMP record?

When generated to satisfy a CGMP requirement, all data become a CGMP record.[13] You must document, or save, the data at the time of performance to create a record in compliance with CGMP requirements, including, but not limited to, §§ 211.100(b) and 211.160(a).

FDA expects processes to be designed so that data required to be created and maintained cannot be modified without a record of the modification. For example, chromatographic data should be saved to durable media upon completion of each step or injection (e.g., peak integration or processing steps; finished, incomplete, or aborted injections) instead of at the end of an injection set, and changes to the chromatographic data or injection sequence should be documented in an audit trail. Aborted or incomplete injections should be captured in audit trails and should be investigated and justified.

It is not acceptable to record data on pieces of paper that will be discarded after the data are transcribed to a permanent laboratory notebook (see §§ 211.100(b), 211.160(a), and 211.180(d)). Similarly, it is not acceptable to store electronic records in a manner that allows for manipulation without creating a permanent record.

13 Under section 704(a) of the FD&C Act, FDA inspections of manufacturing facilities "shall extend to all things therein (including records, files, papers, processes, controls, and facilities) bearing on whether prescription drugs [and] nonprescription drugs intended for human use ... are adulterated or misbranded ... or otherwise bearing on violation of this chapter." Accordingly, FDA routinely requests and reviews records not intended to satisfy a CGMP requirement but which nonetheless contain CGMP information (e.g., shipping or other records that may be used to reconstruct an activity).

You may employ a combination of technical and procedural controls to meet CGMP documentation practices for electronic systems. For example, a computer system, such as a Laboratory Information Management System (LIMS) or an Electronic Batch Record (EBR) system, can be designed to automatically save after each entry. This would be similar to indelibly recording each entry contemporaneously on a paper batch record to satisfy CGMP requirements. The computer system described above could be combined with a procedure requiring data be keyed in or otherwise entered immediately when generated.

For PET drugs, see the "Laboratory Controls" section of the guidance for industry *PET Drugs—Current Good Manufacturing Practice (CGMP).*

13. Why has FDA cited use of actual samples during "system suitability" or test, prep, or equilibration runs in warning letters?

FDA prohibits sampling and testing with the goal of achieving a specific result or to overcome an unacceptable result (e.g., testing different samples until the desired passing result is obtained). This practice, also referred to as testing into compliance, is not consistent with CGMP (see the guidance for industry *Investigating Out-of-Specification (OOS) Test Results for Pharmaceutical Production*). In some situations, use of actual samples to perform system suitability testing has been used as a means of testing into compliance. FDA considers it a violative practice to use an actual sample in *test, prep*, or *equilibration* runs as a means of disguising testing into compliance.

According to the United States Pharmacopeia (USP), system suitability tests must include replicate injections of a standard preparation or other standard solutions to determine if requirements for precision are satisfied (see USP General Chapter <621> *Chromatography*). System suitability tests should be performed according to the firm's established written procedures—which should include the identity of the preparation to be injected and the rationale for its selection—and the approved application or applicable compendial monograph (§§ 211.160 and 212.60).

If an actual sample is to be used for system suitability testing, it should be a properly characterized secondary standard, written procedures should be established and followed, and the sample should be from a different batch than the sample(s) being tested (§§ 211.160, 211.165, and 212.60). CGMP original records must be complete (e.g., §§ 211.68(b), 211.188, 211.194) and subjected to adequate review (§§ 211.68(b), 211.186(a), 211.192, and 211.194(a)(8)).

Transparency is necessary. All data—including obvious errors and failing, passing, and suspect data—must be in the CGMP records that are retained and subject to review and oversight. An investigation with documented, scientifically sound justification is necessary for data to be invalidated and not used in determining conformance to specification for a batch (see §§ 211.160, 211.165, 211.188, and 211.192).

For more information, see the ICH guidance for industry *Q2(R1) Validation of Analytical Procedures: Text and Methodology* and *VICH guidances for industry GL1 Validation of Analytical Procedures: Definition and Terminology and GL2 Validation of Analytical Procedures: Methodology.*[14]

14 VICH=Veterinary International Conference on Harmonisation.

14. Is it acceptable to only save the final results from reprocessed laboratory chromatography?

No. Analytical methods should be accurate and precise.[15] For most lab analyses, reprocessing data should not be regularly needed. If chromatography is reprocessed, written procedures must be established and followed and each result retained for review (see §§ 211.160, 211.165(c), 211.194(a)(4), and 212.60(a)). FDA requires complete data in laboratory records, which includes but is not limited to notebooks, worksheets, graphs, charts, spectra, and other types of data from laboratory instruments (§§ 211.194(a) and 212.60(g)(3)).

15. Can an internal tip or information regarding a quality issue, such as potential data falsification, be handled informally outside of the documented CGMP quality system?

No. Regardless of intent or how or from whom the information was received, suspected or known falsification or alteration of records required under parts 210, 211, and 212 must be fully investigated under the CGMP quality system to determine the effect of the event on patient safety, product quality, and data reliability; to determine the root cause; and to ensure the necessary corrective actions are taken (see §§ 211.22(a), 211.125(c), 211.192, 211.198, 211.204, and 212.100).

FDA invites individuals to report suspected data integrity issues that may affect the safety, identity, strength, quality, or purity of drug products at DrugInfo@fda.hhs.gov. "CGMP data integrity" should be included in the subject line of the email. This reporting method is not intended to supersede other FDA reports (e.g., field alert reports or biological product deviation reports that help identify drug products that pose potential safety threats).

16. Should personnel be trained in preventing and detecting data integrity issues as part of a routine CGMP training program?

Yes. Training personnel to prevent and detect data integrity issues is consistent with the personnel requirements under §§ 211.25 and 212.10, which state that personnel must have the education, training, and experience, or any combination thereof, to perform their assigned duties.

17. Is FDA allowed to look at electronic records?

Yes. All records required under CGMP are subject to FDA inspection. This applies to records generated and maintained on computerized systems, including electronic communications that support CGMP activities. For example, an email to authorize batch release is a CGMP record that FDA may review.

You must allow authorized inspection, review, and copying of records, which includes copying of electronic data (§§ 211.180(c) and 212.110(a) and (b)). See also the guidance for industry *Circumstances that Constitute Delaying, Denying, Limiting, or Refusing a Drug Inspection* and section 704 of the FD&C Act. Procedures governing the review of electronic records are described in chapter 5 of the *Investigations Operations Manual (IOM)* at https://www.fda.gov/iceci/inspections/iom/default.htm.

15 See ICH guidance for industry Q2(R1) Validation of Analytical Procedures: Text and Methodology.

18. How does FDA recommend data integrity problems be addressed?

FDA encourages you to demonstrate that you have effectively remediated your problems by investigating to determine the problem's scope and root causes, conducting a scientifically sound risk assessment of its potential effects (including impact on data used to support submissions to FDA), and implementing a management strategy, including a global corrective action plan that addresses the root causes. This may include retaining a third-party auditor and removing individuals responsible for data integrity lapses from positions where they can influence CGMP-related or drug application data at your firm. It also may include improvements in quality oversight, enhanced computer systems, and creation of mechanisms to prevent recurrences and address data integrity breaches (e.g., anonymous reporting system, data governance officials and guidelines).

These expectations mirror those developed for the Application Integrity Policy. For more detailed information, see *Points To Consider for Internal Reviews and Corrective Action Operating Plans* at http://www.fda.gov/ICECI/EnforcementActions/ApplicationIntegrityPolicy/ucm134744.htm.

CSV

Chapter 28
European Commission
Qualification and Classification of Stand Alone Software Used in Healthcare

July 2016
MEDDEV 2.1/6
European Commission
DG Internal Market, Industry, Entrepreneurship and SMEs Directorate Consumer, Environmental and Health Technologies Unit Health Technology and Cosmetics

GUIDELINES ON THE QUALIFICATION AND CLASSIFICATION OF STAND ALONE SOFTWARE USED IN HEALTHCARE WITHIN THE REGULATORY FRAMEWORK OF MEDICAL DEVICES

FOREWORD

The present guidelines are part of a set of guidelines relating to questions of application of the EU legislation on medical devices. They are legally not binding.

The guidelines have been carefully drafted through a process of consultation of the various interested parties (Competent Authorities, Commission services, industry and Notified Bodies in the medical device sector) during which intermediate drafts were circulated and comments were taken up in the document where appropriate.

Therefore this document reflects positions taken in particular by the aforementioned interested parties.

Due to the participation of the aforementioned interested parties, it is anticipated that these guidelines will be followed within the Member States and, therefore, ensure uniform application of relevant Directive provisions.

INTRODUCTION

The purpose of this document is to define the criteria for the qualification of stand alone software, when used in healthcare setting, as a medical device and the application of the classification criteria to such software.

This document only deals with stand alone software and provides some illustrative examples. Software incorporated in medical devices is outside the scope of this guideline.

The criteria specified in this document apply also to mobile applications.

Directive 2007/47/EC[1] amended the definition of the term "medical device" used in Directives 90/385/EEC[2] and 93/42/EEC[3].

Recital 6 of Directive 2007/47/EC states that "it is necessary to clarify that software in its own right, when specifically intended by the manufacturer to be used for one or more of the medical purposes set out in the definition of a medical device, is a medical device. Stand alone software for general purposes when used in a healthcare setting is not a medical device."

Stand alone software shall be qualified as an in vitro diagnostic (IVD) medical device or as an accessory to an IVD provided that it satisfies the definition of an IVD or of an accessory to an IVD as set out in Directive 98/79/EC[4].

1. Definitions and Abbreviations

Intended purpose: 'intended purpose' means the use for which the device is intended according to the data supplied by the manufacturer on the labelling, in the instructions and/or in promotional materials.[5]

Accessory: 'accessory' means an article which whilst not being a device is intended specifically by its manufacturer to be used together with a device to enable it to be used in accordance with the use of the device intended by the manufacturer of the device[6].

Placing on the market: 'placing on the market' means the first making available in return for payment or free of charge of a device other than a device intended for clinical investigation, with a view to distribution and/or use on the Community market, regardless of whether it is new or fully refurbished[7].

Putting into service: 'putting into service' means the stage at which a device has been made available to the final user as being ready for use on the Community market for the first time for its intended purpose[8].

Medical Device: 'medical device' means any instrument, apparatus, appliance, software, material or other article, whether used alone or in combination, including the software intended by its manufacturer to be used specifically for diagnostic and/or therapeutic purposes and necessary for its proper application, intended by the manufacturer to be used for human beings for the purpose of:

CH 28

- diagnosis, prevention, monitoring, treatment or alleviation of disease,

1 OJ L 247, 5.9.2007, p. 21
2 OJ L 189, 20.7.1990, p. 17
3 OJ L 169, 12.7.1993, p. 1
4 OJ L 331, 7.12.1998, p. 1
5 Article 1(2)g of Directive 93/42/EEC
6 Article 1(2)b of Directive 93/42/EEC
7 Article 1(2)h of Directive 93/42/EEC
8 Article 1(2)i of Directive 93/42/EEC

- diagnosis, monitoring, treatment, alleviation of or compensation for an injury or handicap,
- investigation, replacement or modification of the anatomy or of a physiological process,
- control of conception, and which does not achieve its principal intended action in or on the human body by pharmacological, immunological or metabolic means, but which may be assisted in its function by such means[9];

In Vitro diagnostic medical device: 'in vitro diagnostic medical device' means any medical device which is a reagent, reagent product, calibrator, control material, kit, instrument, apparatus, equipment, or system, whether used alone or in combination, intended by the manufacturer to be used in vitro for the examination of specimens, including blood and tissue donations, derived from the human body, solely or principally for the purpose of providing information:

- concerning a physiological or pathological state, or
- concerning a congenital abnormality, or
- to determine the safety and compatibility with potential recipients, or
- to monitor therapeutic measures[10].

Active medical device: any medical device operation of which depends on a source of electrical energy or any source of power other than that directly generated by the human body or gravity and which acts by converting this energy. Medical devices intended to transmit energy, substances or other elements between an active medical device and the patient without any significant change, are not considered to be active medical devices. Stand alone software is considered to be an active medical device[11].

Active implantable medical device: 'active implantable medical device' means any active medical device which is intended to be totally or partially introduced, surgically or medically, into the human body or by medical intervention into a natural orifice, and which is intended to remain after the procedure[12].

Active therapeutical device: Any active medical device, whether used alone or in combination with other medical devices, to support, modify, replace or restore biological functions or structures with a view to treatment or alleviation of an illness, injury or handicap[13].

Active device for diagnosis: Any active medical device, whether used alone or in combination with other medical devices, to supply information for detecting, diagnosing,

9 Article 1(2)a of Directive 93/42/EEC
10 Article 1(2)b of Directive 98/79/EC
11 Annex IX, section 1.4, of Directive 93/42/EEC
12 Article 1(2)c of Directive 90/385/EEC
13 Annex IX, section 1.5, of Directive 93/42/EEC

monitoring or treating physiological conditions, states of health, illnesses or congenital deformities[14].

Input data: Any data provided to software in order to obtain output data after computation of this data can be considered as an input data. Input data examples (non-exhaustive):

- Data given through the use of a human data-input device such as a keyboard, mouse, stylus, or touch screen;
- Data given through speech recognition;
- Digital document: formatted for general purpose such as Word file or pdf file or jpeg image, formatted for medical purpose such as DICOM file or ECG records or Electronic Health Record, unformatted document. Note that digital documents have to be differentiated from software able to read such documents; Data received from / transmitted by devices.

Output data: Any data produced by a software can be considered as an output data. Output data examples (non-exhaustive):

- Screen display data (such as layout with number, characters, picture, graphics etc.);
- Print data (such as layout with number, characters, picture, graphics etc.);
- Audio data;
- Digital document (formatted for a general purpose such as Word file or pdf file or jpeg image, or formatted for medical purpose such as DICOM file or ECG records or Electronic Health Record, unformatted document).
- Haptic buzzing as an alternative to audio sound

Software: For the purpose of this guideline, "software" is defined as a set of instructions that processes input data and creates output data.

Stand alone software: For the purpose of this guideline 'stand alone software' means software which is not incorporated in a medical device at the time of its placing on the market or its making available.

CH
28

Expert function software: For the purpose of this document, the 'expert function software' means software which is able to analyse existing information to generate new specific information according to the intended use of the software.

Software as a medical device: The term "Software as a Medical Device" (SaMD) is defined as software intended to be used for one or more medical purposes that perform these purposes without being part of a hardware medical device.

Definition of the IMDRF/SaMD WG/N10FINAL:2013 : "Software as a Medical Device (SaMD): Key Definitions".

14 Annex IX, section 1.6, of Directive 93/42/EEC

2. Qualification

2.1 Introduction to criteria for qualification

The purpose of this part of the guidance is to clarify the distinction between different types of medical software, namely medical software that is:

- part of MD or IVD
- accessories
- standalone Software
- not a Medical Device

Stand alone software must have a medical purpose to be qualified as medical device. It should be noted that only the intended purpose as described by the manufacturer of the product is relevant for the qualification and classification of any device and not by virtue of the way it may be called.

Stand alone software that does not meet the definition of a medical device or of an IVD medical device but is intended by the manufacturer to be an accessory to a medical device, or an IVD medical device, falls respectively under the scope of Directive 93/42/EEC or Directive 98/79/EC.

It is to be noted that to be qualified as an IVD medical device, stand alone software must first fulfil the definition of a medical device. Where a given product does not fall under the definition of medical device, or is excluded by the scope of the Directives, other Community and/or national legislation may be applicable.

2.1.1 Qualification criteria as medical device

Software can be used for a large variety of medical purposes[15]. In that respect the arguments do not differ from those used for other medical devices.

Stand alone software can directly control an apparatus (e.g. radiotherapy treatment), can provide immediate decision triggering information (e.g. blood glucose meters), or can provide support for healthcare professionals (e.g. ECG interpretation).

Not all stand alone software used within healthcare can be qualified as a medical device.

Stand alone software may run on different operating systems or in virtual environments. These operating systems or virtual environments do not impact the qualification criteria. Stand alone software might also be an accessory of a medical device.

The risk related to a malfunction of the stand alone software used within healthcare is in itself not a criterion for its qualification or not as a medical device.

It is, therefore, necessary to clarify some criteria for the qualification of stand alone software as medical devices.

The decision diagram (Figure 1) gives some guidance regarding the necessary steps to qualify stand alone software as medical device.

15 MEDDEV 2.1/1: Definitions of "medical devices", "accessory" and "manufacturer"

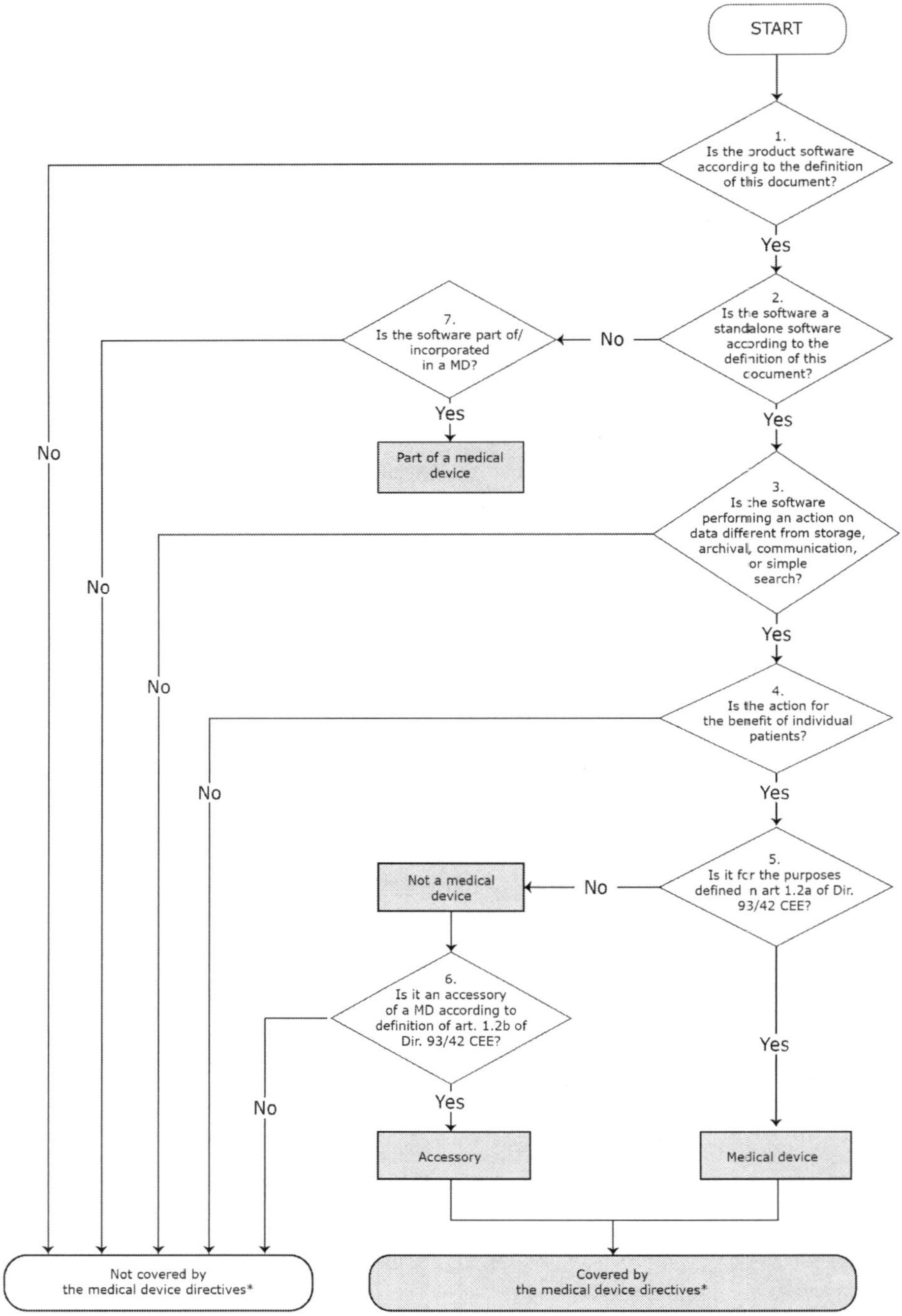

Figure 1: A decision diagram to assist qualification of software as a medical device.

Legend of the flowchart:

MD: Medical Device

*"Medical Device Directives" means the 3 following directives:

- DIRECTIVE 93/42/EEC of 14 June 1993 concerning medical devices
- DIRECTIVE 98/79/EC of 27 October 1998 on in vitro diagnostic medical devices
- DIRECTIVE 90/385/EEC of 20 June 1990 on the approximation of the laws of the Member States relating to active implantable medical devices

Decision step 1: If the product is a software according to the definition of this document, then it may be a medical device; if the product is not a software according to the definition of this document, then it is not covered by the medical device directives..

Decision step 2: if the software is incorporated into a medical device rather than stand alone software, it must be considered as part of that medical device in the regulatory process of that device. If it is stand alone software[16], proceed to decision step 3.

Decision step 3: if the software does not perform an action on data, or performs an action limited to storage, archival, communication[17], 'simple search' or lossless compression (i.e. using a compression procedure that allows the exact reconstruction of the original data) it is not a medical device.

Altering the representation of data for embellishment purposes does not make the software a medical device. In other cases, including where the software alters the representation of data for a medical purpose, it could be a medical device.

'Simple search' refers to the retrieval of records by matching record metadata against record search criteria, e.g. library functions. Simple search does not include software which provides interpretative search results, e.g. to identify medical findings in health records or on medical images.

Software which is intended to create or modify medical information might be qualified as a medical device. If such alterations are made to facilitate the perceptual and/or interpretative tasks performed by the healthcare professionals when reviewing medical information, (e.g. when searching the image for findings that support a clinical hypothesis as to the diagnosis or evolution of therapy) the software could be a medical device.

> ***Note:*** the display of images usually involves alterations to the representation because techniques are used such as contrast stretching, edge enhancement, gray scale manipulation, smoothing, sharpening, zooming and re-sizing. Alterations may include reconstruction, lossy compression, filtering, pattern recognition, modelling, interpolation, transformation, classification (e.g. scoring of tumors against specific criteria), segmentation, registration (e.g. mapping a data set to a model or atlas or to another

CH 28

16 See chapter 2 - Definitions and Abbreviations for a definition of stand alone software.

17 Communication: The flow of information from one point, known as the source, to another, the receiver; Source: IEEE 610.10-1994.

data set, e.g. registering an MRI image on a CT image), calculations, quantification, qualification (e.g. comparison of data against references), rendering, visualisation, interpretation, etc..

Decision step 4: an example of software for the benefit of individual patients is software intended to be used for the evaluation of patient data to support or influence the medical care provided to that patient. Examples of software which are not considered as being for the benefit of individual patients are those which aggregate population data, provide generic diagnostic or treatment pathways, scientific literature, medical atlases, models and templates as well as software for epidemiologic studies or registers.

Decision step 5: if the manufacturer specifically intends the software to be used for any of the purposes listed in Article 1(2)a of Directive 93/42/EEC, then the software shall be qualified as a medical device. However, if only a non-medical purpose is intended by the manufacturer, such as invoicing or staff planning, it is not a medical device.

> ***Note:*** A task such as e-mailing, web or voice messaging, data parsing, word processing, and back-up is by itself not considered as being a medical purpose, according to Directive 93/42/EEC.

Decision step 6: if the software is an accessory to a medical device, it is not a medical device, but it falls under Directive 93/42/EEC. The legal definition of 'putting into service' requires that a device is made available to the final user/operator as being ready for use on the Community market. Software made available to the user over the internet (directly or via download) or via in vitro diagnostic commercial services, which is qualified as a medical device, is subject to the medical devices directives.

2.1.2 Qualification criteria as IVD medical device

Stand alone software fulfilling the definition of medical device and intended to be used for the purpose of providing information derived from *in vitro* examination of a specimen derived from the human body falls under Directive 98/79/EC.

Provided that stand alone software is intended specifically by its manufacturer to be used together with an IVD medical device to enable that device to be used in accordance with its intended purpose, this stand alone falls under the scope of the IVD Directive and shall be treated as an IVD device in its own right.

CH 28

Example: analysis and interpretation

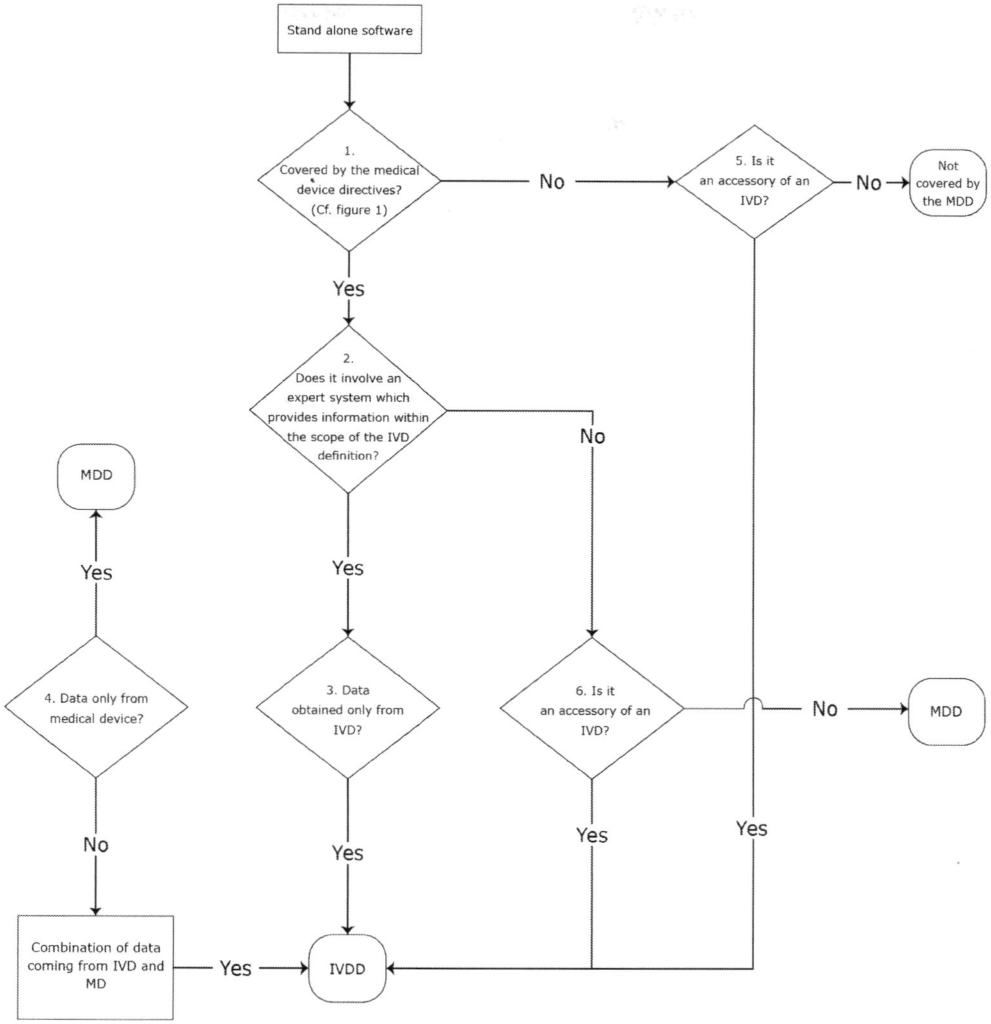

Figure 2: Decision diagram to assist qualification of stand alone software as IVD device

Decision step 1: please, start by making reference to figure 1.

Decision step 2: Stand alone software with expert function:

This stand alone software might provide information on e.g. differential diagnosis, prediction of the risks of developing a disease, prediction of the percentage of efficiency or failure (e.g. of a treatment), identifying species of bacteria.

It may qualify differently based on the fact that the existing information is obtained from either IVD medical devices, other medical devices or both.

Decision step 3: if the information provided by the software is based on data obtained from IVD medical devices only, the software is an IVD medical device or an accessory of an IVD medical device.

If data are obtained from both IVD medical devices and from medical devices are analysed together for the purpose of providing information according to the definition of an IVD medical device, this software is an IVD medical device (e.g. evaluation of the risk of Trisomy 21).

As described in Annex I B 3.1, for stand alone software that is intended for use in combination with other devices or equipment, the whole combination must be safe and must not impair the specified performances of the devices. As a concretization of these general requirements of the IVDD; the clinical evidence of this combined intended use of medical devices shall be performed for each of the medical devices from which the data is obtained.

Decision step 4: if the information provided by the software is based on data obtained from medical devices only, the software would be a medical device.

> ***Note 1:*** Stand alone software that only collects results obtained from one or several IVD devices (directly and/or manually), and transmits without modification this information to a centralised database (e.g. Laboratory Information Management System, LIMS) or to healthcare providers is not an IVD medical device.
>
> ***Note 2:*** Stand alone software (e.g. LIMS) managing the feed-back to an IVD (e.g. retesting of samples) based on collected IVD results is not an IVD medical device as per decision step 5 of figure 1.
>
> ***Note 3:*** Software intended to modify the representation of available IVD results is not considered as an IVD medical device as per decision step 5 of Figure 1, e.g. basic operations of arithmetic (e.g. mean, conversion of units) and/or plotting of results in function of time, and/or a comparison of the result to the limits of acceptance set by the user.
>
> ***Note 4:*** Stand alone software intended for archiving patient results or for transferring results from the home environment to the healthcare provider is not an IVD device.

3. Classification of Stand Alone Software

Stand alone software that meets the definition of a medical device shall be considered as an **active medical device.**[18] This means that rules 9, 10, 11 and 12 of Annex IX to Directive 93/42/EEC may apply.

18 Annex IX, section 1.4, of Directive 93/42/EEC

Clause 2.3 of the implementing rules in Annex IX states that software 'which drives a medical device or influences the use of a device, falls automatically into the same class[19], as the device it drives.

3.1 Software as active therapeutic medical devices

According to rule 9 of Annex IX to Directive 93/42/EEC, all active therapeutic devices intended to administer or exchange energy are in Class IIa unless their characteristics are such that they may administer or exchange energy to or from the human body in a potentially hazardous way, taking account of the nature, the density and site of application of the energy, in which case they are in Class IIb.

All active devices intended to control or monitor the performance of active therapeutic devices in Class IIb, or intended directly to influence the performance of such devices are in Class IIb according to implementing rule 2.3.

Example: radiotherapy planning system used to calculate the dose of ionizing radiation to be administered to the patient, insulin dosage planning stand alone software.

3.1.1 Software intended for diagnosis or therapy

According to rule 10 of Annex IX to Directive 93/42/EEC, active devices intended for diagnosis are in Class IIa:

- if they are intended to image in vivo distribution of radiopharmaceuticals.

Example: Clinical application of registration of PET datasets on CT datasets for follow-up tumour treatment.

- if they are intended to allow direct diagnosis or monitoring of vital physiological processes, unless they are specifically intended for monitoring of vital physiological parameters, where the nature of variations is such that it could result in immediate danger to the patient, for instance variations in cardiac performance, respiration, activity of CNS in which case they are in Class IIb.

Examples: - Software for the presentation of the heart rate or other physiological parameters during routine checkups (Class IIa);

- Software for the presentation of the heart rate or other physiological parameters for intensive care monitoring (Class IIb).

Active devices intended to emit ionizing radiation and intended for diagnostic and therapeutic interventional radiology including devices which control or monitor such devices, or which directly influence their performance, are in Class IIb.

Rule 11 of Annex IX to Directive 93/42/EEC states that all active devices intended to administer and/or remove medicines, body liquids or other substances to or from the body are in Class IIa, unless this is done in a manner:

19 Annex IX, section 2.3, of Directive 93/42/EEC

- that is potentially hazardous, taking account of the nature of the substances involved, of the part of the body concerned and of the mode of application in which case they are in Class IIb.

Stand alone software which drives such medical device or influences the use of such device falls automatically into the same class as the device it drives (implementing rule 2.3).

Rule 12 of Annex IX to Directive 93/42/EEC states that all other active devices are in Class I. Class I stand alone software can also come with a measuring function.

Example: orthopaedic planning software to measure interpedicular distance or sagittal diameter of the spinal canal.

3.2 IVDD AND SOFTWARE IN CONJUNCTION WITH IN-VITRO DIAGNOSTIC DEVICES

Stand alone software qualified as in vitro diagnostic medical devices should be regulated according to Directive 98/79/EC.

When intended for evaluating the risk of trisomy 21, such software are specifically mentioned in Annex II List B of Directive 98/79/EC and shall therefore follow the conformity assessment procedure described in Article 9 of this Directive.

4. MODULES

Some stand alone software may break down into a significant number of applications for the user where each of these applications is correlated with a module. Some of these modules have a medical purpose, some not.

Such software may be intended to cover many needs, *e.g.*:

- Collect and maintain administrative patient details;
- Keep on file the medical history of the patient;
- Invoicing and other accounting functions;
- Provide a link to the social security system for reimbursement;
- Provide a link to drug prescription systems (with possible link to drug dispensing outlets);
- Provide expert system assistance for medical decision making (e.g. radiotherapy dose planner).

This raises the issue as to whether the whole product can be CE marked when not all applications have a medical purpose.

Computer programmes used in healthcare mostly have applications which consist of both medical device and non-medical device modules.

The modules which are subject to the medical device Directives (Figures 1 and 2) must comply with the requirements of the medical device Directives and must carry the CE marking. The non-medical device modules are not subject to the requirements for medical devices.

It is the obligation of the manufacturer to identify the boundaries and the interfaces of the different modules.

The boundaries of the modules which are subject to the medical device Directives should be clearly identified by the manufacturer and based on the intended use.

If the modules which are subject to the medical device Directives are intended for use in combination with other modules of the whole software structure, other devices or equipment, the whole combination, including the connection system, must be safe and must not impair the specified performances of the modules which are subject to the medical device Directives[20].

Annex 1: Illustrative examples of qualification for software used in the healthcare environment

The sector of software pursuing a medical purpose is rapidly evolving. The list of examples provided below is not exhaustive.

The examples have been drafted in the light of today's state of the art, in order to give the reader a better understanding of the application of the principles set out in the guideline.

In the light of the technological progress, further examples will be regularly added into the Manual on borderline and classification in the Community regulatory framework for medical devices[21].

a) Hospital Information Systems

Hospital Information Systems mean, in this context, systems that support the process of patient management. Typically they are intended for patient admission, for scheduling patient appointments, for insurance and billing purposes.

These Hospital Information Systems are not qualified as medical devices. However they may be used with additional modules, as described hereafter.

These modules might be qualified in their own right as medical devices.

b) Decision Support Software

In general, they are computer based tools which combine medical knowledge databases and algorithms with patient specific data. They are intended to provide healthcare professionals and/or users with recommendations for diagnosis, prognosis, monitoring and treatment of individual patients.

Based on steps 3, 4, and 5 of Figure 1, they are qualified as medical devices.

- Radiotherapy treatment planning systems[22] are intended to calculate the dosage of ionizing irradiation to be applied to a specific patient. They are considered to control,

20 i.e. essential requirements 3.1 of Directive 98/79/EC and essential requirements 9.1 of Directive 93/42/EEC
21 http://ec.europa.eu/health/medical-devices/files/wg_minutes_member_lists/borderline_manual_ol_en.pdf
22 See EN 62083 « Requirements for the safety of radiotherapy treatment planning systems »

monitor or directly influence the source of ionizing radiation and are qualified as medical devices.

- Drug (e.g.: Chemotherapy) planning systems are intended to calculate the drug dosage to be administered to a specific patient and therefore are qualified as medical devices.
- Computer Aided Detection systems are intended to provide information that may suggest or exclude medical conditions and, therefore, qualified as medical devices. For example, such systems would be able to automatically read x-ray images or interpret ECGs.

c) Information Systems

Information systems that are intended only to store, archive and transfer data are not qualified as medical devices in themselves. However they may be used with additional modules. These modules might be qualified in their own right as medical devices.

c.1) Electronic Patient Record Systems

Electronic patient record systems are intended to store and transfer electronic patient records. They archive all kinds of documents and data related to a specific patient. The electronic patient records themselves are not computer programs, therefore, they should not be qualified as a medical device i.e. an electronic patient record that simply replaces a patient's paper file does not meet the definition of a medical device. The modules used with electronic patient record system modules that might be qualified in their own right as medical devices are for example:

- an image viewer with functionality for diagnosis based on digital images;
- a medication module.

c.1.1) Clinical Information Systems – CIS / Patient Data Management Systems - PDMS

A CIS/PDMS is a software based system primarily intended for e.g. intensive care units to store and transfer patient information generated in association with the patient's intensive care treatment.

Usually the system contains information such as patient identification, vital intensive care parameters and other documented clinical observations.

These CIS/PDMS are not qualified as medical devices.

Modules that are intended to provide additional information that contributes to diagnosis, therapy and follow-up (e.g. generate alarms) are qualified as medical devices.

c.1.2) Pre-hospital Electrocardiograph (ECG) System

A system for managing pre-hospital ECG is a software based system intended for ambulance services to store and transfer information from patients, which are connected to an ECG monitor, to a doctor at remote location. Usually the system contains information about patient identification, vital parameters and other documented clinical observations. These Pre-hospital Electrocardiograph (ECG) Systems are not qualified as medical devices.

Modules that provide patient's treatment information to the paramedics in the ambulance to start the patient's treatment while the patient is being transported are qualified as Medical Devices.

c.1.3) Radiological Information System (RIS)

A RIS is a software based database used in radiology departments to store and transfer radiological images and patient information. The system normally includes functions for patient identification, scheduling, examination results and imaging identification details.

These Radiological Information Systems are not qualified as medical devices.

However, if such a system includes additional modules they might qualify as medical devices according to step 3 of of Figure 1.

c.1.4) Picture Archive Communication System (PACS)

The Manual on Borderline and Classification in the Community Regulatory Framework for Medical Devices[23], already addresses the issue.

d) Communication Systems

The healthcare sector uses communication systems (e.g. email systems, mobile telecommunication systems, video communication systems, paging etc.) to transfer electronic information. Different types of messages are being sent such as prescriptions, referrals, images, patient records, etc.

Most of the communication systems handle other types of messages other than medical information. This communication system is intended for general purposes, and is used for transferring both medical and non-medical information.

Communication systems are normally based on software for general purposes, and do not fall within the definition of a medical device. Communication system modules might be used with other modules that might be qualified in their own right as medical devices.

Example: software generating alarms based on the monitoring and analysis of patient specific physiological parameters.

d.1) Telemedicine Systems

Telemedicine Systems are intended to allow monitoring and/or delivery of healthcare to patients at locations remote from where the healthcare professional is located.

23 http://ec.europa.eu/health/medical-devices/files/wg_minutes_member_lists/borderline_manual_ol_en.pdf

d.1.1) Telesurgery

Telesurgery is intended to conduct a surgical procedure from a remote location. Virtual reality technology may be used to support a remote surgeon to control a surgical robot performing the surgical procedure.

Telesurgery systems should be qualified as medical devices according to steps 3, 4, and 5 of **Figure 1.**

Remote control software used in combination with telesurgery robots is qualified as a medical device. Communication modules themselves are not medical devices.

Other modules that are intended to influence the surgery procedure are qualified as medical devices.

d.1.2) Video appointment software

Video appointment software is intended to perform remote consultations between clinics and patients. It does not fall under the Medical Devices Directives.

d.1.3) Home care monitoring, wired or mobile

The telecommunication system (mobile, wireless, wire, etc...) is not as such a medical device.

e) Web systems for monitoring of data

A web system for the monitoring of clinical data typically interacts with a medical device (*e.g.* implanted devices or homecare devices), and uses a transmitter to send the information over the internet, a landline telephone or a mobile network.

The information is collected and stored on a web server usually run by an external party who is generally the manufacturer of the system. The information can be reached by authorized health professionals or the patient through an internet connection.

- **Monitoring of performance of medical devices:**

Modules that are intended to monitor the medical performance of medical devices fall under the Medical Devices Directives.

This includes the clinical performance and failures that could affect medical performance of the device. One example of such product is a web system for monitoring of active implants such as pacemakers or Intra cardiac defibrillators (ICDs).

- **Monitoring of non medical performance of medical devices:**

Modules that are intended to monitor non medical performance of medical devices do not fall under the scope of Medical Devices Directives.

Example: software for the monitoring of medical devices in hospital systems for the purpose of maintenance and repair. Software modules on server(s) might be qualified in their own right as medical devices depending on their intended purpose.

f) *In vitro* diagnostic (IVD) software: LIS & WAM

f.1) Laboratory Information Systems (LIS) and Work Area Managers (WAM)

Laboratory Information Systems (LIS) and Work Area Managers (WAM) mean, in this context, systems that support the process from patient sample to patient result. Typically they have pre-analytical functions for ordering, sorting and distribution of test samples.

The main task is the management and validation of incoming information obtained from IVD analysers connected to the system, such as calibration, quality control, product expiry and feedback (e.g. retesting of samples needed) through interconnections with various analytical instruments (technical and clinical validation).

Finally the post analytical process takes care of communication of laboratory results, statistics and optional reporting to external databases.

The software normally supports the following functions:

- Ordering of laboratory tests, samples with labels and sorting;
- Technical and clinical validation, connection to analytic instruments;
- Laboratory results and reports on paper, fax or electronic records that can be directly returned to e.g. the ordering clinic's patient record;
- Analytical instruments can be interfaced with Hospital Information Systems (HIS), Electronic Patient Record Systems, Infectious control databases etc.

Note: Software intended to modify the representation of available IVD results is not considered an IVD medical device, e.g. basic operations of arithmetic (e.g. mean, conversion of units) and/or plotting of results in function of time, and/or a comparison of the result to the limits of acceptance set by the user.

The results are available, readable and understandable without the intervention of the software.

Laboratory Information Systems (LIS) and Work Area Managers (WAM) are not qualified as medical devices in themselves.

However they may be used with additional modules. These modules might be qualified in their own right as medical devices.

CH 28

f.2) Expert system

Where software is intended to capture and analyze together several results obtained for one patient by one or more IVD devices by means of in vitro examination of body samples (possibly combined with information from medical devices) to provide information falling within the definition of an IVD medical device, e.g. differential diagnosis, this software is considered as an IVD in itself.

Examples: - software that integrates genotype of multiple genes to predict risk of developing a disease or medical condition;

- software that uses an algorithm to characterize viral resistances to various drugs, based on a nucleotide sequence generated by genotyping assays. This software serves to generate new information (virus resistance profile) from available information on the genotype of the virus;

- software intended to be used in microbiology for the identification of clinical isolates and/or the detection antimicrobial resistances.

The information provided by the software is based on data obtained with IVD medical devices only or possibly combined with information from medical devices.

The software is an IVD medical device or an accessory of an IVD medical device.

f.3) Interpretation of raw data

In the case where software is necessary to render raw data, obtained from an IVD by means of in vitro examination of body samples, readable for the user, this software is to be considered as an accessory to an IVD when it is specifically intended to be used together with this IVD to enable it to be used in accordance with its intended purpose.

Example: software intended for the analysis and interpretation of ELISA reader optical density results, line patterns or spot patterns of a blot.

f.4) Home care monitoring, wired or mobile

Stand alone software intended for archiving patient results or for transferring results from the home environment to the healthcare provider is not an IVD device. The results are available, readable and understandable by the user without the intervention of the software.

Chapter 29
European Medicines Agency Guideline on Computerised Systems and Electronic Data in Clinical Trials Draft

March 4, 2021
EMA/226170/2021
Good Clinical Practice Inspectors Working Group (GCP IWG)
Start of public consultation: 18 June 2021
End of consultation: 17 December 2021
Effective Date: TBC
Draft

This guideline replaces 'Reflection paper on expectations for electronic source data and data transcribed to electronic data collection tools in clinical trials' (EMA/INS/GCP/454280/2010).

GLOSSARY AND ABBREVIATIONS

Generally used terms

Unless otherwise specified (e.g. "source data" or "source document") and in order to simplify the text, "data" will be used in this guideline in a broad meaning which may include documents (e.g. in electronic trial master files (eTMF)), records or any form of information.

All references to a sponsor in this guideline also apply to a contract research organisation (CRO) to the extent that a CRO has assumed the trial related duties and functions of a sponsor (ICH-GCP 5.2.4).

When a computerised system is implemented by the institution where the investigator is conducting a clinical trial, any reference to the investigator in this guideline also includes that institution, as provided for by ICH-GCP 1.35 (investigator / institution: An expression meaning "the investigator and/or institution, where required by the applicable regulatory requirements"), except for those responsibilities assigned by ICH-GCP to the investigator personally and not to the investigator / institution.

The word "trial participant" is used in this text as a synonym for the term "subject", defined in Directive 2001/20/EC as "an individual who participates in a clinical trial as a recipient of the investigational medicinal product (IMP) or a control".

For the purpose of this guideline, the term "information" reflects meaningful organisation and processing of data and documentation and "data" reflects measurement and assessment of variable parameters relevant to specific outcomes. The "results" are a composition of organised and fit-for-purpose information.

Artificial intelligence

Artificial intelligence (AI) covers a very broad set of algorithms which enable computers to mimic human intelligence. It ranges from simple if-then rules and decision trees to machine learning and deep learning.

Machine learning (ML) is a subset of AI and includes computer algorithms which are trained to classify or predict data, without actually being programmed to do so. ML is divided into supervised and unsupervised learning.

Deep learning (DL) is a subset of ML and contains algorithms which allow software to train itself by exposing multi-layered neural networks to vast amounts of data.

Audit trail (in computerised systems)

"Documentation that allows reconstruction of the course of events." (ICH-GCP 1.9) In computerised systems an audit trail is a secure, computer generated, time-stamped electronic record that allows reconstruction of the course of events relating to the access, creation, modification, and deletion of an electronic record or use of the computerised system itself.

Case report form (CRF)

"A printed, optical, or electronic document designed to record information to be reported to the sponsor on each trial subject." (ICH-GCP 1.11)

Certified copy

"A copy (irrespective of the type of media used) of the original record that has been verified (i.e., by a dated signature or by generation through a validated process) to have the same information, including data that describe the context, content, and structure, as the original." (ICH-GCP 1.63)

Clinical outcome assessment (COA)

COA employs a tool for direct reporting of outcomes by clinicians, trial site staff, trial participants and their caregivers. The term COA is proposed as an umbrella term to cover both single dimension and multi-dimension measures of symptoms, health-related quality of life (HRQL), health status, adherence to treatment, satisfaction with treatment, etc.

Data governance

The totality of arrangements to ensure that data fulfils the ALCOA++ principles (see section 4.5) throughout the entire data life cycle.

Data life cycle

All processes related to the creating, recording, processing, reviewing, analysing, reporting, transferring, storing, migrating, archiving, retrieving and deleting of data.

Dynamic file formats

Dynamic files (e.g. spreadsheets with automatic calculations) include automatic processing and/or enable an interactive relationship with the user to change content (e.g. eCRF). A certified electronic copy may be retained in different electronic file formats to the original record, but the equivalent dynamic nature (including metadata) of the original record should be retained.

Good documentation practice

Good documentation practice is used to describe a standard for creation and maintenance of documentation in order to ensure its integrity. It includes, but is not limited to, that a record is made at the time of the corresponding event, that documents are printed or written (e.g. signed) with indelible and lasting ink, that critical entries are verified by a second person, that pages (e.g. in notebooks) are numbered, that documents, where applicable, are reviewed, approved, signed and dated by appropriate personnel, and that any later alterations are made as 'GxP corrections'. The latter implies that changes include the name and the signature of person who made the change, full visibility of what was changed including both the new and old text (altered text is not obscured), the date and if relevant the time when the change was made, and whenever not completely obvious, the reason or justification why the change was made. These essential characteristics apply equally for both paper and electronic records.

There is a strong bond between good documentation practice and the ALCOA++ principles (see section 4.4) and between GxP corrections and an audit trail (see section 6.2).

Important aspects are implementation of practices such as contracts, change control including version control and traceability, review, approval and distribution processes etc. for critical documents. In general, essential documents should be approved, signed and dated by the relevant/authorised persons.

See also EU GMP Chapter 4.

Patient-reported outcome (PRO)

Any outcome reported directly by the trial participant and based on the trial participant's perception of a disease and its treatment(s) is called patient-reported outcome (PRO). The term PRO is proposed as an umbrella term to cover both single dimension and multi-dimension measurements of symptoms, HRQL, health status, adherence to treatment, satisfaction with treatment, etc. (Source: CHMP Reflection paper on the regulatory guidance for the use of HRQL measures in the evaluation of medicinal products - EMEA/CHMP/EWP/139391/2004)

Qualification

"Action of proving and documenting that equipment or ancillary systems are properly installed, work correctly, and actually lead to the expected results. Qualification is part of validation, but the individual qualification steps alone do not constitute process validation." (ICH Q7 20 Glossary) Expected results for system qualification should be traceable to a system specification, e.g. a User Requirements Specification (URS).

Source data

"All information in original records and certified copies of original records of clinical findings, observations, or other activities in a clinical trial necessary for the reconstruction and evaluation of the trial. Source data are contained in source documents (original records or certified copies)." (ICH-GCP 212 1.51)

Source documents

"Original documents, data, and records (e.g., hospital records, clinical and office charts, laboratory notes, memoranda, subjects' diaries or evaluation checklists, pharmacy dispensing records, recorded data from automated instruments, copies or transcriptions certified after verification as being accurate copies, microfiches, photographic negatives, microfilm or magnetic media, X-rays, subject files, and records kept at the pharmacy, at the laboratories and at medico-technical departments involved in the clinical trial)." (ICH-GCP 1.52)

Static file formats

Static files (e.g. PDF scan) containing information or data that are fixed/frozen and allow no interaction to change the content. Paper document digitised as pdf, e.g. scanned ethics approval letter.

System life cycle

The life cycle of a computerised system includes all phases of the system; i.e. typically 1) the concept phase where the regulated party considers to automate a process and where user requirements are collected, 2) the project phase where a contracted party is selected, a risk-assessment is made and the system is implemented and qualified, 3) the operational phase where a system is used in a regulated environment and changes are implemented in a manner which maintains data confidentiality, integrity and availability, and finally, 4) a retirement phase which includes decisions about data retention, migration or destruction and management of these processes.

Validation

"A process of establishing and documenting that the specified requirements of a computerized system can be consistently fulfilled from design until decommissioning of the system or transition to a new system. The approach to validation should be based on a risk assessment that takes into consideration the intended use of the system and the potential of the system to affect human subject protection and reliability of clinical trial results." (ICH-GCP 1.65)

ABBREVIATIONS

AI	artificial intelligence
BYOD	bring your own device
(e)COA	electronic clinical outcome assessment
(e)CRF	electronic case report form
COTS	commercial of the shelf
CRO	contract research organisation
CTMS	clinical trial management systems
DMP	data management plan
DEXA	dual-energy x-ray absorptiometry

ECG	electrocardiogram
EDC	electronic data collection
EEA	European Economic Area
EU	European Union
GCP	good clinical practice
GCP-IWG	GCP Inspectors' Working Group
GPS	global positioning system
(e)HR	electronic health records
HRQL	health-related quality of life
HTTPS	hypertext transfer protocol secure
IB	investigator brochures
ICH	International Conference on Harmonisation
IMEI	international mobile eEquipment identity
IMP	investigational medicinal product
IaaS	Infrastructure as a service
IQ/PQ	installation qualification/performance qualification
IRT	interactive response technology
IT	information technology
IVRS	interactive voice response system
MEID	mobile equipment identifier
PI	principal investigator
PaaS	Platform as a service
PC	personal computer
SaaS	software as a service
SOP	standard operating procedure
SUSAR	suspected unexpected serious adverse reaction
(e)TMF	electronic trial master file
UAT	user acceptance testing
URS	user requirements specification
UTC	universal time coordinated
VAS	visual analogue scales
VPN	virtual private network

EXECUTIVE SUMMARY

Computerised systems are being increasingly used in clinical research. The complexity of such systems has evolved rapidly during the last years from eCRF, ePROs, to various wearable devices used to continuously monitor trial participants for clinically relevant parameters and ultimately to the use of AI. The latter will be further elaborated on in a future Annex. Changes in trial types (e.g. implementation of fully or partly decentralised trials) will also mean an increased use of computerised systems. Hence there is a need to provide guidance to sponsors, CROs, investigators, and other parties involved in the design, conduct and reporting of clinical trials reflective of these changes in data types and trial types on the use of computerised systems and on the collection of electronic data, as this is important to ensure the quality and reliability of trial data, as well as the safety and wellbeing of the trial participants. This would ultimately contribute to a robust decision-making process based on such clinical data.

1. INTRODUCTION

As described above, the change in data and trial types and thereby the use of computerised systems presents new challenges. The EMA *'Reflection Paper on expectations for electronic source data and data transcribed to electronic data collection tools in clinical trials'* started to address these when it was published in 2010. However, the development of and experience with such systems has progressed. A more up to date guideline is needed.

2. SCOPE

The scope of this guideline is computerised systems, (including instruments, software and services) used in clinical trials in the creation/capture of electronic clinical data and to the control of other processes in the conduct of a clinical trial of investigational medicinal products. These include, but may not be limited to the following:

- Electronic Health Records (eHR), used by the investigator 260 for capture of all health information as per normal clinical practice.
- Tools supplied to investigators/trial participants for recording clinical data by data entry (e.g. COAs).
    - Electronic trial participant data capture devices used to collect ePRO data, e.g. mobile devices supplied to trial participants or applications for the use by the trial participant on their own device (bring your own device (BYOD)).
    - Electronic devices used by clinicians to collect data e.g. mobile devices supplied to clinicians.
- Tools supplied for automatic capture of events such as biometric measures (e.g. blood pressure, respiratory measures or electrocardiogram (ECG) monitoring).
- eCRFs e.g. desktop or mobile device-based programs or access to web-based applications, which may contain source data directly entered, transcribed data or data transferred from other sources, or any combination of these.

- Tools that automatically capture data related to transit and storage temperatures for IMP or clinical samples.
- Tools to capture, generate, handle or store data in a clinical environment where analysis, tests, scans, imaging, evaluations, etc. involving trial participants or samples from trial participants are performed in support of clinical trials (e.g. dual-energy x-ray absorptiometry (DEXA) or X-ray machines and related software).
- eTMFs, which are used to maintain the clinical trial essential documentation.
- Electronic informed consent, for provision of information and/or capture of the informed consent when this is allowed according to national legislation, e.g. desktop or mobile device-based programs supplied to potential trial participants or applications for the use by the potential trial participants on their BYOD or access to web-based applications.
- Interactive Response Technologies (IRT), for management of randomisation, supply and receipt of IMP, e.g. via a web-based application.
- Portals for supplying information from the sponsor to the sites e.g. investigator brochures (IBs), suspected unexpected serious adverse reactions (SUSARs), training material and for documenting site review, training etc.
- Other computerised systems implemented by the sponsor holding/managing and/or analysing data relevant to the clinical trial e.g. clinical trial management systems (CTMS), pharmacovigilance databases, statistical software programming pharmacovigilance databases, statistical software, document management systems and central monitoring software.
- AI used in clinical trials e.g. for trial participant recruitment, determination of eligibility, coding of events and concomitant medication and data clarification and cleaning processes.

The approach towards computerised systems and medical devices used in clinical practice (e.g. regarding validation) should be risk proportionate. The risk-assessment should consider the relevance of the system use for the safety of the participant and the importance and integrity of derived clinical trial data i.e. whether the system is used for standard care and safety measurements for participants or if systems are used to generate primary efficacy data that are relied on in e.g. a marketing authorisation application. Systems used outside approved setting is inherently of higher risk. In case of well-established computerised systems, which are used in line with approval in a routine setting for less critical trial data, the certification by a notified body may suffice as documentation whereas other more critical systems may require a more in-depth validation effort. This decision should be justified pre-trial.

3. Legal and regulatory background

- Directive 2001/20/EC (until repealed by Regulation (EU) No 536/2014)
- Directive 2005/28/EC (until repealed by Regulation (EU) No 536/2014)
- Regulation (EU) No 536/2014
- ICH Guideline 307 for good clinical practice E6(R2), (EMA/CHMP/ICH/135/1995 Revision 2)

This guideline is intended to assist the sponsors, investigators, and other parties involved in clinical trials in complying with the requirements of the current legislation (Directive 2001/20/EC and Directive 2005/28/EC), as well as ICH E6 Good Clinical Practice (GCP) Guideline ('ICH-GCP guideline'), regarding the use of computerised systems and collection of electronic data in clinical trials. The guideline applies to the legal representatives and CROs, which according to the ICH-GCP guideline includes any contracted party such as vendors and service providers to the extent of their assumed trial related duties and functions.

The risk-based approach to quality management also has an impact on the use of computerised systems and collection of electronic data. To ensure continued guidance once the Clinical Trials Regulation (EU) No. 536/2014 ('Regulation') comes into application, this guideline already prospectively considers the specific requirements of the Regulation with respect to these systems and data.

Consideration should also be given to meeting the requirements of any additional current legal and regulatory framework that may in addition apply to the medicinal product regulatory framework, depending on the digital technology. These may include e.g. medical devices, data protection legislation and legislation on electronic identification.

Further elaboration of EU GCP Inspectors' Working group's (GCP IWG) expectations on various topics, including those of computerised systems can be found as GCP Q&As published on the EMA website

4. Principles and definition of key concepts

The following sections outline the basic principles that apply to all computerised systems used in clinical trials.

4.1. Data integrity

CH 29

Data integrity is achieved when data (irrespective of media) are collected and maintained in a secure manner, to fulfil the ALCOA++ principles of being attributable, legible, contemporaneous, original, accurate, complete, consistent, enduring and traceable as described in section 4.5 in order for the data to adequately support robust results and good decision making throughout the data life cycle. Assuring data integrity requires appropriate quality and risk management systems as described in section 4.6., including adherence to sound scientific principles and good documentation practices.

Data governance should address data ownership and responsibility throughout the life cycle, and consider the design, operation and monitoring of processes/systems to comply with the principles of data integrity including control over intentional and unintentional changes to data.

Data governance systems should include staff training in the importance of data integrity principles and the creation of a working environment that enables visibility, and actively encourages reporting of errors, omissions and undesirable results.

Lack of integrity before the mandated retention period can ultimately render the data unusable and is equivalent to data loss/destruction and is considered GCP noncompliant.

4.2. Responsibilities

Roles and responsibilities in clinical trials should be clear. The responsibility for the conduct of clinical trials is assigned via legislation to two parties, which may each have implemented computerised systems for holding/managing data, in the context of clinical trials:

- Investigators and their institutions, laboratories and other technical departments or clinics, generate the data, construct the record and may use their own software and hardware (purchased, part of national or institutional health information systems, or locally developed).
- Sponsors, supplying, and/or, managing and operating computerised systems (including software and instruments) and the records generated by them. The sponsors may do this directly, or via CROs, including organisations providing ePRO, eCRF, or interactive voice response system (IVRS) specialists that collect and store data on behalf of sponsors.

Please refer to Annex 1 regarding the contracting out of tasks related to computerised systems.

4.3. Electronic data

Data consists of collected individual data points. Data becomes information when viewed in context. Metadata is providing context for the data point. Different types of metadata exist such as: variable name, unit, field value before and after change, reason for change, TMF location document identifier, time stamp, user. Typically, these are data that describe the characteristics, structure, data elements and inter-relationships of data e.g. audit trails. Metadata also permit data to be attributable to an individual (or if automatically generated, to the original data source). Metadata form an integral part of the original record. Without the context provided by metadata the data has no meaning.

4.4. Source data

The term source data usually refers to the original reported observation in a source document. However, source data can be processed to a certain degree. Part of the collection process already transforms values e.g. CT scanning images.

Source data files could be e.g. hospital records, clinical and office charts, laboratory notes. Further examples include e-mails, spreadsheets, audio and/or video files, images and tables in databases. An electronic document that contains source data is considered an electronic source document. It is important to ensure that the true source data list is understood, defined and retained.

The location of source documents and the associated source data they contain, should be clearly identified at all points within the data capture process.

Below is an example (figure 1) of a situation where the true source data (e.g. imaging, but could also relate to information from a wearable) is often not used for source data verification, or it is not ensured that it is retained.

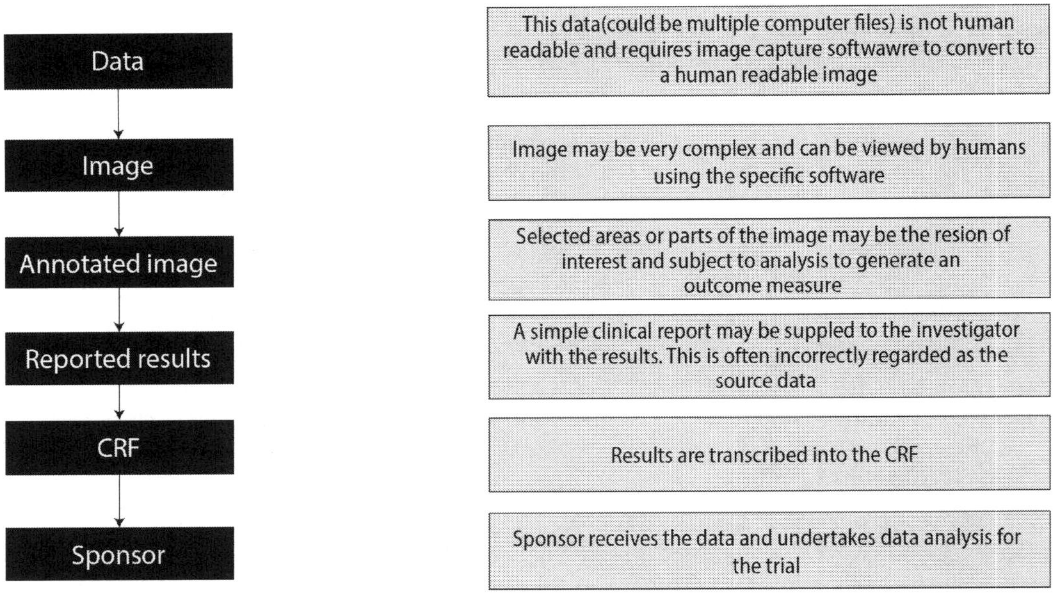

Figure 1

From a practical point of view, the first obtainable permanent data from an electronic data generation/capture should be considered and defined as the electronic source data. This process should be validated to ensure that the source data generated/captured is representative of the original observation and should contain metadata, including audit trail, to ensure data is attributable, legible, complete, original and accurate (see minimum requirements for electronic source data). See section 4.5. The logical location where the source data is first obtained should be part of the metadata.

Below is an example of a typical data flow for the use of ePRO, wearables etc. (figure 2):

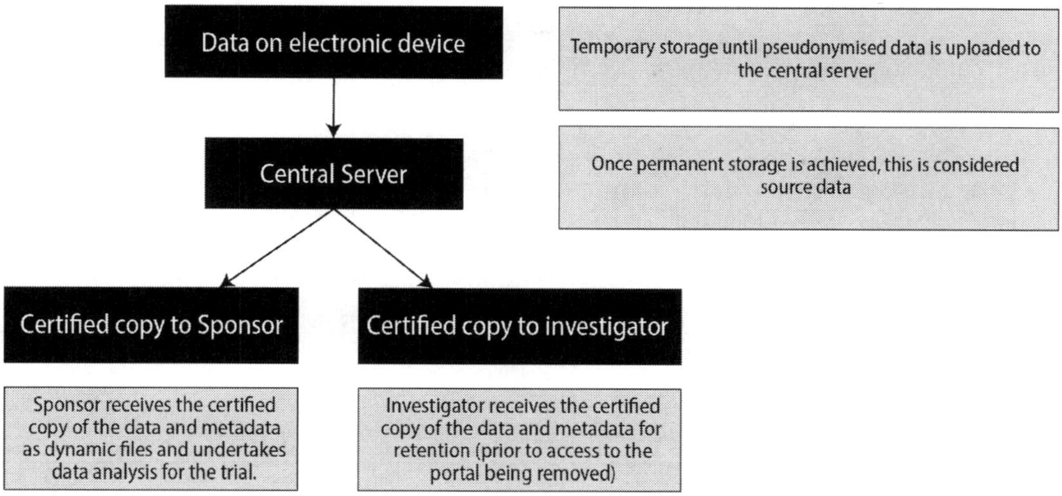

Figure 2

4.5. ALCOA(++) PRINCIPLES

A number of attributes are considered of universal importance to data. These include that the data are:

Attributable

Data should be attributable to the person generating the data. Based on the criticality of the data, it should also be traceable to the system/device, in which the data were generated/captured. The information about originator (e.g. system operator, data originator) and system (e.g. device, process) should be kept as part of the metadata.

Legible

Data should be maintained in a readable form to allow review in its original context. Therefore, changes to data, such as compression, encryption and coding should be completely reversible to facilitate this.

Contemporaneous

Data should be generated by a system or captured by a person at the time of the observation. The information of the timepoint of observation and the time point of permanent save should be kept as part of the metadata, including audit trail. Accurate date and time information should be automatically captured and should be linked and set by an external standard (e.g. universal time coordinated (UTC), central server).

Original

Data should be the original first generation/capture of the observation. Certified copies can replace original data (See section on certified copies: 6.5.). Information that is originally captured in a dynamic state should remain available in that state.

Accurate

The use of computerised systems should ensure that the data are at least as accurate as those recorded by paper means. The coding process, which consists in matching text or data collected on the CRF to terms in a standard dictionary, thesaurus or tables (e.g. units, scales), should be controlled. The process of data transfer between systems should be validated to ensure the data remains accurate. Data should be an accurate representation of the observations made. Metadata should contain information to describe the observations and, where appropriate, it could also contain information to confirm its accuracy.

Complete

To reconstruct and fully understand an event, data should be a complete representation of the observation made and should be represented in the original context and associated metadata, including audit trail. Data where the original context or the metadata, including audit trail, were lost and/or detached is not complete.

Consistent

Processes should be in place to ensure consistency of the definition, generation/capturing and management (including migration) of data throughout the data life cycle. Processes should be implemented to minimise the risk of contradictions e.g. by the use of standardisation, data validation and appropriate training.

Enduring

Data should be maintained appropriately such that they remain intact and durable through the entire data life cycle, as appropriate, according to regulatory retention requirements. (See section on back-up and archiving: 6.8).

Available when needed

Data should be stored at all times in order to be readily available for review when needed.

Traceable

Data should be traceable throughout the data life cycle. Any changes to the data, to the context or metadata should be traceable, should not obscure the original information and should be explained, if necessary. Changes should be documented as part of the metadata (e.g. audit trail).

4.6. Criticality and Risks

ICH-GCP E6(R2) introduces the need for a quality management system with a risk-based approach. Risks should be considered at both the system level e.g. standard operating procedures (SOPs), computerised systems and staff, and for the specific clinical trial e.g. trial specific data and data collection tools or trial specific builds/configurations of systems.

Risks in relation to the use of computerised systems and especially those related to the assurance of data integrity should be identified, analysed and mitigated or accepted throughout the system life cycle. Where applicable, mitigating actions include revised system design, configuration or customisation, increased system qualification or revised SOPs for the use of systems and data governance culture.

In general, risks should be determined based on system used, operator, use of system and data involved. High-risk component parts of any system should always be addressed. For example, a component part of an IRT system that calculates IMP dose based on data input by the investigator would be high risk compared to other functionality such as generation of an IMP shipment report. The complicity between each component should be taken into consideration.

All data collected in the context of an approved clinical trial should be reliable. Consequently, the arrangements for data governance to ensure that data, irrespective of the format in which they are generated, are recorded, processed (including analysis, alteration/imputation, transformation or migration), used, retained (archived), retrieved and destroyed should be considered for data integrity risks and appropriate control processes implemented.

The approach used to reduce risks to an acceptable level should be proportionate to the significance of the risk. Risk reduction activities may be incorporated in protocol design and implementation, system design, build and validation, monitoring plans, agreements between parties defining roles and responsibilities, systematic safeguards to ensure adherence to SOPs, training in processes and procedures etc.

The identification of the most effective and efficient risk-based control, including periodic review of the data and metadata can be determined and implemented.

There are special risks to take into consideration when activities are contracted out. These are further elaborated in Annex 1 on contracts.

4.7. Performing Data Capture in Clinical Trials

The approved clinical trial protocol should specify which data is to be generated/captured by whom and when and which tools or procedures are to be used.

The protocol should identify any data to be recorded directly into the eCRFs and considered to be source data (ICH-GCP 6.4.9). This is equally applicable to other specific data collection systems, such as ePRO. Data directly captured in these tools without prior identification in the protocol to be source data is considered as GCP-noncompliant.

CH 29

Tools used to generate, capture, transfer, manipulate or store data such as a CRF and other instruments such as COA and trial participant diary tools which report clinical data to the sponsor should be an accurate representation of the protocol ensuring capture and transfer of only the data as specified within the protocol.

The sponsor and investigator should maintain a record of the location(s) of their respective essential documents including source documents (ICH-GCP 8.1). Investigators should document source data consistently in accordance with the source data location list.

The source data and their respective capture methods should be clearly defined prior to the recruitment of the trial participants.

A detailed diagram and description of the transmission of electronic data should be available. The sponsor should describe which data will be transferred and in which format, the origin and destination of the data, the parties with access to the transferred data, the timing of the transfer and any actions that may be applied to the data, for example, data validation, reconciliation, verification and review. The use of a data management plan (DMP) is strongly encouraged.

Any data generated/captured and transferred to the sponsor or CRO that is not stated in the protocol or related documents is considered GCP-noncompliant.

There is no requirement or expectation that the sponsors and investigators use computerised systems to collect data; however, the use of electronic data collection (EDC) tools if implemented and controlled to the described standard, offers a wide variety of functions to improve data completeness, consistency and unambiguity, e.g. automatic edit checks, validation checks, assisting information and workflow control.

4.8. Electronic signatures

Whenever an electronic signature is used within a clinical trial to replace a wet-ink signature required by GCP, the electronic signature functionality should meet the expectations stated below regarding *authentication, non-repudiation, unbreakable link and timestamp of the signature*:

The system should thus include functionality to 1) *authenticate* the signatory, i.e. establish a high degree of certainty that a record was signed by the claimed signatory, 2) ensure *non-repudiation*, i.e. that the signatory cannot later deny having signed the record, 3) ensure an *unbreakable link* between the electronic record and its signature, i.e. that the contents of a signed (approved) version of a record cannot later be changed by anyone without automatically being rendered visibly un-signed (unapproved), and 4) provide a *timestamp*, i.e. that the date, time and time zone when the signature was applied is recorded.

Electronic signatures can further be divided into two groups depending on whether the identity of the signatory is known in advance or not; i.e. signatures executed in *closed* and in open systems.

For *closed* systems which constitute the majority of systems used in GCP and which are typically provided by the sponsor, a CRO or an investigator, the system owner knows the identity of all users and signatories and has full control over these. The electronic signature functionality in these systems should be proven during system qualification to have the qualities mentioned above.

However, EU Regulation 910/2014 ("eIDAS") on electronic identification and trust services for electronic transactions is not applicable for closed systems ("eIDAS" clause 21 and article 2.2).

For *open* systems, the signatories (and users) are not known in advance, and hence, identification of a signatory should be based on a personal qualified certificate for electronic signatures. Implementation of electronic signatures in open systems should meet EU Regulation 910/2014 ("eIDAS").

A special case of electronic signatures is *hybrid electronic signatures*, where electronic records in a computerised system are signed using wet-ink signatures on paper. In this case, it follows from the above that there should be an unbreakable link between the 515 electronic record in the computerised system and the signature page on paper, e.g. by means of a checksum (hash code) calculated for the electronic record and printed by the system on the signature page.

Biometric approaches are currently not specifically addressed by ICH-GCP E6(R2). If using biometrics instead of signature or e-signature, investigator and sponsor should ensure that these fulfil the above mentioned requirements and local legal requirements.

4.9. Data protection

"The confidentiality of records that could identify trial participants should be protected, respecting the privacy and confidentiality rules in accordance with the applicable regulatory requirement(s)." (ICH-GCP 2.11). The requirements of Regulation (EU) 2016/679 (General Data Protection Regulation) on the protection of individuals with regard to the processing of personal data and on the free movement of such data should be followed except when specific requirements are implemented for clinical trials e.g. that a trial participant does not have the right to be forgotten (and consequently data deleted) as this would cause bias to e.g. safety data (Regulation 536/2014 recital 76). Trial participants should not be asked to waive their rights by informed consent processes (ICH-GCP section 4.8.4.).

In accordance with Union data protection legislation, the location of personal data processed (both at rest and in transit) must be within the EU/EEA. If personal data is transferred to a third country or international organisation, such data transfer must comply with applicable Union data protection. In summary, this means that the transfer must be either carried out on the basis of an adequacy decision (Article 45 of GDPR, Article 47 of EUDPR), otherwise the transfer must be subject to appropriate safeguards (as listed in Article 46 of GDPR or Article 48 of EUDPR) or the transfer may take only if a derogation for specific situations apply (under Article 49 of GDPR or Article 50 of EUDPR).

4.10. Validation of systems

All computerised systems used within a clinical trial should be subject to processes that confirm that the specified requirements of a computerised system are consistently fulfilled and that the system is fit for purpose. Validation should ensure accuracy, reliability and consistent intended performance, from design until decommissioning of the system or transition to a new system.

The processes used for the validation should be decided upon by the system owner (e.g. sponsors, investigators, technical facilities) and described, as applicable. System owners should ensure adequate oversight of validation activities and documentation (thereon) performed by contracted parties to ensure suitable procedures are in place and that they are being adhered to.

Documentation (including information within computerised systems used as process tools for validation activities) should be maintained to demonstrate that the system is maintained in the validated state. Such documentation should be available for both the validation of the software and for validation of the trial-specific configuration.

Validation of the trial-specific configuration should ensure that the system is consistent with the requirements of the approved clinical trial protocol and robust testing of functionality implementing such requirements is undertaken, for example, eligibility criteria questions in an eCRF, randomisation strata and dose calculations in an IRT system.

See Annex 2.4 for further detail on validation.

4.11. Direct access to computerised systems

All relevant computerised systems should be readily available and directly accessible (this requires a unique username and password) upon request by inspectors of regulatory authorities. If a computerised system is de-commissioned, direct access (with personal username and password) to the data should be still ensured (see section 6.11).

5. Computerised systems

Requirements for validation are described in section 4.10 and Annex 2, requirements for user management in Annex 3 and requirements for IT security in Annex 4 of this guideline.

5.1. Keeping a description of computerised systems

The responsible party should maintain a list of physical and logical location of the data e.g. servers, functionality and operational responsibility for computerised systems and databases used in a clinical trial together with an assessment of their fitness for purpose.

Where multiple computerised systems/databases are used, a clear overview should be available so the extent of computerisation can be understood. System interfaces should be described, defining how the systems interact, including validation status, methods used and implemented security measures.

5.2. Maintaining written procedures for the use of computerised systems

Written procedures should be in place to ensure correct use of computerised systems. GCP requires that sponsors maintain SOPs for using computerised systems (see ICH-GCP 5.5.3b).

5.3. Training requirements for computerised systems

"Each individual involved in conducting a clinical trial should be qualified by education, training, and experience to perform his or her respective task(s)." (ICH-GCP 2.8). This also applies to training in computerised systems. Systems and training should be designed to meet the specific needs of the users (e.g. in sponsors/CROs and investigator). Special considerations should be

considered regarding training of trial participants where they are users (see also Annex 5, section A5.3).

There should be training on the relevant aspects of the legislation and guidelines for those involved in developing, building and managing trial specific computerised systems, for example, those employed at a contract organisation providing eCRF, IRT, ePRO, trial-specific configuration and management of the system during the clinical trial conduct.

All training should be documented, and the records retained in the appropriate part of the investigator site file/sponsor TMF.

5.4. Security

To maintain data integrity and protection of the rights of trial participants, computerised systems, used in clinical trials, should have security processes and features to prevent unauthorised access and accidental or deliberate data changes and maintain blinding of the treatment allocation where applicable.

Checks should be used to ensure that only authorised individuals have access to the system and appropriate permissions (e.g. ability to enter or make changes to data). Records of authorisation of access to the systems, with the respective levels of access clearly documented should be maintained. The system should record changes to user roles and thereby access rights and permissions.

There should be documented training on the importance of security e.g. the need to protect and not to share passwords as well as enforcement of security systems and processes and identification and handling of serious breaches.

See Annex 4 for further guidance on IT security.

6. Electronic data

For each trial, it should be identified what electronic data and records will be collected, modified, imported and exported, archived and how they are retrieved and transmitted. Electronic source data, including its audit trail should be directly accessible to investigators, monitors, auditors and inspectors without compromising the confidentiality of participants' identities (ICH-GCP 1.21).

6.1. Data capture and location

The primary goal of data capture is to collect all data required by the protocol. All pertinent observations should be documented in a timely manner. The location of all source data should be specified prior to the start of the trial and updated during the conduct of the trial where applicable. (ICH-GCP 8.1. Addendum)

6.1.1. Transcription from paper to electronic format

Source data collected on paper (e.g. worksheets, paper CRFs or paper diaries or questionnaires) need to be transcribed either manually or by a validated entry tool into the EDC system or database(s). In case of manual transcription, risk-based methods should be implemented to ensure the quality of the transcribed data (e.g. double data entry and/or data monitoring).

6.1.2. Transfer from electronic sources

Study data are transferred in and between systems on a regular basis. All file and data transfers need to be validated and should ensure that data and file integrity is assured for all transfers.

Data that is collected from external sources and transferred in open networks should be protected from unwarranted changes and secured/encrypted in a way which preclude disclosure of confidential information.

All transfers that are needed during the conduct of a clinical trial need to be pre-specified.

Qualification/validation of transfer should include appropriate challenging test sets and ensure that the process is available and functioning at clinical trial start (e.g. to enable ongoing sponsor review of diary data, lab data or adverse events by safety committees). Data transcribed or extracted and transferred from electronic sources and their associated audit trail should be continuously accessible (according to delegated roles and corresponding access rights) by the sponsor for ongoing review and by the investigator for the entire clinical trial and retention period (ICH-GCP 8.1).

Transfer of source data and records where the original data or file is not maintained is a critical process and appropriate considerations are expected in order to prevent loss of data and metadata.

6.1.3. Direct data capture

Direct data capture also can be done by using electronic data input devices and applications such as electronic diaries, electronic questionnaires and eCRFs for direct data entry. Where treatment-related pertinent information is captured first in a direct data capture tool such as a trial participant diary, a PRO form or a special questionnaire, a written procedure 631 should exist to transfer or transcribe information into the medical record, when relevant. Please also refer to Annex 5.

Direct data capture can be done by automated devices such as wearables or laboratory or other technical equipment (e.g. medical imaging, ECG equipment) that are directly linked to an EDC tool. Such data should be accompanied by metadata concerning the device used (e.g. device version, device identifiers, firmware version, last calibration, data originator, UTC time stamp of events).

6.1.4. Data entry checks

Computerised systems should validate manual and automatic data inputs to ensure a predefined set of validation criteria is adhered to. Data entry checks should be relevant for the protocol and developed and revised as needed. Data entry checks should be validated and implementation of the individual data entry checks should be controlled and documented. If data entry checks are paused at any time during the trial, this should be documented and justified. Data entry checks could be either immediately at data entry (edit checks), run automatically during defined intervals (e.g. daily) or manual.

6.2. Audit trail and audit trail review

6.2.1. Audit trail

An audit trail should be enabled for the original creation and subsequent modification of all electronic data (ICH-GCP 2.10, 4.9.0, 4.9.3 and 5.5.3.c). In computerised systems, the audit trail should be secure, computer generated and time stamped (e.g. UTC).

An audit trail is essential to ensure that changes to the data are traceable. Audit trails should be robust, and it should not be possible for "normal" users to deactivate them. If possible, for an audit trail to be de-activated by "admin users", this should automatically create an entry into a log file (e.g. audit trail). Entries in the audit trail should be protected against change, deletion, and access modification (e.g. edit rights, visibility rights). The audit trail should not be stored outside the system. The responsible investigator, sponsor, and inspector should be able to review and comprehend the audit trail and therefore audit trails should be in a humanly readable format.

Audit trails should be visible at data-point level in the live system and the entire audit trail should be available as an exported dynamic data file in order to allow for identification of systematic patterns or concerns in data across trial participants, sites etc. The audit trail should show initial entry and changes (value - previous and current-) made to what (field, data identifiers) by whom (username, role, organisation), when (date/time stamp), why (reason for change) in a GCP compliant manner.

A procedure should be in place to address the situation when a data originator (e.g. investigator or trial participant) realises that she/he has submitted incorrect data by mistake and wants to correct the recorded data.

It is important that original electronic entries are visible or accessible (e.g. in the audit trail) to ensure the changes are traceable. The audit trail should record all changes made as a result of data queries or a clarification process. The clarification process for data entered should be described and documented. Changes to data should only be performed when justified. Justification should be documented. In case the data originator is the trial participant, special considerations to data clarifications might be warranted. See Annex 5 section A5.1.1.41 for further details.

For certain types of systems (e.g. ePRO) data entered may not be uploaded immediately but may be temporally placed in local memory. Such data should not be edited or changed without the knowledge of the data originator prior to saving. Any changes or edits should be acknowledged by the data originator, should be documented in an audit trail and should be part of validation procedures. UTC date of data entry into the capture tool (e.g. eCRF) and UTC date of data saved to a hard drive should be recorded as part of the metadata. The duration between initial capture in local memory and upload to a central server should be short and traceable (i.e. transaction time), especially in case of direct source data entry.

Data extracts or database extracts for internal reporting and statistical analysis do not necessarily need to contain the audit trail information. However, the database audit trail should capture the generation of data extracts and exports.

Audit trails should capture any changes in data entry per field and not per page (e.g. CRF page). Where edit checks result in a change of data, the edit check should be part of the change rationale captured by the audit trail/event log.

In addition to audit trail, metadata could also include (among others) review of access logs, event logs, queries etc.

Access logs, including user name and user role, are in some cases to be considered important metadata and should consequently be available. This is considered necessary e.g. for systems that contain critical unblinded data.

Care should be taken to ensure that information jeopardising the blinding does not appear in the audit trail accessible to blinded users.

6.2.2. Audit trail review

Procedures for risk-based trial specific audit trail reviews should be in place and performance of data review should generally be documented. Data review should focus on critical data. Data review should be proactive and ongoing review is expected unless justified. Manual review as well as review by the use of technologies to facilitate review of larger datasets should be considered. Data review can be used to (among others) identify missing data, detect signs of data manipulation, identify abnormal data/outliers and data entered at unexpected or inconsistent hours and dates (individual data points, trial participants , sites), identify incorrect processing of data (e.g. non-automatic calculations), detect unauthorised accesses, detect device or system malfunction and detect if additional training is needed for trial participants /site staff etc. Audit trail review can also be used to detect situations where direct data capture has been defined in the protocol but where this is not taking place as described.

In addition to audit trail review, metadata review could also include (among others) review of access logs, event logs, queries etc.

The investigator should receive an introduction on how to navigate audit trail of own data in order to be able to review changes.

6.3. Sign-off of data

The investigators are responsible for data entered into eCRFs and other EDC tools under their supervision (electronic records). Those data should be reviewed and signed-off.

The signature of the principal investigator (PI) or authorised member of the investigator's staff is considered as the documented confirmation that the data entered in the eCRF and submitted to the sponsor are attributable, legible, original, accurate, and complete and contemporaneous (ICH-GCP 4.9.1.). Any member of the staff authorised for sign-off (as per ICH-GCP 8.3.14) should be qualified to do so in order to fulfil the purpose of the review as described below. National law could dictate specific responsibilities, which should then be followed.

The acceptable timing and frequency for the sign-off needs to be defined and justified for each trial by the sponsor and should be determined by the sponsor on a risk-based manner. The sponsor should consider trial-specific risks and provide a rationale for the risk-based approach. Points of consideration are types of data entered, non-routine data, importance of data, data for analysis, length of the trial and the decision made by the sponsor based on the entered data, including the timing of such decisions. It is essential that data are confirmed prior to interim analysis and the final analysis and that important data related to e.g. reporting of SAEs, adjudication of important events and endpoint data, DSMB review, are signed off in a timely manner. In addition, a timely review and sign-off of data that are entered directly into the CRF as source is particularly important.

Therefore, it will rarely be sufficient to just implement one signature immediately prior to database lock. Signing of batches of workbooks is also not suited to ensure high data quality and undermines the purpose of timely and thorough data review.

For planned interim analysis, e.g. when filing a marketing authorisation application, all submitted data (e.g. eCRF pages) need to be signed off by the investigator or her/his designated and qualified representative before extracting data for analysis. The systems should be designed to support this functionality.

To facilitate timely data review and signing by the investigator or her/his designated representative, the design of the EDC tool should be laid out to support the signing of the data at the defined time points.

Furthermore, it is important that the PI reviews the data on an ongoing basis in order to detect shortcomings and deficiencies in the trial conduct at an early stage, which is the precondition to undertake appropriate corrective and preventive actions.

Adequate oversight by the PI is a general requirement to ensure participant safety and data quality and integrity. Oversight can be demonstrated via various means, one of them being review of reported data. Lack of investigator oversight may prevent incorrect data from being corrected in a timely manner and necessary corrective and preventive actions being implemented at the investigator site.

6.4. COPYING DATA

Data can be copied or transcribed for different purposes, either to replace source documents or essential documents or to be distributed amongst different stakeholders as working copies. If essential documents or source documents are irreversibly replaced by a copy, the copy should be certified (ICH-GCP 1.63). See section 6.5.

Copies should contain a faithful representation of the data and contextual information. Source documents and data should allow accurate copies to be made. The method for copying should be practical and should ensure that the resulting copy is complete and accurate, including relevant metadata. See also “Guideline on the content, management and archiving of the clinical trial master file (paper and/or electronic), (EMA/INS/GCP/856758/2018), section 5 for further details on definition.

6.5. Certified copies

When creating a certified copy, the nature of the original document needs to be considered. For example, the content of the file is either static (e.g. PDF document) or dynamic (e.g. worksheet with automatic calculations) or the copy tries to capture the result of an interpreter (e.g. a web page, where a web browser interprets written hypertext mark-up language (HTML), JavaScript among other programming languages). Either way the result of the copy process should be verified either automatically by a validated process or by hand to ensure to have the same information, including data that describe the context, content and structure, as the original.

In case of dynamic files e.g. when a database is decommissioned and copies of data and metadata is provided to sponsors, the resulting file should capture also the dynamic aspects of the original file. In case of files, which are the result of an interpreter, special care needs to be taken not only to consider the informative content of such a file, but also to capture and preserve aspects that are the results of the interactions of the used interpreter(s) and systems settings during the display. For example, window size, browser type, operating system employed and the availability of software dependences (e.g. Java Scripts enabled) can influence the structure and content displayed. Special considerations should be taken whenever copies are to replace original source documents, since (any) deviations of information, including data that describes context, content and structure would be considered GCP non-compliant.

6.6. Hosting and control of data

All data generated at the clinical trial site relating to the trial participants should be available to the investigator at all times during and after the trial. The sponsor should not have exclusive control of the data entered in a computerised system at any point in time. All data held by the sponsor that has been generated in a clinical trial should be verifiable to a copy of these data that is not held (or that has not been held) by the sponsor.

The requirements above are not met if data are captured in a computerised system and the data are stored on a central server under the sole control of the sponsor or under the control of a contracted party that is not considered to be independent from the sponsor or if the sponsor is distributing the data to the investigator instead of the independent third party. This is because the investigator does not hold an independent copy of the data and therefore the sponsor has exclusive control of the data. In order to meet the requirements, the investigator should be able to download a contemporaneous certified copy of the data. This is in addition to the record maintained at an independent third party.

Data entered to EDC tools by the investigator should be available to the investigator throughout the whole legally mandated duration and for the full duration of local legal requirements. This can be ensured either by contemporaneous local copies at the trial site or e.g. by the use of an independent third party. Access to the data may be amended to read only as part of the database lock process. Prior to read-only access to the investigator being revoked, a copy including audit trail should be made available to the investigator in a complete and comprehensive way. In the situation where an independent third party is hosting the data. the copy should not be provided via the sponsor, as this would temporarily provide the sponsor with exclusive control over the data and thereby jeopardise the investigator's control. Copies should not be provided in a way that requires advanced technical skills by the investigators. The period between provision of the copy to the investigator and the closure of the investigators' read only access to the database(s) should allow sufficient time for the investigator to review the copy and access should not be closed until such a review has been performed.

Any contractual agreements regarding hosting should ensure investigator control. If the sponsor is arranging hosting on behalf of the investigators by an independent third party, contracts should ensure the level of investigator control mentioned above.

Investigators delegating hosting of such data to third parties themselves should ensure that the intended use is covered by local legal requirements and in-house rules of the institution.

6.7. Cloud solutions

Irrespective whether a computerised system is installed at the premises of the sponsor, investigator, another party involved in the trial or whether it is made available by a contracted party as a cloud solution, the requirements in this guideline are applicable. There are, however, specific points to be considered as described below.

Cloud solutions cover a wide variety of services related to the computerised systems used in clinical trials. These can range from Infrastructure as a service (IaaS) over Platform as a service (PaaS) to Software as a service (SaaS). Common for these services is, that they provide sponsors and investigators, on-demand availability of computerised system resources over the internet, without having the need or even possibility to directly manage these services.

In case of cloud solution being used the sponsor (ICH-GCP 5.2.1) and/or of the investigator (ICH-GCP 4.2.6) should ensure that the contracted party providing the cloud is qualified (see Annex 4).

By buying in cloud computing, the sponsor and/or investigator are at a certain risk, because many services are managed less visibly by the cloud provider.

Contractual obligations with the cloud solution provider should be detailed and explicit and refer to all GCP relevant topics and to all relevant legal requirements (see Annex 1).

Data jurisdiction may be complex given the nature of cloud solutions and services being shared over several sites, countries and continents; however, any uncertainties should be addressed and solved by contractual obligations prior to the use of a cloud solution.

If the responsible party choses to perform his own qualification of the computerised system, the cloud provider should make a test environment available which is identical to the production environment.

6.8. Adequate back-up of data

Data stored in a computerised system are susceptible to system malfunction, intended or unintended attempts to alter or destroy data and physical destruction of media and infrastructure and are therefore at risk to be lost. Data and configurations should be regularly backed up. Please also refer to Annex 4 for further details on IT security.

The use of replicated servers is strongly recommended. Back-ups should be stored in separate physical locations and logical networks and not behind the same firewall as the original data to avoid simultaneous destruction or alteration.

Frequency of backups (e.g. hourly, daily, weekly) and their retention (e.g. a day, a week, a month) should be determined through a risk-based approach.

Checks of accessibility to data, irrespective of format, including relevant metadata, should be undertaken to confirm that the data are enduring, continue to be available, readable and understandable by a human being. There should be procedures in place for risk-based (e.g. in connection with major updates) restore test from back up of the complete database(s) and configurations and the performed restore tests should be documented.

Disaster mitigation and recovery plans should be in place to deal with events, which endanger data security. Such plans should be regularly reviewed. Disaster mitigation and recovery plans should be part of the contractual agreement where the sponsor subcontracts.

6.9. Migration of data

Migration as opposed to transfer of data (as described in section 6.1.2) is the process of permanently moving existing data (including metadata) from one system into another system e.g. migration of individual safety reports from one safety database to another. It should be ensured that the migration does not adversely affect existing data and metadata.

In the course of design or purchase of a new system and of subsequent data migration from an old system, qualification of the data migration process should have no less focus than qualification of the system itself.

The qualification of data migration should take into consideration the complexity of the task and any foreseen possibilities that may exist to verify the migrated data (e.g. checksum, case counts, quality control of records).

Prior to migration, this process should be planned in detail. A risk analysis identifying the most probable risks should take place and should yield appropriate mitigation strategies. After the planning, the intended procedure should be validated with mock data and results should be considered for risk assessment and mitigation. A data verification focused on key data should be performed post migration.

Verification of migrated data can be simple or rather complex, depending on the different platforms and systems involved. Regardless of effort needed, the migration process should be documented in such detail that throughout all data operations/transformations data changes remain traceable. Mapping from the old system onto the new system should be retained.

Data, contextual information and audit trail should not be separated. In case migration of data into a new system results in a loss of relevant data, adequate mitigating actions should be taken to establish a robust method to join audit trail and data for continuous access by all stakeholders. A detailed explanation is expected, why no system was available, which allowed migration of data and audit trail. Arrangements should ensure that the link between data and metadata can be established. If several parties are involved, contracts should be in place to ensure this.

6.10. ARCHIVING

The investigator and sponsor should be aware of the required retention periods for clinical trial data and essential documents, including metadata. Retention periods should respect the data protection principle of storage limitation. Clinical trial management systems (e.g. TMF) should be in place to keep an inventory of all essential data and documents and corresponding retention periods. It should be clearly defined which data is related to each clinical trial activity and where this record is located and who has access/edit rights to the document. Security controls should be in place to ensure data confidentiality, integrity and availability.

It should be verified that the file remains accessible and depending on the media used for storage and available software through the retention period. This could imply e.g. migration of data (see section 6.9).

Suitable archiving systems should be in place to safeguard the data integrity for the periods established by the regulatory requirements including those in any of the regions where the data may be used for regulatory submissions, and not just those of the country where the data are generated.

Source documents and data should always be available when needed to authorised individuals to meet their regulatory obligations. For direct access please refer to section 4.6.

Data should be maintained in a secure manner and should only be transferred between different (physical) locations in a validated process. Data should be archived in a read only state.

6.11. DATABASE DECOMMISSIONING

After the finalisation of the trial, the database(s) might be decommissioned. It is recommended that the time of decommissioning is decided taking into consideration e.g., whether or not the clinical trial will be used in the terms of a marketing authorisation application in the near future in which case it could be recommended to keep the database(s) live. A dated and certified copy of the database(s) and data should be archived and available on request. In case of decommissioning, the sponsor should ensure (contractually if done by a contracted party) that archived formats provide the possibility to restore the database(s). This includes restoring of dynamic functionality and all relevant metadata (audit trail, event logs, implemented edit checks, queries, user logs, etc.). Where recommissioning is no longer possible, the sponsor should ensure that all the data including metadata files (e.g. audit trails) is available in dynamic data files. The sponsor should review the system to determine the audit trails and logs available in the system and how these would be retained as dynamic files. Where a third party is involved, this should be addressed in the contractual arrangements. Static formats of dynamic data will not be considered adequate. See definitions section regarding static and dynamic formats.

Annex 1 Contracts

Sponsors and investigators outsource an increasing number of tasks in clinical trials, especially in the area of computerised systems where the responsible party might lack internal knowledge or resources or they wish to purchase a product or a service that has been used by others. Sponsors/investigators can delegate tasks to an accomplished third party, but nevertheless the full responsibility for the data integrity, security and confidentiality resides with the sponsor/investigator. (ICH-GCP 4.2.6 and 5.2.1)

Contracts can cover a variety of tasks such as system and trial specific build, provision of license to an application, full clinical trial service including data management tasks e.g. site contact, training, data clarification processes etc., but could also be restricted to hosting services.

The responsible party should ensure that the distribution of tasks is clearly documented and agreed on. It should be ensured that each party has the control of and access to data and information that their legal responsibilities require and that the ethics committees and regulatory authorities approving trials have been properly informed of these activities as part of the clinical trial application process. This should be carefully documented, in the protocol, procedures, contracts or agreements and other documents. It is important to consider who is providing and controlling the computerised system being used. In general, tasks including handling of data under the responsibility of the investigator can only be performed by parties, contractually obligated to the institution or investigator and data under the responsibility of the sponsor can only be handled by parties contractually obligated to the sponsor.

Clear contracts should be in place and appropriately signed by all involved parties prior to provision of services or systems. Contracts should be maintained/updated as appropriate. Sub-contracting and conditions for sub-contracting should be specified.

The responsible parties should ensure oversight of these trial-related duties e.g. by review of defined key performance indicators (KPI) or reconciliations. If appropriate contracts cannot be put in place, e.g. because a contracted party does not allow provision of e.g. access to system requirements specifications, pre-qualification audits or access for GCP inspectors, systems from such a vendor shall not be used in clinical trials.

All parties involved in the conduct of the clinical trial should comply with ICH-GCP and this includes vendors of computerised systems. Therefore, any relevant standards to be followed, e.g. clinical trial legislation and guidance should be specified in the contract. A number of the tasks involve access to, review, collection and/or analysis of data, much of it personal/pseudonymised data. In addition, in specific cases contact with (potential) trial participants and consequently data protection legislation needs to be followed, in addition to the clinical trial legislation and guidance.

The protocol, implicitly, defines part of the specification for system build and there should be consistency between the protocol and the wording of the contract. In addition, it should be clear how subsequent changes to the protocol are handled so that the vendor can implement changes to the computerised system appropriately.

It should be clear from contracts which tasks are delegated also in relation to retaining essential documentation for performed activities. In the context of clinical trials, the retention period for system documentation (including e.g. software/system validation documentation, vendor standard operating procedures (SOPs), training records, issues log/resolutions) as well as Trial Master File (TMF) documentation related to the individual clinical trial (including e.g. helpdesk tickets or meeting minutes) is considerable. It should be clear from the contract which party is retaining and maintaining which documentation and how and in what format that documentation is made available when needed e.g. for an audit or an inspection. There should be no difference in availability of documentation irrespective of whether the documentation is held by the sponsor/investigator or a contracted (or sub-contracted) party. The responsible party is ultimately responsible for e.g. the validation and operation of the computerised system and for providing adequate documented evidence of applicable processes.

Responsible parties should be able to provide the GCP inspectors of the EU/EEA authorities with access to the requested documentation regarding the qualification, validation and operation of computerised systems irrespective of who performed these activities.

It should be specified in contracts that the sponsor or the institution, as applicable, should have the right to conduct audits at the vendor site and that the vendor site could be subject to inspections (by national and/or international authorities) and shall accept these.

The sponsor has a responsibility to escalate serious breaches, including important security breaches, to authorities within short timelines. To avoid undue delay in sponsor reporting from the time of discovery e.g. by a vendor, contracts should specify which information should be escalated and within which (short) deadlines.

As set out in ICH-GCP 8.1 to ensure that the investigator, rather than the sponsor, maintains control over their data, it should be specified in contracts how investigators' access to and control over data is ensured during and after the trial and the revocation of investigator access to data in case of decommissioning should be described. It should also be specified which outputs the involved parties (e.g. sponsor and investigators) will receive during and after the clinical trial and in which formats.

Arrangements about decommissioning of the database(s) should be clear, including the possibility to restore the database(s) to full functionality (including dynamic features) for instance for inspection purposes.

The contracts should address expectations regarding potential system "down-time" and the preparation of contingency plans.

Tasks contracted out could include hosting of data. If data are hosted by a vendor, location of data storage and control of this (e.g. use of cloud services) should be described.

To ensure reliable access to the data, the sponsor/investigator should employ measures to guarantee access to data for the sponsor and investigator in case of foreclosure (bankruptcy), shutdown, disaster of the vendor or for other reasons chosen by the sponsor/investigator (e.g. change of vendor).

Special consideration should be given on training and quality systems. Vendors accepting tasks on computerised systems should not only be knowledgeable on computerised systems and data protection legislation, but also on GCP requirements, quality systems, etc.

Further details on contracts with IT vendors are set up in related Q&A documents.

ANNEX 2 COMPUTERISED SYSTEMS VALIDATION

A2.1 ESTABLISHING REQUIREMENTS AND ENSURING DOCUMENTING CONSISTENT INTENDED PERFORMANCE (VALIDATION)

All responsible parties should ensure appropriate qualification and validation, as per ICH-GCP 5.5.3a, *"the sponsor should ensure and document that the electronic data processing system(s) conforms to the sponsor' established requirements for completeness, accuracy, reliability, and consistent intended performance (i.e. validation)"*. Similarly, investigators or institutions are expected to demonstrate that their computerised systems meet the requirements defined in ICH-GCP 4.9.0.

Validation should include validation of the core software by the vendor for a commercial of the shelf (COTS) and/or software as a service (SaaS) or validation of the software developed by the sponsor or investigator (including the use of open source) and of its subsequent configuration. A further validation may be required where the installed software is then used for specific trials requiring a configuration or build based on the requirements of a specific trial.

The sponsor (or the investigator in case of a system implemented by the investigator's institution) is ultimately responsible for the validation of the computerised systems used in clinical trial processes. They may rely on qualification documentation provided by the vendor if the qualification activities performed by the vendor have been assessed as adequate, but may also have to perform additional qualification/validation activities based on a documented risk-assessment e.g. during pre-qualification audits.

Where the responsible party is using a system (as intended) from a vendor, including the built-in possibilities for configuration, the considerations as described below should be taken into account. Different requirements will apply in cases where the software is changed, or functionalities are added to the system. The system in question may be a system validated by the supplier, but installed at the sponsor/institution, or a system provided as SaaS.

For the responsible party to use the vendor's qualification documentation, they should have a thorough knowledge about the vendor's quality system and qualification activities, which could usually be obtained through an in-depth assessment/audit. This assessment/audit should be performed by qualified staff, with sufficient time spent on the activities and with cooperation from the vendor. The assessment/audit should go sufficiently deep into the actual activities, and a suitable number of examples for relevant activities should be assessed (and documented). The assessment/audit report should document the vendor's qualification documentation to be satisfactory or shortcomings should be mitigated by the responsible party – e.g. by them performing part of the qualification. The responsible party, or where applicable the contract research organisation (CRO) performing these activities for them, should have a detailed knowledge about the qualification documentation and should be able to navigate through it and explain the activities as if they had performed the activities themselves.

As described in Annex 1 on contracts, the qualification documentation should be made available to the inspectors in a timely manner when requested during an inspection, irrespective of whether it is provided by the responsible party, a CRO or the vendor of the system.

Both the responsible party and the vendor should establish full configuration management for qualification and production environments and should be able to fully account for any differences between the vendor's validation environment and the responsible party's production environment. In case of differences, the responsible party should justify that these are considered insignificant.

The responsible party should perform an Installation Qualification/Performance Qualification (IQ/PQ) where the system depends on trained users.

Interfaces between the electronic case report form (eCRF) and other systems should be clearly defined and validated e.g. import of item response theory data, automatically generated emails to safety mailboxes etc.

Documentation supporting the validation of trial specific configurations/builds (e.g. edit checks, auto-calculations) are considered essential documents that form part of the TMF. The documentation for the software validation is also essential and should be retained to be made available, although not required to be in the TMF (see "Guideline on the content, management and archiving of the clinical trial master file (paper and/or electronic), (EMA/INS/GCP/856758/2018)?)

Changes to systems are described in section A.2.8.

A2.2 Requirements documentation (URS, trial specific, edit check specifications)

Independently on whether a system is developed on request by the sponsor/institution, following the traditional V-model or agile principles, is purchased as a COTS product, or is provided as SaaS, all system functionalities intended to be used (including requirement for regulatory authorities' access/review) should be described in a requirements specification, often called a user requirements specification (URS). The URS should form the basis for system design, purchase customisation and configuration, but also for system qualification). In addition, other specification documents should be generated. For example, the use of the software for a trial specific build or configuration will also require specification documentation to be produced. This should make reference to the clinical trial protocol and version for which it was designed. The software development additional documents for functional and design specifications are produced.

The specification documentation should cover all functionality used by or relied on by the sponsor/investigator, including but not limited to operational, functional, data, technical, interface, performance, availability, security, and regulatory requirements.

The sponsor/investigator should take responsibility for the URS. This document should always be reviewed and approved by the sponsor/investigator.

The responsible party should ensure availability of qualification documentation. In case the responsible party cannot rely on a vendor to provide documentation, the responsible party has to requalify the system on the basis of their own and of the vendor's system requirement specifications.

Other specification documentation should be reviewed and approved by the sponsor/investigator as appropriate. For example, where the software is configured for the sponsor's/investigator's use or for trial specific configurations/builds the documentation should be reviewed by the responsible party; however, for COTS or SaaS software the review and approval of the responsible party could be limited to the URS.

The specification documentation should be maintained and updated throughout the system full life cycle as requirements to the system change. For example, there may be software enhancements, bug fixes and for trial specific configurations/builds there could be changes required from protocol amendments. The rationale for such changes to the specification documentation should be documented as part of the change control process.

A2.3 Requirements traceability matrix

For complex systems with a large number of requirements, it is not feasible to keep track of requirements and their corresponding test cases without having a systematic approach of documenting this, e.g. traceability matrix. This document may have many forms and the process may even be automated by software, but it should be created during system development and qualification and be continuously updated as requirements are changed to ensure that for every requirement, there is at least one corresponding test case.

A2.4 Validation plans and test plans/scripts/cases

Validation activities should be planned and documented, for example validation plan and test plan. Test cases and individual test steps should be pre-approved and conducted accordingly. This is required for validation of both core software and trial specific configurations/builds.

Test cases may have many formats and while typically consisting of textual documents including tables with multiple columns corresponding to the elements below, they may be designed and contained in dedicated test management systems, which may even allow automatic execution of test cases (e.g. regression testing). However, expectations to key elements are the same.

Test cases should include exact reference to requirement identity, version of the software being tested (target), any pre-requisites or conditions prior to conducting the test, description of the step taken to test the functionality (input), expected result (acceptance criteria), and require the user to document the actual result as seen in the test step, evidence, if relevant (screen shot), conclusion of the test step (pass/fail), and deviation impact assessment and subsequent decisions regarding the deviations (if applicable).

Test cases for trial specific configurations/builds should ensure that the system meets the specification documentation and therefore the clinical trial protocol requirements.

A2.5 Test execution and reporting

Test execution should follow pre-approved protocols and test cases (see A2.4) and where applicable and required by test cases and test procedures, screen shots should be captured to document test steps and results when relevant. The person performing each test and his access rights (role) should be documented. Where previously passed scripts are not retested along with the testing of fixes for previous fails, this should be risk assessed and the rationale documented.

Testing of the software or trial specific configurations would typically comprise difference components. The software developers would undertake testing (e.g. unit testing/code review) prior to release of the system to user acceptance testing (UAT). The responsibilities for UAT, requirements for UAT test scripts and retention of executed scripts should be defined. There should be a process to control the different system environments and approval for transfer between them (e.g. move from UAT to production environment).

Prior to testing, it should be defined which requirements and tests are related to critical system functionality and consequently should have satisfactorily passed testing prior to deployment. Deviations encountered during system qualification should be recorded and brought to closure. Any failure to meet requirements pre-defined to be critical should be solved prior to deployment or deployment should be justified and potential impact thoroughly assessed. Any known issues with the system on release should be documented in validation report and, where used, release notes.

A2.6 Release into production

Trial specific configurations/builds should only be released into production and made available to trained site users when all the necessary approvals for the clinical trial have been received, e.g. regulatory authority approval and all documentation is in place (e.g. signed protocol, signed agreement with investigator). This includes any updates to the system, e.g., changes to the system resulting from a protocol amendment should only be released into production once it is confirmed that the necessary approvals have been obtained.

There should be a mechanism to record and manage defects and issues raised by the users e.g. via helpdesk or in other ways becoming known (raised by stakeholders). The sponsor/investigator should be informed of any known defects that could potentially constitute a serious breach to ICH-GCP and/or the clinical trial protocol (e.g. through release notes and ad hoc as they arise). Defects/issues should be fixed in a timely manner.

At the end of testing and prior to release to production a validation report should be prepared and approved. At the time of release training materials and other resources for users should be available.

A2.7 Periodic review (maintenance of the validated state)

Validation of a system should be maintained throughout the full life cycle. Periodic (e.g. yearly or related to major updates) system reviews should be conducted to assess and document whether the system can still be considered to be in a validated state, or whether individual parts or the whole system needs re-validation. Depending on the system type and application, the following elements should be evaluated and concluded on, both individually and combined:

- (changes to) hardware/infrastructure;
- changes to operating system/platform;
- application changes;
- configurations, customisations;

- deviations (or recurrence of);
- security incidents;
- newly identified risks;
- new regulation;
- system accesses;
- and failed login attempts.

A2.8 Change control

There should be a formal change control process. Requests for change should be documented and should include details of change, risk-assessment (e.g. for data integrity, regulatory compliance) and testing requirements as a minimum. For trial specific configurations, the change request should include the details of the new version of the protocol if the request relates to a protocol amendment. As part of the change control process, all documentation should be updated as appropriate (e.g. specification documents, training materials, user manuals, test scripts) and a report of the validation activities prepared and approved prior to release into production. There should be version control of the system.

The sponsor/investigator should ensure that any changes to the system do not result in data integrity or safety issues or interfere with the conduct of an ongoing trial. Any updates that result in the changes of a form should be highlighted and provided to the investigator in a comprehensive way and it should be clear when they were implemented.

Any changes to the system itself should be documented, should be attributable and if necessary, the change should be explained. Any significant changes to a data capture system should be authorised in writing by an appropriate decision maker.

Documentation on validation of previous or discontinued versions of systems should be retained (see "Guideline on the content, management and archiving of the clinical trial master file (paper and/or electronic), (EMA/INS/GCP/856758/2018) section 6.3)

The eCRF and/or electronic data collection (EDC) system can change during the course of the trial. Examples could be correction of a question text, change of a visibility rule for a conditional question or the change in number or type of list items in a dropdown field. Any such changes could influence contextual properties that may change data entry behaviour, data interpretation and create issues for statistical analysis and should be sufficiently documented as part of the audit trail system.

Annex 3 User management

A3.1 User management

Organisations should grant, change and revoke system accesses in a timely manner as people begin, change and end their involvement/responsibility in the management and/or conduct of the clinical trial projects.

A3.2 User reviews

At any given time, an overview of current and previous access, roles and permissions should be available from the system. This information concerning actual users and their privileges on systems should be verified at suitable intervals to ensure that only necessary and approved users have access and that their roles and permissions are appropriate. There should be timely removal of access no longer required, or no longer permitted.

A3.3 Segregation of duties

System access should be granted based on a segregation of duties and also the responsibilities of the investigator and the sponsor as outlined in ICH-GCP. For example, a person employed by the sponsor/CRO should not have edit rights to data entered into the eCRF by the investigator.

Users with privileged or "admin access" typically have extensive rights in the system (operating system or application), including but not limited to changing any system setting (e.g. system time), defining or removing users (incl. "admin users"), activate or deactivate audit trail functionality (and sometimes even edit audit trail information) and making changes to data that are not captured in the audit trail (e.g. backend table changes in the database(s)). Users with privileged access should be sufficiently independent from and not be involved in the management and conduct of the clinical trial and in the generation, modification and review of data.

Users of computer clients (e.g. personal computer (PC)) which record or contain critical clinical trial data, should generally not have "admin access" to this equipment and when this is not the case, it needs to be justified.

Unblinded information should only be accessible to pre-identified user roles.

A3.4 Least-privilege rule

System access should be assigned according to the least-privilege rule, i.e. users should not have higher privileges and more access rights than actually necessary for them to undertake their required duties.

A3.5 Individual accounts

All system users should have individual accounts. Sharing of accounts (group accounts) is considered unacceptable and a violation of data integrity and ICH-GCP principles as data should be attributable.

A3.6 Unique user names

System user names should be unique within the system and across full life cycle of the system. User names should be traceable and those assigned to human users should be readily distinguishable from machine accounts.

Annex 4 Security

A4.1 Ongoing security measures, including management of firewalls, patching management, penetration testing etc.

The sponsor/investigator should maintain a security system that prevents unauthorised access to the data (ICH-GCP 2.11, 5.5.3 (d)). Threats and attacks on systems containing clinical trial data and corresponding measures to ensure security of such systems are constantly evolving, especially for systems and services being provided over or interfacing the internet.

A4.2 Physical security

Computerised systems and media containing clinical trial data should be protected against physical damage, unauthorised physical access and unavailability.

The extent of security measures depends on the criticality of the data. In the case where data are transferred from one system to another (e.g. from a hand-held device or local drive to a server), it also depends on whether the transfer has already taken place and on the availability of backups.

The responsible party should ensure an adequate level of security for datacentres as well as for local hardware such as USB drives, hard disks, tablets or laptops.

At a datacentre (e.g. hosting an eCRF system), physical access should be limited to the necessary minimum and be controlled by means of two-factor authentication. The data centre should be constructed to minimise the risk of flooding, there should be pest control and effective measures against fire, i.e. cooling, and fire detection and suppression. There should be emergency generators and uninterruptable power supplies (UPS) together with redundant IP providers. Disposed media (e.g. hard disks) should be properly destructed before being disposed of and in case of co-location (see Cloud services), the servers should be locked up in cages to prevent access from other clients.

Data should be replicated at an appropriate frequency from the primary data centre to a secondary failover site at an adequate physical distance to minimise the risk that the same fire or disaster destroys both datacentres.

A4.3 Firewalls

In order to provide a barrier between a trusted internal network and an untrusted external network and to control incoming and outgoing network traffic (from certain IP addresses, destinations, protocols, applications, or ports etc.), firewall rules should be defined. These should be defined as strict as practically feasible, only allowing necessary and permissible traffic.

CH 29

As firewall settings tend to change over time (e.g. as software vendors and technicians need certain ports to be opened due to installation or maintenance of applications), firewall rules and settings should be periodically reviewed. This should ensure that firewall settings match approved firewall rules and the continued effectiveness of a firewall.

A4.4 Vulnerability management

Vulnerabilities in computer systems can be exploited to perform unauthorised actions, such as modifying data or making data inaccessible to legitimate users. Such exploitations could occur in operating systems for servers, computer clients, tablets and mobile phones, routers and platforms (e.g. databases). Consequently, relevant security patches for platforms and operating systems should be applied in a timely manner, according to vendor recommendations.

Systems, which are not timely security patched according to vendor recommendations, should be effectively isolated from computer networks and the internet.

A4.5 Platform management

Platforms and operating systems for critical applications and components should be updated in a timely manner according to vendor recommendations, in order to prevent their use in the unsupported state. Unsupported platforms and operating systems, for which no security patches are made, are in a vulnerable state. Qualification of applications on the new platforms and operating systems and of the migration of data should be planned ahead and completed in due time prior to expiry of the supported state.

Unsupported platforms and operating systems should be effectively isolated from computer networks and the internet.

It should be ensured that software used in clinical trials, remains compatible with any changes to platforms/operating systems in order to avoid unintended impact on the conduct/management of the clinical trial due to interruption of functionality or requirements for alternative software and data migration.

A4.6 Use of bi-directional devices (e.g. USB devices)

Uncontrolled use of bi-directional devices, which come from or have been used outside the organisation, may intentionally or unintentionally introduce malware and impact data integrity, availability and rights of trial participants. Mitigation using updated antivirus software scans may be attempted.

A4.7 Anti-virus software

Software should be continuously updated with the most recent virus definitions and activated on systems containing critical data in order to identify, pacify and remove known computer viruses. Systems compatibility should be taken into account and monitored prior to the installation of antivirus software.

Part of using anti-viral software is the need to monitor and review the task manager processes to be alerted in case the anti-virus process is terminated.

A4.8 Penetration testing

For systems facing the internet, penetration testing should be conducted at regular intervals in order to evaluate the adequacy of security measures and identify vulnerabilities in system security (e.g. code injection), including the potential for unauthorised parties to gain access to and control of the system and its data. Vulnerabilities identified, especially those related to a potential loss of data integrity, should be addressed and mitigated in a timely manner.

If the security measure requires input data modifications, reversibility and traceability should be considered as some inputs require full traceability (e.g. source data).

A4.9 Intrusion detection system

An effective intrusion detection system should be implemented on systems facing the internet in order to monitor the network for successful or unsuccessful intrusion attempts from external parties and for the design and maintenance of adequate information technology (IT) security procedures.

A4.10 Internal activity monitoring

An effective system for detecting any unusual activity from a user (e.g. excessive file downloads, copying or moving or backend data changes) should be in place.

A4.11 Security incident management

Organisations managing clinical trial data should have and work according to a procedure defining and documenting security incidents, rating criticality of incidents, and where applicable, implementing effective corrective and preventive actions to prevent recurrence. In cases where data have been, or may have been, compromised, the procedures should include ways to report incidents to relevant parties where applicable. When using a third party, the contract should ensure that incidents are escalated to the sponsor in a timely manner for the sponsor to be able to report serious breaches as applicable.

A4.12 Authentication method

The method of authentication on a system should positively identify users with a high degree of certainty. Methods should be determined based on the type of information in the system. As a minimum, an acceptable method would be user ID and password. Further augmentation depends upon criticality of data risk assessment and applicable legislation (including data protection legislation)

A4.13 Remote authentication and password managers Remote authentication

Remote access to clinical trial data, e.g. to cloud-based systems, raises specific challenges. The level of security should be proportionate to the sensitivity and confidentiality of the data (e.g. nominative data in electronic health records are highly sensitive) and to the access rights to be granted (read-only, write or even "admin" rights). A risk-based approach should be used to define the type of access control required. Depending on the level of risk, a two-factor authentication may be appropriate or necessary.

Two-factor authentication implies that two of the following three factors be used:

- something you know, e.g. a user ID and password
- something you have, e.g. a security token, a certificate or a mobile phone and an SMS pass code

- something you are, e.g. a fingerprint or an iris scan (biometrics)

The risk evaluation should take into consideration the potential use of password managers on devices or computers. Password managers represent an increased risk where the use of personal or otherwise uncontrolled equipment to access the computerised system is allowed or where access rights to the equipment itself are insufficiently implemented and controlled. Insufficiently or non-protected user accounts may result in unauthorised access to clinical trial computerised systems due to the automatic suggestion of user credentials. A policy or contractual arrangements banning the use of password managers would not be considered to provide a sufficient level of security, particularly if personal equipment is used.

The risk linked to the potential hacking of user equipment or to key loggers should also be considered.

A4.14 Password policies

Formal procedures for password policies should be implemented. The policies should include but not necessarily be limited to length, complexity, expiry, login attempts, and logout reset. The policies should be enforced by systems and verified during system qualification.

A4.15 Password confidentiality

Passwords should be kept confidential, sharing of passwords is unacceptable and a violation of data integrity. This implies that after a password is received from a manager or "system admin" (e.g. after a vacation), a new password should be set by the user. This should be mandated by the system.

A4.16 Inactivity logout

Systems should include an automatic inactivity logout, which logs out a user after a defined period of inactivity. The inactivity period should be hardcoded, or set by the "system admin", the user should not be able to set the inactivity logout time (outside defined and acceptable limits) or deactivate the functionality. Upon inactivity logout, a re-authentication should be required (e.g. entry of password).

A4.17 Date and time

Where the system captures date, time and time zone and/or the date, time and time zone are required for reconstructions of activities, procedures should be in place to ensure to be consistent irrespective of location and not to be subject to amendment by users (e.g. universal time coordinated (UTC)). This information should be linked to the data as part of the metadata and available throughout the retention period.

A4.18 Remote connection

When remotely connecting to systems over the internet, a secure and encrypted protocol (virtual private network (VPN) and/or hypertext transfer protocol secure (https)) should be used.

Annex 5 Requirements related to specific types of systems, processes and data.

All computerised systems used in clinical trials should fulfil the requirements described in the previous sections, and the general principles apply. The following sub-sections define more specific wording for selected types of systems where the GCP Inspectors' Working Group (GCP-IWG) has found that supplemental guidance is needed e.g. because the type of data collection method relatively new. For eTMFs and interactive response technology (IRT) systems, please refer to separate guidelines on these topics.[1] A few additional clarifications to IRT systems have been added below.

The use of EDC tools offers a wide variety of approaches to increase overall data quality by procedures such as automatic edit checks, validation checks, assisting information and workflow control. However, such approaches should always be limited by necessity, it should not bias data and it should be detectable e.g. when data are changed as a result of a fired edit check and/or notification.

Data entered into the EDC tools should not be changed by an automatic process or by the sponsor (e.g. edit rights given to make "self-evident" corrections) without timely authorisation by the investigator (or delegate) and such changes should be documented. Fields should not be prepopulated or automatically filled in, unless these fields are not editable and derived from already entered data (e.g., body surface area). Any algorithm used for such a process should be documented and validated. Data entered previously into the system may be used to repopulate fields.

Data entered into the eCRF should be consistent with source data, where applicable, and therefore data should be coded in a manner that shows the relation between the original source entry and the coded value. Categorical coding should be pre-specified. However, source data directly entered into an eCRF should be saved in a one to one correspondence.

Completion checks, range checks, sequence checks etc. should be considered to ensure data quality.

A5.1 Electronic clinical outcome assessment (eCOA)

eCOA employs technology for (direct) reporting of outcomes by investigators and trial participants/care givers. This guideline does not address the clinical validation or appropriateness of particular eCOA systems. The guideline aims at addressing the topics specifically related to these eCOA tools being electronic and also to those related to the situation where Bring-your-own-device (BYOD) solutions are used.

Data can be collected by any of several technologies and will be transferred to a server. Data should be made available to involved/responsible parties such as the PIs e.g. via portals, display

1 https://www.ema.europa.eu/en/documents/scientific-guideline/guideline-content-management-archiving-clinical-trialmaster-file-paper/electronic_en.pdf
https://www.ema.europa.eu/en/documents/scientific-guideline/reflection-paper-use-interactive-response-technologiesinteractive-voice/web-response-systems-clinical-trials-particular-emphasis-handling-expiry-dates_en.pdf

of source data on the server, generation of alerts and reports etc. These processes (including access controls) should be controlled and clearly described in the protocol, and all parts of the processes should be validated.

EDC methods may offer more convenience to some trial participants and may increase participant compliance, data quality, reduce variability, reduce the amount of missing data (allowing automatic reminders) and potentially reduce data entry errors. Of importance, whilst use of EDC might be of benefit to some trial participants and patient groups, it may be inconvenient for or even excluding others. This should be considered when using any EDC tool and the choice should be justified.

A5.1.1 Electronic patient reported outcome (ePRO)

A5.1.1.1 System design

The ePRO should be designed to meet the specific needs of the end users. It is recommended to involve site staff and the intended trial participant/patient population in the development e.g. demonstrated usability (such as UAT).

One of the advantages of using an ePRO system is the recording of time stamps of data entry. The date and time should record data entry time and not only data submission/transmission time.

Trial participants should have access to their own previously entered data, unless it is against the purpose of the clinical trial design or the protocol. Therefore, the length of time that data are viewable by the participant should be considered when designing the EDC tool. Decisions about 'view-period' for participants should be based on considerations regarding risk for bias on data to be entered but also considering that if view of recently entered data is not possible by the participant, then there is a risk that the participant could forget if relevant data have been collected – especially if the planned entry is not foreseeable and e.g. just requires e.g. input once daily but e.g. event-driven.

Logical checks should be in place to prevent data changes unreasonable "time travel" e.g. going back (months, years back in time) or forth into the future based on the protocol design.

It is recommended to include a scheduling/calendar component with alerts or reminders to ensure compliance.

A5.1.1.2 Data collection and data transfer

The same GCP standards apply for data collected via ePRO as for any other method of data collection, i.e. that there are processes in place to ensure the quality of the data, and that all clinical information is recorded, handled and stored in such a way as to be accurately reported, interpreted and verified.

An ePRO system typically requires an entry device. Data saved in the device is the original record created by the trial participant. Since the data stored in a temporary memory are at higher risk of physical loss, it is necessary to transfer the data to a durable server at an early stage, by a validated procedure and with appropriate security methods during data transmission. Data should be transferred to the server by a pre-defined timing and procedure. The data saved in the device are considered source data. After the data are transferred to the server via a validated procedure, the data on the server are considered a certified copy. The sponsor should identify the source documents in the protocol and document the timing and locations of source document storage.

Besides the general requirements on audit trail (please refer to section 6.2), if an ePRO system is designed to allow data correction, the data corrections should be documented and an audit trail should record if data saved in the device are changed before submission (if changeable).

Data loss on devices should be avoided. Procedures should be in place to prevent data loss if web access to the trial participant reported data is interrupted, (e.g. server outage, battery in device drained, loss of or unstable internet connection). There should be a procedure in place to handle failed or interrupted data transmission.

It should be ensured/monitored that transmission of data from the ePRO devices are successfully completed.

Important actions should be time stamped in an unambiguous way, e.g. data entries, transfer times and volume (bytes).

A5.1.1.3 Investigator access to ePRO data

Unlike data collected in the eCRF, ePRO source data are not managed (although available to review) by the investigator and are often hosted by a contracted party. The investigator is responsible for the trial participants' data (including metadata). Those should consequently be made available to the investigator in a timely manner. This will allow the investigator to fulfil her or his responsibilities for oversight of safety and compliance and thereby minimise the risk of missed adverse events or missing data.

A5.1.1.4 Data changes

As stated in section 6.2.1 on audit trails, a procedure should be in place to address the situation when a data originator (e.g. investigator or trial participant) realises that she/he has submitted incorrect data by mistake and wants to correct the recorded data.

Data changes for ePRO typically differ from that of other EDC tools because trial participants may not have access to correct data in the application. Hence, procedures need to be in place in order to implement changes when needed. This could be in the form of data clarification processes initiated by trial participants on their own reported data or initiated by investigators.

Data reported should always be reliable and it is not acceptable that data clarification procedures introduced by the sponsor or vendor whether or not described in the protocol do not allow for changes in trial participant data when justified e.g. if the trial participant realises that data has not been entered correctly.

It is expected that the possibility for changes is implemented based on a justified and trial-specific risk assessment and that any changes are initiated in a timely manner by the participant or site staff and in case of the latter is based on solid source at investigator sites e.g. phone notes or emails from trial participants documenting the communication between sites and trial participants immediately after the error was made/discovered. Preferably such notes should be signed by the trial participant to avoid that sites are manipulating data e.g. to make participants/patients eligible for trial participation.

One of the advantages of direct data entry by the trial participant is that recall bias is minimised as the data are entered contemporaneously. Consequently, corrections should not be done at a much later stage without good reason and justification. Whether collected by paper or electronic means, the regulatory requirements are that all clinical data should be accurately reported and should be verifiable in relation to clinical trials.

It is expected that the amount of changes to ePRO data is limited; however, this requires both designs of ePROs that are appropriate to ensure proper understanding by trial participants and appropriate training of trial participants, thereby avoiding entry errors.

A5.1.1.5 Fall back procedures and tracking of devices

There should be fall-back procedures in place in case of device malfunction.

There should be an accountability log of devices handed out to trial participants and this should include the device identification number in order to be reconciled to a particular trial participant. In case of device malfunction or loss of devices, there should be a procedure in place to replace the device and to merge data from several devices of a trial participant without losing traceability.

A5.1.1.6 User name and password

The trial participant's passwords should only be known to the trial participant.

The authentication information should not contain any information, which would allow breach of confidentiality, e.g. trial participants name, trial participants email address, social security number.

In relation to BYOD, sponsors should ensure that basic user access controls are implemented. When mobile applications are used for data entry, access controls need to be in place to ensure attributability. See section A5.1.3 for further guidance on BYOD.

A5.1.1.7 Training

Training should be customised to meet the specific needs of the end users.

A5.1.1.8 User support

Support to the trial participant and the trial site staff should be readily available (e.g. support via phone or e-mail) in order to ensure reliable data and minimise the risk of data loss. Trial participant confidentiality should be ensured at all times, including in the communication process.

Procedures for service desk, user authentication and access restoration should be implemented.

A5.1.2 Clinician reported outcome

Tools to directly collect clinician reported outcomes should generally follow the same requirements as those described for systems in general. The main difference is the user (investigators, other clinicians or independent assessors instead of trial participants), not the system requirements. Special attention should be given to access control in order to avoid jeopardising any blinding, when relevant.

A5.1.3 Bring your own device (BYOD)

Both ePRO data and clinician reported outcome data may be captured by privately owned devices such as mobile phones, tablets, computers and wearables, i.e. BYOD. This can either be achieved via a web application with pre-installed browser applications or by installing an application on the device. Solutions can be either a combination of web and application (hybrid) or coded to the device operating system (native).

It is necessary to provide alternative ways of data collection e.g. devices provided by the sponsor as the trial participants should not be excluded from a trial if not capable or willing to use BYOD.

A5.1.3.1 Technical and operational considerations

When decided to use BYOD, a multitude of devices and operating systems should be considered for the application. It should be ensured that it is not exclusive to one operating system. Qualification activities should also take things like upgrade of operating systems and different screen sizes into account e.g. for visual analogue scales (VAS), where the general presentation should be the same irrespective of device. Because the platform of the BYOD is not under the control of the sponsor, an assessment for updates and change of service terms for the applications and the web-applications should be done.

Measures should be in place to ensure that users cannot change critical settings including captured date and time or deactivate inactivity log out (refer to A4.17 and A4.18).

For each system intended, proper mitigation strategies should be in place and each system configuration should be validated.

Terms of service of the platform provider can be in conflict with ICH-GCP and (local) legal requirements; where such conflicts exist, the device may not be suitable for use.

Procedures and processes should be in place for when the trial participant discontinues the clinical trial or the clinical trial ends and access to applications and data collection should be terminated.

A5.1.3.2 1475 Considerations on security and trial participant confidentiality

The confidentiality of data that could identify trial participants should be protected, respecting the privacy and confidentiality rules in accordance with the applicable regulatory requirements.

A number of challenges for BYOD are related to security and security should be ensured at all levels (mobile device security, data breach security, mobile application security etc.). As mobile devices may be lost or stolen and it cannot be ensured that the trial participants use passwords to secure their device, the security and access control should be at the application level.

Application and operating system (OS) vulnerabilities should be described and the risk minimised. Intentional or unintentional exposure of the data within the app should be prevented and local storage of data should be minimised.

The hardware, operating system and apps are all factors that affect the total security status of the device, and there should be procedures in place regarding e.g., when trial participants/clinicians use less secure devices. Minimum supported device requirements should be defined for personal devices when relevant (e.g. memory capacity, operating system). These should take into account which operating systems are still supported by the manufacturer and for which bug fixes and security patches are released when relevant.

Data capture by BYOD may require the device to be identified to ensure data attributability, including runtime environment information and physical properties (e.g. device details, application details, operation system (OS) details, browser details, screen size, IP address, international mobile equipment identity (IMEI)/ mobile equipment identifier (MEID) number). Only information that is needed for proper identification of and service to the user should be obtained. Trial participant confidentiality should be ensured if device identification information is stored. Access to the application and trial participant data may be protected with multiple barriers (e.g. unlock mobile phone, open application, access data).

If the device's inbuilt possibilities for auto fill formula data and/or using photo, video, and global positioning system (GPS) data etc. are used, this should be described and justified in the protocol, and procedures and processes should ensure that only protocol mandated data are collected and that the confidentiality of data is maintained. In accordance with the principle of 'data minimisation' mobile applications should only collect data which are necessary for the purposes of the data processing (i.e. the performance of the trial) and not access any other information on the person's device. For example, location data should only be collected if this is necessary for the clinical trials activities and the trial participant must be informed about this in the patient information and agree to this in the consent form.

If an app is to be installed on a BYOD, the privacy labels/practices (e.g. regarding tracking data, linked and not linked data) should be clearly communicated to the trial participant upfront.

A5.1.3.3 Installation and support

When using an application, it is recommended that well trained staff assist in the installation even if the application is available through an app-store or service provider platform.

Independently on whether the BYOD solution is based on an application installed on the device or a website/web application, the software and the use should be explained thoroughly in a user manual. Users of the system should have access to user support e.g. from a help desk. There should be a procedure in place in case an application cannot be installed, or the web service is unavailable on a device, if the device has malfunctioned or the participant has purchased a new device. Helpdesk contacts by users should be logged (participant or site staff study ID, purpose of contact, etc.) with due consideration of protecting participant information.

The software and software installation should not limit or interfere with the normal operations of the device. Any unavoidable limitation to the device after installation should be part of the informed consent material.

A5.1.3.4 Ownership of applications and data

Ownership of the clinical trial application and data should be specified.

A5.2 Interactive Response Technology (IRT) System

The GCP-IWG published separate a reflection paper on use of IRT in clinical trials.

A5.2.1 Testing of functionalities

In addition to the content of the IRT reflection paper and section A2.5, A2.8, of the present guideline, sponsors should also consider the issues mentioned below when writing test scripts for UAT.

A5.2.1.1 Dosage calculations

CH 29

Where dosage calculations/assignments are made by the IRT system based on user entered data (e.g., trial participant body surface area or weight), and look up tables (dosage assignment based on trial participant parameters), the tables should be verified against the approved protocol and input data used to test allocations, including test data that would be on a borderline between differing doses. Assigning the incorrect dosage to a trial participant is a significant risk to safety and well-being and should be thoroughly mitigated.

A5.2.1.2 Stratified randomisation

Where the randomisation is stratified by factors inputted by the user, all the combinations of the strata should be tested to confirm the allocation from the correct randomisation table is occurring.

A5.2.1.3 Blinding and unblinding

Unblinded information should only be provided and accessible to pre-identified user roles.

A5.2.2 Emergency unblinding

The process for emergency unblinding should be tested.

Prior to the investigational medicinal product (IMP) being available/shipped at/to the clinical trial site, either of the following should be undertaken:

- Where emergency unblinding is undertaken by a site user, there should be confirmation that the investigator (or delegated personnel) who has the access role and permissions has successfully accessed the system.
- Where the unblinding is undertaken via a specific username/password contained in a sealed envelope provided to the site, its receipt by the site should be documented and confirmed.
- If alternative ways are used for unblinding, those processes should be established as well.

A5.2.3 IRT used for collection of 1550 clinical data from the trial site

Where the IRT system is collecting clinical data, important data should be subject to source data verification and/or reconciliation with the same data collected in the eCRF. For example, the data used for stratification may also be contained in the eCRF. Where clinical data is entered into the IRT system and integrated to the eCRF (electronic data transfer to eCRF) the IRT system meets the definition of an (e)CRF set out in ICH-GCP. In such cases, the additional functionality and GCP requirement concerning eCRFs should be addressed in the IRT system requirements and UAT. For example, investigator control of site entered data, authorisation of data changes by the investigator, authorisation of persons entering/editing data in the eCRF by the investigator.

A5.2.4 Web-based randomisation

Where justified, sponsor or investigator/sponsor may also use a web-based application to create randomisation lists for clinical trials. When using a web-service, the process to evaluate the suitability of the system and GCP compliance as well as the fit-for purpose of the created randomization list should be documented. Where possible the version of the service used, and the seed should be maintained.

Ad hoc randomization via a web-service is not recommended as randomization distribution is unknown and the seed may vary.

The sponsor should ensure that the process of randomisation can be reconstructed via retained documentation and data and that a final randomisation schedule, produced prior to the clinical trial commencing is retained.

A5.3 Electronic informed consent

Ethics committees will review all material related to the informed consent process. Before implementation of an electronic consent procedure is considered, the sponsor should clarify legality and GCP compliance with each country's ethics committees and national regulatory authorities.

The principles of consent as set out in legislation and guidance should be the same whether the process involves a computerised system or not. A hybrid approach could be considered, where national requirements preclude certain parts of an electronic informed consent procedure. At present, in some countries the failure to provide "written on paper" proof of trial participant's informed consent is considered a legal offense.

An electronic informed consent refers to the use of any digital media (e.g. text, graphics, audio, video, podcasts or websites) to firstly convey information related to the clinical trial to the trial participant and secondly document informed consent via an electronic device (e.g. mobile phones, tablets or computers). The electronic informed consent process involves electronic provision of information, the procedure for providing the opportunity to inquire about details of the clinical trial including the answering of questions and/or electronic signing of informed consent. For example, it would be possible for the trial participant to sign informed consent on a paper form following provision of the information electronically or the information and informed consent could be entirely electronic. If using a "wet ink" signature together with an electronic informed consent document (a hybrid approach), the patient information, the informed consent document and the signature should be indisputably linked e.g. by the use of a hash code.

Investigators should be aware that the use of electronic methods may unintentionally discriminate against people who are not comfortable with or who cannot use such technology, and this could introduce bias into the clinical trial. Alternative methods for provision of information and documentation of informed consent should be available for those unable or unwilling to use electronic methods. Any sole use of electronic informed consent should be justified and described in the protocol.

Face to face communication between one or more members of the research team and the potential trial participant is considered essential and could in some countries be mandatory at least for some specific situations (e.g. due to the characteristics of the disease or of trial).

A5.3.1 Provision of information about the clinical trial

The trial participants should have been informed of the nature, objectives, significance, implications, the expected benefit, risks and inconveniences of the clinical trial in an interview with the investigator, or another member of the investigating team delegated by the PI. The interview should take into account the individual disposition (e.g. comorbidities, patient references etc.) of the potential participant. This interview should allow interaction, the asking of questions and allow confirmation of the trial participant's identity and not just simply the provision of information. The interview should be conducted in person or, it could be done remotely where this can be justified and where allowed nationally and if approved by an ethics committee using electronic methods that allow for two-way communication in real time. Whichever method is used it is important that confidentiality is maintained, and therefore communication methods should be private/secure. Consideration should be given as to how the system would be presented documentarily to the ethics committee for approval such that it captures the functionality of the systems and the experience of the potential trial participant using it.

Provision of the information electronically may improve the trial participants' understanding of what taking part in the clinical trial will involve. Computerised system could facilitate features to assess the participant's understanding e.g. via questions at key points, which test the trial participants' understanding as they work their way through the information. This in turn can be used to highlight areas of uncertainty to the person seeking consent so that they can cover this area in more detail with the trial participant.

A5.3.2 Written informed consent

The informed consent of the trial participant should be in writing and electronic methods for documenting the trial participants informed consent should meet this requirement (ICH-GCP 4.8.8): The informed consent form should be **signed** and **personally dated** by at least two (natural) persons; the trial participant or the trial participant's legal representative, and the person who conducted the informed consent discussion. The identity of the persons signing should be ensured.

The method used to record consent should follow national legislation with regards to e.g. acceptability of electronic signatures (see section 4.8) and in some countries "wet ink" signature will be required.

If the use of electronic signatures is allowed by a country, the following applies: date (and where appropriate, time) of signature should be entered by the corresponding signatory. There should be no ambiguity about the time of signature. The system should use UTC for timestamps for the audit trail for the action of signing and dating by the trial participant and investigator, which cannot be manipulated by system settings (e.g. time zones). In cases where entered date and time diverge from the audit trail, a query may be issued, and satisfactory explanation is expected. Any alteration in the document should invalidate the electronic signature.

If an electronic signature is used, it should be possible for monitors, auditors and inspectors to access the signed informed consent forms and all information regarding the signatures, including the audit trail.

Secure archiving should ensure availability and legibility for the required retention period.

A5.3.3 Trial participant identity

It should always be possible to verify the identity of a trial participant with documentation at the trial site. Documentation which makes it possible to demonstrate that the person entering the electronic 'signature' was indeed the signatory, is required. The electronic signing should be captured by the audit trail.

Where consent is given remotely, and the trial participant is required at some point to visit a clinical trial site for the purposes of the trial, verification should be done in person e.g. by using information from an official photo identification if such an ID document is required in the trial site country.

Instead of an electronic signature, a biometric method may be considered.

A5.3.4 Sponsor notification on the consent process

Notification to the sponsor should only contain essential, non-personal identifiable information to allow the sponsor to have an overview of how many trial participants have been enrolled in a clinical trial so far and which versions of the electronic informed consent form have been used. Remote access by the sponsor to personal identifiable information in the electronic consent system should not be permitted. Any unjustified accesses from the sponsor or 3rd parties, which lead to the disclosure of non-pseudonymised information, are likely to be viewed as infringement of data privacy laws.

A5.3.5 Trial participant confidentiality

As for all other computerised systems in clinical trials, the confidentiality of data that could identify trial participants should be protected, respecting the privacy and confidentiality rules in accordance with the applicable national and EU regulatory requirements.

A5.3.6 Trial participant access to the informed consent documentation

Potential trial participants (or, where applicable, their legal representative) should be provided with access to written information about the clinical trial prior to seeking their informed consent. The trial participant should be provided with their own copy of the informed consent documentation (including all accompanying information and all linked information) once their consent has been obtained. This includes any changes to the data/documents made during the process.

The information about the clinical trial should be as a physical hard copy or electronic copy in a form that can be downloaded. The trial participants should also be provided with a copy of their signed and dated written informed consent form (either electronically or on paper). The copy should be available directly.

A5.3.7 Investigator responsibilities

The investigator should take appropriate measures to verify the identity of the potential trial participant (see section A.5.3.3) and ensure that the participant has understood the information given. The informed consent records are essential documentation that should be available at the trial site in the investigator TMF for the required retention period (see section A5.3.9). The investigator should retain control of the informed consent process and documentation (e.g. signed informed consent forms) and ensure that personal identifiable data are not inappropriately disclosed beyond the site. The system used should not limit the investigators ability to ensure that trial participants' confidentiality is protected with appropriate access and retention controls to the system. The investigator should ensure an appropriate process for the copy of the informed consent documentation (information sheet and signed consent form) be provided to the trial participant. All versions of signed and dated electronic consents should be available to the trial participant for the duration of and after the trial. The system used should ensure that the investigator can grant access to the electronic informed consent system to the regulatory authority for inspections and that such access does not require the sponsor's involvement.

A5.3.8 Version control and availability to sites

The electronic informed consent information (electronic trial participant information and informed consent form) are subject to updates and changes during the course of the trial. Regardless of the nature of change or update, the new version containing relevant information has to be submitted to the ethics committee(s) in charge prior to its use for receiving its (their) opinion/approval. Additional information should be made available to the ethics committee(s) in charge concerning technical aspects of the electronic informed consent procedure to ensure continued understanding of the informed consent processes. Only versions approved by the ethics committee(s) in charge should be enabled and used for informed consent process and documentation. Release of electronic trial participant information and informed consent forms to the sites prior to IRB/IEC approval should be prevented. The system should prevent the use of obsolete versions of the information and informed consent document.

A5.3.9 Availability in the investigator TMF

All documents of the informed consent procedure (including all accompanying information and all linked information) are considered to be essential documents and should be archived as such. Replacement of the documents with copies thereof is only acceptable if the copies are certified copies (see section 6.5).

A5.3.10 Withdrawal from the trial

There should be procedures and processes in place for a trial participant to be able to withdraw her/his consent. If there is a possibility for the trial participant to withdraw from the trial through the computerised system, it should be ensured that such a withdrawal of consent generates an alert to the investigator in order to initiate the relevant steps as per protocol and according to the extent of withdrawal. Any withdrawal of informed consent should not affect the results of activities already carried out, such as the storage and use of data obtained on the basis of informed consent before withdrawal.

CSV

Chapter 30
European Medicines Agency
Notice to Sponsors on Validation and Qualification of Computerised Systems Used in Clinical Trials

April 7, 2020
EMA/INS/GCP/467532/2019
Inspections Office, Quality and Safety of Medicines Department

Introduction[1]

The integrity, reliability and robustness of data generated in clinical trials, e.g. data submitted to support marketing authorisation applications (MAAs), are essential to regulators. Most clinical trial data supporting MAAs are now collected through computerised data collection tools, e.g. electronic case report forms (eCRFs) and electronic patient reported outcomes (ePROs). In addition, a wide range of computerised media and systems are used in the conduct of a trial, such as safety databases, systems for electronic interactive response technology (eIRT), clinical trial management systems (CTMSs) etc., the use of which will increase in the future.

Given recent inspection findings and the implications they have had on the integrity, reliability, robustness and acceptability of data in the context of MAAs, the GCP Inspectors Working Group (IWG) in cooperation with the Committee for Medicinal Products for Human Use (CHMP) sees the need to emphasize requirements for sponsors/vendors providing computerised systems or services as well as for the qualification and validation of computerised systems used to manage clinical trial data.

Legal and Regulatory Background

- Directive 2001/20/EC, Article 2(l)
- Directive 2005/28/EC, Article 7
- Regulation (EU) No 536/2014, Recital 51, Articles 2 (30), 2 (31), 47, 71
- ICH Guideline for good clinical practice E6(R2), (EMA/CHMP/ICH/135/1995 Revision 2) sections 1.65, 2.10, 2.13, 5.2.2, 5.5.3

Both Directive 2005/28/EC and Regulation (EU) No 536/2014 contain the provision that regardless whether a sponsor delegates all or part of the clinical trial related activities to an individual or an organization, the ultimate responsibility with regards to the clinical trial conduct — in particular related to the safety of subjects and the integrity, reliability and robustness of the data generated in the clinical trial — remains with the sponsor.

1 Note: This notice should be read in conjunction with Q8 and Q9 from the good clinical practice (GCP) Q&As published on the EMA website: https://www.ema.europa.eu/en/human-regulatory/research-development/compliance/good-clinicalpractice/qa-good-clinical-practice-gcp

The EU legal framework requires that the sponsor of a clinical trial and the investigator ensure that the clinical trial is conducted in accordance to the protocol and with the principles of GCP. Furthermore, the legislation also defines the process of GCP inspection by a competent authority and the coverage of such inspections. Finally, it contains provisions that the information generated should be recorded, handled and stored adequately for the purpose of ensuring effective inspection by Member States.

Validation and Qualification of Computerised Systems

ICH E6(R2) requires that sponsors operating computerised trial data handling or computerised data systems, amongst others, shall validate these systems, maintain an audit trail for initial entry of data and any subsequent changes, maintain a security system to protect against unauthorized access and maintain a list of the individuals authorized to create, access, modify or delete data. Sponsors should set up these computerised systems in such a way that the blinding of clinical trials, when applicable, is maintained (ICH E6(R2), section 5.5.3). In addition, ICH E6(R2) requires that "systems with procedures that assure the quality of every aspect of the trials should be implemented" (section 2.13) and that "all clinical trial information should be recorded, handled and stored in a way that allows its accurate reporting, interpretation and verification" (section 2.10).

Data integrity, reliability and robustness will depend on the design and the validation status of the computerised systems used. Failure to document and therefore demonstrate the validated state of a computerised system is likely to pose a risk to data integrity, reliability and robustness, which depending on the criticality of the affected data may result in a recommendation from the GCP inspectors to the CHMP not to use the data within the context of an MAA.

The term qualification is used in this notice to describe verification of system functionality. The term validation is used to describe the process of establishing and documenting that the specified requirements of a computerised system can be consistently fulfilled from design until decommissioning of the system or transition to a new system (ICH E6(R2), section 1.65), i.e. it operates to defined specifications and defined procedures (SOPs) by a trained user.

Lack of documentation (or access to documentation) of qualification activities:

Recent inspection findings relating to the qualification and validation of computerised systems are of concern, as some sponsors have not been able to provide adequate documentation of the required qualification and validation activities for computerised data collection tools/software during inspections. Computerised systems used in clinical trials can be built by the sponsor but are more typically purchased from a vendor either under a license to use software or as part of a service purchased, which could also include e.g. trial specific builds, hosting of trial data, etc. Qualification activities would consequently be performed by the vendor, by the sponsor or by shared efforts.

The sponsor is ultimately responsible for the validation of the computerised system and for providing adequate documented evidence on the validation process.

Sponsors shall be able to provide the GCP inspectors of the EU/EEA authorities with access to the requested documentation regarding the qualification and validation of computerised systems irrespective of who performed these activities.

The sponsor may rely on qualification documentation provided by the vendor, if the qualification activities performed by the vendor have been assessed as adequate. However, the sponsor may also have to perform additional qualification (and validation) activities based on a documented risk assessment. The conditions for a sponsor to rely on a vendor's qualification documentation are described in Q&A # 9 on expectations regarding qualification documentation published on the EMA website: *https://www.ema.europa.eu/en/human-regulatory/research-development/compliance/good-clinical- practice/qa-good-clinical-practice-gcp*

If the sponsor choses to perform its own full qualification of a system purchased from a vendor, the sponsor should ensure access to the vendor's system requirement specifications to perform its own appropriate qualification of the system. This is necessary, because otherwise the sponsor would not know all the built-in system functionalities and would consequently risk unknown functionalities/actions with unknown impact on their data. Considering the relevant version and configuration of a system, qualification and validation activities should be performed on the basis of all the requirement specifications the system was initially built on and any updates.

Insufficient contractual arrangements:

Clear, written agreements should be in place to document any arrangements between the sponsor and the vendor with regards to qualification and validation. The sponsor remains responsible for ensuring that the conduct of the trial and the final data and data that are submitted to support an MAA comply with relevant legislation.

The GCP IWG has published Q&A # 8 regarding the pitfalls to be aware of regarding contractual arrangements with vendors of electronic systems used in clinical trials: *https://www.ema.europa.eu/en/human-regulatory/research-development/compliance/good-clinical- practice/qa-good-clinical-practice-gcp*

In the framework of a particular MAA, IT vendors could be inspected when they contractually assume clinical trial sponsor-related duties/activities and/or the contract between the sponsor and the vendor contains provisions for inspections/audits of duties/functions performed by the vendor.

According to Article 2(l) of the Directive 2001/20/EC and Art 2.31 of Regulation (EU) No 536/2014, inspectors should be able to inspect third parties who have trial-specific relevant documentation. As qualification documentation of a generic software (a software without trial-specific functionalities or features) does not necessarily fall into this category, the sponsor should ensure access for GCP inspectors in case any such activities are delegated to the vendor, i.e. if the sponsor relies on the vendor for documentation of system requirement specifications, test documentation, etc.

It is not acceptable to use computerised systems in clinical trials for which the validation status is not confirmed or for which appropriate documentation on system validation cannot be made available to GCP inspectors.

If appropriate contracts cannot be put in place, e.g. because a vendor does not allow provision of adequate measures as listed above (access to system requirements specifications, pre-qualification audits, access for GCP inspectors, etc.) and set out in Q&A # 8, systems from such a vendor shall not be used in clinical trials. This is irrespective of the number of sponsors making use of or having used the systems, the number of years such systems have been on the market etc., as serious GCP non-compliances and risks to data integrity, reliability and robustness could exist unnoticed if auditors and GCP inspectors are not allowed access as well as if potential serious breaches are not escalated appropriately by the vendor.

Note: This notice should be read in conjunction with Q8 and Q9 from the good clinical practice (GCP) Q&As.

Q&A: Good clinical practice (GCP)

April 2020
EMA

QUESTION 8

What are the pitfalls to be aware of regarding contractual arrangements with vendors for electronic systems in connection with clinical trials? Rev. April 2020

Sponsors contract out an increasing number of tasks in clinical trials. According to Art 7(1) of Directive 2005/28/EC and Art 71 of the Clinical Trials Regulation (EU 536/2014), any sponsor may delegate any of his trial-related tasks/functions to an individual, company, institution or organization. Nevertheless, where tasks/functions are delegated to third-party, the sponsor remains ultimately responsible for ensuring that the conduct of the trials and the final data generated by those trials comply with the requirements of Regulation (EU) 536/2014 as well as with those of Directive 2001/83/EC in the case of a marketing authorization application. This applies in particular to the safety of the subjects and the reliability and robustness of the data generated in the clinical trial.

Any trial-related tasks/functions that are delegated to a third party should be specified in a written contract and made clear between the sponsor, third party and when relevant, with the investigator (e.g. responsibilities regarding safety reporting, see Q&A 5.4 in Q&A for Clinical Trials regulation).

Sponsors typically lack sufficient internal knowledge or resources to develop and/or manage the electronic systems used in clinical trials, such as systems used for randomisation and investigational medicinal product (IMP) distribution management/accountability (Interactive Response Technology (IRT)) and/or clinical trial data capture (eCRF and ePRO systems). Therefore, very often, sponsors delegate related tasks to third parties. In these cases, sponsors remain responsible to conduct the trial in compliance with the protocol and with principles of good clinical practice (Clinical Trials Regulation Art 47, ICH E6(R2) section 5.2.1).

During good clinical practice (GCP) inspections of commercial as well as academic trials, an increasing amount of deviations from GCP standards have been identified by the inspectors in view of sub-standard contractual arrangements and related procedures. The aim of this Q&A therefore is to highlight aspects with increased frequency of deviations during GCP inspections, which therefore should be prevented by improved contracts between sponsor and vendors of IT systems.

Special consideration should be given on relevant training and quality systems. Experience suggests that vendors accepting tasks regarding electronic systems are frequently knowledgeable about IT systems and sometimes data protection legislation, but not necessarily on ICH E6(R2) requirements, quality systems, etc. This Q&A should be read together with Q&A #2, which contains more general considerations on how contracting should be addressed, and with the Notice to sponsors regarding computerised systems, published on the EMA website in the GCP Q&As section. The examples of deviations are described as bullet points under the following headings: status of contracts, distribution of delegated tasks, standards to be followed, audits and inspections, serious breaches, compliance with the protocol, output and exemptions.

Status of contracts

The following contract-related issues have been identified by GCP inspectors in the context of clinical trial inspections:

Missing contracts or only draft contracts in place.

- Contracts that were not in place at the time when the delegated tasks were initiated.
- Contracts that were not maintained/updated.
- Contracts that were expired and had not been renewed as appropriate.

Distribution of tasks

Due diligence should be exercised from the sponsor to ensure that the distribution of tasks is clearly documented and agreed by the vendor, and that each party has the control and access to the data and information that their legal responsibilities require.

GCP inspectors have observed a lack of clarity with regards to:

- which tasks were defined in the contract (tasks are sometimes partially described or not described at all);
- which party is responsible for carrying out certain task(s) regarding generating, maintaining and archiving the relevant sections of the Trial Master File (TMF): emails, meeting minutes, system documentation such as trial-specific validation documents including documentation for user acceptance testing, specific codings, SOPs, etc.); Inspectors have seen incomplete documentation provided to the sponsor or documents that have been lost due to a lack of clarity concerning the duty of document retention;
- details concerning the retention and sponsor access to non-trial-specific documentation; for example, software/system validation documents, vendor SOPs, training records, issues log/resolutions in helpdesk/IT ticket system, etc.;
- investigator's control of their data and ownership of the data;
- location of data storage and control of this, for example use of cloud solutions;
- addressing potential system "down-time" and the preparation of contingency plans.
- The possibility of sub-contracting by the vendor is not always defined, including how the sponsor maintains oversight of contracted activities.
- The clinical trial applications are frequently incomplete regarding information on contracting out electronic data capture and/or randomisation.

Standards to be followed

The following issues have been observed by GCP inspectors regarding certain standards to be adhered to by the vendor.

- It is unclear/not mentioned according to which standard the vendor will conduct its delegated sponsors' tasks, e.g. current legislation, ICH E6(R2), etc.
- Some vendors are more focused on data protection legislation than ICH E6(R2), which is reflected in standard contracts.

When the vendor fails to formally agree to comply with the applicable national and EU legislation related to the conduct of clinical trials, as well as with ICH E6(R2) requirements, the sponsor should consider whether the use of the vendor is appropriate for the clinical trial.

Audits and inspections

It is sometimes not stated that the sponsor should have access to conduct audits at the vendor site and that the vendor site could be subject to inspections (by national and international authorities) and shall accept these. In addition, it needs to be specified that vendors shall provide necessary documentation (e.g. qualification documentation prepared by the vendor in relation to the system) when requested during a GCP audit/inspection process.

Serious breaches

Reporting of "serious breaches" of GCP/Trial Protocol is already a legal requirement in certain Member States. Once the Clinical Trial Regulation (EU) No 536/2014 will apply, under Art 52 this requirement will become applicable in all Member States, and the EU portal is currently being set up to handle future notification of serious breaches in accordance with the new Regulation.

It is frequently not specified in the contract that the vendor should report potential serious breaches to the sponsor (for assessment and onward reporting) and reporting timescales for such reports are missing.

Compliance with the protocol

The protocol is part of specification for IRT/eCRF builds and therefore should be consistent with the protocol approved by the regulatory authority and given a favourable opinion by the independent ethics committee. Some contracts reviewed had inconsistencies between the protocol and the wording of the contract. Examples have also been seen where contracts referred to the version of the protocol applicable when the contract was signed, however there was no contractual requirement to cover the vendor obtaining any subsequent changes. There is a risk that the vendor could implement changes to the electronic system based on protocol amendments sent by the sponsor that have not been approved by the CA and REC. The contract or the vendor procedures should address how this would be prevented.

Output

In terms of output generated from the clinical trial, the following observations have been made by GCP inspectors:

- Information is often missing about agreed output during and after the trial. Output that in some cases has not been provided to the sponsor includes: metadata, specific types of queries, audit trails on CRF data, history and status of changes to users and their access rights, description of format for delivery of the complete database to sponsors, delivery to investigators, TMF delivery, etc. On several occasions it has been seen during inspections that pdf flat files have been delivered (e.g. the audit trails), which did not facilitate the production of a dataset that could be needed in an inspection.
- Arrangements about decommissioning of the database are not always clear, including the possibility to restore the database to its full functionality for instance for inspection purposes. This has resulted in a difference in how the system can be inspected if it occurred during the live phase of the trial compared to when the trial ended (for example, obtain access to the audit trial and exports of it as datasets).
- Arrangements to ensure an independent investigator copy of the data and to revoke investigator access to data were frequently not described.

Exemptions

It is important to be aware of any exemptions in the contract regarding specific functionalities of the data collection system.

For example, contracts stating, that a data collection system cannot be used in the handling of e.g. serious adverse events, although the same system was actually used for exactly that purpose (i.e. automatically generating emails to safety departments, etc.) have also been noted by the GCP inspectors.

Qualification and validation particulars (Amendment - April 2020)

On the basis of recent GCP inspection findings, inspectors would like to reiterate that sponsors should contractually ensure:

- That all tasks relating to a clinical trial and/or tasks relating to the qualification and validation of a system are clearly described, including which party holds documentation for which activities.
- That sponsor pre-qualification audits or other on-site pre-qualification activities and later audits of the IT vendor can take place. It should also be ensured that these audits and/or other on-site pre-qualification activities are performed with a sufficient amount of time and that sufficiently in-depth review of the vendor qualification documentation is performed in order to establish the qualification and validation status of a system.
- That GCP inspections can take place at the vendor in case the vendor is performing services for the sponsor, when the sponsor has relied fully or partly on the vendor to perform the qualification activities and when it was established during the inspection of the sponsor that part of the documentation can only be verified by inspection of the vendor.
- That any qualification documentation prepared by the vendor in relation to the system should be available for inspection.

- That the sponsor has access to the vendor's system requirement specifications, if the sponsor chose to perform all qualification activities themselves and/or if the vendor does not agree to undertake qualification activities for the sponsor. In case the sponsor retains the full duty/function for the qualification and validation of the software, the sponsor should possess all the necessary information and documentation upfront to be able to carry out this task.
- That the vendor should escalate any potential serious breaches to the sponsor in a timely manner, including security breaches that they become aware of (e.g. by notification from other sponsors using the same system), if they could have any impact on the data integrity, reliability and robustness and on the safety and rights of the trial subjects.

QUESTION 9

What is the level of validation/qualification needed to be performed by a sponsor when using an electronic system previously qualified by a provider? What documentation is required to be available for inspections? Rev. April 2020

This Q&A should be read in conjunction with the 'Reflection paper on expectations for electronic source data and data transcribed to electronic data collection tools in clinical trials ' - EMA/INS/GCP/454280/2010 and any further updates of this guidance. The Q&A aims to address the situation in which a sponsor is using a system (as intended) from a vendor, including the built-in possibilities for configuration. Further useful guidance can be found also in the notice to sponsors regarding computerised systems, published on the EMA website in the GCP Q&As section.

The system in question may be a system validated by the supplier, but installed at the sponsor, or a system provided as software-as-a-service (SaaS or cloud solution).

Different requirements will apply in cases when the sponsor is changing/adding functionalities to the system.

Today, in clinical trial settings, the use of electronic systems, e.g. for data collection, data management, safety data collection and evaluation, treatment allocation and trial management has proved to be more the standard than the exception. A considerable number of electronic Case Report Forms and applications for e.g. collecting Patient Related Outcomes or Clinical Outcome Assessments are provided by, or purchased from, vendors and are customized to varying degrees. GCP inspectors receive an increasing amount of questions from sponsors and deviations are given during GCP inspections regarding the level of validation/qualification needed to be performed by a sponsor when using a system that has already been (or is supposed to have been) validated by the supplier.

According to ICH E6(R2), sections 5.2.1 and 5.5.3.a, respectively, *"the ultimate responsibility for the quality and integrity of the trial data always resides with the sponsor"* and *"the sponsor should ensure and document that the electronic data processing system(s) conforms to the sponsors established requirements for completeness, accuracy, reliability, and consistent intended performance (i.e. validation)."*

According to ICH E6(R2), section 1.65., validation of computerised systems is "a process of establishing and documenting that the specified requirements of a computerised system can be consistently fulfilled from design until decommissioning of the system or transition to a new system."

Furthermore, it is specified that the approach to validation should be based on a risk assessment that takes into consideration the intended use of the system and the potential of the system to affect human subject protection and reliability of trial results. This risk-based approach should be informed by the following guidance given. The risk assessment should be justified by the sponsor and documented.

The sponsor is ultimately responsible for the validation of the clinical trial processes, which is supported by electronic systems and for providing sufficiently documented evidence to GCP inspectors on the validation process and the qualification of the electronic systems. The sponsor may rely on qualification documentation provided by the vendor if the qualification activities performed by the vendor have been assessed as adequate. However, the sponsor may also have to perform additional qualification/validation activities based on a documented risk assessment.

The conditions for a sponsor to use the vendor's qualification documentation include, but are not limited to, the following:

- the sponsor has a thorough knowledge about the vendor's quality system and qualification activities, which will usually be obtained through an in-depth assessment/audit;
- an assessment/audit has been performed by qualified staff, with sufficient time spent on the activities and with cooperation from the vendor;
- an assessment/audit has gone sufficiently deep into the activities and that a suitable number of examples for relevant activities have been looked at (and documented);
- the assessment/audit report determined the vendor's qualification documentation to be satisfactory or that shortcomings can be mitigated by the sponsor- e.g. that the sponsor is performing part of the qualification;
- the sponsor, or when applicable the clinical research organization (CRO) performing these activities for the sponsor, has detailed knowledge about the qualification documentation and can navigate in it and explain the activities as if they had performed the activities themselves;
- when required during a GCP inspection, the qualification documentation is made available to the inspectors in a timely manner irrespective of whether it is provided by the sponsor, CRO or the vendor.
- both the sponsor and the vendor establish full configuration management for qualification and production environments as well as establish that the sponsor can

fully account for any differences between the vendor's validation environment and the sponsor's production environment; subsequently, the sponsor should justify any differences that are considered insignificant. If not, the qualification effort potentially does not justify the use of the system.

- the sponsor performed an Installation Qualification (IQ)/Performance Qualification (PQ) of a system that depends on trained users.

Sponsors and vendors should be aware that if the electronic systems are used for generating/handling relevant clinical trial data or to maintain control and oversight of clinical trial processes, documentation regarding the qualification process and any other relevant documentation on the electronic system maintained at the sponsor level, as well as on the vendor level, and it is the sponsor's responsibility to ensure that these documents are available for inspections by Member States GCP inspectors.

Documentation regarding the validation of processes and qualification of systems is considered essential by GCP inspectors and it is likely to be requested during inspections. This is irrespective of whether the sponsor has contracted out activities related to electronic systems and whether the sponsor choses to consider as an audit the above-mentioned assessment of vendor systems/processes/documentation. GCP inspectors do not consider the documentation/report of these activities as an audit report that falls under ICH E6(R2), section 5.19.3d.

Amendment - April 2020

What should a sponsor do if the sponsor intends to submit an MAA without being able to provide documentation of qualification activities for clinical trial computerised data collection tools/software and access for inspectors is not ensured contractually?

In case a sponsor has relied fully or partly on vendor qualification efforts and documentation for any system function, the sponsor should make sure that such documentation is readily available for inspection if requested. Failure to provide access to the documentation is likely to result in critical findings that will impact the acceptability of the clinical trial data.

A sponsor should amend any contract with vendors to ensure availability of qualification documentation. If a vendor is not willing to amend the contract, the sponsor is responsible to demonstrate that the system concerned is in a validated and qualified state. In case a sponsor cannot rely on a vendor to provide documentation, the sponsor has to requalify the system on the basis of their own and of the vendor's system requirement specifications. In case the trial is ongoing, this should be done without delay; if the trial is completed, this should be undertaken prior to the submission of the MAA. A documented risk assessment is required to assess integrity risks to data captured and held by a computer system that was not in a confirmed qualified/validated state following the retrospective qualification/validation activity. Depending on the outcome of the requalification, the sponsor may need to change to a new vendor/system. The required migration of previously captured clinical trial data should be validated. Findings that are the responsibility of the sponsor are still likely to be issued for the lack of documentation and inadequate vendor assessment prior to trial initiation.

Acronym	Meaning
AAMI	Association for the Advancement of Medical Instrumentation
AI	artificial intelligence
AIMD	active implantable medical devices
ALCOA	attributable, legible, contemporaneously recorded, original, and accurate
ANSI	American National Standards Institute
API	application programing interface
BECS	blood establishment computer software
BIMO	bioresearch monitoring
BYOD	bring your own device
CAD	computer aided detection software
CBER	Center for Biologic Evaluation and Research
CDER	Center for Drug Evaluation and Research
CDRH	Center for Devices and Radiological Health
CFR	Code of Federal Regulation
CFSAN	Center for Food Safety and Nutrition
CHMP	Committee for Medicinal Products for Human Use
CMMI	capability maturity model integration
COTS	commercial off the shelf
CPP	critical process parameters
CQA	critical quality attributes
CRC	cyclic redundancy check
CRO	contract research organizations
CTMS	clinical trial management system
CVM	Center for Veterinary Medicine
DEXA	dual-energy x-ray absorptiometry
DHF	design history file
DHR	device history record
DICE	Division of Industry and Consumer Education
DICOM	Digital Imaging and Communications in Medicine
DMP	data management plan
DMR	device master record
DQ	design qualification
EBR	electronic batch record
ECG	electrocardiogram

Acronym	Meaning
eCOA	electronic clinical outcome assessment
eCRF	electronic case report form
EDC	electronic data collection
EEA	European Economic Area
eHR	electronic health records
eIRT	electronic interactive response technology
EMA	European Medicines Agency
EMC	electromagnetic compatibility
EOL	end-of-life
ePRO	electronic patient reported outcomes
eTMF	electronic trial master file
EU	European Union
FAT	factory acceptance testing
FD&C	Federal Food, Drug, and Cosmetic
FDA	Food and Drug Administration
FDAMA	FDA Modernization Act
FMEA	failure modes and effects analysis
GCAP	good corrective action practices
GCP	good clinical practice
GCP-IWG	GCP Inspectors' Working Group
GHTF	Global Harmonization Task Force
GMP	good manufacturing practice
GPS	global positioning system
GSDP	manufacturer good software development practices
HCT/P	human cells, tissues, and cellular and tissue-based product
HPLC	high performance liquid chromatography
HRQL	health-related quality of life
HTML	hypertext mark-up language
HTTPS	hypertext transfer protocol secure
IaaS	infrastructure as a service
IB	investigator brochures
ICH	International Conference on Harmonisation
IDE	Investigational Device Exemption
IEC	International Electrotechnical Commission

Acronym	Meaning
IEEE	Institute of Electrical and Electronics Engineers
IMDRF	International Medical Device Regulatory Forum
IMEI	international mobile equipment identity
IMP	investigational medical product
IMP	investigational medicinal product
IND	investigational new drug application
IOQ	installation/operation qualification
IQ/OQ/PQ	installation qualification/operational qualification/performance qualification
IQ/PQ	installation qualification/performance qualification
IRB	Institutional Review Boards
IRT	interactive response technology
ISO	International Organization for Standardization
IT	information technology
IVD	in vitro diagnostic
IVRS	interactive voice response system
IWG	Inspectors Working Group
KPI	key performance indicators
LED	light emitting diode
LIMS	laboratory information management system
LIS	laboratory information system
LR-	likelihood ratio negative
LR+	likelihood ratio positive
MDDS	medical device data system
MDR	medical device reporting
MEID	mobile equipment identifier
MES	manufacturing execution system
MAA	marketing authorisation applications
MPCR	master production and control record
NAS	network attached storage
NIST	National Institute of Standards and Technology
NNH	number needed to harm
NNT	number needed to treat
NOS	network operating system
NPV	negative predictive value

Acronym	Meaning
NUREG	Nuclear Regulatory Commission
OC	Office of the Commissioner
ODE	Office of Device Evaluation
OEM	original equipment manufacturer
OOS	out-of-specification
OR	odds ratio
ORA	Office of Regulatory Affairs
OS	operating system
OTS	off-the-shelf
PaaS	platform as a service
PACS	picture archiving and communication system
PAT	process analytical technology
PC	personal computer
PHR	personal health record
PI	principal investigator
PMA	premarket approval
PPV	positive predictive value
QA	quality assurance
QMS	quality management systems
QS	quality system
QSR	quality system record
SaaS	software as a service
SaMD	software as a medical device
SAT	site acceptance testing
SDLC	software development lifecycle processes
SDS	software design specification
SiMD	software in a medical device
SMS	short message service
SOC	system and organization controls
SOP	standard operating procedure
SOUP	software of unknown pedigree
SPLC	software product lifecycle processes
SRS	software requirements specification
SSLC	software system lifecycle processes

Acronym	Meaning
SUSAR	suspected unexpected serious adverse reaction
SWEBOK	software engineering body of knowledge
TMF	trial master file
UAT	user acceptance testing
UDI	unique device identifier
UPC	universal product code
URS	user requirements specification
USP	United States Pharmacopeia
UTC	universal time, coordinated
V&V	verification and validation
VAS	visual analogue scales
VMP	validation master plan
VPN	virtual private network
VV&T	verification, validation, and testing
WAM	work area manager

CSV

Combined Glossary

A	
accessory	*[MEDDEV 2.1/6]* an article which whilst not being a device is intended specifically by its manufacturer to be used together with a device to enable it to be used in accordance with the use of the device intended by the manufacturer of the device.
Act, The	*[21CFR§11]* the Federal Food, Drug, and Cosmetic Act (secs. 201-903 (21 U.S.C. 321-393)) *[21CFR§820]* the Federal Food, Drug, and Cosmetic Act, as amended (secs. 201-903, 52 Stat. 1040 et seq., as amended (21 U.S.C. 321-394)).
active device for diagnosis	*[MEDDEV 2.1/6]* any active medical device, whether used alone or in combination with other medical devices, to supply information for detecting, diagnosing, monitoring or treating physiological conditions, states of health, illnesses or congenital deformities.
active implantable medical device	*[MEDDEV 2.1/6]* any active medical device which is intended to be totally or partially introduced, surgically or medically, into the human body or by medical intervention into a natural orifice, and which is intended to remain after the procedure.
active medical device	*[MEDDEV 2.1/6]* any medical device operation of which depends on a source of electrical energy or any source of power other than that directly generated by the human body or gravity and which acts by converting this energy. Medical devices intended to transmit energy, substances or other elements between an active medical device and the patient without any significant change, are not considered to be active medical devices. Stand alone software is considered to be an active medical device.
active therapeutical device	*[MEDDEV 2.1/6]* any active medical device, whether used alone or in combination with other medical devices, to support, modify, replace or restore biological functions or structures with a view to treatment or alleviation of an illness, injury or handicap.
adaptive maintenance	*[IMDRF/SaMD WG/N10] [ISO/IEC 14764:2006]* the modification of a software product, performed after delivery, to keep a software product usable in a changed or changing environment.

GLOSSARY

Agency	*[21CFR§11]* the Food and Drug Administration.
algorithm	*[IMDRF/SaMD WG/N41]* a finite set of instructions (or rules) that defines a sequence of operations for solving a particular computational problem for all problem instances for a problem set.
analytical validation	*[IMDRF/SaMD WG/N41]* measures the ability of a SaMD to accurately and reliably generate the intended technical output, from the input data.
application	*[Annex 11]* Software installed on a defined platform/hardware providing specific functionality.
architecture changes	*[Deciding When to Submit a 510(k) for a Software Change]* modifications to the overall structure of the software. Examples include but are not limited to: porting to a new OS, software changes to support a new hardware platform, and new middleware.
artificial intelligence (AI)	*[EMA/226170/2021]* a very broad set of algorithms which enable computers to mimic human intelligence. It ranges from simple if-then rules and decision trees to machine learning and deep learning.
audit trail	*[Computerized Systems Used in Clinical Investigations]* a process that captures details such as additions, deletions, or alterations of information in an electronic record without obliterating the original record. An audit trail facilitates the reconstruction of the course of such details relating to the electronic record. *[Computerized Systems Used in Clinical Trials]* a secure, computer generated, time-stamped electronic record that allows reconstruction of the course of events relating to the creation, modification, and deletion of an electronic record. *[Use of Electronic Records and Electronic Signatures in Clinical Investigation - Q&A]* a process that captures details of information, such as additions, deletions, or alterations, in an electronic record without obscuring the original record. An audit trail facilitates the reconstruction of the course of such details relating to the electronic record. *[EMA/226170/2021]* (in computerised systems) a secure, computer generated, time-stamped electronic record that allows reconstruction of the course of events relating to the access, creation, modification, and deletion of an electronic record or use of the computerised system itself. "Documentation that allows reconstruction of the course of events." (ICH-GCP 1.9)

B

basic programming	*[IMDRF/SaMD WG/N41]* problem-solving process used to create a computer program.
bespoke/customized computerised system	*[Annex 11]* a computerised system individually designed to suit a specific business process.

biometrics	*[21CFR§11]* a method of verifying an individual's identity based on measurement of the individual's physical feature(s) or repeatable action(s) where those features and/or actions are both unique to that individual and measurable. *[Use of Electronic Records and Electronic Signatures in Clinical Investigation - Q&A]* a method of verifying an individual's identity based on measurements of the individual's physical features or repeatable actions where those features and/or actions are both unique to that individual and measurable (21 CFR 11.3(b)(3)).
bracketing approach	*[Annex 15]* a science and risk based validation approach such that only batches on the extremes of certain predetermined and justified design factors, e.g. strength, batch size and/or pack size, are tested during process validation. The design assumes that validation of any intermediate levels is represented by validation of the extremes. Where a range of strengths is to be validated, bracketing could be applicable if the strengths are identical or very closely related in composition, e.g. for a tablet range made with different compression weights of a similar basic granulation or a capsule range made by filling different plug fill weights of the same basic composition into different size capsule shells. Bracketing can be applied to different container sizes or different fills in the same container closure system.
bring your own device (BYOD)	*[Use of Electronic Records and Electronic Signatures in Clinical Investigation - Q&A]* the policy of permitting study participants to use their personally owned mobile devices to capture, record, and transmit data in clinical investigations.

C

case report form (CRF)	*[EMA/226170/2021]* "A printed, optical, or electronic document designed to record information to be reported to the sponsor on each trial subject." (ICH-GCP 1.11)
certified copy	*[Computerized Systems Used in Clinical Investigations] [Computerized Systems Used in Clinical Trials]* a copy of original information that has been verified, as indicated by a dated signature, as an exact copy having all of the same attributes and information as the original. *[EMA/226170/2021]* "A copy (irrespective of the type of media used) of the original record that has been verified (i.e., by a dated signature or by generation through a validated process) to have the same information, including data that describe the context, content, and structure, as the original." (ICH-GCP 1.63) *[Use of Electronic Records and Electronic Signatures in Clinical Investigation - Q&A]* a copy (paper or electronic) of original information that has been verified, as indicated by a dated signature, as an exact copy, having all of the same attributes and information as the original.

change control processes	*[Annex 15]* a formal system by which qualified representatives of appropriate disciplines review proposed or actual changes that might affect the validated status of facilities, systems, equipment or The intent is to determine the need for action to ensure and document that the system is maintained in a validated state.
claim	*[IMDRF/SaMD WG/N41]* the objective intent of the manufacturer regarding the use of a product, process or service as reflected in the specifications, instructions and information provided by the manufacturer. *(see also:* intended use/purpose*)*
clarification of requirements – no change to functionality	*[Deciding When to Submit a 510(k) for a Software Change]* changes made to clarify software requirements after a product has received premarket clearance. This clarification may be revised phrasing of an existing requirement or creation of a new requirement altogether, without changing or adding functionality.
cleaning validation	*[Annex 15]* cleaning validation is documented evidence that an approved cleaning procedure will reproducibly remove the previous product or cleaning agents used in the equipment below the scientifically set maximum allowable carryover level.
cleaning verification	*[Annex 15]* the gathering of evidence through chemical analysis after each batch/campaign to show that the residues of the previous product or cleaning agents have been reduced below the scientifically set maximum allowable carryover level.
clinical association	*[IMDRF/SaMD WG/N41]* refers to the extent to which the SaMD's output (concept, conclusion, measurements) is clinically accepted or well founded (existence of an established scientific framework or body of evidence) that corresponds accurately in the real world to the healthcare situation and condition identified in the SaMD definition statement. *(see also:* scientific validity*)*
clinical considerations	*[IMDRF/SaMD WG/N41]* aspects that can raise or lower the potential to create hazardous situations to patients.
clinical data	*[IMDRF/SaMD WG/N41]* defined as safety and/or performance information that is generated from the clinical use of a medical device.
clinical evaluation	*[IMDRF/SaMD WG/N41]* the assessment and analysis of clinical data pertaining to a medical device to verify the clinical safety, performance and effectiveness of the device when used as intended by the manufacturer.
clinical evidence	*[IMDRF/SaMD WG/N41]* an important component of the technical documentation of a medical device, which along with other design verification and validation documentation, device description, labelling, risk analysis and manufacturing information, is needed to allow a manufacturer to demonstrate conformity with the Essential Principles.

clinical outcome assessment (COA)	*[EMA/226170/2021]* COA employs a tool for direct reporting of outcomes by clinicians, trial site staff, trial participants and their caregivers. The term COA is proposed as an umbrella term to cover both single dimension and multi-dimension measures of symptoms, health-related quality of life (HRQL), health status, adherence to treatment, satisfaction with treatment, etc.
clinical performance	*[IMDRF/SaMD WG/N41]* the ability of a device to yield results that are correlated with a particular clinical condition/physiological state in accordance with target population and intended user. *(See also:* clinical validation*)*
clinical research	*[IMDRF/SaMD WG/N41]* use of clinical data generated through clinical use.
clinical trials	*[IMDRF/SaMD WG/N41]* a properly conducted clinical investigation, including compliance to the clinical investigation plan and local laws and regulations, ensures the protection of human subjects, the integrity of the data and that the data obtained is acceptable for the purpose of demonstrating conformity to the Essential Principles.
clinical usability	*[IMDRF/SaMD WG/N41]* the means by which the user and a computer system interact, in particular the use of input devices and software and the evaluation of safety considerations for device users, use environments and user interfaces.
clinical validation	*[IMDRF/SaMD WG/N41]* measures the ability of a SaMD to yield a clinically meaningful output associated to the target use of SaMD output in with the target health care situation or condition identified in the SaMD definition statement. *(see also:* clinical performance*)*
closed system	*[21CFR§11]* an environment in which system access is controlled by persons who are responsible for the content of electronic records that are on the system.
cloud computing	*[Use of Electronic Records and Electronic Signatures in Clinical Investigation - Q&A]* a model for enabling ubiquitous, convenient, on-demand network access to a shared pool of configurable computing resources (e.g., networks, servers, storage, applications, and services) that can be rapidly provisioned and released with minimal management effort or service provider interaction.
commercial off-the-shelf (COTS) software	*[Annex 11]* software commercially available, whose fitness for use is demonstrated by a broad spectrum of users.
commercial off-the-shelf (COTS) systems	*[Use of Electronic Records and Electronic Signatures in Clinical Investigation - Q&A]* commercially available electronic systems (including hardware or software) that can be purchased from third-party vendors.
commit	*[Computerized Systems Used in Clinical Trials]* a saving action, which creates or modifies, or an action which deletes, an electronic record or portion of an electronic record.

GLOSSARY

complaint	*[21CFR§820]* any written, electronic, or oral communication that alleges deficiencies related to the identity, quality, durability, reliability, safety, effectiveness, or performance of a device after it is released for distribution.
component	*[21CFR§820]* any raw material, substance, piece, part, software, firmware, labeling, or assembly which is intended to be included as part of the finished, packaged, and labeled device.
computerized system	*[Computerized Systems Used in Clinical Investigations] [Computerized Systems Used in Clinical Trials]* computer hardware, software, and associated documents (e.g., user manual) that create, modify, maintain, archive, retrieve, or transmit in digital form information related to the conduct of a clinical trial.
computing platforms general purpose (non-medical purpose)	*[IMDRF/SaMD WG/N10]* hardware and software resources (e.g. operating system, processing hardware, storage, software libraries, displays, input devices, programming languages etc.).
concurrent validation	*[Annex 15]* validation carried out in exceptional circumstances, justified on the basis of significant patient benefit, where the validation protocol is executed concurrently with commercialisation of the validation batches.
confidence interval	*[IMDRF/SaMD WG/N41]* an interval about a point estimate that quantifies the statistical uncertainty in the true value being estimated (e.g. an accuracy metric) due to variability in the subject/sample selection process. A $1 - \alpha$ level confidence interval contains the true value in $100(1 - \alpha)$ % of applications, but in any given application either contains it or does not.
continuous monitoring	*[IMDRF/SaMD WG/N41]* collecting post-market information.
continuous process verification	*[Annex 15]* an alternative approach to process validation in which manufacturing process performance is continuously monitored and evaluated.(ICH Q8)
control number	*[21CFR§820]* any distinctive symbWols, such as a distinctive combination of letters or numbers, or both, from which the history of the manufacturing, packaging, labeling, and distribution of a unit, lot, or batch of finished devices can be determined.
control strategy	*[Annex 15]* a planned set of controls derived from current product and process understanding that ensures process performance and product quality. The controls can include parameters and attributes related to drug substance and drug product materials and components, facility and equipment operating conditions, in-process controls, finished product specifications and the associated methods and frequency of monitoring and control. (ICH Q10)

core algorithm changes	*[Deciding When to Submit a 510(k) for a Software Change]* modifications made to an algorithm that directly impact or contribute to the device's intended use. Examples include: alarm algorithms on a monitor, a motor control algorithm for an infusion pump, and a detection module and measurement engine algorithm for an IVD.
corrective maintenance	*[IMDRF/SaMD WG/N10] [ISO/IEC 14764:2006]* the reactive modification of a software product performed after delivery to correct discovered problems.
cosmetic changes – no change to functionality	*[Deciding When to Submit a 510(k) for a Software Change]* changes made to the appearance of the device that do not impact the clinical use of the device. For example, changing the company logo that is displayed on the background of every screen could involve modifying multiple software modules.
critical (situation or condition)	*[IMDRF/SaMD WG/N41]* situations or conditions where accurate and/or timely diagnosis or treatment action is vital to avoid death, long-term disability or other serious deterioration of health of an individual patient or to mitigating impact to public health.
critical data	*[Use of Electronic Records and Electronic Signatures in Clinical Investigation - Q&A]* may include documentation of informed consent, drug accountability and administration information, or study endpoints and protocol-required safety assessments.
critical process parameter (CPP)	*[Annex 15]* a process parameter whose variability has an impact on a critical quality attribute and therefore should be monitored or controlled to ensure the process produces the desired quality. (ICH Q8)
critical quality attribute (CQA)	*[Annex 15]* a physical, chemical, biological or microbiological property or characteristic that should be within an approved limit, range or distribution to ensure the desired product quality. (ICH Q8)
customized electronic systems	*[Use of Electronic Records and Electronic Signatures in Clinical Investigation - Q&A]* systems and software that are specially developed for a specific user, an organization, or a business to meet specific business needs.

D

data	*[EMA/226170/2021]* (1) a broad meaning which may include documents (e.g. in electronic trial master files (eTMF)), records or any form of information. (2)measurement and assessment of variable parameters relevant to specific outcomes.
data element	*[Use of Electronic Records and Electronic Signatures in Clinical Investigation - Q&A]* a single observation associated with a subject in a clinical study. Examples include birth date, white blood cell count, pain severity measure, and other clinical observations made and documented during a study.

data element identifier	*[Use of Electronic Records and Electronic Signatures in Clinical Investigation - Q&A]* the information associated with a data element that includes the origin of the data element, the date and time of entry, and the identification number of the study subject to whom the data element applies. Once set by the electronic system, this value should not be alterable in any way.
data governance	*[EMA/226170/2021]* the totality of arrangements to ensure that data fulfils the ALCOA++ principles (see section 4.5)throughout the entire data life cycle.
data life cycle	*[EMA/226170/2021]* all processes related to the creating, recording, processing, reviewing, analysing, reporting, transferring, storing, migrating, archiving, retrieving and deleting of data.
data originator	*[Use of Electronic Records and Electronic Signatures in Clinical Investigation - Q&A]* an origination type associated with each data element that identifies the source of the data element's capture in the eCRF. This could be a person, a computer system, a device, or an instrument that is authorized to enter, change, or transmit data elements into the eCRF (also, sometimes known as an author).
deep learning (DL)	*[EMA/226170/2021]* subset of machine learning (ML) and contains algorithms which allow software to train itself by exposing multi-layered neural networks to vast amounts of data.
definition statement	*[IMDRF/SaMD WG/N41]* clear and strong statement about intended use that explains how the SaMD meets one or more of the purposes described in the definition of a medical device and describes the SaMD's core functionality.
design history file (DHF)	*[21CFR§820]* a compilation of records which describes the design history of a finished device.
design input	*[21CFR§820]* the physical and performance requirements of a device that are used as a basis for device design.
design level validation	*[Computerized Systems Used in Clinical Trials]* that portion of the software validation that takes place in parts of the software life cycle before the software is delivered to the end user.
design output	*[21CFR§820]* the results of a design effort at each design phase and at the end of the total design effort. The finished design output is the basis for the device master record. The total finished design output consists of the device, its packaging and labeling, and the device master record.
design qualification (DQ)	*[Annex 15]* the documented verification that the proposed design of the facilities, systems and equipment is suitable for the intended purpose.
design review	*[21CFR§820] [General Principles of Software Validation]* a documented, comprehensive, systematic examination of a design to evaluate the adequacy of the design requirements, to evaluate the capability of the design to meet these requirements, and to identify problems.

design space	*[Annex 15]* the multidimensional combination and interaction of input variables, e.g. material attributes, and process parameters that have been demonstrated to provide assurance of quality. Working within the design space is not considered as a change. Movement out of the design space is considered to be a change and would normally initiate a regulatory post approval change process. Design space is proposed by the applicant and is subject to regulatory assessment and approval. (ICH Q8)
design validation	*[21CFR§820]* establishing by objective evidence that device specifications conform with user needs and intended use(s). *(see also:* validation and process validation*)*
device history record (DHR)	*[21CFR§820]* a compilation of records containing the production history of a finished device.
device master record (DMR)	*[21CFR§820]* a compilation of records containing the procedures and specifications for a finished device.
device-MDDS	*[Medical Device Data Systems, Medical Image Storage Devices, and Medical Image Communications Devices]* hardware functions that are solely intended to transfer, store, convert formats, and display medical device data or results.
diagnose (SaMD output to)	*[IMDRF/SaMD WG/N41]* information provided by the SaMD will be used to take an immediate or near term action. *(see also:* treat (SaMD output to)*)*
digital signature	*[21CFR§11]* an electronic signature based upon cryptographic methods of originator authentication, computed by using a set of rules and a set of parameters such that the identity of the signer and the integrity of the data can be verified. *[Use of Electronic Records and Electronic Signatures in Clinical Investigation - Q&A]* an electronic signature based upon cryptographic methods of originator authentication, computed by using a set of rules and a set of parameters such that the identity of the signer and the integrity of the data can be verified (21 CFR 11.3(5)).
direct entry	*[Computerized Systems Used in Clinical Investigations] [Computerized Systems Used in Clinical Trials]* recording data where an electronic record is the original means of capturing the data.
drive clinical management (SaMD output to)	*[IMDRF/SaMD WG/N41]* the information provided by the SaMD will be used to aid in treatment, aid in diagnoses, to triage or identify early signs of a disease or condition will be used to guide next diagnostics or next treatment interventions.
dynamic file formats	*[EMA/226170/2021]* (e.g. spreadsheets with automatic calculations) include automatic processing and/or enable an interactive relationship with the user to change content (e.g. eCRF). A certified electronic copy may be retained in different electronic file formats to the original record, but the equivalent dynamic nature (including metadata) of the original record should be retained.

E

effectiveness	*[IMDRF/SaMD WG/N41]* when it can be determined that a device, based upon valid scientific evidence, that in a significant portion of the target population, the use of the device for its intended uses and conditions of use, when accompanied by adequate directions for use and warnings against unsafe use, will provide clinically significant results. *(see also:* safety, performance*)*
electronic case report form (e-CRF)	*[Computerized Systems Used in Clinical Trials]* an auditable electronic record designed to record information required by the clinical trial protocol to be reported to the sponsor on each trial subject.
	[Use of Electronic Records and Electronic Signatures in Clinical Investigation - Q&A] an auditable electronic record of information that generally is reported to the sponsor on each trial subject, according to a clinical investigation protocol. The eCRF enables clinical investigation data to be systematically captured, reviewed, managed, stored, analyzed, and reported.
electronic data capture (EDC) systems	*[Use of Electronic Records and Electronic Signatures in Clinical Investigation - Q&A]* electronic systems designed to collect and manage clinical trial data in an electronic format.
electronic patient diary	*[Computerized Systems Used in Clinical Trials]* an electronic record into which a subject participating in a clinical trial directly enters observations or directly responds to an evaluation checklist.
electronic record	*[21CFR§11]* any combination of text, graphics, data, audio, pictorial, or other information representation in digital form that is created, modified, maintained, archived, retrieved, or distributed by a computer system.
electronic signature	*[21CFR§11]* a computer data compilation of any symbol or series of symbols executed, adopted, or authorized by an individual to be the legally binding equivalent of the individual's handwritten signature.
electronic systems	*{Use of Electronic Records and Electronic Signatures in Clinical Investigation - Q&A]* systems, including hardware and software, that produce electronic records.
establish	*[21CFR§820]* define, document (in writing or electronically), and implement.
	[General Principles of Software Validation] define, document, and implement.
expert function software	*[MEDDEV 2.1/6]* software which is able to analyse existing information to generate new specific information according to the intended use of the software.

F

finished device	*[21CFR§820]* any device or accessory to any device that is suitable for use or capable of functioning, whether or not it is packaged, labeled, or sterilized.
functionality	*[IMDRF/SaMD WG/N41]* identifies the critical features/functions of the SaMD that are essential to the intended significance of the information provided by the SaMD to the healthcare decision in the intended healthcare situation or condition.

G

general wellness products	*[General Wellness: Policy for Low Risk Devices]* products that meet the following two factors: (1) are intended for only general wellness use, as defined in this guidance, and (2) present a low risk to the safety of users and other persons.
Global Harmonization Task Force (GHTF)	*[IMDRF/SaMD WG/N41]* a voluntary group of representatives from national medical device regulatory authorities and industry representatives. GHTF was disbanded in 2012 and its mission has been taken over by the IMDRF.
good documentation practice	*[EMA/226170/2021]* a standard for creation and maintenance of documentation in order to ensure its integrity. It includes, but is not limited to, that a record is made at the time of the corresponding event, that documents are printed or written (e.g. signed) with indelible and lasting ink, that critical entries are verified by a second person, that pages (e.g. in notebooks) are numbered, that documents, where applicable, are reviewed, approved, signed and dated by appropriate personnel, and that any later alterations are made as 'GxP corrections'.

H

handwritten signature	*[21CFR§11]* the scripted name or legal mark of an individual handwritten by that individual and executed or adopted with the present intention to authenticate a writing in a permanent form. The act of signing with a writing or marking instrument such as a pen or stylus is preserved. The scripted name or legal mark, while conventionally applied to paper, may also be applied to other devices that capture the name or mark.
hazard	*[Off-The-Shelf Software Use in Medical Devices]* a possible source of danger or a condition that could result in human injury.
hazard analysis	*[Off-The-Shelf Software Use in Medical Devices]* identification of hazards and their initiating causes.
hazard mitigation	*[Off-The-Shelf Software Use in Medical Devices]* reduction in the severity of the hazard, the likelihood of the occurrence, or both.
human cell, tissue, or cellular or tissue-based product (HCT/P)	*[21CFR§820]* (regulated as a device) means an HCT/P as defined in 1271.3(d) of 21 CFR Chapter I that does not meet the criteria in 1271.10(a) and that is also regulated as a device.

human cell, tissue, or cellular or tissue-based product (HCT/P) *(cont'd)*	*[21CFR§1271.3(d)]* articles containing or consisting of human cells or tissues that are intended for implantation, transplantation, infusion, or transfer into a human recipient. Examples of HCT/Ps include, but are not limited to, bone, ligament, skin, dura mater, heart valve, cornea, hematopoietic stem/progenitor cells derived from peripheral and cord blood, manipulated autologous chondrocytes, epithelial cells on a synthetic matrix, and semen or other reproductive tissue.
hypothesis	*[IMDRF/SaMD WG/N41]* a supposition or proposed explanation made as a starting point for further investigation. Evidence is not necessary to form a hypothesis.

I

in vitro diagnostic (IVD) medical device	*[IMDRF/SaMD WG/N10] [IMDRF/SaMD WG/N12]* a medical device, whether used alone or in combination, intended by the manufacturer for the in-vitro examination of specimens derived from the human body solely or principally to provide information for diagnostic, monitoring or compatibility purposes.
	[MEDDEV 2.1/6] any medical device which is a reagent, reagent product, calibrator, control material, kit, instrument, apparatus, equipment, or system, whether used alone or in combination, intended by the manufacturer to be used in vitro for the examination of specimens, including blood and tissue donations, derived from the human body, solely or principally for the purpose of providing information: concerning a physiological or pathological state, or concerning a congenital abnormality, or to determine the safety and compatibility with potential recipients, or to monitor therapeutic measures.
independent review	*[IMDRF/SaMD WG/N41]* the process of subjecting a work, research, or ideas to the scrutiny of others who are experts in the same field.
information	*[EMA/226170/2021]* meaningful organisation and processing of data and documentation.
inform clinical management (SaMD output to)	*[IMDRF/SaMD WG/N41]* informing clinical management infers that the information provided by the SaMD will not trigger an immediate or near term action.
input (SaMD)	*[IMDRF/SaMD WG/N41]* one or several defined numeric tables or models accepted by an algorithm.
input data	*[MEDDEV 2.1/6]* any data provided to software in order to obtain output data after computation of this data can be considered as an input data.
installation qualification (IQ)	*[Annex 15]* the documented verification that the facilities, systems and equipment, as installed or modified, comply with the approved design and the manufacturer's recommendations.

intended (medical, purpose, use)	*[IMDRF/SaMD WG/N41]* the objective intent of the manufacturer regarding the use of a product, process or service as reflected in the specifications, instructions and information provided by the manufacturer. *(see also:* claim*)*
intended purpose	*[MEDDEV 2.1/6]* the use for which the device is intended according to the data supplied by the manufacturer on the labelling, in the instructions and/or in promotional materials.
intended use/intended purpose	*[IMDRF/SaMD WG/N10] [IMDRF/SaMD WG/N12]* the objective intent of the manufacturer regarding the use of a product, process or service as reflected in the specifications, instructions and information provided by the manufacturer.
International Medical Device Regulatory Forum (IMDRF)	*[IMDRF/SaMD WG/N41]* a voluntary group of medical device regulators from around the world who have come together to build on the strong foundational work of the Global Harmonization Task Force on Medical Devices (GHTF), and to accelerate international medical device regulatory harmonization and convergence.
investigator / institution	*[EMA/226170/2021]* an expression meaning "the investigator and/or institution, where required by the applicable regulatory requirements."
IT infrastructure	*[Annex 11]* the hardware and software such as networking software and operation systems, which makes it possible for the application to function.

K

knowledge management	*[Annex 15]* a systematic approach to acquire, analyse, store and disseminate information. (ICH Q10)

L

labeling	*[IMDRF/SaMD WG/N41]* the label, instructions for use, and any other information that is related to identification, technical description, intended purpose and proper use of the medical device, but excluding shipping documents.
least burdensome	*[IMDRF/SaMD WG/N41]* addressing a premarket issue that involves the most appropriate investment of time, effort, and resources.
level of concern	*[Guidance for the Content of Premarket Submissions for Software Contained in Medical Devices]* an estimate of the severity of injury that a device could permit or inflict, either directly or indirectly, on a patient or operator as a result of device failures, design flaws, or simply by virtue of employing the device for its intended use.
level of concern, major	*[Guidance for the Content of Premarket Submissions for Software Contained in Medical Devices]* a failure or latent flaw could directly result in death or serious injury to the patient or operator OR could indirectly result in death or serious injury of the patient or operator through incorrect or delayed information or through the action of a care provider.

level of concern, major *(cont'd)*

[Off-The-Shelf Software Use in Medical Devices] the level of concern is major if operation of the software associated with device function directly affects the patient, operator, and/or bystander so that failures or latent flaws could result in death or serious injury to the patient, operator, and/or bystander, or if it indirectly affects the patient, operator, and/or bystander (e.g., through the action of care provider) such that incorrect or delayed information could result in death or serious injury to the patient, operator, and/or bystander.

level of concern, minor

[Guidance for the Content of Premarket Submissions for Software Contained in Medical Devices] failures or latent design flaws are unlikely to cause any injury to the patient or operator.

[Off-The-Shelf Software Use in Medical Devices] the level of concern is minor if failures or latent design flaws would not be expected to result in any injury to the patient, operator, and/or bystander.

level of concern, moderate

[Guidance for the Content of Premarket Submissions for Software Contained in Medical Devices] a failure or latent design flaw could directly result in minor injury to the patient or operator OR could indirectly result in minor injury to the patient or operator through incorrect or delayed information or through the action of a care provider.

[Off-The-Shelf Software Use in Medical Devices] the level of concern is moderate if the operation of the software associated with device function directly affects the patient, operator, and/or bystander so that failures or latent design flaws could result in non-serious injury to the patient, operator, and/or bystander, or if it indirectly affects the patient, operator, and/or bystander (e.g., through the action of the care provider) where incorrect or delayed information could result in non-serious injury of the patient, operator, and/or bystander.

life cycle/lifecycle

[Annex 11] all phases in the life of the system from initial requirements until retirement including design, specification, programming, testing, installation, operation, and maintenance.

[Annex 15] all phases in the life of a product, equipment or facility from initial development or use through to discontinuation of use.

likelihood ratio negative (LR-)

[IMDRF/SaMD WG/N41] (1 – sensitivity) / specificity = ratio of the probabilities of testing negative in patients with and without disease or clinical condition. It can be interpreted as the increase in the odds of disease given a test negative result relative to the pretest odds.

likelihood ratio positive (LR+)

[IMDRF/SaMD WG/N41] sensitivity / (1 – specificity) = ratio of the probabilities of testing positive in patients with and without disease or clinical condition. It can be interpreted as the increase in the odds of disease given a test positive result relative to the pretest odds.

literature search	*[IMDRF/SaMD WG/N41]* use of published clinical data that establishes a valid clinical association.
lot or batch	*[21CFR§820]* one or more components or finished devices that consist of a single type, model, class, size, composition, or software version that are manufactured under essentially the same conditions and that are intended to have uniform characteristics and quality within specified limits.
M	
machine learning (ML)	*[EMA/226170/2021]* a subset of artificial intelligence (AI) and includes computer algorithms which are trained to classify or predict data, without actually being programmed to do so. ML is divided into supervised and unsupervised learning.
machine learning software (incremental)	*[IMDRF/SaMD WG/N41]* software device for which input data is continuously used to automatically extend the existing device's knowledge i.e. to further train the device after it has been released into the market.
management with executive responsibility	*[21CFR§820]* those senior employees of a manufacturer who have the authority to establish or make changes to the manufacturer's quality policy and quality system.
manufacturer	*[21CFR§820]* any person who designs, manufactures, fabricates, assembles, or processes a finished device. Manufacturer includes but is not limited to those who perform the functions of contract sterilization, installation, relabeling, remanufacturing, repacking, or specification development, and initial distributors of foreign entities performing these functions.
	[IMDRF/SaMD WG/N10] any natural or legal person (including legal entities such as a corporation, a partnership or an association) with responsibility for design and/or manufacture of a medical device with the intention of making the medical device available for use, under his name; whether or not such a medical device is designed and/or manufactured by that person himself or on his behalf by another person(s).
manufacturing material	*[21CFR§820]* any material or substance used in or used to facilitate the manufacturing process, a concomitant constituent, or a byproduct constituent produced during the manufacturing process, which is present in or on the finished device as a residue or impurity not by design or intent of the manufacturer.
medical device	*[IMDRF/SaMD WG/N10] [IMDRF/SaMD WG/N12]* any instrument, apparatus, implement, machine, appliance, implant, reagent for in vitro use, software, material or other similar or related article, intended by the manufacturer to be used, alone or in combination, for human beings, for one or more of the specific medical purpose(s) of: (1) diagnosis,prevention, monitoring, treatment or alleviation of disease,

medical device *(cont'd)*	(2) diagnosis, monitoring, treatment, alleviation of or compensation for an injury, (3) investigation, replacement, modification, or support of the anatomy or of a physiological process, (4) supporting or sustaining life, (5) control of conception, (6) disinfection of medical devices, (7) providing information by means of in vitro examination of specimens derived from the human body; and does not achieve its primary intended action by pharmacological, immunological or metabolic means, in or on the human body, but which may be assisted in its intended function by such means. Products which may be considered to be medical devices in some jurisdictions but not in others include: disinfection substances, aids for persons with disabilities, devices incorporating animal and/or human tissues, devices for.in-vitro fertilization or assisted reproduction technologies.
	[MEDDEV 2.1/6] any instrument, apparatus, appliance, software, material or other article, whether used alone or in combination, including the software intended by its manufacturer to be used specifically for diagnostic and/or therapeutic purposes and necessary for its proper application, intended by the manufacturer to be used for human beings for the purpose of: diagnosis, prevention, monitoring, treatment or alleviation of disease, diagnosis, monitoring, treatment, alleviation of or compensation for an injury or handicap, investigation, replacement or modification of the anatomy or of a physiological process, control of conception, and and which does not achieve its principal intended action in or on the human body by pharmacological, immunological or metabolic means, but which may be assisted in its function by such means.
minor injury	*[Guidance for the Content of Premarket Submissions for Software Contained in Medical Devices]* any injury that does not meet the definition of a serious injury as defined in 21 CFR 803.3(w).
mobile application (mobile app)	*[Policy for Device Software Functions and Mobile Medical Applications] [Use of Electronic Records and Electronic Signatures in Clinical Investigation - Q&A]* a software application that can be executed (run) on a mobile platform (i.e., a handheld commercial off-the-shelf computing platform, with or without wireless connectivity), or a web-based software application that is tailored to a mobile platform but is executed on a server. Example: electronic patient-reported outcomes (ePRO)applications on smart phones.
mobile medical app manufacturer	*[Policy for Device Software Functions and Mobile Medical Applications]* any person or entity that manufactures mobile medical apps in accordance with the definitions of manufacturer in 21 CFR Parts 803, 806, 807, and 820.

mobile medical application (mobile medical app)	*[Policy for Device Software Functions and Mobile Medical Applications]* a mobile app that incorporates device software functionality that meets the definition of device in section 201(h) of the FD&C Act; and either is intended to be used as an accessory to a regulated medical device or to transform a mobile platform into a regulated medical device.
mobile platform	*[Policy for Device Software Functions and Mobile Medical Applications] [Use of Electronic Records and Electronic Signatures in Clinical Investigation - Q&A]* commercial off-the-shelf (COTS) computing platforms, with or without wireless connectivity, that are handheld in nature. Examples: smart phones, tablet computers, other portable computers.
mobile technology	*[Use of Electronic Records and Electronic Signatures in Clinical Investigation - Q&A]* portable electronic technology used in clinical investigations that allows for off-site and remote data capture directly from study participants and includes mobile platforms, mobile apps, wearable biosensors and other remote and ingestible sensors, and other portable and implantable electronic devices.

N

negative predictive value (NPV)	*[IMDRF/SaMD WG/N41]* proportion of test negative patients who do not have the disease or clinical condition.
nonconformity	*[21CFR§820]* the nonfulfillment of a specified requirement.
non-device-MDDS	*[Medical Device Data Systems, Medical Image Storage Devices, and Medical Image Communications Devices]* software functions that are solely intended to transfer, store, convert formats, and display medical device data or results.
non-serious (situation or condition)	*[IMDRF/SaMD WG/N41]* situations or conditions where an accurate diagnosis and treatment is important but not critical for interventions to mitigate long term irreversible consequences on an individual patient's health condition or public health.
number needed to harm (NNH)	*[IMDRF/SaMD WG/N41]* number of patients that need to be treated in order have an adverse effect on one patient.
number needed to treat (NNT)	*[IMDRF/SaMD WG/N41]* average number of patients that need to be treated in order to have an impact on one person.

O

odds ratio (OR)	*[IMDRF/SaMD WG/N41]* ratio of the odds of disease or clinical condition given the SaMD test result is S to the odds of disease given the SaMD test result is not S. OR is equivalent to ratio of likelihood ratio positive to likelihood ratio negative.
off-the-shelf software (OTS software)	*[Off-The-Shelf Software Use in Medical Devices]* a generally available software component, used by a medical device manufacturer for which the manufacturer cannot claim complete software life cycle control.

ongoing process verification	*[Annex 15]* (a.k.a. continued process verification). Documented evidence that the process remains in a state of control during commercial manufacture.
open system	*[21CFR§11]* an environment in which system access is not controlled by persons who are responsible for the content of electronic records that are on the system.
operational qualification (OQ)	*[Annex 15]* the documented verification that the facilities, systems and equipment, as installed or modified, perform as intended throughout the anticipated operating ranges.
original data	*[Computerized Systems Used in Clinical Investigations]* those values that represent the first recording of study data.
output	*[IMDRF/SaMD WG/N41]* results obtained from an algorithm.
output data	*[MEDDEV 2.1/6]* any data produced by a software can be considered as an output data.

P

patient-reported outcome (PRO)	*[EMA/226170/2021]* any outcome reported directly by the trial participant and based on the trial participant's perception of a disease and its treatment(s). The term is proposed as an umbrella term to cover both single dimension and multi-dimension measurements of symptoms, HRQL, health status, adherence to treatment, satisfaction with treatment, etc. (Source: CHMP Reflection paper on the regulatory guidance for the use of HRQL measures in the evaluation of medicinal products - EMEA/CHMP/EWP/139391/2004)
perfective maintenance	*[IMDRF/SaMD WG/N10] [ISO/IEC 14764:2006]* the modification of a software product after delivery to detect and correct latent faults in the software product before they are manifested as failures.
performance (essential principles)	*[IMDRF/SaMD WG/N41]* a product's behavior must not cause harm to a person, place or thing if something goes wrong.
performance (metrics)	*[IMDRF/SaMD WG/N41]* measures behaviors, activities and performance.
performance (real world)	*[IMDRF/SaMD WG/N41]* information on real-world device use and performance from a wider patient population than a more controlled study or pertinent literature, and thus provide information that cannot be obtained through such studies. *(see also:* real world performance*)*
performance (studies)	*[IMDRF/SaMD WG/N41]* establish or confirm aspects of device performance which cannot be determined by analytical validation, literature and/or previous experience gained by routine testing.
performance qualification (PQ)	*[Annex 15]* the documented verification that systems and equipment can perform effectively and reproducibly based on the approved process method and product specification.

permanent	*[Guidance for the Content of Premarket* Submissions *for Software Contained in Medical Devices] [Off-The-Shelf Software Use in Medical Devices]* irreversible impairment or damage to a body structure or function, excluding trivial impairment or damage.
placing on the market	*[MEDDEV 2.1/6]* the first making available in return for payment or free of charge of a device other than a device intended for clinical investigation, with a view to distribution and/or use on the Community market, regardless of whether it is new or fully refurbished.
positive predictive value (PPV)	*[IMDRF/SaMD WG/N41]* proportion of test positive patients who have the disease or clinical condition.
post-market surveillance	*[IMDRF/SaMD WG/N41]* the practice of monitoring the safety of a medical device after it has been released on the market.
pre-market	*[IMDRF/SaMD WG/N41]* the period prior to a product being available for purchase.
preventive maintenance	*[IMDRF/SaMD WG/N10] [ISO/IEC 14764:2006]* the modification of a software product after delivery to detect and correct latent faults in the software product before they become operational faults.
process owner	*[Annex 11]* the person responsible for the business process.
process validation	*[21CFR§820]* establishing by objective evidence that a process consistently produces a result or product meeting its predetermined specifications. *(see also:* validation and design validation*)*
	[Annex 15] the documented evidence that the process, operated within established parameters, can perform effectively and reproducibly to produce a medicinal product meeting its predetermined specifications and quality attributes.
product	*[21CFR§820]* components, manufacturing materials, in- process devices, finished devices, and returned devices.
product realisation	*[Annex 15]* achievement of a product with the quality attributes to meet the needs of patients, health care professionals and regulatory authorities and internal customer requirements. (ICH Q10)
professional society guidelines	*[IMDRF/SaMD WG/N41]* practices and documents recommended by leading authorities; use of existing, well-established standards and/or clinical data.
prospective validation	*[Annex 15]* validation carried out before routine production of products intended for sale.
putting into service	*[MEDDEV 2.1/6]* the stage at which a device has been made available to the final user as being ready for use on the Community market for the first time for its intended purpose.

Q

qualification	*[EMA/226170/2021]* "Action of proving and documenting that equipment or ancillary systems are properly installed, work correctly, and actually lead to the expected results. Qualification is part of validation, but the individual qualification steps alone do not constitute process validation." (ICH Q7 20 Glossary) Expected results for system qualification should be traceable to a system specification, e.g. a User Requirements Specification (URS).
qualification, installation	*[Glossary of Computer System Software Development Terminology] (FDA)* establishing confidence that process equipment and ancillary systems are compliant with appropriate codes and approved design intentions, and that manufacturer's recommendations are suitably considered.
qualification, operational	*[Glossary of Computer System Software Development Terminology] (FDA)* establishing confidence that process equipment and sub-systems are capable of consistently operating within established limits and tolerances.
qualification, process performance	*[Glossary of Computer System Software Development Terminology] (FDA)* establishing confidence that the process is effective and reproducible.
qualification, product performance	*[Glossary of Computer System Software Development Terminology] (FDA)* establishing confidence through appropriate testing that the finished product produced by a specified process meets all release requirements for functionality and safety.
quality	*[21CFR§820]* the totality of features and characteristics that bear on the ability of a device to satisfy fitness-for-use, including safety and performance.
quality assurance	*[Glossary of Computer System Software Development Terminology]* (1) *(ISO)* the planned systematic activities necessary to ensure that a component, module, or system conforms to established technical requirements. (2) all actions that are taken to ensure that a development organization delivers products that meet performance requirements and adhere to standards and procedures. (3) the policy, procedures, and systematic actions established in an enterprise for the purpose of providing and maintaining some degree of confidence in data integrity and accuracy throughout the life cycle of the data, which includes input, update, manipulation, and output. (4) *(QA)* the actions, planned and performed, to provide confidence that all systems and components that influence the quality of the product are working as expected individually and collectively.
quality assurance, software	*[Glossary of Computer System Software Development Terminology] (IEEE)* (1) a planned and systematic pattern of all actions necessary to provide adequate confidence that an item or product conforms to established technical requirements. (2) a set of activities designed to evaluate the process by which products are developed or manufactured.

quality audit	*[21CFR§820]* a systematic, independent examination of a manufacturer's quality system that is performed at defined intervals and at sufficient frequency to determine whether both quality system activities and the results of such activities comply with quality system procedures, that these procedures are implemented effectively, and that these procedures are suitable to achieve quality system objectives.
quality by design	*[Annex 15]* a systematic approach that begins with predefined objectives and emphasises product and process understanding and process control, based on sound science and quality risk management.
quality control	*[Glossary of Computer System Software Development Terminology]* the operational techniques and procedures used to achieve quality requirements.
quality policy	*[21CFR§820]* the overall intentions and direction of an organization with respect to quality, as established by management with executive responsibility.
quality risk management	*[Annex 15]* a systematic process for the assessment, control, communication and review of risks to quality across the lifecycle. (ICH Q9)
quality system	*[21CFR§820]* the organizational structure, responsibilities, procedures, processes, and resources for implementing quality management.

R

real world (SaMD) evidence	*[IMDRF/SaMD WG/N41]* evidence derived from aggregation and analysis of real world data elements.
real world data	*[IMDRF/SaMD WG/N41]* product information generated after a product has been released to the market that can provide insight into the performance of the product used in actual clinical settings, in routine medical practice, and by regular use by consumers.
real world performance	*[IMDRF/SaMD WG/N41]* information on real-world device use and performance from a wider patient population than a more controlled study or pertinent literature, and thus provide information that cannot be obtained through such studies. *(See also:* performance (real world)*)*
reengineering	*[Deciding When to Submit a 510(k) for a Software Change]* the examination and alteration of software to reconstitute it in a new form, and includes the subsequent implementation of the new form. It is often undertaken to replace aging legacy software.
refactoring	*[Deciding When to Submit a 510(k) for a Software Change]* a disciplined technique for restructuring a software program's internal structure without changing its clinical performance specification. Refactoring seeks to improve a program structure and its maintainability. In general, reengineering often results in broader and more complex changes, while refactoring is often narrower in scope and less complex.

regulated medical device	*[Policy for Device Software Functions and Mobile Medical Applications]* a product that meets the definition of device in section 201(h) of the FD&C Act and that has been cleared or approved by the FDA review of a premarket submission or otherwise classified by the FDA.
remanufacturer	*[21CFR§820]* any person who processes, conditions, renovates, repackages, restores, or does any other act to a finished device that significantly changes the finished device's performance or safety specifications, or intended use.
requirement	*[General Principles of Software Validation]* any need or expectation for a system or for its software. Requirements reflect the stated or implied needs of the customer, and may be market-based, contractual, or statutory, as well as an organization's internal requirements. There can be many different kinds of requirements (e.g., design, functional, implementation, interface, performance, or physical requirements).
results	*[EMA/226170/2021]* a composition of organised and fit-for-purpose information.
rework	*[21CFR§820]* action taken on a nonconforming product so that it will fulfill the specified DMR requirements before it is released for distribution.
risk analysis	*[Off-The-Shelf Software Use in Medical Devices]* investigation of available information to identify hazards and to estimate risks.
risk assessment	*[Glossary of Computer System Software Development Terminology] (DOD)* a comprehensive evaluation of the risk and its associated impact.
risk categorization framework (SaMD)	*[IMDRF/SaMD WG/N41]* a framework to determine the category of a SaMD based on the significance of the information provided to the healthcare decision and on the state of the healthcare situation or condition that the SaMD is intended for.
risk control	*[Off-The-Shelf Software Use in Medical Devices]* the process through which decisions are reached and implemented for reducing risks to, or maintaining risks within, specified limits.

S

safety	*[IMDRF/SaMD WG/N41]* a product should be designed and manufactured in such a way that, when used under the conditions and for the purposes intended and, where applicable, by virtue of the technical knowledge, experience, education or training, and the medical and physical conditions of intended users, they will perform as intended. *(See also:* effectiveness, performance*)*
	[Off-The-Shelf Software Use in Medical Devices] the probable benefits to health for its intended use when accompanied by adequate directions and warnings against unsafe use, outweigh any probable risks.

safety data	*[IMDRF/SaMD WG/N41]* adverse events and other problems with medical devices that impact the health and safety of patients; safety data may be collected in the same activity as performance data; absence of safety issues during clinical performance testing is an indicator of safety.
scientific validity	*[IMDRF/SaMD WG/N41]* refers to the extent to which the SaMD's output (concept, conclusion, measurements) is clinically accepted or well founded (existence of an established scientific framework or body of evidence) that corresponds accurately in the real world to the healthcare situation and condition identified in the SaMD definition statement. *(see also:* clinical association*)*
secondary data analysis	*[IMDRF/SaMD WG/N41]* use of analyzed data collected for another purpose.
sensitivity	*[IMDRF/SaMD WG/N41]* effectiveness of a SaMD to correctly identifies patients with the intended clinical disease or condition.
serious (situation or condition)	*[IMDRF/SaMD WG/N41]* situations or conditions where accurate diagnosis or treatment is of vital importance to avoid unnecessary interventions (e.g., biopsy) or timely interventions are important to mitigate long term irreversible consequences on an individual patient's health condition or public health.
serious injury	*[21CFR§1271.3(d)] [Guidance for the Content of Premarket Submissions for Software Contained in Medical Devices] [Off-The-Shelf Software Use in Medical Devices]* an injury or illness that:(1) is life-threatening, (2) results in permanent impairment of a body function or permanent damage to a body structure, or (3) necessitates medical or surgical intervention to preclude permanent impairment of a body function or permanent damage to a body structure.
simulated agents	*[Annex 15]* a material that closely approximates the physical and, where practical, the chemical characteristics, e.g. viscosity, particle size, pH etc., of the product under validation.
software	*[MEDDEV 2.1/6]* a set of instructions that processes input data and creates output data.
software as a medical device (SaMD)	*[IMDRF/SaMD WG/N10] [IMDRF/SaMD WG/N12]* software intended to be used for one or more medical purposes that perform these purposes without being part of a hardware medical device.
	[MEDDEV 2.1/6] software intended to be used for one or more medical purposes that perform these purposes without being part of a hardware medical device.
software regression testing	*[Blood Establishment Computer System Validation in the User's Facility]* re-running test cases which a program has previously executed correctly to detect errors caused by changes or corrections made during software development.

software validation	*[Computerized Systems Used in Clinical Trials] [Blood Establishment Computer System Validation in the User's Facility]* confirmation by examination and provision of objective evidence that software specifications conform to user needs and intended uses, and that the particular requirements implemented through the software can be consistently fulfilled.
software verification	*[Blood Establishment Computer System Validation in the User's Facility]* confirmation by examination and provision of objective evidence that specified requirements have been fulfilled. In a software development or manufacturing environment, software verification provides objective evidence that the design outputs of a particular phase of the software development life cycle meet all of the specified requirements for that phase.
source data	*[EMA/226170/2021]* "All information in original records and certified copies of original records of clinical findings, observations, or other activities in a clinical trial necessary for the reconstruction and evaluation of the trial. Source data are contained in source documents (original records or certified copies)." (ICH-GCP 212 1.51)
	[Use of Electronic Records and Electronic Signatures in Clinical Investigation - Q&A] all information in original records and certified copies of original records of clinical findings, observations, or other activities (in a clinical investigation) used for the reconstruction and evaluation of the trial. Source data are contained in source documents (original records or certified copies).
source documents	*[Computerized Systems Used in Clinical Investigations] [Computerized Systems Used in Clinical Trials]* original documents and records including, but not limited to, hospital records, clinical and office charts, laboratory notes, memoranda, subjects' diaries or evaluation checklists, pharmacy dispensing records, recorded data from automated instruments, copies or transcriptions certified after verification as being accurate and complete, microfiches, photographic negatives, microfilm or magnetic media, x-rays, subject files, and records kept at the pharmacy, at the laboratories, and at medico-technical departments involved in a clinical trial.
	[EMA/226170/2021] "Original documents, data, and records (e.g., hospital records, clinical and office charts, laboratory notes, memoranda, subjects' diaries or evaluation checklists, pharmacy dispensing records, recorded data from automated instruments, copies or transcriptions certified after verification as being accurate copies, microfiches, photographic negatives, microfilm or magnetic media, X-rays, subject files, and records kept at the pharmacy, at the laboratories and at medico-technical departments involved in the clinical trial)." (ICH-GCP 1.52)
specification	*[21CFR§820]* any requirement with which a product, process, service, or other activity must conform.

specification *(cont'd)*	*[General Principles of Software Validation]* a document that states requirements.
specificity	*[IMDRF/SaMD WG/N41]* correctly identifies across a range of available measurements patients that do not have the intended disease or condition.
stand alone software	*[MEDDEV 2.1/6]* software which is not incorporated in a medical device at the time of its placing on the market or its making available.
state of control	*[Annex 15]* a condition in which the set of controls consistently provides assurance of acceptable process performance and product quality.
static file formats	*[EMA/226170/2021]* (e.g. PDF scan) containing information or data that are fixed/frozen and allow no interaction to change the content. Paper document digitised as pdf, e.g. scanned ethics approval letter.
system life cycle	*[EMA/226170/2021]* all phases of the system; i.e. typically 1) the concept phase where the regulated party considers to automate a process and where user requirements are collected, 2) the project phase where a contracted party is selected, a risk-assessment is made and the system is implemented and qualified, 3) the operational phase where a system is used in a regulated environment and changes are implemented in a manner which maintains data confidentiality, integrity and availability, and finally, 4) a retirement phase which includes decisions about data retention, migration or destruction and management of these processes.
system owner	*[Annex 11]* the person responsible for the availability, and maintenance of a computerised system and for the security of the data residing on that system.

T

telemedicine	*[Use of Electronic Records and Electronic Signatures in Clinical Investigation - Q&A]* the use of electronic applications, devices, and services, including two-way video, email, smart phones, wireless tools and other forms of telecommunications systems in the provision of health care.
third party	*[Annex 11]* parties not directly managed by the holder of the manufacturing and/or import authorisation.
traditional approach	*[Annex 15]* a product development approach where set points and operating ranges for process parameters are defined to ensure reproducibility.
transmit	*[Computerized Systems Used in Clinical Investigations]* to transfer data within or among clinical study sites, contract research organizations, data management centers, sponsors, or to FDA.
	[Computerized Systems Used in Clinical Trials] to transfer data within or among clinical study sites, contract research organizations, data management centers, or sponsors.

treat (SaMD output to)	*[IMDRF/SaMD WG/N41]* information provided by the SaMD will be used to take an immediate or near term action.
trial participant	*[EMA/226170/2021]* a synonym for the term "subject", defined in Directive 2001/20/EC as "an individual who participates in a clinical trial as a recipient of the investigational medicinal product (IMP) or a control"

U

unique device identifier (UDI)	*[21CFR§820]* an identifier that adequately identifies a device through its distribution and use by meeting the requirements of 21CFR§830.20. A unique device identifier is composed of: (1) a device identifier —a mandatory, fixed portion of a UDI that identifies the specific version or model of a device and the labeler of that device; and (2) a production identifier —a conditional, variable portion of a UDI that identifies one or more of the following when included on the label of the device: (i) the lot or batch within which a device was manufactured; (ii) the serial number of a specific device; (iii) the expiration date of a specific device; (iv) the date a specific device was manufactured. (v) for an HCT/P regulated as a device, the distinct identification code required by 21CFR§1271.290(c).
universal product code (UPC)	*[21CFR§820]* the product identifier used to identify an item sold at retail in the United States.
usability	*[IMDRF/SaMD WG/N41]* the means by which the user and a computer system interact, in particular the use of input devices and software and the evaluation of safety considerations for device users, use environments and user interfaces.
user	*[IMDRF/SaMD WG/N41]* includes patients, healthcare providers, specialized professionals, lay users, consumers.
user interface	*[IMDRF/SaMD WG/N41]* the means by which the user and a computer system interact, in particular the use of input devices and software and the evaluation of safety considerations for device users, use environments and user interfaces.
user requirements specification (URS)	*[Annex 15]* the set of owner, user and engineering requirements necessary and sufficient to create a feasible design meeting the intended purpose of the system.
user validation	*[Blood Establishment Computer System Validation in the User's Facility]* testing new equipment or a new process in the environment where it will be used to ensure that it will reliably produce a product that meets pre-determined qualifications and quality standards.

V

validation	*[21CFR§820]* confirmation by examination and provision of objective evidence that the particular requirements for a specific intended use can be consistently fulfilled. *(see also:* process validation and design validation*)*

validation *(cont'd)*	*[General Principles of Software Validation]* confirmation by examination and provision of objective evidence that software specifications conform to user needs and intended uses, and that the particular requirements implemented through software can be consistently fulfilled.
	[IMDRF/SaMD WG/N41] confirmation through provision of objective evidence that the requirements for a specific intended use or application have been fulfilled.
	[EMA/226170/2021] "A process of establishing and documenting that the specified requirements of a computerized system can be consistently fulfilled from design until decommissioning of the system or transition to a new system. The approach to validation should be based on a risk assessment that takes into consideration the intended use of the system and the potential of the system to affect human subject protection and reliability of clinical trial results." (ICH-GCP 1.65)
vendor	*[Use of Electronic Records and Electronic Signatures in Clinical Investigation - Q&A]* a third-party supplier not regulated by FDA that sells electronic goods and services to sponsors and other regulated entities.
verification	*[21CFR§820]* confirmation by examination and provision of objective evidence that specified requirements have been fulfilled.
	[General Principles of Software Validation] provides objective evidence that the design outputs of a particular phase of the software development life cycle meet all of the specified requirements for that phase. Software verification looks for consistency, completeness, and correctness of the software and its supporting documentation, as it is being developed, and provides support for a subsequent conclusion that software is validated. Examples: software testing, static and dynamic analyses, code and document inspections, walkthroughs.
	[IMDRF/SaMD WG/N41] confirmation through provision of objective evidence that specified requirements have been fulfilled.

W

wearable biosensors	*[Use of Electronic Records and Electronic Signatures in Clinical Investigation - Q&A]* comprise miniaturized sensors worn as on- or in-body accessories (e.g., watches, bracelets, clothing) that allow for continuous monitoring of physiological, biochemical, and motion signals for both diagnostic and monitoring applications. These wearable biosensors may be paired with mobile platforms (e.g., smart phones). Examples of wearable biosensors include accelerometers, activity trackers, wireless heart rate monitors, pulse oximetry sensors, and glucose sensors.
worst case	*[Annex 15]* a condition or set of conditions encompassing upper and lower processing limits and circumstances, within standard operating procedures, which pose the greatest chance of product or process failure when compared to ideal conditions. Such conditions do not necessarily induce product or process failure.

Index

Symbols

A

B

C

INDEX

INDEX

D

E

F

G

H

I

J

K

L

M

N

O

P

Q

R

S

INDEX

INDEX

T

INDEX

INDEX

V

W

INDEX

About the Authors

Mindy Allport-Settle, M.B.A. was born in Beckley and raised in Oak Hill, West Virginia. She moved to North Carolina to attend the N.C. School of the Arts for high school and now lives near Raleigh. Following in the footsteps of Gordon Allport, all of her books are built on a foundation of psychology and sociology with a focus on improving some aspect of industry through research and education.

Her career in healthcare began when she was a teenager working as an emergency medical technician. Since then, she has joined the U.S. Navy's advanced hospital corps, worked in organ and human tissue procurement, specialized in ophthalmology, and moved on to serve as a key executive, board member, and consultant for some of the best companies in the pharmaceutical, medical device, and biotechnology industry. She has provided guidance in regulatory compliance, corporate structuring, restructuring and turnarounds, new drug submissions, research and development and product commercialization strategies, and new business development. Her experience and dedication have resulted in international recognition as the developer of the only FDA-recognized and benchmarked quality systems training and development business methodology.

Her education includes a Bachelor's degree from the University of North Carolina, an MBA in Global Management from the University of Phoenix, and completion of the corporate governance course series in audit committees, compensation committees, and board effectiveness at Harvard Business School.

Dr. Kirstin A. Counts has dedicated over 20 years to patient care, advocacy, and the healthcare industry and is a Board Certified Chiropractic Physician with an additional certification in Functional Medicine Chiropractic Family Practice from the American Chiropractic Association's Council on Diagnosis & Internal Disorders. Focusing on patient care, practice development, compliance strategies, and community outreach, her primary interest is in harmonizing all practical and philosophical approaches to patient care for the unified advancement of the entire healthcare industry.

She received her doctorate degree from Palmer College of Chiropractic in 2000, graduating magna cum laude. She received her BS in Biology with a minor in Modern Dance from the University of South Florida in Tampa and attended high school and her first year of college at the North Carolina School of the Arts in Winston-Salem where she also majored in Modern Dance.

Made in United States
Orlando, FL
04 November 2026

90207649R00339